Encyclopedia of
Survey
Research
Methods

Editorial Board

Encyclopedia of
Survey Research Methods

E D I T O R

Paul J. Lavrakas
Independent Consultant and Former Chief Research
Methodologist for The Nielsen Company

VOLUME

Los Angeles • London • New Delhi • Singapore • Washington DC

A SAGE Reference Publication

For information:

SAGE Publications, Inc.
2455 Teller Road
Thousand Oaks, California 91320
E-mail: order@sagepub.com

SAGE Publications Ltd.
1 Oliver's Yard
55 City Road
London, EC1Y 1SP
United Kingdom

SAGE Publications India Pvt. Ltd.
B 1/I 1 Mohan Cooperative Industrial Area
Mathura Road, New Delhi 110 044
India

SAGE Publications Asia-Pacific Pte. Ltd.
33 Pekin Street #02-01
Far East Square
Singapore 048763

Printed in the United States of America.

Library of Congress Cataloging-in-Publication Data

Encyclopedia of survey research methods/editor, Paul J. Lavrakas.
　　　p. cm.
Includes bibliographical references and index.
ISBN 978-1-4129-1808-4 (cloth)
　　1.　Social surveys—Research—Encyclopedias.　I.　Lavrakas, Paul J.
HN29.E53 2008
300.72′03—dc22　　　　　　　　　　　　　　　　　2008011838

This book is printed on acid-free paper.

08　09　10　11　12　10　9　8　7　6　5　4　3　2　1

Publisher:	Rolf A. Janke
Acquisitions Editor:	Lisa Cuevas Shaw
Assistant to the Publisher:	Michele Thompson
Developmental Editor:	Diana E. Axelsen
Managing Editor:	Jody Smarr
Reference Systems Manager:	Leticia Gutierrez
Production Editor:	Tracy Buyan
Copy Editors:	Colleen Brennan, Pam Suwinsky
Typesetter:	C&M Digitals (P) Ltd.
Proofreaders:	Kevin Gleason, Theresa Kay
Indexer:	Joan Shapiro
Marketing Manager:	Amberlyn Erzinger

Contents

With considerable gratitude to Seymour Sudman, David H. Weaver, and Robert M. Groves for the key support they provided at various times in my career.

List of Entries

Reader's Guide

The Reader's Guide is provided to assist readers in locating articles on related topics. It classifies articles into nine general topical categories: (1) Ethical Issues in Survey Research; (2) Measurement; (3) Nonresponse; (4) Operations; (5) Political and Election Polling; (6) Public Opinion; (7) Sampling, Coverage, and Weighting; (8) Survey Industry; and (9) Survey Statistics.

Ethical Issues in Survey Research

Anonymity
Beneficence
Cell Suppression
Certificate of Confidentiality
Common Rule
Confidentiality
Consent Form
Debriefing
Deception
Disclosure
Disclosure Limitation
Ethical Principles
Falsification
Informed Consent
Institutional Review Board (IRB)
Minimal Risk
Perturbation Methods
Privacy
Protection of Human Subjects
Respondent Debriefing
Survey Ethics
Voluntary Participation

Measurement

Interviewer

Conversational Interviewing
Dependent Interviewing
Interviewer Effects
Interviewer Neutrality

Interviewer-Related Error
Interviewer Variance
Nondirective Probing
Probing
Standardized Survey Interviewing
Verbatim Responses

Mode

Mode Effects
Mode-Related Error

Questionnaire

Aided Recall
Aided Recognition
Attitude Measurement
Attitudes
Attitude Strength
Aural Communication
Balanced Question
Behavioral Question
Bipolar Scale
Bogus Question
Bounding
Branching
Check All That Apply
Closed-Ended Question
Codebook
Cognitive Interviewing
Construct
Construct Validity

Public Opinion

Sampling, Coverage, and Weighting

Survey Industry

American Community Survey (ACS)

American Statistical Association Section on Survey
Research Methods (ASA-SRMS)

Behavioral Risk Factor Surveillance System
(BRFSS)

Bureau of Labor Statistics (BLS)

Cochran, W. G.

Council for Marketing and Opinion Research
(CMOR)

Council of American Survey Research Organizations
(CASRO)

Crossley, Archibald

Current Population Survey (CPS)

Gallup, George

Gallup Poll

General Social Survey (GSS)

Hansen, Morris

Institute for Social Research (ISR)

International Field Directors and Technologies
Conference (IFD&TC)

International Journal of Public Opinion Research
(IJPOR)

International Social Survey Programme (ISSP)

Joint Program in Survey Methods (JPSM)

Journal of Official Statistics (JOS)

Kish, Leslie

National Health and Nutrition Examination Survey
(NHANES)

National Health Interview Survey (NHIS)

National Household Education Surveys (NHES)
Program

National Opinion Research Center (NORC)

Pew Research Center

Public Opinion Quarterly (POQ)

Roper, Elmo

Roper Center for Public Opinion Research

Sheatsley, Paul

Statistics Canada

Survey Methodology

Survey Sponsor

Telemarketing

U.S. Bureau of the Census

World Association for Public Opinion Research
(WAPOR)

Survey Statistics

Algorithm

Alpha, Significance Level of Test

Alternative Hypothesis

Analysis of Variance (ANOVA)

Attenuation

Auxiliary Variable

Balanced Repeated Replication (BRR)

Bias

Bootstrapping

Chi-Square

Composite Estimation

Confidence Interval

Confidence Level

Constant

Contingency Table

Control Group

Correlation

Covariance

Cronbach's Alpha

Cross-Sectional Data

Data Swapping

Design-Based Estimation

Design Effects (*deff*)

Ecological Fallacy

Effective Sample Size

Experimental Design

Factorial Design

Finite Population Correction (fpc) Factor

Frequency Distribution

F-Test

Hot-Deck Imputation

Imputation

Independent Variable

Inference

Interaction Effect

Internal Validity

Interval Estimate

Intracluster Homogeneity

Jackknife Variance Estimation

Level of Analysis

Main Effect

Marginals

Margin of Error (MOE)

Mean

Mean Square Error

Median

Metadata

Mode

Model-Based Estimation

Multiple Imputation

Noncausal Covariation

Null Hypothesis

Outliers

Panel Data Analysis

Parameter

N

n

The sample size is traditionally labeled n, as opposed to the total population size, which is termed N. The sample size, n, can refer to either the original number of population elements selected into the sample (sometimes called the "designated sample size" or "sampling pool"), or it can refer to the final number of completed surveys or items for which data were collected (sometime called the "final sample size" or "final sample"). In the same vein, it could refer to any number in between such as, for example, the number of elements that have been sampled and contacted but not interviewed. Or it could refer to the number of elements for which complete data are available. Another interpretation or use of the term n is the number of elements on the data file and available for analysis.

It is almost always true that n is smaller than N and usually by orders of magnitude. In fact, the ratio (n/N) is often referred to as the *sampling fraction*. Often the population size N is so large relative to n that one can safely assume that with replacement sampling holds even if in practice without replacement sampling is implemented. The relative sizes of n and N also play a role in determining whether the finite population correction factor $[1 - (n/N)]$ is sufficiently different from 1 to play a role in the calculation of sampling variance.

Karol Krotki

See also Element; Finite Population Correction (fpc) Factor; *N*; Population; Sample; Sample Size; Sampling Fraction; Sampling Without Replacement

Further Readings

Kish, L. (1965). *Survey sampling*. New York: Wiley.

N

The total population size is traditionally labeled N, as opposed to the sample size, which is termed n. The population size N refers to the total number of elements in the population, target population, or universe.

N also refers to the number of elements on the sampling frame from which the sample is to be drawn. Since in many cases, the list of population elements contains *foreign elements*, the accurate number of eligible population elements is less than the number of elements on the list. In other cases, the population list not only contains foreign elements but also contains omissions and inaccuracies. These further put into question the validity of the value of N, which should be assessed carefully both before and after sample selection and survey implementation.

In some situations N is unknown, and in fact one of the objectives of the survey is to estimate N and its distributional characteristics. In other situations N is known only approximately, and its estimate is refined based on the information obtained from the survey.

It is almost always true that N is larger than n and usually by orders of magnitude. In fact, the ratio (n/N) is often referred to as the *sampling fraction*. Often the population size N is so large relative to n that we can safely assume that with replacement sampling holds even if without replacement sampling is implemented in practice. The relative sizes of n and N also play a role in determining whether the finite population correction factor $[1 - (n/N)]$ is sufficiently different from 1 to play a role in the calculation of sampling variance.

Karol Krotki

See also Element; Finite Population Correction (fpc) Factor; *n*; Population; Sample; Sample Size; Sampling Fraction; Sampling Frame; Sampling Without Replacement

Further Readings

Kish, L. (1965). *Survey sampling*. New York: Wiley.

NATIONAL COUNCIL ON PUBLIC POLLS (NCPP)

Founded in 1969, the National Council on Public Polls (NCPP) is an association of public opinion polling organizations. Initiated by George Gallup of the American Institute of Public Opinion, the primary goal of NCPP is to foster the understanding, interpretation, and reporting of public opinion polls through the disclosure of detailed, survey-specific information and methods to the general public and the media.

NCPP recognizes that the goal of public opinion polls is to provide reliable, valid, and accurate information. If polls succeed in achieving these goals, scientifically conducted surveys can characterize the public's view on issues, policies, elections, and concerns of the day. But with the enormous amount of polling information available, competing methods of collecting information, and sometimes contradictory results, it is often difficult for the general public and the media to decipher polls that accurately reflect what people think from polls that do not.

NCPP does not pass judgment on specific polls, polling methods, or polling entities but rather advocates that polling organizations whose results reside in the public realm disclose pertinent information

about how their surveys are conducted. NCPP maintains that if provided an adequate basis for judging the reliability and validity of poll results, consumers of surveys may assess these studies for themselves.

It is with this goal in mind that NCPP developed a code for member organizations to abide by when reporting survey findings that are intended for or end up in the public domain. These "Principles of Disclosure" include three levels of disclosure, as described on the NCPP Web site.

Level 1 disclosure requires that all reports of survey findings issued for public release by member organizations include the following information, and, in addition, member organizations should endeavor to have print and broadcast media include these items in their news stories:

- Sponsorship of the survey
- Fieldwork provider (if the member organization did not, itself, conduct the interviews)
- Dates of interviewing
- Sampling method employed (e.g., random-digit dialed telephone sample, list-based telephone sample, area probability sample, probability mail sample, other probability sample, opt-in Internet panel, nonprobability convenience sample, use of any oversampling)
- Population that was sampled (e.g., general population; registered voters; likely voters; or any specific population group defined by gender, race, age, occupation, or any other characteristic)
- Size of the sample that serves as the primary basis of the survey report
- Size and description of the subsample, if the survey report relies primarily on less than the total sample
- Margin of sampling error (if a probability sample)
- Survey mode (e.g., telephone/interviewer, telephone/automated, mail, Internet, fax, email)
- Complete wording and ordering of questions mentioned in or upon which the news release is based
- Percentage results of all questions reported

Level 2 disclosure requires member organizations, in response to any specific written request pertaining to any survey findings they have released publicly, to additionally release any of the following:

- Estimated coverage of target population
- Respondent selection procedure (e.g., within household), if any
- Maximum number of attempts to reach respondent
- Exact wording of introduction (any words preceding the first question)

- Complete wording of questions (per Level 1 disclosure) in any foreign languages in which the survey was conducted
- Weighted and unweighted size of any subgroup cited in the report
- Minimum number of completed questions to qualify a completed interview
- Whether interviewers were paid or unpaid (if interview-administered data collection)
- Details of any incentives or compensation provided for respondent participation
- Description of weighting procedures (if any) used to generalize data to the full population
- Sample dispositions adequate to compute contact, cooperation, and response rates

Level 3 disclosure strongly encourages member organizations to do the following:

- Release raw data sets for any publicly released survey results (with telephone numbers and all other identifying personal information removed)
- Post complete wording, ordering, and percentage results of all publicly released survey questions to a publicly available Web site for a minimum of two weeks
- Publicly note their compliance with these Principles of Disclosure

In keeping with its mission, NCPP established the Polling Review Board (PRB) in 1999 as a source for authoritative comment on good and bad practices of public opinion surveys and/or their public dissemination through the media. Comprised of three member organization representatives, the PRB responds publicly to problems or issues of polling practice, presentation, or media coverage. Comments by the PRB on important polling issues are distributed to the media and are available on NCPP's Web site.

PRB members are also available to provide expert insight and answers to polling questions from politicians, the media, or the general public.

Through expert support and educational activities, NCPP works to advance the public's knowledge about how polls are conducted and how to interpret poll results. NCPP has sponsored seminars, workshops, and press conferences in Washington, D.C., and New York City, and publications to promote understanding and reporting of public opinion polls. One such publication is *Twenty Questions a Journalist Should Ask About Poll Results*, by Sheldon Gawiser and Evans Witt, available by request or online on

NCPP's Web site. It provides a guide for reporters who cover polls.

NCPP recognizes excellence in reporting of polls through its annual Excellence in Media Coverage of Polls Award. Established in 2002, the award encourages accuracy and insight by professional journalists in communicating poll results to the public. Award recipients have included journalists from *The Los Angeles Times*, the Associated Press, *USA Today*, and ABC News.

The National Council on Public Polls Web site provides an opportunity for poll consumers to interact with polling experts and to follow current debates among polling leaders. It includes information about the council, member organizations, NCPP publications, readings, writings, and presentations by member representatives, and a variety of sources about public opinion surveys.

Lee M. Miringoff and Barbara L. Carvalho

See also Gallup, George; Polling Review Board (PRB)

Further Readings

Gawiser, S. R., & Witt, G. E. (1994). *A journalist's guide to public opinion polls*. Westport, CT: Praeger.
National Council on Public Polls: http://www.ncpp.org

NATIONAL ELECTION POOL (NEP)

The National Election Pool (NEP) is a consortium of news organizations—ABC, the Associated Press (AP), CBS, CNN, FOX, and NBC—that conducts exit polls, related surveys of voters, and samples of tabulated vote in U.S. elections. These data allow NEP members to project or "call" winners of many political races earlier than would be possible based on final vote count alone. The voter surveys also allow pool members and subscribers to analyze demographic, attitudinal, and other variables that help explain election outcomes.

Typically the exit polls and sample vote count cover top-of-the-ticket statewide races including those for president, U.S. Senate, and governor, as well as selected ballot initiatives. NEP also conducts a national voter survey in general elections. The NEP exit polls are among the largest one-day survey research undertakings anywhere; in the November

2004 elections, approximately 150,000 interviews were conducted in 1,469 U.S. precincts nationwide.

NEP's roots date to 1990. Before then, several television networks fielded their own exit polls and vote count samples individually. In 1990, the broadcast networks ABC, CBS, NBC, and the then-new cable network CNN formed Voter Research & Surveys (VRS) to pool these functions. In 1993, those networks and the Associated Press, a global news network serving newspapers, broadcasters, and more recently online customers, created the Voter News Service (VNS), which merged the VRS exit polling and sample precinct vote count with the National Election Service (NES), a consortium of news organizations that tabulated vote comprehensively on election nights. The cable network, FOX News Channel, joined VNS after the 1996 presidential primaries.

Exit polls are face-to-face surveys of voters as they exit polling places on Election Day. From the time the polls open until about an hour before they close on Election Day, interviewers approach respondents at a systematic interval and ask them to complete self-administered paper questionnaires, which are kept confidential. Samples of voting precincts—stratified by geography and past vote by party—are selected for the exit polls to be representative of the state, or in a national survey, the entire country. In addition to the exit poll sample, a "superset" random sample of precincts is drawn and news stringers (part-time and/or temporary employees) assigned to report vote count as quickly as possible after polls close. As early and absentee voting began to become more widespread in the United States, VNS started supplementing some exit polls with random-digit dial telephone polling the week before the election to reach voters who would not be covered in the Election Day in-person surveys, and these data are incorporated into projections models and analytical survey cross-tabulations.

In the 2000 general election, VNS and its members became enmeshed in controversy over erroneous or premature calls in the presidential race in several states, particularly in Florida—both early on Election Night, based in part on faulty interpretation of the exit polls, and early the next morning, based on faulty interpretation of the vote count models alone. In a congressional hearing in 2001, the VNS partners vowed to improve their systems, and subsequently they hired a contractor to do so, but the computer overhaul failed in the 2002 midterm election and no exit poll or sample precinct vote data were available that night.

Thereafter, the VNS members disbanded that organization and formed NEP in its place.

Unlike VNS, the new pool did not have its own staff but hired outside vendors—Edison Media Research and Mitofsky International. Under NEP, Edison-Mitofsky used in essence the same survey and sample precinct methodology as VNS (which Warren Mitofsky and Murray Edelman and others had developed at CBS prior to the formation of VRS) but ran the data through new computer systems. However, NEP abandoned the broader VNS vote count function; the AP, which had maintained its own comprehensive vote count during the VNS era—with stringers collecting vote in statewide and down-ballot races in every county in the country (or towns and cities in the New England states, where official vote is not tallied centrally by counties)—became the sole U.S. source of unofficial vote count. AP vote tabulation data are incorporated into the Edison-Mitofsky projections models when it becomes available on Election Night, helping NEP members call winners in races that were too close to be called from early voter surveys, exit polls, and sample precinct vote count alone.

The first election NEP covered was the California gubernatorial recall in November 2003. NEP covered 23 Democratic presidential primaries and caucuses in early 2004; the general election in all 50 states and the District of Columbia in November of that year; and elections in 32 states in the 2006 midterms.

The pool faced controversy again in the 2004 general election when estimates from exit poll interviews early in the day leaked on Web sites and indicated Democrat John Kerry would win the race for president. Even with more complete samples later in the day, some survey estimates fell outside sampling error tolerances when compared to actual vote. Several hypotheses for the discrepancies were offered, and the pool and Edison-Mitofsky took corrective action, including changes to interviewer recruitment and training procedures and measures to stanch leaks of early, incomplete exit poll data. One of those measures, a quarantine room, was established in 2006 and successfully monitored very closely by NEP, which strictly limited the access that NEP's sponsors could have to the exit poll data on Election Day prior to 5:00 P.M. EST, and this resulted in no early leaks in 2006.

NEP planned to cover 23 states in the 2008 Democratic and Republican presidential primaries and all 50 states plus the District of Columbia in the general election in November 2008. The pool now typically supplements the Election Day exit polls with telephone surveys for early or absentee voters in about a dozen states in a presidential general election.

Michael Mokrzycki

See also Election Night Projections; Exit Polls

Further Readings

Traugott, M. W., & Lavrakas, P. J. (2008). *The voter's guide to election polls* (4th ed.). Lanham, MD: Rowman & Littlefield.

NATIONAL ELECTION STUDIES (NES)

The American National Election Studies (NES) are national surveys of voters in the United States that have been conducted by the University of Michigan before and after every presidential election since 1948. For midterm elections, the NES has conducted post-election studies since 1958. The NES has become the standard bearer for election studies. Indeed, international election studies have patterned their approach and question format after the NES. The popularity of the NES is due, in part, to its consistency. It has asked many of the same questions repeatedly since its inception. This has allowed researchers to develop innovative hypothesis testing through the examination of many variables, which has permitted analysis across people, contexts, and time.

History

The NES grew out of the studies created by the Survey Research Center and the Center for Political Studies of the Institute for Social Research at the University of Michigan. The program always lacked sufficient funding, which limited improvement to the study. The funding that it did receive was primarily used to conduct the survey. As a result, there were rarely changes to the core questions of the study. This also meant that those not directly involved in the program had little influence on the types of questions offered.

In 1977, through the initiative of sociologist Warren E. Miller, the National Science Foundation (NSF) formally established the National Election Studies. With sufficient funding, the NES was expected to fulfill two expectations. First, it was expected to continue the time-series collection of core questions. NSF insisted that they continue collecting data on social background, underlying social and political values, opinions on public policy, political predispositions, participation in the political process, and perceptions of groups, leaders, and political candidates. Second, with NSF funding, the NES was also expected to improve the studies' core concepts and questions.

When the NSF began funding the NES, it mandated that NES become a truly national resource. This meant that researchers at the University of Michigan were expected to seek out and accept suggestions from outside sources, primarily researchers at other institutions. This has granted a greater number of scholars access to the NES, which, in turn, has improved the quality and breadth of the study. The NES research agenda undergoes a great deal of evaluation and revision as the principal investigators, board of overseers, and ad hoc committees all have their say in the direction of each project.

Planning the National Election Studies

Planning for the NES typically begins two years prior to the election to be studied. One year prior to the election, the Survey Research Center at the University of Michigan conducts a pilot study. These pilot studies are designed to test new survey questions, which are typically associated with a special theme or important current events. Usually this means that multiple versions of each question are used and later examined for reliability and validity. All NES questionnaires consist of new questions drawn from the pilot studies and the core time-series questions.

The core time-series questions are selected because they are consistently relevant to national elections, public opinion, and civic participation. These questions are included in the NES to serve two purposes. First, it allows the NES to measure the impact of exogenous shocks to the political system. Second, these time-series allow scholarship to examine the nature and causes of political change more closely.

In addition to their time-series questions, the NES created a specific Senate Election Study to allow researchers to analyze senatorial elections. Since only one third of the Senate's seats are up for election in any election cycle, it has always been difficult for national surveys to sample enough respondents to properly analyze these elections. In 1988, 1992, and 1994, the NES created a special survey that specifically sampled states where Senate elections were taking place. They conducted a similar series of studies associated with the presidential nomination process in 1980, 1984, and 1988. These surveys were designed to understand better how Americans make political choices and learn about politics in multi-candidate arenas that sometimes lack partisan cues.

Conducting the National Election Survey

The NES has traditionally been conducted using face-to-face interviews. There have been instances in which telephone interviewing has been used, but the NES has always returned to face-to-face techniques. In presidential election years, pre-election interviews begin the day after Labor Day and end the day before the election. The post-election interviews begin the day after the election and are usually completed between late December and early January. Midterm election interviews also begin the day after the election and end around the start of the new year. The NES uses a multistage area probability design to create its sample.

Research Opportunity

Unlike many public opinion surveys, the NES has been made available to anyone who wants to use it. A researcher can download the individual responses of each person surveyed since 1948. These data sets are available from Inter-university Consortium for Political and Social Research (ICPSR) or directly from the American National Election Studies Web page. The NES also provides a number of other resources, including technical reports, tables, and graphs. To date, there are more than 5,000 entries on the NES bibliography, demonstrating the wide-ranging research options that are available from analysis of these data.

James W. Stoutenborough

See also Election Polls; Face-to-Face Interviewing; Multistage Sample; Perception Question; Pilot Test; Reliability; Telephone Surveys; Validity

Further Readings

American National Election Studies: http://www.electionstudies.org

Franklin, M. M., & Wlezien, C. (Eds.). (2002). *The future of election studies.* Boston: Pergamon.
Johnston, R. (2000). Capturing campaigns in national election studies. In E. Katz & Y. Warshel (Eds.), *Election studies: What's their use?* (pp. 149–172). Boulder, CO: Westview.

NATIONAL HEALTH AND NUTRITION EXAMINATION SURVEY (NHANES)

The National Health and Nutrition Examination Surveys (NHANES) are a group of studies that measure the health and nutritional status of U.S. children and adults. It is conducted by the National Center for Health Statistics (NCHS), Centers for Disease Control and Prevention (CDC). NHANES is the only NCHS survey that gathers objective health measurements based on physical examinations. NHANES contributes to the mission of CDC and the Department of Health and Human Services (DHHS) by collecting standardized data that help shape policies and programs to promote health by preventing and controlling disease and disability. Also, NHANES helps NCHS fulfill its responsibility for producing vital and health statistics for the nation.

Background

The NHANES program began in the early 1960s. The first surveys did not have a nutritional component. They were called the National Heath Examination Surveys (NHES). When nutrition assessments were added in the 1970s, the survey name changed to the National Health and Nutrition Examination Survey (NHANES).

The NHES and NHANES surveys were conducted periodically through 1994 and targeted selected age groups. Since 1999, NHANES has been conducted every year and includes people of all ages.

NHANES is a cross-sectional survey with a stratified, multi-stage probability sample design. The NHANES sample is selected from the civilian, noninstitutionalized U.S. population and is nationally representative. NHANES examines about 5,000 persons annually. Participants are selected in 15 counties across the country each year. These data provide an overview of the health and nutrition of the U.S. population at one point in time. NHANES data are also linked to Medicare and National Death Index records to conduct follow-up studies based on mortality and health care utilization.

Data Collection

NHANES consists of three major pieces: (1) health interviews, (2) medical examinations, and (3) laboratory measures. The health interviews take place in the participants' homes. These are conducted face to face, using computer-assisted personal interviewing (CAPI) software on pen-top computers. CAPI was first used in 1992, during the Third National Health and Nutrition and Examination Survey (NHANES III). Before 1992, NHANES interviews were conducted using pencil and paper.

The home interviews are followed by physical examinations. These are done in the NHANES Mobile Examination Centers (MECs). The MEC is made up of four interconnected 18-wheel tractor trailers. Each of the four trailers houses multiple examination rooms. The MEC visit also includes a dietary recall interview and a health interview covering topics too sensitive to ask in the home.

Laboratory specimens, including blood and urine, are also collected in the MEC. Some laboratory tests are conducted on-site, in the MEC laboratory. Others are done at laboratories across the country. Small amounts of urine and blood are also stored for future testing, including genetic testing.

After the MEC examinations, certain subsets of NHANES respondents participate in telephone interviews. All participants receive a report of the results from selected examination and laboratory tests that have clinical relevance.

The topics covered by NHANES vary over time. Because current NHANES data are released in two-year cycles, survey content is modified at two-year intervals. Some topics stay in the survey for multiple two-year periods. When the data needs for a topic are met, it is cycled out of NHANES, and new topics are added. Rotating content in and out over time has several benefits. It gives NHANES the flexibility needed to focus on a variety of health and nutrition measurements. It provides a mechanism for meeting emerging health research needs in a timely manner. This continuous survey design also makes early availability of the data possible.

Release and Use of Data

NHANES data are used to study major nutritional, infectious, environmental, and other chronic health conditions in the United States. The data are used by federal and state government agencies, community health organizations, private industry, consumer groups, and health providers. NHANES is also an excellent resource for secondary data analysis for college students and academic or private researchers.

Since 2000, NCHS has made NHANES public data sets available on its Web site. Most NHANES data are available to the public at no cost. A small number of NHANES data sets are not publicly available because of confidentiality requirements. These few nonpublic data sets can be accessed through the NCHS Research Data Center (RDC). There are some costs associated with using the NCHS RDC.

A growing number of analysts use NHANES data to study major health conditions in the United States. NHANES data users face certain challenges because of the complexity of the survey design and the vast amount of information in NHANES data sets. To address this issue, NCHS and the National Cancer Institute (NCI) developed a Web-based NHANES tutorial. The tutorial was created to meet the needs of NHANES users regardless of their level of experience with NHANES data or their statistical knowledge. The tutorial has also been accredited for earning credits for Continuing Medical Education (CME), Continuing Education in Nursing (CNE), and Continuing Education Units (CEU).

Natalie E. Dupree

See also Complex Sample Surveys; Computer-Assisted Personal Interviewing (CAPI); Cross-Sectional Data; Multi-Stage Sample; National Health Interview Survey (NHIS)

Further Readings

National Center for Health Statistics. (2004, October). *National Health and Nutrition Examination Survey, 2005–2006.* Retrieved February 15, 2007, from http://www.cdc.gov/nchs/data/nhanes/OverviewBrochure English_May05.pdf

National Center for Health Statistics. (2006, August). *Supporting statement for request for clearance, National Health and Nutrition Examination Survey 2007–2008.* OMB No. 0920-0237. Retrieved February 16, 2007, from http://www.reginfo.gov/public/do/PRAView Document?ref_nbr=200610-0920-003

National Center for Health Statistics. (2007, February). *Current NHANES Web tutorial*. Retrieved February 15, 2007, from http://www.cdc.gov/nchs/tutorials/nhanes/index.htm

National Health and Nutrition Examination Survey: http://www.cdc.gov/nchs/nhanes.htm

NATIONAL HEALTH INTERVIEW SURVEY (NHIS)

The National Health Interview Survey (NHIS) is one of a family of health surveys conducted by the National Center for Health Statistics (NCHS), which is the U.S. government's health statistics agency. The NHIS was authorized in 1956 by an act of Congress—the National Health Survey Act—which stipulated that NCHS was "to provide for a continuing survey and special studies to secure accurate and current statistical information on the amount, disruption, and effects of illness and disability in the United States, and the services received for or because of such conditions." NCHS is now part of the Centers for Disease Control and Prevention (CDC), which is part of the U.S. Department of Health and Human Services.

The NHIS is an annual national household survey, conducted throughout the year, of the civilian noninstitutionalized population of the United States. Following a recent sample size reduction due to budget constraints, the annual NHIS sample now consists of approximately 87,500 persons of all ages who reside in approximately 35,000 households. Trained interviewers from the U.S. Bureau of the Census conduct in-person interviews using computer-assisted personal interviewing.

Core Questionnaire and Supplements

Since its inception in 1957, the NHIS has covered a wide range of health topics, including general health status, acute and chronic conditions, use of health care services, health insurance coverage, and disability and its consequences, as well as basic demographic and socioeconomic information. The NHIS questionnaire was substantially revised in 1997, and its stable core now contains three major submodules, which cover (1) the entire family (about whom a knowledgeable adult responds), (2) a randomly sampled child (about whom a knowledgeable adult responds), and (3) a randomly sampled adult (who responds for him- or herself).

The Family Core questionnaire covers everyone in the family, asking about demographics, general health, and health-related topics. It includes a set of age-appropriate questions on activities of daily living (ADLs) and instrumental activities of daily living (IADLs), and questions on cognitive functioning. Health conditions causing these limitations are identified. Other questions deal with use of medical services, medically attended injuries and poisonings, and disability days. Detailed information on health insurance coverage for each family member is obtained.

The Sample Adult Core covers adults ages 18 and over. Topics include functional limitations and selected conditions, such as heart disease, respiratory conditions, diabetes, arthritis and joint problems, and hearing and visual impairments. Other questions cover mental health status and impact, smoking, drinking, and leisure-time physical activity. Questions are asked about usage of health care services, including having a usual place of health care, hospitalizations, and use of doctor and dentist services.

The Sample Child Core roughly parallels the adult questionnaire; in both, the health conditions covered are age appropriate, and in the former, there are additional questions on developmental problems, school-related difficulties, and mental health.

Each year, supplements—additional questions that go into more detail and/or that cover new topics—are sponsored by other government agencies and added to the NHIS. Examples include several supplements on disability, including longitudinal ones, that were fielded in the 1980s and 1990s. Recent supplement subjects have been health promotion, diabetes, cancer, children's mental health, and complementary and alternative medicine. For example, the 2005 Cancer Control Supplement included topics on diet and nutrition, physical activity, tobacco usage, cancer screening, genetic testing, and family history; this was sponsored by the National Cancer Institute, National Institutes of Health (NIH), and the National Center for Chronic Disease Prevention and Health Promotion at CDC. Another example is the 2004 Children's Mental Health Supplement, which contained the Strengths and Difficulties Questionnaire, 32 questions asked of a parent or guardian about the child, sponsored by the National Institute of Mental Health at NIH. NHIS supplements, or variations of them, are often repeated in different years.

Release of Data

NCHS publicly releases NHIS microdata annually from both the core and supplements. Microdata collected during 2004 were released less than 7 months after the end of the data collection year. Currently, all public use files and supporting documentation for data years 1970 through the year of the most recent release are available without charge from the NHIS Web site. Previous years of public use files from 1963 through 1969 will soon be available for downloading from the NCHS Web site as well.

Since data year 2000, NCHS has been releasing quarterly estimates for 15 key health indicators through its Early Release (ER) Program. After each new quarter of data collection, these estimates are updated and then released on the NCHS Web site 6 months after the data collection quarter. The 15 measures covered by ER include (1) lack of health insurance coverage and type of coverage, (2) usual place to go for medical care, (3) obtaining needed medical care, (4) obesity, (5) leisure-time physical activity, (6) vaccinations, (7) smoking and alcohol consumption, and (8) general health status. For each of these health measures, a graph of the trend since 1997 is presented, followed by figures and tables showing age-specific, sex-specific, and race/ethnicity-specific estimates for the new data quarter. Key findings are highlighted. A separate in-depth report on health insurance is also updated and released every 3 months as part of the ER Program. Both quarterly ER reports are released only electronically, on the NCHS Web site.

In addition to releasing NHIS microdata to the public, NCHS staff members publish their own analyses of the data. Series 10 reports provide results of analyses of NHIS data in substantial detail. Among those series reports are three volumes of descriptive statistics and highlights published annually, based, respectively, on data from the NHIS Family Core, Sample Child Core, and Sample Adult Core. NCHS's series Advance Data From Vital and Health Statistics publishes single articles from the various NCHS programs. NCHS's annual report on the health status of the United States (*Health, United States*) contains numerous tables and other analytic results based on NHIS data.

Multiple years of NHIS microdata are periodically linked to other databases, such as the National Death Index and Medicare records. The National Death Index is an NCHS-maintained central computerized index of state death record information. Linkage to the NDI ultimately provides outcome information about underlying and contributing causes of death.

The NHIS also serves as a sampling frame for the Medical Expenditure Panel Survey (MEPS), which was designed to provide policymakers, health care administrators, businesses, and others with information about health care use and costs and to improve the accuracy of their economic projections. It surveys families and individuals, their medical providers, and their employers across the United States. The MEPS families are a subset of those interviewed within the previous year for the NHIS.

When analysis of NHIS data requires access to confidential microdata that are not released publicly, the NCHS Research Data Center allow researchers meeting certain qualifications to access such data under strict supervision. Researchers must submit a proposal for review and approval. Access may be on-site at NCHS or remotely.

Jane F. Gentleman and Susan S. Jack

See also Computer-Assisted Personal Interviewing (CAPI)

Further Readings

Adams, P. F., Dey, A. N., & Vickerie, J. L. (2005). *Summary health statistics for the U.S. population: National Health Interview Survey*. National Center for Health Statistics. Vital Health Stat Series 10, No. 233. Retrieved April 20, 2008, from http://www.cdc.gov/nchs/data/series/sr_10/sr10_233.pdf

Agency for Healthcare Research and Quality, Medical Expenditure Panel Survey: http://www.meps.ahrq.gov

Barnes, P., & Schiller, J. S. (2006). *Early release of selected estimates based on data from the January–June 2006 National Health Interview Survey*. National Center for Health Statistics. Retrieved April 20, 2008, from http://www.cdc.gov/nchs/nhis.htm

Bloom, B., & Dey, A. N. (2006). *Summary health statistics for U.S. children: National Health Interview Survey, 2005*. National Center for Health Statistics. Vital Health Stat Series 10, No. 231. Retrieved April 20, 2008, from http://www.cdc.gov/nchs/data/series/sr_10/sr10_231.pdf

Cohen, R. A., & Martinez, M. E. (2006). *Health insurance coverage: Early release of estimates from the National Health Interview Survey, January–June 2006*. National Center for Health Statistics. Retrieved April 20, 2008, from http://www.cdc.gov/nchs/nhis.htm

National Center for Health Statistics: http://www.cdc.gov/nchs

National Center for Health Statistics *Advance Data* publications: http://www.cdc.gov/nchs/products/pubs/pubd/ad/ad.htm

National Center for Health Statistics annual *Health, United States* publication: http://www.cdc.gov/nchs/hus.htm

National Center for Health Statistics National Death Index: http://www.cdc.gov/nchs/ndi.htm

National Center for Health Statistics Research Data Center: http://www.cdc.gov/nchs/r&d/rdc.htm

National Center for Health Statistics Series 10 reports: http://www.cdc.gov/nchs/products/pubs/pubd/series/sr10/ser10.htm

National Health Interview Survey: http://www.cdc.gov/nchs/nhis.htm

Pleis, J. R., & Lethbridge-Cejku, M. (2007). *Summary health statistics for U.S. Adults, National Health Interview Survey, 2005*. National Center for Health Statistics. Vital Health Stat 10(232). Retrieved April 20, 2008, from http://www.cdc.gov/nchs/data/series/sr_10/sr10_232.pdf

Schoenborn, C. A., Vickerie, J. L., & Powell-Griner, E. (2006, April 11). *Health characteristics of adults 55 years of age and over: United States, 2000–2003*. National Center for Health Statistics. Advance Data 370. Retrieved April 20, 2008, from http://www.cdc.gov/nchs/data/ad/ad370.pdf

NATIONAL HOUSEHOLD EDUCATION SURVEYS (NHES) PROGRAM

The National Household Education Surveys Program (NHES) is a series of nationally representative telephone surveys of households in the United States sponsored by the U.S. Department of Education's National Center for Education Statistics. The chief purpose of the surveys is to describe the educational activities and experiences of young children, school-age children, and adults. The NHES program conducts several surveys in three main topic areas: (1) adult education, (2) school-age children's education, and (3) education and care of young children. One of the most widely reported estimates from the NHES is the number of children being homeschooled in the United States. NHES is the only scientific sample survey that regularly produces estimates of the prevalence of homeschooling, estimated in 2003 at 1.1 million U.S. homeschooled children. NHES is also an important source of data about trends in the use of school choice in public schools, revealing that the number of children enrolled in chosen public schools, as opposed to assigned schools, rose from 11 to 15% between 1993 and 2003.

The NHES surveys were first conducted in 1991, and subsequent surveys have been administered in 1995, 1996, 1999, 2001, 2003, 2005, and 2007. Data collections have taken place during the period of January through March or April of these years, and most questions refer to the prior 12 months. All interviews are completed using computer-aided telephone interviewing (CATI). In each survey year, two or more surveys are administered concurrently in order to reduce administration costs. A common screener interview is administered to each sampled household. The NHES screener interview includes a roster of all household members and determines each household member's eligibility to be sampled for one of the extended interviews that is being administered.

Six core NHES surveys have been repeated at least twice and are planned for continuing administration: Early Childhood Program Participation; School Readiness; Parent and Family Involvement in Education; After-School Programs and Activities; Adult Education; and Adult Education for Work-Related Reasons. Other surveys have previously been administered but are not planned to be repeated: Civic Involvement; School Safety and Discipline; and the Household and Library Use Survey. Each year's NHES draws an independent cross-sectional sample; NHES is not a longitudinal study, but time-series analysis is possible because many questions have been repeated in different years.

In each NHES survey, interviews are completed with several thousand individuals. The adult surveys describe the population of civilian, noninstitutionalized adults 16 years of age or older and not enrolled in high school or below. Surveys regarding school-age children and very young children are completed by a knowledgeable adult, usually the child's mother.

Response rates on the NHES surveys have been high relative to most telephone surveys. The response rate on the NHES screener interview in 2005 was 67%. The overall weighted response rate for the Adult Education survey in 2005 was 48%, and the overall weighted response rate for both surveys regarding children in 2005 (Early Childhood Program Participation and After-School Programs and Activities) was 56%. The typical response rate pattern observed in NHES surveys is that surveys asking parents to talk about their children achieve a higher response rate than surveys asking adults to talk about their own education. These rates are achieved by using established techniques to maximize response rates, including sending an advance letter to all sampled households for which a vendor is able to determine a valid mailing address, paying a monetary incentive for participation, making repeated call attempts to each household at different times of day over a period of several weeks, and refusal conversion attempts, where sampled individuals who refuse to participate are asked to reconsider.

Like nearly all sample surveys of the general population conducted by the federal government, the NHES uses complex sampling procedures rather than simple random sampling. This means that the classical approaches to hypothesis testing and the estimation of sampling error and confidence intervals (which assume simple random sampling) are not appropriate for NHES data, as these procedures would generally overstate the precision of the estimates and lead researchers to erroneously conclude that the difference between two estimates is statistically significant when it is not.

Matthew DeBell

See also Advance Letters; Complex Sample Surveys; Computer-Assisted Telephone Interviewing (CATI); Incentives; Refusal Conversion

Further Readings

National Household Education Surveys Program: http://nces.ed.gov/nhes

Nolin, M. J., Montaquila, J., Nicchitta, P., Hagedorn, M., & Chapman, C. (2004). *National Household Education Surveys Program: 2001 methodology report*. Washington, DC: U.S. Department of Education, National Center for Education Statistics.

Princiotta, D., & Bielick, S. (2006). *Homeschooling in the United States: 2003*. Washington, DC: U.S. Department of Education, National Center for Education Statistics.

Tice, P., Chapman, C., Princiotta, D., & Bielick, S. (2006). *Trends in the use of school choice: 1993–2003*. Washington, DC: U.S. Department of Education, National Center for Education Statistics.

NATIONAL OPINION RESEARCH CENTER (NORC)

The National Opinion Research Center (NORC) is the oldest and largest university-based survey research organization in the United States. It was founded in 1941 at the University of Denver by Harry H. Field. Field was from Britain and had worked for the Gallup Organization and set up Gallup in Britain. Departing from the model of commercial public opinion firms established by Archibald Crossley, George Gallup, Elmo Roper, and others, Field wanted to conduct survey research in the public interest, to serve the non-profit and government sectors, to improve survey methods, and to advance public opinion research by reviewing and synthesizing results from all organizations. After Field's death in a plane crash in France in 1946, the new director, Clyde Hart, moved NORC in 1947 to the University of Chicago, where it has remained. NORC has played a leadership role in many areas of survey research: organizationally, methodologically, and substantively.

Field organized the first conference ever held in the new field of survey research in Central City, Colorado, in 1946, and this led directly to the founding of the American Association for Public Opinion Research (AAPOR) and the World Association for Public Opinion Research (WAPOR) in 1947.

NORC researchers have pioneered in studying the error structures of surveys and developing methodologies to improve survey quality. These efforts include Herbert Hyman's work in the 1950s on interviewer effects, Norman Bradburn's studies on the measurement of psychological well-being, Bradburn and Seymour Sudman's research on response effects, the studies of context effects by Kenneth Rasinski, Tom W. Smith, and Roger Tourangeau, and the studies conducted of employers, congregations, and voluntary associations using hypernetwork sampling from the General Social Survey (GSS).

NORC has also conducted seminal research in many areas. In 1942, it conducted the first national survey on race relations; this led to a long series on intergroup relations. In 1947, the first national study of occupational prestige was carried out. Measures of occupational prestige were then refined and updated in 1963–65 and in 1989 as part of NORC's GSS. In 1963, immediately following the death of President John F. Kennedy, the Kennedy Assassination Study was fielded. In 2001, in the aftermath of the September 11 terrorist attacks, NORC conducted the National Tragedy Study, drawing on many questions from the Kennedy Assassination Study and from the GSS. In 1970, for the Kinsey Institute, NORC carried out the first national survey to measure many aspects of sexual behavior, including homosexuality. On the 1985

GSS, the first national, egocentric, social network study was completed. In 1985–86, in Chicago, NORC conducted the first systematic probability sample of the homeless. In 1998, the first national sample of congregations was fielded.

Presently NORC has multiple offices in both the Chicago and Washington, D.C., areas. It is divided into three divisions: (1) administrative, (2) survey operations, and (3) academic centers. The administrative division covers basic management functions such as accounting and human resources.

The survey operations division designs and conducts data collection efforts. It is divided into several research departments along substantive lines: Economics, Labor, and Population; Education and Child Development; Health Survey, Program, and Policy Research; Information Technology; International Projects; Statistics and Methodology; and Substance Abuse, Mental Health, and Criminal Justice. Most frequently these departments carry out complex, large-scale, in-person surveys under contract with the federal government.

The academic division consists of several research centers: the Alfred P. Sloan Center on Parents, Children, and Work; the Center on the Demography and Economics of Aging; the Data Research and Development Center; the Ogburn-Stouffer Center for the Study of Social Organization; and the Population Research Center. These centers work with the research departments in designing surveys, conduct some surveys themselves, and analyze results from NORC surveys and other data sources.

One area of special concentration at NORC is panel studies. Over the years these have included such projects as the Midtown Manhattan Study, High School and Beyond, the old and new cohorts of the National Longitudinal Survey of Youth, the National Educational Longitudinal Study, and Baccalaureate and Beyond.

A second area of specialization is studies of societal change. In early years, these included surveys for the Department of State on foreign policy issues and trends on anti-Semitism and race relations. Since 1972, the GSS has monitored societal change with 26 nationally representative surveys and more than 1,000 time series.

A third area has been cross-national and comparative studies, including the Civic Culture Study in 1959, the Soviet Interview Project in 1980, the GSS-related International Social Survey Program from 1985 to the present, and the recent Qatar education project.

A final example of an area of concentration involves the establishment of professional standards for the field of survey research. As noted above, NORC was instrumental in establishing AAPOR and WAPOR. More recently NORC personnel played central roles in the adoption by AAPOR and WAPOR of *Standard Definitions: Final Disposition of Case Codes and Outcome Rates for Surveys*, the work of several National Academies of Science panels, and the formulation of the rules of the International Organization for Standardization for market, opinion, and social research.

NORC's work is very varied and covers many other areas are well. Other examples include the Florida Ballots Project, which counted and analyzed all contested ballots in the 2000 Florida general election; annual rankings of America's best hospitals, which identified the nation's top hospitals by specialty; the National Social Life, Health, and Aging Project, which examined the sexual behavior of older Americans; and Poetry in America, which studied exposure to this literary form.

Tom W. Smith

See also American Association for Public Opinion Research (AAPOR); General Social Survey (GSS); World Association for Public Opinion Research (WAPOR)

Further Readings

Bova, P., & Worley, M. P. (1991). *Bibliography of publications, 1941–1991: A fifty year cumulation.* Chicago: National Opinion Research Center.

Converse, J. M. (1987). *Survey research in the United States: Roots and emergence, 1900–1960.* Berkeley: University of California Press.

Hackett, J. (1992). *America by number: NORC Report 1991.* Chicago: National Opinion Research Center.

National Opinion Research Center: http://www.norc.org

Smith, T. W. (2007). The Midwest and the rise of survey research. In R. Sisson, C. Zacher, & A. Cayton (Eds.), *The American Midwest: An interpretive encyclopedia* (pp. 1723–1724). Bloomington: Indiana University Press.

NETWORK SAMPLING

Network sampling is widely used when rare populations are of interest in survey research. Typically, sampling frames do not exist for rare populations because usually there is little information on the size and magnitude of the population. Two main methods can be employed in a survey with an unknown population: *screening* and *salting*. The first way is to screen for respondents of interest during the interview, and the second approach is to acquire sample units through official records or documents. Both approaches have shortcomings. Screening requires high costs. Salting entails difficulties with obtaining membership information, because official personnel records may be confidential. Network sampling is considered an alternative to the previous ways of estimating rare populations in which sampling frame is almost impossible to obtain.

Network sampling is also called *snowball sampling* or *multiplicity sampling*. This sampling technique is widely used to estimate populations such as the homeless, Korean War veterans, and patients with rare forms of cancer. Particularly, it has been found that network sampling was much more efficient than other conventional sampling methods for estimating the number of cancer patients. Most network samples have employed family members, relatives, and friends as informants; network informants report about all persons in their network; and sizes vary to degree from respondent to respondent.

Indeed, obtaining an initial sampling frame is a prerequisite for any network sampling method, and the quality of that frame is essential for the ultimate success of the method. Although family members or relatives are used as the network for many of the sampling frames, it need not be restricted to them, depending on the topic of a study. For instance, let us suppose that Korean Americans living in Michigan are the target population of a study. Network sampling using families, relatives, friends, and even casual associates may be useful for this case. In addition to blood kinship, membership lists can be used: Korean religion membership lists, Korean association lists, and so on. That is to say, using multiple sources included in the network sampling increases the network frame in quality and coverage.

To estimate the unbiased survey statistics, weighting is necessary for network sampling; the total eligible respondents of a particular network are weighted by the reciprocal of one over the total number of the particular network. Generally, interviewer costs are a primary concern for the network sampling. In this method, interviewers should meet with potential respondents who were identified by informants to see whether the respondents are eligible for a particular survey. This process increases interviewer time and costs, though both depend largely on the size of network. However, this sampling reduces screening costs.

Geon Lee

See also Multiplicity Sampling; Respondent-Driven Sampling (RDS); Snowball Sampling

Further Readings

Sudman, S. (1976). *Applied sampling*. New York: Academic Press.

Sudman, S., & Freeman, H. E. (1988). The use of network sampling for locating the seriously ill. *Medical Care*, *26*(10), 992–999.

NEW YORK TIMES/CBS NEWS POLL

The *New York Times*/CBS News poll was the first newspaper–television polling partnership between two major national news organizations in the United States and was launched with a nationwide telephone survey of nearly 800 adults in early November 1975.

On November 4, 1975, the *CBS Evening News with Walter Cronkite* aired a report regarding the American public's attitudes toward President Ford and his response to the possible default of New York City. The following morning, "Poll Finds Public Thinks Ford Minimizes City Peril," an article by Robert Reinhold, was on page 1 of *The New York Times*.

That first poll evolved from discussions between Henry R. Lieberman, Assistant to the Executive Editor of *The New York Times*, and Warren Mitofsky of CBS News. It was followed by an agreement between the two organizations to conduct a series of monthly national telephone surveys and primary election day exit polls to cover the 1976 presidential election campaign. Both the *Times* and CBS News wanted access to their own political polling in order to add greater dimension to their 1976 political coverage and an independent news stream of exclusive polling data.

The partnership has endured and flourished over the years for a number of reasons. Newspapers and television network news are not in direct competition with each other. Each organization's expertise and their different needs enhance the end result. The partnership saves both organizations money. By sharing the work and the results, a poll essentially costs each partner half as much as a solo effort and guarantees two sets of eyes on every aspect of the polling operation.

That first contract worked out the long-standing agreements about the poll's name and when it would be released. In the paper, the poll is identified as the "*New York Times*/CBS News poll." On the CBS News broadcasts, it is the "CBS News/*New York Times* poll."

A joint poll is usually released first on the *CBS Evening News*, broadcast in the East at 6:30 p.m. At that time, CBS also releases the poll to their network radio and Web site. Their press release for the poll is then emailed to a wide audience, including the news wires and other media outlets.

The *Times* publishes the poll article in the paper the following morning. But, after 6:30 p.m. the evening before, the *Times* is free to post the poll story on its Web site. Some poll stories are also printed in *The International Herald Tribune*. The full question wording and results are also posted on both newspapers' Web sites.

Initially, responsibilities were divided for practical reasons. CBS already had an election unit in place, with statisticians and computer programmers, and so provided the sampling, weighting, and technical expertise.

From the beginning, the *Times* and CBS News handled their own fieldwork and continue to do so. The *Times* is in charge of hiring and training the interviewers and managing the data collection. When the surveys were conducted on paper, the interviewing was conducted on West 43rd Street in the advertising department of the *Times*—a large room with desks, telephones, and an advertising staff that cleared out by 5:00 p.m. and did not work weekends. Desks for weekday interviewing were located throughout the newsroom.

The introduction of CATI interviewing in 1991 necessitated the relocation of the interviewing operation to the CBS offices on West 57th Street. Currently, there is a dedicated survey room in the CBS Broadcast Center, with space for about 50 interviewers with monitoring capability and supervisor stations. The *Times* remains responsible for hiring and training the interviewers and maintaining records. But, as with many aspects of the *Times*/CBS News poll, the organizations work together on staffing issues.

There have been changes in the methodology and procedures over time. About the same time as the interviewing was switched to CATI technology, the sampling changed from Mitofsky-Waksberg sampling to list-assisted sampling. The weighting program has been adjusted over time. Some exit polls conducted by CBS News were joint projects with the *Times* until the major television networks first joined forces to conduct exit polls in 1990.

Both the *Times* and CBS News have small departments that create the questionnaires, manage the data collection, and analyze the poll results. The CBS News Election and Survey Unit works directly with executive producers and producers of the *Evening News*, *60 Minutes, The Early Show*, radio, and the Web. The News Surveys Department of the *Times* works directly with the national editor, the Washington Bureau, the Foreign and Metro News desks, and other department heads.

Teams from the *Times* and CBS News develop the questionnaire together, with each bringing subjects and questions to the table, often after consulting with reporters, editors, and producers. Usually the *Times*/CBS polls deal with national politics and policy, but polls often also contain questions on other topics, including business, sports, travel, and culture. Occasionally, polls are conducted with samples of respondents other than national adults, including state and local surveys and polls of convention delegates, business executives, and teenagers.

Although the questionnaire design and data collection are joint operations, the *Times* and CBS News go their separate ways once the survey is completed. Each organization receives tables with banners of standard variables and has access to an interactive system for generating custom tables. Every poll receives two simultaneous but independent analyses by separate teams. That can, and sometimes does, lead to different emphasis in the resulting broadcasts and articles.

Through the decades of collaboration, each side may (and does) conduct polls outside the partnership, often because of lack of interest in a specific polling topic or issue or an outlet by one of the partners. For example, polls in the New York metropolitan area or polls for special series in the *Times* are frequently conducted by the *Times* without CBS. CBS often does surveys without the *Times* for its own special broadcasts.

After more than 30 years interviewing about a half-million respondents in nearly 450 surveys, the partnership is still going strong.

Marjorie Connelly

See also List-Assisted Sampling; Media Polls; Mitofsky-Waksberg Sampling; Random-Digit Dialing (RDD)

Further Readings

Kagay, M. R. (1991). The use of public opinion polls by *The New York Times:* Some examples for the 1988 presidential election. In P. J. Lavrakas & J. K. Holley (Eds.), *Polling and presidential election coverage.* Newbury Park, CA: Sage.

Kagay, M. R. (1995). The evolving use of public opinion polls by *The New York Times:* The experience in the 1992 presidential election. In P. J. Lavrakas, M. W. Traugott, & P. V. Miller (Eds.), *Presidential election polls and the news media.* Boulder, CO: Westview.

Kagay, M. R. (2000). Continuing evolution in the use of public opinion polls by the *New York Times:* The 1996 presidential election experience. In P. J. Lavrakas & M. W. Traugott (Eds.), *Election polls, the news media, and democracy.* New York: Chatham House/CQ Press.

NEYMAN ALLOCATION

Stratified samples are commonly used when supplementary information is available to help with sample design. The precision of a stratified design is influenced by how the sample elements are allocated to strata. Neyman allocation is a method used to allocate sample to strata based on the strata variances and similar sampling costs in the strata. A Neyman allocation scheme provides the most precision for estimating a population mean given a fixed total sample size.

For stratified random sampling, the population is divided into H mutually exclusive strata. In each stratum, a simple random sample is drawn without replacement. Neyman allocation assigns sample units within each stratum proportional to the product of the population stratum size (N_h) and the within-stratum standard deviation (S_h), so that minimum variance for a population mean estimator can be achieved. The equation for Neyman allocation is

$$n_h = \frac{N_h S_h}{\sum_{h=1}^{H} N_h S_h} n,$$

where n_h is the sample size for stratum h and n is the fixed total sample size. The effect of Neyman allocation is to sample more heavily from a stratum when (a) the population size of the stratum is large; (b) the variability within the stratum is large, so that the heterogeneity needs to be compensated.

Of note, Neyman allocation is a special case of optimal allocation whose objective in sample allocation is to minimize variance of an estimator for a population mean for a given total cost. It is employed when the costs of obtaining sampling units are assumed to be approximately equal across all the strata. If the variances are uniform across all the strata as well, Neyman allocation reduces to proportional allocation where the number of sampled units in each stratum is proportional to the population size of the stratum. When the variances within a stratum are different and are specified correctly, Neyman allocation will give an estimator with smaller variance than proportional allocation.

The major barrier to the application of Neyman allocation is lack of knowledge of the population variances of the study variable within each stratum. In some situations, historical estimates of strata variances can be used to provide good approximation to Neyman allocation for the current survey sample. For example, the Medical Expenditure Panel Survey Insurance Component (MEPS IC) is an annual survey of establishments that collects information about employer-sponsored health insurance offerings. To implement Neyman allocation, stratum variance estimates were obtained from the 1993 National Employer Health Insurance Survey for the initial MEPS IC 1996 and later from prior MEPS IC surveys.

In situations where estimated population variances within each stratum are not easily available, an alternative is to find a surrogate variable (a proxy) that is closely related to the variable of interest and use its variances to conduct a Neyman allocation. For example, the U.S. Government Accountability Office conducted a survey in 2004–2005 to estimate the average and median purchase prices of specified covered outpatient drugs (SCODs) in a population of 3,450 hospitals. Since a direct measure of purchase prices for SCODs was not available at the time of sample selection, the total hospital outpatient SCOD charges to Medicare was used as a proxy to carry out the Neyman allocation.

In practice, Neyman allocation can also be applied to some selected strata instead of all strata, depending on specific survey needs. For example, the National Drug Threat Survey 2004 was administered to a probability-based sample of state and local law enforcement agencies. The sample frame of 7,930 law enforcement agencies was stratified into a total of 53 strata. Of those 53 strata, 50 strata were formed based on the geographic locations of the local law enforcement agencies. A Neyman allocation was used to allocate sample to these strata. The remaining three strata were constructed to represent specific groups of state and local law enforcement agencies, including all state-level and large local law enforcement agencies. To ensure a thorough analysis of the domestic drug situation, these three strata were sampled with certainty.

Ranked set sampling (RSS) is another sampling protocol that can benefit substantially from the implementation of Neyman allocation. In RSS, the various rank order statistics serve the role of strata in a stratified sampling approach. Neyman allocation in RSS assigns sample units for each rank order statistic proportionally to its standard deviation. That is,

$$n_h = \frac{S_h}{\sum\limits_{h=1}^{H} S_h} n.$$

Here, H refers to the total number of rank order statistics and S_h denotes the standard deviation for the hth rank order statistic.

Haiying Chen

See also Optimal Allocation; Proportional Allocation to Strata; Ranked-Set Sampling; Stratified Sampling

Further Readings

Cochran, W. G. (1977). *Sampling techniques* (3rd ed.). New York: Wiley.

Takahasi, K., & Wakimoto, K. (1968). On unbiased estimates of the population mean based on the sample stratified by means of ordering. *Annals of the Institute of Statistical Mathematics, 20,* 1–31.

900 Poll

A 900 poll is a one-question unscientific "survey" that typically is taken by having television viewers or radio listeners call into a 1-900-number that *involves a cost to the caller*—sometimes a considerable cost. A different 900-number is given for each "response" that the poll allows the self-selected respondents to choose as their answer to whatever the survey question is. These polls are typically sponsored over a brief period of time—often an hour or less, for example, within a television program or shortly after it ends. For example,

callers who prefer Contestant A (or Position A on an issue) and those who prefer Contestant B (or Position B on an issue) use separate 900-numbers. It is possible to offer callers more than two answer choices, and thus more than two 900-numbers, but typically these polls utilize only two or three choices.

Such polls have no scientific standing because there is no way to know what target population is represented by those who choose to dial in. Since this is a nonprobability sample, there is no valid way to calculate the size of the sampling error. Additional threats to their validity include the possibility that the same person will call in more than once.

Nonetheless these polls offer a vehicle for media organizations to provide their audience with a feeling of involvement in the programming, since the poll results are typically reported during the show and/or used to make some decision as part of the programming—for example, who won the competition. They also can serve as a source of revenue for the organization that conducts them, and, depending on how much is the charge to call in and how many people respond, they can generate a good deal of profit as they are relatively inexpensive to run.

Paul J. Lavrakas

See also 800 Poll; Nonprobability Sampling; Self-Selected Listener Opinion Poll (SLOP)

Nominal Measure

A *nominal measure* is part of taxonomy of measurement types for variables developed by psychologist Stanley Smith Stevens in 1946. Other types of measurement include ordinal, interval, and ratio. A nominal variable, sometimes referred to as a *categorical variable*, is characterized by an exhaustive and mutually exclusive set of categories. Each case in the population to be categorized using the nominal measure must fall into one and only one of the categories. Examples of the more commonly used nominal measures in survey research include gender, race, religious affiliation, and political party.

Unlike other types of measurement, the categories of a variable that is a nominal measure refer to discrete characteristics. No order of magnitude is implied when comparing one category to another. After the relevant attributes of all cases in the population being

Table 1 Example of three types of descriptive statistics appropriate for nominal measures

	Count	Proportion	Percentage (%)	Ratio (Males to Females)
Male	651	0.484	48.4	0.938
Female	694	0.516	51.6	
TOTAL	1345	1.000	100.0	

measured are examined, the cases that share the same criteria are placed into the same category and given the same label, for example, "Female" or "Male."

Numbers can be used as labels, but great care should be used when using the variable in statistical analyses. The number assignment in place of a more descriptive label is completely arbitrary. Because the categories of a nominal variable are without mathematically measurable relationship to each other, there is no measure of standard deviation to apply to such a measure. As a result, the types of statistical analysis that can be used with such variables are limited. The only appropriate measure of central tendency is the mode; the mean or median of such a variable is meaningless.

For each of the categories of a nominal variable, one can calculate a proportion, a percentage, and a ratio. The proportion would be the number of cases having the selected value of the variable divided by the total number of cases resulting in a value of zero (none of the cases), one (all of the cases), or a value in between. The percentage for the same category would simply be the proportion multiplied by 100. The ratio is a measure of two categories of the variable in relation to one another. Ratios are calculated by dividing one category by another category. Table 1 illustrates these three types of descriptive statistics appropriate for nominal measures.

Measures of the strength of the relationship between two nominal variables, often called *contingency tests*, can be calculated using a chi-square test, which compares the observed counts in each category to the expected values if there were no relationship. The Fisher's Exact test is appropriate when both nominal variables are dichotomous (have only two values). A variety of other nonparametric tests are available that are appropriate for a variety of situations, including empty cells in a cross-tabulation of two nominal variables, sensitivity to extremely large marginal counts, and other

factors that can disturb the underlying assumptions of the more commonly used chi-square and Fisher's Exact tests.

James Wolf

See also Chi-Square; Contingency Table; Interval Measure; Level of Measurement; Ordinal Measure; Ratio Measure

Further Readings

Stevens, S. S. (1946, June 7). On the theory of scales of measurement. *Science, 103*(2684), 677–680.

NONATTITUDE

Nonattitude refers to the mental state of having no attitude or opinion toward some object, concept, or other type of stimulus. In survey research, this is manifested by an overt *no opinion* or *don't know* response to an attitude question, but it may also be hidden by a random or guesswork choice of answers to avoid appearing ignorant. Additionally, it is likely that not all *no opinion* or *don't know* responses reflect nonattitudes. This makes it hard to estimate how many respondents have nonattitudes toward the object.

How the Problem Was Uncovered

The nonattitude problem became prominent when the National Election Survey (NES) reinterviewed panels of Americans at 2-year intervals in the 1950s. Political scientist Philip Converse observed the low *stability* of individuals' answers given 2 years apart on issues that had been widely discussed by political leaders and the media. Question reliabilities ranged from .23 to .46. He also noted a lack of constraint or structure in responses to different policies: Most people did not consistently choose liberal or conservative policies within a single survey. The mean correlation between domestic policy responses was .23. A survey of congressional candidates of the two parties, interviewed with the same questions, found a mean interitem correlation of .53. Later NES panel studies of political elites showed that their responses had much more reliability over time as well as much greater interitem correlation. These findings were confirmed by panel studies in the 1970s and surveys since in many countries.

Converse concluded that a great many people had no opinions on major issues of the day and were concealing this by randomly choosing responses rather than answer "Don't know," "Undecided," or "No opinion" even when these alternatives were offered in a nonjudgmental manner. The observed (low) correlations over time and between issues could be produced by one stratum holding real opinions, which were highly stable and consistent, and another stratum of covert nonopinion-holders expressing pseudo-opinions. Assuming no real attitude change over the 2-year periods, he estimated the percentage of covert non-opinion-holders on each question from the number of changed answers, added in the overt nonopinions, and argued that from 20% to 80% of the public had nonattitudes on a wide range of policy questions. This cast doubt on the meaning of most reported opinion survey results, and on the ability of much of the public to form meaningful opinions on the political issues of the day and influence elite decision making. It also led to a major methodological, theoretical, and ideological controversy.

Alternative Models With Latent Attitudes

Critics analyzing the same data rejected the idea that a large part of the public had nonattitudes on leading public issues. Alternative theories to explain the observed instability and incoherence of responses include the following:

1. Measurement error produced by vague and ambiguous questions, concealing real attitudes, which could be revealed by better questions

2. The influence of temporary stimuli—events in the news or in personal life—leading to wide variations in momentary feelings around underlying attitudes

3. The possibility that each object has a variety of elements or considerations about which the individual has positive or negative feelings, but "samples" unsystematically in answering the questions—perhaps randomly, perhaps in response to recent events or cues given by question wording or sequence

4. Those who more systematically inventory the considerations they hold in mind may have a near balance of positive and negative feelings—an ambivalence making their answers unstable from

time to time or under different question wordings, although they have strong feelings about the issue.

Critics of the nonattitude hypothesis have used structural equation models to show that the pattern of observed (low) correlations could be the result of most people having stable underlying attitudes, albeit very weakly connected to their responses to the particular questions. According to some estimates, these *latent attitudes* were quite stable, with correlations over 2-year periods ranging from .8 to .9. Instead of a public made up of people with attitudes and people without, public responses in a particular issue area might come from a *latent continuum* of attitude holding, ranging from those with highly reliable and inter-related opinions (such as those found in elites), through those with general pre-dispositions producing only modest degrees of reliability and structure, to a residue with total absence of attitudes, admitted or concealed. Another model uses the idea of *issue publics*—that there are small groups of people with stable, organized ideas in particular issue areas but with only loose underlying attitudes, or none at all, toward policies in other areas. The rest of the public may have poorly structured attitudes in all of the areas, or nonattitudes in some or all. Because political elites have to inform themselves, discuss, and take stands on a wide range of issues, they develop consistent attitudes, based on a general ideology or party loyalty linking many issues.

All these alternative models find stable underlying attitudes in the public at the expense of admitting that public responses to specific policy questions are unstable and only loosely connected to real attitudes. Since the same questions produced stable and coherent answers from political elites and were worded in the terms found in the political discourse of the media, candidates, and decision makers, the large error terms calculated for the questions can be interpreted as reflecting the weakness of public opinion, not the survey technique.

Do Nonattitudes Matter?

A public poorly equipped to relate its underlying attitudes to current policy issues would seem little more likely to have a strong influence on policy than one with nonattitudes. Benjamin Page and Robert Shapiro counter that the nonattitudes or weakly connected attitudes to specific issues do not cripple democracy, because *collective public opinion*, the aggregate of favorable and unfavorable attitudes toward policies and candidates, is rather stable and changes rationally to respond to social and economic problems. They admit imperfections in the process, including failures of the information-providing system, elite misleading or manipulation, and the biasing effects of economic inequality on the "marketplace of ideas," but consider the past 50 years of American experience as evidence that public opinion matters. Comparative research across societies is needed to show which kinds of parties, media institutions, and social organization do better at overcoming the nonattitude problem and improve the correspondence of policies with the public's interests and values.

How Surveys Can Deal With the Nonattitude Problem

Remedies for the survey researchers' nonattitude problem are of several kinds:

1. Screening questions can cut down the number of pseudo-opinions that obscure the picture of actual public opinion.

2. Multi-item scales within issue areas reduce reliance on unreliable single questions. They allow factor and latent attitude analysis to identify underlying attitude dimensions and test the extent to which these dimensions are related to particular policy or candidate choices.

3. Given enough items, the consistency of respondents' attitudes can be measured by the spread of item responses around the respondent's mean position. Using intercorrelation of items to measure attitude constraint at the group level can be misleading if the group has low variance; low intercorrelations may result from high consensus rather than nonattitudes.

4. Nonopinions that slip through the screening questions can be detected by asking questions that reveal contradictory answers and open-ended probes that reveal empty responses.

5. Ideally, the same people should be reinterviewed, preferably several times over a period of years, to check on stability of answers and underlying attitudes and to distinguish stable attitude change from measurement error and weak attitudes.

6. For some purposes, researchers may be interested in what people's attitudes would be, or whether

nonattitudes would be replaced by attitudes, if they were exposed to new information or arguments. One can postulate a universe of *potential opinion response* under different conditions and set up survey experiments to sample from that universe. Every opinion poll is an "experiment" on how people respond to certain formulations of issues, given their exposure to certain experiences, information, recent news, and guidance by opinion leaders. What people were actually thinking before the interviewer arrived can only be approximated by surveys. What they would think if better informed or encouraged to deliberate more seriously may also be worth trying to approximate.

Allen H. Barton

See also Attitude Measurement; Attitudes; Cognitive Aspects of Survey Methodology (CASM); Deliberative Poll; Don't Knows (DKs); Measurement Error; Reliability; Validity

Further Readings

Converse, P. E. (1970). The nature of belief systems in mass publics. In D. E. Apter (Ed.), *Ideology and discontent* (pp. 206–261). New York: Free Press.

Page, B. I., & Shapiro, R. Y. (1992). *The rational public*. Princeton, NJ: Princeton University Press.

Saris, W. E., & Sniderman, P. M. (Eds.). (2004). *Studies in public opinion: Attitudes, nonattitudes, measurement error, and change*. Princeton, NJ: Princeton University Press.

Smith, T. W. (1984). Nonattitudes: A review and evaluation. In C. F. Turner & E. Martin (Eds.), *Surveying subjective phenomena* (Vol. 2, pp. 215–255). New York: Russell Sage Foundation.

Zaller, J. R. (1992). *The nature and origins of mass opinion*. Cambridge, UK: Cambridge University Press.

NONCAUSAL COVARIATION

Although correlation is a necessary condition for causation, it is not a sufficient condition. That is, if X and Y can be shown to correlate, it is possible that X may cause Y or vice versa. However, just because correlation is established between the two variables, it is not certain that X causes Y or that Y causes X. In instances when X and Y are correlated but there is no empirical evidence that one causes the other, a researcher is left with a finding of *noncausal covariation*. A researcher can speculate that one variable causes the other, but unless there is empirical evidence demonstrating an internally valid casual relationship, the researcher has no solid ground upon which to claim the relationship is causal.

In survey research, researchers rarely have valid evidence upon which to base conclusions of causation. Many researchers forget this and often interpret and report their results as though a causal relationship does exist between variables. For example, a researcher may find a correlation between minority status and the willingness to cooperate in a survey when sampled. However, merely finding that minority status is correlated with someone's response propensity is not sufficient to claim that being a racial or ethnic minority person "causes" one to be less likely to participate in surveys. Instead, it is likely that some other variables that are correlated with both being a minority and not being as willing to participate in surveys, such as educational attainment, are the real causal agents.

To demonstrate a causal relationship using a research design with strong internal validity, a true experiment is necessary. Experiments require that random assignment of respondents be carried out with exposure to different levels of the independent variable that the researcher controls. Then, in its simplest form, the experiment will show whether the group assigned to one level of the independent variable shows statistically different levels of the dependent variable than does the group exposed to the other level of the independent variable. If it does, then a causal relationship has been identified. For example, if survey respondents were randomly assigned to one of two levels of prepaid incentives ($5 or $10), then the researcher could determine whether the difference in incentives changed the response rate of the group getting the higher incentive. If it did, then the researcher has evidence of causation, not merely correlation.

Unfortunately, there are many relationships that survey researchers are interested in studying that do not readily lend themselves to experimentation. Although there are other statistical techniques that can be used to investigate whether a correlational relationship is likely to also represent a casual relationship, without an experimental design, a researcher cannot be as confident about drawing cause-and-effect conclusions and often must resign herself or himself to acknowledging that the relationship is one of noncausal correlation.

Paul J. Lavrakas

See also Dependent Variable; Experimental Design; Independent Variable; Internal Validity; Random Assignment

Further Readings

Babbie, E. (2006). *The practice of social research* (11th ed.). Belmont, CA: Wadsworth.

Campbell, D. T., & Stanley, J. C. (1963). *Experimental and quasi-experimental designs for research*. Boston: Houghton-Mifflin.

NONCONTACT RATE

The noncontact rate for a survey measures the proportion of all sampled cases that are *never contacted* despite the various efforts that the researchers may set in motion to make contact. By default, if a sampled case is never contacted, then no original data for the survey can be gathered from it, other than observations an in-person interviewer might make of the housing structure or neighborhood. For surveys in which the initial sampling unit is a household or business and then there is a respondent sampled within that unit, a noncontact rate can be calculated both at the unit level and at the within-unit (respondent) level. In theory, a noncontact rate of zero (0.0) means that every eligible sampled case was contacted, whereas a noncontact rate of one (1.0) means none of the sampled eligible cases were contacted. Neither of these extreme conditions is likely to occur in a survey. However, the best of commercial, academic, and government surveys in the United States achieve noncontact rates of less than 2%, meaning that more than 49 of every 50 eligible sampled cases are contacted at some point during the field period.

In face-to-face and telephone surveys of the general public, businesses, or specifically named persons, noncontacts result from no human at a household or business ever being reached by an interviewer during the survey's field period, despite what is likely to be many contact attempts across different days of the week and times of the day or evening. In mail and Internet surveys, noncontacts result from the survey request never reaching the sampled person, household, or business due to a bad address, transmittal (delivery) problems, or the person never being at the location to which the survey request is sent during the field period.

Calculating a noncontact rate is not as straightforward as it may first appear due to the many sampled cases in almost all surveys for which the researcher is uncertain (a) whether they are eligible and/or (b) whether they really were "contacted" but did not behave in such a way that provided the researcher with any certainty that contact actually occurred.

Unit-Level Noncontact Rate

At the unit level (household or business), the numerator of the noncontact rate can be computed by tallying up all those sampled units for which the researchers are certain contact attempts were made. In addition to these cases, the researchers must make an informed decision about what portion of the units for which it is uncertain if contact was made also should be included in the numerator (and the denominator). This uncertainty differs when the survey is interviewer-administered versus when it is done via mail or Internet. In the case of in-person surveys, interviewers who approach homes or businesses can make informed judgments about whether the unit looks to be occupied. If it is determined to be occupied and no contact is ever made with an occupant, then that unit must be included in the numerator (and the denominator) of the noncontact rate calculation. If it is determined the unit is not occupied then that unit is not counted as a noncontact and thus not counted in the numerator (and may or may not be counted in the denominator depending on whether all sampled cases or only "eligible" cases are included in the denominator). This estimation of eligibility (referred to as e) of which additional units to count as noncontacts is further complicated when a survey has unusual eligibility criteria (e.g., only adults aged 35–49 years), because some of the apparent noncontacts would have been found to actually be ineligible had contact been made. In these surveys, the researchers must make informed (and defensible) decisions about how to estimate which of these cases should be included in the numerator of the unit-level noncontact rate calculation. The denominator of the unit-level noncontact rate can be calculated either by including all cases, or by including all known eligible cases, or by including all known eligible cases plus an estimate (e) of the portion of unknown eligibility cases that are judged to be eligible. As noted above, for mail and Internet surveys, sampled cases from which there is no reply whatsoever to the researchers are very difficult to classify as to whether contact ever was made. Again, the researchers need to make a reasonable judgment about what proportion of these cases should be counted as eligible and what portion of these should be counted as being implicit refusals rather than as noncontacts in the noncontact rate calculation. Any of these cases that are counted as refusals should *not* enter into the noncontact rate numerator.

Respondent-Level Noncontact Rate

When a survey samples a specific respondent within a unit, then a respondent-level noncontact rate also can be calculated. The respondent-level rate differs from the unit level in that some of the contacted units will end the field period as a noncontact at the respondent level, but not at the unit level. That is, even though contact has been made with some other person at the home or business, no contact is ever made with the selected respondent. Because of this, the respondent level noncontact rate will almost always be higher than the unit-level rate and will never be lower. Apart from this, the considerations that apply when calculating a unit-level noncontact rate are essentially the same ones that apply when calculating the rate at the respondent level.

Paul J. Lavrakas

See also *e*; Eligibility; Field Period; Noncontact; Standard Definitions; Unit Level

Further Readings

AAPOR. (2006). *Standard definitions: Final dispositions of case codes and outcome rates for surveys.* Retrieved April 21, 2008, from http://www.aapor.org/uploads/ standarddefs_4.pdf

NONCONTACTS

Noncontacts are a disposition that is used in telephone, in-person, mail, and Internet surveys both as a temporary and a final disposition. Two primary types of noncontacts can occur in surveys. The first type occurs when a researcher makes contact with a household or other sampling unit, and no one is present to receive the contact. The second type of noncontact occurs when a researcher makes contact with a household or other sampling unit, but the selected respondent is unavailable to complete the questionnaire.

For example, the first type of noncontact occurs during in-person surveys when an interviewer visits a household unit and finds no one there (but does find clear evidence that the unit is occupied). Noncontacts also occur when contact is made with a household or other sampling unit but the selected respondent is not available to complete the questionnaire at the time of contact. For example, this type of noncontact occurs with in-person surveys when an interviewer visits a sampled address, determines that the address is a household (or other sampled unit), administers the introductory script and respondent selection procedures to someone at the address, and then learns that the selected respondent is not available to complete the interview. This type of noncontact is very similar for telephone surveys and occurs whenever an interviewer dials a case, reaches a household, administers the introductory script and respondent selection procedures for the survey, and learns that the designated respondent is not available at the time of the call. Because contact has been made with someone within the designated sampling unit, cases that result in this type of noncontact usually are considered eligible cases and thus are included when computing survey response rates.

Noncontacts may also occur in mail and Internet surveys, but the nature of these surveys makes it very difficult for researchers to know when this is happening and makes it almost impossible to differentiate between the two types of noncontacts. For example, in a mail survey, the questionnaire may be delivered to a household when the residents are away for the entire field period of the survey. Similarly, in an Internet survey the respondent may be away from email and the Internet for the entire field period, or the questionnaire may be sent to an email address that the respondent does not check during the field period of the survey. Only if the researcher receives information (such as, in the case of an Internet survey, an automated email reply noting that a respondent is away) specifying that the survey questionnaire was sent to and received by the named respondent is the survey researcher able to determine conclusively that a noncontact has taken place.

Because noncontacts usually are considered to be eligible cases or cases of unknown eligibility (depending on the type of noncontact), researchers continue to process these cases throughout the field period. In order to better manage survey sampling pools, many researchers assign different disposition codes to the two different types of noncontacts. These disposition codes allow researchers to manage the sample more

precisely. For example, noncontacts in which no contact is made with anyone at the household or other sampling unit often are recontacted on a variety of days and times (or after a specified period of time in a mail or Internet survey) to increase the chances of making contact with someone at the household or other sampling unit. For cases in which contact is made with someone in a household or other sampling unit (but the selected respondent is not available), the researcher can work to identify a good time to recontact the selected respondent. Because these types of noncontacts are a temporary disposition, it is important that researchers learn as much as possible about when to try to contact the selected respondent and then use any information learned to optimize the timing of additional contact attempts and, in doing so, to maximize the chances of converting the noncontact disposition into a completed interview.

Noncontact also can be used as a final disposition if (a) it occurs on the final contact attempt for a case, (b) previous contact was made during the field period but there was no success in completing the questionnaire at that time, and (c) there was never a previous refusal outcome for the case. If there was a previous refusal outcome, the case should be given the final disposition of "refusal" even if the last contact attempt resulted in a "noncontact."

Matthew Courser

See also Busies; Callbacks; Final Dispositions; Response Rates; Temporary Dispositions

Further Readings

American Association for Public Opinion Research. (2006). *Standard definitions: Final dispositions of case codes and outcome rates for surveys* (4th ed.). Lenexa, KS: Author.
Lavrakas, P. J. (1993). *Telephone survey methods: Sampling, selection, and supervision* (2nd ed.). Newbury Park, CA: Sage.

Noncontingent Incentives

Noncontingent incentives are traditionally used in survey research as a way of increasing survey response rates. The concept of noncontigent versus contingent incentives is that a noncontigent incentive is given to the respondent regardless of whether the survey is completed, whereas a contingent incentive is given *contingent* on the respondent's cooperation in completing the survey. Typically, the noncontingent incentive would be given at the time the respondent receives the request to complete the survey. This type of incentive is most commonly used with mailed surveys, although it can be used in any survey mode. The most common type of noncontingent incentive in survey research is a monetary incentive paid in the form of cash or as a cash alternative, such as a check. The recent introduction of cash cards and gift cards have made them another viable option for monetary incentive use in surveys. Many nonmonetary incentives have been used to enhance response rates in surveys. Some examples of nonmonetary incentives that can be given as a noncontingent incentive include sweepstakes entries, videos, gas cards, coupons, online credits, small household appliances, books, electronic devices, small gadgets, and knickknacks.

Don Dillman advises that the proper use of noncontingent monetary incentives is one of the most important strategies a researcher can use to improve survey response rates. Social exchange theory postulates that small (i.e., token) noncontingent incentives make the respondent feel socially obligated, that is, "They already gave me something, so now I should do the survey for them."

The scholarly literature shows a clear consensus that the use of a small noncontingent monetary incentive will increase cooperation rates in surveys significantly and is more effective than contingent incentives of considerably greater value. When considering which type of incentive, if any, to use in a particular survey, the researcher should consider the type of survey instrument (mailed, phone, Internet, intercept), the relative importance of the response rate, the level of effort required to complete the survey, the probable motivation of respondents, and the possible need to *differentially incent* members of some hard-to-reach demographic subgroups. For simple and short mailed surveys, short phone interviews, and short Internet surveys, an incentive is not likely to be needed. As the length and complexity of the survey increase or respondent engagement (e.g., level of interest) decreases, the need to consider the use of a noncontingent incentive is likely to increase. Care should be taken to ensure that the incentive offered is appropriate for the respondents being surveyed and does not introduce bias into the behavior of the respondent. An example of an inappropriate incentive would be a free DVD rental offered for participation in a television viewing survey. The respondent behavior that was being measured would most likely be impacted and the results may be biased.

The amount of incentive offered to the respondent should not be out of proportion to the effort required to complete the survey. A respondent who is given "too high" a noncontingent incentive amount as the sole motivating factor in the decision to cooperate in the survey may not answer the survey as accurately as someone else who received a noncontingent incentive of more modest value. Researchers should be aware of this *buying cooperation* phenomenon, which may cause some respondents to provide answers they think the researcher wants from them rather than providing accurate answers. Conversely, some respondents may have become so accustomed to receiving a noncontingent incentive when sampled for a survey that they may dismiss any survey request that does not offer one.

Norm Trussell

See also Contingent Incentives; Economic Exchange Theory; Incentives; Social Exchange Theory

Further Readings

Dillman, D. A. (1991). The design and administration of mail surveys. *Annual Review of Sociology, 17,* 225–249.

Dillman, D. A. (2000). *Mail and Internet surveys: The tailored design method.* New York: Wiley.

James, J. M., & Bolstein, R. (1990). The effect of monetary incentives and follow-up mailings on the response rate and response quality on mail surveys. *Public Opinion Quarterly, 54,* 346–361.

Singer, E., Van Hoewyk, J., Gebler, N., Trivellore, T., & McGonagle, K. (1999). The effect of incentives on response rates in interviewer-mediated surveys. *Journal of Official Statistics, 15,* 231–250.

Singer, E., Van Hoewyk, J., & Maher, M. P. (2000). Experiments with incentives in telephone surveys. *Public Opinion Quarterly, 64,* 189–205.

Trussell, N., & Lavrakas, P. J. (2004). The influence of incremental increases in token cash incentives on mail survey response: Is there an optimal amount? *Public Opinion Quarterly, 68,* 349–367.

Noncooperation Rate

Noncooperation occurs when a research unit is able to cooperate but clearly demonstrates that it will *not* take required steps to complete the research process. The noncooperation rate compares the number of research units that refuse to cooperate to the number of all potentially eligible units. Noncooperation, along with noncontacts, compromises the majority of survey nonresponse. In survey research, noncooperation often takes three basic forms:

1. *Household refusals* refer to the refusals that occur shortly after the household has been requested to participate in the research and before a designated respondent has been selected from within the household. The reasons of household refusals often involve "Not interested," "Don't have time," and "Don't do surveys." No comment hang-ups during a telephone interviewer's introduction of the survey often occur, especially when the interviewer is speaking English and the respondent lives in a non-English-speaking household.

2. *Respondent refusals* refer to a refusal to participate by the designated respondent selected within the household. Respondent refusals might be harder to convert, since the refusal was given by the person who should be interviewed and not by a gatekeeper within the household.

3. *Breakoffs*, which are a form of partial completion, refer to instances in which the respondent does not continue through the major part of the questionnaire. Breakoffs are different from other partial interviews because the proportion of questions completed in other partials may be considered as sufficient response, depending on the definition of response rate used. The standard of being a sufficient partial response is pre-determined by the researchers; the researcher should always provide a clear definition. For example, legitimate partial completions might be defined as cases with 50% to 94% of the questions answered. Breakoffs are considered as noncooperation, similar to refusals, as some of these are respondents merely hang up on the interviewer after questioning has started without saying anything more.

The most common way to calculate noncooperation rate (NCR) is to use the proportion of all cases in which a sample unit refuses to complete an interview out of all potentially eligible cases; this is comparable to a refusal rate. The numerator includes cases in which the household refuses to start the questionnaire, or the identified respondent refuses to start, or the identified respondent refuses to complete the interview. The denominator is the number of all eligible cases, as indicated in the following formula:

$$NCR1 = (Household\ Refusals + Respondent\ Refusals$$
$$+ Breakoffs)/(Interviews + Partials$$
$$+ Household\ Refusals + Respondent\ Refusals$$
$$+ Breakoffs + Noncontacts$$
$$+ Other\ Eligible\ Nonresponse$$
$$+ Unknown\ Eligibility)$$

NCR1 is the most conservative approach to calculating the noncooperation rate.

Other versions of the noncooperation rate differ in the composition of the denominator. The following formula (NCR2) includes estimates of the proportion of cases of unknown eligibility that actually are eligible. By estimating such a proportion (i.e., *e*), researchers aim to make a more precise computation of all potentially eligible units. However, the estimation of *e* must be guided by the best available scientific information on what share the eligible cases make among the unknown cases, and one must not select a proportion simply in order to decrease the noncooperation rate. The basis for the estimate must be explicitly stated and detailed.

$$NCR2 = (Household\ Refusals + Respondent\ Refusals$$
$$+ Breakoffs)/(Interviews + Partials$$
$$+ Household\ Refusals + Respondent\ Refusals$$
$$+ Breakoffs + Noncontacts$$
$$+ Other\ Nonresponse$$
$$+ [e * Unknown\ Eligibility])$$

A third type of noncooperation rate calculation (NCR3) discards all cases of unknown eligibility. It means either a special case of NCR2, in which *e* is assumed to be zero (i.e., that there are no eligible cases among the cases of unknown eligibility) or the rare case in which there are no cases of unknown eligibility. This formula generates the maximum nonresponse rate, since the denominator is the smallest among the three computations:

$$NCR3 = (Household\ Refusals + Respondent\ Refusals$$
$$+ Breakoffs)/(Interviews + Partials$$
$$+ Noncooperation + Noncontacts$$
$$+ Other\ Nonresponse)$$

Weiyu Zhang

See also Completion Rate; Cooperation Rate; Designated Respondent; *e*; Hang-Up During Introduction (HUDI); Household Refusal; Noncooperation; Nonresponse Rates; Partial Completion; Refusal Rate; Respondent Refusal; Response Rates

Further Readings

American Association for Public Opinion Research. (2006). *Standard definitions: Final dispositions of case codes and outcome rates for surveys* (4th ed.). Lenexa, KS: Author.

Groves, R. M., Dillman, D. A., Eltinge, J. L., & Little, R. J. A. (2002). *Survey nonresponse*. New York: Wiley.

NONCOVERAGE

Every scientific survey has a target population that is operationalized by a sampling frame. Ideally, all units in the sampling frame should match those in the target population on a one-to-one basis. In reality, misalignment between the two occurs and is termed *coverage error*. Noncoverage is one of the elements of coverage error arising from the imperfectness of a sampling frame that fails to include some portion of the population. Because these frames cover less than what they should, noncoverage is also termed *undercoverage*. Noncoverage is the most frequently occurring coverage problem, and it may have serious effects because this problem cannot be recognized easily in the given frame. Because the target population is defined with extent and time, the magnitude of noncoverage depends on the maintenance of the frame. Depending on whether the households or people covered by the frame differ from those not covered, noncoverage may introduce biases (coverage error) in survey estimates.

The classic example of noncoverage is the *Literary Digest* poll predicting Alf Landon as the overwhelming winner over the incumbent president, Franklin D. Roosevelt, in the 1936 election. Although it had surveyed 10 million people, their frame was comprised of the *Literary Digest* readers, a list of those with telephone service, and a list of registered automobile owners. Although the general voter population was the target population of the poll, the sampling frame excluded a large proportion of the target population and, more important, an unevenly higher proportion of the middle- and low-income Democratic voters. The general voter population was more likely to differ in their preference of presidential candidate than those who were covered in the frames. Because the sampling frame failed to represent the target population, the poll results favoring Landon's victory were in error.

There are two main sources of noncoverage error in general population surveys. The first is the problem of covering housing units and the second of covering people within housing units. The effect of these sources in noncoverage differs by survey mode. Telephone surveys are discussed more frequently than other surveys with respect to noncoverage error. Between the two noncoverage sources, coverage of people within housing units in telephone surveys has not been found to be as problematic as coverage of housing units. This is because the landline (wired) telephone survey frames are constructed using a directory listing, random-digit dialing, or a combination of the two. No matter which frame is used, telephone surveys cover households that own a telephone and subscribe to a telephone service. Because ownership of a landline telephone is found to be associated with socioeconomic status, it is acknowledged that the telephone is not the ideal mode for surveys in which the socioeconomically disadvantaged population is an important component of the sample. Since 2002, households in the United States with only cellular (mobile) phones have emerged as another noncoverage problem in traditional telephone surveys whose frames are based on landline telephone numbers. Because the cellular phone–only population in the United States (estimated to exceed 20% of adults in 2008) has distinctive characteristics and its proportion in the general population is continuing to grow, the survey research field is making a concerted effort to alleviate this problem.

Face-to-face and mail surveys use area frames with lists of geographical units or list frames based on addressees or other household identifiers. Frames for face-to-face surveys are further developed by enumerating members in those units. The completeness of the latter component has found to be more problematic than housing unit coverage. This is because enumeration requires the asking about specific members of the unit oftentimes before adequate rapport has been established with whomever answers the door. Interviewers' behavior at the door and the information from the responding member affects the completeness of the enumeration. Males, ethnic and racial minorities, and younger people are more subject to within-unit noncoverage than others.

Noncoverage is a major hurdle for Internet and Web surveys of the general population because a substantial proportion does not have Internet access. The coverage of the Internet is uneven across certain demographic and socioeconomic variables, such as age, education, income, and race/ethnicity. This systematic difference adds complexities and errors in Internet surveys arising from noncoverage. This also results in another distinctive problem, in that it is not feasible even to create a reliable frame for general population Internet surveys.

Sunghee Lee

See also Coverage Error; Internet Surveys; Post-Stratification; Random-Digit Dialing (RDD); Sampling Frame; Target Population; Undercoverage; Unit Coverage; Web Survey, Within-Unit Coverage

Further Readings

Groves, R. M. (1989). *Survey costs and survey errors.* New York: Wiley.

NONDIFFERENTIATION

Survey respondents are routinely asked to answer batteries of questions employing the same response scale. For example, in an effort to understand consumer preferences, respondents might be asked to rate several products on a scale of 1 to 5, with 1 being "very poor" to 5 being "very good." *Nondifferentiation* (sometimes called "straight-lining") occurs when respondents fail to differentiate between the items with their answers by giving identical (or nearly identical) responses to all items using the same response scale. That is, some respondents might give a rating of 2 to all products, producing nondifferentiated answers.

In the survey literature, nondifferentiation is identified as a very strong form of satisficing. According to the notion of satisficing, when respondents are unable to or unwilling to carefully go through all the cognitive steps required in answering survey questions, they may satisfice by looking for an easy strategy or cues to provide a satisfactory (but not optimal) answer. Nondifferentiation is such an easy response strategy that it saves cognitive effort; respondents presumably do *not* retrieve information from memory and do *not* integrate retrieved information into a judgment (or estimation). Instead, they may interpret each

question within a battery superficially and select a reasonable point on the response scale and stick with that point for all items in the battery. The answers are thus selected without referring to any internal psychological cues relevant to the specific attitude, belief, or event of interest.

Like other satisficing behaviors, nondifferentiation is most likely to occur when (a) respondents do not have the ability to answer optimally, (b) respondents are not motivated to answer carefully, and/or (c) the questions are difficult to answer. Studies have demonstrated empirically that nondifferentiation is more common among respondents with lower levels of cognitive capacity (such as respondents with less education or with less verbal ability) and more prevalent toward the end of a questionnaire. In addition, nondifferentiation is more prevalent among respondents for whom the question's topic is more personally important.

Nondifferentiation may occur regardless of the mode of data collection. However, there is evidence suggesting that nondifferentiation is more likely to occur with modes that do not promote respondent motivation or use more difficult response tasks. For instance, Web surveys have been shown to promote nondifferentiating responses, especially when questions are displayed in a grid format (i.e., a tabular format where question stems are displayed in the left-most column and response options are shown along the top row). In addition, Web surveys appear to lead to more nondifferentiation than interviewer-administered modes. Within interviewer-administered modes, respondents are found to give more nondifferentiating responses to the telephone surveys than to the face-to-face interviews.

Nondifferentiation is a form of measurement error and thus decreases data quality (both validity and reliability). Of considerable concern, the presence of nondifferentiating responses artificially inflates intercorrelations among the items within the battery and thus suppresses true differences between the items. Therefore, measures should be taken to reduce the extent of nondifferentiation in a survey. Survey researchers, for example, should take measures to help increase respondent motivation to provide thoughtful answers (e.g., interviewers instructing or encouraging respondents to think carefully before answering a survey question) or to lessen the task difficulty (e.g., avoiding a grid format in a Web survey and avoid placing a battery of similar items toward the end of a survey) in order to reduce the extent of nondifferentiation in a survey.

Ting Yan

See also Cognitive Aspects of Survey Methodology (CASM); Measurement Error; Respondent Burden, Respondent Fatigue; Respondent-Related Error; Response Bias; Retrieval; Satisficing; Web Surveys

Further Readings

Fricker, S., Galesic, M., Tourangeau, R., & Yan, T. (2005). An experimental comparison of Web and telephone surveys. *Public Opinion Quarterly*, 69, 370–392.

Holbrook, A. L., Green, M. C., & Krosnick, J. A. (2003). Telephone versus face-to-face interviewing of national probability samples with long questionnaires: Comparisons of respondents satisficing and social desirability responses bias. *Public Opinion Quarterly*, 67, 79–125.

Krosnick, J. A. (1991). Response strategies for coping with the cognitive demands of attitude measures in surveys. *Applied Cognitive Psychology*, 5, 213–236.

Krosnick, J. A. (1999). Survey research. *Annual Review of Psychology*, 50, 537–567.

NONDIRECTIVE PROBING

Probing inadequate survey answers for the additional information that may be necessary to fully meet a question's goal(s) is an important element of standardized survey interviewing. In training interviewers to probe effectively, an important distinction should be drawn between nondirective and directive forms of this technique. Unlike directive probing, nondirective probing is designed to encourage and motivate respondents to provide clarifying information without influencing their answers. That is, this approach is specifically designed to be neutral in order to avoid increasing the probability that any specific type of answer is encouraged, or discouraged, from respondents. When nondirective probing is employed, an answer is never suggested by the interviewer. Some examples of nondirective probing of closed-ended questions include slowly repeating the original question or repeating the full set of response options (e.g., "Is that a 'Yes' or a 'No'?"). When asking open-ended questions, some nondirective probe examples include repeating respondent answers, using neutral statements such as, "Could you tell me a little bit more about that?" "I'm not sure I understand what you mean here," "So why do you feel that way?" and "Is there anything else you wanted to say about this?" or simply pausing while respondents collect their thoughts.

Nondirective probing is also important when requesting numerical information. Useful strategies when probing answers to these types of questions include asking respondents to provide more exact information (e.g., "I need a more precise figure if possible"), asking them to select a single number from a range of values initially reported (e.g., "Would you say 2 or would you say 3?"), and asking them to perform any necessary calculations when they provide information using a format other than what was requested (e.g., question: "How old are you?"; answer: "I was born in 1955"; probe: "So how old would that make you?").

In contrast, directive probes are not neutral. They may inadvertently bias respondent answers by limiting the potential range of responses available or by suggesting that some answers are more preferable than others. In probing a closed-ended question, an example of a directive probe would be presenting a truncated range of response options (e.g., answer: "My health is on the low side"; probe: "So, would you say your health is 'only fair' or 'poor'?"). Interviewers often also will construct directive probes to open-ended questions by attempting to reword a respondent's initial answer (e.g., "In other words, you are opposed to income taxes because they are a disincentive to work?"). Similarly, an example of a directive probe to a numeric question might be, "So that means you were 12 when you first smoked a cigarette?". These latter two examples highlight the fact that directive probes can often be answered with a "Yes" or "No" answer.

Although an important element of standardized interviewing, nondirective probes themselves ironically can be only partially standardized and hence are both employed and worded to some extent at the discretion of the interviewer. This variability should also be considered a potential source of measurement error, one that is best confronted through careful training of interviewers regarding the critical nature of their role in conducting standardized survey interviews, as well as the specific goals of each question included in the survey instrument.

Timothy Johnson

See also Bias; Closed-Ended Question; Interviewer Monitoring; Interviewer Neutrality; Interviewer Training; Measurement Error; Open-Ended Question; Probing; Standardized Survey Interviewing

Further Readings

Fowler, F. J. (1990). *Standardized survey interviewing: Minimizing interviewer-related error.* Newbury Park, CA: Sage.

Gwartney, P. A. (2007). *The telephone interviewer's handbook: How to conduct standardized conversations.* New York: Jossey-Bass/Wiley.

NONIGNORABLE NONRESPONSE

When patterns of nonresponse (either unit or item nonresponse) are significantly correlated with variables of interest in a survey, then the nonresponse contributes to biased estimates of those variables and is considered *nonignorable*. Recent trends of increasing survey nonresponse rates make the question whether nonresponse is ignorable or not more salient to more researchers.

Since data are only observed for responders, researchers often use participating sample members or members for whom there are complete responses to make inferences about a more general population. For example, a researcher estimating the average income of single parents might use income data observed for single-parent responders to make generalizations about average income for all single parents, including those who did not participate or who refused to answer the relevant questions. The underlying assumption is that single-parent sample members who do not respond or respond with incomplete data are similar to single-parent sample members who participate fully. This implies that the units with missing data or incomplete data are a random subsample of the original sample and do not differ from the population at large.

If this assumption is spurious (i.e., it is *not* true)— that is, units with missing or incomplete data are different in meaningful (nonignorable) ways from the rest of the sample on key variables of interest—then inferences with missing data can lead to biased estimates. For example, if lower-earning single parents have high unit nonresponse rates because they are more difficult to locate and contact, then the estimate of income, the key variable, will be upwardly biased.

Thus, when survey participation rates are correlated with key variables, unit nonresponse is likely to be nonignorable.

Essentially every survey has some nonresponse either because of an inability to locate or contact a sample member, or because of a sample member's refusal to participate or to answer certain questions. When researchers make inferences from their sample to the population, then survey response rates are considered an indicator of the representativeness of the data, making the response rate an important criterion of data quality. Because of this, declining response rates make the question of whether or to what extent the nonresponse is ignorable especially important.

The growing problem of nonresponse has led researchers to increase efforts to reduce nonresponse and measure possible nonresponse error. Nonresponse due to noncontact is usually dealt with by improving tracking and locating efforts and by increasing the number of contact attempts at different times of day and days of week to maximize the probability of contact. Survey organizations may provide interviewer training in avoiding or converting refusals. Incentives are used to increase contact rates and decrease refusal rates. Efforts to maintain contact with sample members are used between waves in longitudinal studies to minimize sample attrition. Where nonresponse is due to a physical or mental limitation of the sample member, proxy interviews (e.g., by a family member) may provide key data. In some rare instances, researchers are able to compare survey responses to administrative data in order to measure the impact of nonresponse. Finally, researchers will also make statistical adjustments using external benchmarks such as census data to estimate the impact of nonresponse on their estimates.

Since these can be costly enterprises, they may be inefficient if nonresponse is in fact ignorable—that is, the measures (in the aggregate) that are missing from nonresponders are not different enough from the measures (in the aggregate) taken from responders to change the survey statistics in any appreciable (meaningful) way. Thus there is great interest in separating nonresponse into its components in order to focus on the largest parts of nonresponse that contribute to bias. Targeting resources at a particular component of nonresponse can help minimize bias if the researcher expects the cause of this component of nonresponse to be correlated with key variables.

Danna Basson

See also Ignorable Nonresponse; Missing Data; Nonresponse
Error; Nonresponse Rates

Further Readings

Curtin, R. (2005). Changes in telephone survey nonresponse
over the past quarter-century. *Public Opinion Quarterly*,
69, 87–98.

de Leeuw, E., Hox, J., & Huisman, M. (2003). Prevention
and treatment of item nonresponse. *Journal of Official
Statistics*, *19*, 153–176.

Groves, R. M. (2006). Nonresponse bias in household
surveys. *Public Opinion Quarterly*, *70*(5), 646–675.

Journal of Official Statistics: http://www.jos.nu

Singer, E. (2006). Introduction: Nonresponse bias in
household surveys. *Public Opinion Quarterly*,
70(5), 637–645.

NONPROBABILITY SAMPLING

Sampling involves the selection of a portion of the
finite population being studied. Nonprobability sampling does not attempt to select a random sample from
the population of interest. Rather, subjective methods
are used to decide which elements are included in the
sample. In contrast, in probability sampling, each element in the population has a known nonzero chance
of being selected through the use of a random selection procedure. The use of a random selection procedure such as simple random sampling makes it
possible to use design-based estimation of population
means, proportions, totals, and ratios. Standard errors
can also be calculated from a probability sample.

Why would one consider using nonprobability
sampling? In some situations, the population may not
be well defined. In other situations, there may not be
great interest in drawing inferences from the sample
to the population. Probably the most common reason
for using nonprobability sampling is that it is less
expensive than probability sampling and can often be
implemented more quickly.

Nonprobability sampling is often divided into three
primary categories: (1) quota sampling, (2) purposive
sampling, and (3) convenience sampling. Weighting
and drawing inferences from nonprobability samples
require somewhat different procedures than for probability sampling; advances in technology have influenced some newer approaches to nonprobability
sampling.

Quota Sampling

Quota sampling has some similarities to stratified
sampling. The basic idea of quota sampling is to set
a target number of completed interviews with specific
subgroups of the population of interest. Ideally, the
target size of the subgroups is based on known information about the target population (such as census
data). The sampling procedure then proceeds using
a nonrandom selection mechanism until the desired
number of completed interviews is obtained for each
subgroup. A common example is to set 50% of
the interviews with males and 50% with females in
a random-digit dialing telephone interview survey. A
sample of telephone numbers is released to the interviewers for calling. At the start of the survey field
period, one adult is randomly selected from a sample
household. It is generally more difficult to obtain
interviews with males. So, for example, if the total
desired number of interviews is 1,000 (500 males and
500 females), and the researcher is often able to
obtain 500 female interviews before obtaining 500
males interviews, then no further interviews would be
conducted with females and only males would be
selected and interviewed from then on, until the target
of 500 males is reached. Females in those latter sample households would have a zero probability of
selection. Also, because the 500 female interviews
were most likely obtained at earlier call attempts,
before the sample telephone numbers were thoroughly
worked by the interviewers, females living in harder-to-reach households are less likely to be included in
the sample of 500 females.

Quotas are often based on more than one characteristic. For example, a quota sample might have
interviewer-assigned quotas for age by gender and by
employment status categories. For a given sample
household, the interviewer might ask for the rarest
group first, and if a member of that group were present in the household, that individual would be interviewed. If a member of the rarest group were not
present in the household, then an individual in one of
the other rare groups would be selected. Once the
quotas for the rare groups are filled, the interviewer
would start to fill the quotas for the more common
groups.

Quota sampling is sometimes used in conjunction
with area probability sampling of households. Area
probability sampling techniques are used to select primary sampling units and segments. For each sample

segment (e.g., city block) the interviewer is instructed to start at a corner of the segment and proceed around the segment contacting housing units until a specific number of interviews are completed in the segment.

In another example, one might select an area probability sample of housing units using multi-stage sampling. At the segment level, the interviewers would be supplied with quotas for adults, assuming one adult is interviewed in each household. The instructions might consist of something simple as alternating between interviewing available males and females in the households they make contact with. In random-digit dialing, a probability sample of telephone numbers can be drawn and a quota sampling method can be used to select one adult from each sample household. In telephone surveys conducted under tight time constraints, the selection of a male or female adult from the household can be limited to adults who are at home at the time the interviewer calls. This eliminates the need for callbacks.

The most famous limitation of this type of quota sampling approach is the failure of the major pre-elections polls, using quota sampling, to accurately predict the results of the 1948 presidential election. The field interviewers were given quotas (with estimates based on 1940 census figures) to fill based on characteristics such as age, gender, race, degree of urbanicity, and socioeconomic status. In addition to the inaccurate quotas, the interviewers were then free to fill the quotas without any probability sampling mechanism in place. This subjective selection method resulted in a tendency for Republicans being more likely to be interviewed within the quota groups than Democrats. The sample thus contained too many Republicans, causing the pre-election polls to incorrectly predict Thomas E. Dewey (the Republican candidate) as the winner.

A major problem with quota sampling is the introduction of unknown sampling biases into the survey estimates. In the case of the 1948 presidential election, the sampling bias was associated with too many Republicans being selected. Another problem with quota sampling is that the sampling procedure often results in a lower response rate than would be achieved in a probability sample. Most quota samples stop attempting to complete interviews with active sample households once the quotas have been met. If a large amount of sample is active at the time the quotas are closed, then the response rate will be very low.

Purposive Sampling

Purposive sampling is also referred to as *judgmental sampling* or *expert sampling*. The main objective of purposive sampling is to produce a sample that can be considered "representative" of the population. The term *representative* has many different meanings, along the lines of the sample having the same distribution of the population on some key demographic characteristic, but it does not seem to have any agreed-upon statistical meaning. The selection of a purposive sample is often accomplished by applying expert knowledge of the population to select in a non-random manner a sample of elements that represents a cross-section of the population. For example, one might select a sample of small businesses in the United States that represent a cross-section of small businesses in the nation. With expert knowledge of the population, one would first decide which characteristics are important to be represented in the sample. Once this is established, a sample of businesses is identified that meet the various characteristics that are viewed as being most important. This might involve selecting large (1,000 + employees), medium (100–999 employees), and small (<100 employees) businesses.

Another example of purposive sampling is the selection of a sample of jails from which prisoner participants will be sampled. This is referred to as two-stage sampling, but the first-stage units are not selected using probability sampling techniques. Rather, the first-stage units are selected to represent key prisoner dimensions (e.g., age and race), with expert subject matter judgment being used to select the specific jails that are included in the study. The opposite approach can also be used: First-stage units are selected using probability sampling, and then, within the selected first-stage, expert judgment is employed to select the elements from which data will be collected. "Site" studies or evaluation studies will often use one of these two approaches. Generally, there is not interest in drawing inferences to some larger population or to make national estimates, say, for all prisoners in U.S. jails.

A clear limitation of purposive sampling is that another expert likely would come up with a different sample when identifying important characteristics and picking typical elements to be in the sample. Given the subjectivity of the selection mechanism, purposive sampling is generally considered most appropriate for the selection of small samples often from a limited geographic area or from a restricted population definition, where inference to the population is not the highest priority. Clearly, the knowledge and experience of the expert making the selections is a key aspect of the "success" of the resulting sample, but it would be difficult to quantify that characteristic of a sample.

Convenience Sampling

Convenience sampling differs from purposive sampling in that expert judgment is not used to select a representative sample of elements. Rather, the primary selection criterion relates to the ease of obtaining a sample. Ease of obtaining the sample relates to the cost of locating elements of the population, the geographic distribution of the sample, and obtaining the interview data from the selected elements. Examples of convenience samples include *mall intercept interviewing*, unsystematically recruiting individuals to participate in the study (e.g., what is done for many psychology studies that use readily available undergraduates), visiting a sample of business establishments that are close to the data collection organization, seeking the participation of individuals visiting a Web site to participate in a survey, and including a brief questionnaire in a coupon mailing. In convenience sampling, the representativeness of the sample is generally less of a concern compared to purposive sampling.

For example, in the case of surveying those attending the Super Bowl using a convenience sample, a researcher may want data collected quickly, using a low-cost method that does not involve scientific sampling. The researcher sends out several data collection staff members to interview people at the stadium on the day of the game. The interviewers may, for example, carry clipboards with a questionnaire they may administer to people they stop outside the stadium an hour before the game starts or give it to people to have them fill it out for themselves. This variation of taking a convenience sample does not allow the researcher (or the client) to have a clear sense of what target population is being represented by the sample. Although convenience samples are not scientific samples, they do on occasion have value to researchers and clients who recognize their considerable limitations—for example, providing some quick exploration of a hypothesis that the researcher may

eventually plan to test using some form of probability sampling. On the other hand, some researchers naively treat such samples as equivalent to simple random samples and calculate standard errors based on simple random sampling. Doing this does not produce valid statistical information.

Weighting and Drawing Inferences From Nonprobability Samples

One issue that arises with all probability samples and for many nonprobability samples is the estimation procedures, specifically those used to draw inferences from the sample to the population. Many surveys produce estimates that are proportions or percentages (e.g., the percentage of adults who do not exercise at all), and weighting methods used to assign a final weight to each completed interview are generally given considerable thought and planning. For probability sampling, the first step in the weight calculation process is the development of a base sampling weight. The base sampling weight equals the reciprocal of the selection probability of a sampling unit. The calculation of the base sampling weight is then often followed by weighting adjustments related to nonresponse and noncoverage. Finally, post-stratification or raking is used to adjust the final weights so that the sample is in alignment with the population for key demographic and socioeconomic characteristics. In nonprobability sampling, the calculation of a base sampling weight has no meaning, because there are no known probabilities of selection. One could essentially view each sampling unit as having a base sampling weight of one.

Sometimes nonresponse and noncoverage weights are developed for nonprobability samples, but the most common technique is to use a weighting procedure such as post-stratification or raking to align the nonprobability sample with the population that one would ideally like to draw inferences about. The post-stratification variables are generally limited to demographic and socioeconomic characteristics. One limitation of this approach is that the variables available for weighting may not include key characteristics related to the nonprobability sampling mechanism that was employed to select the sampling units. The results of weighting nonprobability samples have been mixed in the situation when benchmarks are available for a key survey outcome measure (e.g., the outcome of an election).

Recent Developments in Nonprobability Sampling

Finally, it should be mentioned that newer versions of nonprobability sampling have appeared in recent years, some driven by changes in technology. These have generally been labeled *model-based sampling approaches*, and to some degree the use of the term *model-based sampling* has replaced the term *nonprobability sampling*. Web surveys are one new example of nonprobability sampling. Web surveys are generally convenience samples of households or adults recruited to participate in surveys delivered over the Web. The samples are usually set up as panels, that is, a recruited household or adult is asked to respond to some number of surveys over their tenure in the sample. At the recruitment phase, characteristics of the households or adults can be collected. This makes it possible to limit future surveys to households or adults with a specific characteristic (e.g., persons ages 18–24 years, female executives, retirees). Because respondents use the Web to complete the questionnaire, these nonprobability sample Web surveys can often be conducted much more quickly and far less expensively than probability samples.

Another new type of nonprobability sampling is based on selecting email addresses from companies that compile email addresses that appear to be associated with individuals living in households. Some companies set up email panel samples through a recruitment process and allow clients to send a questionnaire to a sample of email addresses in their panel. For both email and Web panel samples, the estimation methods used to attempt to draw inferences from the sample to the population are a very important consideration. The use of propensity scores and post-stratification or raking has been explored by some researchers. The calculation of standard errors, as with all nonprobability samples, is problematic and must rely on model-based assumptions.

Another relatively new nonprobability sampling method is known as *respondent-driven sampling*. Respondent-driven sampling is described as a form of snowball sampling. Snowball sampling relies on referrals from an initial nonprobability or probability sample of respondents to nominate additional respondents. It differs from multiplicity sampling in that no attempt is made to determine the probability of selection of each subject in the target population. Snowball samples are sometimes used to select samples of members of a social network in the situation when no complete list of such members exists and the costs of doing a probability sample would be prohibitive. Respondent-driven sampling has most often been employed for surveys of very rare populations in relatively small geographic areas, such as a city or county.

The use of probability sampling, as championed by Leslie Kish and other important statisticians, has resulted in probability sampling being employed in most surveys conducted by the U.S. government. For commercial research, probability sampling methods and nonprobability sampling methods have been employed. More recently, as the cost of collecting data has risen, a considerable amount of the commercial research conducted in the United States has moved to nonprobability sampling methods. For surveys conducted for the federal government, model-based sampling methods have been used in some situations. During the coming years, it is possible that the use of probability sampling will decline further. It is therefore important that more research be conducted to further assess biases from using nonprobability samples and devise strategies to both measure and adjust for these biases.

Michael P. Battaglia

See also Area Probability Sample; Convenience Sampling; Design-Based Estimation; Kish, Leslie; Mall Intercept Survey; Model-Based Estimation; Multiplicity Sampling; Multi-Stage Sample; Probability Sample; Propensity Scores; Purposive Sample; Quota Sample; Raking; Random Sampling; Respondent-Driven Sampling (RDS); Sample; Sampling; Simple Random Sample; Snowball Sampling; Stratified Sampling; Weighting; Web Survey

Further Readings

Cochran, W. G. (1977). *Sampling techniques*. New York: Wiley.

Henry, G. T. (1990). *Practical sampling*. Newbury Park, CA: Sage.

Kish, L. (1965). *Survey sampling*. New York: Wiley.

NONRESIDENTIAL

Nonresidential dispositions occur in telephone and in-person surveys of the general public when a case contacted or called by an interviewer turns out to be a business or other type of nonresidential location such as a hospital, government office, or library. The nonresidential disposition also usually includes institutions such as prisons, sanitariums, work camps, and group quarters such as military barracks and college dormitories. Nonresidential cases are considered ineligible for a survey of the general public survey because conducting an interview with these cases would violate critical assumptions of probability sampling. Although the proportion of nonresidential cases in a telephone or in-person sample varies based on the sampling area, the nonresidential survey disposition tends to be fairly common, with nonresidential numbers comprising up to a significant minority of the telephone numbers in a landline telephone random-digit dial (RDD) sample. More recent technologies that are capable of screening out numbers in an RDD sample without interviewers calling the number have substantially reduced the proportion of nonresidential numbers in many telephone survey samples.

One special challenge in telephone surveys is call forwarding technology, which allows one telephone number to be transferred to another number. For example, if a residential telephone number is transferred to another telephone number within the same household, the case may still remain eligible if the survey uses weighting techniques to adjust for unequal probabilities of selection (since the residential unit contacted effectively has an additional telephone line, and thus, a greater chance of being sampled). If a nonresidential telephone number is forwarded to a residence (e.g., a business number being forwarded to the owner's home residence), the case should be considered ineligible. More detailed rules may be needed for special (but uncommon) cases in which the number for a residence outside the sampling area is forwarded to another residence inside the sampling area. Finally, a residence and a business occasionally may share the same telephone number; these cases should be treated as eligible for the interview. Only numbers that ring exclusively to a business or other nonresidential unit should be given the nonresidential disposition.

For in-person surveys, two special cases can make it more difficult to determine whether a case is truly nonresidential. For example, although the primary unit at an address might be a business or an institution, it is important to ensure that there is not a residential housing unit within the larger unit (such as an apartment above a business or a warden's house on the grounds of a prison). An additional challenge is posed by vacation and other seasonal homes, and special rules may need to be developed to properly determine the disposition of these housing units.

The challenges and special cases mentioned illustrate that at times it may be difficult to determine whether a telephone number or housing unit is residential. Although these instances are fairly uncommon, it important to ensure that there is definitive evidence that the case is nonresidential before applying the nonresidential disposition to a case. Obtaining this evidence may require additional investigation (such as talking to neighbors or documenting visible signs that the unit is uninhabited or not used as a residence). In surveys of the general public, a nonresidential outcome is treated as final and ineligible and thus is not used in response rate calculations.

Matthew Courser

See also Call Forwarding; Dispositions; Final Dispositions; Response Rates; Temporary Dispositions

Further Readings

American Association for Public Opinion Research. (2006). *Standard definitions: Final dispositions of case codes and outcome rates for surveys* (4th ed.). Lenexa, KS: Author.

Lavrakas, P. J. (1993). *Telephone survey methods: Sampling, selection, and supervision* (2nd ed.). Newbury Park, CA: Sage.

NONRESPONSE

Nonresponse refers to the people or households who are sampled but from whom data are not gathered, or to other elements (e.g., cars coming off an assembly line; books in a library) that are being sampled but for which data are not gathered. The individual nonrespondents on a survey contribute to the *nonresponse rate*, the aggregate tally of how many did not provide data divided by how many "should" have. One minus the nonresponse rate is, of course, the overall response rate.

Classification

Calculating nonresponse is not as simple as it initially seems. One survey may have mainly nonrespondents who could not be reached (i.e., contacted) by the researchers. Another reaches most of the sampled persons, but a large proportion refuse the survey. A third has an easily reached, cooperative set of people in a sampling frame, but many do not possess a characteristic that is part of the definition of the desired survey population. These reasons for nonresponse, usually termed *noncontact, refusal,* and *ineligibility,* respectively, are differentiated within most classification procedures for nonresponse, such as the *Standard Definitions* established by the American Association for Public Opinion Research (AAPOR). The components of nonresponse may differ across the various contact types or modes of survey. For example, the noncontact count may be higher on a telephone survey in which calls to some numbers are never answered than on a postal survey in which a letter mailed is presumed to be a contact, except for a few nondeliverables returned by the post office. On the street, as distinguished from the logical world of survey methodology research articles and textbooks, the distinctions among noncontact, refusal, and ineligibility are not always watertight. Is a foreign-born person who opts out of a survey due to language problems, or an elderly citizen with impaired hearing or eyesight, an ineligible or a refusal? Only the person himself or herself really knows. What of those who, in a face-to-face household survey, recognize the approaching person as a survey taker and decline to answer the doorbell? Refusal or noncontact?

Predictability

Nonresponse, like many social behaviors, is only weakly predictable at the level of the individual yet becomes more ordered at the aggregate. Any experienced survey methodologist, told the type of population to be sampled, the mode of contact (i.e., telephone, in-person, mail, Web, or multi-mode), the length and content of the questions, the resources available for callbacks and follow-ups, and whether or not payments or other incentives are to be used, can give an informed estimate of the final response and nonresponse rates. Information on the sponsor, and whether the fieldwork is to be conducted by a government agency, a survey unit at a university, or a commercial firm, will add further precision to the estimates. At the same time, and in most cases, the attempt at prediction of whether one person versus another will respond or not generates only slight probabilities. Always depending on the particulars of the survey, people of greater

or lesser education, male or female, racial majority or minority, young or old, may be disproportionately among the nonrespondents. Such effects often appear in surveys, but few generalities are possible. Perhaps the safest is the tendency for middle, rather than upper or lower, socioeconomic status people to respond: the *middle-class bias* sometimes attributed to surveying. Even this, however, is not a certainty. For example, on a survey whose results will help generate funds for social programs, the lower socioeconomic strata may have good reason to respond. If the survey is conducted by an agency of government, there may be some deference to the authority of the sponsor among the lower strata, also contributing to probability of response. Offsetting those advantages might be a subcultural hesitancy and anxiety about participating in surveys. The probability of an individual responding to a survey remains inherently hard to predict, because so many factors enter the mix. (An exception being panel surveys in which response behavior in a previous wave can be highly predictive of subsequent wave participation.)

A Historical Perspective on Survey Nonresponse

It used to be firmly believed by survey methodologists that the response versus nonresponse rates on a survey accurately indicated the quality of the data. One rule of thumb, to which several generations of students were exposed via a widely used textbook by Earl Babbie, was that a mailed survey with 50% response was "adequate," 60% "good," and 70% "very good." These notions were advanced in the early 1970s, when the highest quality surveys still tended to be face-to-face and the telephone survey was still under development. Face-to-face ("personal") interview surveys of the national population in the United States, if of high quality, were expected in this era to have nonresponse rates of only some 20 to 25%. By the mid-1970s, however, a growing number of voices were detecting erosion in response rates to personal interview surveys. The issue even was noted in *The New York Times* on October 26, 1975. The telephone survey was meanwhile gaining acceptance among survey researchers as they perfected the generation of sampling frames via random-digit dialing (RDD). Research was also under way during the 1970s on enhancing the validity of mailed surveys, led by Don Dillman's comprehensive strategy known as the "total design method" or TDM.

By the end of the 1990s, a second crisis in survey response rates had developed. This time, the center of attention was the telephone survey, for face-to-face household interview surveys had become rare due to their astronomical cost when fielded to a national population. Telephone surveys by commercial firms, when dealing with topics not deemed highly salient by the public, were now highly unlikely to breach the 50% response mark, the guideline used some 30 years earlier to define adequate quality in a survey. Further, as the proportion of U.S. households with cell phone only (no landline) approached 10% in 2005, problems of sample coverage on telephone surveys were mounting.

Declining Response Rates and Implications

As one report of declining responses followed another, as the pattern was detected not just in the United States and Canada, but throughout Europe as well, researchers began to reevaluate the consequences of high nonresponse for the validity of a survey. Studies appeared with examples in which nonresponse was *ignorable*, that is, did not seem to seriously bias results from the survey. To be sure, these results did not mean that nonresponse no longer mattered, but they did challenge the simple rule of thumb that, if a survey were to be trusted, a majority of those who could respond should respond. By 2008, it is more clearly realized that one survey could have low, but seriously biasing nonresponse, another much higher but more ignorable nonresponse. A survey, for example, on a rare deviant behavior might be nonthreatening for abstainers but precipitate heavy nonresponse among practitioners. If the population sampled were somewhat "captive," such as students in a school, the response rate could be high, but the nonrespondents who refused to sign permission slips might be precisely the respondents most urgently needed for the survey estimates to be accurate. Nonresponse would, in contrast, prove ignorable if nonrespondents were a near-random subset of the sample, even if the proportion of nonrespondents to respondents were very high.

Although the notion of ignorable nonresponse has provided some reassurance about the continuing usefulness of the survey method for evidence-based social policy, academic studies, and market research, rising nonresponse rates still require attention. When there are nonrespondents in a survey, the researcher can never be certain that bias does not exist for at least some variables.

Current Theories

Survey methodologists thus put considerable resources into the quality of survey fieldwork. Since part of the problem of high survey nonresponse in the 21st century is lifestyle based—for example, the diminished predictability of when a householder will be reachable by telephone at home—the number of repeat calls or "callbacks" has had to be increased for high-quality telephone surveys. Survey research organizations are also now more involved in attempts at "conversion" of initial refusers than they may once have been. Considerable experimentation has been conducted with incentives for surveys. Modest gifts or small sums of money work especially well on the self-enumerated modes of survey, such as mailed or Web contact. The incentive can be delivered up-front, "pre-paid," not conditional on the response taking place. Somewhat counterintuitively, pre-paid rewards prove more effective than the "post-paid" rewards given only after the survey is successfully collected from the respondent. Naturally all such techniques add to the costs of surveying and tend to slow down the speed at which data can be collected.

Especially for commercial survey firms, who must watch the balance sheet, it is difficult to maintain response rates near historical norms. To be sure, surveys via the Internet—the *Web survey*—hold some promise for controlling the spiraling costs of survey research. Since the year 2000, growing attention to the Web mode has been evident in the research journals. At the moment, Web surveys work best for well-defined subpopulations having known email addresses. University students, for example, are routinely being surveyed by university administrators and academic researchers, with response rates in the 40s when carefully conducted. NSSE, the National Survey of Student Engagement, is one well-known example. The general public is harder to survey adequately via the Web. A survey questionnaire simply dumped onto an Internet site for those Web passers-by who wish to answer (sometimes as many times as they like!) is not a serious option. Better-quality Web surveys mimic the traditional mailed survey. A sampling frame exists, consisting in the Web case of email addresses, and a sequence of contacts is carried out. Provision is made via passwords to prevent one person answering several times. It is imaginable that convergence will take place between the methods of the mailed survey and telephone RDD. That is, if plausible, randomly generated email addresses were created, with a filtering system to capture the working ones, it would be possible to field Web surveys of general populations. Technical issues would arise around defining exactly what this population was, for the samples would sprawl across national boundaries. The method might be no more uncertain, however, than the current interest in creating "panels" of reusable respondents.

If one answer to declining response rates is thus technological innovation, another draws from the traditional conceptual tools of the social sciences. The growing resistance to surveys, especially those by telephone, has prompted renewed theorizing about what kind of behavior is involved when people do or do not respond to a survey. Many theoretical approaches appear within the research literature, but two main approaches are especially prominent. *Social exchange theory*, that dates to the mid-1970s and as applied to survey nonresponse, asks if response decisions are best understood as reasoned actions reached after a mental processing of relative costs and benefits. The cognitive heuristics people use in decision making received increasing attention toward the end of the 1980s. Here response behavior is viewed as somewhat impulsive action largely bypassing the consciousness.

Along with decision-making styles, survey methodologists theorize about the role of cultural factors. Do people, for example, hold attitudes toward the survey method in general, accepting or declining specific surveys largely on the basis of the attitude, or is the behavior "situational," mainly determined by what else is going on when a respondent is contacted? Research on attitudes toward the survey method has intensified in the new century. Such attitudes do tend to relate with survey response behavior, but the ties are weak, making it an overstatement to say that the respondents on any particular survey are only those in favor of the method. On the other hand, when it does occur, this is highly nonignorable, biasing nonresponse. The main determinant of who does and does not participate in a survey seems to lie within the multitude of contingent, situational circumstances. People may be busy or idle when the telephone rings; the fieldworker may succeed or fail in striking an instant rapport with the prospective interviewee. These are closer to random events, which more likely result in less-biasing nonresponse.

Complicating these attempts at theoretical interpretation of survey nonresponse is the heterogeneity of human populations. Not all topics hold the same interest for all people—quite the opposite. Research by Robert M. Groves and colleagues shows that response rates can exceed the norm by tens of percentage points when the topic of the survey and the subpopulation being sampled match up well. It follows from this "leverage-saliency" interpretation of nonresponse that techniques such as cash incentives will be proportionately most effective when the topic–population match, thus the salience of the topic, is weak. As such research accumulates, it is increasingly realized that just knowing how many of the eligible people in a sample responded to a survey is insufficient information. People assessing the validity of a survey need to know why people responded and why others did not.

The study of survey nonresponse is thus both a technical issue for methodologists and a rich conceptual puzzle for social science. Ideas about survey nonresponse adapt to the tectonics of social change, making this research topic a living, changing body of ideas rather than a cemetery of textbook certainties.

John Goyder

See also American Association for Public Opinion Research (AAPOR); Leverage-Saliency Theory; Nonresponse Error; Nonresponse Rates; Panel; Random-Digit Dialing (RDD); Social Exchange Theory; Standard Definitions; Total Design Method (TDM)

Further Readings

de Leeuw, E., & de Heer, W. (2002). Trends in household survey nonresponse: A longitudinal and international comparison. In R. M. Groves, D. A. Dillman, J. L. Eltinge, & R. J. A. Little (Eds.), *Survey nonresponse* (pp. 41–54). New York: Wiley.

Dillman, D. A. (1978). *Mail and telephone surveys: The total design method for surveys*. New York: Wiley.

Dillman, D. A. (2000). *Mail and Internet surveys: The tailored design method*. New York: Wiley.

Goyder, J., Boyer, L., & Martinelli, G. (2006). Integrating exchange and heuristic theories of survey nonresponse. *Bulletin de Méthodologie Sociologique*, *92*, 28–44.

Groves, R. M. (2006). Nonresponse rates and nonresponse bias in household surveys. *Public Opinion Quarterly*, *70*, 646–675.

Groves, R., Singer, E., & Corning, A. (2000). Leverage-salience theory of survey participation: Description and an illustration. *Public Opinion Quarterly*, *64*, 299–308.

Stoop, A. L. (2005). *The hunt for the last respondent: Nonresponse on sample surveys*. The Hague, Netherlands: Social and Cultural Planning Office.

NONRESPONSE BIAS

Nonresponse bias occurs when sampled elements from which data are gathered are different on the measured variables in nonnegligible ways from those that are sampled but from which data are not gathered. Essentially, all surveys are likely to have some degree of nonresponse bias, but in many cases it occurs at a very small and thus a negligible (i.e., ignorable) level. The size of the bias is a function of (a) the magnitude of the difference between respondents and nonrespondents and (b) the proportion of all sampled elements that are nonrespondents. Thus, even if only one of these factors is large, the nonresponse bias may well be nonnegligible.

There are three basic types of survey nonresponse. The first is refusals, which occur when sampled individuals or households decline to participate. The second is noncontacts, when sampled individuals are never reached. The third type of nonresponse consists of situations in which the interviewer cannot communicate with the sampled person because of a language barrier or some mental or physical disability. Most nonresponse is the result of refusals and noncontacts.

It has long been thought that response rates are a good indicator of survey quality and nonresponse bias; however, recent research has challenged this notion. This is encouraging news for researchers because it means that surveys with lower response rates are not necessarily more biased than those with higher response rates. But this does not mean that nonignorable nonresponse bias cannot or will not occur. Nonresponse bias will be present when the likelihood of responding is correlated with the variable(s) being measured, and this correlation can vary across variables even within the same survey.

Nonresponse bias has been a growing concern to survey researchers as response rates have declined over the years. There are a variety of reasons for this, including an increase in refusals with the rise of telemarketing and an increase in technologies to screen calls such as answering machines, voicemail, and caller ID. It is important to consider nonresponse due to refusals and noncontacts separately because the characteristics of refusers can be different from those who are difficult to reach.

Researchers can use several methods to maximize response rates; much recent research has focused on the correlation between response rates and nonresponse bias; and strategies for reducing nonresponse bias are being designed.

Maximizing Response Rates

Researchers can try to maximize response rates in various ways. For refusals, interviewers can be trained on refusal avoidance strategies, and refusal conversions can be conducted in an attempt to include the less cooperative in the sample. For noncontacts, repeated contacts (in the case of in-person surveys) and callbacks (in the case of telephone surveys) can be made at different times of day and on different days of the week, so that people who are more difficult to reach are included. And language barriers can be overcome by using bilingual interviewers. Repeated reminder mailings in the case of mail surveys and Internet surveys can also be deployed to reduce nonresponse in those types of surveys. Other techniques have been used to increase response rates, such as sending advance letters and using incentives.

Recent Research

Through the 1990s, a common assumption in the field of survey research was that surveys with higher response rates always were more accurate (i.e., had lower nonresponse bias) than those with lower response rates. But this assumption has been challenged by recent research on opinion questions in telephone polls and exit polls. In telephone polls, Scott Keeter and his colleagues, and separately Richard Curtin and his colleagues, have found that fairly large changes in response rates had a minimal impact on their survey estimates. Using a large number of in-person exit polls over different election cycles, Daniel Merkle and Murray Edelman found little or no relationship between response rates and survey bias.

This research has been encouraging to survey researchers because it shows that surveys with lower response rates are not necessarily less accurate. However, this does not mean that survey researchers do not need to worry about nonresponse bias. Robert Groves conducted an extensive review of previous nonresponse studies, most of which focused on non-opinion variables, and found a number of instances in which nonresponse bias was present, even in some surveys with very high overall response rates. He found that response rates were not a good predictor of such bias, consistent with the previous research mentioned. Groves also found that the magnitude of nonresponse bias even differed across variables *within the same survey*, further pointing out the limitation of using a survey's response rate as a measure of data quality and as an indicator of the presence of nonresponse bias.

One reason that response rates are not good predictors of nonresponse bias is that they tell researchers nothing about the second critical component of what determines the magnitude of bias: the size of the difference on key survey measures between respondents and nonrespondents. For variables on which respondents are not different than nonrespondents, surveys with lower response rates will be as accurate as those with higher response rates. The difficult part is knowing when this is the case, because researchers often do not have data on nonrespondents.

Groves explains this by noting that nonresponse bias is a function of the correlation between the survey variable(s) of interest and peoples' likelihood of participating in the survey, called *response propensity*. When there is no relationship between the survey variable and response propensity, then there will not be any nonresponse bias. Nonresponse bias increases as the correlation between response propensity and the survey variable increases.

For example, if one were conducting a survey in the evenings measuring the frequency of dining out, there would be a negative correlation between the survey variable (frequency of dining out) and the likelihood of responding to the survey. Those who dine out more often would be less likely to be home at the time of the survey contact and therefore would be less likely to participate. In this case, the survey would understate the amount that people dine out, because those who do so more often would be less likely to be available to respond.

Reducing Nonresponse Bias

Nonresponse bias can be reduced by *decreasing the correlation* between response propensity and the survey variable. This could be done in the dining-out example by extending the survey calling times to other parts of the day in addition to evenings. The correlation between the frequency of dining out and

response propensity would decrease and so would the magnitude of the nonresponse bias on this variable.

It is also possible for procedures designed to increase response rates to actually increase nonresponse bias. This will occur when the mechanism designed to increase response rates *increases the correlation* between response propensity and the survey variable. For example, consider a survey situation in which people with lower incomes are initially more likely to respond, and the researcher includes a monetary incentive in the survey design as a way to increase the response rate. If the appeal of the monetary incentive is negatively correlated with income, the incentive could increase the response rate but also increase nonresponse bias on variables related to income.

Another important way survey researchers try to decrease nonresponse bias is by applying weighting adjustments to the data, called *post-stratification*. A common approach is to weight survey data to match census demographics such as age, race, gender, and education. These types of adjustments assume that respondents and nonrespondents in a given demographic group are similar on the other survey variables measured. When this is the case, such weighting adjustments will decrease bias on variables that are highly correlated with the weighting variables. Weighting adjustments that can take into account factors that influence response propensity will be more successful at reducing or eliminating bias.

Daniel M. Merkle

See also Callbacks; Ignorable Nonresponse; Noncontacts; Nonignorable Nonresponse; Nonresponse Error; Nonresponse Rate; Post-Stratification; Post-Survey Adjustments; Refusals; Refusal Avoidance Training (RAT); Refusal Conversion; Refusal Rate; Response Propensity; Response Rates

Further Readings

Curtin, R., Presser, S., & Singer, E. (2000). The effects of response rate changes on the Index of Consumer Sentiment. *Public Opinion Quarterly, 64,* 413–428.

Groves, R. M. (2006). Nonresponse rates and nonresponse bias in household surveys. *Public Opinion Quarterly, 70,* 646–675.

Keeter, S., Miller, C., Kohut, A., Groves, R., & Presser, S. (2000). Consequences of reducing nonresponse in a large national telephone survey. *Public Opinion Quarterly, 64,* 125–148.

Merkle, D. M., & Edelman, M. (2002). Nonresponse in exit polls: A comprehensive analysis. In R. M. Groves, D. A. Dillman, J. L. Eltinge, & R. J. A. Little (Eds.), *Survey nonresponse* (pp. 243–258). New York: Wiley.

NONRESPONSE ERROR

During the past decade, nonresponse error—which occurs when those units that are sampled but from which data are not gathered differ to a nonignorable extent from those sampled units that do provide data—has become an extremely important topic to survey researchers. The increasing attention given to this part of the total survey error is related to the observation that survey participation is decreasing in all Western societies. Thus, more efforts (and cost expenditures) are needed to obtain acceptably high response rates.

In general, the response rate can be defined as the proportion of eligible sample units for which an interview (or other form of data collection) was completed. The calculation of the standard response rate is straightforward: the number of achieved interviews divided by the number of sample units for which an interview could have been completed. These are eligible sample units: completed interviews, partial interviews, noncontacted but known eligible units, refusals, and other noninterviewed eligible units.

Simple Model

Although the nonresponse rate is important information used to evaluate the nonresponse error, that rate is only one component of the nonresponse error. The biasing effect of nonresponse error is also related to the difference between respondents and nonrespondents. A simple model for a sample mean can be used to illustrate this point.

Given a sample with n units, r of these n units participated in the survey and nr units did not: $n = r + nr$. Y is a metric characteristic, and $\overline{Y}_r =$ mean estimated for the r respondents, $\overline{Y}_n =$ mean estimated for all n sample units, and $\overline{Y}_{nr} =$ mean estimated for the nr nonrespondents. The estimated mean for all the units in the sample $(\overline{Y}_n)$ equals to a weighted sum of the estimated mean for the respondents $(\overline{Y}_r)$ and the estimated mean for the nonrespondents $(\overline{Y}_{nr})$. The latter is weighted by the nonresponse rate $\left(\dfrac{nr}{n}\right)$, the

former by the response rate $\left(\dfrac{r}{n}\right)$. This results in the following formal specification:

$$\overline{Y}_n = \frac{r}{n}\overline{Y}_r + \frac{nr}{n}\overline{Y}_{nr}$$
$$= \left(1 - \frac{nr}{n}\right)\overline{Y}_r + \frac{nr}{n}\overline{Y}_{nr}$$
$$= \overline{Y}_r - \frac{nr}{r}(\overline{Y}_r - \overline{Y}_{nr})$$
$$\overline{Y}_r = \overline{Y}_n + \frac{nr}{r}(\overline{Y}_r - \overline{Y}_{nr})$$

This expression makes it clear that the estimated mean for the respondents is equal to the estimated mean for all units in the sample plus a factor that expresses the biasing effect of the nonresponse error. When there is no nonresponse, then $(nr = 0 \rightarrow r = n)$: $\overline{Y}_r = \overline{Y}_n$. In this situation, the estimated mean for the r respondents is equal to the mean estimated for all n sample units. This signifies that there is no nonresponse error. This is also the case when the estimated mean of the respondents and the nonrespondents are equal: $\overline{Y}_r = \overline{Y}_{nr}$. In this case, the decision to participate is uncorrelated with Y, and as far as Y is concerned, there is no difference between the group of respondents and the group of nonrespondents.

Although this nonresponse model for a sample mean is simple, it shows that the reduction of nonresponse error operationally is not straightforward. For example, with an incentive one can increase the response rate, but it is possible that some persons are more susceptible to the incentive than others. When the susceptibility to incentives is related to a substantive relevant characteristic, the use of the incentive will *increase* the difference between respondents and nonrespondents with respect to that characteristic, thus increasing nonresponse error. In this situation, a higher response rate due to the incentive does not result in a smaller nonresponse error; instead, just the opposite occurs.

The model also illustrates that for the evaluation of the nonresponse error one must both compare the respondents with the nonrespondents and calculate the response rate. After defining some additional basic concepts, the information necessary for this evaluation follows.

Basic Concepts

Until now, the sample units in the example given were divided or classified into two general groups:

respondents and nonrespondents. The respondents are eligible sample units with a completed interview; nonrespondents are eligible units that are not interviewed. *Ineligible units* in a sample of individuals include those that are deceased; emigrated or have left the country for a long period of time; units residing in an institution and unoccupied or demolished premises. In a sample of households or addresses, the ineligible units include the following: unoccupied or demolished premises; premises under construction; nonresidential addresses; addresses occupied, but no resident households; and addresses occupied by resident households, but no eligible respondents. For some units there is not enough information; these units are classified as units of *unknown eligibility* (e.g., unknown whether an eligible person is present in an existing housing unit).

In a standard in-person household survey, there are two main reasons for nonresponse: refusal and noncontact. Mostly, interviewers are instructed to contact sampling units according to a prescribed contact procedure. For example, the contact procedure may specify at least four contact attempts, including at least one visit in the evening and one during the weekend, and that these visits should be spread over at least two different weeks. Even then it is not always possible to contact all the units in the sample. These units that are not contacted at the end of the contact procedure receive the final disposition of "noncontact." Refusals are contacted sample units with a negative reaction to the request to participate in a survey. Given these two main reasons for nonresponse, one can further segment the group of nonrespondents into three subclasses: (1) refusals, (2) noncontacts, and (3) other nonrespondents. The concepts just defined can be represented in a simple diagram (see Table 1).

The classification shown in Table 1 is useful to define and calculate some rates that are relevant to evaluating nonresponse error. As already mentioned, the response rate is the total number of respondents divided by the number of eligible sampling units. Among the group classified as "unknown eligibility" (*ue*) one can estimate the proportion of eligible units (*pe*) by using the current survey. This proportion (*pe*) equals $e/(e + ie)$.

Using these definitions, the calculation of the *response rate* is straightforward: $r/(r + rf + nc + on + (pe \times ue))$. One can also calculate the proportion of nonrespondents in the group of eligible units: $nr/(e$ nonresponse rate $+ (pe \times ue))$. It is a standard practice to calculate the *refusal rate* as $r/(r + rf)$.

Information to Evaluate Nonresponse Error

Information from all the units in the sample (respondents and nonrespondents) is needed to evaluate the nonresponse error in a survey. This is the case both to calculate the rates discussed previously and to compare the group of respondents with the group of nonrespondents. Obtaining information from nonrespondents seems at first a contradiction in terms. Although it is a difficult task to collect information from the nonrespondents, there are some opportunities. Sometimes one can use the sampling frame. The sampling frame is the listing of all units in the target population. Sometimes the sampling frame (e.g., national register, staff register) contains information about some basic sociodemographic characteristics of the units (e.g., age, gender, civil status, educational level, professional group). When this kind of information is available, it offers an excellent opportunity to compare respondents and nonrespondents using some relevant background characteristics. Another extremely useful source of information

Table 1 Classification of final fieldwork outcomes in a survey

Sampling Units (n)			
Eligible (e)		*Unknown Eligible (ue)*	*Ineligible (ie)*
Respondents (*r*)	Nonrespondents (*nr*)		
	- Refusals (*rf*)		
	- Noncontacts (*nc*)		
	- Other nonrespondents (*on*)		

to evaluate the nonresponse error is the *paradata* collected by means of the case control form. A case control form is an essential instrument for monitoring the field work or interviewer activities of a survey. A case control form is filled out by the interviewer; it contains information about all contact attempts and contacts—date, day of the week, time, mode of the visit (personal, personal but only intercom, telephone, etc.)—and outcome of contact (interview, appointment, no contact, refusal, etc.). Also, the reason for refusal mentioned by the respondent (e.g., bad timing, not interested, don't know enough about the topic, too difficult for me) can be registered on the contact form or on a separate refusal report form. Sometimes in-person interviewers are also asked to record on these forms a number of observable area and dwelling characteristics (e.g., type of dwelling, physical state of dwellings in the area), as well as observable characteristics and other information about the person who refuses.

It is important that the case control form is filled out for all the eligible units in the sample and that the information is available for both respondents and nonrespondents. The information from the case control form is essential for calculating the response rates. (One can say that a case control form of some description is a vital part of a well-designed and organized survey.) Without information from the case control form, a profound evaluation of the nonresponse error is really not possible. One must realize that using a case control form makes the requirements of the field work activities in a survey more severe and complex. For example, an increase of the survey cost is a logical consequence.

Reducing Nonresponse Error

Although the structure of the simple model of nonresponse error makes it clear that reduction of nonresponse error is not just a matter of increasing the response rate, much of nonresponse research is related to factors that can have a positive effect on the decision to participate in a survey interview. In a frequently cited model of survey participation developed by Robert M. Groves and Mick P. Couper in the late 1990s, the (doorstep) interaction between the interviewer and the respondent is the only factor with a direct effect on the respondent's decision to cooperate or to refuse. Other factors in the model have an indirect effect through the interaction. These factors can be classified into two categories: (1) factors out of researcher control and (2) factors under researcher

control. The factors out of researcher control are related to the general social context in which the survey is organized (political and economic conditions, survey-taking climate, neighborhood characteristics) and to respondent's characteristics (sociodemographic characteristics, knowledge of the topic, experience with surveys, psychological predisposition). Survey design features (respondent selection, survey topic, mode of administration) and interviewer characteristics (sociodemographic characteristics, experience, expectation, ability) are factors that the researcher can control.

Given the central role in the model of the interaction between interviewer and respondent, the interviewers' training to obtain positive reactions to the request to participate is one important factor in increasing survey participation. During the training, interviewers must become familiar with adequate doorstep strategies. Two techniques must be mentioned in this context: *tailoring and maintaining* interaction. In contrast with the idea that interviewer behavior must be standardized, the initial interaction with the respondent is not directed by a standard script. Interviewers must tailor their interaction with the respondent. They must read the cues from the respondents and adapt their interviewing approach, thereby averting a refusal. Some respondents, for example, are more sensitive to the topic of the questionnaire; others are more willing to participate if they believe that others will also participate. During the interaction, the interviewer must play upon the reasons that are important in the respondent's decision process. To obtain information about which reasons will dominate the respondent's decision, a second interaction principle, maintaining interaction, must be applied. Interviewers should try to avoid provoking a quick negative reaction from the respondent. It is important that they try to prolong the interaction as long as possible, so that they get enough information to persuade the respondents adequately. In this way, maintaining interaction is vital to the tailoring principle. Increasing the number of contact attempts can also be considered as a special kind of maintaining interaction.

It is not only important to train the interviewers to achieve contact and to persuade the respondents, but also to closely monitor the interviewer's field work activities (e.g., contact strategies, response rate, contact rate, and refusal rate for each interviewer) so that information can be used to improve fieldwork performance.

It is clear that a few interviewers with exceptionally high refusal and noncontact rates can have a serious impact on the field work results. Detection of these rates at an early stage in the field work is crucial.

In addition to the interviewer's training and follow-up, it is generally accepted that an advance letter (or other form of advance contact) to the sample units has a positive effect on the response rate. In the advance letter, the topic and the intention of the survey interview are introduced, the field work organization and the responsible authority are mentioned, and privacy and confidentiality are emphasized. When incentives are used, one can announce the incentive in the advance letter. Pre-paid (noncontingent) cash incentives in particular can increase the willingness of a sample unit to cooperate.

Refusal conversion, that is, obtaining information from initially reluctant respondents, is another strategy that one can use to increase the response rate. It is typical that an experienced interviewer with good response rates is used to try to make a refusal conversion attempt with any reluctant respondents. This means that a refusal is recontacted by another interviewer and asked again to participate in the survey. Due to privacy reasons, this procedure is illegal in some countries.

A well-organized field work for a survey offers possibilities to minimize nonresponse error during the data collection period and to assess the nonresponse error at the end of the field work. In a well-organized survey, an adequate sampling frame is available; interviewers are well trained to contact and persuade the respondents; an informative and carefully edited advance letter is used; a well-designed case-control form is filled out after each contact attempt with each sample unit; if necessary and possible, a refusal conversion procedure is implemented; and accurate and timely monitoring of the field work is organized. All these characteristics are not only relevant to decrease and to evaluate nonresponse error but also are very useful to improve survey data quality in general.

Geert Loosveldt

See also Advance Contact; Advance Letter; Control Sheet; Error of Nonobservation; Ignorable Nonresponse; Incentives; Ineligible; Interviewer Monitoring; Interviewer Training; Noncontact; Nonignorable Nonresponse; Nonresponse Rates; Paradata; Refusal; Refusal Avoidance Training (RAT); Refusal Conversion; Refusal Report Form (RRF); Response Rates; Sampling Frame; Standard Definitions; Tailoring; Total Survey Error (TSE); Unknown Eligibility

Further Readings

American Association for Public Opinion Research. (2006). *Standard definitions: Final dispositions of case codes and outcome rates for surveys* (4th ed.). Lenexa, KS: Author.

Biemer, P. P., & Lyberg, L. E. (2003). *Introduction to survey quality.* New York: Wiley.

Groves, R. M. (2006). Nonresponse bias in household surveys. *Public Opinion Quarterly, 70*(5), 646–675.

Groves, R. M., & Couper, M. (1998). *Nonresponse in household interview surveys.* New York: Wiley.

Groves, R. M., Dillman, D. A., Eltinge, J. L., & Little, R. J. A. (Eds.). (2002). *Survey nonresponse.* New York: Wiley.

NONRESPONSE RATES

The nonresponse rate is defined as the percentage of all potentially eligible units (or elements) that do not have responses to—at least a certain proportion of—the items in a survey questionnaire. Thus, a nonresponse rate can be calculated at the unit level (in which all data from a sampled respondent are missing) and/or the item level (in which only data for certain variables from a sampled respondent are missing).

The nonresponse rate is not the same as nonresponse error. Nonresponse error occurs when nonrespondents in a survey are systematically different from respondents in nonnegligible ways that are germane to the objects of the study. For example, if the survey attempts to assess public opinion on the president's new plan for the Iraq War, then nonresponse error would occur if citizens who express their opinions on the issue were significantly more likely to oppose the plan than were those who were sampled but from whom no data were gathered. As such, the nonresponse rate alone does not tell whether there is nonresponse error or how much error exists in the survey. However, knowing the nonresponse rate is a necessary step toward estimating the nonresponse error.

All sampled cases in a survey can be categorized into one of four major groups: (1) eligible cases with sufficient data to be classified as *responses*, (2) eligible cases with no sufficient data (i.e., *nonresponses*), (3) cases of *unknown eligibility*, and (4) *ineligible cases*.

Responses

Cases that are treated as responses can also be divided into two groups: complete responses and partial responses. Standards that are widely used to define partial responses versus complete responses include the following: (a) the proportion of all applicable questions completed; (b) the proportion of essential questions completed; and (c) the proportion of all questions administered. Essential questions may vary, depending upon the purposes of a survey. In the case of the previously mentioned survey about public approval of the new war plan, the crucial variables may include attitudes toward the plan, party identification, and so on. Survey researchers should define what constitutes a complete versus a partial response based on one of the standards or a combination of the standards prior to data collection. Complete responses, for example, could be defined as cases that have answers to 95% or more of essential questions, whereas partial responses might be defined as cases with answers to 50–94% of such questions. Cases with fewer than 50% of the essential questions answered could be treated as *breakoffs*, which is a form of nonresponse. By this definition, only cases with data for at least 50% of crucial questions would be deemed as responses or partial responses.

Nonresponses

Nonresponses can result from noncooperation or refusals, noncontacts, and from other factors. The situations in which instances of nonresponse occur vary across surveys and across different sampling or data collection modes. Refusals happen in random-digit dialing (RDD) telephone or in-person surveys of households when a household has been contacted and either a responsible household member or the designated respondent has refused to participate in the study. Breakoffs refer to a premature termination from an interview. In mail or online surveys, refusals occur when contact has been made with a specifically named respondent or with a household or organization where the respondent works or lives, and the respondent or a responsible member of the household or organization has refused to participate. However, researchers often are not certain when this has happened as they typically receive no direct evidence to this effect. A breakoff occurs when partially completed questionnaires are returned with some notification suggesting that the respondent refused to complete the rest of the questionnaire. The distinction between breakoffs and partial responses should be pre-determined by researchers using the criteria defining a complete response versus a partial response, as previously mentioned.

Noncontacts in RDD telephone surveys of households refer to cases in which a telephone number is confirmed as a residential household, but the selected member of the household is never available to speak with an interviewer. In in-person surveys, noncontacts happen when the interviewers cannot reach the respondents, either because they cannot enter the building where the respondents live or work or because the respondents are not there and available at the time. In the case of mail or online surveys, noncontacts refer to the cases in which a questionnaire is returned after the deadline or researchers are notified that the respondent is not available during the time when the study is in the field. Here also, researchers rarely have firm evidence that this, if fact, has occurred. In mail and Internet surveys, there are relatively few instances in which the researchers learn that the sampled respondent was never contacted (e.g., receiving a notification from the postal service or an Internet server that the packet or email was undeliverable).

Other types of nonresponse include cases in which the respondent is or was eligible and did not refuse to participate in the study, but no data were collected for reasons of health, language, literacy, and so on.

Unknown Eligibility

Unknown eligibility occurs in RDD telephone surveys of households when it is not known if a sampled telephone number belongs to a residential household or whether there is an eligible respondent living in the household. In in-person household surveys, a case is categorized as unknown eligibility when it is unknown whether an eligible household is located at the sampled address or whether an eligible respondent lives in the place. In mail or online surveys, unknown eligibility includes cases in which nothing is known about whether a questionnaire has reached the respondent or whether the respondent is eligible.

Ineligible Cases

In landline RDD telephone surveys of households, ineligible cases may include phone numbers of households that are located outside of the geographical area of interest. For example, researchers may be interested in

Wisconsin residents' opinions about the seat belt law, but some telephone numbers selected by the computer may reach residents of Illinois or Minnesota and therefore should be considered as ineligible. Often with U.S. cell phone RDD samples this is even more problematic. Ineligible cases in RDD surveys also include telephone numbers of fax machines, nonresidential households, and/or out-of-service numbers. In in-person household surveys, ineligible cases result from the situation in which there is no household located at the sampled address or no eligible respondents within a sampled household. A case is deemed as ineligible in mail or online surveys when the researchers have evidence that a respondent fails to pass the screening questionnaire designed to assess eligibility.

Formulae to Calculate Nonresponse Rates

The calculation of nonresponse rates varies depending upon what are considered as potentially eligible units. The first formula of nonresponse rate (NRR1) generates the minimum nonresponse rate because the potential eligible cases include all cases of responses, all cases of nonresponses, and all cases of unknown eligibility:

$$NRR1 = nonresponses/(responses$$
$$+ nonresponses + unknown\ eligibility).$$

The second way of calculating the nonresponse rate (NRR2) requires researchers to estimate the proportion of cases with unknown eligibility (separately by type, e.g., for answering machines, for ring–no answers, for busy signals) that may be actually eligible—that is, the e term in the formula NRR2—based on the best available scientific evidence. By doing so, researchers can make a more accurate estimate of eligible units, thereby having a better estimate of the nonresponse rate. When using NRR2, the evidence used for the estimation must be provided in detail. For instance, researchers might know that 40% of cases with "ring–no answer" in an RDD telephone survey actually are eligible according to past survey experience. Then they can set the value of e as 0.4 for the ring–no answer final dispositions and calculate the rate using the estimate.

$$NRR2 = nonresponses/(responses + nonresponses$$
$$+ [e \times unknown\ eligibility]).$$

A third type of nonresponse rate calculation (NRR3) does not treat cases of unknown eligibility as potentially eligible cases. Thus, NRR3 can be considered as a special case of NRR2, in which e equals zero (i.e., it is assumed that there are no eligible cases among those whose eligibility is unknown). NRR3 may also be used in rare situations in which the eligibility of all cases is known. This formula generates the maximum nonresponse rate because the denominator is the smallest among the three computations:

$$NRR3 = nonresponses/(responses + nonresponses).$$

Complex surveys require more complicated ways to calculate nonresponse rates. There are three general situations of complex design, including (1) single samples with unequal probabilities of selection, (2) multi-wave panels, and (3) surveys that use a listing from a previous survey as a sample frame. In single-stage designs in which the units are sampled with unequal probabilities, the rates should be weighted by base weights that are the inverse of the selection probabilities or a number that is proportional to the inverse. In multiple-wave designs, the rates for the units that are sampled at the last stage should incorporate nonresponse at the earlier stages. For example, a three-wave, longitudinal survey should report both the nonresponse rate for the third wave and the cumulative nonresponse rate across the three waves. In two-phase designs that subsample respondents from a previously existing frame, the nonresponse rate of the current survey should be reported, and so should be the nonresponse rate that incorporates the previous sample (i.e., one that calculates nonresponse from both the current and the previous sample).

Weiyu Zhang and Xiaoxia Cao

See also Completed Interview; Complex Sample Surveys; *e*; Item Nonresponse; Noncontact; Nonresponse; Nonresponse Bias; Nonresponse Error; Partial Completion; Refusal; Response Rates; Standard Definitions; Unit Nonresponse

Further Readings

American Association for Public Opinion Research. (2006). *Standard definitions: Final dispositions of case codes and outcome rates for surveys* (4th ed.). Lenexa, KS: Author.

Curtin, R., Presser, S., & Singer, E. (2002). Changes in telephone survey nonresponse over the past quarter-century. *Public Opinion Quarterly, 69*, 87–98.

Groves, R. M. (2006). Nonresponse rates and nonresponse bias in household surveys. *Public Opinion Quarterly, 70,* 646–675.

Groves, R. M., Dillman, D. A., Eltinge, J. L., & Little, R. J. A. (2002). *Survey nonresponse.* New York: Wiley.

Lavrakas, P. (1993). *Telephone survey methods: Sampling, selection, and supervision* (2nd ed.). Newbury Park, CA: Sage.

NONSAMPLING ERROR

Nonsampling error is a catchall phrase that refers to all types of survey error other than the error associated with sampling. This includes error that comes from problems associated with coverage, measurement, nonresponse, and data processing. Thus, nonsampling error encompasses all forms of bias and variance other than that associated with the imprecision (variance) inherent in any survey sample.

Coverage error refers primarily to the bias and variance that may result when the sampling frame (the list from which the sample is drawn) used to represent the population of interest fails to adequately "cover" the population, and the portion that is missed differs in nonignorable ways from the portion that is included on the frame. Coverage error also includes bias and variance that can result when a within-unit respondent selection technique is used that does not adequately represent the population at the level of the individual person. *Nonresponse error* refers to the bias and variance that may result when not all those who are sampled have data gathered from them, and these nonresponders differ in nonignorable ways from responders on variables of interest. Item-level nonresponse error includes the bias and variance that may result from cooperating respondents who do not provide answers (data) to all the variables being measured if the data they would have provided differ in nonignorable ways from the data that the other respondents are providing on those variables. *Measurement error* refers to bias and variance that may result related to the questionnaire, the behavior of the person who gathers the data, the behavior of respondents, and/or the mode of data collection. *Data processing errors* refer to the bias and variance that may result from mistakes made while processing data, including the coding and recoding of data, the transformation of data into new variables, the imputation of missing data, the weighting of the data, and the analyses that are performed with data.

Researchers concerned with nonsampling error can take two different strategies to try to deal with it. First, they can implement numerous methodological and other quality control techniques to try to reduce the amount of nonsampling error that results in their studies; this typically adds to the costs of the research study. Second, they can build in methodological studies to try to measure the nature and size of the nonsampling errors that cannot be reduced to negligible levels; this also adds to the project cost but often not as much as the first approach.

Many people appear to think that nonsampling error applies only to research studies that use the survey method of data collection. However, each type of error that makes up nonsampling error has its counterpart in any form of social research, be it qualitative or quantitative, including experiments and quasi-experiments, content analysis, observational research, cognitive interviewing, and focus groups.

Paul J. Lavrakas

See also Bias; Content Analysis; Coverage Error; Measurement Error; Nonresponse Error; Sampling Error; Sampling Frame; Total Survey Error (TSE); Variance

Further Readings

Groves, R. M. (1989). *Survey errors and survey costs.* New York: Wiley.

NONTELEPHONE HOUSEHOLD

Telephone surveys became an acceptable mode of data collection in the United States in the 1970s, when approximately 90% of households in the United States had a telephone. According to the 2000 Census, 98% of U.S. households contained a telephone. However, the 2000 Census did not distinguish between wireline and wireless service, so having a "telephone" could mean having a landline phone, a wireless phone, or both. In each year since the 2000 Census, more and more households began to substitute wireless telephone service for their wireline or landline telephone service. This phenomenon, often referred to as "cutting the cord," has introduced additional coverage bias in traditional wireline random-digit dial (RDD) samples, as in 2008 approximately 20% of U.S. households had only a cell phone.

By 1986, only a little more than 7% of households were without a telephone. Analysis of National Health Interview Survey (NHIS) data by Owen Thornberry and James Massey in 1988 showed that certain sociodemographic cohorts were disproportionately represented among the nontelephone population, particularly families and persons living in poverty. If information on low income, or any correlates of low income, was an important objective of a telephone survey, researchers were encouraged not to use a telephone sample for data collection. As the number of households without a telephone declined into the 1990s, concerns about bias diminished but did not disappear.

In 1995, Scott Keeter proposed a method for minimizing the bias associated with the exclusion of households without a telephone. Keeter showed that interruption of telephone service is usually episodic in nature. Based on this observation, he proposed using survey data collected from respondents reporting interruption of telephone service to make adjustments for the nontelephone population.

Based on the 2006 NHIS data and data from Mediamark's 2006 national syndicated survey, only 2% of households have no phone of any kind. Findings from the 2007 NHIS survey show 15% cell phone only and another 10% as being "cell phone mostly" (i.e., they have a landline and a cell phone but essentially do not use their landline for incoming calls). This shift in telephone ownership away from landline telephones means that a traditional RDD sample today will represent only 87% of all households. In 2006, E. Deborah Jay and Mark DeCamillo experimented with a Keeter-like approach for adjusting for cell phone only households. In their study, they asked about interruption of telephone service and whether the household had cell phone service during that interruption. As with the Keeter study, the demographics of recent cell phone only households were similar to published demographics of cell phone only households. The authors proposed using data collected from respondents that reported a recent cell phone only status to adjust estimates for noncoverage of the cell phone only population.

Including households with no telephone service of any kind is not a viable option for RDD surveys. However, cell phone only households can be included in telephone surveys. Frames exist for sampling cell phone numbers, and there has been a significant amount of ongoing research related to sampling cell phones both in the United States and around the world. Many methodological issues remain to be solved, and in the United States sampling cell phones is uniquely complicated by Telephone Consumer Protection Act (TCPA) regulations that prohibit dialing a cell phone with an autodialer.

Linda Piekarski

See also Cell Phone Only Household; Cell Phone Sampling; Dual-Frame Sampling; Telephone Consumer Protection Act of 1991; Telephone Households; Telephone Penetration; Telephone Surveys

Further Readings

Frankel, M. R., Srinath, K. P., Hoaglin, D. C., Battaglia, M. P., Smith, P. J., Wright, R. A., et al. (2003). Adjustments for non-telephone bias in random-digit-dialing surveys. *Statistics in Medicine, 22,* 1611–1626.

Jay, E. D., & DeCamillo, M. (2006, May). *Identifying recent cell phone-only households.* Paper presented at 2006 Annual Conference of the American Association for Public Opinion Research, Montreal, Canada.

Keeter, S. (1995). Estimating telephone non-coverage bias with a telephone survey. *Public Opinion Quarterly, 59*(2), 196–217.

Kim, S. W., & Lepkowski, J. L. (2002). Telephone household non-coverage and mobile telephones. *2002 Proceedings of the Section on Survey Research Methods, American Statistical Association* (pp. 1845–1850). Alexandria, VA: American Statistical Association.

Lavrakas, P. J., Steeh, C., Boyle, J., Blumberg, S., Callegaro, M., et al. (2008). *Guidelines and considerations for survey researchers when planning and conducting RDD and other telephone surveys in the U.S. with respondents reached via cell phone numbers.* Lenexa, KS: American Association for Public Opinion Research. Retrieved June 1, 2008, from http://www.aapor.org/uploads/Final_AAPOR_Cell_Phone_TF_report_041208.pdf

Thornberry, O. T., & Massey, J. T. (1988). Trends in United States telephone coverage across time and subgroups. In R. M. Groves, P. P. Biemer, L. E. Lyberg, J. T. Massey, W. L. Nicholls II, & J. Waksberg (Eds.), *Telephone survey methodology* (pp. 25–49). New York: Wiley.

NONVERBAL BEHAVIOR

Nonverbal behavior is physical action that complements, supplements, or takes the place of spoken words or sounds. Examples include, but are not limited to, facial expressions, body postures, and gestures.

Data collection in survey research may include the cataloging (observing and coding) of nonverbal behavior in order to help put verbal data—written or spoken words or other utterances—into context for more in-depth analysis and interpretation. For example, a study based on personal interviews of people who are reluctant to speak with the interviewer may gauge the level of rapport that the interviewer was able to establish by examining the nonverbal behavior of respondents. If these respondents are frowning, turning their backs to the interviewer, or otherwise demonstrating discomfort, this information could be used to gauge the credibility of the answers of those interviewed.

Nonverbal behavior can change, alter, enhance, supplement, complement, or contradict the meaning of an act of verbal communication. Nonverbal behavior sometimes contradicts or confuses the meaning of verbal communication. For example, if an individual tells an interviewer that they enjoy an activity but they frown as they say so—the frown communicates something different than a smile or a neutral expression. In this case, the respondent may be providing a socially desirable yet inaccurate verbal answer. A researcher could work toward producing more valid data by recording the nonverbal behavior that accompanies the verbal communication.

Survey researchers also need to be concerned about the nonverbal behavior that interviewers exhibit. Interviewers who are expected to remain neutral while administering a questionnaire may keep their voice and language neutral but may inadvertently demonstrate nonverbal signals that could bias a respondent's answers. Thus, interviewer training, especially in the case of in-person (face-to-face) interviews, should emphasize interviewers being aware of their own nonverbal behavior.

Nonverbal communication and its meanings can vary across cultures and groups. For example, whether a speaker looks at a listener in his or her eyes during conversation has different meanings in different cultures. In some cultures, looking into the eyes of the person to whom you are speaking is considered respectful and desirable behavior. In other cultures, a direct gaze is thought to be a sign of disrespect. In addition, recent studies of eye gazing and human communication have found that eye gazing may not be only a cultural phenomenon but also a physiological one. People with differing brain structures—for example, some people with autism spectrum disorders—look at areas on faces other than the eyes because direct eye gaze can provoke a physiological fear response for them.

The conditional and contingent meanings of nonverbal behavior as a complement to verbal communication can make coding and analyzing the information a challenging, but potentially very useful, aspect of research.

Heather H. Boyd

See also Attitude Measurement; Behavior Coding; Coding; Face-to-Face Interviewing; Interviewer Neutrality; Interviewer Training; Measurement Error; Social Desirability

Further Readings

Ekman, P., & Friesen, W. V. (2003). *Unmasking the face: A guide to unmasking the emotions from facial cues.* Cambridge, MA: Malor Books.

NULL HYPOTHESIS

A null hypothesis is one in which no difference (or no effect) between two or more variables is anticipated by the researchers. This follows from the tenets of science in which empirical evidence must be found to disprove the null hypothesis before one can claim support for an alternative hypothesis that states there is in fact some reliable difference (or effect) in whatever is being studied. The null hypothesis is typically stated in words to the effect that "A equals B." The concept of the null hypothesis is a central part of formal hypothesis testing.

An example in survey research would be a split-half experiment that is used to test whether the order of two question sequences within a questionnaire affects the answers given to the items in one of the sequences, for example, in crime surveys where fear of crime and criminal victimization experience are both measured. In this example, a researcher could hypothesize that different levels of fear would be reported if the fear items followed the victimization items, compared to if they preceded the victimization items. Half the respondents would be randomly assigned to receive one order (fear items, then victimization items), and the other half would receive the other order (victimization items, then fear items). The null hypothesis would be that the order of these question sequences makes no difference in the answers given to the fear of crime items. Thus, if the null hypothesis is true, the researcher would not expect to observe any reliable (i.e., statistically significant) difference in levels of fear reported under the two question ordering conditions. If results indicate a statistically reliable difference in fear under the two conditions, then the null hypothesis is rejected and support is accorded to the alternative hypothesis, that is, that fear of crime, as reported in a survey, is affected by whether it precedes or follows victimization questions.

Another way of understanding the null hypothesis in survey research is to think about the crime survey example and the confidence intervals that can be calculated around the fear of crime measures in the two ordering conditions. The null hypothesis would be that the 95% confidence intervals for the fear measures under the two orders (conditions) would overlap and thus not be reliably (significantly) different from each other at the .05 (alpha) level. The alternative hypothesis would be that the confidence intervals would not overlap, and thus the fear measures gathered under one order are reliably different from the same fear measures gathered under the other order.

Rejecting a null hypothesis when it is in fact true is termed a *Type I error*. Not rejecting a null hypothesis when it is fact false is termed a *Type II error*.

Paul J. Lavrakas

See also Alpha, Significance Level of Test; Alternative Hypothesis; Confidence Interval; Experimental Design; *p*-Value; Split-Half; Statistical Power; Type I Error; Type II Error

Further Readings

Babbie, E. (2006). *The practice of social research* (11th ed.). Belmont, CA: Wadsworth/Cengage Learning.

Campbell, D. T., & Stanley, J. (1966). *Experimental and quasi-experimental designs for research*. Chicago: Rand-McNally.

NUMBER CHANGED

When a telephone survey is conducted, some dialings will result in a message stating that the number they have dialed has been changed. The message often includes the new number. "Number changed" dispositions in RDD samples are normally classified as ineligible, but there are some circumstances for which

the researcher might want to considered such numbers eligible and call the new number.

When a household changes its landline phone number, it is usually because that household has moved to a new location. If the move was to a location outside the exchange boundaries of the old telephone number, a U.S. household traditionally had to obtain a new telephone number in an exchange serving their new address. However, number portability has changed this by allowing people to keep their telephone number when they move. A household also might change its number without relocating. For example, they might want to replace their directory-listed number with a new, unlisted number. Or a household might elect to change their service provider to a competitive local exchange carrier or to a provider of Voice over Internet Protocol (VoIP) services. In areas where number portability is not available, the household would be required to get a new telephone number in order to change service providers.

Usually numbers that result in a "Number changed" message are removed from a random-digit dialed (RDD) sample because the new geographic location makes them ineligible for the survey. A more important reason for their exclusion is that an RDD sample could have allowed both numbers—the old number and the new number—to be eligible for selection. If researchers elect to call the new number, they must also apply a weight to correct for the multiple probabilities of selection of that household.

However, for telephone surveys that sample specifically named persons—for example, when working from a client-supplied list of customers—it often will be appropriate to call the new number. Other instances in which it would be appropriate to call a changed number would be (a) recontacting a respondent for a follow-up interview and (b) conducting longitudinal surveys of the same respondents. In such cases, multiple probabilities of selection usually would not be a concern.

Linda Piekarski

See also Dispositions; Final Dispositions; Hit Rate; Number Portability; Random-Digit Dialing (RDD); Telephone Surveys

Further Readings

American Association for Public Opinion Research. (2006). *Standard definitions: Final dispositions of case codes and outcome rates for surveys* (4th ed.). Lenexa, KS: Author.

Retrieved April 21, 2008, from http://www.aapor.org/uploads/standarddefs_4.pdf

NUMBER PORTABILITY

Number portability is the ability of users of telecommunications services in the United States and most other countries to keep their existing telephone number when changing from one local service provider to another. Under Federal Communications Commission (FCC) rules, the implementation of local number portability (LNP) in the United States has caused some problems for telephone survey researchers. In the early days of wireline-to-wireline portability, both numbers associated with a porting request could be dialed successfully. When wireline-to-wireless porting was implemented, there were concerns that this would influence the ability of researchers and telemarketers to comply with the portion of the Telephone Consumer Protection Act (TCPA) of 1991 that limited calls to certain types of phone numbers, including wireless phone numbers.

In 1996, the U.S. Congress amended the Telecommunications Act of 1934 to establish a framework that would promote competition and reduce regulation in all telecommunications areas. It was recognized that certain barriers to competition would need to be eliminated, specifically the inability of customers to switch from one service provider to another and retain the same phone number. New FCC rules were enacted that gave consumers the ability to switch from one service provider to another and keep their existing telephone numbers. The rules were applicable only locally, that is, only within a local exchange or rate center. If a person moved from one geographic area to another, the number would not be portable. Telephone companies were allowed to charge a fee to cover their porting costs. However, because of these costs, most small landline companies were not required to port numbers to wireless carriers until the FCC had completed a study about the effects of porting rules on small companies.

Local number portability in the United States was implemented in phases. Portability between local landline (wire) service providers was implemented in 1998. The FCC had also required that three categories of CMRS (commercial mobile radio service) providers—cellular providers, broadband personal communications service (PCS) providers, and covered specialized mobile radio (SMR) providers—also provide number portability. The commission concluded that requiring them to do so would promote competition between and among local landline and wireless services. A separate timetable for compliance was established for CMRS providers. LNP between wireless service providers was finally implemented in November 2003 and between landline and wireless services in early 2005.

Porting in the United States requires two 10-digit numbers. One is the original subscriber number, which is no longer a valid local routing number or switch, and the other is a number in a prefix or 1000-block belonging to the new carrier that is used for rerouting a call to the correct end-user location and for accounting. A 1000-block is a block of 1,000 consecutive local numbers within a prefix, all starting with the same seven digits (e.g., 203-255-1XXX). Within a prefix, 1000-blocks can belong to different service providers offering different types of service. Since the subscriber's new carrier can also provide telephone service to new or existing customers as well as customers that are changing carriers, these remote porting numbers can and do occur in 100-blocks found on list-assisted RDD databases. A 100-block is a block of 100 consecutive numbers starting with the same eight digits (203-333-65XX). List-assisted RDD frames normally contain only 100-blocks with one or more directory-listed numbers from which RDD samples are generated by appending a random number between 00 and 99 to selected 100-blocks. Once a new subscriber (e.g., 203-333-6555) appears in a telephone directory, the 100-block 203-333-65XX becomes eligible for RDD samples. During the generation of an RDD sample, both kinds of numbers—those belonging to regular subscribers and those belonging to subscribers that have ported their number to this new carrier—can be generated during random number assignment.

As part of local number portability in the United States, a special database, currently maintained by NeuStar (the FCC-designated administrator of the U.S. database of ported numbers), and software were developed for telecommunications carriers to use. The database contains each ported number and the new number associated with that ported number. The software allows any telecommunications carrier to query the database before connecting a telephone call. If the number a customer has dialed is on the database, the carrier will be provided with the information required to redirect that call to the correct switch and location routing number (LRN). In the early years of LNP, the required databases and software were not in place everywhere. During that period, portability was sometimes handled using traditional call-forwarding techniques. Since both numbers, the number being ported and the number associated with the new switch, could be randomly generated in an RDD sample, both numbers would be "working" and would connect to the same residence. This caused what has been frequently referred to as *ghost numbers*, the telephone numbers associated with the new service provider but not recognized by a respondent to a survey.

Ghost numbers created two problems for researchers using RDD samples. First, a household that had ported its number would only report one telephone number, the number that they ported to a different provider. But in reality they had two numbers, the number they had ported and the number belonging to their new service provider. This meant that they had two chances of selection. Second, if contact was made on the telephone number belonging to the new service provider, the respondent would not recognize that number as being their telephone number. This meant that it was unclear to an interviewer whether the number had been dialed incorrectly or whether the number was a ghost number. Although call-forwarding techniques may still be used in areas that are transitioning to local number portability, the vast majority of competitive LRNs will not connect if dialed directly. However, their presence as disconnects or nonworking numbers in RDD samples will contribute to reduced sample productivity.

By 2005, full portability had been implemented in the United States, allowing porting between wireless and landline services. At this point, telephone survey research was further affected because a landline telephone number ported to a wireless phone number might easily appear in an RDD landline sample. This was a particular concern, because dialing wireless numbers in the United States using automated telephone equipment is a violation of TCPA regulations. The FCC was lobbied to provide a method for identifying these numbers. NeuStar, and the FCC agreed to license this information for an annual fee. Licensees have access to two files of ported numbers that are updated daily: a file of wireless-to-wireline telephone numbers and a file of wireline-to-wireless.

According to data from the FCC, by December 2004, 30.5 million numbers had been ported from one landline carrier to another, and more than 10 million numbers had been ported from one wireless carrier to another. By contrast, only 818,000 numbers had been ported from landline service to wireless service and only 10,000 from wireless service to landline service. Based on the NeuStar databases, as of July 2006, 2.4 million landline numbers have been ported to a wireless service provider, while only about 90,000 wireless numbers have been ported to landline service.

The porting of numbers between landline and wireless service providers can create coverage bias in RDD frames. In order to protect clients from inadvertent violation of the TCPA regulations, most sample providers routinely remove numbers ported to a wireless service and known wireless numbers (which would include those that have ported their wireless number to landline service) from their databases and telephone samples. Conceptually, the wireless-to-wireline file and the wireline-to-wireless file could be used to eliminate this bias. However there are strict prohibitions on the use of these files. Subscribers are contractually obligated to use this information solely to "meet the requirements and conditions of the TCPA." Therefore, using these numbers to augment a telephone frame could be in violation of these restrictions, unless they are pre-identified and hand-dialed by a qualified subscriber.

Ongoing analysis of this file by Survey Sampling International suggests that the coverage bias is minimal. On average, only about 14% of these ported numbers appear in a list-assisted frame, representing only 0.03% of the total frame. This file changes on a daily basis. On the other hand, research firms or call centers usually dial telephone sample numbers for days or weeks following their selection; researchers are encouraged to subscribe to the service and do their own scrubbing on a daily basis if they want to avoid all legal issues.

Another serious problem caused by number portability that U.S. telephone surveys face is the fact that some numbers for area codes and prefixes in a particular local area may reach people living in other geographic areas. This can happen when a landline number has been ported to a wireless service provider or a provider of Voice over Internet Protocol (VoIP). In these cases the cell phone or VoIP router and/or computer can be *transported* from one geographic location to another. Additionally, some VoIP service providers offer subscribers a telephone number (for inbound calls only) in a totally different area code. As the frequency of this transporting increases, telephone surveys will need to devise cost-effective ways to screen for the geographic eligibility of the household or respondent.

Linda Piekarski

See also Access Lines; Call Forwarding; Cell Phone Only Household; Cell Phone Sampling; Geographic Screening; Prefix; Random-Digit Dialing (RDD); Telephone Consumer Protection Act of 1991

NUMBER VERIFICATION

The verification of a telephone number in a telephone survey is done by an interviewer who confirms with a respondent that the number that was ostensibly dialed is in fact the number that was reached. The need to do this has been reduced over the years as more landline telephone surveys have come to be conducted with computer-assisted telephone interviewing (CATI) systems that include software and hardware to place the calls to the sampled telephone numbers, as opposed to having interviewers manually dial the numbers. However, the need for number verification has not been eliminated completely, as even with automatic dialing equipment mistakes sometimes occur. Furthermore, in the United States and due to current federal telecommunications regulations, all cell phone numbers that are sampled for a telephone survey must be hand-dialed—unless the cell phone owner has given the survey organization prior consent to be called—and thus interviewers will need to verify whether they have dialed the sampled number correctly.

There are several reasons that a landline (or cell phone) telephone survey may not reach the correct number, even when using equipment to place the calls. For example, national and local telephonic systems are subject to occasional error when "wires get crossed" (the electronic signals get mixed up), thus leading to a call reaching another number than the one to which it was intended. Call forwarding, whereby one telephone number is programmed by its owner to ring at another number, can also lead to the "wrong" number being reached. This is problematic when a business number that appears in an RDD sample is forwarded to a residential number. In this case, the household would not be eligible unless one of its residential numbers also was sampled. However, if a business number were reached because the residential number that was sampled in RDD was forwarded to it, then the resident reached via her or his forwarded home number would remain eligible. If the telephone survey has sampled "named persons," then reaching them on a different number than what was dialed does not make them ineligible. In these instances of number verification, the interviewer will learn whether the number dialed is not the number reached, and if it is, then the interview may continue or may be politely terminated and coded as out-of-sample depending on the manner of forwarding that took place. Using manual dialing will lead to errors made by the interviewers who are placing the calls. Thus, whenever interviewers are hand-dialing sampled numbers, a verification that the correct number was reached always should be included in the introduction of the survey before the questionnaire is administered. Typically, this verification is done after cooperation has been gained, because it is assumed that doing it too soon after initial contact will lead to an increase in nonresponse.

Paul J. Lavrakas

See also Call Forwarding; Cell Phone Sampling; Out of Sample; Random-Digit Dialing (RDD); Standard Definitions; Telephone Surveys

Further Readings

Lavrakas, P. J. (1993). *Telephone survey methods: Sampling, selection, and supervision* (2nd ed.). Newbury Park, CA: Sage.

O

Open-Ended Question

The selection of question structure is fundamental to the process of questionnaire construction. The open-ended question is one type of structure; the other, more commonly used alternative is the closed-ended question. The open-ended question does not provide answer categories. The person (respondent) who is asked an open-ended question formulates the answer and gives the response in his or her own words. Although this structure gives the respondent more freedom in crafting an answer, it also increases the cognitive effort. Without answer choices as cues to aid in understanding the question and deciding on an answer, the respondent has to perform additional cognitive tasks before he or she responds.

Reasons to Use Open-Ended Questions

All open-ended questions are alike in that the respondent is not given answer choices. However, the reasons for using this structure and the level of cognitive effort needed to respond can vary. The following are seven examples that illustrate different reasons for open-ended questions.

1. *Build rapport and encourage participation.* Asking an easy-to-answer question at the beginning of the questionnaire signals expressing an opinion as a benefit of survey participation and acknowledges the importance of what the respondent has to say. Sometimes initial quesstions used for this purpose are considered "warm-up" questions because one of the main objectives is to engage the respondent (e.g., *In your opinion, what is the most important issue facing the United States today?*).

2. *Get factual information.* When there is a wide range of answers expected to provide individual factual information, an open-ended structure can address the problem of having a list of more response choices than it is practical to include in a questionnaire. Factual information may be a request for a verbatim or for a numeric response (e.g., *What is your occupation? How much do you plan to spend on holiday gifts? Last year, what was your total annual household income?*).

3. *Expand a list.* When a closed-ended question offers a list of specific items or response choices (e.g., places where people get their news), a follow-up question asking about additional information can ensure that the pre-listed choices have not omitted any options (e.g., *Are there any others?*).

4. *Explain a prior answer.* An open-ended question can deepen the understanding of the response to a preceding question by obtaining additional details on the reason for the answer choice (e.g., *Why were you satisfied/ dissatisfied with your last doctor's appointment?*).

5. *Establish knowledge.* A test question can distinguish between more and less informed respondents to enhance the understanding of opinion formation (e.g., *Who are the U.S. senators from your state?*).

6. *Clarify terminology.* Asking respondents to define a key word in a question documents their level of understanding. It can also inform the variation in the meanings of words used among the respondents

who gave an answer (e.g., *What does* welfare *mean to you?*).

7. *Explore new topics.* The questionnaire can be an opportunity to get suggestions for future survey topics that are especially salient to the respondent. In particular for longitudinal studies, this information can inform the development of future questionnaires (e.g., *Questionnaires by their nature are limited. What city services, not included in this questionnaire, should be evaluated in future surveys?*).

Data Quality Considerations

When an open-ended question is used, particular attention must be paid to other aspects of the survey process that can affect the data quality and are specifically related to this structure: method of data collection, coding verbatim responses, and time and expenditure trade-offs.

Method of Data Collection

There are two basic methods used to collect information: self-administered (the respondent self-records answers by writing on a paper questionnaire or by entering a response into a computer) and interview (the respondent answers questions that are read and then recorded verbatim by another person, i.e., the interviewer). With the self-administered method, the respondent is responsible for providing a quality answer. The types of respondent-related errors specific to the open-ended structure are (a) missing answers; (b) incomplete responses; (c) misunderstood terminology; and (d) illegible writing. The format of a self-administered paper or electronic questionnaire can provide some assistance in reducing these errors. For example, the size of the space provided is a visual cue on how much information the respondent is expected to report—a smaller space results in less information, while more information is provided when there is a larger space. When there is a request to write in numeric factual information (e.g., *What was the last date you saw your doctor?*), clear instructions on how to provide the month, day, and year will reduce the variation, and possible errors, on how respondents report this information.

An interview can reduce some of the self-administered errors because an interviewer guides the respondent; however, there are other data quality considerations that need attention. The types of errors that can result from interviewer effects are biased answers as result of leading probes; answers given in order to provide socially desirable responses; and inaccurate verbatim recording. Specific interviewer training on how to ask open-ended questions is essential to minimize these types of errors.

In general, compared to the self-administered mode, more complete and accurate information can be expected when an interview method is used. When a survey includes both methods to give respondents a choice on how to participate, the variation in responses associated with each method needs to be considered.

Coding Verbatim Responses

Coding verbatim responses is necessary with open-ended questions. While one of the main advantages of using an open-ended structure is getting specific, individual information, the lists of verbatim answers need to be organized to be useful for data analysis and reports. Developing numeric codes to accurately represent the verbatim responses is challenging. The quality of open-ended data is diminished when careful attention is not given to code development. Errors can also occur when a person reads a verbatim answer and has to make a judgment about the most appropriate code to assign. Thorough training on how to make these judgments improves the accuracy and the confidence in reliable coding results. When multiple people are coding verbatim responses, the quality of the data also depends on intercoder reliability. To minimize the amount of coding that is needed on a questionnaire completed with an interviewer, a list of precoded answers can be provided. While the question is still asked using an open-ended structure, the interviewer uses the precoded list to classify a verbatim answer. There are two possible sources of error associated with a list of precoded choices: the reliability of the interviewer's judgment in selecting the appropriate answer and the accuracy of the items on the precoded list.

To obtain quality information, open-ended questions require sufficient time and financial resources to support the actions required for data quality. Time needs to be allowed when the questions are being answered and for coding the answers after the completed questionnaires are returned. A typical open-ended question can take two or three times longer for a respondent to complete than a closed-ended question because of the cognitive process associated with formulating a response and the extra time required to record a complete, legible verbatim answer. Also, because coding is needed to organize and quantify open-ended questions for data analysis and reporting, additional time has to be allocated for this process. Including open-ended questions means additional funds are needed to provide training for interviewers and coders and for professional time used to develop a coding system and to monitor the quality of the codes.

Janice Ballou

See also Closed-Ended Question; Coding; Interviewer Effects; Interviewer-Related Error; Mode Effects; Precoded Question; Questionnaire Design; Questionnaire Length; Respondent Burden; Respondent-Related Error; Verbatim

Further Readings

Biemer, P. P., & Lyberg, L. E. (2003). *Introduction to survey quality*. Hoboken, NJ: Wiley.

Bradburn, N. M., & Sudman, S. (1979). *Improving interview method and questionnaire design*. San Francisco: Jossey-Bass.

Dillman, D. A. (2000). *Mail and Internet surveys*. New York: Wiley.

Payne, S. P. (1951). *The art of asking questions*. Princeton, NJ: Princeton University Press.

Schuman, H., & Presser, S. (1981). *Questions and answers in attitude surveys*. New York: Academic Press.

OPINION NORMS

From a social science perspective, public opinion is much more than an aggregation of polling statistics. While individual survey responses are an instrumental component of understanding public opinion as a social force, the context in which the individual operates (e.g., media environment, typical discussion patterns) is an equally important consideration in obtaining a better understanding of the evolution of public opinion. Recognizing the normative aspects of a public opinion climate allows researchers to understand better how individuals come to possess opinions and how those opinions are shared with others.

Past work on behavioral norms offers insight as to how contextual forces, or "climates of opinion," can influence the actions and expressions of group members. Such social norms can be classified into two main categories, descriptive and injunctive. *Descriptive* norms are informational and describe the way things *are* within a given social setting, whereas *injunctive* norms possess a sanctioning function and prescribe the way things *ought* to be. Individuals who violate injunctive norms (i.e., engage in *proscribed* behavior) run the risk of alienating themselves from those around them.

By making use of interactions with important reference groups and exposure to available media, individuals are able to get a sense of what is socially acceptable when expressing political views and opinions. This iterative process establishes the normative environment surrounding opinion expression—it is within this climate that individuals may feel more or less inclined to express their own view. Respondents' perceptions of congruity between their own opinion and the perceived opinion of a given reference group can either encourage or dissuade opinion expression, much like behavioral norms influence the actions of those within a given social context.

Individual perceptions of this climate are an important and quantifiable aspect of understanding the impact that normative environments can have on individual behavior and expression. Aggregated perceptions of public opinion, such as those generated from survey data, constitute a "social barometer" that quantifies both the extremity and the amount of agreement among actors as related to these prevailing social forces.

Researchers interested in capturing the normative aspects of public opinion should account for the following opinion characteristics: (a) the valence and the strength of individual opinion (e.g., *Do you approve or disapprove of* X?, and *To what degree?*); and (b) perceptions of the valence and strength of the group opinion (e.g., key reference groups, such as members of your community, residents of this state). Within a survey context, questionnaires need to be geared toward respondents' perceptions of the climate of opinion and can included questions such as, *In your judgment, what would the reaction be if someone expressed* strong support *for* Candidate X *during the course of a conversation among people in your neighborhood: Very positive, somewhat positive, neutral, somewhat negative, or very negative?* While survey items such as these tap into individual perceptions of the context in which opinions are expressed, they also allow for simple (experimental) manipulations of key variables within the question (e.g., substituting candidates or discussion topics, level of support or opposition, and reference groups named within the question).

With this response data in hand, Jay Jackson's Return Potential Model (RPM) provides one example for quantifying the normative opinion climate. Normative "intensity" can be evaluated using the RPM by calculating the mean group deviation from a midpoint or neutral response option. This measure specifies the approval or disapproval associated with an opinion as well as the extremity or strength with which a norm is held (e.g., slight approval versus strong approval of expressing a specified opinion). It is quantified by using the following equation:

$$I_i = x_i - m,$$

where intensity (*I*) is the mean deviation from the researcher's specified midpoint value (*m*). It is important to note that intensity is a bidirectional concept that can apply to strong disapproval as well as strong approval. In other words, the degree to which a certain opinion norm is characterized by negative intensity (i.e., an opinion is strongly opposed) is related to the probable level of social sanctions for expressing that opinion. For high-intensity norms, violation will most likely result in some form of social isolation. On the other hand, expressing opinions associated with low-intensity norms may be seen as odd but will likely bear little social cost.

When measuring the normative opinion climate, it also is important to know how much agreement exists within a specified group. The RPM model also captures normative "crystallization," which quantifies the amount of consensus associated with a norm. Specifically, this assessment of crystallization measures the level of agreement regarding what opinions are appropriate to express. Mathematically, crystallization is *inversely* associated with variance among respondents' normative views and therefore becomes greater when there is relatively more agreement about public opinion. To properly derive crystallization (*C*), the following equation is used:

$$C_i = 1/(x_i - x_{mean}),$$

where C_i is the inverse of the deviation from the mean approval rating among all respondents. Highly crystallized opinion norms are well understood and solidified. Low crystallization is likely to be associated with normative ambiguity. For example, if it is perceived that everyone in a certain group strongly supports Candidate X, it is safer for group members to speak highly of that candidate without fears of social sanctions. Because such a normative environment is unambiguous (i.e., highly crystallized), group members are better able to anticipate the reactions of others.

With intensity and crystallization available as quantifications of normative opinion climates, researchers are able to generate predictions related to subsequent opinion expression, willingness to deliberate, and any number of communication behaviors that may fall under the sway of public opinion as a social force.

Carroll J. Glynn and Michael Huge

See also Experimental Design; Opinions; Public Opinion; Social Isolation; Spiral of Silence

Further Readings

Glynn, C. J. (1997). Public opinion as a normative opinion process. *Communication Yearbook, 20,* 157–183.

Jackson, J. M. (1975). Normative power and conflict potential. *Sociological Methods and Research, 4,* 237–263.

Price, V., Nir, L., & Capella, J. N. (2006). Normative and informational influences in online political discussions. *Communication Theory, 16,* 47–74.

Rimal, R. N., & Real, K. (2005). How behaviors are influenced by perceived norms. *Communication Research, 32*(3), 389–414.

OPINION QUESTION

Opinions that individuals hold about an issue are potentially quite complex, considering how opinions comprise beliefs, feelings, and values on that issue. As a result, survey questions designed to assess a respondent's opinion on an issue can tap a combination of the respondent's feelings and thoughts. As composite measures, however, opinions are gauged through a variety of opinion items.

The most basic opinion question, sometimes called an "attitude question," is designed to measure the direction of opinion. That is, where does the respondent stand on the issue or attitude object? Such opinion items, typically closed-ended, can be dichotomous in nature (e.g., *Do you support or oppose abortion?* Answer categories: Support; Oppose. *Are you in favor of the death penalty for a person convicted of murder?* Answer categories: Yes; No). Opinion items also can employ a scale that measures not only the direction of one's opinion but also the respondent's intensity of opinion (e.g., *To what extent do you support or oppose abortion?* Answer categories: Strongly oppose; Somewhat oppose; Somewhat support; Strongly support).

Open-ended questions can be used as well to measure opinions, but these can be more effective in shedding light on why respondents hold the opinions they hold. For instance, respondents in the American National Election Studies who express their intention to vote for a particular candidate are asked, *Is there anything in particular about [Politician X] that might make you want to vote for him?* Other open-ended items, such as the "Most Important Problem" question (*What do you believe is the most important problem facing the nation today?*), do not offer respondents an opportunity to articulate reasons why they volunteered a particular issue. However, like the aforementioned opinion questions, responses to Most Important Problem items can be used to shape public policy, campaign efforts, or marketing strategies.

Regardless of the issue under study, how an opinion question is asked can have a significant impact on its response. Hence survey researchers routinely take into consideration a number of concerns when crafting their questionnaires. First, are nonattitudes a potential problem? Also known as "false positives" (i.e., errors of commission), nonattitudes occur when respondents report an opinion on an issue about which they know nothing or really have no attitude. To circumvent the problem of nonattitudes, survey researchers can employ a filter question immediately before the opinion question such that only respondents who report knowledge or awareness of the issue are asked their opinion about that issue. Another way to reduce nonattitudes is to offer respondents a "Don't Know" option or a middle response category (e.g., "Neither support nor oppose"). Though common, the inclusion of a middle response category can have the unintended consequence of generating "false negatives" (i.e., errors of omission), the reporting of no opinion when in fact one exists.

A second consideration in the crafting of opinion items concerns how the question and response categories are worded. The question should include a clearly specified attitude object and should not be double-barreled; put another way, respondents should not be asked to express their opinion about two attitude objects (e.g., *Do you support abortion and health care reform?*). In addition, questions should not include double negatives, colloquialisms, or leading terms such that respondents feel pressured to provide a socially desirable answer. Response alternatives, the construction of which should follow these same guidelines, also should be balanced and include a sufficient range of variation.

Content of the specific opinion question aside, survey researchers need to be mindful of the order in which the item appears in the instrument. After all, responses to opinion questions concerning a general attitude object are influenced by top-of-mind considerations. For instance, respondents asked several questions about the environment will weigh this issue more heavily than other issues when asked subsequently about how they view the president's current performance. Respondents also can try to answer opinion questions such that they appear consistent. The order of the response alternatives also can shape how individuals reply to a given question. This is important because some respondents are predisposed to select the first (*primacy effect*) or last (*recency effect*) response option. Survey researchers thus have begun to rely on rotating or randomizing response order within a given sample.

Because individuals' opinions reflect their psychological states and are measured by self-reports, the validity of responses to opinion questions is of utmost importance. Fortunately, researchers in a number of disciplines are working on theoretical and methodological fronts to better understand how responses to opinion questions are shaped.

Patricia Moy

See also Attitude Measurement; Attitudes; Attitude Strength; Closed-Ended Question; Contingency Question; Double-Barreled Question; Double Negative; Error of Commission; Error of Omission; National Election Studies (NES); Nonattitude; Open-Ended Question; Opinion Norms; Opinions; Primacy Effect; Questionnaire Order Effects; Random Order; Recency Effect; Respondent-Related Error; Response Alternatives; Response Order Effects; Self-Reported Measure; Social Desirability

Further Readings

Bishop, G. F. (2005). *The illusion of public opinion: Fact and artifact in American public opinion polls*. Lanham, MD: Rowman & Littlefield.

Glynn, C. J., Herbst, S., O'Keefe, G. J., & Shapiro, R. Y. (1999). *Public opinion*. Boulder, CO: Westview.

Schuman, H., & Presser, S. (1996). *Questions and answers in attitude surveys: Experiments on question form, wording, and context*. Thousand Oaks, CA: Sage.

Sudman, S., & Bradburn, N. M. (1982). *Asking questions: A practical guide to questionnaire design*. San Francisco: Jossey-Bass.

OPINIONS

Opinions in survey research can be defined as subjective attitudes, beliefs, or judgments that reflect matters of personal (subjective) preference. Some opinions may not be confirmable or deniable by factual evidence (e.g., a person's attitude toward the use of capital punishment), whereas others may be (e.g., the belief that a particular presidential candidate will be elected). Moreover, the strength of one's opinions may depend on one's level of knowledge or attentiveness on a subject.

The term *opinion* is often used interchangeably with *attitude* and *belief*, but opinions are a broader category that includes both attitudes and beliefs. One's subjective position on the truth of a subject is a belief, such as whether global warming is the result of human-made activity or if abstinence education lowers the rate of teenage pregnancies. Some beliefs could, at some point, be resolved with finality through science. Attitudes are a type of opinion that have an evaluative component—that is, they refer to a positive or negative evaluation of a person, idea, or object. Attitudes are latent, subjective constructs that cannot be observed directly and cannot be confirmed or denied with factual information.

Opinions are measured in surveys, which is just one way that opinions can be expressed. Opinions can also be expressed via other behaviors such as voting, participation in marches or demonstrations, or attempting to influence another person's opinion. Although surveys involve measures of individuals' opinions, surveys typically are designed to measure public opinion, which can be defined as the aggregate of opinions across the public.

Opinion Formation and Change

Opinions can be formed and changed through a number of routes including direct experience, parental influence, group determinants, elite discourse, and information from the mass media or other sources. Direct experiences strongly influence opinions and opinions based on direct experiences may be stronger than those formed via other mechanisms. Salient incidents, especially traumatic ones, can lead to indelible views on a subject, such as when a child is bitten by a dog and subsequently dislikes dogs throughout life, or when a person undergoes a religious conversion that leads to radical changes in his or her perspective on an array of topics. Researchers also find that repeated exposure to a stimulus object is sufficient to enhance a person's opinion of the object. This theory underlies strategies used in advertising and marketing and can be seen at work, for example, in political campaigns in which greater candidate name recognition increases the probability that a candidate will win the election.

Although a person's opinions depend much on his or her personal experience, the source of many of these experiences is through parental teaching and modeling of parents' behavior. Gender role and racial opinions are two prominent areas where parental influence is often observed. Researchers have found that children's opinions toward gender are strongly influenced by their parents. Mothers who worked outside the home, for example, tend to have daughters who hold less traditional views toward work roles than those raised by mothers who were housewives. Researchers have also found that by the age of 4, many children tend to hold opinions that reflect cultural stereotypes about race, and that children tend to adopt their parents' racial prejudices. Parental influence on opinion formation has also been found to be significant in the development of political attitudes or political socialization, although as a child ages this influence wanes.

Other important influences on opinions are through institutions and social groups with which a person has contact, for example, schools, peers, and other reference groups. Schools tend to have an indoctrinating effect by disseminating not only knowledge required to formulate an opinion but also culture and values that constrain those opinions. For example, children may develop favorable feelings toward the president or the police as a result of classroom experiences. Peer groups tend to have a reinforcing effect on one's opinions. Voters, for example, often cite that they spoke with people in their social network about their vote decision and that their decision is similar to those of their friends. Finally, an individual's opinions can be influenced by the opinions of others in groups to which he or she belongs. However, this effect depends on two factors: (1) the degree of closeness a person feels to the group, and (2) the importance that person places on membership within the context of other groups that he or she belongs to.

Elite discourse (i.e., idea exchange among politicians, journalists, scholars, etc.) can also influence opinions. During periods of elite agreement, individuals tend to receive one-sided information on the topic, therefore increasing the likelihood that public opinion will reflect elite consensus. During elite disagreement, the individual receives two-sided information, leading to more varied opinions among the public. When the elite discourse is two-sided, people may attend to and be influenced by messages from elites whom they like or trust and disregard messages from elites whom they dislike or distrust. The elite discourse during the Vietnam War has been cited as one example of this effect. During the early years of the war, most of the political elites agreed on a containment strategy in Vietnam, but in the later years, as casualties mounted, elites disagreed, and public support for the war declined substantially.

With several thousand television, radio, and print media outlets in the United States, the mass media also has a significant role in affecting opinions. The majority of research today supports indirect effects of the media—although the media provides information on a range of topics, this information often does not substantially change public attitudes. The media does, however, influence public opinion indirectly via agenda setting, whereby media coverage influences which issues are salient to the public.

A person's attentiveness to information about an issue during opinion formation and change and his or her subsequent knowledge about the issue can have a significant impact on the strength of his or her opinion on that issue. Researchers have found that people tend to form fickle opinions when they do not attend to information about the issue and have little information on the topic. In contrast, a person's opinion on a subject may be more stable if it is based on a large body of evidence.

Jamie Patrick Chandler

See also Agenda Setting; Attitudes; Issue Definition (Framing); Opinion Norms; Opinion Question; Public Opinion

Further Readings

Asher, H. (2007). *Polling and the public* (7th ed.). Washington, DC: CQ Press.

Erikson, R. S., & Tedin, K. L. (2007). *American public opinion: Its origins, content, and impact.* New York: Pearson Longman.

Oskamp, S. P., & Schultz, W. (2004). *Attitudes and opinions.* Mahwah, NJ: Lawrence Erlbaum.

Taber, C. S. (2003). Information processing and public opinion. In D. O. Sears et al. (Eds.), *Oxford handbook of political psychology* (pp. 433–476). New York: Oxford University Press.

Zaller, J. R. (1992). *The nature and origins of mass opinions.* New York: Cambridge University Press.

OPTIMAL ALLOCATION

Optimal allocation is a procedure for dividing the sample among the strata in a stratified sample survey. The allocation procedure is called "optimal" because in a particular survey sampling design (stratified simple random sampling) it produces the smallest variance for estimating a population mean and total (using the standard stratified estimator) given a fixed budget or sample size.

A sample survey collects data from a population in order to estimate population characteristics. A stratified sample selects separate samples from subgroups (called "strata") of the population and can often increase the accuracy of survey results. In order to implement stratified sampling, it is necessary to be able to divide the population at least implicitly into strata before sampling. Given a budget that allows gathering data on n subjects or a budget amount $\$B$, there is a need to decide how to allocate the resources for data gathering to the strata. Three factors typically affect the distribution of resources to the strata: (1) the population size, (2) the variability of values, and (3) the data collection per unit cost in the strata. One also can have special interest in characteristics of some particular strata that could affect allocations.

In a stratified simple random sample, a sample of size n_h is selected from strata or subpopulation h, which has a population size of N_h ($h = 1, 2, \ldots, H$). The standard estimator of the population total is $\sum_{h=1}^{H} N_h \bar{y}_h$, where $\bar{y}_h$ is the mean (arithmetic average) of the sample values in stratum h and $\sum$ denotes summation across strata $h = 1, 2, \ldots, H$. The variance of the estimator is $\sum_{h=1}^{H} N_h^2 \left(1 - \frac{n_h}{N_h}\right) \frac{S_h^2}{n_h}$, where S_h^2 is the variance of the values in stratum h. If the rate of sampling is small in all strata, then (ignoring the finite population correction terms $\left(1 - \frac{n_h}{N_h}\right)$) the variance is approximately $\sum_{h=1}^{H} N_h^2 \frac{S_h^2}{n_h}$. Suppose the cost to collect data from one element (person, unit, etc.) in stratum h is C_h. If there is a budget of B, then the entire budget is spent when $B = \sum_{h=1}^{H} n_h C_h$. Then the variance (ignoring the finite population correction terms) of the estimated population total is minimized when the sample size in stratum h is $n_h = n N_h S_h / \sqrt{C_h} / \sum_{g=1}^{H} N_g S_g / \sqrt{C_g}$, where the summation in the denominator is over all strata, S_h is the standard deviation (square root of the variance) of the values in stratum h, and n is the total sample size. This formula implies that one should sample more in large subpopulations (strata), more in strata with large variances, and more in strata with small cost. If costs of per unit data collection are the same in all strata, then the optimal allocation in stratum h is $n_h = n N_h S_h / \sum_{g=1}^{H} N_g S_g$. If in addition variances (and standard deviations) are constant, then $n_h = n N_h / \sum_{g=1}^{H} N_g$, which is the allocation known as *proportional allocation* to strata. If the n_h's

are not integers, then one must round the numbers to integers for sample selection. Rounding does not necessarily move all values to the closest integer for all strata, because the total sample size n needs to be allocated.

Suppose one wanted to collect data on students at a large public university. Questions of interest could be hours worked per week; amount of money expended per semester on textbooks; amount of time spent eating at restaurants in a week; number of trips to the airport in a semester; and whether or not friends smoke cigarettes. The students selected for the survey could be contacted via their university email addresses and asked to complete an online Web survey. A survey can be preferable to contacting every student, because for a sample better efforts can often made to encourage response and check data quality. Administrative records contain college year designations (first, second, third, fourth) for each student in the target population; college years can be used as strata. Suppose the total sample size is allowed to be 1,600 students. Equal allocation to strata would sample 400 students from each year. Table 1 presents allocations of students to the four strata based on total enrollments by college year; these numbers are similar to 2006 enrollment at Iowa State University. The hypothetical variable being considered is hours worked per week. It is assumed that students in higher years have more variable employment situations than students in earlier years, hence the increasing standard deviation. It also is assumed that more attempts are needed to contact students in later years than in earlier years. As can be seen in the table, the stratum of fourth-year students receives the largest sample ($n_4 = 731$), whereas the stratum of first-year students receives the smallest ($n_1 = 224$).

Table 1   Optimal allocation of 1,600 students to four strata defined by college year

Year	Population Size: Total Enrollment	Standard Deviation: S_h	Per Unit Data Collection Cost: C_h	Sample Size: $n_h = \dfrac{n N_h S_h / \sqrt{C_h}}{\sum_{g=1}^{H} N_g S_g / \sqrt{C_g}}$	Sample Size: Rounded Values
First	5,000	2.9 hours	1.0	223.8	224
Second	4,058	4.4 hours	1.1	262.8	263
Third	4,677	5.8 hours	1.2	382.3	382
Fourth	6,296	8.9 hours	1.4	731.1	731
Total	20,031			1,600.0	1,600

If, instead of being unequal, the costs per stratum were constant, then even more sample would be allocated to the strata with more advanced students. The first- through fourth-year strata would receive 201, 247, 376, and 776 students, respectively. If one planned to report on the four strata separately, then some compromise between optimal allocation and equal allocation would be advisable so that sample sizes in all strata remain reasonably large.

In practice, the costs associated with data collection and the variances (and standard deviations) in the various strata are unlikely to be known exactly. Instead, a preliminary small survey (a *pilot survey*) might be used to test methods of data collection and to collect data in order to estimate information needed for more efficient allocation. Alternatively, information that has been published or that is available in administrative records might be useful, or past experience in other surveys might be used.

Optimal allocations determined by one outcome variable, such as hours worked per week, are not necessarily the same as those determined using a different outcome variable, such as grade point average or body mass index. If several variables are considered important outcomes for a survey, then one could determine optimal allocations for each based on available data and select a compromise among the various allocations. It is likely that the average or compromise among allocations will be closer to proportional allocation than the most extreme allocations determined by optimal allocations based on the several variables.

Michael D. Larsen

See also Disproportionate Allocation to Strata; Elements; Finite Population Correction (fpc) Factor; Proportional Allocation; Strata; Stratified Sampling

Further Readings

Cochran, W. G. (1977). *Sampling techniques* (3rd ed.). New York: Wiley.

Kish, L. (1965). *Survey sampling*. New York: Wiley.

Lohr, S. L. (1999). *Sampling: Design and analysis*. Pacific Grove, CA: Duxbury.

Ordinal Measure

Within the context of survey research, *measurement* refers to the process of assigning values to characteristics of individuals to indicate their position on an underlying construct, such as their level of satisfaction with the government or their political party affiliations. Ordinal measures are used to produce ordered rankings among values. For example, measurements or responses to the question, *In general, would you say your health is: excellent, very good, good, fair, or poor?* can be sorted and ordered from healthiest ("excellent") to least healthy ("poor"). Ordinal measures convey information about the relationship between values—that one value is greater than another—but they do not indicate how much greater a value is. Although "excellent" is greater in value than "very good," one cannot say with certainty that the distance between those two values is the same, less, or more than the distance between "very good" and "good."

Of the four levels of measurement, ordinal measures are more sophisticated than nominal measures but less statistically powerful than interval or ratio measures. With nominal measures (e.g., political party identification), numbers may be assigned arbitrarily to categories to distinguish among them, as the numbers themselves do not have an inherent value. With interval measures (e.g., IQ scores), the distance between values is equivalent, but unlike ratio-level measures (e.g., age), they do not include a true zero as a value. Characteristics of scales generally determine the appropriate statistics. Ordinal scales are best suited for nonparametric statistics such as modes and chi-square, but they often also are used for correlations, analyses of variance, and in mathematical models. Technically, means are not meaningful measures because of the categorical nature of ordinal data; that is, medians should be used as central measures of tendency. However, means and other statistics appropriate for interval data are used by many researchers willing to accept the uncertain differences between ordinal ranks. Ordinal scales with fewer than 5 points should probably not be treated as interval level, because the small number of data points may mask large differences between scale values.

Ordinal measures are typically obtained with ordinal scales that include closed-ended response categories in which the categories are labeled using words, numbers, or some combination of both. Key decisions in obtaining ordinal measures include how many categories or scale points to administer and how to label the points. Ordinal scales typically range from 3 to 11 points (e.g., 0–10 scale). In general, data quality is higher when measured using 5 to 7 points. A guiding principle in constructing ordinal scales is to develop categories that are balanced and approximately equal distance from one another. Likert scales, a popular type of ordinal scale, demonstrate this balance well. Likert scales are bipolar and include categories with both positive and negative values. A typical example is one in which respondents are asked their level of agreement with a particular statement, with response options ranging from "strongly disagree," "somewhat disagree," "neither," "somewhat agree," to "strongly agree." With regard to labeling, decisions include whether to label all of the categories or just the end points with verbal descriptions, or whether to label the categories with a combination of verbal descriptions and numbers. Overall, data quality is optimized when every scale point is represented by a verbal description.

Jennifer Dykema, Steven Blixt, and John Stevenson

See also Balanced Question; Bipolar Scale; Closed-Ended Question; Interval Measure; Level of Measurement; Likert Scale; Nominal Measure; Ratio Measure

Further Readings

Babbie, E. (2006). *The practice of social research* (11th ed.). Belmont, CA: Wadsworth/Thomson Learning.
Krosnick, J. A., & Fabrigar, L. R. (in press). *The handbook of questionnaire design*. New York: Oxford University Press.

OUTBOUND CALLING

Telephone calls involving call centers are classified as inbound or outbound, depending on whether the call is being received by the call center (inbound) or initiated in the call center (outbound).

Any telephone survey that starts with a list of telephone numbers involves outbound calling, although telephone surveys often use inbound calling in support functions and can also be entirely inbound.

The list of numbers used might be randomly generated, such as a random-digit dialed (RDD) sample, created from public listings such as the white pages or from prior respondent contact (for example, a customer satisfaction survey might use the phone numbers provided by the customer at the point of purchase).

Particularly with RDD surveys, only a small proportion of dials made will result in live connects, and therefore the efficiency of outbound calling can be significantly improved by using dialer technology. Functions of particular value to conducting outbound surveys include the following:

1. *Autodispositioning*, in which the outcome of certain types of calls (e.g., busy, fax, disconnected) can be automatically detected from the signal tones, saving interviewer time and increasing accuracy in the assignment of dispositions, and

2. *Autodialing*, where the act of dialing is performed automatically on some trigger, such as
   - A keystroke instruction from an interviewer
   - The interviewer logging into the system or completing an interview, or
   - In the case of predictive dialers, some combination of the probability of a dial being answered and the probability of an interviewer being free to handle a connected call

Outbound calling is often more successful when supported by pre-survey notification to the selected sample, such as by an advance letter sent to numbers in the sample that can be matched to an address. For some numbers that cannot be associated with any postal address, pre-survey notification is still possible using text messaging or pre-recorded voice messages (some dialers have the ability to automatically dial and leave a pre-recorded message on any line that answers), although there have been mixed findings on whether these nonletter forms of pre-notification help or harm response rates.

The use of caller ID is another feature for which there is a varying impact on response rates. Some data suggest that a well-known survey name embedded in the caller ID can help response, and it is known that some exchange systems and household systems will not receive calls that do not have a caller ID associated with them. Other data suggest that households are more likely to answer the phone on a refusal conversion call if the caller ID is suppressed or different from that used on earlier dials. Finally, most calls go through many exchanges between the call center from which the call originates and the target telephone number that can change or transform the ID transmitted, introducing additional uncertainty about the impact of caller ID on the success of an outbound call.

Jenny Kelly

See also Advance Contact; Advance Letter; Caller ID; Directory Sampling; Inbound Calling; List-Assisted

Sampling; Matched Number; Predictive Dialing; Random-Digit Dialing (RDD); Refusal Conversion

Further Readings

Kelly, J., Link, M., Petty, J., Hobson, K., & Stork, P. (2008). Establishing a new survey research call center. In J. Lepkowski, C. Tucker, M. Brick, E. de Leeuw, L. Japec, P. Lavrakas, et al. (Eds.), *Advances in telephone survey methodology* (pp. 317–339). New York: Wiley.

Trussell, N., & Lavrakas, P. J. (2005, May). *Testing the impact of caller ID technology on response rates in a mixed mode survey*. Paper presented at the 60th annual American Association for Public Opinion Research Conference, Miami Beach, FL.

OUTLIERS

An *outlier*, as the term suggests, means an observation in a sample lying outside of the "bulk" of the sample data. For example, the value "87" is an outlier in the following distribution of numbers: 2, 5, 1, 7, 11, 9, 5, 6, 87, 4, 0, 9, 7. This original meaning has been expanded to include those observations that are influential in estimation of a population quantity. Influence of an observation in estimation is intuitively understood as the degree to which the presence or absence of that observation affects the estimate in terms of the variance.

The notion of outliers is common in all statistical disciplines. However, it has a distinctive meaning in sample surveys for mainly two reasons: (1) sample surveys mostly deal with finite populations, often without assuming a parametric distribution; and (2) sample surveys often employ complex sample designs with unequal inclusion probabilities. Moreover, the meaning and handling of outliers differ also, depending on the stage of the survey process at hand: sample design stage, editing stage, and estimation stage.

The occurrence of outliers is frequently unavoidable when a multi-purpose survey is conducted. It may be nearly impossible to make the design efficient for all variables of interest in a large-scale multi-purpose survey. The outliers that have the most impact come from sample units that have a large sample value coupled with a large sampling weight. Probability proportional to size sampling (PPS) or size stratification is often used in the design stage to prevent such a situation from occurring. If the measure of size (MOS) is not reliable, it is difficult to eliminate outliers entirely, unless a census or a sample survey with a high sampling rate is used. This problem is especially pronounced when dealing with a volatile population such as businesses in economic surveys. A typical situation is that a unit with a small MOS, and thus assigned a small probability, has grown to have a medium or large value at time of observation, resulting in a huge weighted value.

In the editing stage of a survey process, outlier detection is performed to find extreme values that may be due to some survey error (response error or keying error during data entry). Such outliers are detected by comparing individual data values with others using a standardized distance measure defined as the absolute difference of the value from the center of the data (location) divided by a dispersion measure (scale). Using the sample mean and sample standard deviation to define the distance tends to mask outliers. To avoid the *masking effect*, estimates that are robust (insensitive) to outliers should be used. For example, one may use the median to estimate location and either the interquartile range (w), the difference between the third quartile (i.e., 75th percentile) and the first quartile (i.e., 25th percentile), or the mean absolute difference—which is the median of observations' absolute differences from the sample median. Weighted values of these quantities rather than unweighted values may be used if the sampling weights are available. Once the standardized distance is defined, a criterion by which an outlier is detected is set as the *tolerance interval* of the standardized distances; if an observation falls outside of the interval, it is declared as an outlier. The interval can be symmetric, nonsymmetric, or one-sided, depending on the underlying population distribution.

In the estimation stage, the impact of outliers is evaluated and treated. The influence of an observation depends on the estimator, and so outliers that were detected in the editing stage may or may not influence the values of the estimator. There are basically three approaches for treating outliers: (1) trimming or discarding of outliers, (2) *Winsorization* of outliers (i.e., replacing outliers with the largest or smallest "inliers" (which fall in the tolerance interval), (3) down-weighting of outliers. Trimming is seldom used in survey sampling. Winsorization can be effective if the weights are equal or similar. A variant of Winsorization is sometimes applied using pre-determined cutoff values (e.g., tolerance interval boundaries) instead of using the observed values to replace the outliers. When Winsorization is applied to the weighted data, it defines a hybrid method that modifies the sample values and weights simultaneously in a systematic way. Down-weighting can be achieved in various ways. Sometimes, post-stratification is used to create a post-stratum of outliers and their weights are reduced. A robust estimation technique such as *M-estimation* can be applied, which automatically detects outliers and down-weights them. It is preferable to limit the modified sampling weights to no less than unity because each sample observation should represent at least itself.

From the design-based perspective, any treatment of outliers in estimation introduces some bias in exchange for reduction of the sampling variance, and thus it can be seen as a bias–variance trade-off. Therefore, the mean square error (MSE) criterion is a good guiding principle by which to choose an estimator. Based on this principle, some people try to define an estimator that minimizes estimated MSE. Bayesian methodology is sometimes employed to achieve a bias–variance trade-off. However, it should be noted that often it is notoriously difficult to estimate the MSE reliably.

The influence of an outlier in estimation depends on the sample size. If the sampling rate is large or the sample size is large, the problem of outliers may be less troublesome because the variability in the estimator will be small. However, even with a large sample, outliers can cause a problem for domains with small domain sample sizes, where estimators may be less stable (i.e., more variable). In a multi-purpose survey, a set of weights that is too volatile can create an outlier situation for any variable. To control the variability of weights without considering a particular variable, weight trimming is often used. It should not be confused with the trimming technique that involves discarding of observations. The weight trimming simply reduces extreme weights to an appropriately chosen cutoff to control the weight variability. The technique itself resembles Winsorization, and it may be better to call it "weight Winsorization" rather than "weight trimming."

Hyunshik Lee

See also Design-Based Estimation; Finite Population; Mean Square Error; Probability of Selection; Probability Proportional to Size (PPS) Sampling

Further Readings

Lee, H. (1995). Outliers in business surveys. In B. G. Cox, D. A. Binder, B. N. Chinnappa, A. Christianson, M. J. Colledge, & P. S. Kott (Eds.), *Business survey methods* (pp. 503–526). New York: Wiley.

Out of Order

The out of order survey disposition is used in telephone surveys when the telephone number dialed by an interviewer is nonworking or not in service. Although each local telephone company in the United States handles out-of-order telephone numbers differently, most companies in urban and suburban areas include a recording on these numbers that says something like, "The number you have dialed is a nonworking number," or "The number you dialed is not in service at this time." Some telephone companies in rural areas also include these recordings as standard practice. Thus, interviewers dialing out-of-order numbers in these areas may hear nothing, or the number may ring and ring, making it difficult to determine whether these numbers should be coded using the out of order disposition or as a ring–no answer noncontact.

In most telephone surveys, a case with an out of order disposition would be considered ineligible. Out of order dispositions are considered final dispositions and typically are not redialed again during the field period of a survey.

One other exception to these rules occurs if a telephone number in the sampling pool is temporarily disconnected or temporarily out of service, or if the number has a recording that indicates that the line is being checked for trouble. If there is clear evidence that a number in the sampling pool is temporarily out of order, this number should not be considered ineligible but instead should be considered a case of unknown eligibility. Assuming the field period permits it, most survey organizations will wait a few days and attempt to redial numbers that appear to be temporarily out of service.

Matthew Courser

See also Final Dispositions; Missing Data; Noncontacts; Response Rates; Temporary Dispositions; Unknown Eligibility

Further Readings

American Association for Public Opinion Research. (2006). *Standard definitions: Final dispositions of case codes and outcome rates for surveys* (4th ed.). Lenexa, KS: Author.

Lavrakas, P. J. (1993). *Telephone survey methods: Sampling, selection, and supervision* (2nd ed.). Newbury Park, CA: Sage.

OUT OF SAMPLE

The out of sample survey disposition is used in all types of surveys, regardless of mode. Cases with out of sample dispositions are considered ineligible and are not contacted again. As a result, the out of sample disposition is considered a final disposition.

In a telephone survey, out of sample dispositions usually occur when the telephone number dialed by an interviewer rings to a household, business, or individual that is outside of the geographic sampling area for a survey. For example, in a random-digit dial (RDD) survey of the general public, this is most common when the survey is sampling relatively small geographic areas such as counties, towns or villages, or neighborhoods for which telephone prefix boundaries do not conform exactly (or even closely) to geopolitical boundaries. Out-of-sample cases usually are discovered only if the questionnaire for the telephone survey includes screening questions that verify that the respondent or household is located within the geographic area being sampled for the survey.

In an in-person survey, out-of-sample cases include ineligible housing units that were listed as being within the sampling area but actually are outside of it. Out-of-sample cases in these surveys also can include other households or businesses that were incorrectly included in a list sample—any unit that is not properly part of the target population for the survey.

In a mail or Internet survey of named respondents, out-of-sample cases occur when the named respondent is found to be ineligible to participate in the survey based on screening information he or she provides on the questionnaire. For example, a respondent who indicates that he or she is not a doctor would be considered out of sample in a mail or Internet survey of physicians.

Matthew Courser

See also Final Dispositions; Ineligible; Response Rates; Temporary Dispositions

Further Readings

American Association for Public Opinion Research. (2006). *Standard definitions: Final dispositions of case codes and outcome rates for surveys* (4th ed.). Lenexa, KS: Author.

OVERCOVERAGE

Overcoverage occurs in survey sample frames when the frame contains more than enough sample records. This primarily results from two situations. In one case, there are records in the sample frame that do not contain respondents or members of the target population. In other cases, the same respondent is targeted by duplicate or multiple records in the sample frame. In either case, the sample frame contains sample records that should be interviewed.

Different types of overcoverage are commonly referred to as "ineligible units" or "multiple records." Different researchers use the term *overcoverage* inconsistently, so it is important to consider whether overcoverage in a given sample frame is caused by ineligible units, multiple records, or both.

Sample frames ideally contain a perfect one-to-one correspondence between sample records and members of the target population for a survey. In some cases, multiple records refer back to a single member of the target population. This type of overcoverage is sometimes called a "multiplicity of elements." In other cases, sample records fail to lead to members of the target population. These cases are sometimes referred to as "blanks" or "foreign elements."

Multiple sample records that refer to a single member of the target population are common in sample frames. In cases in which directories or lists are used as sampling frames, respondents can be included more than once if lists are compiled from multiple sources. More commonly, multiple records lead back to a single respondent when the sample frame and target populations are measured (covered) inconsistently. For example, if telephone numbers are sampled for a survey of households, a household with multiple telephones will be included multiple times. If sales records are used as a source for a consumer survey, then consumers who have made multiple purchases might be included in a sample multiple times.

Overcoverage caused by duplicate or multiple records can be adjusted for either by cleaning the sample frame or by providing sample weights to adjust for different probabilities that a respondent is included in the sample frame. Frame cleaning can be accomplished either before or during the survey field process. Cleaning before involves checking the sample frame for duplicate or multiple records and eliminating them. This "de-duping" is a basic part of constructing and checking a sample frame and is made enormously easier and more practicable by increased computer power.

The second type of overcoverage, in which sample records do not contain valid members of the target population, is present in almost all sample frames. This occurs for a variety of reasons. In some cases, sample records do not correspond to anything similar to the target population. For example, telephone samples often contain disconnected telephone numbers or numbers that have not been assigned. Household surveys may send an interviewer to an empty lot. A business directory might contain mailing addresses for establishments that went out of business many years ago. These listings are referred to as "blanks," "empty records," "empty listings," or more colloquially as "bad records" or "duds." In other cases, the sample record reaches a unit that can be screened for eligibility, but the record turns out to not be a member of the target population for the survey. For example, a survey of eligible voters may reach nonvoters, a survey that targets telephone households in one city instead may reach some households in a neighboring town, or a survey of college students may reach some recent graduates. These records are called "foreign elements," "out-of-scope units," or, colloquially, "screen-outs."

Survey researchers attempt to identify blanks or foreign elements by screening to determine whether they are eligible for the survey. In some cases, this can be done automatically. For example, residential telephone samples can be screened against databases of known business households, and other electronic matching can identify other foreign elements. In many cases, however, an interviewer or other field staff member needs to contact a sample record to determine if it is an eligible member of the survey's target population. This is especially true for studies that utilize general population sample frames to identify rare subpopulations. For example, a survey of parents with disabled children who live at home may need to contact and screen all households in the sample to locate the eligible households, even though the majority of households do not have children living there and most others have children who are not disabled. These low-incidence samples can add great cost to a survey.

Blanks and foreign elements generally do not lead to biased or distorted survey results, but they often result in a loss of both sample and economic efficiency. Surveys that desire a specific degree of statistical precision need to increase (inflate) initial sample sizes to account for these records. More important for many researchers, the cost implications of conducting surveys that contain many ineligible units make interviews with many rare or low-incidence populations impracticable.

Chase H. Harrison

See also Coverage Error; Duplication; Eligibility; Sampling Frame; Survey Costs

Further Readings

Biemer, P., & Lyberg, L. (2003). *Introduction to survey quality*. Hoboken, NJ: Wiley.
Groves, R. M. (1989). *Survey errors and survey costs*. New York: Wiley.
Kish, L. (1965). *Survey sampling*. New York: Wiley.
Lessler, J. T., & Kalsbeek, W. D. (1992). *Nonsampling error in surveys*. New York: Wiley.

OVERREPORTING

In many surveys, respondents tend to report more socially desired behaviors than they actually performed. In addition to this type of misreporting—called "overreporting"—respondents are also inclined to understate that they have engaged in socially undesirable behaviors, which is called "underreporting." Similar to underreporting, overreporting is assumed to be connected to social desirability bias and thus occurs on the cognitive editing stage of the question–answer process.

Among other topics, overreporting of voting and being registered to vote has been in the focus of methodological research for decades. Since respondents in national- and state-level and local election polls tend to overly state that they have voted in the election, voter turnout has traditionally been overestimated. Usually, overreporting is identified applying post-survey validations using record checks (like in the National Election Study).

Since not every survey can afford a cost-intensive validation study, several attempts have been made in order to reduce vote overreporting, either by softening the question wording so that respondents will not feel embarrassed to admit that they have not voted or by a set of preceding questions on voting behavior in other, prior elections. It was assumed that respondents would be more willing to admit that they have not voted in the most recent past election if they were able to report voting in previous elections. However, neither tactic succeeded—the proportion of vote overreporting remained unaffected.

Overreporting is associated with respondent characteristics. Respondents who hold strong positive opinions on a particular behavior are more likely to falsely report this behavior in a survey.

Marek Fuchs

See also Cognitive Aspects of Survey Methodology (CASM); Errors of Commission; Record Check; Respondent-Related Error; Sensitive Topics; Social Desirability; Underreporting

Further Readings

Belli, R. F., Traugott, M. W., Young, M., & McGonagle, K. (1999). Reducing vote overreporting in surveys: Social desirability, memory failure, and source monitoring. *Public Opinion Quarterly, 63*(1), 90–108.

Presser, S. (1990). Can changes in context reduce vote overreporting in surveys? *Public Opinion Quarterly, 54*(4), 586–593.

Tourangeau, R., Rips, L. J., & Rasinski, K. (2000). *The psychology of survey response*. Cambridge, UK: Cambridge University Press.

P

PAIRED COMPARISON TECHNIQUE

The paired comparison technique is a research design that yields interval-level scaled scores that are created from ratings made by each respondent for all possible pairs of items under consideration. The basis for the method dates back to its first reported use in the mid-1800s. Although the technique is a very powerful approach for producing a highly reliable ranking of the rated items, it is underutilized by survey researchers due to the amount of data that often must be gathered, and thus its cost and the burden it places on respondents.

At the simplest level, paired comparisons (i.e., simultaneously comparing two things with each other) are made by each respondent among a set of items using a binary scale that indicates which of the two choices are most preferred, most pleasant, most attractive, or whatever other judgment the respondent is asked to make in comparing the two. However, more complex judgments can be generated by having respondents indicate their choices along a continuum of response choices rather than a simply binary choice (A or B).

For example, if a political pollster wanted to determine the relative ordering of voter preferences among five Republican primary candidates, a paired comparison design would yield the most valid data. In this design, each candidate would be paired with each of the other candidates, and each respondent would judge each pair on some criterion. Typically this

would be done by using a scaled response format such as *Strongly Prefer Candidate A; Prefer Candidate A; Slightly Prefer Candidate A; Slightly Prefer Candidate B; Prefer Candidate B; Strongly Prefer Candidate B*. Generally the midpoint of the preference scale—which in this example would be, "Prefer Neither Candidate A nor Candidate B"—is not offered to respondents because it is reasoned that the likelihood that there is complete indifference between the two is extremely low. Providing this "no preference" choice may encourage some respondents to satisfice and use the middle option too readily.

Scoring using paired comparison data is straightforward. In the previous example a "Strongly Preferred" response would be scored with a 3, a "Preferred" response would scored with a 2, and a "Slightly Preferred" response would be scored with a 1. If Candidate A were paired with Candidate D, and Candidate A were "strongly preferred" over Candidate D by a given respondent, then the respondent would be assigned a $+3$ score for Candidate A for that pairing, and the respondent would get a -3 score for Candidate D for that pairing. The scaled scores for a specific candidate for each respondent would be the sum of the respondent's individual scores from each of the pairings in which that candidate was included. In the example of five candidates being paired in all possible ways, there would be $((c(c-1))/2)$ possible paired comparisons, with c representing the number of things being paired. Thus in this example there are $((5(5-1))/2)$ or 10 pairs: AB, AC, AD, AE, BC, BD, BE, CD, CE, and DE. (The pairings would be presented in a random order to respondents.) Each pairing would require a separate question in the survey; thus, this five-candidate comparison would require 10 questions being asked of each respondent. If one of the candidates in this example were "strongly preferred" by a specific respondent over each of the other four candidates she or he was paired with, that candidate would get a score of +12 for this respondent. If a candidate were so disliked that every time she or he was paired with one of the other four candidates a given respondent always chose "Strongly Preferred" for the other candidates, then the strongly disliked candidate would be assigned a scaled score of –12 for that respondent. Computing scale scores for each thing that is being rated is easy to do with a computer, and these scaled scores provide very reliable indications of the relative preferences a respondent has among the different items being compared. That is, asking a respondent to rank all of the things being compared in one fell swoop (i.e., with one survey question) will yield less reliable and valid data than using a paired comparison design to generate the ranking.

Unfortunately, increasing the numbers of things being compared in a paired comparison design quickly causes many more pairings to be required for judgment by each respondent. Thus, if a researcher wanted 10 things to be compared, a total of 45 pairings would need to be judged by each respondent. In instances when a large number of pairings are to be made by respondents, a researcher is wise to add some reliability checks into the set of pairings. This is done by randomly selecting some of the pairs and reversing the order of the things within those pairings. For example, if the AF pairing were randomly chosen as one of the reliability checks, and if A was compared with F earlier in the question sequence by the respondent, then later on in the sequence F would be compared with A. The respondent is not likely to recall that she or he had already made this comparison if the set of items being compared is large. Adding such reliability checks allows the researcher to identify those respondents who are not taking the task seriously and instead are answering haphazardly.

Paul J. Lavrakas

See also Interval Measure; Ranking; Rating; Respondent Burden; Satisficing

Further Readings

Brown, T. C., Peterson, G. L., & Brink, G. E. (2007). *An enquiry into the method of paired comparison: Reliability, scaling, and Thurstone's law of comparative judgment.* Fort Collins, CO: Rocky Mountain Research Station, U.S. Forest Service. Retrieved June 4, 2008, from http://www.fs.fed.us/rm/value/brown.html

David, H. A. (1988). *The method of paired comparisons* (2nd ed., Vol. 41). New York: Oxford University Press.

Lavrakas, P. J. (1975). Female preferences for male physiques. *Journal of Research in Personality, 9,* 324–334.

Thurstone, L. L. (1927). A law of comparative judgment. *Psychology Review, 34,* 273–286.

Thurstone, L. L. (1927). The method of paired comparisons for social values. *Journal of Abnormal Social Psychology, 21,* 384–400.

PANEL

A panel refers to a survey sample in which the same units or respondents are surveyed or interviewed on two or more occasions (*waves*). Panels can give information about trends or changes in the characteristics of a given population over a period of time. A panel usually can measure changes in the characteristics of interest with greater precision than a series of independent samples of comparable size. A survey using a panel design is often called a "longitudinal survey," which is one particular type of repeated survey.

The sample design for a panel is very different from the one for an independent sample or a series of independent samples. In the sample design for a panel, more stable stratification variables over time can (and should) be employed than when using independent samples, because whereas a panel design may be statistically efficient in a short run, it may not be over a longer period of time. Also, the design for a panel should incorporate the changes in the population that the panel is meant to represent, such as births and other additions and deaths and other removals of sample units, in an optimal way so as not to cause disruption to the ongoing survey operations at different points of time or waves.

Advantages and Disadvantages

There are clear advantages to using a panel rather than using a series of independent samples in studying a target population. Some of these include the following:

1. A panel provides the details on the nature of change. For example, suppose that from one independent sample to another the prevalence of a disease changes from 5% to 15%. We know the

simple change of 10 percentage points, but do not know whether the incidence of new cases is 0% or 10% or something in between 0% and 10%. Using a panel, the percentage of new cases is easily obtained.

2. It reduces the variability for estimates of change at different points in time. For example, if P_1 and P_2 are the estimated proportion of unemployed people at Time 1 and Time 2, respectively, then the estimate of change is $P_2 - P_1$. When using a panel, the variance of $P_2 - P_1$ is reduced relative to the one for two independent samples.

3. It often reduces the observational errors by interviewers or respondents. For example, as the surveys are repeated, interviewers have a better experience of administering the interviews and respondents have a better understanding of the questionnaire.

4. It gives information on the dynamic behavior of respondents over time. For example, it is possible to explain the fact that the same people experiencing an event in the past, say unemployment, tend to experience it in the future.

However, there also are disadvantages to using a panel:

1. Analysis of a panel data is more complicated due to differential unit and item nonresponse and wave nonresponse, as well as the complexity of sample design. *Wave nonresponse* occurs when one or more waves of panel data are missing for a sample unit that has responded for at least one wave. Weighting, imputation, or a combination of weighting and imputation can be employed to compensate for missing wave data.

2. Measuring changes in individuals from one year to another year may be unreliable because reluctant respondents may give poor answers to repeated interviews, or respondents may refuse to be interviewed several times due to panel fatigue, resulting in higher nonresponse over time.

3. Respondents' answers to questions in previous waves may affect their answers in subsequent waves; this is termed *panel conditioning*.

4. It is difficult to keep the panel representative during a long period of time because the target population can change over time.

5. It may be too expensive to locate all respondents a year later or after a certain period of time, due to travel costs and the obstacles to following and finding some respondents who have moved without any new contact information.

6. It can be difficult to identify the same sample units over time. For example, identification of the same family units can be complicated when the family composition is changed by births, deaths, marriages, divorces, and so on.

Rotating Designs

Even if a panel is a "bad" sample, that is, if it does not well represent a given population over time, the organization carrying out the panel survey may have to continue to maintain that panel. But there is a solution to such a problem of the panel. It is a *rotating panel design*, in which a part of the panel sample is replaced at each subsequent point in time. This design is intermediate (i.e., a hybrid) between a panel sample and independent samples. As the simplest example, one may choose a panel design involving overlaps of half of the sample elements, as shown by AB, BC, CD, DE, EF, and so on at different points of time. In this example, the B panel sample appears in the first and second waves of data collection; the C panel sample appears in the second and third waves, and so on. Such rotating designs not only reduce respondent burden but also provide an opportunity to refresh the sample at each point of time with cases that better reflect the current makeup of the target population.

Examples

A number of panel surveys with economic or social science focus have been conducted around the world. One of the oldest panel surveys is the Panel Study of Income Dynamics (PSID) conducted by the Survey Research Center at the University of Michigan. This panel study has collected information on the dynamic aspects of economic and demographic behavior, including sociological and psychological measures. The panel of the PSID is a representative sample of U.S. family units and individuals (men, women, and children). The panel, originating in 1968, consisted of two independent samples: a cross-sectional national sample and a national sample of low-income families. The cross-sectional sample, which yielded about 3,000 completed interviews, was an equal probability sample of households from the 48 contiguous states. The national sample of low-income families came from the Survey of Economic Opportunity (SEO) conducted by the U.S. Bureau of the Census. This second sample consisted of about 2,000 families from SEO respondents with heads under the age of 60. The original core sample combined by the two samples was increased to approximately 6,168 in 1997 and nearly 7,400 in 2005. These changes were to reflect the changing nature of immigration in the United States. The PSID was collected in face-to-face interviews using paper-and-pencil questionnaires between 1968 and 1972. Thereafter, the majority of interviews were conducted by telephone, and in the 1999 wave, 97.5% of the interviews were conducted by computer-assisted telephone interviewing.

Sun Woong Kim

See also Attrition; Item Nonresponse; Longitudinal Studies; Panel Conditioning; Panel Data Analysis; Panel Survey; Respondent Burden; Rotating Panel Design; Wave

Further Readings

Hill, M. S. (1992). *The panel study of income dynamics: A user's guide.* Newbury Park, CA: Sage.

Kasprzyk, D., Duncan, G. J., Kalton, G., & Singh, M. (Eds.). (1989). *Panel surveys.* New York: Wiley.

Kish, L. (1995). *Survey sampling.* New York: Wiley.

Panel Conditioning

Panel conditioning is an effect sometimes observed in repeated surveys when a sample unit's response is influenced by prior interviews or contacts. Various possibilities have been suggested to explain the cause. Panel conditioning can affect the resulting estimates by introducing what is sometimes called "time-in-sample bias" or "rotation group bias."

In many surveys, the household, business, or other sample unit is contacted more than once over a period of time, usually to reduce the total survey cost, to produce longitudinal estimates, or to decrease the standard error of the estimate of change in the items of interest. In various documented studies, the levels of unemployed persons, expenditures, illness, victimizations, house repairs, and other characteristics were significantly higher or lower in earlier survey contacts than in later ones.

Potential scenarios to explain this behavior are extensive. At times a respondent recalls the answer to a question from a prior interview and repeats it, even when there is a change. Respondents can learn from their past experience answering a questionnaire. In some surveys, certain responses—for example, receiving some type of income or being a victim of a crime—may elicit a lengthy set of follow-up questions or probes. Over time, a respondent may observe this tendency and adjust her or his response to avoid being asked the follow-up sequence. On the other hand, the concepts or questions in a questionnaire may become clearer to a respondent after one or more contacts, producing responses based on better understanding or recall. In these instances, the conditioning can lead to more accurate data.

In surveys that ask for opinions, attitudes, or projected behavior, the person in a sample may become more informed or aware of the issues through a series of interviews. This can affect a later outcome by causing the respondent to explore the topic before the next interview or to change his or her behavior, for example, to vote for a specific candidate or simply to vote.

The effects of panel conditioning are not always initiated by the respondent. The procedures for conducting a repeated survey can differ from one interview to the next. For example, when the household or business is first contacted, additional relevant questions might be asked that are omitted in later interviews. This omission can influence the subsequent responses. Further, the interviewer may have access to responses from prior interviews and may change the way he or she conducts the next interview based on this information.

In a repeated survey, the effects of panel conditioning on the estimates are difficult to measure and correct for, in part because the effects may be confounded with actual change, panel attrition, the mode of data collection, or other factors. One way to study the effects is to operate a repeated panel simultaneously with independent cross-sections of the same population and compare the results at fixed points in time. Another approach is to compare responses to reliable administrative records and gauge the accuracy over the life of the panel.

Statistically, the group or panel of sample units responding for the first time will exhibit a bias if the mean of their responses differs from the true value based on the entire population. In the same way, the estimate from the panel responding for the second or third time can suffer from bias of a different value. Often this time-in-sample bias is measured by comparing a panel's value to the average over all panels, with the latter as a proxy for the "truth." However, without additional studies, the true bias of each panel cannot be determined; it can only be expressed relative to a number such as the average.

The relative effects among the panels may be studied under a balanced rotating panel design, in which the set of times in sample is the same in every period. Under such a design, if the time-in-sample biases are additive and remain constant over time, the biases can cancel each other relative to the truth when estimating change over time.

Patrick J. Cantwell

See also Attrition; Panel; Panel Fatigue; Panel Survey; Reinterview; Response Bias; Rotating Panel Design

Further Readings

Bailar, B. A. (1975). The effects of rotation group bias on estimates from panel surveys. *Journal of the American Statistical Association, 70*, 23–30.
Kasprzyk, D., Kalton, G., Duncan, G., & Singh, M. P. (Eds.). (1989). *Panel surveys.* New York: Wiley.

PANEL DATA ANALYSIS

Panel data analysis refers to the statistical analysis of data sets consisting of multiple observations on each sampling unit. This could be generated by pooling time-series observations across a variety of cross-sectional units, including countries, firms, or randomly sampled individuals or households. This also encompasses longitudinal data analysis in which the primary focus is on individual histories. Two well-known examples of U.S. panel data are the Panel Study of Income Dynamics (PSID) and the National Longitudinal Surveys of Labor Market Experience (NLS). European panels include the German Socio-Economic Panel, the British Household Panel Survey, and the European Community household panel.

Benefits and Limitations

Some of the benefits and limitations of using panel data for statistical analysis include a much larger data set, because panel data are multiple observations on the same individual. This means that there will be more variability and less collinearity among the variables

than is typical of cross-section or time-series data. For example, in a demand equation for a given good (say, gasoline), price and income may be highly correlated for annual time-series observations for a given country or state. By stacking or pooling these observations across different countries or states, the variation in the data is increased and collinearity is reduced. With additional and more informative data, one can get more reliable estimates and test more sophisticated behavioral models using less restrictive assumptions.

Another advantage of panel data is their ability to control for individual heterogeneity. Not controlling for these unobserved individual specific effects leads to bias in the resulting estimates. For example, in an earnings equation, the wage of an individual is regressed on various individual attributes, such as education, experience, gender, race, and so on. But the error term may still include unobserved individual characteristics, such as ability, which is correlated with some of the regressors, such as education. Cross-sectional studies attempt to control for this unobserved ability by collecting hard-to-get data on twins. However, using individual panel data, one can, for example, difference the data over time and eliminate the unobserved individual invariant ability. Panel data sets are better able to study complex issues of dynamic behavior. For example, with cross-section data, one can estimate the rate of unemployment at a particular point in time. Repeated cross-sections can show how this proportion changes over time. Only panel data sets can estimate what proportion of those who are unemployed in one period remains unemployed in another period.

Limitations of panel data sets include problems in the design, data collection, and data management of panel surveys. These include the problems of coverage (incomplete account of the population of interest), nonresponse (due to lack of cooperation of the respondent or because of interviewer error), recall (respondent not remembering correctly), frequency of interviewing, interview spacing, reference period, the use of bounding to prevent the shifting of events from outside the recall period into the recall period, and time-in-sample bias.

Another limitation of panel data sets is distortion due to measurement errors. Measurement errors may arise because of faulty response due to unclear questions, memory errors, deliberate distortion of responses (e.g., prestige bias), inappropriate informants, misrecording of responses, and interviewer effects. Although these problems can occur in cross-section studies, they are aggravated in panel data studies. Panel data sets may also exhibit bias due to sample selection problems. For the initial wave of the panel, respondents may refuse to participate, or the interviewer may not find anybody at home. This may cause some bias in the inference drawn from this sample. Although this nonresponse can also occur in cross-section data sets, it is more serious with panels because subsequent waves of the panel are still subject to nonresponse. Respondents may die, move, or find that the cost of responding is high. The rate of attrition differs across panels and usually increases from one wave to the next, but the rate of increase typically declines over time.

Applications

Most panel data applications have been limited to a simple regression with error components disturbances, such as the following:

$$y_{it} = x'_{it}\beta + \mu_i + v_{it}, \quad i = 1, \ldots, n; \quad t = 1, \ldots, T,$$

where y_{it} may denote log(wage) for the ith individual at time t, and x_{it} is a vector of observations on k explanatory variables such as education, experience, race, sex, marital status, union membership, hours worked, and so on. In addition, β is a k vector of unknown coefficients, μ_i is an unobserved individual specific effect, and v_{it} is a zero mean random disturbance with variance σ^2_v. The error components disturbances follow a one-way analysis of variance (ANOVA). If μ_i denote fixed parameters to be estimated, this model is known as the *fixed-effects* (FE) model. The x_{it}'s are assumed independent of the v_{it}'s for all i and t. Inference in this case is conditional on the particular n individuals observed. Estimation in this case amounts to including $(n-1)$ individual dummies to estimate these individual invariant effects. This leads to a large loss in degrees of freedom and attenuates the problem of multi-collinearity among the regressors. Furthermore, this may not be computationally feasible for large sample size panels. In this case, one can eliminate the μ_i s and estimate β by running least squares of $\tilde{y}_{it} = y_{it} - \bar{y}_{i.}$ on the $\tilde{x}_{it}$s similarly defined, where the dot indicates summation over that index and the bar denotes averaging. This transformation is known as the *within transformation*, and the corresponding estimator of β is called the *within estimator* or the *FE estimator*. Note that the FE estimator cannot estimate the effect of any time-invariant variable such as gender, race, or religion. These variables are wiped out by the within transformation. This is a major disadvantage if the effect of these variables on earnings is of interest.

If μ_i denotes independent random variables with zero mean and constant variance σ^2_μ, this model is known as the *random-effects* (RE) model. The preceding moments are conditional on the x_{it}s. In addition, μ_i and v_{it} are assumed to be conditionally independent. The RE model can be estimated by generalized least squares (GLS), which can be obtained using a least squares regression of $y^*_{it} = y_{it} - \theta\bar{y}_{i.}$ on x^*_{it} similarly defined, where θ is a simple function of the variance components σ^2_μ and σ^2_v. The corresponding GLS estimator of β is known as the *RE estimator*. Note that for this RE model, one can estimate the effects of individual-invariant variables. The best quadratic unbiased (BQU) estimators of the variance components are ANOVA-type estimators based on the true disturbances, and these are minimum variance unbiased (MVU) under normality of the disturbances. One can obtain feasible estimates of the variance components by replacing the true disturbances by OLS or fixed-effects residuals.

A specification test based on the difference between the fixed- and random-effects estimators is known as the *Hausman test*. The null hypothesis is that the individual effects are not correlated with the x_{it}s. The basic idea behind this test is that the fixed-effects estimator $\tilde{\beta}_{FE}$ is consistent, whether or not the effects are correlated with the x_{it}s. This is true because the fixed-effects transformation described by $\tilde{y}_{it}$ wipes out the μ_i effects from the model. However, if the null hypothesis is true, the fixed-effects estimator is not efficient under the random-effects specification because it relies only on the within variation in the data. On the other hand, the random-effects estimator $\hat{\beta}_{RE}$ is efficient under the null hypothesis but is biased and inconsistent when the effects are correlated with the x_{it}s. The difference between these estimators $\hat{q} = \tilde{\beta}_{FE} - \hat{\beta}_{RE}$ tends to zero in probability limits under the null hypothesis and is nonzero under the alternative. The variance of this difference is equal to the difference in variances, $\text{var}(\hat{q}) = \text{var}(\tilde{\beta}_{FE}) - \text{var}(\hat{\beta}_{RE})$ because $\text{cov}(\hat{q}, \hat{\beta}_{RE}) = 0$ under the null hypothesis. Hausman's test statistic is based on $m = \hat{q}'[\text{var}(\hat{q})]^{-1}\hat{q}$ and is asymptotically distributed a chi-square with k degrees of freedom under the null hypothesis.

Special Panel Data Sets

Space limitations do not allow discussion of panel data models that include treatment of missing observations, dynamics, measurement error, qualitative limited dependent variables, endogeneity, and nonstationarity of the regressors. Instead frequently encountered special panel data sets—namely, pseudo-panels and rotating panels—are discussed. *Pseudo-panels* refer to the construction of a panel from repeated cross-sections, especially in countries where panels do not exist but where independent surveys are available over time. The United Kingdom Family Expenditure Survey, for example, surveys about 7,000 households annually. These are independent surveys because it may be impossible to track the same household across surveys, as required in a genuine panel. Instead, one can track cohorts and estimate economic relationships based on cohort means. Pseudo-panels do not suffer the attrition problem that plagues genuine panels and may be available over longer time periods.

One important question is the optimal size of the cohort. A large number of cohorts will reduce the size of a specific cohort and the samples drawn from it. Alternatively, selecting few cohorts increases the accuracy of the sample cohort means, but it also reduces the effective sample size of the panel.

Rotating panels attempt to keep the same number of households in the survey by replacing the fraction of households that drop from the sample in each period with an equal number of freshly surveyed households. This is a necessity in surveys in which a high rate of attrition is expected from one period to the next. Rotating panels allow the researcher to rest for the existence of time-in-sample bias effects. These correspond to a significant change in response between the initial interview and a subsequent interview when one would expect the same response.

Other Considerations

Panel data are not a panacea and will not solve all the problems that a time-series or a cross-section study could not handle. For example, with macro-panels made up of a large number of countries over a long time period, econometric studies argued that panel data will yield more powerful unit root tests than individual time-series. This in turn should help shed more light on the purchasing power parity (PPP) and the growth convergence questions. This led to a flurry of empirical applications, along with some skeptics who argued that panel data did not save the PPP or the growth convergence problem.

Also, collecting panel data is quite costly, and there is always the question of how often one should interview respondents. For example, some economists argue that economic development is far from instantaneous, so that changes from one year to the next are probably "too noisy" (i.e., unreliable) and too short term to really be useful. They conclude that the payoff for panel data is over long time periods, 5 years, 10 years, or even longer. In contrast, for health and nutrition issues, especially those of children, one could argue the opposite case—that is, those panels with a shorter time span—are needed in order to monitor the health and development of these children.

Users of panel data argue that these data provide several advantages worth their cost. However, as with survey data in general, the more we have of it, the more we demand of it. The survey researcher using panel data, or any data for that matter, must know the data's strengths and limitations.

Badi H. Baltagi

See also Analysis of Variance (ANOVA); Attrition; Cross-Sectional Data; Longitudinal Studies; Measurement Error; Panel; Panel Conditioning; Panel Fatigue; Panel Survey; Repeated Cross-Sectional Design; Rotating Panel Design

Further Readings

Kalton, G., & Brick, M. (2000). Weighting in household panel surveys. In D. Rose (Ed.), *Researching social and economic change: The uses of household panel studies* (pp. 96–112). New York: Routledge.

Kasprzyk, D., Duncan, G. J., Kalton, G., & Singh, M. P. (Eds.). (1989). *Panel surveys.* New York: Wiley.

PANEL FATIGUE

Panel fatigue refers to the phenomenon in survey research whereby the quality of data that is gathered from a particular member of a survey panel diminishes if she or he is expected to stay in the panel for too long a duration (i.e., for too many waves) of data collection. In the extreme, panel fatigue leads to premature panel nonresponse for particular panel members prior to their tenure in the panel officially expiring. That is, the respondent drops out of the panel early and thereafter is a source of *panel attrition*. Panel fatigue also contributes to item nonresponse (i.e., missing data), to increases in satisficing as a mode of response, and to other forms of lower quality of data. Because panel fatigue does not occur uniformly across all types of respondents, it often leads to *differential panel attrition*. Old adults and young adults, those with less educational attainment, and/or minorities are most likely to display panel fatigue.

The effects of panel fatigue are best countered by researchers making informed and reliable decisions about how long is "too long" for panel members to stay in a panel survey. These data quality considerations must be balanced with the cost implications of having to turn over (i.e., refresh) the panel more often than is desirable from a cost standpoint. For example, a conservative but expensive approach would be to determine when nonnegligible panel fatigue starts for the 20% or so of panel members who are the first to experience panel fatigue, and then limit all panel membership to that lower duration. Panel fatigue also can be countered by not timing waves of subsequent data collection too closely together; or by rotating random subsets of panel members in and out of data collection (e.g., every other wave, or every two of three waves).

Extra attention paid to panel members also may help counter panel fatigue. This includes friendly "staying in touch" communications from the researchers between waves of data collection that show sincere interest in the well-being of the panel members and subtly stress the importance of remaining active panel members. Use of contingent (performance-based) incentives also has been shown to be effective in reducing the negative effects of panel fatigue.

Paul J. Lavrakas

See also Attrition; Contingent Incentives; Missing Data; Panel; Panel Conditioning; Panel Survey; Rotating Panel Design; Satisficing; Wave

Further Readings

Holden, R., Heng, L. M., Lavrakas, P. J., Bell, S., & Flizik, A. (2006, May). *Personal contact and performance-based incentives to raise long-term panel compliance and to reduce missing data.* Paper presented at the 61st annual conference of the American Association for Public Opinion Research, Montreal, Quebec.

Kasprzyk, D., Duncan, G., Kalton, G., & Singh, M. P. (Eds.). (1989). *Panel surveys.* New York: Wiley.

Lansdowne, J. (1970). The mailed questionnaire in panel research: Some empirical observations. *Social Forces,* *49*(1), 136–140.

PANEL SURVEY

The essential feature of a longitudinal survey design is that it provides repeated observations on a set of variables for the same sample units over time. The different types of longitudinal studies (e.g., retrospective studies, panel surveys, and record linkages) are distinguished by the different ways of deriving these repeated observations. In a panel survey, repeated observations are derived by following a sample of persons (a panel) over time and by collecting data from a sequence of interviews (or waves). These interviews are conducted at usually fixed occasions that in most cases are regularly spaced.

There are many variations under this general description of a panel survey, including (a) cohort panel surveys, (b) household panel surveys, and (c) rotating panel surveys. These three types of panel surveys can be distinguished, first, by the sampling units and the population the survey aims to represent. The focus can be entirely on individuals or on individuals within their household context. A second distinction is between surveys comprising a single panel of indefinite life and surveys comprising multiple overlapping panels of fixed life. Choosing the appropriate design for a panel survey depends on the priorities and goals of the (potential) data users and requires an assessment of the benefits of the different sorts of information collected and the costs required for deriving them.

Cohort Panel Surveys

A cohort panel survey is the simplest example of a single panel of indefinite life. It is an individual-level panel focusing on a population subgroup that has experienced the same event during the same time period (a cohort), such as having been born in a particular month, being a high school graduate in a given year, or having been married during the same year.

Cohort panel surveys are also called "fixed panel surveys," since the definition of membership of the cohort is fixed and cannot change over time. The rules for following the sample units in subsequent waves are simple: At each wave of the cohort panel survey, interviews are attempted with all original cohort members. After the initial sample selection, no additions to the sample are made.

Cohort panels are often set up to study long-term change and individual development processes, such as transitions into adulthood and marital or other union formation and dissolution. The data of the 1970 British Cohort Study (BCS70), for example, provide researchers with an opportunity to study the life-course experiences of a group of individuals representative of all men and women born in the 1970s in Great Britain. More specifically, the BCS70 follows more than 17,000 men and women born in Great Britain in a specific week in 1970. Since the first wave of data collection in 1970 (age 0), there have been six other major data collection waves, in 1975 (age 5), 1980 (age 10), 1986 (age 16), 1996 (age 26), 1999/2000 (age 29/30), and 2004/2005 (age 34/35). This cohort panel survey collected data on many aspects of the health, social development, and education of the cohort members as they passed through childhood and adolescence. In the more recent waves, the information collected covers transitions into adult life, including leaving full-time education, entering the labor market, setting up independent homes, forming partnerships, and becoming parents.

In cohort studies, individuals are sometimes followed through their entire life course, and because of this cohort studies often have longer times in between interviews or waves (e.g., 5 or 10 years for BCS70). However, a longer inter-interview period might result in a larger proportion of the sample that drops out because of panel attrition. This happens because the proportion of sample units who have moved increases for longer intervals and because the difficulties of tracking movers since the last wave become more severe when the intervals are longer. Some cohort panel surveys reduce some of the problems of tracing sample units by using more frequent interviewing. For example, the National Longitudinal Survey of Youth 1979 (NLSY79), a U.S. nationally representative sample of approximately 13,000 young men and women who were 14 to 22 years of age when first surveyed in 1979, interviewed cohort members annually through 1993 and bi-annually since 1994.

Household Panel Surveys

When the only objective of a panel survey is to facilitate longitudinal research at the individual level, it may be sufficient to adopt a cohort approach that simply follows the initial sample selected for the first wave. However, when cross-sectional population estimates for the life of the study are also important, it is necessary to update the sample at each wave to represent new entrants to the population of interest. The typical household panel survey has an indefinite life and is set up to study individual and household change; individuals are interviewed at fixed intervals, usually a year, and information is collected about them and the households in which they reside. The best-known household panel surveys may be the U.S. Panel Study of Income Dynamics (PSID), the British Household Panel Study (BHPS), and the German Socio-Economic Panel (*Das Sozio-oekonomische Panel*—SOEP). The PSID is considered the "grandfather" of all modern household panel surveys, as it originated in 1968. After a decade and a half of experience gained from the PSID, the German SOEP was established in 1984, followed by the British BHPS in 1991.

The main difficulty with household panel surveys is thus that they require a more complicated design to remain representative across time for both the individuals and the households in which they reside. The composition of nearly every population of interest, whether of individuals or households, changes over time. Individuals enter the population when they are born, immigrate or attain the age or another status that is used to define the population of interest, and depart when they die, emigrate, move to institutions, such as a home for the elderly, or in some other way lose that eligibility status. At the same time, families are "born" when children leave their parents and set up their own independent households or when a divorce or separation breaks up a family into two, and families "die" when all members of the original household die or when two households are merged into one through marriage or other living arrangements. In a household panel survey, in addition to making decisions about the sample design for the initial wave, important decisions need to be made about which sample units are to be retained in the panel at each wave to remain representative of a population that changes composition as a consequence of birth, death, and mobility during the life of the panel.

Following-rules are those rules that are designed to follow up and to update the initial sample, so as to ensure that on every wave throughout the survey's time span, the sample remains cross-sectionally representative of the population of interest. Following-rules are thus used to add new members to the sample and to remove members from the sample in the same way as persons are added to or removed from households in the broader population. In most household panels, all adults and children in the representative sample of households in the first wave are defined as *original* or *continuous sample members* (OSMs). A child born to or adopted by an OSM also counts as an original sample member. Temporary sample members (TSMs) are individuals who join the household of an original sample member after the initial wave. For example, a new partner who moves in with an OSM, or an elderly person who becomes dependent and moves in with a family member who is an OSM, would be considered a TSM. Most household panel surveys have adopted the rule that, at the second and subsequent waves, attempts are made to interview all adult members of all households containing either an OSM or an individual born to an OSM, whether or not they were members of the original sample. In practice, this means that split-off OSMs, such as children leaving the parental home or an ex-spouse who leaves the original household after a divorce, are followed in all subsequent waves. Similarly, these split-off persons are also followed when they reunite with members of their former households, as when a couple separates but then reunites or a child returns to the parental home after a "false" start in an independent household. However, TSMs are only followed in the subsequent wave on the condition that they continue to live with an original sample member.

The main advantage of household panel surveys is the rich set of variables that they provide. For example, the BHPS, a nationally representative sample of more than 5,000 households and 10,000 individual interviews, was originally designed as a research resource to further understanding of social and economic change at the individual and household levels in Britain. In addition, as the duration of the BHPS lengthens, new analyses become feasible. After more than 15 years of data collection, and with both parents and children as sample members in their own right, it becomes possible to conduct analyses of intergenerational influences and intergenerational mobility.

Household panels typically use the same sort of instruments to collect this rich set of variables about each household and its members. Questions about the household itself (e.g., type of dwelling, housing costs, enumeration of household members, and the relationships between the household members) are answered by the household head or some other designated adult. For some household panel surveys, this designated adult also responds to questions about the individual household members; however, in most household panel surveys each adult member of each household responds to an individual questionnaire that asks about personal characteristics and behavior. Typical components of this individual questionnaire are personal income, employment, health, time use, and attitudes on various subjects.

Rotating Panel Surveys

A repeated panel survey is made up of a series of individual panel surveys. When there is overlap in the time periods covered by the individual panels, and individual panel members are rotated into and out of the panel over a relatively short time period, we speak of a *rotating panel survey*. An initial sample of respondents is selected and interviewed for a predetermined time, from a few months to several years, but at intervals shorter than for most household panels. During the life of this first panel, a new panel is selected, followed, and interviewed in the same way as in the first panel. Third and subsequent panels are constructed similarly. Each individual panel has a pre-determined fixed life, although the overall rotating panel survey usually has an indefinite life.

Rotating panels are used to provide a series of cross-sectional estimates (e.g., unemployment rates and changes in those rates), but they also have a focus on short-term longitudinal measures (e.g., durations of spells of unemployment). For example, the Survey of Labour and Income Dynamics (SLID) provides national data on a whole range of transitions, durations, and repeated occurrences of individuals' financial and work situations. The SLID is a Canadian rotating panel that started in 1993, consisting of a succession of overlapping panels each with a duration of 6 years and with each new panel introduced 3 years after the introduction of the previous one. Each panel of the SLID consists of roughly 15,000 households and about 30,000 adults, and respondents are interviewed annually.

The rules for following respondents in rotating panels are similar to those in household panels. However, by restricting the duration of each panel to a shorter period, problems of attrition are reduced and representativeness is more easily maintained. In addition, using the combined data from the constituent panels with overlapping measurement periods, rotating panel surveys as a whole can provide better cross-sectional information at each point in time. Another advantage of rotating panel surveys is that the shorter interval between the interviews can reduce recall error. The longer the time between waves, and thus, the longer the reference period, the more recall errors that occur. For example, the U.S. Survey of Income and Program Participation (SIPP), with individual national panel with a sample size ranging from approximately 14,000 to 36,700 interviewed households and a duration that ranges from two and a half years to four years, interviews panel members every 4 months and uses a recall period of 4 months to collect data about the source and amount of income, labor force information, program participation, and eligibility data.

Femke De Keulenaer

See also Attrition; Longitudinal Studies; Panel; Panel Data Analysis; Rotating Panel Design; Wave

Further Readings

Kalton, G., & Citro, C. F. (1993). Panel surveys: Adding the fourth dimension. *Survey Methodology, 19*(2), 205–215.
Kasprzyk, D., Duncan, G. J., Kalton, G., & Singh, M. P. (Eds.). (1989). *Panel surveys.* New York: Wiley.

PAPER-AND-PENCIL INTERVIEWING (PAPI)

Prior to the 1980s, essentially all survey data collection that was done by an interviewer was done via paper-and-pencil interviewing, which came to be known as PAPI. Following the microcomputer revolution of the early 1980s, computer-assisted interviewing (CAI)—for example, computer-assisted personal interviewing (CAPI), computer-assisted self-interviewing (CASI), and computer-assisted telephone interviewing (CATI)—had become commonplace by the 1990s, essentially eliminating most uses of PAPI, with some exceptions. PAPI still is used in instances where data are being gathered from a relatively small sample, with a noncomplex questionnaire, on an accelerated start-up time basis,

and/or the time and effort it would take to program (and test) the instrument into a computer-assisted version simply is not justified. PAPI also serves as a backup for those times when computer systems go down and interviewers would be left without work if there were not a paper version of the questionnaire to fall back to on a temporary basis. (Of note, mail surveys typically use paper-and-pencil questionnaires, but since they are not interviewer-administered surveys, mail questionnaires and that mode of data collection are not discussed here.)

PAPI is markedly inferior to CAI in many ways. The most important of these are (a) how sample processing is done with PAPI and (b) the limits of the complexity of the questionnaires that can be implemented via PAPI. Processing sample cases in PAPI traditionally was done manually. This required a supervisory person or staff to hand-sort "call sheets" or "control sheets" that were printed on paper, on which the interviewers filled out information each time an attempt was made to complete a questionnaire with a sampled case (e.g., at a telephone number or household address). This manual approach put practical limits on the complexity of the sample management system that could be used to sort and reprocess the active sample. It also relied entirely on the behavior and memory of the sample coordinator, which of course was fallible.

Questionnaires in PAPI cannot practically deploy complex randomization schemes that are easily programmed into and controlled by CAI. Although randomization can be built into PAPI, it typically requires that multiple versions of the questionnaire be created, printed, and randomly assigned to sampled cases. And, while randomized "starts" to question sequences can also be implemented in PAPI, interviewer error in implementing that type of randomization accurately is much more prevalent in PAPI. True randomization of the order of items within a question sequence is a nightmare to implement—if not outright impossible—accurately in PAPI when there are more than two items to randomize. The use of questions that use "fills" from answers previously given by the respondent (e.g., *Earlier you said that you had gone to the hospital X times the past 3 months . . .*) is also much more difficult to implement accurately in PAPI, whereas there are essentially no limits to its use in CAI. PAPI also has no assured way to control an interviewer from entering an "out-of-range" value to a particular question, whereas in CAI valid value ranges are programmed into each question asked.

The legibility of answers recorded by interviewers to open-ended questions in PAPI always is more problematic than what is captured via CAI. All in all, there is a great deal more potential for certain types of interview-related error in data collection in PAPI than is the case with CAI.

Data processing with PAPI is more time consuming and error prone than with CAI, given the answers that are recorded on paper by interviewers must be transformed into some computer-readable format via data keypunching. Data archiving also is much more problematic with PAPI, as even a small-sized survey organization must store boxes and boxes of completed questionnaires for some period of time after the completion of a survey project. However, although computer files can become corrupted and important past data can be lost, PAPI questionnaires are rarely destroyed, unless a fire or water damage occurs, until they are purposely thrown away.

There are some important benefits that occur from PAPI and do not routinely occur with CAI that have been forgotten or not realized by many researchers, especially those who started their careers after 1990. The most important of these is the level of attention that the average interviewer pays to the questions being asked and the answers being given in PAPI. In PAPI, there is a greater cognitive burden on the interviewer to negotiate the questionnaire, and a successful PAPI interviewer quickly learns that she or he must pay close attention to what she or he is asking the respondent and to what the respondent is replying. Often, this causes good PAPI interviewers to be more alert to problems and inconsistencies a respondent is creating than is typical of successful CAI interviewers. The PAPI interviewers then can try to probe to clarify or otherwise remedy these issues. In CAI, too many "successful" interviewers appear to take a mindless approach to interviewing and simply allow the computer lead them through the interview without really paying attention to the substance of what the respondent is saying. PAPI does not guarantee that this benefit will result, nor does CAI guarantee it will not result, but with PAPI, experience shows that interviewers are more likely to be intellectually engaged in the interviewing task than with CAI.

A second "benefit" of PAPI over CAI is that the same questionnaire, all other factors being equal, is completed more quickly if the interviewer uses a paper version of the questionnaire. Some have estimated the time difference to be 10%–20% longer with CAI than

with PAPI. The reason underlying this phenomenon is that PAPI interviewers have much more active control over the pace of going from question to question than do interviewers using CAI. In PAPI, the "next" question generally is on the same page right below the current question, and the interviewer does not have to wait for the computer to display the next question before going on to it. In fact, in PAPI, interviewers often start reading the next question as they are recording the answer to the previous question. This does not occur as readily in CAI, since the computer software does not display the next question until after the answer to the current question has been entered by the interviewer.

Paul J. Lavrakas

See also Call Sheet; Computer-Assisted Personal Interviewing (CAPI); Computer-Assisted Self-Interviewing (CASI); Computer-Assisted Telephone Interviewing (CATI); Control Sheet; Interviewer-Related Error; Random Order; Random Start; Sample Management

PARADATA

Paradata, also termed *process data* (but not to be confused with metadata), contain information about the primary data collection process (e.g., survey duration, interim status of a case, navigational errors in a survey questionnaire). Paradata can provide a means of additional control over or understanding of the quality of the primary data (the responses to the survey questions).

Collecting Paradata

Since paradata are defined simply as data describing the primary data collection process, paradata can be collected in every survey mode. However, the amount, type, and level of detail of the captured paradata will vary depending on whether the data have to be manually recorded or whether they are automatically logged by computer software. A crude distinction can also be made between paradata describing the data collection process as a whole (calls, follow-up procedures, etc.) and more specific paradata referring to how a survey questionnaire was filled in.

Case management software (such as that used in centralized computer-assisted telephone interviewing [CATI] facilities) can record a wide array of paradata about the survey process as a whole. The software is capable of logging the time, duration, and outcome of each call to a sample unit, although some of this information may need to be supplied by the interviewer (e.g., call outcome). In noncomputerized settings, paper call sheets filled in by the interviewers can serve to collect paradata.

The most efficient way of collecting paradata on how a survey questionnaire is filled in is to use a computerized survey questionnaire with software that logs meaningful actions such as ticking response options, navigating through the questionnaire, and so on. This could be viewed as an automatic behavior-coding system.

Whether and which paradata can be collected depends on the software used to create the survey questionnaire. Many CAI software packages allow the recording of paradata. For Web surveys, JavaScript code has been developed to collect detailed paradata similar to keystroke data generated by CAI software. (Apart from these data, Web server logs can also be used to collect less-detailed paradata.)

Uses of Paradata

Paradata can assist survey questionnaire pretests. For instance, data on how long it took to answer survey questions could be of importance in this phase. Long response latencies could indicate problems with particular questions. Paradata from keystroke files can reveal where errors were made, which may indicate poor interface design.

Paradata can also be collected during the actual field work. Recently, researchers have used paradata to adapt the survey design while the field work is still ongoing in order to improve survey cost efficiency and to achieve more precise, less biased estimates (these are so-called responsive design surveys).

In interviewer-administered surveys, paradata can be used to evaluate interviewer behavior. Time data can help identify interviewers who administered all or parts of the questionnaire too quickly. As in pretests, keystroke data can reveal where errors are being made. If these analyses are conducted during the field work, corrective measures can still be implemented in this phase.

When conducting experiments in a survey (e.g., within the questionnaire), researchers can use paradata as an additional source of information about the effects of the experimental treatment. Apart from a test of the effect of the treatment (e.g., survey instructions) on the dependent variable (e.g., omission errors in a self-administered questionnaire), paradata allow the researcher to see the effects of the treatment on the response behavior itself. This may provide additional insight into the reason why a specific treatment is effective or not.

Data Preparation

If the researcher has clear a priori assumptions about which information is important, paradata can be stored in conventional matrix form data sets. This, for instance, is the case when call sheets are used or when simple survey question durations are recorded. The variables are pre-defined, and the interviewer or computer software is instructed to compute and record their values. These variables can then be used in conventional analyses.

If some variables cannot be pre-defined, the data can be collected in a relatively unstructured way. Keystroke data are of this type. Data are collected by adding each action to a data string. Since not every interviewer or respondent will perform the same number of actions, or in the same sequence, these data strings will be of different lengths and their structure will vary from one observation to the next. In addition, different parts of the data strings could be important depending on the focus of the analysis. SAS macros or other software capable of recognizing string patterns can be used to extract the useful information from the strings before the actual analysis.

Dirk Heerwegh

See also Computer-Assisted Personal Interviewing (CAPI); Computer-Assisted Self-Interviewing (CASI); Computer-Assisted Telephone Interviewing (CATI); Response Latency; SAS; Web Survey

Further Readings

Bassili, J. N., & Fletcher, J. F. (1991). Response-time measurement in survey research: A method for CATI and a new look at nonattitudes. *Public Opinion Quarterly*, 55, 331–346.

Groves, R. M., & Heeringa, S. G. (2006). Responsive design for household surveys: Tools for actively controlling survey errors and costs. *Journal of the Royal Statistical Society: Series A (Statistics in Society)*, *169*, 439–457.

Heerwegh, D. (2003). Explaining response latencies and changing answers using client side paradata from a Web survey. *Social Science Computer Review*, *21*, 360–373.

Jeavons, A. (1999). Ethology and the Web: Observing respondent behaviour in Web surveys. *Marketing & Research Today*, *28*, 69–76.

PARAMETER

A parameter is a numerical quantity or attribute of a population that is estimated using data collected from the population. Parameters are to populations as statistics are to samples. For example, in survey research, the true proportion of voters who vote for a presidential candidate in the next national election may be of interest. Such a parameter may be estimated using a sample proportion computed from data gathered via a probability sample of registered voters. Or, the actual annual average household "out-of-pocket" medical expenses for a given year (parameter) could be estimated from data provided by the Medical Expenditures Survey. Or, the modal race of students within a particular school is an example of an attribute parameter that could be estimated using data acquired via a cluster sample of classrooms or students from the particular school. An important parameter in the realm of survey nonresponse is the likelihood of the response. The binary event "respond or not respond" can be modeled as a Bernoulli random variable with unknown parameter, p, which can vary by sampling unit as a function of demographic, socioeconomic, or other variables.

Parameters may also refer to specific aspects of a sampling distribution of a test statistic or reference distribution. For example, when estimating the mean weight loss for subscribers of a particular weight loss plan (the parameter), the most straightforward point estimate is the sample mean. The corresponding confidence interval is then computed with respect to a reference distribution—usually approximated by a normal distribution with a location and a scale parameter. The location parameter—or mean of the sampling distribution of the sample mean—has the same value as the population mean (parameter); the scale parameter, or standard deviation, is equal to the population standard deviation divided by the square root of the sample size. In general, the statistical parameters for the approximate sampling distribution of a statistic end up being equal to a function of the actual population parameters themselves.

While parameters are generally of direct interest in both estimation and inference, they can also serve as "auxiliary" inputs for statistical techniques to improve estimates of target or primary parameters. For example, in the most current random-digit dial (RDD) survey practice, landline RDD samples of households may be augmented with a screened sample of cell phone numbers identified as "cell phone only." A reliable estimate of the distribution of "type of phone ownership" (a nontarget parameter) is then used to adjust the initial survey weights via raking techniques to provide overall unbiased estimates of these population totals. The true number of patients diagnosed with a particular stage of cancer as well as the actual number of patients of each gender within a state are auxiliary parameters or universe counts that can be used to adjust the base survey weights so that representation by stage and sex may be achieved for a state registry-based survey that aims to estimate the percentiles of the distribution of quality-of-life scores for patients diagnosed with lung or skin cancer. These auxiliary parameters can also be used in calibration estimators to adjust for survey nonresponse.

Parameters can be univariate, bivariate, or multivariate quantities that, in turn, can be estimated appropriately by univariate, bivariate, or multivariate statistics. The regression parameters for the impact of income and education on average number of hours spent watching television give an example of several parameters that are estimated simultaneously from sample data via finite population regression. Multivariate collections of parameters can also be more complex, to include variances and covariances of a collection of measured variables contained in a survey questionnaire, along with path coefficients or factor loadings of latent variables in the context of factor or latent class analysis.

Trent D. Buskirk

See also Confidence Interval; Nonresponse; Point Estimate; Population; Raking; Sample; Statistic

Further Readings

Yates, D., Moore, D., & McCabe, G. (1999). *The practice of statistics*. New York: W. H. Freeman.

PARTIAL COMPLETION

The partial completion survey disposition is used in all types of surveys, regardless of mode. In a telephone or in-person interview, a partial completion results when the respondent provides answers for some of the questions on the survey questionnaire that were asked by the interviewer but is unable or unwilling to allow the interviewer to administer all of the questions in the interview (item nonresponse). Partial completions in telephone or in-person surveys can occur when an appointment or other commitment prevents the respondent from completing the interview or when the respondent begins the interview but then refuses to complete the entire interview process (called a "breakoff"). In a mail survey, a partial completion results when the respondent receives a paper-and-pencil survey questionnaire, answers only some of the questions on the questionnaire, and returns the questionnaire to the researcher. In an Internet survey, a partial completion occurs when the respondent logs into the survey, enters answers for some of the questions in the questionnaire, and submits the questionnaire electronically to the researcher. If a partial is not a hostile breakoff, most survey firms attempt to recontact the respondent who completed the partial interview (by telephone, mail, or Internet, depending on the survey mode) in order to attempt to get a completed interview.

In practice, the difference between completed interviews, partial completions, and breakoffs is that completed interviews contain the smallest number of item nonresponses, while breakoffs contain the largest number of item nonresponses. Most survey organizations have developed rules that explicitly define the difference among breakoffs, partial completions, and completed interviews. Common rules used by survey organizations to determine whether an interview with item nonresponse can be considered a completed interview include (a) the proportion of all applicable questions answered, and (b) the proportion of critically important or essential questions administered. For example, cases in which a respondent has answered fewer than 50% of the applicable questions might be defined as breakoffs;

cases in which the respondent has answered between 50% and 90% of the applicable questions might be defined as partial completions; and cases in which the respondent has answered more than 90% of applicable questions might be considered completed interviews.

Matthew Courser

See also Breakoff; Completed Interview; Final Dispositions; Item Nonresponse; Response Rates; Temporary Dispositions

Further Readings

American Association for Public Opinion Research. (2006). *Standard definitions: Final dispositions of case codes and outcome rates for surveys* (4th ed.). Lenexa, KS: Author.

PERCENTAGE FREQUENCY DISTRIBUTION

A percentage frequency distribution is a display of data that specifies the percentage of observations that exist for each data point or grouping of data points. It is a particularly useful method of expressing the relative frequency of survey responses and other data. Many times, percentage frequency distributions are displayed as tables or as bar graphs or pie charts.

The process of creating a percentage frequency distribution involves first identifying the total number of observations to be represented; then counting the total number of observations within each data point or grouping of data points; and then dividing the number of observations within each data point or grouping of data points by the total number of observations. The sum of all the percentages corresponding to each data point or grouping of data points should be 100%. The final step of creating a percentage frequency distribution involves displaying the data.

For example, as part of a study examining the relationship between number of trips to a physician and socioeconomic status, one might survey 200 individuals about the number of trips each made to a physician over the past 12 months. The survey might ask each individual to choose from the following responses: "0 times during the past year," "1–3 times during the past year," "4–6 times during the past year," "7–9 times during the past year," and "10 or more times during the past year."

If 10 respondents were to select the first response, 80 were to select the second, 50 were to select the third, 40 were to select the fourth, and 20 were to select the fifth, then the percentage frequency distribution would be calculated by dividing the number of responses for each choice by the total number of responses, or 200. The percentage frequency of each would be 5%, 40%, 25%, 20%, and 10%, respectively. The percentage frequency distribution is shown in table form (Table 1) and in bar graph form (Figure 1).

Alternatively, one could aggregate—or group—data points. For instance, in the previous example, a percentage frequency distribution could group the number of trips to the doctor into three distinct categories, such as "0 times," "1 to 6 times," and "7 or more times." When grouping the responses, the total percentage of each category of response is merely the sum of the percentages for each response. When grouped in this manner, the frequency percentage of "0 times" would remain unchanged at 5%, the total for "1 to 6 times" would be 65% (the sum of 40% and 25%), and the total for "7 or more times" would be 30% (the sum of 20% and 10%).

Most statistical software programs can easily generate percentage frequency distributions and provide visual representations in table or graph form.

Joel K. Shapiro

See also Frequency Distribution; Relative Frequency; Unit of Observation

Further Readings

Kvanli, A. H., Guynes, C. S., & Pavur, R. J. (1986). *Introduction to business statistics*. St. Paul, MN: West.

Table 1   Percentage frequency distribution

Response	Percentage (%) of Respondents Selecting Response
0 times during the past year	5
1–3 times during the past year	40
4–6 times during the past year	25
7–9 times during the past year	20
10 or more times during the past year	10

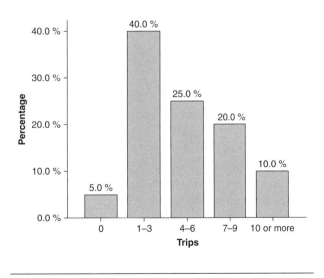

Figure 1   Percentage frequency distribution

PERCENTILE

A percentile is a statistic that gives the relative standing of a numerical data point when compared to all other data points in a distribution. In the example $P_{.84} = 66$, $P_{.84}$ is called the *percentile rank* and the data point of 66 is called the *percentile point*. The .84 in the percentile rank of $P_{.84}$ is a proportion that tells us the relative standing of the percentile point of 66 compared to all other data points in the distribution being examined. Reporting percentiles can be a useful way to present data in that it allows an audience to quickly determine the relative standing of a particular data point.

By itself, a raw score or data point says little about its relative position within a data set. Percentiles provide a number expressing a data point's relative position within a data set. At a glance, the percentile shows the reader whether a particular numerical data point is high, medium, or low in relation to the rest of the data set. Salaries, IQ scores, standardized test scores such as the SAT, GRE, body mass index (BMI), height, and weight are all frequently expressed as percentiles.

Some percentile values commonly used in reporting are the median, $P_{.50}$, below which 50% of the cases fall; the lower quartile, $P_{.25}$, below which 25% of the cases fall; and the upper quartile, $P_{.75}$, below which 75% of the cases fall. The area between the lower quartile and the middle quartile is called the "interquartile range," which contains the middle 50% of values in a distribution.

There are two basic definitions of the proportion expressed in the percentile rank. One definition used in some introductory statistics textbooks calculates the percentile rank as the proportion of cases falling *below* the percentile point. Using this definition, the maximum obtainable percentile must be less than 1.0, because there is no number in a data set that falls below itself. The second definition of percentile rank is the proportion of cases *at or below* the percentile point. Using this second definition, the 100th percentile is the maximum obtainable percentile, because 100% of the data falls at or below the largest number in a data set. The definition of *percentile* is dependent on the formula used to calculate the percentile rank.

Using our example $P_{.84} = 66$, the first definition of percentile rank calculates the percentile rank of .84 to mean 84% of the cases in the distribution fall *below* the percentile point of 66. A relatively simple way to calculate percentiles using this definition can be obtained with the formula $p(N)$ where p is the desired percentile rank and N is the number of cases in the distribution. This calculation gives the position within the distribution where the percentile point is located once the data points in the distribution are ordered from lowest to highest. If $p(N)$ results in a fractional number, round up to the next highest number for the percentile point position within the distribution. Once the position within the data set is determined, count up from the bottom of the distribution to the number obtained from the calculation $p(N)$. The mean of that number in the data set and the number value in the next highest position in the distribution is the percentile point corresponding to the percentile rank.

The calculation given is by no means the only way to calculate percentiles; however, it is one of the simplest. Statistical software programs such as Statistical Package for the Social Sciences (SPSS) and SAS and spreadsheet programs such as Microsoft Excel allow the user to calculate percentiles quickly. SPSS and SAS allow the user to choose from a variety of different formulas that will calculate the percentile values in slightly different ways, yielding slightly different results, depending on the user's needs.

Dennis Dew

See also Mean; Median; SAS; Stata; Statistic; Statistical Package for the Social Sciences (SPSS)

Further Readings

McCall, R. B. (2001). *Fundamental statistics for behavioral sciences* (8th ed.). Belmont, CA: Wadsworth.

PERCEPTION QUESTION

Perception is the subjective process of acquiring, interpreting, and organizing sensory information. Survey questions that assess perception, as opposed to those assessing factual knowledge, are aimed at identifying the processes that (a) underlie how individuals acquire, interpret, organize, and, generally make sense of (i.e., form beliefs about) the environment in which they live; and (b) help measure the extent to which such perceptions affect individual behaviors and attitudes as a function of an individual's past experiences, biological makeup, expectations, goals, and/or culture.

Perception questions differ from other types of survey questions—behavioral, knowledge, attitudinal, or demographic—in that questions that measure perception ask respondents to provide information on how they perceive such matters as the effectiveness of programs, their health status, or the makeup of their community, among other specific measures assessing biological, physiological, and psychological processes.

Broadly, research on perception is driven by many different kinds of questions that assess how individual senses and perceptions operate; how and why individuals are susceptible to perceptions or misperceptions; which structures in the brain support perception; and how individual perceptions acquire meaning. Research on the psychology of perception suggests that the actions of individuals are influenced by their perceptions of the opinions, values, and expectations of others, including those individuals identified as important by the respondent. This is of particular import to survey methodologists, because an individual's perceptions may influence her or his survey responses and, moreover, may be inaccurate. When this inaccuracy is systematic (biasing) rather than random, such inaccuracy has consequences for interpreting the survey data collected. Theory development on perception indicates that the accuracy of reported perceptions is related to communication mode, coordination efforts, and the salience of the percept. Other research finds that perceptions may be distorted by intimate relationships, attraction, personality traits, or indirect cues or interviewer effects, among other influences. Such influences may induce social desirability bias, where perception questions are improperly drafted or fail to account for question wording and ordering effects within the instrument and administration mode.

Including perception measures in a survey instrument enables researchers to investigate both qualitative and quantitative empirical hypotheses by incorporating open-ended and closed-ended measures that assess the way the respondent acquires, interprets, and organizes information, questions about the relationships among the respondent's perceptions, and the meaning of reported perceptions. To this end, introspection, experimental psychology, and neuroscience research are used to study perception in fields ranging from cognitive to computer science; each use different questions to measure perception. The method of introspection asks respondents to examine and report their conscious thoughts, reasoning, or sensations, such as the questioning used in cognitive interviewing. Here, respondents may be asked how their perceptions compare with the perceptions of other people.

The subjective nature of perception, however, presents a reliability problem. Because the survey interviewer or researcher cannot often easily or reliably identify whether a respondent is being truthful or accurate in her or his reports of a subjective experience, it is not possible to tell whether a particular word used to report an experience is being used to refer to the same kind of experience reported by another respondent. Thus, the reliability of introspection and the data collected using this method should be scrutinized carefully. Methods in experimental psychology include questions that prompt the participant to report, for example, object recognition, motion detection, visual illusions, and the like. In some cases, this report follows the participant performing a perceptual task. Neuroscience research uses perception questions to study attention and memory systems to identify how individuals store, organize, and retrieve perceptions as a way to understand information processing generally.

Finally, it is important, given the subjective nature of perception questions, to minimize the error in survey statistics by choosing wisely those design and estimation methods that are likely to reduce error.

Traci Lynne Nelson

See also Behavioral Question; Cognitive Aspects of Survey Methodology (CASM); Cognitive Interviewing; Construct; Construct Validity; Context Effect; Experimental Design; Gestalt Psychology; Interviewer Effects; Knowledge Question; Measurement Error; Question Order Effects; Respondent-Related Error; Saliency; Social Desirability

Further Readings

Blake, R., & Sekuler, R. (2005). *Perception* (5th ed.). Columbus, OH: McGraw-Hill.

Groves, R. M., Fowler, F. J., Couper, M. P., Lepkowski, J. M., Singer, E., & Tourangeau, R. (1989). *Survey methodology*. New York: Wiley.

PERTURBATION METHODS

Perturbation methods are procedures that are applied to data sets in order to protect the confidentiality of survey respondents. The goal of *statistical disclosure control* (SDC) is to provide accurate and useful data—especially public use data files—while also protecting confidentiality. Various methods have been suggested, and these may be classified two ways: (1) methods that do not alter the original data but reduce the amount of data released; and (2) methods that alter individual values while maintaining the reported level of detail. The first set of methods may be described as *data coarsening;* the second set of methods may be described as *statistical perturbation methods*.

Perturbation methods have the advantage of maintaining more of the actual data collected by survey respondents than data coarsening. Variables selected for perturbation may be those containing sensitive information about a respondent (such as income) or those that may potentially identify a respondent (such as race). These methods can be used for data released at the microdata level (individual respondent records) or at the tabular level (in the form of frequency tables). Depending on the data, their values, and method of data release, researchers may select one perturbation method over another, use multiple perturbation techniques, or use these techniques in addition to data coarsening.

Examples of perturbation methods are described below, with a focus primarily on perturbation of microdata. This is not an exhaustive list, as new methods are continually being developed.

Data swapping. In this method, selected records are paired with other records in the file based on a predetermined set of characteristics. Data values from some identifying or sensitive variables are then swapped between the two records. The sampling rate is designed to protect the confidentiality of the data without affecting the usability of the data set. This method introduces uncertainty to an intruder as to which reported values were provided by a particular respondent.

Rank swapping, a method similar to data swapping. With rank swapping, pairs are created that do not exactly match on the selected characteristics but are close in terms of the ranks of the characteristics.

Adding random noise. This method is a way of masking sensitive items by adding or multiplying by random numbers. The random numbers are selected from a pre-specified distribution with a mean of 0 and a selected standard deviation, so that the value is altered as little as possible but enough to prevent reidentification.

Replacing values with imputed data. With this method, specified sensitive values on a randomly selected set of records are replaced with imputed values from other, similar records. This approach will introduce some uncertainty as to whether the sensitive items on a record were actually reported by a particular respondent.

Data synthesis. Values are replaced with those predicted from models developed to generate multiple imputations that allow for valid statistical inference. All values for all records may be replaced (full synthesis), or a subset of variables on a subset of records (partial synthesis).

Blurring. In this method, small groups of records are formed based on the proximity of their values of a sensitive variable or other variables related to the sensitive variable. Aggregate (usually average) values are calculated from the individual responses for the sensitive item in that group. The aggregate value may be used in place of one (for example, the middle) or all individual responses for the group on the released data file.

Microaggregation. This is similar to blurring. However, the records are grouped so they are similar in terms of all sensitive variables of interest. This same grouping is used to "blur" all the sensitive variables.

Supersampling and subsampling. Records from the original file are sampled with replacement and added to it. The result is a file that is larger than the original microdata file. The larger file is then subsampled to produce the final microdata file. This method reduces the appearance of actual sample uniques (since they may not be sampled for the final file) and creates others (since a value and its duplicate may not both be selected).

Post-randomization method (PRAM). For each record on the data file, the values of one or more categorical variables are changed to already existing values on the file. These changes are made independently of other records using a pre-determined probability distribution. The level of protection depends on the probability matrix, the values, and their frequencies in the original data.

Data shuffling. This method is similar to data swapping. However, rather than have data values exchanged between records, a value for a sensitive variable on record a is replaced with the value from record b. The value from record b is then replaced with the value from record c, and so on, based on the conditional distribution of the sensitive variable.

Rounding. This is a perturbation method appropriate for tabular data. With random rounding, the decision to round a value up or down (to a pre-determined base) is made at random. Controlled rounding is similar, but the adjustments are such that the original marginal totals of the table are preserved.

Sylvia Dohrmann

See also Confidentiality; Data Swapping; Privacy; Suppression

Further Readings

Elliot, M., Hundepool, A., Nordholt, E. S., Tambay, J.-L., & Wende, T. (2006). The new glossary on statistical disclosure control. *The Survey Statistician, 54,* 26–36.

Federal Committee on Statistical Methodology, Subcommittee on Disclosure Limitation Methodology. (1994). *Report on statistical disclosure limitation methodology.* Statistical Policy Working Paper 22. Washington, DC: Office of Management and Budget, Executive Office of the President.

PEW RESEARCH CENTER

The Pew Research Center is a nonpartisan research center based in Washington, D.C. There are seven separate projects within the Pew Research Center, most of which employ sample surveys as a primary research tool. In addition to relying on surveys for much of its research, the Pew Research Center also conducts research on survey methodology.

The oldest of the projects is the Pew Research Center for the People & the Press, which was founded in 1987 as the Times Mirror Center for the People & the Press. The Times Mirror Center was originally created by the Times Mirror Company, a media corporation that owned *The Los Angeles Times* and other major newspapers and communications properties. Its mission was to conduct in-depth research that would illuminate the connections among the public policy world, the press, and the public, and to disseminate the research widely and without cost. In 1995, the Pew Charitable Trusts became the primary source of funding for the center, which was renamed the Pew Research Center for the People & the Press. In 2004, several other Pew-funded research projects were combined under the umbrella organization of the Pew Research Center. The Pew Charitable Trusts is a Philadelphia-based public charity.

The president of the Pew Research Center is pollster Andrew Kohut, who was president of the Gallup Organization from 1979 to 1989 and who served as the research director for the Times Mirror Center when it was founded. He subsequently became its director in 1993. When funding from Times Mirror ended, Kohut obtained funding from Pew to continue the center's operations. In subsequent years, he oversaw the creation of the Pew Internet and American Life Project, which extended the People & the Press's previous work on the Internet. He also forged research partnerships with the Pew Forum on Religion & Public Life and the Project for Excellence in Journalism, Pew-funded projects that are now part of the Pew Research Center.

The Pew Research Center for the People & the Press conducts monthly polling in the United States on policy issues, public interest in the news, and political parties and elections. Among its regular but less frequent projects are (a) a biennial survey on news consumption; (b) a survey of foreign policy attitudes among the public and several groups of foreign policy elites; (c) a survey of U.S. journalists, conducted with the Project for Excellence in Journalism, regarding issues facing the news industry and journalism; (d) an annual survey on religion and politics conducted with the Pew Forum on Religion & Public Life; (e) surveys

on the political values of the public; and (f) methodological research focused on issues facing the survey research community. The center also conducts extensive polling during national elections, typically including a broad "scene-setter" poll during the summer prior to the election, several polls during the fall focused on the issues and candidate images, a predictive survey conducted the weekend before the election, and a post-election survey to gauge the public's reaction to the outcome of the election and expectations for the future. In conjunction with the Pew Internet & American Life Project, the People & the Press Center also conducts a post-election survey on the public's use of the Internet to follow and participate in the election campaigns.

The Pew Internet & American Life Project, founded in 1999, uses surveys to study the social and political impact of the Internet in the United States. Most of its work consists of random-digit dialed (RDD) telephone surveys of the general public and special populations, but it also uses Internet surveys and qualitative methods in some of its research. Its director is Lee Rainie, a former journalist who served as managing editor of *U.S. News & World Report.* The project conducts regular tracking surveys to monitor trends in Internet use for a range of activities, including email use, broadband adoption, search engine use, blog creation and readership, and use of the Internet in such areas as health care, hobbies, the arts, social interaction, education, shopping, decisions about major purchases, and political activity.

The Pew Hispanic Center makes extensive use of survey research to study the Hispanic population of the United States and its impact on the country. The center conducts regular RDD telephone surveys of the Hispanic population, focusing on such topics as political engagement, employment, identity, education, and remittances. It also conducts extensive secondary analysis of U.S. Census surveys such as the decennial census, the Current Population Survey, and the American Community Survey. Its founding director is Roberto Suro, a former journalist who served as reporter for *The Washington Post, Time* magazine, and *The New York Times.*

In addition to partnering with the People & the Press Center on annual surveys of religion and politics in the United States, the Pew Forum on Religion & Public Life also had used surveys to study Pentecostalism in Asia, Latin America, and Africa as well as in the United States. It also has worked with the Pew Hispanic Center on a survey of Hispanics regarding religious beliefs and practices and is undertaking an effort to track the size and composition of religious groups in the United States. The Pew Forum's director is Luis Lugo, a former professor of political science and director of the religion program for the Pew Charitable Trusts.

The Global Attitudes Project, founded in 2002 by Andrew Kohut, conducts public opinion polling internationally on a range of topics including politics, religion, economics, social life, and foreign affairs. Among the subjects of its surveys has been the rise of anti-American sentiment, opinions about Islamic extremism, views of democracy among Muslim publics, and opinions about the impact of globalization.

Scott Keeter

Further Readings

Pew Research Center: http://pewresearch.org

PILOT TEST

Pilot tests are "dress rehearsals" of full survey operations that are implemented to determine whether problems exist that need to be addressed prior to putting the production survey in the field. Traditional pilot tests are common and have been a part of the survey process since the 1940s. In recent years, by the time a pilot test is conducted, the questionnaire has frequently already undergone review (and revision) through expert review, focus groups, and/or cognitive interviews.

The terms *pretest* and *pilot test* are sometimes used interchangeably; however, in recent years *pretest* has taken on the meaning of testing within a survey laboratory, rather than in the field with the general population. Some organizations or survey researchers now refer to pilot tests as *field pretests*. Pilot testing is one of the most critical aspects of a successful survey operation resulting in good survey data. Going into the field for a full production survey without knowing whether the questionnaire and/or field interviewer procedures work is a recipe for disaster.

Objectives

In surveys, nonsampling measurement error can be caused by problems associated with interviewers, respondents, and/or the questionnaire. The objective of a pilot test is to identify potential problems and address them prior to the production survey to reduce the amount of nonsampling measurement error produced by the survey.

Procedures

The pilot test procedures should mirror the procedures that will be used in the production survey. For pilot tests, the sample size is typically 50–100 cases. In fact, *sample* is an inappropriate term to use, since a nonrandom convenience sample rather than a random sample is typically used. It is important to have a "sample" that is as similar in characteristics as the respondents in the production survey sample. But due to costs and staff efficiencies, pilot tests are frequently done in one to three locations in the country, in particular when data collection is face-to-face, with a relatively small interview staff. If a project involves surveying persons with unique characteristics, it is extremely important that persons with the targeted characteristics be included in the pilot test sample.

All of the procedures used in the production survey should be used in the pilot test. This includes modes of survey administration, respondent rules, interviewer staffing, and interviewer training.

It is not beneficial to include only the best or most experienced interviewers in the pilot test. Those interviewers often have enough experience that they know how to make a problematic question work, but their solutions sometimes lie outside of standardized interviewing practices and are therefore inconsistent from case to case. Using some inexperienced and/or low-caliber interviewers allows problematic situations to arise naturally and be evaluated. If the situation arises during the pilot test, it is likely it will be encountered in the production survey. It is better to find out about the problem during the pilot test, so that the problem can be addressed prior to production interviewing.

Implementation

When the pilot test is implemented, an estimate of average interview time for questionnaire completion can be obtained that has implications on the survey budget. If the interview time exceeds that which is allowed or budgeted for, then decisions will need to be made about reducing the number of the questions in the survey, reducing the sample size, or changing interview procedures. If there are deep or rare paths of questioning in the questionnaire, reducing the sample size may result in not having enough cases for meaningful analyses of the characteristics associated with the rare paths. The pilot test will also provide information about question comprehension, sensitivity, difficulty, and/or item nonresponse related to specific questions. The pilot test permits issues related to question sequencing and transitional lead-ins to surface. It is important to know whether a lead-in works to segue between questionnaire sections or to serve as a buffer just prior to sensitive questions. Information on case or unit refusals as well as item refusals or other nonresponse is produced through pilot tests. The pilot test provides information about interviewer difficulties related to survey administration and also improvements that may be needed for interviewer training.

Evaluation Methods

The most common form of evaluation of a pilot test is interviewer debriefings. Interviewer debriefings usually consist of the pilot test interviewers meeting together and along with the project manager; they go through the questionnaire question by question, identifying what problems they encountered. Feedback on interviewer training and interviewer procedures is also solicited, so that revisions can be made prior to the production survey. Relying solely on interviewers for feedback about the questionnaire is insufficient to gain an objective view, however. Some interviewers may have difficulty separating the problems the respondents encountered from issues about the questionnaire that the interviewers do not like. And some interviewers are more vocal than others, and the problems they perceive exist with the questionnaire may actually be less consequential than problems observed with different items by a less vocal interviewer.

Interviewer evaluation of pilot tests has expanded during the past 20 years to include standardized rating forms. With these forms, interviewers consider their pilot test experience and provide ratings as to whether, and the extent to which, the question was problematic. This allows all interviewers to weigh in equally on problem identification and provides empirical data for the researcher to analyze.

During the past 20 years, additional methods have been used to evaluate pilot tests. These include behavior coding, respondent debriefing, and vignettes. Behavior coding is used to evaluate interviewer and respondent interactions to determine if there are problems with specific questions. The information from behavior coding is even richer if coders make notes about the interviewer–respondent exchange whenever any problematic behaviors occur. The notes can assist the questionnaire designer when he or she is working to revise the question to improve it for the production survey. The notes often provide insights about the nature of the problem, and not just that a problem exists.

The respondent debriefing method has been used to obtain information about problematic concepts or questions to aid in identifying the problem source. A respondent debriefing consists of probing questions that are administered at the end of the interview to obtain additional information about earlier survey questions. Pilot tests provide the opportunity to probe for question comprehension from a larger and more representative sample of persons than laboratory testing due to greater sample selectivity with laboratory subjects than with pilot test respondents.

In some cases, the number of respondents in the pilot test is not large enough to adequately cover all the concepts and question paths in the questionnaire. With vignettes, short examples of specific situations related to critical concepts or questions in the survey instrument are presented to pilot test respondents. Respondents are asked how they would answer a particular question given the "story" in the vignette. Examining responses to vignettes helps to determine if a problem exists with specific questions or concepts of interest.

It is critical that the project schedule allow sufficient time for pilot test data evaluation so necessary revisions can be made and, if possible, retested to ensure that the revisions don't introduce a new set of problems. Time must be allowed for the benefit of the pilot test to be realized.

Implications

It is very important for survey organizations to build pilot testing into their timelines and budgets for each survey. Pilot testing is frequently the first activity to get cut when budget and time run tight, yet unknown problems of the questionnaire or interviewer procedures may lead to increased nonsampling measurement error and subsequently lower-quality survey data. Incorporating pilot tests into the routine procedures for survey development and planning is vital in order to identify weaknesses in the questionnaire and interviewer procedures prior to the production survey.

Jennifer M. Rothgeb

See also Behavior Coding; Convenience Sampling; Interviewer Debriefing; Measurement Error; Questionnaire Design; Questionnaire Length; Respondent Debriefing; Survey Costs

Further Readings

Groves, R. M., Fowler, F. J., Couper, M. P., Lepkowski, J. M., Singer, E., & Tourangeau, R. (Eds.). (2004). *Survey methodology*. Hoboken, NJ: Wiley.

Lyberg, L., Biemer, P., Collins, M., de Leeuw, E., Dippo, C., Schwarz, N., et al. (Eds.). (1997). *Survey measurement and process quality*. New York: Wiley.

Presser, S., Rothgeb, J., Couper, M., Lessler, J., Martin, E., Martin, J., et al. (Eds.). (2004). *Methods for testing and evaluating survey questionnaires*. Hoboken, NJ: Wiley.

Schwarz, N., & Sudman, S. (1996). *Answering questions*. San Francisco: Jossey-Bass.

Sudman, S., & Bradburn, N. (1982). *Asking questions*. San Francisco: Jossey-Bass.

POINT ESTIMATE

Point estimates are single numeric quantities (i.e., "points") that are computed from sample data for the purpose of providing some statistical approximation to population parameters of interest. For example, suppose surveys were being designed to estimate the following population quantities: (a) the proportion of teenagers within a school district who consumed at least one alcoholic beverage last year, (b) the mean number of candy bars consumed last week by county hospital nurses within a state, (c) the total number of text messages sent by cell phone customers of a particular cell phone provider within the last month, (d) the correlation between education and annual expenditures on magazine subscriptions within the past year for U.S. citizens. In every case, a single numeric quantity, or statistic, can be computed from collected sample data to estimate the population parameters of interest. In contrast to point estimates, *interval estimates* are computed using point estimates to provide an estimated range of values for the parameter.

Point estimates generally have a form that is consistent with the population parameter they are intending to estimate; for example, a sample mean is used to estimate a population mean; a sample proportion is used to estimate a population proportion; a sample correlation coefficient is used to estimate the population correlation coefficient. Within the context of survey research, point estimates can also be computed with or without survey weights. Moreover, point estimates are subject to sampling variability in that the values of the point estimates for a given parameter may vary from different samples of the same size selected from the same population.

For example, consider a sample of 10 students selected from a school district using a multi-stage probability sampling design to estimate the mean number of days absent from school during the most recent semester. These data are provided in Table 1.

One unweighted point estimate for the population parameter is given simply by the sample mean computed by dividing the sum of all 10 data points by 10. From the table, the sum of all the data points (sum of second column) is 47, so the unweighted point estimate given by the sample mean is 4.7 days absent for the semester. Because of the survey design, a weighted point estimate could also be computed using the Horvitz-Thompson estimator, which divides the weighted sum of all 10 data points by the sum of

Table 1   Student absentee data from a hypothetical sample of 10 students

Student	Number of Days Absent Last Semester	Survey Weights	Weighted Values
1	3	40	120
2	5	40	200
3	1	40	40
4	6	18	108
5	9	18	162
6	7	18	126
7	8	18	144
8	4	18	72
9	2	15	30
10	2	15	30
Column Sum	47	240	1032

the weights. From the table, the numerator of the weighted point estimate is 1,032 (column 4 sum) and the denominator is 240 (column 3 sum), so the weighted point estimate is given by $1032/240 = 4.3$ days absent for the semester.

Trent D. Buskirk

See also Interval Estimate; Population Parameter; Weighting

Further Readings

Feld, A. (2005). *Discovering statistics using SPSS.* Thousand Oaks, CA: Sage.

Lohr, S. L. (1999). *Sampling: Design and analysis.* Pacific Grove, CA: Brooks/Cole.

POLITICAL KNOWLEDGE

Political knowledge has long been considered an integral part of public opinion, as well as a topic of survey research interest in its own right for many decades. While many definitions of political knowledge exist, most reflect an understanding of it as factual information about politics and government that individuals retain in their memory.

Political knowledge is similar to, but somewhat narrower than, "political awareness," "political sophistication," or "political expertise." Political knowledge is an important source of the considerations people draw upon when asked to respond to an attitude or opinion question and is thus an integral aspect of many theories of public opinion formation and change. It also is a key concept in democratic theory, with scholars and philosophers since the time of Plato debating whether the public knows, or could know, enough to play an appropriate role in the governance of a society.

Political knowledge is typically measured in surveys with questions asking respondents to recall specific facts or to recognize names or events. There also are questions asking respondents to rate their own level of knowledge, either in general or on specific subjects. Related to these are questions that ask whether the respondent has heard or read anything about an event, person, or issue. Another type of measure is an interviewer rating of the respondent's level of knowledge. In the absence of these kinds of measures, researchers sometimes use other surrogates, such as level of formal education. While such surrogates may be correlated with political knowledge, they have significant limitations.

Knowledge questions began appearing on national surveys soon after the invention of the modern sample survey. One of the oldest knowledge questions appearing in the Roper Center's comprehensive database of survey questions is a January 1937 item that asked a national Gallup poll sample, *In your estimation, how much is the national debt today*? Soon thereafter, Gallup was regularly including knowledge questions on its national polls. Other survey organizations, including some located in government agencies, began asking knowledge questions in the late 1930s.

Despite the long interest by survey researchers in the concept, there was little sustained scholarly attention to the measurement of knowledge until the 1980s. Vincent Price's 1999 review of the topic for a major handbook on the measurement of political attitudes notes that the 1968 edition of the handbook identified only four developed scales, with limited evidence of reliability and validity. By 1999, there was an increased interest in political knowledge.

Most research finds that overall levels of political knowledge held by the public are quite low. Political scientist Philip E. Converse succinctly summed up a vast body of literature when he noted that the variance in political information is very high although the mean level is very low. There is no consensus among scholars as to how much knowledge the public needs to function effectively in a democratic system, but there is agreement that much of the public lacks adequate knowledge to participate effectively. Research has found that there has been relatively little change over time in the overall levels of knowledge held by the public, despite increases in education and changes in the mass media environment that arguably could have raised knowledge levels.

A consistent research finding is that there are dramatic differences in knowledge levels across groups in the population, supporting Converse's observation of variance in levels of political knowledge, with the well-educated more knowledgeable than the less-educated, whites more knowledgeable than racial minorities, men more knowledgeable than women, and middle-aged people more knowledgeable than the young or the very old. These differences apply to most types of political knowledge, but not to all. For example, women are at least as knowledgeable as men, if not more so, on many questions about local government and politics.

Research also confirms that political knowledge and political engagement are highly correlated, with more knowledgeable people far more likely to vote and take part in other political activities. More knowledgeable people also are more likely to vote for candidates who take positions on issues consistent with those of the voter.

Survey researchers have worried that testing respondents' knowledge about politics (or about any other topic) has the potential to harm the rapport between the interviewer and the respondent and even lead respondents to terminate the interview. There is little solid evidence that this is a serious problem, and anecdotal evidence suggests that response rates for surveys containing knowledge questions are not lower than for other surveys.

How best to measure political knowledge has been the subject of considerable debate among survey researchers. Assuming that *political knowledge* is defined as factual information about politics retained in memory, asking factual questions of a random sample of the population of interest would be the most appropriate method. But which questions? How many? What kind? Should respondents guess if they are unsure? Scholars have relied upon the experience of educational testing for guidance on many of these issues, such as the idea that tests of knowledge should include many questions, cover most or all important subdomains of knowledge, and have varying levels of difficulty.

It is generally agreed that a larger number of questions can provide more reliable measurement, whether of knowledge or opinion. But practical considerations in most surveys limit the space that can be devoted to knowledge measures, and thus careful selection of items that discriminate well is essential. Fortunately, considerable research indicates that general political knowledge is not a particularly multidimensional concept, in that different kinds of knowledge—such as knowledge of the institutions and processes of government, the candidates and parties, and the major issues of the day—tend to be highly correlated with one another. This greatly simplifies the survey researcher's task, allowing a relatively smaller number of questions to produce knowledge scales of acceptable reliability as assessed through measures such as Cronbach's alpha.

Scott Keeter

See also Cronbach's Alpha; Election Polls; Knowledge Question; Media Polls; Public Opinion

Further Readings

Converse, P. E. (2000). Assessing the capacity of mass electorates. *Annual Review of Political Science, 3,* 331–353.

Delli Carpini, M. X., & Keeter, S. (1996). *What Americans know about politics and why it matters.* New Haven, CT: Yale University Press.

Mondak, J. J. (2001). Developing valid knowledge scales. *American Journal of Political Science, 45*(1), 224–238.

Price, V. (1999). Political information. In J. P. Robinson, P. R. Shaver, & L. S. Wrightsman (Eds.), *Measures of political attitudes* (pp. 591–640). New York: Academic Press.

Zaller, J. R. (1992). *The nature and origins of mass opinion.* New York: Cambridge University Press.

POLL

Poll is a term commonly used to refer to a public opinion survey in which the main purpose is to collect information concerning people's opinions, preferences, perceptions, attitudes, and evaluations of public opinion issues. The performance of public officials, confidence in public and private institutions, enacted policies on topics such as poverty, education, taxes, immigration, public safety, the war on terror, same-sex marriage, abortion, or gun control are only some of the topics that polls typically focus upon. Also, the term *poll* is associated with the measurement of current presidential and congressional vote intention, using either candidates' actual names or generic references such as "Democrat" or "Republican" in order to forecast election results.

A poll is conducted on the basis of sampling principles; that is, a representative group of persons from a specific population is interviewed in order to generalize results to the whole population. A common practice in a poll is to establish an approximate *confidence interval*, also known as *sampling error* or *margin of error*. For instance, a poll may be reported stating that "with 95% confidence the margin of error is plus/minus 3% around the estimated percentage, given a sample size of 1,000 cases." This type of statement means that if the poll were taken repeatedly with different samples of the same size, one might expect that 95% of the time (i.e., 19 times out of 20) the poll estimate would be within the confidence interval.

A poll may be conducted using self-administered or interviewer-administered methods or a combination of both, depending on the survey aims as well as budget constraints. Telephone and face-to-face modes are the predominant interviewer-administered methods used for public opinion polling. Mailing, computer- and Web-based methods are self-administered modes that are also used. Such interviewing modes are used either because of financial reasons, time constraints, or at times when public issues are highly controversial or socially (un)desirable. By removing the interviewer's presence, a pollster may elicit more truthful answers; however, having no live interviewers may considerably reduce the willingness of a respondent to participate.

Question wording plays a critical role in a poll; variations in the question stem may achieve different results. For instance, a question asking, *Would you vote or not for making marijuana legally available for doctors to prescribe in order to reduce pain and suffering?* may yield very different results than a question worded, *Do you support legalizing marijuana for medical use?* Question order is also an important feature in opinion polling, because respondents tend to answer polling questions within the context in which they are asked; hence, the content of preceding questions may affect subsequent answers.

Mostly, polling questionnaires have closed-ended questions with either ordered response scales or categorical response options. Sometimes polls also include a few open-ended questions, which usually are follow-up questions from previous closed-ended questions. Thus, respondents are provided statements or alternatives among which they can choose, as simple as a "Yes/No" format and as extensive as a numeric 11-point scale ranging from 0 to 10 and anchored with "Extremely Dissatisfied" and "Extremely Satisfied." Also, differences in the way response options are presented may yield different patterns of response even when the question wording is kept constant. For instance, providing explicit response option categories such as "Don't Know," "No Opinion," or "Neutral" may change the overall distribution of the other response options.

The order of response options also matters in opinion polling, because in some interviewing modes, respondents tend to select the response option listed either in the first or last position—known as a *primacy effect* and *recency effect*. Furthermore, other elements such as field work timing, weighting procedures, and nonresponse may lead to simultaneous publication of apparently contradictory poll results. Overall, polls are useful for gathering public opinion information, but careful attention must be given to sampling and non-sampling errors when data are reported and analyzed.

René Bautista

See also Closed-Ended Question; Confidence Interval; Election Polls; Margin of Error; Media Polls; Nonsampling Error; Open-Ended Question; Primacy Effect; Question Order Effects; Recency Effect; Response Order Effects; Sampling Error; Social Desirability

Further Readings

Traugott, M. W., & Lavrakas, P. J. (2008). *The voter's guide to election polls* (4th ed.). Lanham, MD: Rowman & Littlefield.

POLLING REVIEW BOARD (PRB)

The Polling Review Board (PRB) is part of the National Council on Public Polls (NCPP), an association comprised of survey organizations from academia, the media, market research, and the news, among other industries. The Polling Review Board supports the NCPP's mission by monitoring the conduct and reporting of polls by member and nonmember organizations. Established in 1969, the NCPP has undertaken to set professional standards on polling and to educate the media, politicians, and the general public on polling, reporting poll results, and the interpretation of reported polls. The NCPP publishes principles of survey disclosures and maintains a Speaker's Bureau and an interactive Web site.

The Polling Review Board publishes reports, available on the NCPP's Web site, that distinguish different types of polls and clarify issues of interest to those in and outside of the polling organizations that make up the NCPP's membership. The paragraph that follows details the NCPP's Principles of Disclosure, the guide used by the NCPP and the Polling Review Board to ensure that consumers of surveys are able to understand reported survey results.

The NCPP's Principles of Disclosure are aimed at ensuring that publicly available survey results disclose methodological information which will enable consumers of surveys to assess the reliability and validity of the results reported. The Principles of Disclosure are organized according to three levels of reporting. Level One stipulates the information that all reports of survey findings from member organizations must contain if issued for public release. Level Two disclosure includes information which is provided by a member organization in response to a written request for additional information pertaining to reported survey results publicly released by a member organization. Member organizations are encouraged to provide Level Three disclosures, which include the release of raw datasets, the posting of complete survey wordings, question ordering and percentage results for publicly released survey questions, and a note regarding the survey organization's compliance with NCPP Principles of Disclosure.

Beyond these disclosure levels, the NCPP also details in its Principles of Disclosure a review procedure employed by the NCPP officers and the Committee on Disclosure in which a question is raised regarding member compliance with NCPP Principles of Disclosure and/or where an individual or organization questions the survey methods employed by a member organization's publicly available survey. The Principles of Disclosure were last revised in 2006.

Traci Lynne Nelson

See also Call-In Polls; Deliberative Poll; Election Polls; Exit Polls; Gallup Poll; Internet Pop-Up Polls; Log-In Polls; Media Polls; National Council on Public Polls (NCPP); Poll; Push Polls; Straw Polls; Tracking Polls

Further Readings

Polling Review Board. (2003, March). *Reporting international surveys*. National Council on Public Polls. Retrieved August 22, 2007, from http://www.ncpp.org/?q=node/30

Polling Review Board. (2004, September). *Finding the elusive voter*. National Council on Public Polls. Retrieved August 22, 2007, from http://www.ncpp.org/?q=node/28

POLLSTER

A pollster is a person who measures public attitudes by conducting opinion polls. Pollsters design, conduct, and analyze surveys to ascertain public views on various subjects. Pollsters typically conduct this work on behalf of clients, including corporations, news organizations, and candidates for public office.

Time magazine first used the term in May 1939, referring to "Dr. George Horace Gallup, punditical pollster of public opinion." But the term appeared only rarely in print until after the infamous presidential Election Night ordeal of 1948 sent the polling profession temporarily reeling. The three major pollsters of the day—Gallup, Elmo Roper, and Alfred M. Crossley—each forecast an Election Day sweep for New York Gov. Thomas E. Dewey, so when President Harry S. Truman won, the *Detroit Free Press* ran the box-score "Truman 304, Pollsters 0."

In the year before the 1948 debacle, there were 15 references to pollsters in *The Washington Post* and *The New York Times*. The Dewey mishap helped put the term into more popular usage; those papers used the term 139 times during the next year. (There were nearly 500 such mentions in 2006.)

After 1948, Gallup and others updated their methodologies, employing probability samples in their estimates. But many had already begun to use the word *pollsters* pejoratively. Lindsay Rogers, a professor of public law at Columbia University, wrote *The Pollsters*, a scathing book, hoping to equate the new profession with a bunch of "hucksters."

For some, the negative label stuck. In 1976, Gallup called the term "sort of denigrating." Roper never used the title, also insisting that his work be called "surveys," not polls. Richard Wirthlin, a Republican consultant, once said the term made him "shudder."

However, *pollster* regained its more neutral meaning on the heels of pollsters' successful implementation of new opinion-gathering techniques following the famous early failure. "Pollsters Bask in the Limelight," the AP wire rang in 1960. "The Pollsters Come Through," read a *New York Times* editorial in 1968.

By then, pollsters had become integral to political campaigns. President John F. Kennedy was the first to hire a pollster when he commissioned Louis Harris to conduct private campaign polls. (Columnist Stewart Alsop called Harris a "pulse-feeler.") President Bill Clinton titled his advisor Stanley Greenberg "Pollster to the President," and a popular movie during the Clinton era, *The American President*, included prominent roles for the actress and actors playing the White House's public opinion advisors and pollster. And in 2004, the presidential candidates spent about $5.5 million on polling, and those running for their party's nomination in 2008 were well on pace to shatter that amount before the first primary votes had been cast.

Most political pollsters also gather opinion data for commercial clients and/or interest groups. Many major media companies and some think tanks also employ pollsters. According to the Bureau of Labor Statistics, which also eschews the term *pollster*, there were approximately 24,000 people employed as "survey researchers" in 2006.

Despite their prominence in politics and market research, pollsters have been little noted in popular culture. Only one major motion picture features a "poll-taker" as a protagonist. In *Magic Town* (1947), Jimmy Stewart turns around a failing polling operation by finding a town whose demographics perfectly mirror that of the nation's.

And the term still confuses many. Democratic pollster Peter Hart recounts a relative-to-be's glee at hearing there was to be an "upholsterer" in the family. One *Washington Post* pollster was complimented on his "Pulitzer" at a gala.

Jon Cohen

See also Crossley, Archibald; Election Polls; Gallup, George; Media Poll; Poll; Probability Sample; Public Opinion; Public Opinion Research; Roper, Elmo

Further Readings

Gallup, G. H. (1940). *The pulse of democracy: The public opinion poll and how it works.* New York: Simon & Schuster.

Moore, D. (1995). *The superpollsters: How they measure and manipulate public opinion in America.* New York: Four Walls Eight Windows.

Rogers, L. (1949). *The pollsters: Public opinion.* New York: Knopf.

POPULATION

All definitions of the population start with a definition of an individual, the elementary units about which inferences are to be drawn. The population is then the collection or aggregation of the individuals or other elements about which inferences are to be made.

In statistical usage, a *population* is any finite or infinite collection of individual elements. That inferences are to be made to the collection of individuals is implied by this definition. The term *universe* is also used in statistics for infinite or hypothetically infinite set of elements.

In survey usage, a *population* is strictly a finite collection of the units from which information is sought in the survey, with additional specification. The term *universe* is avoided, because it implies the infinite and hypothetical; survey research is materially oriented.

There are dimensions of the definition required for implementation purposes. Survey research also often defines populations that are mixtures of units, often where the different types of units are hierarchically ordered. For example, a survey could be designed to collect data from schoolchildren, teachers, and schools in the same survey. All three types of units are part of the population, an aggregate of different types of units.

A population description in survey usage includes the content, the units, the extent, and a temporal dimension. For example, a survey of student performance in a national measurement of educational attainment could specify the population as all students (content), grouped in classrooms (units), in schools in the United States and its territories (extent), in 2008 (temporal dimension). This population is clearly countable and potentially subject to census rather than survey collection.

A population definition often must be modified to meet operational constraints, leading to several types of populations that must be specified. There are different overlapping terms applied to these populations. A *population of inference* may be constrained by operational considerations to a target population. For example, the resources available to the survey may require the elimination of elements that are costly or impractical to reach. A *target population* may consist of all students (content) in public schools (units) in the 50 states, the District of Columbia, and Puerto Rico (extent), enrolled at the time of data collection during the 2007–2008 school year (temporal).

Further restrictions arise as materials are obtained to select the sample. The collection of materials used to select the sample is referred to as a *frame*, and the aggregate of units in the frame is sometimes referred to as the *frame population*. For example, the frame may include only schools known to be in operation at the beginning of the school year; schools opened during that year are excluded.

Some survey researchers define yet another reduction of the population that accounts for nonresponse. For example, not all students may respond to a request to provide information for the survey; students may be absent repeatedly on survey administration days at a school; or parental permission was not obtained for all students selected for study. A *survey population* is sometimes used to describe this latter collection of individuals, implying all elements that would have responded to the survey request rather than only those in the sample that did respond. In principle, the population of inference, the target population, and the frame population can be delineated and counted outside the framework of the survey. The survey population is delineated within the conduct of the survey, less precisely.

The extent of the population will vary within use of data for a particular survey. Surveys are seldom designed to yield information only for the total population. *Subclasses* are subpopulations within the target population for which separate estimates are prepared. A subclass is thus a portion of the sample for which inferences are to be made to the totality of subclass elements in the population. In other words, a subclass is a population with a different extent, or limits. For example, the survey of educational attainment will undoubtedly present findings for male, female, elementary, and other subgroups of students. Each subgroup is itself a population with a different extent than the overall survey population.

The definition of the term *population* is not standardized in the field. Some authors use different terminology to define each of these groups. For example, many textbooks use the term *target population* for *population of inference* used here. *Sampled population* is used to refer to the target population. Careful attention should be given to the definitions used by the authors of survey documents.

James M. Lepkowski

See also Elements; Frame; Population of Inference; Sampling Frame; Target Population; Universe

Further Readings

Cochran, W. G. (1977). *Sampling techniques.* New York: Wiley.

Kish, L. (1965). *Survey sampling.* New York: Wiley.

POPULATION OF INFERENCE

The population of inference refers to the population (or universe) to which the results from a sample survey are meant to generalize. Surveys are used to study characteristics of, and make generalizations about, populations. There are different terms that are used to describe the population, but the most commonly used is the *target population*, which is a finite set of elements to be studied. However, the term *population of inference* (or *inferential population*) is used more often during the conceptualization stage of research studies and surveys.

The target population is specified with the content of the study elements (e.g., general population, students), the units to which the elements belong (e.g., household, school classroom), the geographic boundaries (e.g., country, state), and the time periods (e.g., month, year). In contrast, the population of inference is rather loosely defined in that the specificities of these design elements are not addressed in detail. However, one may argue that the population of inference is more explicitly specified than the *population of interest*.

To illustrate how these terms are related, consider the following example. A research project may proceed as follows: (a) the population of interest is defined as the general population of the United States; (b) the population of inference for the survey is conceptualized to fulfill the research intent by refining the time scope to the year 2008; (c) the target population is operationalized as the noninstitutional civilian persons residing in the conterminous United States between March 1, 2008, and September 30, 2008, who speak English or Spanish. Notice that the definition of the population becomes more crystallized, the breadth of the study population becomes narrower, and the population itself becomes more operationalizable through this process. Of course, these three "populations" may coincide in some cases, for instance, when studying members of certain associations or employees of certain corporations.

Note also that the term *universe* is also often used as a synonym of *population*. The main difference between the universe in statistics and the population considered in surveys is that the former contains a hypothetical infinite set of elements generated by a theoretical statistical model, while the latter is more tangible, as it is a finite set of elements existing in real life. Because surveys are operationalized on the concept of finite populations, the term *universe* is not frequently used in survey research and statistics literature.

Although the conceptualization of each survey is carried out for one specific population of inference and the data collection is conducted on one target population, there may be multiple populations of inference when collected survey data are used. For instance, the

Current Population Survey (CPS) in the United States is conducted to provide official statistics for the employment and economic situation of the U.S. population. However, individual studies using the CPS data make inferences not only about the general population but also its various subgroups, such as female workers, senior citizens ages 65 and older, households living under the U.S. federal poverty threshold, non-Hispanic whites, rural residents, and so on.

Sunghee Lee

See also Current Population Survey (CPS); Finite Population; Frame; Population; Population of Interest; Sampling Frame; Target Population; Universe

Further Readings

Kish, L. (1965). *Survey sampling*. New York: Wiley.
Lessler, J. T., & Kalsbeek, W. D. (1992). *Nonsampling error in surveys*. New York: Wiley.
Särndal, C.-E., Swensson, B., & Wretman, J. (1992). *Model-assisted sampling*. New York: Springer.

POPULATION OF INTEREST

Most scientific research has some specific groups of interest and attempts to make generalizations about the characteristics of those groups. This is what is termed the *population of interest*. For example, a public health study assesses medical needs among senior citizens; an educational study examines the relationship between high school students' academic performance and their parents' academic attainment; and a marine biology project attempts to investigate the life cycle of humpback whales. The population of interest in the first study is the senior citizens; the second high school students; and the third humpback whales. The same applies to applied social science studies that employ surveys.

While closely related to one another, the population of interest is more loosely defined than the *population of inference* and the *target population*. In fact, the definition of the population of interest is too loose to be directly implemented in survey data collection. In the case of the senior citizen study, who constitutes the senior citizens? Is there any age criterion? What is the reference time period for the survey? The age criterion applied to the scope of senior citizens yields different sets of people depending on the selected ages and time

period chosen. Are all U.S. senior citizens eligible for the survey? What about U.S. senior citizens living abroad at the time of the survey? What about those living in nursing homes? These kinds of questions must be answered in order to make the survey operationalizable. The answers to these questions narrow the population of interest to the population of inference and then narrow it further to the target population.

Strictly speaking, survey results cannot be generalized to the population of interest unless it is perfectly aligned with the target population. This, however, is not necessarily practiced in reality. For example, the target population of the General Social Survey (GSS) in the United States is defined as "all non-institutionalized English-speaking persons 18 years of age or older living in the U.S." Most studies based on the GSS data use the results to explain behaviors and attitudes of "American adults," which is different from the target population. This type of misalignment is common, reflecting the gap between the ideal and practical study settings.

Surveys are conducted using fixed resources, so often the budget will not allow for a survey design that reaches every person in the population of interest. It is costly to develop questionnaires in languages other than English and hire and train interviewers for non-English interviews, and it may not be the most effective way to allocate resources given that the proportion of non-English speakers in the general population is not large. Also, even in the unlikely case where there were essentially "unlimited" resources, one may not have access to all of the population elements. For example, it may be impractical, if not impossible, to try to reach prison and jail inmates for general population surveys, or U.S. residents abroad. Errors coming from these factors, however, often do not hamper the generalizability of survey findings when the noncovered portion of the population is relatively small.

Sunghee Lee

See also Finite Population; Frame; Population; Population of Inference; Sampling Frame; Target Population

POPULATION PARAMETER

Population parameters, also termed *population characteristics*, are numerical expressions summarizing various aspects of the entire population. One common example is the population mean,

$$\bar{Y} = \frac{\sum_{i=1}^{N} Y_i}{N},$$

where Y_i is some characteristic of interest observed from the element i in the population of size N. Means, medians, proportions, and totals may be classified as descriptive parameters, while there are parameters measuring relationships, such as differences in descriptive parameters, correlation, and regression coefficients.

Although population parameters are sometimes considered unobservable, they are taken to be fixed and potentially measurable quantities using survey statistics. This is because sampling statistics are developed for well-specified finite populations that social science studies attempt to examine and that the population parameters depend on all elements in the population. Before any sort of data collection, population parameters actually are not known. When a census is conducted, all members of the population are observed (in theory), and the "exact value" of the population parameters becomes obtainable. And, by default, the measures taken by a census come to define what is the population "parameter," even if the census is not likely to be exactly accurate. In reality, however, the census is a special case and is not a feasible option for measuring most population parameters.

Instead, social science studies use samples drawn from the population of interest. The population parameters are estimated using estimators. One example is the mean of the sample elements,

$$\bar{y} = \frac{\sum_{j=1}^{n} y_j}{n},$$

where y_j is the same characteristics described previously but measured on the element j in the sample of size n. The sample mean, $\bar{y}$, is used as an estimator of the population parameter, $\bar{Y}$, and a sample mean calculated from a particular sample is an estimate of the population parameters. The key feature of the sample statistics is their representativeness (or unbiasedness) of the population parameters, which is generated mathematically via a probability sample design. Because the sample elements are selected under a random mechanism in probability sampling, $E(\bar{y}) = \bar{Y}$ is ensured, in theory.

It also should be noted that the sample statistics themselves are a random variable with a probability or sampling distribution and are dependent upon the sample design and the realized sample. Unlike population parameters that are constant, estimates from a particular sample may be different from those of another sample drawn from the same population, due to sampling variance and simply because a different set of sample units is selected. This is related to the fact that the unbiasedness of the sampling statistic (e.g., $E(\bar{y}) = \bar{Y}$) is a property of the entire sampling distribution, not of a particular sample. Standard errors associated with the sample estimates measure this sampling variability.

A census provides parameter estimation without sampling errors, but it does not automatically imply that the parameters are measured without error, as the quantities calculated from census data are still subject to nonsampling errors, namely coverage, nonresponse, and/or measurement errors. For example, population values calculated from census data collected using inadequately trained interviewers and plagued by low response rates well may have larger errors than sample estimates from well-designed and administered survey data. In many cases, resources used for a census can be redistributed for a sample survey with better quality control—especially with respect to nonresponse and measurement errors. The sample estimates for population parameters are likely to be more accurate than the population values from a census. Apart from the cost issue, this is another reason why sample surveys are more widely used to study population parameters rather than a census.

Sunghee Lee

See also Finite Population; Population; Population of Inference; Survey; Target Population

Further Readings

Cochran, W. G. (1977). *Sampling techniques.* New York: Wiley.

Kish, L. (1965). *Survey sampling.* New York: Wiley.

Särndal, C.-E., Swensson, B., & Wretman, J. (1992). *Model-assisted sampling.* New York: Springer.

POSITIVITY BIAS

Positivity bias refers to the phenomena when the public evaluates individuals positively even when they have negative evaluations of the group to which that individual belongs. It is commonly seen within the political science literature that examines positive respondent evaluations of individual political leaders in spite of that respondent's negative views on government in general. This phenomenon has been seen for more than 70 years.

It has been suggested that the public will generally evaluate specific individuals more favorably than impersonal objects or groups. Poll results evaluating political leaders suggest that this positivity bias can be found regardless of the leader's party, ideology, or relative fame. The positivity bias has also been seen in evaluations of individuals in careers as wide ranging as Hollywood actors and actresses to athletes to union leaders.

This phenomenon seems to exist regardless of the amount or quality of information a respondent has for the object of evaluation. Studies indicate that the positivity bias is even seen when the respondent has never heard of the individual he or she is evaluating. In this situation, some suggest that the respondent assumes a favorable evaluation because he or she presumes that the person must be famous in order to be included in the survey. Research has also revealed that a positivity bias can be found in any subpopulation categorized by demographics like age, gender, race, and religion.

Examples

Within public opinion research, there are many examples of positivity bias to draw from. For instance, during the Watts riots in Los Angeles in August 1965, a survey of African Americans revealed that only 2 of the 13 political leaders assessed received negative evaluations. This was unexpected since the riots were in response to racially motivated brutality by the police department. Although evaluations of the police department and city government were low, the political leaders were generally held in relatively high regard.

Another example comes from surveys conducted in the middle of the Watergate scandal in the 1970s. Even in the midst of a scandal, only 4 of the 18 leaders assessed received negative evaluations. Once again, the public generally held the government in relatively low regard, yet 77% of the leaders evaluated received positive evaluations.

Positivity bias has a long history of scholarly research in the social sciences. It is still common to see published research examining these phenomena, but it is rare to see it explicitly referred to as *positivity bias*. This phenomenon has drawn the interest of a host of scholars seeking to understand why the public

loves their congressional representatives, yet hates Congress.

Source

The source of the positivity bias is debatable. Within psychology, some believe that these biases are a part of the consistency paradigm, while others suggest it is more closely associated with the person perception literature. Political scientists tend to think of it in terms of perceived similarity, such that respondents believe the individuals they are evaluating are more similar at the individual level than the group to which the individual belongs.

Research has also attempted to determine whether the positivity bias is an artifact of the survey instrument. In a battery of experimental tests, research has shown that this bias is not associated with a respondent's desire to please the interviewer regardless of the instrument used. Another possible explanation is the way these evaluations are measured. These types of questions typically use a Likert-based, bipolar scale. Research has been conducted to determine if measurement options explain the positivity bias. Studies also sought to determine if the use of the subject's official title influenced a respondent's evaluation. In the end, results consistently suggest that the survey instrument is not responsible.

James W. Stoutenborough

See also Approval Rating; Bipolar Scale; Demographic Measure; Likert Scale; Respondent; Social Desirability

Further Readings

Lau, R. R., Sears, D. O., & Centers, R. (1979). The "positivity bias" in evaluations of public figures: Evidence against instrument artifacts. *Public Opinion Quarterly, 43*, 347–358.

Sniderman, P. M., Brody, R. A., Siegel, J. W., & Tannenbaum, P. H. (1982). Evaluative bias and issue proximity. *Political Behavior, 4*, 115–131.

POST-STRATIFICATION

Stratification is a well-known sampling tool built on the premise that like units in a population should be treated similarly. It is a statistical fact that grouping similar units, when sampling, can generally reduce the variance of the survey estimates obtained. Stratification can be done when selecting units for study, or it can be carried out afterward. The latter application is usually termed *post-stratification*.

Illustration

To illustrate the differences between stratification and post-stratification, assume a researcher is interested in the total poundage of a population that consisted of 10,000 baby mice and one adult elephant. Suppose, further, that the average baby mouse weighted 0.2 pounds but the elephant weighted three and one-half tons or 7,000 pounds. This would mean, if the whole population were to be enumerated, that the researcher would obtain a total of

$$(10,000) \times (0.2) + (1) \times (1) \times (7000)$$
$$= 2000 + 7000 = 9,000 \text{ pounds.}$$

Now, if the researcher drew a sample of size $n = 2$ from this population, she or he would not get a very good estimate of the poundage, unless she or he took the elephant as one of the selections. So, naturally the researcher would stratify, taking the one elephant plus one of the mice at random.

If the researcher took account of population sizes, then she or he would multiply the poundage of the mouse selected by $N_1 = 10,000$ and add it to the poundage of the $N_2 = 1$ elephant, and the estimated total poundage over repeated samples would be 9,000 pounds (as shown in the preceding formula). Of course the individual mice vary in size (with a standard error of 0.005 pounds, say), so the researcher would not expect to hit the total "dead on" each time, but she or he might come very close, even with this small a sample (i.e., 9,000 pounds on the average would be the estimate with a standard error of 50 pounds).

How does this example change if the researcher post-stratified? Put another way, what if the researcher decided to stratify *after*, *not before*, she or he had selected the sample of $n = 2$? Suppose, to be specific, that the researcher had taken a simple random sample without separate strata for elephants and mice?

Well, first of all, of the $(10,001) \times (10,000)/2$ or approximately 50 million samples of two elements, only 10,000 will have exactly one elephant and one mouse. All the other samples will have two mice, and there would be no way to get a good estimate from these samples no matter what the researcher did—a big price

to pay for not stratifying before selection. To be specific, if two mice are selected, the expected estimate is

$$(10,001/2) \times (0.2) + (10,001/2) \times (0.2) = 2,000.2.$$

The remaining 10,000 samples, with one elephant and one mouse, do even more poorly unaided. For them the researcher will have an unadjusted expected estimate of

$$(10,001/2) \times (0.2) + (10,001/2)$$
$$\times (7,000) = 35,004,500.1.$$

This second result, however, can be "saved" by post-stratification in the same way as was previously illustrated for stratification, since each sample has one mouse and one elephant. The calculations here are

$$[10,000/(10,001/2)]/(10,001/2) \times (7,000)$$
$$+ [1/(10,001/2)]/(10,001/2) \times (.2) = 9,000.$$

In this case, the researcher gets back what the stratified estimator provided, but there is clearly a big risk that she or he might get a sample that would not be usable (i.e., that post-stratification cannot save).

Implications of the Illustration

Sometimes even a simple illustration like this makes clear some of the general issues. Three will be mentioned:

1. Stratification and post-stratification can often give the same results.

2. If a researcher can stratify beforehand, usually it is wise to do so. That way she or he can better control the sample sizes in each stratum and guarantee any efficiency gains that the stratification may achieve.

3. Stratification can be used to oversample subsets of a population. If post-stratification is used, the sample sizes cannot be enlarged over what they would have been in its absence.

Generalizations

Both stratification and post-stratification can be used with designs that run the gamut from a simple random sample to a complex multi-stage one. All that is needed is to have a usable population total Y that can be estimated from the sample, say, by y. For each such pair

(Y, y) to post-stratify, a researcher simply adjusts or post-stratifies the original sample estimates by factors of the form $w = Y/y$. In the previous illustration they were

$$Y_1/y_1 = [10{,}000/(10{,}001/2)] \text{ and}$$
$$Y_2/y_2 = [1/(10{,}001/2)].$$

When the application of stratification and post-stratification were first introduced in a data-poor and information-poor world, there were very few known or assumed-to-be-known values Y. But, as early as the 1940s, the problem of trying to handle multiple (Y, y) pairs arose. For example, suppose a researcher wanted to post-stratify an area probability household sample by age, gender, race, and state. The Current Population Survey (CPS) comes to mind. Suppose further that the researcher only had, as is typical, usable marginal totals for some of these values, not a complete cross-classification of all of them. Raking, or raking ratio estimation, was invented for situations like this.

Raking is an extension of standard post-stratification. It works as follows. Under regularity constraints, raking operates in the same way as post-stratification, but iteratively. First, one post-stratifies on one set of marginals (say, age); then, using the newly adjusted data, one post-stratifies again, but this time on a second set of marginals (say, gender); and so forth. Methods differ here, but most practitioners of raking cycle back to the beginning and repeat the process until they have achieved the desired degree of closeness. When W. Edwards Deming and F. F. Stephan first invented the method, "computers" were still human beings, so only simple problems could be handled. Today, there have been examples of raking in which up to 60 or more marginals have been employed.

Issues with raking arise when trying to employ many marginals. Most important among these is that the process may not converge, or, if it does, there can be an attenuation of the post-stratified weights. One standard diagnostic employed in raking or even simpler forms of post-stratification is to calculate the relative variance of the weights themselves, before and after adjustment. As the relative weight variance grows, the possibility may exist that the sample is not very representative of the population or that it is simply too small to simultaneously fit all the population marginals required of it. Standard advice in post-stratification would be to collapse

marginals with effective sample sizes of less than 20 or 30.

Post-stratification sometimes can only be done after the data are collected—for example, as in the CPS example, stratifying by gender is best done after selection. The use of post-stratification to better align a sample with known outside information can have three distinct goals:

1. *Reducing sampling error.* The implication in some sampling texts is that variance reduction is the key reason post-stratification is used. In most cases although this is valuable, it is the second and third goals that predominate.

2. *Handling differential nonresponse.* While variance reduction can arise here too, usually it is bias reduction that is the goal and sometimes comes at the expense of variances.

3. *Adjusting for undercoverage.* This type of adjustment might be done to bring surveys from incomplete frames up to some common level. One example might be post-stratifying interviews obtained by using random-digit dialing selections from a frame of landline telephone numbers that was brought up to age, gender, and race totals from the CPS (which uses a frame that includes households without landlines).

Practitioners often use post-stratification to achieve several of these objectives at the same time. The variety of approaches used goes well beyond what is discussed here. Good case studies are found in the survey metadata systems of major government programs sponsored by national statistical offices. Applications by the major polling organizations also should be sought out, as these are usually good examples.

Fritz Scheuren

See also Current Population Survey (CPS); Post-Survey Adjustments; Raking; Strata; Stratified Sampling

Further Readings

Cochran, W. (1977). *Sampling techniques.* New York: Wiley.

Deming, W. E. (1942). *The statistical adjustment of data.* New York: Dover.

Hansen, M., Hurwitz, W., & Madow, W. (1953). *Sample survey methods and theory* (Reprinted ed., 2 vols.). New York: Wiley.

Lohr, S. (1999). *Sampling: Design and analysis.* Pacific Grove, CA: Duxbury.

POST-SURVEY ADJUSTMENTS

Post-survey adjustments refer to a series of statistical adjustments applied to survey data prior to data analysis and dissemination. Although no universal definition exits, post-survey adjustments typically include data editing, missing data imputation, weighting adjustments, and disclosure limitation procedures.

Data Editing

Data editing may be defined as procedures for detecting and correcting errors in so-called raw survey data. Data editing may occur during data collection if the interviewer identifies obvious errors in the survey responses. As a component of post-survey adjustments, data editing involves more elaborate, systematic, and automated statistical checks performed by computers. Survey organizations and government statistical agencies may maintain special statistical software to implement data editing procedures.

Data editing begins by specifying a set of *editing rules* for a given editing task. An editing program is then designed and applied to the survey data to identify and correct various errors. First, missing data and "not applicable" responses are properly coded, based on the structure of the survey instrument. Second, range checks are performed on all relevant variables to verify that no invalid (out-of-range) responses are present. Out-of-range data are subject to further review and possible correction. Third, consistency checks are done to ensure that the responses to two or more data items are not in contradiction. In computerized data collection, such as Computer-Assisted Telephone Interviewing (CATI), Computer-Assisted Personal Interviewing (CAPI), or Web surveys, real-time data editing is typically built into the data collection system so that the validity of the data is evaluated as the data are collected.

Missing Data Imputation and Weighting Adjustments

Imputation and weighting adjustments are standard tools for dealing with missing data in surveys. Missing data result from two types of nonresponse: unit nonresponse and item nonresponse. *Unit nonresponse* occurs when no data are collected from a sampled unit, while *item nonresponse* occurs when no data are obtained for some items from a responding unit. In general, imputation is employed for item nonresponse, while weighting is reserved for unit nonresponse.

Imputation is the substitution of missing data with estimated values. Imputation produces a complete, rectangular data matrix that can support analyses where missing values might otherwise constrain what can be done. The statistical goal of imputation is to reduce the potential bias of survey estimates due to item nonresponse, which can only be achieved to the extent that the missing data mechanism is correctly identified and modeled.

Many imputation techniques are used in practice. *Logical imputation* or *deductive imputation* is used when a missing response can be logically inferred or deduced with certainty from other responses provided by the respondent. Logical imputation is preferred over other imputation methods because of its deterministic nature. Hot-deck imputation fills in missing data using responses from other respondents (donor records) that are considered similar to the respondents' missing data with respect to some characteristics. In cold-deck imputation, the donor may be from a data source external to the current survey. In regression imputation, a regression model is fitted for the variable with missing data and then used to predict the missing responses.

Both deck imputation and regression imputation could lead to underestimation of the variance, because the imputed values are either restricted to those that have been observed or they tend to concentrate at the center of the distribution. The multiple imputation method provides a valuable alternative imputation strategy because it supports statistical inferences that reflect the uncertainty due to imputation. Instead of filling in a single value for each missing response, the multiple imputation method replaces each missing value with a set of plausible values. The multiply imputed data sets are then analyzed together to account for the additional variance introduced by imputation.

Weighting adjustments increase the weight of the respondents to compensate for the nonrespondents. Weighting adjustments typically begin with the calculation of the *base weight* to account for the sample design. The base weight, defined as the reciprocal of the probability of selection, accounts for the unsampled cases in the sampling frame. Various adjustments may be made to the base weight to derive the final analysis weight for the respondents. In random-digit dial (RDD) surveys, for example, the base weight may be adjusted for multiple telephone lines, nonresolution of released telephone numbers, screener nonresponse, eligibility rate, within-household selection probability, nonresponse, and so on.

Many sample surveys target a specific subpopulation. If the survey fails to determine the eligibility status for a proportion of the sample, an eligibility adjustment may be made to the base weight by distributing the base weight associated with cases of unknown eligibility status to cases for which the eligibility status is known.

Nonresponse adjustments are typically done in most surveys to compensate for eligible nonrespondents. In weighting class nonresponse adjustments, respondents and nonrespondents are classified into weighting classes based on pertinent information available for both groups. Within each weighting class, the weight of each respondent is increased by a factor equal to the inverse of the response rate in the weighting class. The weighting classes are typically defined by variables that are correlated to response propensity as well as the variables of analytical interest. Response propensity scores are sometimes used to define weighting classes or to derive the adjustment factor directly.

Weighting adjustments often involve additional steps to adjust for discrepancies between the sample and population distributions. Raking ratio adjustments make the marginal distributions of the weighted sample conform to those of the population. When the joint distribution of some population characteristics is known, post-stratification adjustments may be carried out to ensure that the joint distribution of the weighted sample match that of the population.

Disclosure Limitation Procedures

Government agencies and their contractors often are required by law or established policies to protect the confidentiality of the respondents if the survey data are to be released to the public in the form of microdata files or statistical tables. The required protection is achieved by the application of statistical disclosure limitation procedures to the survey data before public release. Specific disclosure limitation procedures depend on the nature of the data to be released. Common procedures include suppression, removing identifiers,

sampling, swapping or switching, rounding, adding random noise, top or bottom coding, generation of simulated or synthetic data, and so on.

Y. Michael Yang

See also Computer-Assisted Personal Interviewing (CAPI); Computer-Assisted Telephone Interviewing (CATI); Disclosure Limitation; Hot-Deck Imputation; Imputation; Item Nonresponse; Multiple Imputation; Post-Stratification; Raking; Raw Data; Response Propensity; Suppression; Unit Nonresponse; Weighting

Further Readings

Federal Committee on Statistical Methodology. (1994). *Report on statistical disclosure limitation methodology.* Statistical Working Paper 22. Washington DC: Office of Management and Budget.

Kalton, G. (1983). *Compensating for missing survey data.* Ann Arbor: University of Michigan, Institute for Social Research, Survey Research Center.

Rubin, D. B. (1987). *Multiple imputation for nonresponse in surveys.* New York: Wiley.

PRECISION

Precision in statistical surveys relates to the variation of a survey estimator for a population parameter that is attributable to having sampled a portion of the full population of interest using a specific probability-based sampling design. It refers to the size of deviations from a survey estimate (i.e., a survey statistic, such as a mean or percentage) that occurs over repeated application of the same sampling procedures using the same sampling frame and sample size. While *precision* is a measure of the variation among survey estimates, over repeated application of the same sampling procedures, *accuracy* is a measure of the difference between the survey estimate and the true value of a population parameter. Precision and accuracy measure two dimensions for a survey estimate. A sampling design can result in survey estimates with a high level of precision and accuracy (the ideal). In general, sampling designs are developed to achieve an acceptable balance of accuracy and precision.

The sampling variance is a commonly used measure of precision. Precision can also be represented by the standard error (the square root of the sampling variance for a survey estimate), the relative standard error (the standard error scaled by the survey estimate), the confidence interval width for a survey estimate (using the standard error and the values from an assumed probability density function for the survey estimate), and difference between estimated percentiles for a population parameter (for example, the intraquartile range for the survey estimate).

The sampling variance is conceptually the squared difference between the estimate for a specific sample and the expected value of the estimate summed over all possible samples selected in the same fashion with the same sample size using the same sampling scheme. The sampling variance is different from the classical "population" variance (a measure of the variation among the observations in the population) in the sense that the population variance is a constant, independent of any sampling issues, while the sampling variance becomes smaller as the sample size increases. The sampling variance is zero when the full population is observed, as in a census.

Because only a single sample is selected and the expected value of an estimate is unknown, sampling theory has provided formulae to estimate the sampling variance from a single sample. To allow for the computation of a sampling variance, the sample scheme must be reproducible, that is, it can be completely replicated. Moreover, to compute an unbiased estimate of the sampling variance, (a) every unit in a sampling frame needs to have a positive chance of being selected (the unit selection probability is greater than zero), and (b) every pair of units must have a positive chance of being in a sample (the joint selection probability for any pair of units is greater than zero).

The sampling variance is a function of the form of the statistic, the underlying population, and the nature of the sampling design, and it is called the "design-based sampling variance." The design-based variance generally assumes the use of a sampling weight, which is computed from the inverse of the probability of selection of the sample.

A statistical sample survey has two general forms of statistics: (a) linear combinations of the survey data (for example, a total) and (b) nonlinear combinations of the survey data. Nonlinear combinations include the ratio of two estimates (for example, a mean or a proportion in which both the numerator and the denominator is estimated) and more complex combinations such as regression coefficients. For linear estimates with simple sample designs (such as a stratified or unstratified simple random sample) or complex designs (such as stratified multi-stage designs), explicit equations are available to compute the sampling variance. For the more common nonlinear estimates with simple or complex sample designs, explicit equations are not generally available, and various approximations or computational algorithms are used to provide an essentially unbiased estimate of the sampling variance.

Two primary forms of sampling variance estimators are available for complex sample designs: (a) the procedures based on the Taylor series linearization of the nonlinear estimator, using explicit sampling variance equations, and (b) the procedures based on forming pseudo-replications of the sample or pseudo-replicates of the survey estimates. The first method uses the classical Taylor series linearization of a nonlinear estimator to construct an analytic variable representing the first-order linearized form of the survey estimator using weighted totals and the data from individual sample members. This linearized analytic variable is used in the explicit sampling variance equations to estimate the sampling variance. Within the class of pseudo-replication procedures, the balanced repeated replication (BRR) procedure, the jackknife procedure, and the bootstrap procedure are most widely used or discussed. The pseudo-replication procedures compute a number of survey estimates using partial subsamples selected from the single sample. The sampling variance is then estimated as a function of the variance among these pseudo-replicated survey estimates. Both forms of sampling variance estimators generate similar estimates of the sampling variance, and the use of one form may be more desirable for specific survey estimators and situations.

The precision for survey estimates is a function of number components in a survey. In general, sampling designs are developed to achieve a balance of precision relative to the population, the information required, and the available resources for the survey.

Frank Potter

See also Balanced Repeated Replication (BRR); Bootstrapping; Census; Confidence Interval; Jackknife Variance Estimation; Parameter; Population; Probability Sample; Sample Size; Sampling Frame; Sampling Variance; Standard Error; Statistic; Taylor Series Linearization; True Value

PRECISION JOURNALISM

Precision journalism is a term that links the application of social science research methods (including survey research methods) to the practice of gathering information for the news purposes of journalists. Similar to a social scientist, a precision journalist discloses the data collection methodology well enough that another precision journalist or researcher could replicate the research studies and ostensibly would reach the same conclusions.

The term was coined by Everette E. Dennis in 1971 as part of seminar he taught at the University of Oregon. The concept then was explicated by one of his students, Neil Felgenhauer, in a term paper that later became a book chapter. Most of the "new journalism" of the time that inspired Dennis's seminar was the creation of talented writers (e.g., Tom Wolfe) who used fiction techniques to construct powerful narratives about current events. The class discussion compared this semi-fictional approach to journalism with precision journalism techniques. As Dennis and William Rivers noted in a 1974 report, although other journalists are pushing news reporting toward more of an art, precision journalists are pushing it toward more of a science. The origins of precision journalism go back to the first public opinion polls that used systematic sampling methods instead of just gathering readily available person-on-the-street interviews. George Gallup based a newspaper column on his national polls that used rigorous survey methods, which, for example, led to a much more accurate pre-election prediction of the 1936 Landon-Roosevelt election than that of the more well-known and much larger unscientific poll conducted by the *Literary Digest* magazine.

Other early users of precision journalism were the television networks wanting to be first to announce the presidential winner on Election Day, although not all their early usage of these new reporting techniques proved reliable or accurate. For example, in 1960, CBS used a statistical model based on the timing of and results from the pre-election polls they had been conducting. The model captured the candidate standings at given points in time and compared them to the presidential candidate standings at the same points in times in the previous election. The initial findings from the model proved to be incorrect, and the resulting bias produced an incorrect early call for Richard Nixon as the projected winner over John F. Kennedy.

In the 1960s, news coverage of the civil rights and anti-war movements fueled the need for new reporting techniques. Standard journalism traditionally was focused on gathering information from the most visible spokespersons for the respective movements—a top-down approach—and thus tended to place too much importance on what was said by these elite sources, who often had their own personal agendas. In contrast, *Newsweek* magazine commissioned pollster Louis Harris to do special civil rights surveys among black citizenry to uncover a broader and more accurate understanding of the attitudes held by the black community.

In 1967, when there were race riots in Detroit, the Knight Newspapers sent Philip Meyer from their Washington bureau to help *The Detroit Free Press* cover the ongoing story. Meyer stayed in Detroit to conduct a survey of residents in the affected neighborhoods in order to measure the grievances held by blacks and thus the root causes of the riot. (Meyer had learned these research techniques as a Nieman Fellow at Harvard University in the previous academic year.) The news stories that resulted from the surveying were one of several factors that earned the *Free Press* the 1968 Pulitzer Prize for general local reporting. Following this, Meyer was assigned to study Miami to further utilize precision journalism methods to aid news coverage of racial problems there before and after the 1968 assassination of Dr. Martin Luther King, Jr. In 1969, the Russell Sage Foundation sponsored Meyer to take a leave of absence from Knight Newspapers and direct a project to prepare a precision journalism handbook for journalists, which resulted in the publication of the first edition of Meyer's book, *Precision Journalism*.

Sometimes precision journalism is confused with *computer-assisted reporting* (including using the Internet to do information searches), because precision journalism often does involve large-scale data collection and analyses aided by computers. But computers are neither necessary nor sufficient for the conduct of precision journalism. Precision journalism includes myriad social science research methods and is not limited to survey research. Over the years, its practitioners have used content analysis of public records, experimental designs, and other quantitative and qualitative behavioral science methods.

In the mid-1970s, the National Science Foundation helped the acceptance of precision journalism by sponsoring two training programs at Northwestern University for midcareer journalists. Reporters from *The New York Times* and *The Washington Post* participated and followed up with related projects at their home newspapers, which helped introduce precision journalism to many other editors and reporters across the country. By the late 1970s, journalism students at Northwestern's Medill School of Journalism and elsewhere were being taught the methods of precision journalism both at the undergraduate and graduate levels. Subsequently, the National Institute for Computer-Assisted Reporting (NICAR) incorporated precision journalism concepts in its training coursework. By the present decade, the use of precision journalism methods is considered fairly routine for most major and many smaller news organizations.

Paul J. Lavrakas

See also Exit Polls; Gallup, George; Horse Race Journalism; Media Poll

Further Readings

DeFleur, M. H. (1997). *Computer-assisted investigative reporting.* Mahwah, NJ: Lawrence Erlbaum.
Dennis, E. E., & Rivers, W. L. (1974). *Other voices: The new journalism in America.* San Francisco: Canfield Press.
Meyer, P. (2002). *Precision journalism: A reporter's introduction to social science methods* (4th ed.). Lanham, MD: Rowman & Littlefield.

PRECODED QUESTION

Precoded questions refer to survey items for which response categories may be identified and defined exhaustively, or very nearly so, prior to data collection activities. Precoding questions involves specifying the coding frame (i.e., the set of possible answers) and associating each response category within the frame with a value label (which is typically, but not necessarily, numeric).

The term *precoded* also refers to a type of question that is asked by interviewers as though it is an open-ended question, but it has precoded responses that interviewers are to use to match (code) respondents' answers rather than copy down the verbatim given by the respondent. This also is referred to as *field coding*.

The use of precoded questions delivers two important benefits to the survey researcher. First, their use minimizes the time to prepare the answers for statistical analysis following the completion of data collection activities. Second, because the data are coded as

they are collected, their use is thought to reduce coder variance.

Value Labels

Value labels for precoded questions are typically assigned in a manner that coincides with the measurement level (nominal, ordinal, interval, or ratio) implied by the item in order to aid interpretive analysis of the survey data. For example, value labels assigned to response possibilities that correspond to interval or ratio level measures typically are numerical, with the set of numbered values chosen to reflect the ordered and evenly spaced characteristics assumed by these measurement levels. When ordinal measures are involved, numerals are typically used for the value label codes, and the number values chosen appear in a consecutive sequence that is directionally consistent with the ordinal character of the measure's response categories. (Although the use of alphabetical characters would be equally effective in communicating the directional sequence of the response categories, use of numerals is almost always preferred because manipulation of alphabetical or "string" value labels by statistical analysis software applications typically is far more cumbersome than when numeric value labels are used.) In contrast, *code value labels* for items featuring nominal levels of measurement may be assigned in an arbitrary manner, as they bear no meaning or relationship to the response categories themselves. Therefore, while sequenced numerals or letters may be used for these value labels, these often are assigned in an order corresponding to the sequence in which the response choices are documented in the research instrumentation.

These guidelines are reflected in the self-administered questionnaire examples in Figure 1, shown with the code value labels represented by the small numerals near the check boxes corresponding to the response choices offered.

It is worth observing that, since the value labels for a nominal measure item are arbitrary and meaningless, it often is functional to use alphabetical value labels to aid the analyst's memory in associating the value labels with the code definitions themselves. In the nominal measurement item shown in Figure 1, for example, the letter O (for Own) might have been chosen for the value label instead of 1, R (for Rent) might have been assigned instead of 2, and A (for Another) might have been used instead of 3.

Interval-Level Measurement	"Not including today, on how many of the past seven days have you read that day's edition of a newspaper?"
	7 ☐ All, Seven Days
	6 ☐ Six Days
	5 ☐ Five Days
	4 ☐ Four Days
	3 ☐ Three Days
	2 ☐ Two Days
	1 ☐ One Day
	0 ☐ None, Zero Days
Ordinal-Level Measurement	Please indicate how strongly you agree or disagree with the following statement: "Looking back on my life, I am fairly well satisfied."
	7 ☐ Completely Agree
	6 ☐ Mostly Agree
	5 ☐ Slightly Agree
	4 ☐ Neither Agree nor Disagree
	3 ☐ Slightly Disagree
	2 ☐ Mostly Disagree
	1 ☐ Completely Disagree
Nominal-Level Measurement	Do you own your home, rent your home, or do you have some other living arrangement?
	1 ☐ Own home
	2 ☐ Rent home
	3 ☐ Another living arrangement

Figure 1   Examples of precoded labels for items having alternative levels of measurement

Types

Precoded questions may be either closed-ended (where response categories are specified exhaustively prior to data collection), partly closed-ended (where nearly all response categories can be and are specified prior to data collection, but a response category of "Other (specify):" is included to accommodate unanticipated or unusual responses), or open-ended (where responses are expected to be spontaneously self-generated by the respondent). Still, because of the difficulty of anticipating the responses that respondents will provide to an open-ended question, precoded questions most often are closed-ended or partly closed-ended. Furthermore, researchers often want the richer detail provided by full verbatim responses to an open-ended question rather than losing this detail and having interviewers choose a precoded response.

There are two varieties of open-ended question for which precoding is common, however. The first is the self-coding open-ended question. These are questions in which the form of the respondent's answer is implied and logically restricted by the question itself. *How many books did you read last month?* would be an example of such a question. Logically, a respondent either must provide an answer like "None" (i.e., zero) or some other whole number or must fail to provide an

answer by saying "I don't know" or refusing to respond to the item. The whole number answers self-code to that numeric value and the Don't Know and Refused possibilities may be assigned unlikely number values, such as, for example, 88 and 99, respectively.

The second type of precoded open-ended question has response "categories" that are clear within a given culture and thus easily anticipated. A routinely used item asking the respondent to describe his or her formal education, such as *What is the highest grade or level of school you have completed?*, is a good example of this kind of question. In this case, the range of possibilities can easily be anticipated, and the interviewer can be expected to code the respondent's answer reliably as soon as it is given. For example, the following set of response categories and corresponding code value labels might be used by interviewers:

No formal education = 00,

Less than high school graduate = 01,

High school graduate or G.E.D. = 02,

Some college, but no degree = 03,

Two-year college degree (associate's degree) = 04,

Four-year college degree (e.g., B.A. or B.S.) = 05,

Some graduate school = 06,

Master's degree (M.A., M.S., M.B.A., etc.) = 07,

Doctoral degree (M.D., D.O., Ph.D., J.D., etc.) = 08,

Don't know = 88, and

Refused = 99.

Jonathan E. Brill

See also Closed-Ended Question; Coder Variance; Coding; Field Coding; Interval Measure; Level of Measurement; Nominal Measure; Open-Ended Question; Ordinal Measure; Ratio Measure; Verbatim Responses

PREDICTIVE DIALING

Predictive dialing is a telephone call placement technology that is used in survey research to improve utilization of interviewer time during computer-assisted telephone interviewing (CATI) surveys. In random-digit dialing (RDD) surveys, typically fewer than 15% of dialings are answered by a human; for the remaining 85%, and when predictive dialing is not used by a telephone research center, interviewers must disposition unanswered numbers, data or fax lines, disconnects, and answering machines. With predictive dialing, the dialer will handle many of these unproductive calls in the "background," passing calls to interviewers only when a call connects with a human being. The resulting increase in the proportion of "talk time" for the interviewer—time spent by the interviewer persuading and/or interviewing respondents—not only provides direct cost savings, with less interviewer time needed in total for the same number of interviews, but may provide an indirect gain because, in theory, interviewers remain more focused and engaged in the core of their work (i.e., speaking with respondents).

Predictive Versus Nonpredictive Dialing

From an operational standpoint, what distinguishes predictive dialing from nonpredictive dialing is the elimination of the 1:1 interviewer-to-call ratio. If one call is placed for one available interviewer, then the interviewer will be idle while the call is placed and the signal returned, which could be for 30 seconds or more. Autodialing (mechanized dialing while still using a 1:1 ratio), along with automatic signal recognition for engaged (busy), fax, disconnected, and unanswered lines, will partially reduce nonproductive time and increase interviewers' talk time. Predictive dialers include these autodialing technologies but also allow for the probability that not all call results will require interviewer intervention, so typically there are a great many more calls being placed than the number of interviewers available to take them, with the dialer handling the calls that do not require interviewer involvement.

Predictive dialing algorithms utilize time-series or queuing methods, and the variables utilized vary by manufacturer: for example, interviewers in the queue, those nearing the end of a call, connect rates, average call length, and so on. Ideally, all predictive dialing systems strive to make the number of connects equal to the number of interviewers available. Variation from this ideal has two possible results: first, there are more connects than interviewers, leading to either *abandoned calls* or "dead air"—and ultimately alienated respondents. Second, there are too few connections, which results in a decrease in a call center's

productivity and an increase in its costs. The extent to which the predictive algorithm errs on the side of "wait time" versus increased "abandonment" (i.e., dropping a call that the dialer detects has been answered by a human since no interviewer is available) is determined by setting the *maximum abandonment rate* parameter on the dialer. At its most conservative setting (i.e., "zero abandonment"), the dialing ratio will be 1:1 (in effect, removing the predictive element). Most survey companies operate with the abandonment rate set under 3% (meaning 3 out of every 100 connects will be abandoned). Of note, research has suggested that setting the abandonment rate too high in telephone surveys is counterproductive, as respondents who have had too many prior contact calls abandoned by a predictive dialer may become frustrated, which increases their likelihood to refuse when a "live" interviewer comes onto the line during a subsequent call attempt.

Telemarketing Versus Research Applications

Predictive dialing originated in the telemarketing industry and is still extensively used there; however, most predictive dialers used by survey research companies operate quite differently than their telemarketing counterparts. Specifically, the algorithms used to predict how many telephone numbers to dial do not utilize *interviewer wait time* as a criterion but instead use the quantity of numbers that need to be dialed to yield connects for already waiting interviewers. This difference is significant both in terms of operation and the designed intention to minimize abandoned calls. Obviously, both algorithms result in abandoned calls, but the research approach is much more conservative.

Another significant difference between telemarketing applications and research applications is the "dead air" that respondents often hear after answering their phone to a telemarketing call, which is the delay between the moment a potential respondent answers the telephone and says "Hello" to the time an interviewer is routed the call and can reply to the respondent, which is the signal that a human is actually on the other end of the line. This delay can arise from several sources:

1. *The switching process.* If the dialer sends a case to an interviewer before the dial is made, there is in effect a complete circuit between the interviewer and

the respondent. During any predictive process (even set at zero abandonment), that circuit needs to be established. If an interviewer is already waiting and both hardware and software configured to minimize the delay, the link is established in milliseconds and will be essentially undetectable by the respondent who picks up a handset from the cradle, although it may be just noticeable by the respondent who has a headset already on his or her ear. The more hardware and software intervention there is between the "connect" signal received by the dialer and an actual switch by the dialer of the audio to the interviewer (e.g., if the call is being routed through a separate switch, as may occur with geographically dispersed systems), the longer this connection will take, and the more noticeable the delay will be.

2. *The queuing process.* As an alternative to abandoning a connection, some systems will queue up the additional connections for which an interviewer is not immediately available and then establish the connections with an interviewer as soon as one becomes available. The delay can be short or long, depending on the system; for example, if there are many interviewers and the average connection time is short, then the probability of an interviewer becoming free in the next few seconds will be very high and the average wait quite short. For situations in which longer delays are more common, some systems have provisions for playing a recorded message to the respondent during the wait for an interviewer to become available.

3. *Automatic answering machine detection (AMD).* The proportion of calls to households that are actually picked by a resident as opposed to answered by an answering machine or voicemail system is in the minority and is declining each year, so substantial cost savings can be made if calls connecting to an answering machine or voicemail can be handled by the dialer rather than an interviewer. The problem is that AMD systems rely on the pause after the respondent says "Hello" to distinguish a human from an answering machine (where the greeting is rarely so brief before the pause occurs). The delay required by this (to hear "Hello" and then the telltale pause) is then often compounded by placing the call in a queue to wait for the next available interviewer. In addition to causing delays, AMD has the further disadvantage of being error prone in detection of answering machines, sometimes adding answering machines to the queue waiting

for interviewers because the answering machine has been mistaken for a human, and other times, more seriously, mistaking a human for an answering machine and hanging up on the person after keeping her or him waiting several seconds.

There is no doubt that these delays annoy respondents and increase the likelihood of the respondent hanging up before the interviewer can engage him or her. In the telemarketing industry, this is not viewed as such a problem that it outweighs the substantial cost benefits, since the telemarketer's objective is to maximize sales, which is done by maximizing interviewer talk time, and the pool of numbers to churn through is practically endless. In survey research, however, scientific sampling and the need for high response rates means such alienation cannot be risked, and therefore most survey research applications do not use AMD and instead configure their dialers to eliminate as far as possible any remaining dead air, even though doing so reduces the cost savings that could otherwise be delivered by the predictive dialer.

Yet another downside to predictive dialing, unless it is matched with *preview dialing*, is that it makes it impossible for an interviewer to study the call history for a given number or household before she or he engages that household in the next call attempt to try to gain a completed interview. This is especially disadvantaging in refusal conversion attempts, where past history with the household can be very important for the interviewer to prepare her or his best approach to trying to convert a previous refusal. Preview dialing occurs when a case is sent to an interviewer before the dial is made, so the interviewer can review the case history and any pertinent call notes (such as details of any prior refusal) before initiating the dial. Many dialing systems are flexible, allowing modes to be combined in different ways based on previous results with the sample number or household in order to enhance productivity while maintaining excellent survey practice. For example, one could start all numbers off in preview mode and pass on to predictive dialing only those cases that have had no contact at all in for the first *n* dials (where *n* is typically in the range 4–8), since only a very small proportion of such cases will ultimately be identified as households. Alternatively, one might start all cases in predictive mode, but as soon as a sample number is identified as a household, all subsequent dials could be assigned to utilize preview mode.

Jenny Kelly and Dale W. Kulp

See also Computer-Assisted Telephone Interviewing (CATI); Do-Not-Call (DNC) Registries; Outbound Calling; Random-Digit Dialing (RDD); Refusal Conversion; Telemarketing

Further Readings

Hansen, S. E. (2008). CATI Sample Management Systems. In J. Lepkowski, C. Tucker, M. Brick, E. de Leeuw, L. Japec, P. J. Lavrakas, et al. (Eds.), *Advances in telephone survey methodology* (pp. 340–358). New York: Wiley.

Kelly, J., Link, M. W., Petty, J., Hobson, K., & Cagney, P. (2008). Establishing a new survey research center. In J. Lepkowski et al. (Eds.), *Advances in telephone survey methodology* (pp. 317–339). New York: Wiley.

PRE-ELECTION POLLS

One of the most common and visible applications of survey research is pre-election polling. These polls typically include one or more trial heat questions, which ask respondents how they will vote in the upcoming election, along with other measures of voter knowledge, attitudes, and likely voting behavior. Unlike most polls, the validity of pre-election polls can be assessed by comparing them with actual election outcomes.

Numerous organizations in the United States and around the world conduct pre-election polls, and the number and frequency of such polls has been growing. Many pre-election polls are public, conducted by news organizations, academic institutions, and nonprofit organizations. Many others are privately conducted by partisan party organizations and campaigns to assist in candidates' message development, resource allocation, and overall strategy. The results of most of these private polls are not made public.

Accuracy

Pre-election polls in the United States have a generally good record of accurately forecasting the outcome of elections. According the National Council on Public Polls (NCPP), the average candidate error for national polls in the 2004 presidential election was 0.9 percentage point; in 2000, the average error was 1.1 percentage points. Polls in state-level races were also very accurate. The average candidate error in 2004

across 198 state polls reviewed by the NCPP was 1.7 percentage points.

But inaccurate polls attract a great deal of attention and tend to be remembered for a long time. Modern polling's most spectacular failure occurred in 1948, when public polls incorrectly forecast the defeat of President Harry S Truman by Thomas Dewey. The problems that led to the 1948 polling debacle were soon addressed, and it is highly unlikely that an error of that magnitude could occur again.

History

Election polling has a long history that precedes the development of modern probability sampling. Straw polls of the 19th century were a popular means by which public opinion in elections was gauged, and an early 20th-century magazine, the *Literary Digest*, conducted a very large and widely followed straw poll in several presidential elections through 1936. The *Literary Digest* poll's spectacular failure in the presidential election of 1936, in which it incorrectly forecast the defeat of President Franklin Roosevelt by the Republican candidate, Alf Landon, by a large margin, discredited straw polls. Despite having more than 2,000,000 respondents, the self-selected nature of the mail survey respondents and the fact that the sampling frame was biased toward more affluent voters led to a gross overrepresentation of Republican voters in the *Literary Digest* sample. A Gallup poll based on a sample that more closely conformed to the principles of probability sampling was quite accurate in the 1936 election and helped to affirm the legitimacy of modern polling methods.

Purposes

Conducting pre-election polls entails many decisions, each of which can affect the accuracy of the poll: (a) the timing of the poll, (b) the sampling method, (c) the determination of likely voters, (d) the trial heat question employed, and (e) the choice of other measures to be included in the poll. Pre-election polls are conducted throughout the election cycle but are considered appropriate for forecasting the election outcome only if taken very close to Election Day. But pre-election polls are conducted for many purposes other than forecasting. Some are conducted at the beginning of a campaign to provide information about the public interest in the election, awareness of the potential candidates, voter views on issues including the importance of different issues, and the likely receptivity of the voters to different messages. Polls conducted during the campaign can provide all of this information as well as reactions of the public to the candidates and events in the campaign. Polls in the latter stages of the campaign are used by the candidates and parties in making decisions about how to allocate campaign resources geographically or in targeting different demographic groups.

Methods for Conducting Pre-Election Polls

Most U.S. pre-election polls are conducted by telephone, though a growing number are conducted via Internet. Telephone samples are typically either random-digit dial (RDD) or from lists of registered voters (so-called registration-based sampling [RBS]). Each method has its advantages and disadvantages. RDD theoretically reaches all potential voters who have a landline telephone but also reaches many people who are not citizens, are not registered, or who are uninterested in politics and very unlikely to vote. The exclusion of voters who do not have landlines but may have cell phones is an increasing limitation of most RDD surveys. Most polling organizations do not routinely include cell phone samples as a part of their RDD telephone surveys as of 2008. Cell-only adults constituted 20% of the population at the end of 2007 and also tend to be younger than other adults and more likely to be Hispanic, characteristics associated with lower levels of voter turnout. But the number of cell-only adults is expected to continue to grow, which may affect the accuracy of RDD samples used for making pre-election forecasts.

RBS samples eliminate many of these problems because they include only those individuals who are actually registered and may include useful information, such as past voting history, that can assist pollsters in estimating the likelihood that an individual will vote in a given election. The quality of RBS samples varies from state to state, however, and telephone numbers are often outdated or not included for many records. As a result, polls based on RBS samples can sometimes be biased by overrepresenting the kind of individuals who are willing to provide telephone numbers or who remain living at a single residence for a long period of time.

One special type of pre-election poll is the *tracking poll*. Tracking polls attempt to document changes in

the support of candidates by interviewing a sample of voters every day over a few weeks or more. The typical design for a tracking poll interviews a mix of respondents from a new sample called for the first time on a given day and respondents from a sample first called one or two days before. Responses from interviews over a 2- to 4-day period are weighted together, averaged, and reported. While not as rigorous in design as the typical pre-election poll, tracking polls provide a view of changes in the campaign that may be very useful to journalists and campaign professionals.

Challenges

Perhaps the most difficult challenge for pre-election polls is determining which respondents will actually vote. Average turnout of the voting age population in U.S. presidential elections during the past several elections has been a little more than 50%. But in most pre-election polls, significantly higher percentages of respondents say they intend to vote. This difference reflects both biases in the pool of survey respondents and the fact that voting is a socially desirable behavior that is apt to be overreported.

The political views of likely voters and nonvoters often diverge, and thus it is critical for polls to distinguish those who are likely to vote from those who will not. Considerable research has focused on locating the questions that best discriminate likely voters from others. As a result, most organizations use a combination of questions that include measures of voter registration, voting intention (sometimes on a scale from 0 to 10, or a verbal scale), past voting activity, interest in the campaign, and knowledge of how to vote.

The process of identifying likely voters is relatively straightforward. Typically, a scale combining the turnout measures is created and respondents are ranked on the scale. Separately, an estimate of the likely turnout percentage is made for the election, based on an assessment of voter interest in the current election and a comparison with past elections with similar characteristics. That estimated turnout percentage is used to determine how many of the respondents on the survey's turnout scale will be classified as likely voters. For example, if the predicted turnout percentage is 55%, respondents in the top 55% of survey respondents in the distribution of the turnout scale will be classified as likely voters. For elections with lower turnout, the standard will be more stringent.

Pre-election polls can include a very wide range of content, including interest in the election, knowledge and awareness of the candidates, opinions about the candidates on various dimensions, campaign activities engaged in by the respondent (including donations, volunteer work, efforts to persuade others), importance of various issues, opinions on the issues, and of course, likely vote choice.

Pre-election polls can be valuable whenever they are conducted during the campaign cycle. But only those polls conducted close to the election can have a reasonable assurance of accuracy in predicting a winner of a given race. Many voters pay little attention to a campaign until very close to Election Day, and thus polling several weeks or even several days prior to the election can be inaccurate. One of the main reasons for polling's notorious failure in the 1948 presidential election between Harry S Truman and Thomas Dewey was the fact that most organizations stopped polling days or weeks before the election. Many observers believe that Truman's aggressive efforts at the end of the campaign helped him convert enough voters to eke out a victory, and that this shift in sentiment was not picked up by the polls. Similarly, the failure in the public polls to predict Ronald Reagan's substantial 1980 presidential victory was due at least in part to their stopping data collection on the Sunday before the election, when in fact many voters did not make the final decision whether they would vote for Carter or for Reagan until the day of the election. As such, most polling organizations that offer a final poll forecasting the outcome of the election gather their data through the weekend of the election, and sometimes even through the day before the election. In 1996, the accuracy of presidential polls was correlated with how close to the election they polled.

Scott Keeter

See also Election Polls; National Council on Public Polls (NCPP); Gallup, George; Likely Voter; Overreporting; Random-Digit Dialing (RDD); Registration-Based Sampling (RBS); Sampling Frame; Social Desirability; Straw Polls; Tracking Poll; Trial Heat Question

Further Readings

Crespi, I. (1988). *Pre-election polls: Sources of accuracy and error.* New York: Russell Sage Foundation.

Herbst, S. (1993). *Numbered voices: How public opinion has shaped American politics.* Chicago: University of Chicago Press.

Lavrakas, P. J., & Traugott, M. T. (Eds.). (2000). *Election polls, the news media and democracy.* New York: CQ Press.

Traugott, M. W., & Lavrakas, P. J. (2008). *The voter's guide to election polls* (4th ed.). Lanham, MD: Rowman & Littlefield.

PREFIX

Understanding how telephone numbers are assigned is very important when you are designing or implementing a telephone sample. Telephone numbers in the United States, Canada, and the Caribbean consist of 10 digits divided into three components. The first three digits are the area code or Numbering Plan Area (NPA). Area codes usually cover large geographic areas. The next three digits represent smaller geographic areas within an area code and are referred to as the *prefix* (NXX). The term *prefix* is also used to refer to the first three digits of the seven-digit local numbers. When the NXX is combined with the final four digits of a phone number, the result is a unique seven-digit local number that is associated with a unique end user within an NXX. In most areas of the United States, local seven-digit dialing of landlines is the norm. Within these areas, the area code component of a 10-digit number need not be dialed, and calls are switched using only the prefix. Although area codes are unique, prefixes are unique only within an area code. Thus, in making a long-distance telephone call or a call to a different area code, the area code is required in order to define a unique prefix. Not all prefixes are available for assignment of local numbers. Some are reserved for other uses, such as directory assistance (555) and special services such as 911 and 411.

Although the terms *prefix, wire center, rate center, central office,* and *exchange* are frequently used interchangeably, there are distinctions. The wire center, rate center, or central office is the building containing the telephone equipment and switches where individual telephone lines are connected and through which calls to and from individual local numbers are routed. The term *exchange* usually refers to the geographic area served by a particular rate center or wire center. Thus an exchange can be serviced by multiple prefixes (NXX codes). In some areas of the United States, these prefixes might belong to different area codes.

Each prefix contains 10,000 possible local numbers (0000–9999). Within prefixes, local telephone companies assign four-digit local telephone numbers. During the past 20 years the demand for telephone numbers has dramatically increased, driven by technological advances and governmental regulations relating to cell phones, pagers, ATMs, faxes, computers, Internet access, and local number portability. In order to meet this demand, the North American Numbering Plan (NANP) was modified to allow for what became known as *interchangeable area codes*. Originally an area code could not be the same as a prefix number, and a prefix number could not be the same as an area code number. Starting in 1973, prefix codes could be any number in the format NXX where N is a number between 2 and 9 and X a number between 0 and 9. In 1995, area codes were allowed to be any number in the same format (NXX).

Interchangeable area codes are also allowed for area code overlays, where two or more different area codes can service the same geography. In some areas, the borders for new area codes have been drawn to conform to legal geographic boundaries, such as city or county lines. Instead of moving entire prefixes to a new area code, prefixes were "partitioned" into two or three pieces across two or three different area codes. Today, an exchange can be serviced by prefixes in multiple area codes, in which case 10-digit dialing is mandatory. For this reason, many people refer to the NPA-NXX as the prefix.

Historically, a prefix was assigned to a single service provider. In order to conserve the pool of available telephone numbers, 1000-block pooling was introduced, requiring that unused blocks of local numbers be made available for reassignment to other service providers. A 1000-block is a block of 1,000 consecutive local numbers within a prefix, all starting with the same digit; for example, 203-255-1000 through 203-255-1999. As a result, a single prefix may now contain multiple carriers, providing different types of service to different-sized exchange areas.

Linda Piekarski

See also Access Lines; Number Portability; Suffix Banks

PRE-PRIMARY POLLS

Pre-primary polls are those conducted before primary elections in an attempt to measure voters' preferences.

They present a number of difficult challenges for pollsters.

Voters in primary elections can be volatile in their preferences, often because many candidates are relatively unknown and voters have limited information about them. This is especially true in early primary states in U.S. presidential campaigns, when the field of candidates is often wide and there are many lesser-known candidates struggling to gain momentum. With little information, voters can be highly susceptible to the dynamics of the campaign, and every time a candidate starts a new ad campaign or launches a micro-targeting effort, poll numbers can move in response.

Primary electorates are made up of partisans of one party (or of independents who lean toward a party) and thus tend to be relatively homogeneous as compared to the electorates in general elections. It can be easier to predict the outcomes of general elections because partisans of one party generally choose to vote for their party's candidates, making their votes relatively easy to predict. Pollsters in general elections can focus on studying how independents and swing voters will behave on Election Day. But in primary elections, voters base their decisions on a complex set of preferences that go beyond basic party affiliations and are much harder to quantify.

Primary elections also often have low or variable turnout, making turnout projections difficult. While turnout in heavily contested primaries early in the presidential cycle sometimes can rival turnout in general elections, turnout in primaries is usually much lower. Many primaries are uncontested or are not very competitive, because incumbents are rarely challenged. Thus when a competitive primary comes along, there is often little voting history that can be useful in predicting future turnout. Turnout models for general elections that place importance on past voting behavior often are not as good at predicting turnout in primaries. And when competitive primaries happen in areas that have not seen competition in a while, they often draw large numbers of people who have not voted in a primary before. The behavior of first-time voters can be difficult to predict.

U.S. election laws and party regulations related to the administration of primary elections and party caucuses vary dramatically across states, adding to the complexity of preprimary polling. For example, some states allow only voters registered with a given party to vote in that party's primary. These primaries are called "closed primaries." Other states have "open primaries" that allow any voter to choose the primary in which he or she will vote. This makes it important to include political independents in pre-primary polls in open primary states. The fact that independents can change their minds at the last minute about which party's primary they will choose makes it a challenge to predict the composition of each party's electorate.

The fact that primary electorates are made up of one party's partisans also presents difficulties for sampling. Most pre-primary polls use screening techniques to determine eligibility to vote in a particular primary, and such screening techniques can be expensive to administer. In states with closed primaries and party registration, lists of registered voters can be used to draw samples of party registrants, but the quality of such lists varies dramatically by state. Lists can be out of date or lack contact information for the voters. It can also be challenging to develop appropriate weighting schemes for pre-primary polls, because it is difficult to find good estimates of the demographic profiles of a particular primary electorate that can be used as weighting benchmarks.

Polling in caucus states presents special challenges. For example, in Iowa's Democratic Party caucuses, participants gather to select delegates to the party convention in a multi-stage process, which involves an initial stage intended to narrow the field of candidates to a small number of "viable" candidates. Participants who initially supported one candidate upon entering the caucus may realign and choose another candidate to support after the viable candidates are selected. Thus pre-caucus polls must anticipate the second choice of caucus-goers in predicting the outcome of the caucuses.

Many media organizations conduct pre-primary polling as part of their election coverage, but budgets for pre-primary polls are often lower than those for general election polling. Thus media pre-primary polls are often based on small samples, are conducted with limited frequency and with less sophisticated turnout models, all of which can contribute to their volatility and affect their accuracy. Media organizations often conduct pre-primary polling using national samples, which can be useful for analyzing the dynamics of the campaign across all the states but have little predictive power when it comes to the races in individual states.

On the other hand, the national attention focused on early primary and caucus states like Iowa and New Hampshire means that residents of those states are polled early and often by media organizations and candidates alike. Multiple and often contradictory polls are reported in these early primary states. Pollsters compete with campaigns for the time and attention of voters, who by some accounts are driven crazy by telephone calls and emails. The increasing cacophony of polling and electioneering in early presidential primary states presents new problems for pre-primary polling.

Trevor N. Tompson

See also Election Polls; Horse Race Journalism; Leaning Voter; Likely Voter; Media Polls; Pre-Election Polls

Further Readings

Traugott, M. W., & Lavrakas, P. J. (2008). *The voter's guide to election polls* (4th ed.). Lanham, MD: Rowman & Littlefield.

PRIMACY EFFECT

The *primacy effect* is one aspect of a well-known phenomenon called the "serial position effect," which occurs when one is asked to recall information from memory. The other aspect of the serial position effect is the *recency effect*. Psychologists discovered these effects more than a century ago; for example, in the 1890s, Mary Whilton Calkins experimented with these effects while she was a student of William James. Essentially, the serial position effect means that the recall of a list of items is easiest for a few items at the end of the list and for a few items at the beginning of the list. The recall of items in the middle of the list is generally poor. The primacy effect refers to the recall of items at the beginning of the list, while the recency effect refers to the recall of items at the end of the list. If one graphed the number of recalled items as a function of position in the list, one would obtain a U-shaped function.

Suppose that an experiment were performed in which the following list of 24 words was read aloud at the rate of one word per second to a group of persons:

apple, basketball, cat, couch, potato, book, bus, lamp, pencil, glasses, guitar, truck, photo, rose, apartment, movie, clock, car, dog, bowl, shoe, bicycle, plane, university

The individuals who had listened to the words being read aloud were then asked to write down all the words that they could remember. According to the serial position effect, the recency effect would predict that the terms *university, plane*, and *bicycle* would be easily recalled; in addition, the primacy effect would predict that the terms *apple, basketball*, and *cat* would also be easily recalled. However, items in the middle of the list, such as *guitar, movie, photo*, and *rose* would be least likely to be remembered.

The only exception to this principal occurs when an item in the middle of the list is extremely well known. For instance, suppose that one were asked to write down all the presidents of the United States that one could recall. The primacy and recency effects are still in evidence; that is, the current president and a few preceding ones are easily recalled, as are several of the first few presidents of the United States. But in this case, Abraham Lincoln is so famous that although his presidency occurred in the middle of the list, he tends to be very easily recalled. And because he is so well known, the presidents associated with him chronologically also tend to have elevated probabilities of being recalled. In this case, the graph of the recall frequency of presidents in chronological order includes two U-shaped graphs, one following the other, where Lincoln represents the peak in the middle of the list of presidents. This is known as the *von Restorff effect* and was discovered in 1933. It does not matter whether research participants are asked to write down all of the presidents that they can remember (a free recall task) or whether they are asked to write down the presidents in order of their respective terms in office; in both cases, the von Restorff effect occurs.

It is important for survey researchers to know about the serial position effect because it can cause response order effects in closed-ended questions. For example, suppose a survey related to an upcoming presidential election includes an item that lists seven Democratic contenders and asks, *For whom would you vote?* If the question is always asked with the candidates' names in the same order, it is likely that one would obtain a U-shaped distribution of responses. To avoid the serial position effect, one needs to use multiple forms of the item so that candidates' names are rotated.

Carla R. Scanlan

See also Measurement Error; Recency Effect; Response Order Effects

Further Readings

Roediger, H. L., & Crowder, R. G. (1982). A serial position effect in recall of United States presidents. In U. Neisser (Ed.), *Memory observed: Remembering in natural contexts* (pp. 230–237). San Francisco: W. H. Freeman.

PRIMARY SAMPLING UNIT (PSU)

In sample surveys, primary sampling unit (commonly abbreviated as PSU) arises in samples in which population elements are grouped into aggregates and the aggregates become units in sample selection. The aggregates are, due to their intended usage, called "sampling units." *Primary sampling unit* refers to sampling units that are selected in the first (primary) stage of a multi-stage sample ultimately aimed at selecting individual elements.

In selecting a sample, one may choose elements directly; in such a design, the elements are the only sampling units. One may also choose to group the elements into aggregates and choose the aggregates in a first stage of selection and then elements at a later stage of selection. The aggregates and the elements are both sampling units in such a design. For example, if a survey is selecting households as elements, then counties may serve as the primary sampling unit, with blocks and households on those blocks serving as the sampling units in subsequent sampling stages of the survey. Thus, *sampling unit* is a term that combines sample selection with the units used as potential selections at any point in the sampling process. For example, in a systematic selection of elements from a list, the elements are the sampling units. The sampling unit contains only one element. But in order to reduce cost of sample selection and data collection, samples may be drawn in multiple stages. Elements are grouped into aggregates (e.g., households on blocks in counties), and a sample of aggregates (e.g., counties) is selected at the first stage. Later elements (e.g., households on blocks) are selected from elements in selected aggregates (e.g., blocks). The aggregates selected at the first stage (e.g., counties) are called "primary sampling units." In multi-stage samples, another level of aggregation may occur within selected primary sampling units, and the aggregates at the second stage (e.g., blocks) are selected, that is, the second stage units. The procedure of creating and selecting aggregates within previously selected aggregates may proceed through several levels of a hierarchy until, at the last stage, the individual element (e.g., households) is selected. The selected elements are chosen only within already chosen aggregates within the hierarchy.

Primary sampling units are not necessarily formed from a list of elements or individuals. They may be conceptual representations of groups for which lists could be obtained, one from each primary sampling unit. For example, suppose a sample of adults living in a large country with widespread population is to be selected, and no list of adults of sufficient quality (e.g., good coverage, covering nearly all adults) is available. Aggregation of adults on an existing list cannot take place. However, units can be formed that are for all intent aggregates of adults within them. A common procedure, *area sampling*, uses geographic areas at successive levels of a geographic hierarchy as sampling units, with implicit aggregation of adults (or other elements) who usually reside within them.

For example, in the United States, a common area primary sampling unit is the county. Within counties, geographic areas such as towns or townships or other administrative units defined by geographic borders can be identified. Within towns or other administrative units, the geography may be further divided into smaller units, such as city blocks or enumeration areas with boundaries formed by streets or highways, rivers, and other relatively permanent, readily identified features. These blocks or enumeration areas are created by a government statistical agency for the purpose of providing census counts of various types of units within them.

The geographic hierarchy from county to town to block may be used as successive sampling units in a survey aimed at ultimately selecting elements that can be associated uniquely with the final stage area unit.

In the first stage of selection to obtain a sample of adults, a sample of counties is selected. The counties from which sample counties are selected are primary sampling units. The selected counties are sometimes called "primary selections."

One could, in principle, create a list of all adults in selected counties and select adults who usually reside in the selected counties in a second and final stage of selection. However, the cost of creating lists of adults at the county level would be prohibitive.

Additional area units—blocks—become sampling units within selected counties and are second-stage

sampling units. The hierarchy of units and selection may continue to households and persons within households. At some point, lists of units may need to be created at a stage of selection to continue the process. For example, households within selected blocks and persons within selected households can be listed manually. In such a design, counties, blocks, households, and adults are all sampling units, even though some units are defined and listed by a government agency while others are defined and listed by the survey organization. Only counties are primary sampling units in the sample.

James M. Lepkowski

See also Area Probability Sample; Elements; Multi-Stage Sample; Unit

Further Readings

Cochran, W. G. (1977). *Sampling techniques.* New York: Wiley.

Kish, L. (1965). *Survey sampling.* New York: Wiley.

PRIMING

Priming is a psychological process in which exposure to a stimulus activates a concept in memory that is then given increased weight in subsequent judgment tasks. Priming works by making the activated concept accessible so that it can be readily used in evaluating related objects. For example, hearing news about the economy may prime individuals to focus on economic considerations when assessing a president's performance because economic concepts are activated, accessible, and presumably relevant for this type of evaluation. In this way, priming affects the opinions that individuals express, not by changing their attitudes, but by causing them to alter the criteria they use to evaluate the object in question.

Priming is a widely used concept with applications in the fields of psychology, political science, and communication. It is also relevant to survey researchers in that priming can inadvertently occur within questionnaires and interviewing, and surveys can be used to study the priming process.

Survey researchers recognize that their instruments may be susceptible to producing unintended priming effects that could bias key measurements. Inadvertent priming can occur when information presented in one part of the survey activates ideas that are then given increased weight in answering subsequent questions. Research in the Cognitive Aspects of Survey Methodology (CASM) movement suggests that respondents may use cues found within a survey as a way of addressing the cognitive challenges of survey participation. This can happen because respondents often do not have well-formed opinions on many survey topics and therefore have to contemplate a mixture of thoughts that come to mind when a question is posed. Ideally, respondents would search their memories for relevant information that could be used to generate a precise summary judgment. However, respondents may choose instead to reduce their cognitive effort by answering with whatever seemingly relevant information is immediately accessible, including information that may have been primed in earlier parts of the survey. By satisficing in this way, respondents can efficiently generate a serviceable, if not necessarily accurate, response by using little more than the ideas they have recently encountered.

To reduce the potential for inadvertent priming within a survey, researchers often carefully consider decisions about question order, wording, and format. A common strategy is to ask open-ended questions before related closed-ended questions so that the open-ended response is not a mere reflection of the ideas primed by the closed-ended form of the question. For example, political surveys typically ask respondents to assess "the biggest problem facing the nation today" before posing more specific questions about particular policies or political events. This ensures that the initial open-ended response is a measure of perceived major problems that does not inadvertently reflect recently primed considerations. Researchers also may take steps to ensure that the phrasing of their questions does not prime thoughts that will bias responses. They may even proactively seek to reduce priming effects by explicitly asking respondents to consider a number of factors before answering a question.

Surveys have also proven valuable in the study of priming, not only as measurement tools but as means to further understand the priming process. In fact, many survey experiments have used controlled manipulations of question order, wording, and format to measure the strength and effectiveness of priming in various situations. Other studies have reorganized surveys to test past findings that may have been biased by inadvertent priming within the survey. Indeed, survey research has been critical in measuring priming effects and illuminating our understanding of the priming process.

Michael Parkin

See also Closed-Ended Question; Cognitive Aspects of Survey Methodology (CASM); Open-Ended Question; Question Order; Saliency; Satisficing

Further Readings

Krosnick, J. A. (1991). Response strategies for coping with the cognitive demands of attitude measures in surveys. *Applied Cognitive Psychology, 5,* 213–236.

Krosnick, J. A., & Kinder, D. R. (1990). Altering the foundations of support for the president through priming. *The American Political Science Review, 84,* 497–512.

Tourangeau, R., Rips, L. J., & Rasinski, K. (2000). *The psychology of survey response.* Cambridge, UK: Cambridge University Press.

PRIOR RESTRAINT

Prior restraint refers to a legal principle embodied in the First Amendment to the U.S. Constitution that relates to guarantees of freedom of the press. At the most fundamental level, it provides protection against censorship by the government, and it is particularly relevant to survey research because of legal disputes about the presentation of exit poll results on Election Night.

Prior restraint actually refers to any injunction that would prohibit the publication of information, an infringement on the so-called freedom of the press. Many consider it an especially serious issue because it prevents the dissemination of information to the public, as distinct from an injunction issued after the information has been released that prohibits further dissemination or provides for some kind of relief as in the instance of libel, slander, or defamation of character.

The case law history of the principle is generally credited as starting with *Near v. Minnesota,* in which the U.S. Supreme Court decided in 1931 that a small Minnesota paper could not be prevented in advance from publishing information about elected officials. In this 5–4 decision, the Justices left open the possibility of prior restraint in some cases, especially those involving national security. Censorship was practiced during World War II, but the issue of national security was not addressed explicitly until *The New York*

Times Co. v. United States, a case in which the Nixon administration went to the court in 1971 to prohibit the publication of the Pentagon Papers by *The Washington Post* and *The New York Times*. The Court decided that an injunction was not warranted.

Another important area of litigation involved censorship of artistic content in the theater and films, usually related to obscenity. In order to avoid new legislation and formal constraints, many industry groups developed so-called voluntary codes that circumscribed content. This approach was adopted in the film and comic book industries, and a rating system developed by the Motion Picture Association of America is still in force. Many content producers do not see any significant difference between a formal law and the prior restraint that results from such practices.

It is in this context that the states and the Congress have unsuccessfully attempted to limit or prohibit the collection and dissemination of exit poll data since 1980. This contentious issue arose from a number of considerations. They include the geopolitics of American presidential elections, the role of the Electoral College, and the fact that the election takes place across four time zones in the continental United States and six time zones if Alaska and Hawaii are included. The exit poll data are used to project the outcome of the presidential contest in each state, since the Electoral College generally involves a "winner takes all" allocation of a state's electoral votes, and then each state projection is added to a running total of each candidate's electoral votes. In recent presidential elections, the Democrats have done well on the east and west coasts and contested the Great Lakes region. The Republicans have done well in the South, Midwest, and West, not including the west coast, and they have contested the Great Lakes too.

This geography is obviously closely aligned with the time zones in the United States, and if the Democratic candidate has not built a sizable electoral vote lead by 9 or 10 p.m., they generally cannot achieve a majority. And herein lies the problem, as the television networks can call one state at a time as their polls close and then eventually a projected winner before the voting is completed on the west coast and beyond. In the 1980 presidential election, for example, Ronald Reagan was projected as the winner by NBC at 8:15 EST (5:15 PST), and Jimmy Carter conceded the election an hour and a half later, more than one hour before the polls closed on the west coast. While the Democrats cried "foul" because they believed that turnout on the west coast was depressed because of the early call, Carter's concession after all three major networks came to the same conclusion took them off the hook somewhat. But in the 2000 election, it was the Republicans' turn to claim injury after Florida was called relatively early for Al Gore, and then the call was reversed, and then reversed again. Florida actually votes in two time zones, so the claim was made that turnout in the western panhandle of the state dropped off in the last hour of voting.

There is variety of polling data that show that Americans are opposed to the use of exit polls as part of Election Night coverage and would support restrictions on their use, including banning them altogether. Starting after the 1980 election, buoyed by their own partisan concerns about their accuracy and impact, members of Congress and various state legislatures began to consider legislation to either prohibit exit polling outright or to limit the mode of data collection in a way that made it less feasible and more prone to error. These state and local laws required exit poll interviewers to stay far enough away from a polling place so as to make the systematic sampling of voters leaving the precinct impractical, because voters could not be intercepted efficiently before they got to their vehicles and left the area.

The main defense of the networks was their First Amendment right to gather and disseminate news and the case law opposed to prior restraint except under the direst circumstances. Several bills were introduced in Congress to eliminate exit polls or to restrict the dissemination of news based upon data collected through them. None of these laws passed, mainly because of the clear understanding of their unconstitutionality under the prior restraint doctrine. As a second tack, Congress also considered federal changes to election law to stipulate a standard closing hour for the polls across the nation, a proposal supported by the networks. However, Congress does not have much authority to regulate elections because they are generally considered a state matter. And there is also considerable disagreement over what would be the best set of standardized hours to hold elections.

Some states passed laws that would have kept exit poll interviewers at least 300 feet from a polling place, but this was declared unconstitutional as a constraint on collecting information about political views and disseminating them to citizens, a form of protected speech. This principle has been endorsed repeatedly in a series of state court decisions. On the other hand, a House Concurrent Resolution passed in 1985 that asked the networks to refrain from projecting the outcome in any single race until the polls were closed. This proposal was not very different from a pledge that network executives had already made not to call a state until all or most of the polls in a state were closed. But in effect, an agreement for self-restraint proved to be an acceptable solution to a problem in which Congress and the states were essentially powerless to intervene because the networks were protected by the principle of prior restraint.

Michael W. Traugott

See also Election Night Projections; Election Polls; Exit Polls

Further Readings

Prior Restraints. (2003). *The First Amendment handbook.* Arlington VA: Reporters Committee for Freedom of the Press. Retrieved December 29, 2006, from http://www.rcfp.org/handbook/c05p01.html

Seager, S. E., & Handman, L. R. (2001). *Congress, the networks, and exit polls.* American Bar Association, Forum on Communication Law. Retrieved December 29, 2006, from http://www.abanet.org/forums/communication/comlawyer/winter01/seager.html

Traugott, M. W., & Lavrakas, P. J. (2008). *The voter's guide to election polls* (4th ed.). Lanham, MD: Rowman & Littlefield.

PRIVACY

Within the realm of survey research, privacy consists of the right to control access to one's self and one's personal information. Private behavior occurs in a context in which an individual can reasonably expect that no observation or recording is taking place. Privacy is distinct from *confidentiality* in that privacy refers to the protection of the right of individuals, whereas confidentiality refers to the protection of the data collected.

Identity, health and financial information, criminal justice involvement and court records, education, and work performance data are commonly regarded as private, despite the fact that many are commonly accessible through credit-reporting background check agencies.

The distinction between public and private behaviors is often ambiguous. Some information that becomes part of public record, such as a person's phone number, marital status, or income, would be considered private information and in the United States is covered by a federal law, the Family Educational Rights and Privacy Act, also known as FERPA or the Buckley Amendment. Some behaviors that occur in the public realm, such as a person's presence in a "red-light district," hospital emergency room, stock brokerage, or welfare office may also be considered private.

An individual's ability to control access to their personal information is often determined by socioeconomic status, age, and other circumstances. For example, information about receiving welfare or credit history is public, whereas account balances are not, unless you are a government official. Minors have generally fewer rights to privacy than do adults. Institutionalized persons may have significant limitations on their ability to control personal information.

The Health Insurance Portability and Accountability Act (HIPAA) Privacy Rule regulates the disclosure of information about health status, provision of health care, or payment for health care that can be linked to an individual. Student education records are protected by the FERPA. In the United States, however, there is no comprehensive federal law protecting all the private records and information of individuals. In contrast, the European Directive on Data Protection requires countries in the European Union (EU) to have government data protection agencies, requires registration of databases with those agencies, and in some cases requires prior approval before personal data processing begins. In order to bridge these different privacy approaches and provide a streamlined means for U.S. organizations to comply with the directive, the U.S. Department of Commerce in consultation with the European Commission developed a "safe harbor" framework. The safe harbor—approved by the EU in July 2000—provides direction for U.S. companies to help them comply with European privacy laws.

Institutional review boards (IRBs) provide critical oversight for human subjects research to ensure that research does not constitute an invasion of privacy. An individual's right to privacy from research, including survey research, is generally protected by the right to refuse to participate in research or to refuse to answer any individual question with a survey or interview. Controversy issues arise when investigators wish to use personally identifiable records or observe behavior without obtaining consent. In general, if data are publicly available and cannot be linked to any identifiable subjects, there are no privacy concerns.

Federal regulations require IRB review of government-funded research studies that include observations of public behavior that could identify individual subjects and, if made public, could reasonably place the subject at risk of criminal or civil liability or cause damage to the subject's financial standing, employability, or reputation. The IRB will generally weigh these risks against the value of the knowledge to be gained.

Once private data are collected, secure storage becomes an important obligation of the researcher. In accordance with HIPAA requirements, private data should be protected by storing backups in a separate location, securing computers (both workstations and servers) and storage devices with locks, protecting computers and electronic media with "sign-on" passwords, and by using encryption software to encode private data.

Amy Flowers

See also Certificate of Confidentiality; Confidentiality; Informed Consent; Institutional Review Board (IRB); Perturbation Methods; Voluntary Participation

PRIVACY MANAGER

The privacy manager sample disposition is specific to telephone surveys. Privacy manager services are telecommunications technologies that are available to households and businesses as an optional subscription from most local U.S. telephone companies. Many privacy manager services work with caller identification (caller ID) services to identify and block incoming calls that do not display a telephone number that the household has identified as a known number. Because very few households or businesses will have the name or telephone number of a telephone survey interviewing organization as a "known" number, privacy manager technologies make it significantly more difficult for telephone interviewers to contact households that subscribe to these services.

In addition to blocking calls from "unknown" numbers, most privacy manager services also block calls whose identification is displayed as anonymous, unavailable, out of area, or private. Callers with blocked numbers usually have the option to temporarily unblock

their numbers so their calls can be connected. When interviewers dial a number that has privacy manager services, the interviewer will hear something like, "The person you are trying to reach does not accept unidentified calls. Your caller ID/telephone number was not received/known." Interviewers then have the opportunity to identify who is calling. If the interviewer announces his or her name and organization, usually the phone then will ring and the household or business will hear the identification provided by the interviewer. At that point, the household or business can choose to accept the call, reject the call, send the call to a voice-mail system or answering machine, or send a "solicitor's rejection," such as notifying the caller that "telemarketing calls are not accepted."

The number of households and businesses with privacy manager services has increased as the number of telemarketing calls has grown in the past decade and as the cost of these services has dropped. As a result, many survey organizations have established "privacy manager" as a unique survey disposition—both to track the prevalence of these call outcomes and to help ensure that cases with these outcomes are managed properly. Finally, because privacy manager technologies make it more difficult to screen numbers in a sample, cases that have a call outcome of privacy manager usually are considered cases of unknown eligibility (because many times it is difficult or impossible for telephone interviewers even to determine whether the case is a household or not). Existing evidence suggests that the level of cooperation that eventually can be gained from repeated calling attempts to households with privacy manager is very low (<5%).

Matthew Courser

See also Caller ID; Dispositions; Final Dispositions; Nonresidential; Response Rates; Temporary Dispositions

Further Readings

American Association for Public Opinion Research. (2006). *Standard definitions: Final dispositions of case codes and outcome rates for surveys* (4th ed.). Lenexa, KS: Author.

PROBABILITY

In general, probability is a numerical representation of how likely is the occurrence of certain observations.

Whenever an empirical investigation involves uncertainty, due to sampling, insufficient understanding of the actual procedure or of the laws governing the observed phenomena, or for any other reason, the concept of probability may be applied.

The concept of probability developed from the investigation of the properties of various games, like rolling dice, but in addition to the very practical desire of understanding how to win, it also incorporates deep philosophical thought. Currently, most scholars consider probabilities as objectively existing values that can be best revealed by observing long sequences of potential occurrences of events and using the relative frequencies of the events to approximate their probabilities. Another, also objective, view of probability is that it can be calculated as the ratio of the possible number of observations when an event occurs to the total number of possible observations. Some other scholars think that probability is subjective: It expresses the degree of belief a certain person has in the occurrence of an event. Fortunately, all these approaches lead to probabilities that have essentially the same properties.

A simple illustration is rolling a fair die with all outcomes being equally likely. Then, each outcome has probability equal to 1/6. More precisely, this may be a subjective belief of an observer, or the assumption of the experimenter, or may be empirically tested by observing the results of long sequences of rolls. In either case, the probability of having a value less than 4 (i.e., 1, 2, or 3) is equal to ½, and the probability of having an even outcome (i.e., 2, 4, or 6) is also ½. The probability of having an outcome less than 4 *and* even is 1/6, as this only happens for 2. There are however, events that are possible but cannot occur at the same time. For example, having a value less than 4 and greater than 5 is not possible. The event that cannot occur is called the "impossible event" and is denoted by $\emptyset$.

Probability theory has many applications in the social sciences. It is the basis of random sampling, where the units of the population of interest, usually people, are selected into the sample with probabilities specified in advance. The simplest case is simple random sampling, where every person has the same chance of being selected into the sample and the steps of the selection process are independent from each other. In such cases, probability models with all outcomes having equal probability may be relevant, but the more complex sampling schemes often used in practice require other models. Probabilistic methods are also used to model the effects of errors of a measurement and, more generally, to model the effects of not measured or unknown factors.

Theory of Probability

In a precise theory, the events associated with the observation of an experiment possess probabilities. To define the properties of probability, one has to define certain operations on these events. The product of two events A and B occurs if both A and B occur and is denoted by AB. For example, one event may be, when rolling a die, having a value less than 4; another event may be having an even value. The product of these is having a value that is less than 4 and is even, that is, 2. Or, an event may be hitting the right-hand side of a circular target, another may be hitting its upper half, and the product is hitting the upper right-hand-side quarter. If two events cannot occur at the same time, their product is the impossible event, $\emptyset$. Another operation is the sum of two events, denoted as A + B. The sum occurs if at least one of the two original events occurs. The sum of having a value less than 4 and of having an even value is having anything from among 1, 2, 3, 4, and 6. The sum of the right-hand-side of the target and of its upper half is three quarters of the target, obtained by omitting the lower left-hand-side quarter.

There are three fundamental rules governing probabilities:

1. The probability of an event is a number between 0 and 1:

$$0 \leq P(A) \leq 1.$$

2. If an event occurs all the times (surely), its probability is 1:

$$P(S) = 1.$$

3. If two events are such that they cannot occur at the same time, then the probability of their sum is the sum of their probabilities:

$$P(A + B) = P(A) + P(B), \text{ if } AB = \emptyset.$$

The last property may be extended to cover the sum of infinitely many events. To see that this may be necessary, think of how many times a die needs to be rolled to have the first 6. Let A1 be that once, A2 that twice, and so on. One cannot say that at most A10 or A1000 cannot occur. The event that one has a 6 is A1 + A2 + A3 + ⋯ A more general form of 3 postulates:

3. If a sequence of events A1, A2, A3,... is such that no two events can occur at the same time, then the probability of their sum is the sum of their probabilities, that is, $P(A1 + A2 + A3 + \ldots) = P(A1) + P(A2) + P(A3) + \ldots$ if $AiAj = \emptyset$ for $i \neq j$.

Independence

The events A and B are independent, if

$$P(AB) = P(A)P(B).$$

In the die-rolling example, the events of having an even number and of having a value less than 5 are independent, because the former (2,4,6) has probability 1/2 and the latter (1,2,3,4) has probability 2/3, while the intersection (2,4) has probability 1/3, that is, the product of 1/2 and 2/3. On the other hand, the events of having an even number and having something less than 4 are not independent, because the former has probability 1/2, the latter has probability 1/2, and their product has probability 1/6. The interpretation of this fact may be that within the first three numbers, even numbers are less likely than among the first six numbers. Indeed, among the first six numbers, three are even numbers; among the first three, only one is even.

Conditional Probability

The conditional probability shows how the probability of an event changes if one knows that another event occurred. For example, when rolling the die, the probability of having an even number is 1/2, because one half of all possible outcomes are even. If, however, one knows that the event of having a value less than 4 has occurred, then, knowing this, the probability of having an even number is different, and this new probability is called the "conditional probability" of having an even number, given that the number is less than 4. Because there is only one even number out of the first three, this conditional probability is 1/3.

The conditional probability of A given B is denoted by P(A | B) and is precisely defined as

$$P(A|B) = P(AB)/P(B),$$

that is, the probability of the product of the events, divided by the probability of the condition. We have

seen that the probability of having a value that is even and also less than 4 is 1/6, and the probability of having a value less than 4 is 1/2, and their ratio is 1/3.

It follows from the definition directly that if A and B are independent, then P(A | B) = P(A), that is, conditioning on the occurrence of B does not change the probability of A, if these are independent. Indeed, if A and B are independent,

$$P(A|B) = P(AB)/P(B) = P(A)P(B)/P(B) = P(A),$$

where the first equality is the definition of conditional probability and the second one is based on the definition of independence. Therefore, independence of events means no relevance for each other.

Applications

The foregoing simple examples are not meant to suggest that formulating and applying probabilistic models is always straightforward. Sometimes even relatively simple models lead to technically complex analyses. Further, the inference based on a probabilistic model is only relevant if, in addition to the correct analysis of the model, it is also based on a model that appropriately describes the relevant aspects of reality. The results will largely depend on the choice of the model.

Tamás Rudas

See also Frequency Distribution; Percentage Frequency Distribution; *p*-Value; Random Error; Random Sampling; Relative Frequency; Simple Random Sample

Further Readings

Bennett, D. J. (1998). *Randomness*. Cambridge, MA: Harvard University Press.

Feller, W. (1968). *An introduction to probability theory and its applications* (3rd ed.). New York: Wiley.

Rudas, T. (2004). *Probability theory: A primer*. Thousand Oaks, CA: Sage.

Rudas, T. (Ed.). (2007). *Handbook of probability theory with applications*. Thousand Oaks, CA: Sage.

PROBABILITY OF SELECTION

In survey sampling, the term *probability of selection* refers to the chance (i.e., the probability from 0 to 1)

that a member (element) of a population can be chosen for a given survey. When a researcher is using a probability sample, the term also means that every member of the sampling frame that is used to represent the population has a known nonzero chance of being selected. That chance can be calculated as a member's probability of being chosen out of all the members in the population. For example, a chance of 1 out of 1,000 is a probability of 0.001 $(1/1,000 = 0.001)$. Since every member in a probability sample has some chance of being selected, the calculated probability is always greater than zero. Because every member has a known chance of being selected, it is possible to compute representative unbiased estimates of whatever a researcher is measuring with the sample. Researchers are able to assume with some degree of confidence that whatever they are estimating represents that same parameter in the larger population from which they drew the sample. For nonprobability samples (such as quota samples, intercept samples, snowball samples, or convenience samples), it is not feasible to confidently assess the reliability of survey estimates, since the selection probability of the sample members is unknown.

In order to select a sample, researchers generally start with a list of elements, such as addresses or telephone numbers. This defined list is called the "sampling frame." It is created in advance as a means to select the sample to be used in the survey. The goal in building the sampling frame is to have it be as inclusive as possible of the larger (target) population that it covers. As a practical reality, sample frames can suffer from some degree of undercoverage and may be plagued with duplication. Undercoverage leads to possible coverage error, whereas duplication leads to unequal probabilities of selection because some elements have more than one chance of being selected. Minimizing and even eliminating duplication may be possible, but undercoverage may not be a solvable problem, in part because of the cost of the potential solution(s).

In designing a method for sampling, the selection probability does not necessarily have to be the same (i.e., equal) for each element of the sample as it would be in a simple random sample. Some survey designs purposely oversample members from certain subclasses of the population to have enough cases to compute more reliable estimates for those subclasses. In this case, the subclass members have higher selection probabilities by design; however, what is necessary in

a probability sample is that the selection probability is knowable.

Depending on the method of data collection, the final selection probability may not be known at the outset of data collection. For example, in household surveys, such as those selected via random-digit dialing (RDD), additional information such as the number of eligible household members needs to be collected at the time of contact in order to accurately compute the final selection probability. The more eligible members in the household, the lower is the selection probability of any one member; for example, in a household with a wife, husband, and two adult children, each has a probability of selection within their household of 1/4. Furthermore, in RDD landline telephone surveys of the general public, it is common to ask how many working telephone numbers are associated with a household. If there are two working landline telephone numbers, then the household has twice the chances of being selected compared to households with only one working landline number, and thus a weighting adjustment can be made for households with two or more numbers. Similarly, in mail survey questionnaires that are not sampling specifically named people, a question about household size regarding eligible members is generally asked. In a systematic sample (e.g., exit polls), the probability of selection is the inverse of the sampling interval.

Selection weights, generally the inverse of the selection probability for each case, are calculated to adjust for differential selection probabilities due to features of the sample design (e.g., stratification) or sampling strategies like oversampling subclasses. To compensate for most complex design features, special statistical software solutions need to be employed. In a similar fashion, using the inverse of the selection probabilities, response rates should also be weighted when unequal selection probabilities exist.

Mario Callegaro and Charles DiSogra

See also Complex Sample Surveys; Convenience Sampling; Coverage Error; Duplication; Element; Mall Intercept Survey; Nonprobability Sample; Overcoverage; Post-Stratification; Probability; Probability Sample; Quota Sampling; Response Rates; Sampling; Sampling Frame; Sampling Interval; Simple Random Sample; Snowball Sampling; Systematic Sampling; Target Population; Undercoverage; Weighting

Further Readings

Levy, P. S., & Lemeshow, S. (2008). *Sampling of populations: Methods and applications* (4th ed.). Hoboken, NJ: Wiley.

PROBABILITY PROPORTIONAL TO SIZE (PPS) SAMPLING

Probability proportional to size (PPS) sampling includes a number of sample selection methods in which the probability of selection for a sampling unit is directly proportional to a size measure, X_i, which is known for all sampling units and thought to be approximately proportional to the unknown Y_i. The X_i must all be strictly greater than 0. In single-stage sampling it can be used to reduce the variance of survey estimates. If the observed values, Y_i, are exactly proportional to X_i, the variance of an estimated total will be exactly 0. When the Y_i are approximately proportional to the X_i, the variance can still be greatly reduced relative to equal probability sampling schemes. PPS sampling is also used in the early stages of multi-stage samples to achieve equal probability samples of the final-stage sampling units or EPSEM samples.

In all cases, suppose one is estimating a population total for a variable Y_i with N units.

$$Y = \sum_{i=1}^{N} Y_i.$$

There are a wide variety of sampling schemes that have PPS properties. Only a few of them are discussed here for illustration.

PPS With Replacement Sampling

The simplest PPS sampling method is *PPS with replacement* sampling. In this case, the single-draw probability of selection, p_i, on each independent sample draw is proportional to X_i, that is,

$$p_i = \frac{X_i}{\sum_{i=1}^{N} X_i}.$$

Note that unless $N = 1$, the individual probabilities will be less than 1. The with replacement estimator is

$$\hat{Y}_{wr} = \frac{1}{n} \sum_{i=1}^{n} \frac{y_i}{p_i},$$

where y_i represent the observed values indexed over the sample of n draws. Note that the same population unit may be selected at more than one draw. The variance of this estimator is

$$V(\hat{Y}_{wr}) = \frac{1}{n} \sum_{i=1}^{N} p_i \left(\frac{Y_i}{p_i} - Y \right)^2.$$

The replacement variance estimator has a simpler form:

$$v(\hat{Y}_{wr}) = \frac{1}{n(n-1)} \sum_{i=1}^{n} \left(\frac{y_i}{p_i} - \hat{Y}_{wr} \right)^2.$$

An unbiased estimate of the variance can be obtained for all samples of size 2 draws or greater.

To select a PPS with replacement sample, the following procedure is followed for each sample draw. Select a uniform (0,1] random number, R. Assume the N population elements are ordered and indexed by I. Compute the partial sums $S_i = \sum_{j=1}^{i} p_j$. Select the unit i if $S_{i-1} < r \le s_i$; in simpler terms, the unit selected will be the first one whose partial sum equals or exceeds R.

PPS Without Replacement Sampling

In practice, *PPS without replacement* sampling is more commonly used, particularly in the first stage of multi-stage samples. Since sampling is without replacement, the sample size n now represents unique population units selected into the sample. Let S be the set of all $\binom{N}{n}$ samples of size n from the population of size N and is indexed by s and $\sum_{s \in S} P_s = 1$. P_s represents the probability of a particular sample s. The probability of selecting any particular unit i in a sample of size n is formally defined as $\pi_i = \sum_{s \supset i} P_s$. Summation is over all samples of size n that contain the population element i. Many creative methods have been developed to select PPS without replacement samples that satisfy the property $\pi_i = np_i$ where p_i is as defined previously for with replacement sampling. It often happens that $np_i \ge 1$ for some i. A common fix for this problem is to select unit

i with probability 1 and select a PPS without replacement sample of size $n - 1$ from the remaining elements.

The commonly used estimator associated with PPS without replacement sampling is the *Horvitz-Thompson estimator*, $\hat{Y}_{wpr} = \sum_{i=1}^{n} \frac{y_i}{\pi_i}$.

In order to compute the variance of the Horvitz-Thompson estimator, it is also necessary to know the pairwise selection probabilities. These probabilities, denoted by π_{ij}, are the probabilities that population units i and j both get selected in the same sample. Similarly to the formal definition for the unit probabilities, the pairwise selection probabilities are defined in terms of the sum over a subset of sample selection probabilities; in this case, the summation is limited to samples that contain both unit i and unit j:

$$\pi_{ij} = \sum_{s \supset (i,j)} P_s.$$

The Yates-Grundy form of the variance of the Horvitz-Thompson estimator is

$$V(\hat{Y}_{wor}) = \frac{1}{2} \sum_{i=1}^{N} \sum_{j \neq i}^{N} (\pi_i \pi_j - \pi_{ij}) \left(\frac{Y_i}{\pi_i} - \frac{Y_j}{\pi_j} \right)^2.$$

This form of the variance is only defined for samples of size 2 or greater. Samples of size 1 meet the PPS with replacement definition.

The variance estimator has similar form:

$$v(\hat{Y}_{wor}) = \frac{1}{2} \sum_{i=1}^{n} \sum_{j \neq i}^{n} \frac{(\pi_i \pi_j - \pi_{ij})}{\pi_{ij}} \left(\frac{y_i}{\pi_i} - \frac{y_j}{\pi_j} \right)^2.$$

Unbiased estimates of the variance can be obtained only if the pairwise probabilities, π_{ij}, are positive for all pairs of units.

PPS Methods for Small Samples

A number of sampling schemes have been developed for selecting PPS without replacement samples that have all positive pairwise probabilities. Since PPS sampling is often used in conjunction with stratification, samples of size 2 per stratum are not uncommon. For samples of size 2, simply select the pair with probability

$$\pi_{ij} = K \pi_i \pi_j \left[\frac{1}{1 - \pi_i} + \frac{1}{1 - \pi_j} \right] \text{ where}$$

$$K = \left[2 + \sum_{i=1}^{N} \frac{1}{1 - \pi_i} \right]^{-1}.$$

M. R. Sampford's rejective method may be applied to larger samples and also produces positive pairwise probabilities. In this method of selection, an initial draw is made with PPS exactly as in the method used for each draw in PPS with replacement sampling with probabilities p_i. The remaining $n - 1$ selections are also drawn using PPS with replacement with probabilities proportional to $\lambda_i = \frac{p_i}{1 - np_i}$. If the first n draws yield unique elements, then one retains the sample. Otherwise, one repeats the entire process until a sample of n unique elements is selected.

PPS Systematic

PPS systematic sampling provides a relatively simple method for selecting larger PPS samples but does not provide for unbiased variance estimation since most pairwise probabilities will be 0. For larger samples, the ordering of the frame before selecting the sample is often desirable, since it imposes an implicit stratification along the ordering dimension. For example, some socioeconomic balance can be achieved in a sample by ordering counties or other geographic units based on percentage above or below a specified income level in the most recent decennial census. Approximate variance formulas that recognize the implicit stratification are often used.

PPS sample selection is relatively simple. Note that

$$\pi_i = \frac{nX_i}{\sum_{i=1}^{N} X_i},$$

and the π_i sums to n. To select a PPS systematic sample from an ordered list, select a uniform $(0,1]$ random number, R. Then form partial sums of the ordered list $S_i = \sum_{j=1}^{i} \pi_j$. Select the n units i that satisfy $S_{i-1} < r + k - 1 \leq s_i$ for $k = 1, 2, \ldots, n$.

Of note, PPS systematic sampling can be viewed as a sequential sampling method.

James R. Chromy

See also EPSEM Sample; Equal Probability of Selection; Multi-Stage Sample; Sampling Without Replacement;

Sequential Sampling; Stratified Sample; Systematic Sampling; Unit

Further Readings

Brewer, K. R. W., & Hanif, M. (1983). *Sampling with unequal probabilities.* New York: Springer.

Hansen, M. H., Hurwitz, W. N., & Madow, W. G. (1953). *Sample survey methods and theory.* New York: Wiley.

Horvitz, D. G., & Thompson, D. J. (1952). A generalization of sampling without replacement from a finite universe. *Journal of the American Statistical Association, 47,* 663–685.

Sampford, M. R. (1969). A comparison of some possible methods of sampling from smallish populations with units of unequal size. In N. L. Johnson & H. Smith, Jr. (Eds.), *New developments in survey sampling.* New York: Wiley-Interscience.

PROBABILITY SAMPLE

In gathering data about a group of individuals or items, rather than conducting a full census, very often a sample is taken from a larger population in order to save time and resources. These samples can be classified into two major groups describing the way in which they were chosen: *probability samples* and *nonprobability samples*. Both types of samples are made up of a basic unit called an individual, observation, or elementary unit. These are the units whose characteristics are to be measured from a population. In probability samples, each member of the population has a known nonzero probability of being chosen into the sample. By a random process, elements are selected and receive a known probability of being included in the sample; this is not the case in nonprobability sampling.

In order to estimate some quantity of interest with a desired precision from a sample, or to contrast characteristics between groups from a sample, one must rely on knowing to whom or to what population one is referring. Well-designed probability samples ensure that the reference population is known and that selection bias is minimized. The best samples are simply smaller versions of the larger population. The process by which a sample of individuals or items is identified will affect the reliability, validity, and ultimately the accuracy of the estimates and inferences made.

Underlying Concepts

The concepts behind probability sampling underlie statistical theory. From the finite population of N elements, all possible samples of size n are identified. For example, if the population consisted of 6 elements, and samples of size 2 are to be chosen, there would be 15, $\binom{6}{2}$, possible samples to consider. In theory, prior to selection, the probability of each of these samples being chosen is known. Therefore, the selection probability of each individual is also known. Summing the probabilities of all samples containing an individual element will compute the individual's probability of appearing in the sample. By knowing the probability of selecting each unit, a statistical weight can be assigned by which population estimates can be calculated. The statistical weight is defined as the inverse of the probability of selection into the sample, allowing each sampled unit to represent a certain number of units in the population. Most often, the goal of a probability sample is to estimate certain quantities in the population using these statistical weights.

Reliability and Validity

From a probability sample, the quantities that are estimated, such as population totals, means, proportions, and variances, have certain properties that can be evaluated. For instance, over repeated sampling, estimators from the probability sample can be evaluated for how reproducible or reliable they are (variance) and if, on average, the estimates from the sample are similar to the true value of the population quantity (unbiasedness or validity). Combining the ideas of reliability and validity, the accuracy, or how far away on average the estimator is from the true value (mean squared error), can also be evaluated on the sample estimator.

None of these desirable properties can be determined from estimates derived from nonprobability samples. Nonprobability samples are used in many unscientific surveys, market research, and public opinion polls, often because they are easier and less expensive to conduct. These types of surveys include purposive or deliberate, quota, and snowball samples. As an example, imagine that interviewers are attempting to question shoppers as to their political views at a local supermarket in order to describe future poll results for a city. In quota sampling, the interviewer may be asked to "find" a certain number of individuals in various demographic groups, such young women, older women, black men, and white men. The individuals that are found by the interviewer may be of only one political leaning or of one socioeconomic group simply because they are easy to find and shop at the particular market. Without a systematic plan for sampling, the decision about whom to interview is left up to the interviewer, likely creating bias in the sample. In certain circumstances, such as in populations that are hard to reach, probability samples may not be feasible. Thus, as long as they are not used to make inference to a larger population, some non-probability samples are useful.

In order to draw a probability sample, a list of sampling units must be organized from which to sample. In hard-to-reach populations, this sampling frame may not be available. The sampling frame must allow every unit in the population to have a chance of selection; otherwise coverage error could result. For example, the sampling frame may consist of all medical records within a certain time period. A sample can be drawn from the medical record numbers. Alternatively, the sampling frame may be an enumerated list of city blocks from which a household, and eventually an individual, will be chosen. Using the sampling frame, the sample can be selected in numerous ways.

Sampling Designs

Simple Random Sampling

The simplest design used to sample units is called a "simple random sample." Simple random sampling can either be done *with replacement* or *without replacement*. In sampling with replacement, the unit sampled can be selected more than once, since it is returned to the pool once sampled. In practice, nearly all probability samples are performed without replacement, having each element appear only once in the sample. Simple random samples without replacement consist of selecting n units from a population of N elements, each possible subset having the same probability of selection. For example, if numbers 1 to 100 were placed in an urn, and 10 numbers were drawn without replacing them after each turn, this would be a simple random sample. The units or people associated with these 10 numbers would constitute the sample from the population of size 100.

In fact, simple random samples are not often used alone as the sample design for a survey. Enumerating every element of a population is a tedious and time-consuming process. In addition, once this list is compiled it may be out of date. Perhaps a study's interest is in estimating a certain health characteristic of high

school students in a city. If one were to enumerate all high school students in the city today, students may leave or enter the school tomorrow. Moreover, performing a simple random sample design for a population that covers a large geographic area is not practical. Since each element will have the sample probability of selection, it may require traveling many miles between elements. For all of these reasons, simple random sampling is rarely used alone; however, it provides the basis for comparison to other more commonly used designs.

Systematic Sampling

In some situations, it is not possible to construct a sampling frame before sampling has to occur, but a very good estimate of the number of records in a certain interval may be known. In situations like these it is possible to take a probability sample comprised of every kth element in the population. This is called "systematic sampling." Suppose characteristics of patients presenting to an emergency room is being planned and, from previous observation, it is known that 1,000 patients will come to the emergency room in a given week. If we would like to collect information on 100 patients using a systematic sample, we will survey every 10th patient. A random number is selected between 1 and 10, and every 10th element after that is included in the sample. Systematic sampling is an extremely popular sampling method due to its ease of implementation.

Stratified Random Sampling

One way to improve the precision of estimates over what is possible with simple random sampling is to carry out what is called a "stratified random sample." In this type of sample, elements of a population may also be categorized into distinct groups, called "strata." Within each stratum, a sample of units can then be drawn using simple random or systematic sampling. In general, stratification by a characteristic will reduce variability in the resulting population estimates, especially when the characteristic is related to the measurement of interest. Often, it will also allow reliable estimates to be made about each stratum. Following from the previous example, the individuals to sample may be either male or female. Separately, a simple random sample of men and a simple random sample of women can be chosen, stratifying the sample by gender. Disadvantages of stratified random sampling still exist, including the cost of constructing a sampling frame for each stratum before drawing the sample and then a probability sample from each. This may actually increase the costs of selecting the sample over what would be the case for a simple random sample, but the increased precision may justify the additional time and cost.

Cluster Sampling

One common variation in designing a probability sample is called "cluster sampling." In this type of sampling, the sampling frame enumerates listing units that are not the individuals or elements, but are larger groupings called "clusters." For instance, it may be easier to enumerate city blocks and sample these blocks rather than enumerate all individuals to conduct a survey describing the health of individuals in an area. Once blocks are chosen, dwelling units can be sampled and individuals selected within each unit. Cluster sampling may dramatically reduce cost and time; however, these designs usually have a trade-off in precision. As opposed to simple random sampling, sampling frames are much easier to construct for cluster samples. Only the elementary units of the chosen clusters will have to be listed for sampling. This may entail counting the number of houses on a city block or students in a particular classroom as opposed to the entire city or school. Although clusters may be chosen randomly, most often they are chosen with probability proportional to some measure of the cluster's size (PPS). In general, cluster sampling with PPS reduces variability in estimates as compared to cluster sampling with equal probability, when the size of clusters varies greatly. Moreover, since cluster samples greatly decrease travel costs, the decreased precision for a fixed sample size compared to simple random sampling is outweighed by the ability to sample a greater number of individuals for a fixed cost, ultimately resulting in more precise estimates for a fixed budget. Cluster sampling is feasible in many situations where simple random sampling is not.

Some common *random-digit dialing* (RDD) techniques are, in fact, cluster samples. The most straightforward random-digit dialing method simply randomly selects phone numbers from a frame: a simple random sample. However, only 20% of the phone numbers may be household phone numbers. RDD methods based on sampling combinations of the area code, the exchange, and blocks of the remaining four numbers are cluster samples. *Blocks* are groups of 100 numbers

with the same first two digits. For example, 555-444-12XX would be considered one 100-block listed on the sampling frame. Once a household is found in an area code + exchange + block, all of the numbers in the particular block are called, dramatically reducing the number of nonhousehold calls, as is done in the Mitofsky-Waksberg approach to RDD sampling.

Importance of Well-Designed Probability Surveys

The elements of design, including stratification, clustering, and statistical weights, should not be ignored in analyzing the results of a probability sample survey. Ignoring the sampling design may underestimate variability, affecting potential inferences. Software has advanced greatly in recent years and has become more accessible to researchers wishing to estimate population characteristics and their associated standard errors using sample survey data. This should encourage researchers to carry out well-designed probability surveys to attain their study objectives and to use appropriate methods to analyze their data.

Erinn M. Hade and Stanley Lemeshow

See also Census; Cluster Sample; Coverage Error; Elements; Finite Population; Mitosky-Waksberg Sampling; Multi-Stage Sample; *n*; *N*; Nonprobability Sample; Probability Proportional to Size (PPS) Sampling; Purposive Sample; Quota Sampling; Random; Random-Digit Dialing (RDD); Random Sampling; Replacement; Sampling Frame; Simple Random Sample; Snowball Sampling; Strata; Stratified Sampling; Systematic Sampling; Target Population; Unbiased Statistic; Unit of Observation; Validity; Variance

Further Readings

Levy, P. S., & Lemeshow, S. (1999). *Sampling of populations: Methods and applications* (3rd ed.). New York: Wiley.

Lohr, S. L. (1999). *Sampling: Design and analysis.* Pacific Grove, CA: Duxbury.

Probable Electorate

The *probable electorate* is defined as those citizens who are registered to vote and who very likely will vote in an upcoming election. In election polling and surveying, this concept is operationalized as a sample of pre-election survey respondents whose candidate preferences have been weighted by the respondents' estimated likelihood of voting.

One ongoing challenge in election polling lies in ascertaining which respondents will actually turn out to vote. The distribution of candidate support among the sample in the aggregate, while revealing, is essentially irrelevant when it comes to making predictions about election outcomes. What matters are the choices of those respondents who will actually vote on (or in some cases before) Election Day. If survey researchers had a crystal ball, they could determine with precision which respondents would actually be voters (but then, of course, they could dispense with the pre-election survey altogether and simply foretell the outcome of the election). In the real world, techniques are necessary to carve out a probable electorate upon which to base pre-election predictions.

Estimating a probable electorate requires either the creation of a binary turnout screener, by which survey respondents are assigned voting probabilities of either 0 or 1, or the use of a weighting method in which respondents are assigned estimated probabilities on a continuum that can range anywhere between 0 and 1. However, few pollsters provide detailed information on how, exactly, they construct their likely voter estimates, treating their procedures like a secret (proprietary) formula. What is known about how probable electorates are constructed in practice is based on a relatively slim store of publicly available information.

Turnout screening (i.e., a series of survey questions that helps the researcher estimate the likelihood a given respondent will vote) aims to differentiate voters and nonvoters, taking into account the candidate preferences of the former, but not the latter, when making election predictions. Turnout screens can take multiple forms, some simple, some exceedingly complex. On the simple side, a screen might be based on a self-reported turnout intention, asking respondents how likely they are to vote in an upcoming election, then counting only the preferences of those who say they will "definitely" or "probably" vote.

Of course, not everyone who says they plan to vote will actually do so (although most of those who say they will not, do not). More sophisticated screeners take into consideration registration status, past voting behavior, campaign interest, knowledge about the location of polling places, or some combination. Some turnout screeners are based on as many as a dozen questions or more, although research suggests that a screener that includes 15 questions is not much more accurate than screeners based on eight or fewer items.

Using multi-item indices to construct a turnout screening method produces estimated levels of voting likelihood (a "turnout score") that require the application of some threshold or cut-point: for example, should respondents scoring a 6 or above on a 10-point likelihood scale be counted as probable voters, or only those scoring 7 or higher? The answer depends in part on a priori estimates of what turnout will be on Election Day. Higher anticipated turnout entails including more respondents in one's probable electorate.

An alternative to imposing a threshold in order to create a binary screener involves assigning turnout probabilities (ranging from 0 to 1, like a propensity score) for every respondent in one's sample. Doing so requires deriving estimates from out-of-sample models, usually involving "validated" reports of voter turnout. Such models include demographic, behavioral, and in some cases attitudinal factors and yield weights that can be applied to respondents in any given pre-election survey that includes the same questions.

Once a respondent's voting probability has been calculated, his or her candidate preference is simply weighted accordingly. The preferences of those deemed more likely to vote are thus counted more than those of respondents with little chance of turning out. Respondents who say they do not intend to vote, or those who are not registered, can be assigned a probability of 0. For others, though, this method recognizes that even those unlikely to vote have some chance of casting a ballot while acknowledging that not all "likely voters" are created equal.

Paul Freedman

See also Election Polls; Likely Voter; Pre-Election Polls; Propensity Scores

Further Readings

Crespi, I. (1988). *Pre-election polling: Sources of accuracy and error.* New York: Russell Sage Foundation.

Daves, R. (2000). Who will vote? Ascertaining likelihood to vote and modeling a probable electorate in preelection polls. In P. Lavrakas & M. Traugott (Eds.), *Election polls, the news media, and democracy* (pp. 206–223). New York: Chatham House.

Perry, P. (1960). Election survey procedures of the Gallup Poll. *Public Opinion Quarterly 24*, 531–542.

PROBING

Probing involves the use of specific words or other interviewing techniques by an interviewer to clarify or to seek elaboration of a person's response to a survey question. When respondents provide incomplete or irrelevant answers to survey questions, it becomes necessary for interviewers to query respondents further in an effort to obtain a more complete or specific answer to a given question. Although survey researchers may take great care in constructing questionnaires in terms of the wording of both questions and response options, some respondents may not provide a response in the format pre-specified by the researcher, especially when answering closed-ended questions. Likewise, respondents may offer vague or overly simplistic replies to open-ended questions, that is, questions with no predetermined response categories. Additionally, respondents may simply provide the response, "I don't know," which the researcher may or may not want to accept as a valid response.

The following are examples of responses requiring probing:

> Interviewer question: *In the past 12 months, has a doctor, nurse, or other health professional given you advice about your weight?* [The valid response options are "Yes" or "No."]
>
> *Irrelevant respondent answer:* "My husband is on a diet."
>
> *Unclear respondent answer:* "People are always telling me I need to gain some weight."

To elicit an acceptable response to a given item, interviewers should use an appropriate neutral, unbiased, or "nondirective" probe. Interviewers should take care to elicit the information needed without suggesting or leading the respondent to a particular response. Researchers should include suggested wording for potential probes in their questionnaires, in an effort to equip interviewers to handle these situations. Although every situation is different, there are some basic techniques and general rules that most interviewers find successful when probing respondents for information.

1. *Repeat the question.* When respondents appear to have misunderstood or misinterpreted a survey question, repeating the question is the best probe. This technique is used with the expectation that after hearing the survey question a second time, the respondent will understand what information the question is intended to collect.

2. *Silent probe.* Interviewers may also use a silent probe, which is a pause or hesitation intended to indicate to a respondent that the interviewer may be waiting for additional information or clarification on a response. Oftentimes, interviewers will utilize this technique during later stages of an interview, once a respondent's habits or response patterns have become more obvious.

3. *Neutral question or statement.* When a respondent offers an inadequate response, interviewers use neutral questions or statements to encourage a respondent to elaborate on their initial response. Examples of good neutral probes are "What do you mean?" "How do you mean?" "Please tell me what you have in mind," "Please tell me more about …" Note that these probes maintain neutrality and do not lead the respondent by asking things such as "Do you mean you don't support the bill?"

4. *Clarification probe.* When a response to an item is unclear, ambiguous, or contradictory, interviewers will use clarification probes. Examples of good clarification probes are "Can you give me an example?" or "Could you be more specific?" Whereas these probes are helpful, interviewers must be careful not to appear to challenge the respondent when clarifying a statement. Interviewers must know when to draw the line between probing a respondent for more or better information and making the respondent feel pressured to answer an item, which could lead to an outright refusal to continue participation in the rest of the survey.

Most interviewers will agree that "I don't know" is the response to survey items requiring probing that occurs most frequently. Because a "don't know" response is vague and can mean any number of things, interviewers are often challenged with the need to choose the correct probe. Interviewers are also challenged to not cross the line between probing and pressuring in this situation as well. Interviewers are trained to remind respondents that participating in a survey is not a test, and that there are no right and wrong answers. A good practice for interviewers is encouraging a given respondent who provides a "don't know" response to an item to give his or her "best estimate," or "best guess." Encouraging the respondent to answer an item and reminding them that their answers, no matter what they are, are the "right answers" to a given question will likely lead to better consideration of the question and a higher quality response.

David James Roe

See also Bias; Closed-Ended Question; Interviewer Effects; Interviewer Neutrality; Interviewer-Related Error; Nondirective Probing; Open-Ended Questions

Further Readings

Weisberg, H. F., Krosnick, J., & Bowen, B. (1996). *An introduction to survey research, polling and data analysis* (3rd ed.). Thousand Oaks, CA: Sage.

PROPENSITY SCORES

Propensity scoring was developed as a statistical technique for adjusting for selection bias in causal estimates of treatment effects in observational studies. Unlike randomized experiments, in observational studies researchers have no control over treatment assignment, and, as a result, individuals who receive different treatments may be very different in terms of their observed covariates. These differences, if left unadjusted, can lead to biased estimates of treatment effects. For example, if smokers tend to be older than nonsmokers, then comparisons of smokers and nonsmokers will be confounded with age. Propensity scores can be used to adjust for this observed selection bias.

Survey researchers have used propensity scores to adjust for nonresponse bias, which arises when respondents and nonrespondents differ systematically in terms of observed covariates, and to adjust for selection (coverage) bias, which arises when some of the population is systematically omitted from the sample.

Estimating Treatment Effects in Observational Studies

In the context of estimating causal effects in observational studies, the *propensity score* is the conditional probability that an individual belongs to a specific treatment group (e.g., the treated group or the control group) given a set of observed covariates. Propensity scores are balancing scores, meaning that within subclasses that are homogeneous in the propensity score, the distributions of the covariates are the same for treated and control units (i.e., are "balanced"). This makes it possible to estimate treatment effects, controlling for covariates, by matching or subclassifying on the propensity score since comparisons of individuals with different treatments made within these matched pairs or groups are not confounded by differences in observed covariate distributions. An unbiased estimate of the average treatment effect is obtained when researchers have controlled for all relevant covariates (the so-called strongly ignorable treatment assignment assumption).

Propensity scores are usually estimated by logistic regression, although other models can be used. Most of the propensity score literature focuses on the binary treatment case (e.g., treated vs. control); however, propensity score methods have been extended more recently to accommodate multiple treatment groups. Propensity scores can be used for stratification, matching, or as a covariate in future analyses.

Adjusting for Nonresponse Bias in Surveys

Propensity scores have been used in survey research to adjust for nonresponse bias. In this case, the propensity score is the probability of being a respondent given observed characteristics. These propensity scores can be used in post-stratification, weighting adjustments, and imputation.

Post-stratification using propensity scores is useful when there are a substantial number of variables available for post-stratification, as there might be in panel surveys where information from a previous wave is available for nonrespondents. In this situation, standard post-stratification methods that form weighting cells by complete cross-classification of all the control variables are not practical, since the number of weighting cells would be very large and could include cells with nonrespondents but few or no respondents. If there are no respondents in a cell, the nonresponse weight adjustment is infinite. An alternative is to estimate the propensity to be a respondent using the available observed variables and then to group these estimated propensities into a reasonable number of weighting classes. This takes advantage of the propensity score's ability to adjust for a large number of covariates simultaneously using only a single scalar summary (the propensity score).

Propensity scores can also be used directly in nonresponse weighting adjustments. To adjust for nonresponse, survey weights can be multiplied by the inverse of the estimated propensity score for that respondent. This avoids the assumptions involved with grouping together respondents with similar but not identical response propensity scores into weighting classes. However, this method relies more heavily on the correct specification of the propensity score model, since the estimated propensities are used directly in the nonresponse adjustment and not just to form weighting cells; and this method can produce estimators with very large variances, since respondents with very small estimated propensity scores receive very large weights.

Propensity scores can also be used for imputation for nonresponse through propensity-matching techniques. The idea here is similar to that of *nearest neighbor imputation* or *predictive-mean-matching imputation*. Nonrespondents are matched to respondents with similar propensity scores, and then these respondents serve as "donors" for the nonrespondents' missing information. This can be done using single or multiple imputation. For single imputation, the respondent who is closest in terms of estimated propensity score can be chosen as the donor or can be selected at random from a pool of donors who are all relatively close. For multiple imputation, a pool of potential donors can be created by specifying tolerances for the difference in propensity scores between the nonrespondent and the respondents, or by grouping together the nearest k respondents, or by stratifying on the estimated propensity scores. The approximate Bayesian bootstrap can then be used to create "proper" multiple imputations that correctly approximate the uncertainty in the imputed values. To do this, a bootstrap sample of potential donors is selected at random with replacement from the available pool of potential donors for each nonrespondent. Imputation donors for each nonrespondent are then selected at random with replacement from this bootstrap sample. This process is repeated to create multiple imputations for each nonrespondent.

Adjusting for Selection Bias in Surveys

Propensity scores have also been used in survey research to adjust for selection (coverage) bias. For example, propensity scores have been used to adjust for the selection bias that arises in Web surveys because not all members of the target population have Internet access. For this approach to be successful, it is necessary to have a *reference survey* that does not have the selection bias problems of the Web survey. For example, the reference survey could be a telephone survey, assuming that the entire population of interest has telephone service. The reference survey and the Web survey are combined to estimate the propensity to be a Web respondent (as opposed to a telephone respondent), given observed covariates. The reference survey can be a very short survey, containing only questions about characteristics, attitudes, or behaviors that are hypothesized to differ between the Web population and the telephone population. The resulting estimated propensities can be used for poststratification as described previously, except that instead of each cell containing respondents and nonrespondents, each cell contains Web respondents and telephone respondents. Weight adjustments are made so that the Web survey's weighted proportion of respondents in each cell matches the reference survey's estimated proportion in each cell.

Elaine L. Zanutto

See also Bootstrapping; Coverage Error; Experimental Design; Imputation; Multiple Imputation; Nonresponse Bias; Panel Survey; Post-Stratification; Propensity-Weighted Web Survey; Wave; Weighting

Further Readings

D'Agostino, R. B., Jr. (1998). Propensity score methods for bias reduction in the comparison of a treatment to a non-randomized control group. *Statistics in Medicine, 17*, 2265–2281.

Lavori, P. W., Dawson, R., & Shera, D. (1995). A multiple imputation strategy for clinical trials with truncation of patient data. *Statistics in Medicine, 14*, 1913–1925.

Little, R. J. A. (1986). Survey nonresponse adjustments for estimates of means. *International Statistical Review, 54*, 139–157.

Rosenbaum, P. R. (1987). Model-based direct adjustment. *Journal of the American Statistical Association, 82*, 387–394.

Rosenbaum, P. R., & Rubin, D. B. (1983). The central role of the propensity score in observational studies for causal effects. *Biometrika, 70*, 41–55.

Schonlau, M., Zapert, K., Payne Simon, L., Haynes Sanstad, K., Marcus, S., Adams, J., et al. (2004). A comparison between responses from a propensity-weighted Web survey and an identical RDD survey. *Social Science Computer Review, 22*, 128–138.

PROPENSITY-WEIGHTED WEB SURVEY

Because Web surveys are often convenience samples, traditional methods for statistical inference do not readily apply. Propensity scoring is one attempt to correct for the selection bias of a nonrandom Web sample. Broadly speaking, the propensity scoring adjustment is accomplished by reweighting the convenience sample such that the distribution of so-called propensity variables corresponds to that of a reference sample. *Propensity variables* (or *propensity questions*) can be any survey questions that have been answered both by the Web survey participants and by the respondents of the reference sample. *The reference sample* is a separate probability sample (e.g., a random-digit dialed [RDD] phone survey) from a possibly much shorter survey that contains only the propensity questions.

History

Propensity scoring has traditionally been applied in biostatistics to estimate causal effects. Harris Interactive, a New York–based Web survey business, first applied propensity scoring to correct for selection bias in Web surveys. Harris Interactive uses special "Webographic" questions as propensity variables. Webographic questions—also called "lifestyle," "attitudinal," or "psychographic" questions—are meant to capture the difference between the online and the offline population.

The Practice of Propensity Scoring

In practice, the Web sample and the reference sample are combined to form a single data set. An indicator variable, indicating whether a respondent is from the Web sample, is regressed on the propensity questions, usually via logistic regression, representing the probability that respondents within certain characteristics are from the Web sample. The propensity scores are computed as the predicted values from this logistic regression. The propensity scores can be used in a variety of ways, including as weights for stratification and matching techniques (research). Using the inverse propensity scores as adjustment weights is appealing because the concept of reweighting is familiar and because standard survey software

can be used to conduct statistical tests. Another popular method is to stratify the propensity scores into quintiles and to use the resulting five-level categorical variable in a post-stratification step.

Limitations

First, it is not possible to adjust for unbalanced, unobserved variables that correlate with outcomes unless the unobserved variable strongly correlates with observed variables. Second, to calibrate the Web survey, the propensity scoring approach requires a reference sample. For example, Harris Interactive conducts regular RDD phone surveys for that purpose. This requirement currently limits the appeal of this method and makes it most useful for panel surveys. Propensity scoring attempts to achieve balance. That is, after the propensity weighting adjustment, the distribution of the propensity variables should be the same for both the Web sample and the reference sample. The traditional goal to find a logistic regression model that fits the data well is therefore not necessarily useful. Instead, the researcher should verify whether balance was achieved. Preliminary research seems to indicate that the propensity adjustment reduces the bias considerably but does not remove it altogether for all outcome variables. One direction for future research is to find out which set of propensity variables works best for which set of outcomes. Of additional note, propensity scoring has also been applied to adjust for nonresponse bias when data are available for both nonrespondents and respondents of a survey.

Matthias Schonlau

See also Convenience Sampling; Nonresponse Bias; Post-Stratification; Probability Sample; Propensity Scores; Psychographic Measures

Further Readings

Schonlau, M., Van Soest, A., Kapteyn, A., Couper, M., & Winter, J. (in press). Selection bias in Web surveys and the use of propensity scores. *Sociological Methods and Research.*

Schonlau, M., Zapert, K., Payne Simon, L., Sanstad, K., Marcus, S., Adams, J., et al. (2004). A comparison between a propensity weighted Web survey and an identical RDD survey. *Social Science Computer Review, 22*(1), 128–138.

PROPORTIONAL ALLOCATION TO STRATA

Proportional allocation is a procedure for dividing a sample among the strata in a stratified sample survey. A *sample survey* collects data from a population in order to estimate population characteristics. A *stratified sample* selects separate samples from subgroups of the population, which are called "strata" and can often increase the accuracy of survey results. In order to implement stratified sampling, it is necessary to be able to divide the population at least implicitly into strata before sampling. Given a budget that allows gathering data on n subjects or a budget amount $B, there is a need to decide how to allocate the resources for data gathering to the strata. Three factors typically affect the distribution of resources to the strata: (1) the population size, (2) the variability of values, and (3) the data collection per unit cost in the strata. One also can have special interest in characteristics of some particular strata that could affect allocations.

Assuming the goal of the survey is to estimate a total or average for the entire population, the variability of values are not known to differ substantially by strata, and data collection costs are believed to be roughly equal by strata, one could consider allocating sample size to strata proportional to strata population sizes. That is, if there are H strata with population size N_h in stratum h, $h = 1, 2, \ldots, H$, and one can afford to collect data on n units, then the proportional allocation sample size for stratum h is $n_h = n(N_h/N)$, where $N = \sum_{h=1}^{H} N_h$ is the total population size. As a result, strata with large numbers of units in their populations receive more sample, whereas small strata receive less sample. With roughly equal per-unit data collection costs, a budget amount $B corresponds to a total sample size n. If the n_h's are not integer, then one must round the numbers to integers for sample selection. Rounding does not necessarily move all values to the closest integer for all strata, because the total sample size n needs to be allocated.

Suppose you want to collect data on students at a large public university. Questions of interest could be hours worked per week, amount expended per semester on textbooks, amount of time spent eating at restaurants in a week, number of trips to the airport in a semester, and whether or not friends smoke cigarettes. The students selected for the survey could be contacted via their university email addresses and asked to complete an online Web survey. A survey can be preferable to contacting every student, because better efforts can often be made for a sample to encourage response and check data quality. Administrative records contain college year designations (1st, 2nd, 3rd, 4th) for each student in the target population; college years can be used as strata. Suppose the total sample size is allowed to be 1,600 students. Equal allocation to strata would sample 400 students from each year. Table 1 presents proportional allocations of students to the four strata based on total enrollments by college year; these numbers are similar to 2006 enrollment at Iowa State University. As can be seen in the table, the stratum of fourth-year students receives the largest sample ($n_4 = 503$), where as the stratum of second-year students receives the smallest ($n_2 = 324$).

Proportional allocation of the sample in stratified sampling can yield more precise estimates of means (e.g., average amount spent on textbooks) and totals (e.g., number of trips to the airport) of characteristics in the population than *equal allocation* to strata with the sample total sample size (n) when strata are of very unequal sizes. In fact, if data collection costs per unit and the variance of values are the same across strata, then proportional allocation is optimal under *stratified simple random sampling*. Suppose 1,600 students are to be chosen from the population for a survey, and the college (Agriculture, Business, Design, Engineering, Human Sciences, and Liberal Arts & Sciences) of enrollment within the university is used to stratify students into groups. Table 2 presents an example for which some strata would have much larger or smaller samples than others.

Table 1 Proportional allocation of 1,600 students to four strata defined by college year

Year	Population Size: Total Enrollment	Sample Size: $n_h = nN_h/N$	Sample Size: Rounded Values
First	5,000	399.4	399
Second	4,058	324.1	324
Third	4,677	373.6	374
Fourth	6,296	502.9	503
Total	20,031	1,600.0	1,600

Table 2   Proportional allocation of 1,600 students to six strata defined by college

College	Population Size: Total Enrollment	Sample Size: $n_h = nN_h/N$	Sample Size: Rounded Values	Sample Size: Adjusted to 200 Minimum
Agriculture	2,488	198.7	199	200
Business	3,247	259.4	259	246
Design	1,738	138.8	139	200
Engineering	4,356	347.9	348	331
Human Sciences	2,641	211.0	211	201
Liberal Arts & Sciences	5,561	444.2	444	422
Total	20,031	1,600.0	1,600	1,600

If variances in strata are quite different or costs of data collection vary by strata, then one could consider *optimal allocation* and probably produce more precise estimates of population means and totals. If one plans to make inferential statements about all strata separately, then it might be a good idea to adjust sample sizes to be closer to equal than suggested by proportional allocation. The right-most column of Table 2 presents a compromise between proportional and equal allocation to strata. The minimum sample size per stratum was increased to 200, and the remaining sample sizes were ratio adjusted so that the full sample size is still 1,600. In this example, one could, of course, stratify by college year and college simultaneously, thereby producing 24 strata.

Michael D. Larsen

See also Disproportionate Allocation to Strata; Optimal Allocation; Stratified Sampling

Further Readings

Cochran, W. G. (1977). *Sampling techniques* (3rd ed.). New York: Wiley.
Kish, L. (1965). *Survey sampling*. New York: Wiley.
Lohr, S. L. (1999). *Sampling: Design and analysis*. Pacific Grove, CA: Duxbury.

PROTECTION OF HUMAN SUBJECTS

In most instances, survey research requires human participation and the self-report of opinions, facts, behaviors, and/or experiences. Some survey research also requires the collection of physiological samples. It may also involve the use of administrative data if the researcher has access to Social Security records, health records, military service information, and the like. Past abuses of human research participants have led to the development of a set of ethical guidelines to which researchers must adhere in order to protect human subjects from physical, mental, and emotional harm.

Historical Perspective on the Abuse of Human Subjects in Research

One of the earliest examples of the abuse of human subjects was the infamous Tuskegee Syphilis Study that was conducted from 1932 to 1972 in Macon County, Alabama. The purpose of the study was to observe the progression of untreated syphilis in black men. A total of 399 black men with syphilis and 201 black men without it were recruited. The men were told that they were receiving treatment when in fact they were not. In addition, the physicians in the county were told not to treat these men since it would interfere with the study. When penicillin became the established treatment for syphilis in 1947, the treatment was withheld from the men in the study known to have syphilis. The men and the course of their illnesses were documented and observed until they died. Their spouses caught the disease from them and children were born infected with it. Yet their diagnosis and treatment was withheld. Finally, a front-page article in *The New York Times* exposed what was going on, and the public became outraged. Consequently, a panel was appointed by the Department of Health and Scientific Affairs to review the study. Although the men had freely consented to participate, the panel discovered that they were never told of the considerable risks to their health and to the health of their families. In October 1972, the panel advised that the study be discontinued because the men had not been told about the risk of physical harm, which was necessary for the men to have given informed consent. One month later, the Assistant Secretary of Health and Scientific Affairs announced that the study was ended. The termination of the study was followed by a lawsuit brought by the National Association for the Advancement of Colored People (NAACP), which resulted in an award of $9 million to the participants as well as free medical care and burials for those who were still living.

A second example of the abuse of human research participants was the Willowbrook Hepatitis Study that was carried out from 1963 through 1966 at the Willowbrook State School of New York. Here, mentally disabled individuals were intentionally infected with hepatitis in order to study the disease and a possible treatment, gamma globulin. These individuals were all children who by reason of their mental status could not legally give consent themselves. Parents who wished to have their children admitted to the institution were told that there was no room for their child unless they agreed to have the child participate in the hepatitis studies. The investigators claimed that most of the children at Willowbrook would eventually become infected with hepatitis anyway. The public became outraged that the parents and their children were forced to enter the hepatitis research program or else admission to the institution would be denied.

There were also numerous studies that involved radiation in order to discover its effects; however, in some of these studies participants were not warned about the potential risk of cancer. For example, some of the studies involved prison inmates at Oregon State Prison and Washington State Prison who received radiation to the testicles but were not warned of the risk of testicular cancer; these studies took place from 1963 to 1971. In the late 1940s, the impact of radiation on fetal development was studied at the Vanderbilt University; 800 pregnant women were exposed to radiation. In 1998, the participants were awarded a large settlement.

In addition, there were the atrocities committed by Nazis such as Dr. Josef Mengele at Auschwitz, who was infamous for his "research" on twins. For example, the Nazis prized blonde hair and blue eyes; therefore, a major focus of Mengele's work was to experiment with changing hair and eye color. On Mengele's orders, chemicals were put in children's eyes with eye drops or needles in an attempt to change their eye color. Afterward, the children could not see for several days. Since the children were incarcerated in a death camp, they had no choice but to submit to the painful experiments.

These cases highlight a number of the issues that needed to be addressed in the creation of a code to protect human research participants.

Codes of Research Ethics

The first attempt at a code of research ethics was the Nuremberg Code, and it was created in response to the war crimes committed by the Nazis. The 10 points of the Nuremberg Code are paraphrased in Table 1.

Table 1   Summary of the Nuremberg Code

1. Participation must be completely voluntary and the participant must have the legal capacity to consent. The person must be fully informed of the nature and duration of the research.

2. The research must be of benefit to society and the findings cannot be obtained by any other method.

3. The research should have a sound foundation in animal research and with knowledge of the history of the problem under study.

4. Unnecessary physical or psychological harm must be avoided.

5. No research shall be performed that may cause death or disability to the participant.

6. The degree of risk must not exceed the expected benefit of the research.

7. Proper plans must be made and adequate facilities must be provided to protect the research participant from even remote possibilities of injury, death, or disability.

8. Research may only be conducted by highly qualified, trained scientists.

9. During the research, the participant is free to stop participating at any time.

10. The researcher must be prepared to end the experiment if it becomes clear to the researcher that continuing will harm the participants.

This laid the foundation for most of the current ethical standards in research. The American Psychological Association (APA) began writing ethical guidelines in 1947, and its first ethical code was published in 1953. Numerous revisions of the APA ethical guidelines for the protection of human participants have taken place over the years, and the latest revision occurred in 2002. Note that APA guidelines address more issues than the Nuremberg Code did; one difference is the issue of research with children who are not yet old enough to give legal consent to participate. Table 2 provides a summary of the current APA ethical guidelines for the protection of human participants.

Carla R. Scanlan

See also Certificate of Confidentiality; Debriefing; Deception; Ethical Principles; Informed Consent; Voluntary Participation

---

Table 2 Summary of the 2002 American Psychological Association guidelines for the protection of human research participants

1. Research proposals submitted to institutional review boards (IRB) must contain accurate information. Upon approval, researchers cannot make changes without seeking approval from the IRB.

2. Informed consent is usually required and includes: (a) the purpose of the research, expected duration, and procedures; (b) the right to decline to participate and to withdraw once the study has begun; (c) the potential consequences of declining or withdrawing; (d) any potential risks, discomfort, or adverse effects; (e) any potential research benefits; (f) the limits of confidentiality; (g) incentives for participation; (h) whom to contact for questions about the research and participants' rights. Researchers provide opportunity for the participants to ask questions and receive answers.

3. When research is conducted that includes experimental treatments, participants shall be so informed at the beginning of the study of (a) the experimental nature of the treatment, (b) the services that will or will not be available to the control group(s) if appropriate; (c) the means by which assignment to treatment or control group is made; (d) available treatment alternative if the person does not want to participate or withdraws after the study has begun; (e) compensation for costs of participating.

4. Informed consent shall be obtained when voices or images are recorded as data unless (a) the research consists only of naturalistic observations taking place in public places and the recording is not anticipated to cause harm; or (b) the research design includes deception, and consent for the use of the recording is obtained during debriefing.

5. When psychologists conduct research with clients/patients, students, or subordinates as participants, steps must be taken to protect the participants from adverse consequences of declining or withdrawing from participation. When research participation is a course requirement, or an opportunity to earn extra credit, an alternative choice of activity is available.

6. Informed consent may not be required where (a) research would not be reasonably expected to cause distress or harm and (b) involves (i) the study of normal educational practices, curricula, or classroom management methods in educational settings; (ii) only anonymous questionnaires, archival research, or naturalistic observations that would not place participants at risk of civil or criminal liability nor damage financial standing, employability, or reputation, and confidentiality is protected; or (iii) the study of organizational factors conducted in the workplace poses no risk to participants' employability and confidentiality is preserved.

7. Psychologists make reasonable efforts to avoid offering excessive or inappropriate financial or other inducement for research participation that would result in coercion.

8. Deception in research shall be used only if it is justified by the study's significant prospective scientific value and nondeceptive alternatives are not feasible. Deception shall not be used if it will cause physical pain or severe emotional distress.

9. (a) Participants shall be offered promptly supplied information about the outcome of the study; (b) if delay or withholding of the study outcome is necessary, reasonable measures must be taken to reduce the risk of harm; (c) when researchers realize that research procedures have harmed a participant, they take reasonable steps to minimize the harm.

Further Readings

The Belmont Report: http://www.hhs.gov/ohrp/
humansubjects/guidance/belmont.htm

Bordens, K. S., & Abbott, B. B. (2005). *Research design and
methods* (6th ed.). New York: McGraw-Hill.

Cases of Unethical Research: http://www.clarion.edu/
academic/adeptt/bpcluster/cases.htm

Institutional Review Board Guidebook: http://www.hhs.gov/
ohrp/irb/irb_appendices.htm

Lagnado, L. M., & Dekel, S. C. (1991). *Children of the
flames*. New York: Morrow.

The Tuskegee Timeline: http://www.cdc.gov/nchstp/od/
tuskegee/time.htm

Willowbrook Hepatitis Study: http://hstraining.orda.ucsb.edu/
willowbrook.htm

PROXY RESPONDENT

If a respondent reports on the properties or activities of another person or group of persons (e.g., an entire household or a company), the respondent is said to be a *proxy* respondent. In some cases, proxy responses may be a part of the design of the survey. In the U.S. Current Population Survey, for example, a single responsible adult is asked to report for all members of the household 14 years of age or older. In many surveys, adults are asked to report for children. In other cases, proxy responses are used only when there is a particular reason that the targeted person cannot report. In household travel surveys, for example, data are typically sought directly from each adult member of the household. Only if a particular adult is on extended travel, has language or medical difficulties that would interfere with responding, or some similar reason, would a proxy respondent be used.

Since a proxy response is treated the same as a self-reported response, an obvious benefit of allowing proxy responses is to increase the response rate. If the targeted person is unavailable for the entire survey period, the only way to get a response may be to accept a proxy response. In surveys in which information is sought about all members of a household, the lack of a response from one member, if only self-reported data are permitted, could jeopardize the utility of the information from the others.

Not allowing proxy responding also may increase nonresponse bias. Those unavailable to respond for themselves are more likely to be on long trips, in the hospital, or away at college, and so on, than those who are available. If these factors are related to the purpose of the survey, then the use of proxy respondents should be considered.

Because the proxy respondent will have a different perspective and set of memories than the targeted person, proxy responding can be expected to affect measurement error in the survey. Proxy respondents may record fewer less salient events (e.g., smaller purchases or short trips) than respondents reporting for themselves. On the other hand, there are instances when proxy responses may be more accurate than reports from self-respondents, for example, the main record keeper in a household reporting for other household members.

Some survey items do not lend themselves to proxy responding because measurement error is apt to be particularly great. A noteworthy case is attitudinal items. Even if the proxy respondent knows the targeted person extremely well, the attitudes of the proxy respondent will likely be confounded with the attitudes of the targeted person in the responses.

Michael P. Cohen

See also Eligibility; Measurement Error; Nonresponse; Nonresponse Bias; Respondent-Related Error; Response Rates; Unit; Unit Nonresponse

Further Readings

Groves, R. M. (1989). *Survey errors and survey costs*.
New York: Wiley.

PSEUDO-POLLS

The term *pseudo-poll* refers to a number of practices that may appear to be legitimate polls but are not. A legitimate poll uses scientific sampling to learn about the opinions and behaviors of a population. Pseudo-polls include unscientific (and thus, unreliable) attempts to measure opinions and behaviors as well as other practices that look like polls but are designed for purposes other than legitimate research.

A variety of techniques are used to conduct unscientific assessments of opinion, all of which are considered pseudo-polls. These can be used by media and other organizations as an inexpensive way to measure public opinion and get the audience involved. However, they are very problematic from a data quality standpoint and should not be referred to as polls.

One common approach is the *call-in poll*. This is a method used when audience members or newspaper readers are invited to call a phone number and register their opinions. This is also to referred as a *SLOP*, a term coined by survey researcher Norman Bradburn, which stands for "self-selected listener opinion poll." A similar technique is used by newspapers and magazines that publish questionnaires and ask their readers to fill them out and mail them in. A newer approach, called a *log-in poll*, is where Web sites post questions for people to click on to register their opinions, with the aggregate results being displayed instantly.

A major problem with all of these types of pseudo-polls is that the participants are entirely self-selected. Only those people who tuned in to that particular broadcast at that time or read that newspaper or went to that Web site can be included. Further, those who make the effort to participate are often very different from those in the audience who do not. Those who participate are often more interested in the topic or feel very strongly about it.

Another big problem with pseudo-polls is that they are open to manipulation by those with a vested interest in the topic. With call-in polls there is no limit on the number of calls that can be placed, so people can (and do) call multiple times and groups can set up elaborate operations to flood the phone line in support of their point of view. Manipulation is also a problem with Internet log-in polls. For example, multiple clicks can be possible, and it is common for political campaigns to direct their supporters to Web sites that have log-in polls to boost their position's and/or candidate's standing.

For these reasons, these types of pseudo-polls often produce biased results and should be ignored. Legitimate pollsters who are concerned with poll accuracy avoid these types of bias by selecting respondents using probability sampling techniques. Although survey researchers know that these pseudo-polls should not be taken seriously, many members of the public do not make a distinction between these and the real thing. In fact, pseudo-polls may be incorrectly seen as even more credible than real polls because they often have much larger sample sizes.

There are other types of pseudo-polls for which the purpose is not opinion collection. One of these is called a "push poll." This is not a poll at all, but rather a sneaky and unethical telemarketing trick used by some candidates' political campaigns. Large numbers of people are called and are asked to participate in what appears to them to be a legitimate poll. In the process people are told negative, often false, things about the opposing candidates. The purpose is to shift or "push" people's opinions about the candidates rather than to collect data.

Sales and fundraising calls designed to look like polls are other types of unethical pseudo-poll not designed to collect data. SUGing, which stands for "selling under the guise" of survey research, takes people through what appears to be a legitimate poll to try to get them to purchase something. The information obtained in the purported survey later may be used to hone the ultimate sales pitch.

FRUGing is similar and stands for "fundraising under the guise" of survey research. Respondents are administered a bogus survey whose purpose is to obtain donations for the given cause. Often the questionnaire is targeted to those with a certain point of view, and the question wording is biased in favor of that point of view in an effort to increase the respondent's chances of contributing.

The purpose of legitimate polling and survey research is to provide accurate information about a population's opinions and behaviors. Call-in polls and similar efforts using mail, Internet, or fax may attempt to provide this information but fail because the procedures they employ yield biased data. Other types of pseudo-polls, such as push polls and SUGing and FRUGing efforts, are deceptive practices designed to manipulate people and are condemned by professional survey research associations.

Daniel M. Merkle

See also Call-In Polls; 800 Poll; FRUGing; Log-In Polls; 900 Poll; Probability Sample; Push Poll; Self-Selected Listener Opinion Poll (SLOP); Self-Selected Sample; Self-Selection Bias; SUGing; Survey Ethics; Telemarketing

Further Readings

Gawiser, S. R., & Witt, G. E. (2002). *20 questions journalists should ask about poll results*. Retrieved June 12, 2008, from http://www.ncpp.org/?q=node/4

Traugott, M. W., & Lavrakas, P. J. (2008). *The voter's guide to election polls* (4th ed.). Lanham, MD: Rowman & Littlefield.

Psychographic Measure

A psychographic measure is a variable that represents a personal characteristic of an individual that is not a physical trait, as are demographic measures (age, gender, height, etc.). Rather, psychographic variables include personality traits, lifestyle preferences or interests, values or beliefs, and attitudes or opinions.

Because psychographics are not directly observable, as are many demographics, nor do they have a "factual" basis as do demographics, their measurement is less precise. Surveys are routinely used to measure psychographics, and they can serve as powerful independent variables in helping explain many dependent variables of interest. For example, in political science, understanding why people vote for the presidential candidates they do is heavily explained by psychographics such as party affiliation, socioeconomic class, religion, veteran status, sexual orientation, and other values, beliefs, and attitudes.

Psychographic characteristics often are measured by scales formed from a set of Likert items in which a series of statements are made and the respondent indicates the extent to which she or her agrees or disagrees with each statement. Factor analysis and other scaling techniques can then be used to identify the most reliable set of items to make up a scale for a particular psychographic measure.

Including psychographic measures in a questionnaire often increases the richness of one's survey database because they often are powerful predictors of other variables of interest. Psychographics are used routinely by market researchers. There are myriad scales that measure various psychographics; many are in the public domain, while others are highly proprietary and are quite expensive to access. In the latter case, many companies have devised and validated proprietary psychographic scales that require a researcher to send her or his raw survey data to the company. Then, for a fee, the company "scores" the raw data, thereby creating the psychographic variables for each respondent the researcher has in her or his data set.

Paul J. Lavrakas

See also Attitudes; Demographic Measure; Likert Scale; Opinions

Further Readings

Goldberg, M. (1976). Identifying relevant psychographic segments: How specifying product functions can help. *The Journal of Consumer Research, 3*(3), 163–169.

Kahle, L., & Chiagouris, L. (1997). *Values, lifestyles, and psychographics.* Mahwah, NJ: Lawrence Erlbaum.

PUBLIC OPINION

Public opinion is one of the oldest and most widely invoked concepts in the social sciences and has many meanings and controversies associated with it. The concept of public opinion has evolved during the past three millennia as the notion of democracy evolved. Public opinion plays a central role in democracy, and, as such, the ability to "measure" public opinion accurately has become a critical endeavor for modern-day democracies.

Historical and Philosophical Background

The concept has origins in early political philosophy dating to the writings of Plato, who was mainly concerned about the mercurial nature of crowds and the problems associated with direct democracy. Aristotle is often cited on the point of the collective wisdom of the group being wiser than individuals', but he was not in general a reliable advocate for rationality of the common people.

The controversies about the competence and rationality of people continued throughout the history of Western philosophy, through the Middle Ages to the present day. From the perspective of our contemporary representative democracies, public opinion is considered with reverence as "the will of the people." But such representations are often accompanied by doubts about the extent of the public's competencies, levels of knowledge, ability to weigh contradictory information, and level of emotion.

The origin of public opinion is often portrayed as an achievement of Western culture and civilization, coming together in word and deed on the eve of the French Revolution. Informed people met frequently in the upper-class salons of the day to discuss public affairs. Records of this era are clear about the frequency and quality of these conversations and their importance in influencing events in that time and place. Coming together were the developments in popular information, regular venues for conversation and deliberation of the issues of the day, and people self-consciously interested in being a part of a public. Jean-Jacques Rousseau, the philosopher, and Jacques Necker, the French finance minister, were setting out their philosophical ideas justifying public opinion and its relationship to governance as well as coining the phrase *public opinion*.

The true origins of public opinion as we understand it today are more properly attributed to 17th-century England than to 18th-century France. England was a country profoundly influenced by the Reformation, which set off a burst of creativity in the printing industry. This led to economic and political conditions that produced a wide range of printed products, such as pamphlets and early newspapers, for a wide swath of society. England had a vigorous popular press and an egalitarian pub culture in which people of many diverse classes, informed by the pamphlets and early newspapers, met and discussed issues of the day. Framing the contemporary issues and providing concrete avenues for political activity was a vibrant system of petitions. These petitions, which were inexpensively produced and reproduced in large numbers by the commercial printers of the day, were debated in pubs across the country. Signed petitions representing the outcomes of these conversations were presented at court. Kings and their advisers for their own reasons felt duty-bound to reply to these petitions. This was not the elite salon culture of 18th-century France, but a broad-based social movement. English culture lacked the eloquence of Rousseau's philosophical arguments and the concise elegance of the French phrase *l'opinion publique*. But English society developed a working system of public opinion, based on a system of news and popular information, about a century before the French.

The American Revolution was influenced indirectly and directly by the experiences of both England and France. The American experiment in democracy settled on representative democracy under a constitution that guaranteed and safeguarded fundamental human rights of freedom of speech, press, petition, and religion. Also recognized were the rights of assembly and limited government power over individuals, establishing the principle of innocent until proven guilty to protect individuals from state power. The constitution also established a system of checks and balances among the various branches of government and procedures that empowered people but kept this power carefully controlled and subject to administrative and judicial approvals at various stages. This was the American solution to the issue of competence of public opinion. The republic was founded on the natural rights of people to self-govern, but governance itself was accomplished through layers of representatives

under a constitution that protected fundamental liberties and human rights.

What Is Public Opinion?

Public opinion deals with opinions that people are willing to share with others, in contrast to their private opinions. Thus, communication emerges as a central variable in public opinion. Opinions formed but not shared are considered private or perhaps "secret opinions." Public opinion derives its force from people's willingness to express preferences "in public" and even to offer dissent from established policies. It is intimately related to issues of governance, and through public opinion people have asserted the right to self-government. This suggests that public opinion is primarily about "bottom-up communication" from citizens to their government. To the extent that government prevents the flow of such information or does not allow these claims, public opinion does not exist. The historian Richard J. Evans argued in his book *The Third Reich in Power* that public opinion was effectively extinguished in Germany in the 1930s by a series of repressive measures aimed at the news media, rival political parties, and even private conversation by Hitler's government. This suggests that public opinion cannot be just a collection of individual, privately held opinions.

However, if it is not just the aggregation of individual private opinions, what else can it be? Rousseau wrote of a concept he called "the General Will" or will of the nation. Some understand this as public opinion, but they are not synonymous. General Will is a highly abstract and mystical notion of a kind of supra-individual "mind of the nation" supposedly based on fully informed, rational thinking in the public's best interest. This concept was used to justify repression of dissenters during the French Revolution, and a century later arguably formed the basis for totalitarian regimes' control of people against their individual will. Rousseau himself contrasted the General Will with a more mathematical concept of a majority vote of the people, that is, as a result of an imaginary election in which individuals participated.

Gabriel Tarde, a criminologist, was also an early social theorist who was careful to explicitly link the emerging mass medium of newspapers to interpersonal communication and the development of the idea of a rational public. Tarde was profoundly concerned with both mass communication as able to channel what he called "currents of opinions" through the literate population without mass meetings and crowds intervening. Tarde noted the conditions for a "public" as being a group of readers—not just scholars—dispersed across a wide territory who were joined together by their shared thoughts on certain topics that were created by their reading of the same news reports. Tarde thus inextricably linked the public and the institution of journalism.

In the early 1990s, pioneering social psychologist Charles Horton Cooley defined *public opinion* not as the "mere aggregation of opinion" but as a "social product," that is, a result of communication and reciprocal influence. Cooley wrote an extensive treatise on his theory of public opinion in which he made clear that it was the product of coordinated communication in which people give time and attention to studying a problem individually. A nation can be said to have a form of public opinion when individuals must take into consideration their own ideas but also fresh ideas that flow from others engaged in thinking about the same topics. The outcome of the process for Cooley was not agreement but "maturity and stability of thought" that resulted from sustained attention and discussion about a topic. In other words, people might not agree after deliberation more than they did before, but their differences after careful consideration are better thought out and less changeable. Cooley believed that after such deliberation, people would know what they really think about a topic as well as what others around them think. To Cooley, this was the important difference between true opinion and simply one's casual impression. Today, we would refer to this as "opinion quality."

James Bryce was an early theorist of public opinion whose views, from the late 1880s, are of particular importance because of their influence on George Gallup, who did more than anyone in his era to bring together survey research, public opinion, and democracy. Bryce theorized that the history of democracy was best explained by stages in which political regimes took public opinion seriously. The first stage reflects systems in which public opinion is theoretically acknowledged as the basis of governance but the public is passive and allows a dominant group to exercise authority. The second stage moves theory into practice, such as when the early United States adopted a constitution built on the principle of the consent of the governed and the people begin to exercise power. The third stage reflects public opinion

through regular, periodic elections in which people can shape government's direction by their votes. But Bryce acknowledged that voting was an imprecise way of forming public opinion and communicating it to the government. The fourth stage, according to Bryce, involved continuous monitoring of public opinion without the filtering of representatives or voting. The result would be popular sovereignty that no longer needed voting. Bryce's fourth stage was purely theoretical, however, largely because there was no practical way to achieve such continuous monitoring, and at the time he was writing he was doubtful such a process could ever be carried out in practice.

Gallup believed survey research and the resulting science of public polling were the tools to bring Bryce's understanding of the ultimate stage of democracy into existence, although he was careful to say that the purpose of polls was not to sabotage representative government but rather to provide "technical assistance" that would supplement and enhance the work of representatives. As Gallup explained, accurate public opinion polls would replace informal soundings of public preferences with a systematic, scientific set of procedures for knowing what people's opinions and preferences were. Thus, it is hard to overestimate Gallup's influence on contemporary thinking about public opinion, how it is measured, and its intimate relationship to survey research in contemporary life. Although there are many research tools available to provide information about public opinion, survey research is by far the most dominant, and Gallup was a leading figure in the development of the survey research industry.

Problems of Public Opinion and Its Measurement

Contemporary democracies measure their successes in various ways, chief among them on the nature and breadth of the population that constitutes the polity. Other measures include the equal treatment of all members of the society, the level of effective consultation or voice that citizens have influencing government actions, and the degree of legal protection citizens have from governmental intrusions or abuses. All of these criteria have something to do with public opinion. In fact, each democratic attribute raises significant questions about public opinion, at least indirectly. Some key questions in the study of public opinion through the ages are presented in the following subsections that directly or indirectly relate to the nature of democratic systems.

Who Is "the Public" and How Representative Are Opinion Polls?

Does the electorate include men and women? Are minorities included proportional to their numbers in the population? Although at the time of the American Revolution the public was defined narrowly to exclude women and African American slaves, full citizenship rights were eventually extended to all citizens and the right to vote for all guaranteed. However, even nowadays not all people are equally likely to respond to public opinion polls and surveys (e.g., opinion polls typically have differential nonresponse among the less educated strata of society), which therefore begs the question of how well opinion polls can measure public opinion in a society.

How Competent Are the People to Live Up to the Requirements of Democratic Systems?

This is perhaps the oldest and most important question about public opinion, and it has been asked since ancient times. Some of the early social scientists took a very dim view of the competency of public opinion. Gustav LeBon, one of the early writers of mass psychology, was a famous skeptic who took a dim view of "popular capabilities." Walter Lippmann was skeptical of the capabilities of public opinion. His influential books, *Public Opinion* and *The Phantom Public*, make the point clearly that democratic theory requires too much of ordinary people. Furthermore, the press, in Lippmann's view, was not adequate to the task of public enlightenment as required in democratic society.

When the issue of public competence is raised, it is useful to determine whether the supposed incompetence is attributed to inherent limitations of people, or is it more properly limited to the public's level of literacy and educational attainment? Other possibilities include the type and amount of communication that is available to the masses, the role models and values conveyed to the public about expectations related to civic virtues, whether the public actually has the requisite skills such as how to participate in dialogue, debate, and deliberation of political choices. Lippmann's chief critic was the philosopher and educational reformer

John Dewey. His 1927 book, *The Public and Its Problems*, argued that the public was fully capable but that too many people lacked the required levels of communication and the quality of public media needed for informed decision making.

Do Majorities Exercise Tyranny Over Minorities?

Tyranny of the majority is a third enduring problem of public opinion. The fear is that people whose views are in the majority will use their power to oppress those holding minority views. This raises questions of civil liberties such as the protections of freedom of expression and assembly as well as protections for speakers from retribution. There has emerged in the literature of public opinion over the years considerable attention to social pressures that hinder people's willingness to speak their mind on controversial issues. These constraints range from people's unwillingness to be out of step with others to real fear of repercussions or reprisals from employers or government officials.

Are People Too Gullible in the Face of Persuasion?

Susceptibility to persuasion has emerged as a key issue for public opinion in the media age, since if the mass public is too gullible in the face of propaganda, the competence of the masses cannot be assured. Much of the vast literature on media effects is at least to some extent guided by this concern. In addition to the standard mass persuasion literature, newer work on framing raises the issue in a new way. Framing effects have been shown to be very powerful in influencing people's reactions to issues and political figures, although the vast majority of framing effects studies are performed in laboratories and use stimuli that are carefully balanced in ways that natural political discourse is not.

Opinion Quality and Public Opinion Measurement

One of the newest questions in contemporary public opinion research harkens back to the oldest literature on the role of conversation and deliberation in helping to create fully informed citizens with well-thought-out, stable opinions. To address questions of opinion quality, a number of measurement approaches have been advanced in recent years, ranging from the Choice Questionnaire to Deliberative Polls and to sophisticated experiments incorporating opportunities for people to discuss and deliberate before having their opinions measured.

Choice Questionnaire

Many issues facing policymakers involve complex scientific or policy information or difficult concepts about which the public has not had the opportunity to learn. In such circumstances, standard polling will provide unsatisfactory results, since only a tiny portion will have opinions and most will say they have never thought of the questions. Long sets of questions about which people have no experience will not be tolerated well by most survey respondents. The Choice Questionnaire is a type of survey that attempts to incorporate opportunities for the public to learn about the issue being surveyed before questions are asked. This must be done in a manner sensitive to the nature of the framing of the alternatives so that that the information presented does not result in decision bias.

Deliberative Polls

As described by James F. Fishkin, deliberative polls are a type of research in which randomly selected individuals are invited to participate in in-person events during which they will be presented with various oral and written briefing materials about topics to be considered. Participants are surveyed about their views on the topics when they are sampled and again at the end of the process. After considering the information presented, the participants are divided into groups for discussion and deliberation about the topics. No control groups are typically specified for such gatherings, but some investigators have effectively utilized control groups to be able to investigate the effects from the briefing materials separately from the effects of deliberation. As discussed extensively in the vast literature of deliberative democracy, deliberation is generally believed to have beneficial effects on quality opinion formation because opinions formed under conditions of deliberation will presumably have been carefully considered, be based on considerations of relevant facts, and have resisted challenges by others. This is thought to lead to more stable opinions that are more resistant to change than opinions formed in less rigorous circumstances.

Gerald M. Kosicki

See also Attitude; Attitude Stability; Deliberative Poll; Differential Nonresponse; Issue Definition (Framing); Gallup, George; Opinions; Poll; Public Opinion Research

Further Readings

Baker, K. M. (1990). *Inventing the French Revolution.* Cambridge, UK: Cambridge University Press.

Barone, M. (2007). *Our first revolution: The remarkable British upheaval that inspired America's founding fathers.* New York: Crown.

Bishop, G. F. (2005). *The illusion of public opinion.* Boulder, CO: Rowman & Littlefield.

Bryce, J. (1888/1995). *The American commonwealth.* Indianapolis, IN: Liberty Fund.

Cooley, C. H. (1909/2005). *Social organization.* New Brunswick, NJ: Transaction.

Dewey, J. (1927). *The public and its problems.* Athens, OH: Swallow Press.

Evans, R. J. (2005). *The Third Reich in power.* New York: Penguin.

Fishkin, J. S. (1995). *The voice of the people: Public opinion and democracy.* New Haven, CT: Yale University Press.

Gallup, G., & Rae, S. F. (1940). *The pulse of democracy: The public opinion poll and how it works.* New York: Simon & Schuster.

LeBon, G. (1896/1982). *The crowd: A study of the popular mind.* Marietta, GA: Cherokee.

Lippmann, W. (1922). *Public opinion.* New York: Free Press.

Lippmann, W. (1927/2004). *The phantom public.* New Brunswick, NJ: Transaction.

Neijens, P. (1987). *The choice questionnaire: Design and evaluation of an instrument for collecting informed opinions of a population.* Amsterdam: Free University Press.

Price, V., & Neijens, P. (1997). Opinion quality in public opinion research. *International Journal of Public Opinion Research, 9,* 336–360.

Rousseau, J. J. (1762/1997). *The social contract and other later political writings.* Edited by V. Gourevitch. Cambridge, UK: Cambridge University Press.

Sniderman, P. M., & Theriault, S. M. (2004). The structure of political argument and the logic of issue framing. In W. E. Saris & P. M. Sniderman (Eds.), *Studies in public opinion: Attitudes, nonattitudes, measurement error and change* (pp. 93–132). Princeton, NJ: Princeton University Press.

Tarde, G. (1901/1969). The public and the crowd. In T. N. Clark (Ed.), *On communication and social influence: Selected papers* (pp. 277–294). Chicago: University of Chicago Press.

Weissberg, R. (2002). *Polling, policy and public opinion: The case against heeding the "voice of the people."* New York: Palgrave Macmillan.

Zaret, D. (2000). *Origins of democratic culture: Printing, petitions and the public sphere in early modern England.* Princeton, NJ: Princeton University Press.

PUBLIC OPINION QUARTERLY (POQ)

Public Opinion Quarterly (POQ) is the journal of the American Association for Public Opinion Research (AAPOR). Founded in 1937 at Princeton University, the journal is an interdisciplinary publication with contributors from a variety of academic disciplines, government agencies, and commercial organizations. The mission of the journal is to advance the study of public opinion and survey research. At this writing, POQ is the premier journal in this field, with high citation rankings in political science, interdisciplinary social science, and communication.

POQ was originally focused on the impact of the mass media on public opinion and behavior. The conjunction of two developments contributed to the journal's founding: the consolidation of channels of mass communication (at that time, print, motion pictures, and radio) and the growth of social science research on human behavior. The mid-1930s was a time of intense concern about the impact of messages distributed simultaneously to mass audiences. Franklin Roosevelt's "fireside chats," Father Coughlin's radio commentaries, and Adolf Hitler's speeches from Nuremburg were exemplars of the new phenomenon of a single persuasive voice reaching millions of people across the spectrum of society at the same time. This era also saw the consolidation of commercial interest in the opportunities presented by the mass media to influence public views and consumer behavior. Advertising and public relations had become significant societal institutions. By this time, too, it was standard for government entities to have press offices and information bureaus to attempt to affect public views of policies and programs. Public opinion polls, commercial ventures supported by media concerns, had become a significant focus of attention in elections and in commercial research. The rationale for POQ, presented in the editorial foreword to the first issue, was that mass opinion had become a major

societal force whose genesis, shifting trends, and effects needed careful scientific study.

Those interested in the study of public opinion included academics across a range of fields—political science, psychology, sociology—as well as researchers employed in government and commercial organizations. POQ was established as a meeting place for these varied interests. Although the journal was housed at Princeton University and edited by academics at several universities, articles by advertising executives, playwrights, government ministers, and employees of media organizations also were published. Papers were devoted to the study of both elite, opinion-shaping organizations as well as to the understanding of mass opinion. Articles on propaganda could be found alongside papers on new developments in public relations. Descriptions of recent poll findings, examination of polling methods, and commentary on the impact of polls were common features. Thus, the journal combined analysis and critique with how-to lessons on measuring and influencing public opinion. It blended theoretical arguments with applied investigation.

In subsequent decades, POQ's mix of content has remained broadly the same, though the relative size of subject categories has shifted. The societal and technological forces that stimulated interest in the study of public opinion in the 1930s were transformed over time, just as the scholarly world evolved in new directions. The early research focus on channels of mass communication and their impact on mass opinion and behavior gave way by the 1960s to more complex and nuanced conceptualizations of public opinion formation and change. The journal tracked this evolution in articles published by members of Paul Lazarsfeld's Columbia School, including authors such as Elihu Katz and Joseph Klapper. At the same time, the world of social science publishing expanded. Newer journals (e.g., *Journal of Communication, Journal of Advertising, Journal of Advertising Research, Journal of Broadcasting and Electronic Media, Journal of Consumer Research, Journal of Marketing Research, Journal of Public Relations Research, Communication Research, Political Psychology, Political Behavior*) began to publish submissions on mass media effects and public opinion that might once have appeared in POQ.

Articles examining survey methodology, though present in the journal from the first issue, gained greater prominence over time. In the 1930s and

1940s, the focus of many papers was on methods of interviewing, as polling and survey organizations transitioned from the use of mail questionnaires, discredited particularly by the failure of the *Literary Digest* Poll in 1936 to accurately predict the outcome of the presidential election. Interviewer rapport and the match between interviewers and respondents on demographic characteristics were investigated by such scholars as Daniel Katz and Paul Sheatsley. In addition, there was discussion of question design and sampling methods and on the general "failure of the polls" in the 1948 Dewey-Truman election. Methodological concerns beyond the commercial polls were evidenced in Philip Hauser's paper on the design of the 1950 Census and by Hugh Parry and Helen Crossley's classic 1950 examination of response validity in their Denver community survey.

The 1960s brought a focus on survey methods in studies of race that has continued to this day. Papers by Howard Schuman and others on race of interviewer effects were particularly notable. The 1970s and 1980s featured a blossoming of research on survey methods, including the earlier focus on interviewers plus many papers on question wording and order and a major push on mode of interview effects (telephone vs. face-to-face contacts).

The prominence of survey methodology in POQ now routinely incorporates all of the preceding themes, plus sampling, post-survey adjustment, and the always present and increasingly crucial issue of nonresponse. Work on mode of interview now concerns Internet surveys and cellular phones as well as the older landline telephone, face-to-face, and mail varieties. The design of self-administered questionnaires, whether paper or Web based, is undergoing a major examination. The survey contexts in which these methodological studies occur include a wide range of substantive concerns, certainly more than would be conjured up by the term *public opinion*. The increasing output of strong methodological studies has led POQ to expand the number of its pages by 25% and to add a fifth topical issue devoted to some special and important aspect of survey methodology. This issue, in turn, serves as the basis for an annual AAPOR methods workshop. Moving forward, the journal should keep pace with the demand for methodological education.

Peter V. Miller

See also American Association for Public Opinion Research (AAPOR)

Further Readings

Katz, E. (1957). The two-step flow of communication: An up-to-date report on a hypothesis. *Public Opinion Quarterly, 21,* 61–78.

Klapper, J. T. (1957). What we know about the effects of mass communication: The brink of hope. *Public Opinion Quarterly, 21,* 453–474.

Parry, H., & Crossley, H. (1950). Validity of responses to survey questions. *Public Opinion Quarterly, 14,* 61–80.

Public Opinion Quarterly: http://poq.oxfordjournals.org/

Schuman, H., & Converse, J. M. (1971). The effects of black and white interviewers on black responses in 1968. *Public Opinion Quarterly, 35,* 44–68.

PUBLIC OPINION RESEARCH

Public opinion research is an applied social science activity that features prominently in various academic disciplines, including communication, political science, psychology, public policy, and sociology. Public opinion research often has as its goal the quantification and description of preferences of large numbers of people in carefully described geographic areas such as cities, states, or nations. Often the specific time frame under study is particularly important, and typically public opinion is assessed on a recurring basis by firms and organizations specializing in such tasks. Some of these involve media organizations that use the results of public opinion research as the basis for news stories or to comment upon political or social events, policies, and people.

Use of Survey Research to Assess Public Opinion

Most often, public opinion as the object of empirical research is studied using some variation on the methods of survey research. A great deal of emphasis is typically placed on estimating the proportion of the adult or registered voter population holding certain attitudes toward various public affairs topics or evaluations of various public officials. Breakdowns by political party affiliation and various demographics are commonly presented. The accuracy of political polling is often verified by comparisons of poll results to election results. Although that works in an acceptable manner for polls that measure voter intention and are taken close to Election Day, it is less helpful for standard measures of political attitudes, for which there are no real-world indicators.

Much public opinion research is descriptive, that is, it attempts to estimate population parameters of various benchmark indicators such as presidential approval, the state of consumer confidence, and general levels of trust and confidence in government, among other standard questions. Such research is often done on a periodic basis, and recent results are compared to the running time-series of results of similar surveys done by the same organization. An alternative is to round up similar questions taken at the same time by different organizations, but such results are often difficult to compare directly because of slight variations in question wording, sampling and weighting strategies, various field work considerations, and other types of "house effects" that subtly influence survey results. Because such characteristics of polls or surveys tend to be consistent within the organization that produced the poll, it is usually considered most appropriate to compare results at a given time with previous results of the same poll.

Criticisms and Controversies

Public opinion research can be criticized in various ways, including that many results are less than fully useful because people have not considered the questions carefully or do not have well-formed opinions on particular matters and so invent an answer on the fly in response to a survey question. For years this sparked controversy among scholars and users of public opinion polling as the "pseudo-opinion" problem. More recent scholarly work that is informed by cognitive models addresses this by noting that such results may not be quite as serious of a problem as previously believed, largely because people may invent opinions on the spot but they do so using their values, social positions, and demographic background factors that are relatively stable. According to these "online processing models," such responses may have substantial validity even though people have not previously considered the issue.

Another criticism of contemporary public opinion research comes from Daniel Yankelovich, a leading pollster, social critic, and advocate of deliberative democracy who is chairman and cofounder of Public Agenda. In his 1991 book, *Coming to Public Judgment*, Yankelovich said that there is a missing concept in the way surveys currently are used to measure public opinion. What is missing is a way to measure the "quality" of the opinions that people express in surveys. To Yankelovich, high-quality public opinion is stable, consistent, and for which a respondent expressing the opinions recognizes their implications and takes responsibility for them. Since Yankelovich's critique, a number of scholars have conducted research to try to create ways to assess the quality of the opinions expressed by respondents in opinion polls, but to date no best practice has been agreed upon for doing this.

Various technical considerations of public opinion assessment have been controversial in recent years. Telephone polling became the dominant method of opinion assessment by the mid-1980s, replacing in-person interviewing, when landline telephone penetration became nearly universal. Random-digit dialing (RDD) technology combined with computerized programs that automate dialing and many other aspects of survey questionnaire administration revolutionized public opinion assessment and drove costs lower. However, other technological trends have continued to chip away at the dominance of telephone surveys and presented new challenges to methodologists, including the widespread use of automatic telephone answering machines, privacy managers, and caller identification systems, and other ways to screen telephone calls have made gaining survey responses by telephone more difficult and expensive. Patterns of assigning telephone numbers to electronic devices such as fax machines and computers have also made sampling populations by RDD more difficult. The widespread availability of wireless telephone technology and the migration of landline numbers to wireless devices have added complications. As residential consumers have switched from landline telephones to mobile ones, concerns about the adequacy of standard RDD sampling frames have increased. While the survey industry is developing reasonable solutions to these problems as they have appeared, it is not clear that public understanding has kept up. This may cause problems for the credibility of public opinion research among some consumers.

Other Ways to Assess Public Opinion

Public opinion research is nearly synonymous with *survey research*, but the two are not identical. In fact, public opinion can be assessed in many other ways besides survey research, and there are other schools of thought about the problem of public opinion. There are a number of alternatives to survey research, including qualitative interviews such as focus groups, content analysis, historical methods, and mass observation. None has the widespread use, flexibility, or quantitative nature of survey research. However, a popular public opinion textbook argues that survey research alone is an insufficient way to study public opinion and recommends a series of tools including content analysis, focus groups, and controlled laboratory experiments. In fact, considering the whole of public opinion, scholars from diverse disciplines use a wide range of evidence to make claims about public opinion, including focus groups, systematic analysis of mass media content, and other, more exotic tools as described following.

Experiments

In the past several decades, public opinion research has been enriched theoretically by the infusion of cognitive theory. Along with this has come increased interest in using the power of controlled laboratory experiments to help understand the psychological processes by which opinions are formed. Some of the best of these are careful about recruiting more representative samples than often is the case with experimental designs (e.g., subjects from the citizenry at large), but many rely on convenience samples of college students. Experimental studies tend to be particularly useful for understanding the processes by which people incorporate new information, such as media messages, and for building cognitive theory. Moving ideas back and forth between experiments and survey research seems to be a key characteristic of the growing subfield known as *political psychology*. Another use of experimental logic and design also has increased dramatically in recent years due to the advent of computerized data collection systems that make it relatively easy to provide alternative question forms to randomly selected subgroups within the main survey sample. This has facilitated a burgeoning interest in question-wording experiments and has hastened the acceptance of cognitive models into the survey research literature.

Focus Groups

Focus groups are a type of qualitative research tool that relies on moderated group interviews of 6 to 12 people at a time. Typically lasting an hour or two, focus groups are often transcribed or recorded on audio or video for further study. The experience is organized with a carefully planned conversation guide to move people through the various topics under consideration. Moderators must be able to create a nonthreatening tone for the conversation and encourage everyone to share their opinions while preventing talkative participants from dominating the conversation. Focus groups develop a unique group dynamic based on the individuals who participate in any given session, and this needs to be accounted for in any analysis of focus group data. Focus groups are used as aids in designing more systematic survey questionnaires, but they have often proved valuable in helping explain polling results and explore processes uncovered in survey research. The best focus groups typically use random sampling to select participants.

Content Analysis

Content analysis is a systematic, rigorous, and quantitative analysis of printed or visual materials. Because of the intimate connection between public opinion and popular media, many scholars believe that systematic analysis of media content helps provide clues about what material informed public opinion in a given time and place. Carroll J. Glynn and her coauthors argue that media content can reveal valuable evidence about public opinion because their popularity indicates that they "resonate with cultural norms, values and sentiments." For example, Media Tenor, a leading global firm based in Germany, specializes in content analysis of the world's media for a wide range of corporate and government clients.

Historical Methods

There is intense interest in understanding public opinion at key points in history. For historical periods for which there is survey research available, the problems are mainly to locate the original raw data and translate it in such a way that it can be analyzed by contemporary computers and software. Early survey data were produced using certain data coding conventions that are no longer used, including multi-punched data that were designed to accommodate more than 10 symbols in a single digit space. This was accomplished by adding extra, nonnumerical symbols such as @, &, or # to the data field. In an era when data were entered onto computer cards and sorted by machine, this would have helped reduce sorting and thus provided increased efficiencies in data processing, and such systems were used by some polling firms at least into the 1980s. Other issues with reanalyzing older data relate to the nature of the quota and other nonprobability sampling procedures that were popular at the time. This may require special weighting and analysis procedures. A surprising amount of data from earlier times survives and is available for reanalysis at major data archives such as the Interuniversity Consortium for Political and Social Research (ICPSR) at the University of Michigan, and the Roper Center for Public Opinion Research at the University of Connecticut. A major data source for Europe and the United Kingdom is the UK Data Archive at the University of Essex.

For time periods that pre-date the availability of survey data, historians have become adept at finding other types of data with which to pursue studies of public opinion. Typical source material includes diaries and records, political petitions, legislative records, letters, and other materials limited only by imagination and availability. Robert Darnton, a leading historian of the French Revolution, for example, has uncovered a rich trove of records of expressed opinion in France on the eve of the French Revolution in the basements of the Bastille. These investigative records were created by secret police employed by Louis XV as he tried to hold on to power in the final years leading up the revolution. They include records of overheard conversations in public places, restaurants, and other settings where people gathered to discuss public affairs. There is a fast-growing historical literature examining public opinion at various key points in history by resorting to a wide variety of data sources in order to make inferences. For example, David Zaret has made a career examining the use of popular petitions in England in the 17th century to understand popular resentments and problems that were brought to the attention of monarchs. One advantage of these petitions as raw data for the analysis of public opinion is that they were signed by people of all social classes and in many cases were acted upon favorably by the king. Public opinion during the American Civil War is another example. Much of the professional work of popular historian Stephen Ambrose on World War II soldiers was conducted via oral histories of the men and women who served in the American military during the war.

Mass Observation

Emphasizing the study of expressed opinion—that is, opinions that people shared with one another in public settings—was a major goal of an organization known as Mass Observation that was active in Britain starting in the 1930s. The group used anthropological-style field methods to observe people in conversations in public places, measuring what opinions people expressed in public about topics of concern. The group was founded by journalist Charles Madge, poet and filmmaker Humphrey Jennings, and self-taught anthropologist Tom Harrisson. The three men envisioned Mass Observation as a scientific organization for the assessment of public life. Over the years it grew into a type of social movement, at its high point involving thousands of volunteers. The organization benefited from contracts from the British government during World War II to gather systematic evidence about morale and the life of citizens as impacted by war and continued to exist after the war. The movement eventually became a private firm engaging mainly in consumer market research and eventually merged with BMRB International, a large British advertising agency. Mass Observation continues to exist to this day as a data archive at the University of Sussex. The Sussex group continues to solicit participants in its panel of writers. In recent years a number of reports from the original Mass Observation project have been reissued, and several new ones compiled. Unlike survey research, which gathers self-reports of individuals' private opinions expressed only to an interviewer, Mass Observation gathered the comments and opinions that people actually expressed in public settings.

Gerald M. Kosicki

See also Approval Ratings; Consumer Sentiment Index; Content Analysis; Convenience Sampling; Experimental Design; Focus Group; Media Polls; Nonattitude; Precision Journalism; Public Opinion; Random-Digit Dialing (RDD); Roper Center for Public Opinion Research; Trust in Government

Further Readings

Berinsky, A. J. (2006). American public opinion in the 1930s and 1940s: The analysis of quota-controlled sample survey data. *Public Opinion Quarterly, 70,* 499–529.

Calder, A. (1985). Mass observation 1937–1949. In M. Bulmer (Ed.), *Essays on the history of British sociological research* (pp. 121–136). Cambridge, UK: Cambridge University Press.

Campbell, D. A. (2003). *English public opinion and the American Civil War*. London: Royal Historical Society Boydell Press.

Darnton, R. (2004). Madamoiselle Bonafon and the private life of Louis XV: Communication circuits in eighteenth-century France. *Representations, 87*, 102–124.

Glynn, C. J., Herbst, S., O'Keefe, G. J., Shapiro, R. J., & Linderman, M. (2004). *Public opinion* (2nd ed.). Boulder, CO: Westview.

Herbst, S. (1993). *Numbered voices: How opinion polling has shaped American politics*. Chicago: University of Chicago Press.

Hubble, N. (2006). *Mass-observation and everyday life: Culture, history, theory*. London: Palgrave Macmillan.

Iyengar, S., & McGuire, W. J. (Eds.). (1993). *Explorations in political psychology*. Durham, NC: Duke University Press.

Sirkin, M. G., Herrmann, D. J., Schechter, S., Schwarz, N., Tanur, J. M., & Tourangeau, R. (1999). *Cognition and survey research*. New York: Wiley.

Yankelovich, D. (1991). *Coming to public judgment: Making democracy work in a complex world*. Syracuse, NY: Syracuse University Press.

Zaret, D. (2000). *Origins of democratic culture: Printing, petitions and the public sphere in early-modern England*. Princeton, NJ: Princeton University Press.

PURPOSIVE SAMPLE

A purposive sample, also referred to as a *judgmental* or *expert sample*, is a type of nonprobability sample. The main objective of a purposive sample is to produce a sample that can be logically assumed to be representative of the population. This is often accomplished by applying expert knowledge of the population to select in a nonrandom manner a sample of elements that represents a cross-section of the population.

In probability sampling, each element in the population has a known nonzero chance of being selected through the use of a random selection procedure. In contrast, nonprobability sampling does not involve known nonzero probabilities of selection. Rather, subjective methods are used to decide which elements should be included in the sample. In nonprobability sampling, the population may not be well defined. Nonprobability sampling is often divided into three categories: purposive sampling, convenience sampling, and quota sampling.

An example of purposive sampling would be the selection of a sample of universities in the United States that represent a cross-section of U.S. universities, using expert knowledge of the population first to decide with characteristics are important to be represented in the sample and then to identify a sample of universities that meet the various characteristics that are viewed as being most important. For example, this might involve selecting large, medium, and small public and private universities. This process is referred to as *two-stage sampling*, but the first-stage units are not selected using probability sampling techniques. This kind of two-stage sampling should not be confused with *stratified sampling*, which is a probability method of sampling. Instead, in this example of purposive sampling, such "strata" (size of university and type of university) are used without the scientific rigor of probability sampling. Nonetheless, they are used to assure a more representative mix of elements than may otherwise occur if the expert were not explicitly choosing universities of different sizes and types.

Another example of purposive sampling could be the selection of a sample of food stamp offices from which participants will be sampled. Here, the first-stage units are selected to represent key food stamp recipient dimensions, with expert subject matter judgment used to select the specific food stamp offices that are included in the study.

One limitation of purposive sampling is that another expert would likely come up with different sampled elements from the target population in terms of important characteristics and typical elements to be in the sample. Given the subjectivity of the selection mechanism, purposive sampling is generally considered most appropriate for the selection of small samples often from a limited geographic area or from a restricted population definition, when inference to the population is not the highest priority.

Michael P. Battaglia

See also Convenience Sampling; Nonprobability Sample; Probability Sample; Quota Sampling; Stratified Sampling

Further Readings

Henry, G. (1990). *Practical sampling*. Newbury Park, CA: Sage.

PUSH POLLS

A push poll is a form of negative persuasion telephone calling during a political campaign that is meant to simulate a poll but is really intended to convince voters to switch candidates or to dissuade them from going to the polls to vote. To an unskilled recipient of such a call, it sounds like a traditional telephone survey at the start, but the tone and content of the questioning soon changes to the provision of negative information about one of the candidates. A distinguishing characteristic of a push poll is that often none of the "data" are analyzed; the purpose of the call is to "move" voters away from a preferred candidate. Push polling is so antithetical to legitimate polling that in 1996 the American Association for Public Opinion Research (AAPOR), the American Association of Political Consultants (AAPC), and the National Council on Public Polls (NCPP) issued a joint statement condemning the practice. Since then, the Council for Marketing and Opinion Research (CMOR) has joined in this denunciation.

The support of the AAPC was important because campaigns often test thematic content or different approaches to arguments for the purposes of developing campaign strategy. In these circumstances, the polling firm is collecting data for analysis to determine which themes or approaches are most effective. But in a push poll, no data are analyzed; the calls are made with the intent of getting voters to switch their support from one candidate to another or to so turn them off from the political process that they will decide to stay home on Election Day rather than vote. And a great many more people are contacted than are needed in the standard sample size for a legitimate election campaign poll.

In a period of declining response rates, polling and survey research organizations are always concerned about establishing good rapport with respondents, in the short term with an eye toward completing a specific interview and, more generally, with the purpose of maintaining a positive image of the industry that will promote future cooperation in surveys. Having a bad experience with something that seems like a very biased poll is harmful to both of these interests.

In general, push polling efforts occur late in the campaign, when public disclosure is more problematical. Many of those called cannot distinguish between a legitimate call from an established polling firm for a telephone interview and a push poll call, so they stay on the phone. If the push poll campaign is not brought to light quickly, Election Day arrives and news coverage wanes right after a winner is declared in the contest; so the push poll succeeds in its intent without disclosure. Because there is little regulation of the polling industry, and none in real time, the most effective antidote to push polling is disclosure through the media. But this requires learning of the push polling through those who have received the calls and then trying to track down the source of the calls. Those who are most sensitive to push polls and likely to be sources of disclosure are pollsters and campaign workers. However, any single person is very unlikely to receive such a call to begin with.

Push poll calls are typically very short and involve only a few questions, unlike the typical telephone interview that lasts at least 5 minutes and sometimes up to half an hour. The questions often involve significant distortions of one candidate's record or positions. Push polls sometimes involve tens of thousands of calls being made in a state where there is a presidential primary taking place, or just a few thousand calls for a smaller constituency. Of course, no individual who receives such a call can tell from their own experience that they are part of a larger campaign, making detection of the negative calling campaign more difficult.

In their original form, these calls were made by interviewers who worked from a script. With the advances of technology, they can now be produced on a computer that does both the dialing and reading of the script. This means that more calls can be made in a shorter period of time and at a lower cost per call.

Michael W. Traugott

See also American Association for Public Opinion Research (AAPOR); Council for Marketing and Opinion Research (CMOR); National Council on Public Polls (NCPP); Poll; Pseudo-Polls

Further Readings

American Association for Public Opinion Research. (2007, June). *AAPOR statement on "push" polls.* Retrieved June 12, 2008, from http://www.aapor.org/aaporstatement onpushpolls

American Association of Political Consultants. (n.d.). *AAPC board of directors declaration regarding "push polling."*

Retrieved June 12, 2008, from http://www.theaapc.org/about/pushpolling/

Council for Marketing and Opinion Research. (n.d.). *What is research? Differences between research and sales.* Retrieved from http://www.cmor.org/research/differences.cfm

National Council on Public Polls. (1995, May 22). *Push polls.* Retrieved June 12, 2008, from http://www.ncpp.org/?q=node/41

p-VALUE

The probability value (abbreviated "*p*-value"), which can range from 0.0 to 1.0, refers to a numeric quantity computed for sample statistics within the context of hypothesis testing. More specifically, the *p*-value is the probability of observing a test statistic that is at least as extreme as the quantity computed using the sample data. The "probability" is computed using a reference distribution that is generally derived using the null hypothesis. The phrase *extreme* is usually interpreted with respect to the direction of the alternative hypothesis—if two tailed, then the *p*-value represents the probability of observing a test statistic that is at least as large in absolute value as the number computed from sample data. Put another way, the *p*-value can be interpreted as the likelihood that the statistical result was obtained by chance alone.

P-values often are reported in the literature for analysis of variance (ANOVA), regression and correlation coefficients, among other statistical techniques. The smaller the *p*-value, the more the evidence provided against the null hypothesis. Generally, if the *p*-value is less than the level of significance for the test (i.e., α), then the null hypothesis is rejected in favor of the alternative and the result is said to be "statistically significant."

In the context of survey research, interest may be given in comparing the results of a battery of questionnaire items across demographic or other groups. For example, a sequence of *t*-tests may be conducted to compare differences in the mean ages, education level, number of children in the home, annual income, and so on, for people who are surveyed from rural areas versus those from urban areas. Each test will generate a test statistic and a corresponding two-sided *p*-value. Comparing each of these separate *p*-values to .05 or .10, or some other fixed level of alpha, can give some

indication for the significance of the hypotheses tests that the mean levels of age, education, and so on, are equal for citizens living in urban and rural areas versus the alternative hypothesis that these means are different. However, using the separate *p*-values alone inflates the Type I error rate of the entire sequence of tests. To avoid this inflation, adjusted *p*-values are often used to provide an overall error rate that is equal to the nominal alpha level specified by the researcher. The most straightforward of these adjustments is the Bonferroni adjustment, which compares either the *p*-value to alpha divided by the number of tests or compares the *p*-value multiplied by the number of tests to the nominal alpha level. If the adjusted *p*-values are less than alpha, then the specific null hypothesis is rejected.

The computation of *p*-value can be illustrated using data obtained from a single survey item that asks a random sample of 20 households the following question: *How many children live full time within your household?* The null hypothesis is that an average of 2 children live full time per household; the alternative hypothesis posits the average number exceeds 2. The reference distribution for the sample mean values for samples of size 20 is provided in Table 1.

The sample mean computed from the 20 sampled households was 2.5 children per household. In this case the hypothesis is one-tailed and the *p*-value is literally interpreted as the probability that the sample

Table 1   Distribution of the sample mean number of children per household for possible samples of 20 households randomly selected from the population

Possible Values for $\bar{X}$	*Proportion of Samples Having This Value for $\bar{X}$*
0	5%
1	10%
1.5	15%
2	35%
2.5	20%
3	10%
3.5	5%

mean is 2.5 or larger. To compute this probability, we use the reference distribution from Table 1 as follows:

$$p\text{-}value = \text{Probability } (\bar{X} \geq 2.5)$$
$$= \text{Probability } (\bar{X} = 2.5, 3 \text{ or } 3.5)$$
$$= .20 + .10 + .05 = .35.$$

In this case, the result is interpreted as not statistically significant since the *p*-value was .35, which exceeds nominal alpha levels of .05 or .10.

Trent D. Buskirk

See also Alpha, Significance Level of Test; Alternative Hypothesis; Null Hypothesis; *p*-Value; Statistic; Type I Error

Further Readings

Le, C. T. (2001). *Health and numbers* (2nd ed.). New York: Wiley-Liss.

Yates, D., Moore, D., & McCabe, G. (1999). *The practice of statistics*. New York: W. H. Freeman.

Q

QUALITY CONTROL

The term *quality control* refers to the efforts and procedures that survey researchers put in place to ensure the quality and accuracy of data being collected using the methodologies chosen for a particular study. Quality-control efforts vary from study to study and can be applied to questionnaires and the computerized programs that control them, sample management systems to ensure proper case processing, the monitoring of appropriate interviewer behavior, and other quality-control aspects of the survey process, all of which can affect the quality of data and thus the results.

Training Interviewers

In surveys that use interviewer-administered questionnaires, proper training of interviewers is often seen as the heart of quality control. To become successful and effective, interviewers first must be introduced to the survey research process through a general training, in which fundamental concepts such as basic interviewing techniques, obtaining cooperation, and maintaining respondent confidentiality are covered. Following general training, interviewers should be trained on the specifics of an individual project. Training sessions should strive to maximize active participation. Topics covered should be reinforced with group discussion and interaction, trainer demonstrations, and classroom practice and discussion. Role playing and practice are also key elements of effective basic project training.

Assessment of the knowledge gained and retained by interviewers is also a part of survey quality control.

Monitoring Interviews

In surveys that use interviewer-administered questionnaires, monitoring interviews has become a standard quality-control practice. Telephone interviewer monitoring is accomplished by using silent monitoring equipment so that neither the interviewer nor the respondent is aware of it. In addition, facilities may use equipment that allows the monitors to listen to an interview and simultaneously visually observe the progress of an interview on a computer screen. Monitoring serves four objectives, all aimed at maintaining a high level of data quality. These objectives include (1) obtaining information about the interview process (such as procedures or interview items) that can be used to improve the survey, (2) providing information about the overall data quality for the survey in order to keep the data collection process in statistical control, (3) improving interviewer performance by reinforcing good interviewing behavior, and (4) detecting and preventing data falsification.

Generally speaking, there are two different types of telephone monitoring conducted: *quality assurance monitoring* and *interviewer performance monitoring*. Quality assurance monitoring involves the use of a coding scheme that allows monitors to score interviewers on a variety of aspects such as proper question delivery, use of nondirective probing, and correct entry of responses. Interviewer performance monitoring takes more of a qualitative approach. Under this process, monitors record any observations that might be useful in subsequent evaluation of the interviewing staff. Monitors will make observations that focus on appropriate administration of items, remaining neutral, tone of voice, pace, and so on, and will provide feedback, both in the form of positive reinforcement and constructive criticism with potential retraining as warranted.

While monitoring telephone interviewers is an efficient and nonintrusive activity, conducting monitoring of face-to-face interviews in the field is more challenging. Traditionally monitoring face-to-face interviews in the field is done in one of two ways. First, direct observations can be made by field supervisors who accompany field interviews during data collection. During these periods, supervisors will observe and evaluate field interviewers on adherence to survey protocols while noting areas requiring improvement. Second, tape recordings are used to record portions of interviews and are reviewed after the fact to evaluate interviewers on quality, proper administration of the survey, and so forth. While effective in capturing quality information, these two methods have traditionally come with a cost, as they are both intrusive and cumbersome. Recent advancements in digital recording have made monitoring possible without the need to carry recording equipment such as microphones and tapes. *Computer audio-recorded interviewing* allows for the recording of portions of interviews for quality control on computer-assisted personal interviewing (CAPI) laptops, eliminating the need for external equipment.

Supervisory Meetings

During field and telephone data periods, supervisors often hold regularly scheduled meetings, sometimes referred to as *quality circle meetings*, to discuss data collection issues. These sessions are conducted to build rapport and enthusiasm among interviewers and supervisory staff while assisting in the refinement of an instrument and providing ongoing training for the staff. Such meetings have the potential to identify previously unrecognized problems with an instrument, such as questions that respondents may not understand or questions that are difficult to administer. In addition these sessions may reveal computer-assisted interviewing software problems and issues with data collection procedures and operations.

Verification Interviews

In addition to monitoring for quality and conducting regular meetings with interviewers, many data collection supervisors take an additional step to ensure data quality and prevent falsification. Verification by telephone and reviewing interview timing data are particularly useful and important for field interviews where data are not collected in a central facility; when data are collected this way, it makes the interviewers more susceptible to falsification, also known as "curb stoning."

Telephone verification is conducted by first telling respondents who have just completed face-to-face interviews that they may be contacted at a later date for quality-control purposes. Telephone interviewers will then contact selected respondents to verify the face-to-face interview was completed properly and with the correct sample member. Any suspicious results are then conveyed to the data collection supervisors for investigation.

Some face-to-face surveys also review questionnaire timing data as part of standard quality-control procedures. Under this method, as interviews are completed and transmitted from the field, timing data are captured for each module or section within the instrument, along with overall timing data on the overall length of the study. By recording and analyzing this information, researchers can create reports that can be used to detect suspiciously short interview administration times. This quality-control method allows for early detection and resolution of problems, leading to more complete and accurate data for analysis.

Examining Systems and Data for Quality

In addition to training and implementing procedures to ensure quality control through interviewers, and regardless of the mode of data collection and whether or not the questionnaire is interviewer administered, researchers must also take steps to verify that the systems and procedures being used to collect and process data are functioning properly. By using systematic testing plans, researchers can verify routes through the computerized questionnaire and ensure that a program is working as specified in terms of display, skip pattern logic, and wording. Researchers should also review frequencies of the collected data throughout data collection (especially early in the field period) to ensure skip patterns are being implemented properly and to identify and address any questions that have higher-than-expected rates of item-level nonresponse. Logic checks should be deployed to evaluate the likely accuracy of the final data set before analyses begin. If coding of open-ended responses is conducted, quality-control measures must be deployed to ensure inter-coder reliability. Finally, reliability checks should be conducted on all analyses that are performed.

David James Roe

See also Coding; Computer-Assisted Personal Interviewing (CAPI); Computer-Assisted Telephone Interviewing (CATI); Face-to-Face Interviewing; Falsification; Field Period; Frequency Distribution; Intercoder Reliability; Interviewer Monitoring; Interviewer Training; Missing Data; Supervisor; Validation; Verification

Further Readings

Biemer, P., & Lyberg, L. (2003). *Introduction to survey quality*. Hoboken, NJ: Wiley.

Fowler, F., & Mangione, T. (1990). *Standardized survey interviewing: Minimizing interviewer-related error*. Newbury Park, CA: Sage.

Lavrakas, P. (1993). *Telephone survey methods: Sampling, selection, and supervision*. Newbury Park, CA: Sage.

QUALITY OF LIFE INDICATORS

Two types of survey measures fall under the quality of life domain. The first is *psychological measures* used to assess satisfaction in response to a life situation, typically an individual-level measure of quality of life in the context of the mental health of persons living with chronic health diseases. The second is a *social indicator*, designed to assess life quality for the purpose of creating aggregated indices for making systemic comparisons. Though the former has received a higher volume of research, the latter is more central to public opinion research.

Assessing the well-being of individuals and communities may be one of the most important contributions public opinion researchers can make. By providing benchmarks, researchers can elucidate the antecedents and consequences of individual life satisfaction as well as assess the progress of communities over time. At the same time, measuring quality of life is extremely complex as it encompasses myriad dimensions, including both material conditions and psychological orientations.

The challenge for social indicators researchers has been to come up with objective measures that are both comprehensive, in terms of capturing the various relevant dimensions of quality of life, and non-ethnocentric, in that they do not reflect researcher biases in terms of what constitutes life quality. However, any attempt to measure quality of life inherently involves making subjective decisions about what constitutes "quality." As such, these measures will always be subject to charges of ethnocentricity. However flawed such measures are, they do serve as a point of comparison and a yardstick against which to measure progress.

The unit of analysis is one important consideration in the assessment of life quality. That is, will the measure describe differences in the life quality of individuals, communities, or nations? At the micro level, measures attempt to assess the psychological and material well-being of individuals. Other indicators have been designed to assess the quality of life afforded by a particular community or nation. Macro-level indices most often are based on indicators that are aggregated and reported in terms of mean levels; however, when it comes to larger social units, the dispersion of such aggregated measures is also significant in order to take into account inequality in the distribution of resources that contribute to quality of life.

Quality of life measurement has typically involved a combination of economic, psychological, and social conditions. Economic indicators include estimates of standard of living, disposable income, wages, savings, bankruptcy rates, and other such criteria. Among the dimensions of social conditions are measures of crime, education, employment, crowding, pollution, aesthetic surroundings, housing quality, birth rates, infant mortality, longevity, doctors per capita, and health care. Psychological dimensions include assessments of happiness, life satisfaction, self-esteem, self-efficacy, marital satisfaction, family life, friendships, health, housing, jobs, housework, neighborhoods, communities, education, standard of living, financial state, and life in general. These measures may be classified into two groups: external measures, which refer to measures of the structural conditions that impinge upon an individual (often referred to as *social indicators*), and internal measures, which refer to indicators based on respondents' perceptions of their own life situations (often referred to as *measures of social well-being*).

Some prominent examples of quality of life measures are Cantril's Self-Anchoring Scale; Campbell, Converse, and Rogers's Domain Satisfactions and Index of Well-Being; Andrews and Withey's Global Well-Being Index; and Deiner's Quality of Life Index. Among the measurement challenges in this area are the following: the positivity bias (the tendency for respondents to use the high end of the scale for perceptual measures of psychological indicators), the ethnocentrism bias (indicators that reflect values of the researchers), the subjectivity bias (a reliance on non-objective perceptual indicators), the quantitative bias (a reliance on quantitative measures that may be less meaningful than qualitative indicators), measurement biases (such as response set and social desirability), weighting biases (problems of determining the relative importance of indicators), and measurement complexity (because there are so many important dimensions of life quality, measurement is cumbersome).

Douglas M. McLeod

See also Bias; Level of Analysis; Perception Question; Positivity Bias; Public Opinion; Social Desirability

Further Readings

Andrews, F. M., & Withey, S. B. (1976). *Social indicators of well-being: American perceptions of life quality.* New York: Plenum Press.

Campbell, A., Converse, P. E., & Rodgers, W. L. (1976). *The quality of American life.* New York: Russell Sage Foundation.

Cantril, H. (1965). *The pattern of human concerns.* New Brunswick, NJ: Rutgers University Press.

Deiner, E. (1995). A value based index for measuring national quality of life. *Social Indicators Research, 36,* 107–127.

QUESTIONNAIRE

The questionnaire is the main instrument for collecting data in survey research. Basically, it is a set of standardized questions, often called *items*, which follow a fixed scheme in order to collect individual data about one or more specific topics. Sometimes questionnaires are confused with interviews. In fact, the questionnaire involves a particular kind of interview—a formal contact, in which the conversation is governed by the wording and order of questions in the instrument. The

questionnaire often is administered in a standardized fashion, that is, in the same way to all the respondents of the survey. The logic behind the standardization of questions and answers is that only if a stimulus is the same for all the respondents of a survey can it be, at least theoretically, possible to get the same (symbolic, cognitive, psychological, social) reaction from it. Responses obtained across individuals should be comparable to one another.

This entry discusses the construction, format, and layout of questionnaires, along with question wording and types. Lastly, this entry addresses the importance of pretesting and the various ways questionnaires can be administered.

Questionnaire Construction

When questionnaires are constructed, four primary requirements must be met:

1. Theoretical knowledge of the topic of research, achieved through the reconnaissance of the relevant literature (if such exists) and/or in-depth interviews or other qualitative methods of research (ethnographies, focus groups, brainstorming, etc.) that may serve as pilot studies.

2. Valid and reliable operationalization of concepts and hypotheses of research. Most questionnaire items, in fact, originate from the operationalization phase. To check the validity (the degree to which an item or scale measures what it was designed to measure) and reliability (the consistency or replicability of measurements) of a set of items, various techniques can be used: external, construct, and face validity, among others, in the first case; and parallel forms, test–retest, split-half, intercoder techniques, in the case of reliability.

3. Experience in writing a questionnaire, or at least the availability of good repertoires of published questionnaires.

4. A knowledge of the target population. This is crucial information: The target population must be able to answer to the questions accurately.

Questionnaires are usually composed of three main parts: the cover letter (or introduction), the instructions, and the main body. Usually, they finish with thanking the respondents for their valuable collaboration.

The *cover letter* (or its equivalent in interviewer-administered surveys) introduces the research and tries to motivate the respondents to cooperate with the survey task. It also explains the aims of the research, informs about its contractors and sponsors, and, above all, guarantees the anonymity or at least the confidentiality of the respondents. It is a sort of "contract," where the costs and benefits for collaboration between the respondent and the researcher are defined. The cover letter is one of the key elements in improving the response rate.

Instructions are especially important when the questionnaire is self-administered. Instructions contain all the rules the respondents must follow to answer the questions (e.g., how to check the boxes, which part of the questionnaire has to be skipped in certain cases, etc.). These rules should be as simple as possible. They can be categorized as (a) general instructions, (b) section introductions, (c) question instructions, and (d) "go to" instructions for contingency questions.

Finally, the *main body* includes the actual questions. There are many types of questions: questions about what people are (demographic data and attributes, such as gender, age, education, occupation), do (behaviors, such as buying records or traveling), think (beliefs, opinions, or judgments), or remember. These ingredients must be arranged in a structure that takes into account the attention, memory, sensibility, motivations, and background characteristics of the respondents.

Questionnaire Structure and Format

The structure of the questionnaire must be logical and the questions adequately linked and arranged together (e.g., grouping all the questions about the same subject together or using linking sentences when passing from one topic to another). Moreover, the length of the questionnaire must be reasonable: Only questions that are absolutely necessary should be included. With respect to questionnaire layout, at least these basic rules should be followed: (1) Each questionnaire must have an identification code, number, or both; (2) each question must have its own progressive number, and the space and graphic style of questions and response categories must be legible; and (3) the numerical values or codes for closed-ended questions (e.g., from the codebook) should be embedded into the questionnaire, in order to facilitate data entry into a case-by-variable matrix. In short, each response alternative must have its corresponding code (see examples in the following section of this entry). Of course, this does not apply to open-ended questions.

Generally, the ordering of items within a questionnaire follows this pattern: (a) general and neutral questions (to build rapport and thereby obtain the respondent's confidence), (b) questions that require greater effort (e.g., complex, core questions), (c) sensitive questions, and (d) demographic questions. This general pattern has been found to increase data quality for most surveys.

Nevertheless, the order in which questions are organized and the use of filter questions can yield various shapes, for example, funnel format (from general to specific questions), inverted funnel format (from specific to general questions), diamond format, X-format, box format, and mixed formats. The researcher will need to choose the form that best fits his or her goals. Classic and recent studies confirm that the order of the questions is an important contextual factor that influences respondents' answers.

Questionnaire Wording and Question Types

A general rule, in constructing questions, is to be *clear* in terminology and *simple* in structure. More specifically:

- Questions should use simple vocabulary.
- Their syntax should be simple, without subordinate clauses and without double negatives.
- They should not contain two questions in one (double-barreled questions).
- Questions must be concrete with respect to time and events.
- They should not lead the respondent to particular answers.
- The number of response alternatives should be limited unless additional visual cues are employed.
- All the alternatives of response should appear acceptable, even the most extreme.
- The response alternatives should be exhaustive and mutually exclusive.

Basically, two broad types of questions can be distinguished: *open-ended* and *closed-ended* (or *fixed alternative*) questions. The latter are more frequent in survey research. Open-ended questions are suitable when the researcher thinks it would be better to leave the respondents free to express their thoughts with their own words. However, they require a subsequent postcoding, for instance through content analysis, lexical correspondence analysis, or a qualitative treatment.

The difficulties and costs in the coding and analysis of open-ended questions have long limited their use in questionnaires. Today, given the huge advances in the field of (automatic) textual analysis, this limitation has lessened. On the other hand, closed-ended questions allow immediate statistical treatment. Unfortunately, sometimes the respondent cannot find a suitable answer among the alternatives proposed. In short, closed-ended questions require particular attention in providing relevant response alternatives.

There are many types of closed-ended questions. The following are examples of the most common:

- Selection among nominal categories, as in the following example:

  What is your religion?
  Christian [ ]₁
  Jewish [ ]₂
  Muslim [ ]₃
  Other [ ]₄
  Atheist/Agnostic [ ]₅

- Checklists, as in the following example:

  What kind of TV programs do you like watching? (Please check all the answers that apply.)
  News [ ]₁
  Sports [ ]₂
  Telefilms [ ]₃
  Soap operas [ ]₄
  Movies [ ]₅
  Talk shows [ ]₆
  None of the above [ ]₇

- Selection among ordinal categories, as in the following example:

  How many times did you go shopping last week?
  Three or more [ ]₄
  Twice [ ]₃
  Once [ ]₂
  Never [ ]₁

- A particular kind of selection among ordinal categories is the degree of agreement or disagreement with a statement, as in the next example, known as a Likert-type question:

  Please indicate how much you agree or disagree with the following statement: "I find much of my job repetitive and boring."
  Strongly Agree [ ]₅
  Agree [ ]₄

Neither Agree nor Disagree [ ]₃
Disagree [ ]₂
Strongly Disagree [ ]₁

- Ranking of personal preferences, as in the following example:

  Please rank from 1 (most favorite) to 5 (least favorite) the following drinks, using each number only once:
  a. Wine _____
  b. Beer _____
  c. Cola _____
  d. Water _____
  e. Lemonade _____

- Semantic differential scaled responses, as in the following example:

  How happy are you with the government's choice of diminishing funds for military research?
  Very Happy 7…6…5…4…3…2…1 Very Unhappy

- Interval-level or ratio-level responses, as in the following example:
  How many children under the age of 18 do you have? _____

As noted earlier, when choosing the alternatives of response for each item, two conditions must be fulfilled. Categories should be (1) *exhaustive* (i.e., all possible responses must find a place in one of the options proposed); and (2) *mutually exclusive* (i.e., each response should correspond to only one precoded category, unless differently specified).

Pretesting the Questionnaire

Before administering a questionnaire to the actual sample of respondents, it is necessary to carry out at least one pretest (pilot test) to verify that it is well understood and does not yield obvious bias effects. The output of a pretesting phase can lead the researcher to (a) aggregate, specify, or better articulate the response alternatives, (b) revise or delete questions that raise many "I don't know," "I don't remember," "I don't want to answer" observations, specifications, explanations, or criticisms; (c) delete those questions that appear to have no variance; (d) integrate missing topics; (e) create a new order for the questions; and (f) verify the timing of the interview.

Pretests can be carried out in many ways: recording the reactions of the respondents during the interview, interviewing or debriefing the respondents *ex post*, asking the advice of a panel of experts, or mixing these methods. This phase should not be skipped, and a particular study could require more than one pretest before the questionnaire is finalized.

Administering the Questionnaire

Final questionnaires can be administered in many ways. In interviewer-administered questionnaires, particular care must be addressed to the training and monitoring of the interviewers. Another important distinction is the mode of data collection: face-to-face, telephone, mail, computer, and Internet data collection in their various forms (CATI, CAPI, CASI, etc.). Each one has its own advantages and drawbacks, in terms of costs, quickness, intrusiveness, anonymity guarantees, general design of the questionnaire, types of questions allowed and quality of the responses, return rates, and data entry. The researcher must find the right trade-off among costs and benefits with respect to all these factors.

Many new studies have focused on the role of the Internet in survey data collection. At least three big advantages characterize the use of the Internet in survey research: (1) the possibility to reach a huge population at a relatively low cost, (2) the possibility to minimize the intrusiveness of the interviewer and his or her instruments, and (3) the possibility to provide standardized multi-media stimuli (e.g., audio-visual content) as part of the questionnaire. These advantages to Web questionnaire notwithstanding, there also are many problems to take into account when using the Internet for data collection: the quality of the samples, verifying the eligibility of the respondents, the contexts in which questionnaires are completed, and so forth. Currently, it seems that a mix of traditional and innovative methods is necessary.

Finally, questionnaires can be administered on a single occasion (*cross-sectional design*) or at intervals over a period of time. In this second case, there are two alternatives: *trend* or *repeated cross-sectional* studies (when the same questionnaire is administered to different samples during the chosen period) and *longitudinal* studies (when the same questionnaire is administered to the same units). The most common type of longitudinal study is the *panel*, in which the same respondents are interviewed more than once,

using a questionnaire that is identical, or at least very similar, to that used in each wave of the panel.

Alberto Trobia

See also Anonymity; Check All That Apply; Closed-Ended Question; Codebook; Computer-Assisted Personal Interviewing (CAPI); Computer-Assisted Self-Interviewing (CASI); Computer-Assisted Telephone Interviewing (CATI); Confidentiality; Construct Validity; Content Analysis; Contingency Question; Cover Letter; Cross-Sectional Survey Design; Double-Barreled Question; Double Negative; Exhaustive; Interval Measure; Interviewer Monitoring; Interviewer Training; Likert Scale; Longitudinal Studies; Mode of Data Collection; Mutually Exclusive; Nominal Measure; Open-Ended Question; Ordinal Measure; Panel Survey; Pilot Test; Precoded Question; Questionnaire Design; Questionnaire Length; Questionnaire-Related Error; Question Order Effects; Question Wording as Discourse Indicators; Ratio Measure; Reliability; Repeated Cross-Sectional Design; Respondent Debriefing; Respondent–Interviewer Rapport; Response Alternatives; Self-Administered Questionnaire; Semantic Differential Technique; Sensitive Topics; Validity; Wave

Further Readings

Alreck, P. L., & Settle, R. B. (1995). *The survey research handbook: Guidelines and strategies for conducting a survey.* Burr Ridge, IL: Irwin.

Converse, J. M., & Presser, S. (1986). *Survey questions: Handcrafting the standardised questionnaire.* London: Sage.

Couper, M. (2000). Web surveys: A review of issues and approaches. *Public Opinion Quarterly, 64*(4), 464–494.

Dillman, D. A. (1978). *Mail and telephone surveys: The total design method.* New York: Wiley.

Foddy, W. H. (1993). *Constructing questions for interviews and questionnaires: Theory and practice in social research.* Melbourne, Australia: Cambridge University Press.

Fowler, F. J., Jr. (1995). *Improving survey questions: Design and evaluation.* Thousand Oaks, CA: Sage.

Newell, R. (1993). Questionnaires. In N. Gilbert (Ed.), *Researching social life* (pp. 94–115). London: Sage.

Presser, S., Rothgeb, J., Couper, M., Lessler, J., Martin, E., & Singer, E. (2004). *Methods for testing and evaluating survey questionnaires.* New York: Wiley.

Singer, E., & Presser, S. (1989). *Survey research methods: A reader.* Chicago: University of Chicago Press.

Sudman, S., & Bradburn, N. M. (1983). *Asking questions.* San Francisco: Jossey-Bass.

Tourangeau, R., Rips, L. J., & Rasinski, K. (2000). *The psychology of survey response.* Cambridge, UK: Cambridge University Press.

QUESTIONNAIRE DESIGN

Questionnaire design is the process of designing the format and questions in the survey instrument that will be used to collect data about a particular phenomenon. In designing a questionnaire, all the various stages of survey design and implementation should be considered. These include the following nine elements: (1) determination of goals, objectives, and research questions; (2) definition of key concepts; (3) generation of hypotheses and proposed relationships; (4) choice of survey mode (mail, telephone, face-to-face, Internet); (5) question construction; (6) sampling; (7) questionnaire administration and data collection; (8) data summarization and analysis; (9) conclusions and communication of results.

One goal of the questionnaire design process is to reduce the total amount of measurement error in a questionnaire. Survey measurement error results from two sources: *variance* and *bias*. Question wording (including response alternatives), ordering, formatting, or all three, may introduce variance and bias into measurement, which affects the reliability and validity of the data and conclusions reached. Increased variance involves random increases in distance between the reported survey value from the "true" survey value (e.g., attitude, behavior, factual knowledge). Increased bias involves a systematic (directional) difference from the "true" survey value. Questionnaire-related error may be introduced by four different sources: the interviewer, the item wording/format/ordering, the respondent, and the mode of data collection. Careful questionnaire design can reduce the likelihood of error from each of these sources.

Goals, Objectives, and Hypotheses

The process of designing a questionnaire begins with a definition of the goals and objectives of the study. A clearly defined purpose acts as an anchor that sets the stage for questionnaire format and question construction or ordering. In what concepts and phenomena is the researcher interested? What does he or she want to learn? To what population are the results to generalize? These are all questions that should be asked during the initial phase of questionnaire design. Each item included in the questionnaire should meet the criteria that it will provide useful information related to the goals and research questions of the survey; parsimony is a virtue in questionnaire design. To properly define goals and research questions, key concepts of interest need to be detailed. A list of concepts of interest and how they relate to one another aids in selecting specific questions to include. These concepts are transformed into (i.e., operationalize as) survey questions that measure the concept in some way, proceeding from abstract concepts to specific measurements. Once the goals and objectives of the survey have been established, it is possible to generate specific research questions and, possibly, directional hypotheses based on theory and previous findings. The items used in the questionnaire should produce data that are appropriate to the desired analyses.

Questionnaire Format

The layout of a questionnaire, no matter what type, should reduce the cognitive burden of respondents (and interviewers) and contain an intuitive and logical flow. For example, in most cases, questions on related topics should be grouped together and questions should maintain the chronology of events. Questionnaire format should be as easy as possible to understand and use for the interviewer or the respondent depending on the mode of administration. Questions should be numbered individually, clearly spaced, and visually distinct from one another. It is especially important that self-administered questionnaires provide clear and concise instructions and have a simple layout (e.g., common question format, visual instructions for skipping questions). For interviewer-administered questionnaires, instructions that are to be read aloud to respondents should be visually distinct from instructions that are for only the interviewer; for example, set off by *italics*, CAPS, **bold type**, or parentheses ( ). Ideally, important questions should appear early in a questionnaire to avoid the possible negative effects of respondent fatigue on motivation, recall, and item nonresponse.

Questionnaires that have a professional appearance are taken more seriously by respondents (e.g., displaying professional affiliations). Social validation is also an important factor; questionnaires that end by thanking respondents for their time and effort and reminding respondents of the usefulness of the data they have provided are rated as more enjoyable by respondents.

Questionnaire length is an important issue for both cost reasons and effects on respondent behavior. First, longer questionnaires place a greater burden on respondents and are more costly. Second, longer questionnaires can have many significant effects on respondent behavior. Refusal rates rise with the length of the questionnaire; respondents may be willing to spend time on a 20-minute interview but may feel a 45-minute interview is far too long. In addition, greater attrition, measurement error, and satisficing may occur due to fatigue with longer questionnaires.

The contingencies that are built into a questionnaire, even when the questionnaire is computer assisted, must be designed with impeccable logic. Furthermore, when the questionnaire is not administered via computer and is self-administered (i.e., paper-and-pencil questionnaires), these so-called skip patterns must be explained in very clear and uncomplicated language, graphics, or both.

Question Wording

Unclear concepts, poorly worded questions, and difficult or unclear response choices may make the questionnaire difficult for both respondents and interviewers. Questionnaires should contain items that are both reliable and valid. Reliability is the consistency of the measurement; that is, the question is interpreted and responded to similarly over repeated trials. Construct validity is whether or not the measurement, as worded, properly reflects the underlying construct of interest.

Questions may be troublesome for respondents with respect to comprehension, retrieval, and response formation. First, the respondent must be able to understand the question. Questions should use simple (enough) terms and concepts that respondents are likely to know, and they should not contain vague and ambiguous terms; in other words, questions should be worded appropriately for the reading and knowledge level of the respondents. Questions should avoid unnecessary complexity, such as compound sentences, double-barreled questions (two questions within one), and double negatives. Longer questions that provide sufficient detail (without becoming convoluted) and are explicit generally will enhance comprehension.

Even though questions may be perfectly understandable for respondents, there may be problems with retrieval of the desired information from respondents' memory. Questions should ask for information that is as recent as possible and provide cues that match the original encoding context. Question

construction may be either personal or impersonal in form: The choice depends on what kind of information, personal or general, the question is designed to elicit. Shorter recall periods (or reference periods) are easier for respondents to handle. Cues that are distinctive and personally relevant to the respondent also aid retrieval. Questions that ask for information that is general or was initially superficially encoded in the brain are prone to greater error in comparison to questions with appropriate, specific cues.

Terms that have multiple possible interpretations should have brief definitions provided in the question. Questions that define concepts for respondents work better if the definition of the concept precedes the actual question. Likewise, reference periods are also more effective when they are provided before the question. Event history calendars are useful for asking about similar events over a long period of time. It is also a good idea to avoid sensitive questions if possible (e.g., questions about income, religion, or sexual behavior). Any questions relating to sensitive information should be clearly necessary, and respondents should understand this need.

Response Alternatives

Responses can be either open-ended or closed-ended. *Open-ended* questions provide no predetermined response categories and allow the respondent to answer with whatever information he or she considers relevant. This answer format is more cognitively demanding for respondents, but it often results in more detailed and informative responses. Open-ended questions are good for gathering information on a topic for which there is no clear set of response categories. Open-ended questions work better with interviewer-administered questionnaires than in surveys that use self-administered questionnaires. An open-ended response format may result in a great deal of information, but it may be information that is not easily comparable or easily codable. Open-ended data also can be quite time-consuming and very costly to process.

Closed-ended questions ask respondents to select among a predetermined set of response categories. These response categories must be exhaustive and mutually exclusive. The closed-ended method reduces the cognitive burden of the respondent and enhances the ability to compare responses. The data are already coded (assigned a numerical value) and can be easily quantified, which saves data processing time and money. Closed-ended questions are ideal for self-administered questionnaires because they avoid the greater subjectivity and volatility of open-ended questions. However, if the researcher is not careful, the selection of response alternatives may bias respondents by framing thinking and by predetermining what are considered "appropriate" answers.

Response categories for event information may be divided by occurrence, absolute frequency (actual amount), relative frequency (quantifiers that denote more or less of something, such as "always," "most of the time," "sometimes," "basically never"), regularity, and specific dates. Attitude answers may take the form of ratings, rankings, agree–disagree scales, and forced choice. Attitude questions essentially require an evaluation of some phenomenon (e.g., approval/disapproval of the president). In selecting terms to use to describe attitudes, it is best to use terms that are simple and easy to understand, as well as terms that are likely to be interpreted similarly by all respondents.

Response scales require decisions concerning the length of scale, whether or not to include midpoint or explicit "don't know" options, and whether to use verbal labels, numbers, or both. A very common scale for closed-ended survey items is a Likert scale (e.g., "strongly agree," "somewhat agree," "neither agree nor disagree," "somewhat disagree," or "strongly disagree"). Rating scales can be presented as either a verbal description (e.g., strongly agree, strongly disagree), numbers (e.g., 1 to 5), or a combination of both. Meaningful verbal labels with relatively equal intervals provide a linguistic reference point for numerical scales, which significantly aids respondents.

Including a middle category is desirable when there is a readily identifiable and meaningful midpoint to a scale (e.g., increase, remain the same, decrease). The number of response options should attempt to maximize discrimination between response categories while maintaining the usefulness and meaningfulness of response categories. Research shows that five to nine response categories is best. There is tremendous debate over the usefulness of explicitly including "don't know" responses. Some argue that questionnaire designers are incorrect in assuming respondents always have an opinion and that surveys often force respondents to artificially produce an opinion. The lack of opinion regarding a topic has been referred to as displaying a "nonattitude." Others argue that explicit "don't know" response choices encourage respondents to satisfice and thereby not make the mental effort required to answer questions accurately. If given the chance, respondents with a low level of motivation will opt to get through a survey quickly and often choose the "don't know" response to facilitate this process, when otherwise they would have produced an opinion by not being offered a "don't know" option and thus been forced to put a little more effort into answering the question. A good situation in which to include an explicit "don't know" option is on unfamiliar topics where respondents are much more likely to have no knowledge or information about the subject and thus truly may have no opinion.

Question Testing Methods

Survey methodologists have developed several different methods of testing questionnaires to detect problems before they go out in the field. Question testing methods include the following: expert panels, traditional interviewer debriefing, behavior coding, cognitive interviewing, focus groups, and split-half experiments. Using one or some combination of methods improves the quality of a questionnaire.

Conventional pretesting involves interviewers conducting a relatively small number of interviews with a draft version of the questionnaire, followed up by an informal group debriefing session. Conventional pretesting accurately identifies problems that interviewers may have with the delivery of questions, but it is not as good at diagnosing respondent difficulties.

Behavioral coding standardizes the method of observing and recording the respondent–interviewer interaction. Behaviors that occur during the question–answer process are categorized (i.e., respondent asks for repetition of the response categories), and their frequency of occurrence is recorded. Behavioral coding aids in the identification of problems in question wording and question ordering and conceptual ambiguities. This method generates more reliability and consistency across interviewers in coding the question answering process because it uses a method that results in quantifiable data. One drawback to behavioral coding is that it does not yield any information for the *reasons* behind question problems.

Cognitive interviewing techniques are adept at revealing the largely invisible cognitive processes respondents engage in while answering questionnaires. Respondents may be asked to "think aloud" while answering questions, or respondents may be asked specific standardized question probes (e.g., "What did you count as 'exercise' when I asked you, *On average how many times do you exercise per week?*") designed to reveal the thinking process. This method is useful for identifying problems with question comprehension, recall strategies, sensitivity of questions, response selection, and vagueness of reference periods. The most common criticism of cognitive interviewing techniques is that they are somewhat artificial, sometimes causing the respondent to engage in behavior and thinking patterns they would not normally engage in when responding to a question.

Expert panels gather substantive and methodological experts to critique questionnaires. These panels are a relatively inexpensive and quick alternative to the other question testing methods. Experts have "seen it all" over the years and can easily point out troublesome aspects of questionnaires.

Focus groups, that is, small groups of respondents asked to discuss survey questions, are able to generate a large amount of information in a short amount of time. However, this technique sometimes may result in a skewed group consensus due to group dynamics.

Split-half experiments examine the effects of different question wording, ordering, or format by randomly assigning different forms of a question to different respondents. However, these tests can be costly and may require larger sample sizes than a survey otherwise needs.

Gregory G. Holyk

See also Attitude Measurement; Behavior Coding; Bias; Closed-Ended Question; Cognitive Interviewing; Construct Validity; Contingency Question; Event History Calendars; Exhaustive; Focus Group; Forced Choice; Interviewer Debriefing; Mutually Exclusive; Nonattitude; Open-Ended Question; Paper-and-Pencil Interviewing (PAPI); Questionnaire; Questionnaire Length; Questionnaire-Related Error; Question Wording as Discourse Indicators; Reliability; Respondent Burden; Response Alternatives; Satisficing; Validity; Variance

Further Readings

Aday, L. A. (2006). *Designing and conducting health surveys: A comprehensive guide* (3rd ed.). San Francisco: Jossey-Bass.

Dillman, D. A. (2006). *Mail and Internet surveys: The tailored design method* (2nd ed.). New York: Wiley.

Fowler, F. J., Jr. (1993). *Survey research methods* (2nd ed.). Newbury Park, CA: Sage.

Fowler, F. J., Jr. (1995). *Improving survey questions: Design and evaluation.* Thousand Oaks, CA: Sage.

Oppenheim, A. N. (1999). *Questionnaire design, interviewing, and attitude measurement.* New York: Pinter.

Schaeffer, N. C., & Presser, S. (2003). The science of asking questions. *Annual Review of Sociology, 29,* 65–88.

QUESTIONNAIRE LENGTH

Questionnaire length refers to the amount of time it takes a respondent to complete a questionnaire. Survey instruments can vary in length from less than a minute to more than an hour. The length of a questionnaire is important because it can directly affect response rates, survey costs, and data quality. Longer questionnaires result in higher data collection costs and greater respondent burden and may lead to lower response rates and diminished quality of response. However, practical experience and experimental data suggest that below a specific threshold, questionnaire length bears little relationship to response rate or data quality and has only a minor impact on survey costs.

For telephone and online surveys, although longer questionnaires will result in higher data collection costs, it is generally recognized that questionnaire length is a major factor for these modes only when it exceeds 20 minutes. The field cost of increasing the length of a telephone interview 1 minute beyond the 20-minute mark is 2 to 3 times as high as the cost of adding another minute to a 15-minute telephone interview. This higher cost reflects the lower response rates associated with longer interviews (due to the effects of the increase in respondent burden) and the greater number of interviewer hours needed to achieve the same sample size. The cost of administering a Web survey is similarly increased when the length of interview exceeds 20 minutes. In this case, additional monetary incentives and rewards must be offered to prompt respondents to complete a longer interview. For mail surveys, questionnaire length has a small impact on field costs compared to phone and online surveys. Longer mail questionnaires may require more postage and data entry will be more expensive, but these cost increases are generally not as large as those for other modes of data collection. With in-person interviewing, respondents do not appear to be as affected by the length of the questionnaire as they do by the length of other survey modes.

Questionnaire length also affects data quality. For telephone surveys, long questionnaires get lower response rates than short questionnaires and may therefore be subject to more potential nonresponse bias. The length of a telephone questionnaire affects response rates in two ways. First, when interview length is specified in the respondent introduction or otherwise disclosed by interviewers prior to the first substantive question, the number of refusals tends to be higher for a longer questionnaire than for a shorter one. Second, the more time an interview takes, the greater the chance that a respondent will break off the interview because of disinterest, to attend to personal business, or for some other reason. Refusals and break-offs can be recontacted in order to complete an interview, but this adds time and cost to a survey research project. There is also evidence that both respondents and interviewers can get fatigued toward the end of a long telephone survey, possibly compromising data quality, for example, through an increased tendency to satisfice. Mail survey data quality can also be affected by questionnaire length through lower response rates, but there is no widely accepted threshold beyond which a mail survey's response rate declines significantly.

As noted earlier, face-to-face interviewing is less affected by length of interview than are other methodologies, partly because respondents' initial agreement to allow interviewers into their homes tends to make them more receptive to making a major time commitment. Before telephone surveys became the most popular methodology, the norm was to conduct interviews face-to-face. The main cost incurred with in-person interviewing often was associated with sending the interviewer out into the field and not necessarily how long the interviewer remained at a particular household once he or she was there. These in-person surveys often ranged in interview length from 45 minutes to an hour. But even this methodology is subject to limits in questionnaire length; in-person surveys that take as long as 75 minutes to administer are reported to have lower response rates than those that can be completed in 45 minutes.

Questionnaire length is only one of many factors that influence a survey's data quality. For example, long questionnaires are less likely to have low response rates when respondents are engaged and interested in the survey topic, and long, mail survey questionnaires that are well-designed can result in higher response rates than shorter questionnaires that are not

as attractive to respondents. By adding steps to the data collection process, such as advance letters, incentives, and reminder mailings or phone calls, researchers can match or even exceed the boost in response rate that would be obtained by shortening a questionnaire.

Larry Hugick and Jonathan Best

See also Partial Completion; Questionnaire; Questionnaire Design; Response Rates; Respondent Burden; Satisficing

Further Readings

Dillman, D. A. (2000). *Mail and Internet surveys: The tailored design method*. New York: Wiley.

QUESTIONNAIRE-RELATED ERROR

Error related to the questionnaire is one component of total survey error. This type of error is traditionally viewed as being a discrepancy between the respondent's answer and the "true" score or answer. Questionnaire-related errors may stem from the content of the questionnaire (the wording, ordering, and/or formatting of the questions themselves), the method of delivery (whether by interviewer, by telephone, on paper, by computer, or some other mode), the materials that accompany the questionnaire (such as show cards in a face-to-face survey), or all of these things. The focus in this entry is primarily on response error by respondents, although these other factors can be considered secondary aspects of questionnaire-related error.

Recent work on questionnaire error draws on cognitive psychology to inform the design of standardized instruments. One prominent framework of the survey response process (or the mental steps a person undergoes when answering survey questions), advanced by Roger Tourangeau, Lance Rips, and Ken Rasinski, consists of four major components: (1) comprehension and interpretation of the question; (2) retrieval of relevant information from memory; (3) judgment, or deciding on an answer; and (4) response, including mapping the answer to response categories and reporting the answer.

Errors may arise at any step, and the questionnaire may affect the likelihood and extent of those errors. Although there are many design principles that minimize error, often there are trade-offs that researchers need to consider when adopting any given solution.

Comprehension

Taking steps to ensure question comprehension by respondents is often the first stage in developing a questionnaire that minimizes error due to misunderstanding or misinterpreting questions. In general, the more complex or ambiguous the task, the more error there will be. Questions may contain words unfamiliar to the respondent, may have complex syntax, or may assume a higher level of respondent cognitive ability than is warranted. Sometimes researchers use specialized terminology rather than colloquial language. Respondents may also not pay close attention and may miss part of the question.

One difficulty is that many words in natural language are ambiguous, and researchers often must use vague quantifiers that have an imprecise range of application. Some examples include categories of words denoting frequency (e.g., *never, sometimes, pretty often, very often*), probability expressions (e.g., *very unlikely, somewhat unlikely, likely*), amounts (e.g., *none, some, many, all*), and strength (e.g., *extremely dissatisfied, very dissatisfied, somewhat dissatisfied*). There is evidence that respondents have varied associations with words that denote frequency, regularity, or size. For example, *How often ...?* results in variability based on how respondents interpret the word *often*. It is advisable to use more specific quantifiers, such as *On how many days ...?* or *How many times in the last week/month/year ...?*

Simple words or categories that appear to have common understandings, such as *household* or *sibling*, can be interpreted differently. When possible, such terms should be defined so as to minimize variability in how respondents interpret them. For example, *household* can include persons who use the address as their permanent address but who are not physically living there, such as college students who live in dormitories, individuals on military duty, or individuals who may reside at that address for only part of the year. *Sibling* may include biological siblings, half siblings, and adopted or stepsiblings.

Retrieval of Events and Behaviors

The retrieval stage of the response process involves bringing information from long-term memory to working memory. Though respondents occasionally may have the opportunity and the inclination to refer to documents for their answers, they most often need to rely on memory. In general, the more complex the memory task is, the less accurate the respondents' answers will be, thereby contributing to questionnaire-related error.

Most questions are time-bound so time frames or reference periods should be specified, partly to avoid ambiguity and partly to ease the recall task. For example, when asking how many people live in the household, the time span should be clear (e.g., *during the last 12 months, since [month] of last year*). Similarly, it should be clear if the reference period is calculated in days or is defined by the calendar (e.g., the last 30 days or the most recent calendar month). Longer reference periods increase both the time over which respondents have to remember events and the number of events respondents have to remember, both of which decrease accuracy. Because more recent events are easier to recall than older events, asking about more recent reference periods increases accuracy.

As the retention interval becomes longer, respondents rely less on direct recall and more on inference in answering questions. Thus respondents may be subject to *forward telescoping*, or mistakenly reporting events that happen before the reference period, as well as to *backward telescoping*, or omitting events that occur during the reference period. One method for reducing telescoping is *bounded recall*, which involves enumerating for respondents critical events that may have occurred at the boundaries for the reference period.

Questions asking for dates may be particularly difficult to answer accurately because dates (especially for common events such as going to the grocery store) are not normally kept in memory. Instead, respondents will infer dates from other life events they may use to anchor their memories (e.g., "in the spring, after my child was born ..."). For example, college students may organize events in memory around the academic school year calendar (e.g., fall semester, homecoming weekend, Christmas break, spring break, freshman year). Questionnaire experts recommend using calendars and noting personal landmarks to promote recall. Distinctive or emotionally involving events (e.g., purchase of a new home) are easier to recall than nonsalient, frequent, and typical events (e.g., going to the ATM to withdraw money).

Smaller categories of events also help recall accuracy. For example, asking about time spent on housework during the past 7 days may be more manageable if respondents are asked separately about time spent cleaning, time spent cooking, and time spent washing and ironing (or other household activities). Providing multiple cues and decomposing the task can improve recall. In addition, spending more time on the task gives respondents more time to search memory. Thus longer introductions and a slower interviewing pace can be beneficial. Finally, some research suggests it is possible to motivate respondents to search their memories more carefully by highlighting the importance of accurate information; the impact of this, however, is normally small.

Threatening and Socially Desirable Behaviors

The likelihood and extent of respondent error may be correlated with the nature of the event being asked about and the respondent characteristics being measured. For example, a question asking respondents about the number of sexual partners they have had may be answered more accurately by respondents with few partners and less accurately by respondents with more partners because the latter have more to remember. In addition, this question may be sensitive; it may be perceived as socially desirable or undesirable to report a certain number of sexual partners. Questions about illegal behaviors, such as cocaine usage, may also be perceived as threatening and may result in underreporting of behaviors, whereas questions about behaviors perceived as socially desirable, such as voting, may result in overreporting of behaviors.

Minimizing error often involves reassuring the respondent of confidentiality, an action that encourages accurate reporting. However, while part of the error may be due to intentional misrepresentation, the social desirability of a behavior may interact with memory so that socially undesirable behaviors are remembered as occurring less frequently, and socially desirable behaviors are remembered as occurring more frequently. Thus memory aids can increase accuracy in the reporting of such behaviors.

Subjective Phenomena Questions

As in questions about events and behaviors, accuracy for subjective questions necessitates comprehension on the part of the respondent. Subjective questions may be poorly worded or confusing, leading to variability in respondent interpretations of certain words or phrases. Questions may also be double-barreled, making it difficult to respond to them. However, while events and behaviors generally are thought to entail recall from long-term memory, questions asking about attitudes involve a combination of memory and inference.

Traditionally, attitudes were thought to be long-term values that were recalled from memory at the moment when asked. Recent research on attitudes suggests that there may be instances when attitudes are recalled from memory and other instances when they are formed anew each time they are called for. That is, rather than search the mental "file cabinet" for one's rating of the president or one's attitude on foreign policy, respondents integrate the bits of information in working memory into an attitude, for example, each time they are asked about the president or foreign policy. Respondents may use previous evaluations, impressions, general values, specific beliefs, or even information from prior survey questions to form their responses.

Thus the notion of accuracy in reports of subjective phenomena differs from accuracy in reports of events and behaviors. Accuracy often means that responses were not unduly swayed in one direction, that the question and response alternatives were balanced, and that biasing information was not conveyed to the respondent. In addition, the context in which the question was asked (e.g., what other question or questions closely preceded it) is important to how respondents answer because information provided earlier may frame the context for current questions.

When researchers report the results of attitude questions, they must make the question wording and context available to the reader. It is impossible to talk about accuracy or error without knowing the wording and context in which the question was asked. Furthermore, results related to attitude stability or reliability need to be interpreted with caution. Such statistics may help point out questions that need to be improved, but low stability or reliability scores are not necessarily artifacts of measurement. They may also be substantively informative about people's attitudes on a given topic.

Trade-Offs

Although the questionnaire design principles mentioned earlier minimize many errors, they may introduce yet others and need to be balanced against other considerations, namely, interview time, respondent burden, and cost. The more strategies that are used to help respondents remember, the more likely it is that the questionnaire will encourage recall of events and behaviors that occur outside the time frame of interest. Similarly, providing examples may help the respondent understand what is meant by the question, but it may focus the respondent exclusively on the examples provided. In asking how many days the respondent reads a news magazine, one might provide examples (e.g., . . . *such as* Time, Newsweek, *or* US News and World Report) at the risk of focusing the respondent entirely on the examples and excluding other news magazines that are not in the question text. Thus specificity in the question may reduce error due to comprehension or interpretation problems, but it may introduce other types of error, such as errors of omission.

In addition, many of the solutions to increase accuracy also increase cost. Providing examples in the question text lengthens the question; decomposing all events and behaviors in a questionnaire could lengthen the interview considerably; and using event history calendars adds extra time to administer. When multiplied over many questions, this may increase questionnaire length and respondent burden. When multiplied over many respondents, this can increase costs. Researchers must decide which trade-offs are most appropriate for their particular survey. In addition, the more tasks there are for interviewers to administer, the more interviewer variability is introduced as a source of error.

Questionnaire design that minimizes error is often thought of as being part art and part science. Good questionnaires generally combine good design principles (the "art") and insights from cognitive psychology (the "science"). Researchers continue to strive to make questionnaire design more of a science; however, there are many particularities in how people remember and report events and subjective experiences in different areas of their lives, and there is unfortunately no overarching theory of questionnaire design. In general, it is good to invest resources in developing appropriate questions using ethnographic techniques, in evaluating comprehension and interpretation using cognitive interviewing, and in testing and evaluating questionnaires prior to fielding them. Pilot surveys are invaluable and provide an opportunity for behavior coding to systematically count the occurrence of problematic interviewer or respondent behaviors. Finally, interviewing protocols and other aspects of instrumentation (such as visual layout of a questionnaire) also need to be considered.

Danna Basson

See also Bounding; Cognitive Aspects of Survey Methodology (CASM); Cognitive Interviewing; Confidentiality; Context Effect; Double-Barreled Question; Errors of Omission; Interviewer-Related Error; Measurement Error; Mode-Related Error; Pilot Test; Questionnaire Design; Questionnaire Length; Question Order Effects; Reference Period; Respondent Burden; Respondent-Related Error; Social Desirability; Telescoping; Total Survey Error (TSE); True Value; Visual Communication

Further Readings

Bradburn, N. M., Sudman, S., & Wansink, B. (2004). *Asking questions: The definitive guide to questionnaire design for market research, politics, and social and health questions.* San Francisco: Jossey-Bass.

Presser, S., Rothgeb, J. M., Couper, M. C., Lessler, J. T., Martin, E., Martin, J., et al. (2004). *Methods for testing and evaluating survey questionnaires.* Hoboken, NJ: Wiley-Interscience.

Schuman, H., & Presser, S. (1996). *Questions and answers in attitude surveys: Experiments in questions form, wording, and context.* Thousand Oaks, CA: Sage.

Sirken, M. G., Hermann, D. J., Schechter, S., Schwarz, N., Tanur, J. M., & Tourangeau, R. (Eds.). (1999). *Cognition and survey research.* New York: Wiley.

Tourangeau R., Rips, L. J., & Rasinski, K. (2000). *The psychology of the survey response.* Cambridge, UK: Cambridge University Press.

Zaller, J., & Feldman, S. (1992). A simple theory of the survey response: Answering questions or revealing preferences? *American Journal of Political Science, 36,* 579–616.

QUESTION ORDER EFFECTS

The order in which questions are asked in a questionnaire can have a significant effect on the results. The preceding questions provide the context in which the respondent answers an item, and changing this context can make a large difference in the survey results.

There are a number of ways in which items that appear earlier in a questionnaire can affect responses to later questions. One is by establishing a norm of reciprocity or fairness, a frequently cited example of which is provided by the work of Herbert Hyman and Paul Sheatsley from more than 50 years ago. These researchers varied the order of two questions: one on whether the United States should allow communist reporters from other countries to come to the United States and send back to their newspapers the news as they saw it and another on whether a communist country like Russia should let American newspaper reporters come in and send back to America the news as they saw it. Changing the order resulted in a difference of 37 percentage points in the percentage of "yes" responses to the question on communist reporters and a 24 percentage point difference in the results for the American reporters item. When either of the items was asked second, the context for the item was changed as a result of the answer to the first, and the responses to the second were more in line with what would be considered "fair," based on the previous response.

Another way in which the earlier questions in a survey can affect results is by altering the frame in which a question is interpreted. For example, if respondents are asked about their interest in politics as the first item in a series, their reported level of interest is likely to be higher than if this question appears after a series of potentially difficult political knowledge items, such as whether they happen to remember anything special that their U.S. Representative had done for their district or how they had voted on any particular legislative bill. When the "interest in politics" item is asked first, respondents answer in terms of their general experience and may report a fairly high level of interest based on watching the network news regularly or talking about politics with their friends. Asking the knowledge questions first changes the meaning of "interest in politics"; respondents are more likely to interpret this in terms of having specific knowledge about how their member of Congress has acted. Because most respondents cannot remember any such specific information, the context of the question leads them to report a lower level of political interest.

Question order can also change the salience of various alternatives. In surveys that ask about the most important problem facing the country, for example, this question generally will be one of the first items asked. In this position, respondents are more likely to provide an answer based on their recent experience. If they are first asked a series of questions about some

issue such as immigration or public education, the percentage of respondents who cite this issue as "the most important problem" will be higher. By making immigration or public education more salient to the respondent, this question order will change the context in which they interpret the "most important problem" item, and these different question orders will produce different results.

Another type of question order effect that has been identified is termed a *part–whole contrast effect*. Such an effect can occur when a series of items on a particular topic includes both a rather general item and a more specific question. When the general and specific items are asked in different orders, the results for the specific item are generally unaffected, whereas those for the general item change significantly. In these situations, agreement with the more general item implies agreement with the more specific item, but the reverse is not true. When respondents are asked the general item after the more specific one, they may "subtract" their response to the specific question, altering the distribution of responses to the general item when it is asked after, rather than before, the more specific one.

Series of questions that have the same response format are also subject to effects due to question order. Items in such series may be affected by the content of the items that precede them in the list or potential response set bias among respondents. For example, in a survey about city services in which respondents are asked to rate various services as either excellent, good, fair, poor, or very poor, ratings for garbage collection services may differ depending on whether this item is asked before or after other services such as police protection, fire protection, or arts and cultural activities. One way in which researchers have attempted to address this issue is through randomization of these items, in which each of them is presented first to some respondents, each presented last to others, and at all positions in between across respondents. Through randomization, all possible orders of this set of items may be presented. Although this technique does not necessarily eliminate potential question order effects, randomization is thought to distribute any such effects across the set of items, so that no particular item is either relatively advantaged or disadvantaged by its position in the list.

There are no technical procedures for eliminating question order effects. Not every question can be first in the questionnaire, and questions asked early set the context in which later questions are interpreted. Question order effects are also persistent, and separating items for which there is likely to be an order effect with questions on unrelated topics generally does not eliminate such effects. In designing any questionnaire, therefore, careful consideration must be given to the potential for question order effects. Conducting cognitive interviews and a thorough pretest of the questionnaire also will help to identify such possible effects. Procedures such as randomization of sets of items or systematically varying the order of questions will serve to minimize the impact of question order or enable the researcher to specify the magnitude of such effects.

It is difficult to identify in advance the contexts in which question order effects will occur, and some effects will certainly arise despite the best efforts of the designers of survey questionnaires to minimize them. Identifying such effects is important in any analysis, but it may be of particular consequence in trend analyses, in which the focus is on change in opinions or attitudes. Even when the identical question is asked at different points in time, varying results may be due not to actual change but rather to the different order (context) in which the questions were asked.

Robert W. Oldendick

See also Cognitive Interviewing; Context Effect; Pilot Test; Random Order; Random Start; Response Bias; Topic Saliency

Further Readings

Bishop, G. F., Oldendick, R. W., & Tuchfarber, A. J. (1984). What must my interest in politics be if I just told you "I don't know"? *Public Opinion Quarterly, 2,* 510–519.

Hyman, H., & Sheatsley, P. (1950). The current status of American public opinion. In J. C. Payne (Ed.), *The teaching of public affairs: Twenty-first Yearbook of the National Council of Social Studies* (pp. 11–34). Washington, DC: National Council for the Social Studies.

Schuman, H., Kalton, G., & Ludwig, J. (1983). Context and contiguity in survey questionnaires. *Public Opinion Quarterly, 1,* 112–115.

Schuman, H., & Presser, S. (1996). *Questions and answers in attitude surveys.* Thousand Oaks, CA: Sage.

Sigelman, L. (1981). Question-order effects on presidential popularity. *Public Opinion Quarterly, 2,* 199–207.

QUESTION STEM

A question stem is the part of the survey question that presents the issue about which the question is asking. With closed-ended questions, the stem can perhaps best be defined as the first half of a survey question that consists of two parts: (1) the wording or text that presents the issue the respondent is being asked to consider (along with any instructions, definitions, etc.) and (2) the answer options (response alternatives) from which a respondent may choose.

Survey researchers must strive to craft question stems that meet a number of important criteria. First and foremost, question stems must be written so that, to the degree that this can be controlled, all respondents understand the question being posed to them as meaning the same thing. If a given question is perceived differently by different types of respondents, it essentially becomes multiple questions capturing different things, depending on respondent perception. Because of this, survey researchers must make every attempt to word question stems simply and write to the population of interest. Question designers should consider providing definitions of terms and any guidance they can in a given question stem to ensure uniform understanding of concepts and terms.

Although questions including definitions, examples, and so forth, are created with the best of intentions, they may be too cumbersome for respondents. Survey researchers should avoid question stems that are too long and wordy; question stems should be as succinct as possible. Survey researchers are encouraged to break up complex issues into separate questions in order to aid respondent understanding. In doing so, the creation of double-barreled questions is also avoided.

In addition to being worded to ensure respondents' understanding, question stems must also be carefully worded to avoid affecting the results of a given item. Question stems should be written without the use of inflammatory phrases and should not purposely contain emotional or slanted language that could influence respondents and bias results. As the survey research industry continues to move toward the use of mixed-mode data collection and the full conversion of surveys from one mode to another, question stems must be checked carefully for mode appropriateness as well. Different modes rely on different words, instructions, and phrasing to communicate ideas, and question stems must be constructed in ways that do not confuse respondents. For example, closed-ended question stems offered in mail surveys, where respondents are able to see answer choices below question text, often must be altered for telephone surveys, where the categories must become part of the question stem that is read to respondents.

Although it is simple to define a question stem in theory, survey researchers may find it difficult in practice to develop a question stem that is appropriate, adequate, and understood by respondents. Many attempt to develop high-quality question stems in an effort to capture information on a respondent's attitude or beliefs toward a given issue but fall short due to a number of pitfalls. For this reason, experts have encouraged researchers for decades to design question stems based on quality items already developed and tested.

David James Roe

See also Bias; Closed-Ended Question; Mode of Data Collection; Open-Ended Question; Questionnaire Design

Further Readings

Fowler, F. J., Jr. (1995). *Improving survey questions: Design and evaluation.* Thousand Oaks, CA: Sage.

Schuman, H., & Presser, S. (1996). *Questions and answers in attitude surveys: Experiments on question form, wording and context.* Thousand Oaks, CA: Sage.

Sudman, S., & Bradburn, N. (1982). *Asking questions: A practical guide to questionnaire design.* San Francisco: Jossey-Bass.

QUESTION WORDING AS DISCOURSE INDICATORS

Many of the questions used by survey researchers serve to solicit people's opinions on topical issues, and the distribution of the answers to survey questions makes up what is usually considered to be the "public's opinions." Thus, most research on survey questions treats these questions as "stimuli" and focuses on their communicative and evocative functions. As such, scholars examine response biases associated with certain question formats or wordings, the cognitive processes underlying these biases, and the flow and conversational logic of the interviewing process. But survey questions also may be viewed as

responses, where those who formulate the questions are responding to meaningful social forces and conditions. Thus, survey questions can be excellent indicators for public discourse.

From this perspective, *the wording of survey questions* becomes the focus of analysis, and when studied systematically over time, question wording indicates the evolving discourse packages of important public issues. This entry introduces the notion of question wording as discourse indicators, develops its rationale, proposes content-analytic methods and concepts for such discourse analysis, and provides empirical examples of this approach.

Survey Questions as Indicators of Social Discourse

Public opinion and public discourse are often viewed as two parallel systems interacting with each other to provide interpretation and meaning to relevant events and policies. Discourse analysis reveals the evolving culture of issues and events in terms of their interpretive frames. The analysis of public opinion provides a glimpse into how individuals adopt such frames and which perspectives prevail on the aggregate. Frequency distributions of public opinion polls provide the latter. Public discourse packages of important public issues can be captured extremely well by content analysis of questions in public opinion polls through systematic examination of the language of survey questions.

It is commonly accepted that question–answer situations must be understood in the social context in which they take place. This contextual approach applies to the interview setting as well as to the content and form of the questions themselves, which must be seen as segments of the ongoing social discourse. In fact, survey questions and the way they frame issues are increasingly viewed as part of the elite discourse and political debate, which effectively shape popular discourse and thinking. Pollsters who design surveys are in the same position as public officials, editors, journalists, and newsmakers of all sorts: All choose how public issues are to be framed, and their choices have consequences.

Indeed there are good reasons to think of survey questions as useful indicators of social discourse on a specific issue. First, to be valid and reliable and to engage respondents, thus not adding to nonresponse, survey questions must be formulated in a way that carries widely shared meaning. Thus, pollsters often use words that respondents would use themselves in the same context, or they define key concepts in the questions in terms familiar to the respondents. Either way, the choice of wording reflects the ongoing political debate and, eventually, public discourse. Second, public opinion surveys and polls tend to focus on topical issues and current events and are likely to share similar choice criteria used by editors to decide what is news. Just like news items, they tend to concentrate on salient events and to reflect critical discourse moments. Third, when pollsters change question wording—often a hard decision for pollsters to make—they usually intend to either adapt to meaningful social changes or to write a better question. But writing better questions often means simply fine-tuning the questions so as to fit into a frame of reference perceived, by the pollster, as dominant or most relevant. Sometimes changes in questions are made to increase respondents' capability or willingness to respond. These changes do not occur arbitrarily but often indicate pollsters' assumptions about the salience of an issue, the public's level of knowledge, and the prevailing social norms affecting willingness to respond. In short, the reasons for introducing changes in question form and wording may, in fact, reflect developments in public discourse.

In addition to changes in question wording over time, there also may be differences in the wording and format used by separate research organizations and distinct studies of the same issue at a given point in time. These differences are often seen as nuisances by researchers who attempt to grasp public opinion on an issue. But for discourse analysis, these variations only enrich knowledge of the competing discourse frames and packages they may represent. Moreover, when such differences diminish and pollsters converge on similarly worded questions, this may indicate the emergence of a dominant discourse frame.

Content Analysis of Survey Questions

Various content-analytic methods and concepts may be applied to discourse analysis of question wording. Linguistic approaches offer especially profound and valuable tools for grasping the meaning embedded within the text without compromising reliability and generalizability. One such approach is that of Roberto Franzosi, which utilizes a semantic text grammar to organize textual data around a simple but flexible structure of Subject-Action-Object and their modifiers. The scheme reliably organizes textual data both hierarchically and relationally, with explicit links between important elements of discourse such as actors and actions. It is most useful for analyzing changes in the role and type of actors over time, in the nature of actions, and in their relationships with other elements of text. This fits the structure of many survey questions, which present respondents with alternative situations, scenarios, positions, or policies involving actors and a range of possible actions.

In addition to *semantic text grammar coding*, syntactic features that define the surface structure of the text (e.g., the use of passive or active voice) may provide valuable discourse indicators for the ideological leaning and cultural biases embedded in texts.

The deep structural schema of survey questions differs from that of other texts such as news reports. Importantly, even more than other types of text, standardized survey questions must presuppose respondents' social knowledge and integrate or supplement that knowledge in their wording. Coding question presuppositions offers especially valuable and compact indications of the "taken for granted" in public discourse, mutually known to all participants and often linked to ideological stances.

An illustration of the use of survey questions as discourse indicators may be given from a study of Israeli discourse on the Israeli–Arab conflict. Jacob Shamir, Neta Ziskind, and Shoshana Blum-Kulka built a comprehensive database of questions on peace and the territories. The data were collected systematically from the principal polling organizations, academic studies, and the leading daily newspapers. The study covered a 25-year period from June 1967, immediately after the Six-Day War, to October 1991 when the Madrid peace conference was convened. The study found a self-centered and self-serving discourse, which viewed Israel as the key actor in the conflict. Arab states and Palestinians were mainly action recipients and sometimes secondary initiators. Most noticeable was the marginal role of the Palestinian actor in Israeli discourse. Over time, the analysis revealed two major shifts in discourse on the territories. One was a transition from a general, abstract, and simplistic "territories for peace" frame to a concrete and policy-oriented approach referring to specific policy options. At the same time, the focus of discourse frames shifted from land to people: from a virtually exclusive focus on the territories to greater awareness of the Palestinian inhabitants in the territories. These two changes were not unrelated and coincided with a gradual increase in attention in the discourse to conflicting values in the political culture.

Summary

Public opinion surveys provide a natural arena in which discourse frames thrive and can be traced. Surveys closely follow current events and issues in the news. They constitute a key discourse domain of ongoing social action, a kind of self-contained system of communication highly indicative of the world of political discourse in general. They provide critical historical instances in the form of mini-texts, in which major themes on the public agenda, assumptions, and ideologies are crystallized in the form of questions. Therefore, content analysis of question wording provides an appealing approach for the study of political discourse.

Jacob Shamir

See also Content Analysis; Poll; Pollster; Public Opinion; Questionnaire; Questionnaire Design

Further Readings

Franzosi, R. (2004). *From words to numbers: Narrative, data, and social science.* Cambridge, UK: Cambridge University Press.

Gamson, W. A., & Modigliani, A. (1989). Media discourse and public opinion on nuclear power: A constructionist approach. *American Journal of Sociology, 9,* 1–37.

Kinder, D. R., & Sanders, L. M. (1990). Mimicking political debate with survey questions: The case of white opinion on affirmative action for blacks. *Social Cognition, 8,* 73–103.

Shamir, J., Ziskind, N., & Blum-Kulka, S. (1999). What's in a question: A content analysis of survey questions. *Communication Review, 3,* 353–377.

Quota Sampling

Quota sampling falls under the category of nonprobability sampling. Sampling involves the selection of a portion of the population being studied. In probability sampling each element in the population has a known nonzero chance of being selected through the use of a random selection procedure such as simple random sampling. Nonprobability sampling does not involve known nonzero probabilities of selection. Rather, subjective methods are used to decide which elements should be included in the sample. In nonprobability sampling the population may not be well defined. Nonprobability sampling is often divided into three categories: purposive sampling, convenience sampling, and quota sampling.

Quota sampling has some similarities to stratified sampling. The basic idea of quota sampling is to set a target number of completed interviews with specific subgroups of the population of interest. The sampling procedure then proceeds using a nonrandom selection mechanism until the desired number of completed interviews is obtained for each subgroup. A common example is to set 50% of the interviews with males and 50% with females in a random-digit dialing telephone interview survey. A sample of telephone numbers is released to the interviewers for calling. At the start of the survey, one adult is randomly selected from a sample household. It is generally more difficult to obtain interviews with males. So for example, if the total desired number of interviews is 1,000 (500 males and 500 females), and interviews with 500 females are obtained before interviews with 500 males, then no further interviews would be conducted with females and only males would be randomly selected and interviewed until the target of 500 males is reached. Females in those sample households would have a zero probability of selection. Also, because the 500 female interviews were most likely obtained at earlier call attempts, before the sample telephone numbers were thoroughly worked by the interviewers, females living in harder-to-reach households are less likely to be included in the sample of 500 females.

Quotas are often based on more than one characteristic. For example, a quota sample might have interviewer-assigned quotas for age by gender by employment status categories. For a given sample household the interviewer might ask for the rarest group first, and if a member of that group is present in the household, that individual will be interviewed. If a member of the rarest group is not present in the household, then an individual in one of the other rare groups will be selected. Once the quotas for the rare groups are filled, the interviewer will shift to filling the quotas for the more common groups.

The most famous example of the limitations of this type of quota sampling approach is the failure of the pre-election polls to predict the results of the 1948 U.S. presidential election. The field interviewers were given quotas to fill based on characteristics such as age, gender, race, degree of urbanicity, and socioeconomic status. The interviewers were then free to fill the quotas without any probability sampling mechanism in place. This subjective selection method resulted in a tendency for Republicans being more likely to be interviewed within the quota groups than Democrats. This resulted in the sample containing too many Republicans and causing the pre-election polls to incorrectly predict Thomas Dewey (the Republican candidate) as the winner.

Quota sampling is sometimes used in conjunction with area probability sampling of households. Area probability sampling techniques are used to select primary sampling units and segments. For each sample segment (e.g., city block) the interviewer is instructed to start at a corner of the segment and proceed around the segment, contacting housing units until a specific number of interviews are completed in the segment.

A major problem with quota sampling is the introduction of unknown sampling biases into the survey estimates. In the case of the 1948 U.S. presidential election, the sampling bias was associated with too many Republicans being selected. Another problem with quota sampling is that the sampling procedure often results in a lower response rate than would be achieved in a probability sample. Most quota samples stop attempting to complete interviews with active sample households once the quotas have been met. If a large amount of sample is active at the time the quotas are closed, then the response rate will be very low.

Michael P. Battaglia

See also Convenience Sampling; Nonprobability Sampling; Probability Sample; Purposive Sample; Simple Random Sample; Stratified Sampling

Further Readings

Henry, G. (1990). *Practical sampling.* Newbury Park, CA: Sage.

Kish, L. (1965). *Survey sampling* (2nd ed.). New York: Wiley.

R

RADIO BUTTONS

A radio button is a type of survey response format used in electronic questionnaire media such as Web surveys, email surveys, personal digital assistant (PDA) applications, and other electronic documents. The radio button response format allows respondents to select one, and only one, of a set of two or more mutually exclusive response options. Respondents select the response option of interest by using a mouse pointer, keyboard key, or touch-screen stylus. The term *radio button* is a reference to the punch-in buttons invented years ago on radios to choose a preset station, such as in an automobile; as each new button is pressed, the previously pressed button is returned to the neutral position.

Radio buttons are often displayed as a series of open circles with a value or value label shown next to each button. They can be listed vertically, horizontally, or in a grid or matrix. Other electronic response formats include (a) drop-down boxes for longer lists of options, (b) check boxes for check-all-that-apply questions, and (c) text input fields for open-ended responses. Radio buttons, like other on-screen electronic response formats, require the respondent to exercise care when selecting the option of interest, making the format susceptible to careless respondent error. This is particularly true for respondents with less extensive computer experience.

Although drop-down boxes require less screen space than do radio buttons, the latter more closely resemble the format used in paper-based questionnaires. Additionally, while all radio button options are immediately visible to the respondent, drop-down boxes require a series of actions by the respondent to open the drop-down list, scroll through the full set of options, and select a response. This difference can result in greater respondent burden, increased cognitive difficulty for the respondent, and response distribution differences due to primacy effects.

Adam Safir

See also Drop-Down Menus; Internet Surveys; Mutually Exclusive; Primacy Effects; Questionnaire Design; Respondent Error; Web Survey

Further Readings

Heerwegh, D., & Loosveldt, G. (2002). An evaluation of the effect of response formats on data quality in Web surveys. *Social Science Computer Review, 20* (4), 471–484.

Tourangeau, R., Crawford, S., Conrad, F. G., & Couper, M. P. (2004). What they see is what we get: Response options for Web surveys. *Social Science Computer Review, 22* (1), 111–127.

RAKING

Raking (also called raking ratio estimation) is a post-stratification procedure for adjusting the sample weights in a survey so that the adjusted weights add up to known population totals for the post-stratified classifications when only the marginal population totals are known. The resulting adjusted sample weights provide a closer match between the sample and the population across these post-strata than the original sample. Raking, however, assumes that nonrespondents in each post-stratum are like respondents. Nonetheless, when implemented with care, raking improves the mean squared error of sample estimates.

The term *raking* is used to describe this statistical technique because the raking ratio—the ratio of the population total (or control) total for a given post-stratum to the marginal row (or column) total from the sample for that same post-stratum—is calculated and then applied to each of the cells in that row (or column). This is done for each of the post-strata and repeated iteratively multiple times until the marginal row and column totals converge to the population totals. In essence, the raking ratio is "raked" over the cells in the respective rows and columns until convergence to the population totals is achieved, hence the term.

Raking was developed by W. Edwards Deming and Frederick F. Stephan in the late 1930s and used with the 1940 U.S. Census to ensure consistency between the census and samples taken from it. The computational procedure is the same as *iterative proportional fitting* used in the analysis of contingency tables, but the latter is not typically formulated in terms of weight adjustment.

The Two-Variable Raking Procedure

In two-variable (or two-dimensional) raking, population totals are known for the strata of two distinct variables. This situation can be represented by a rectangular array of cell estimates based on the initial sample weights with the "true" population row and column totals, called the row and column control totals, known. One objective is to adjust the cell entries so that both the row and column sums of the cell entries add up to the control totals.

The initial sample weights reflect the probabilities with which the sample units were selected and may incorporate a nonresponse adjustment as well. To preserve the original sample design and possible nonresponse adjustment, one objective of the raking procedure is to change the initial cell estimates as little as possible, subject to their adding up to the control totals in both dimensions.

The steps in raking are as follows. For the first variable (the row variable in a two-dimensional cross-tabulation), multiply the first row by the control total for row 1 divided by the sum of the cell entries for row 1. This adjustment will now make the cell entries for row 1 sum to the control total for that row. Then do the corresponding adjustment (multiplying the appropriate raking ratio for row 2 by each row 2 entry) to row 2. Continue in this way until all rows have been adjusted with each row summing to its respective control total.

For the second variable, multiply the first column by the control total for column 1 divided by the sum of the cell entries for column 1. At this point column 1 adds up to the control total for column 1, but the rows may no longer add up to their respective control totals. Continue multiplying each column by its respective raking ratio until all columns add up to their respective control totals. Then repeat the raking ratio adjustments on the rows, then the columns in an iterative fashion. (The appropriate raking ratios for the rows and columns will likely change in each iteration until the process converges.) Raking stops when all the rows *and* columns are within a pre-specified degree of tolerance or if the process is not converging. If raking converges, the new sampling weight for a sampling unit in a particular cell is the initial sampling weight times the raking-adjusted cell estimate divided by the initial cell estimate.

Because raking adjusts by a series of multiplications, any zero cell entry will remain zero. This property is advantageous in the case of structural zeros: cells that must be zero by definition or that are known to be zero in the entire population. In other cases, if the initial sample estimate for a cell is zero, but the population value may be positive, for example, the number of people suffering from a rare disease in a geographic area, it may be advisable to replace the initial zero estimate for the cell by a small positive value.

For two-variable raking, the process is known to converge if all initial cell entries are nonzero. If there are zero cells, for some configurations the process will not converge.

The Many-Variable Raking Procedure

Raking can also be performed when there are more than two distinct variables. For three variables, one has control totals for rows, columns, and pillars. The rows are adjusted to add up to the control totals, then the columns, then the pillars. These raking steps are repeated until convergence occurs. Raking is similarly specified for more than three control variables. Convergence is difficult to ascertain in advance, but the presence of zero cells is an important factor.

The Closeness Property

One of the properties of raking is that the raking-adjusted cell estimates are as close, in a specific sense, to the initial cell estimates as is possible subject to the raking-adjusted cell estimates adding up to the controls. For two-variable raking, let c_{ij} and r_{ij} denote, respectively, the initial and raking-adjusted cell estimates for the cell in row i and column j. Early researchers speculated that raking minimizes (subject to the constraints of the control totals) the weighted least squares distance between the c_{ij} and r_{ij}. In fact, raking minimizes (subject to the constraints of the control totals) $\sum_i \sum_j r_{ij} \log(r_{ij}/c_{ij})$ where the sum is over all cells ij with $c_{ij} > 0$. It can be verified that the sum is always nonnegative and only zero when $r_{ij} = c_{ij}$ for $c_{ij} > 0$. The corresponding conditions hold for more-than-two variable raking.

Practical Considerations

Raking is often employed when the control totals are not known exactly but can be estimated with higher accuracy than can the cell estimates. For example, for household surveys in the United States, demographic estimates from the Current Population Survey or the American Community Survey may be deemed accurate enough to use as control totals.

Much experience and fine tuning are needed in raking to determine the number of control variables to use and the number of cells. Too many control variables may lead to convergence problems or highly variable weights resulting in increased variance. In addition, if the variables used in the raking are not highly correlated with all the variables in the sample, then the variances for the uncorrelated variables can increase. Too few control variables may result in sample estimates that do not match the population as closely as otherwise could be achieved.

Michael P. Cohen

See also Bias; Mean Square Error; Post-Stratification; Weighting

Further Readings

Bishop, Y. M. M., Feinberg, S. E., & Holland, P. W. (1975). *Discrete multivariate analysis: theory and practice.* Cambridge: MIT Press.

Deming, W. E. (1943). *Statistical adjustment of data.* New York: Wiley.

Deming, W. E., & Stephan, F. F. (1940). On a least squares adjustment of a sample frequency table when the expected marginal totals are known. *Annals of Mathematical Statistics, 11,* 427–444.

Kalton, G. (1983). *Compensating for missing survey data.* Ann Arbor: University of Michigan, Institute for Social Research.

RANDOM

A process is *random* if its outcome is one of several possible outcomes and is unknown prior to the execution of the process; that is, it results merely by chance. Some survey operations are carried out as random processes because of advantages resulting from multiple possible outcomes or from the absence of advance knowledge about the outcome. Such survey operations are said to be *randomized* and are discussed in more detail later in this entry. *Random numbers* are the realized outcomes of a numeric-valued random process. They are used by researchers or survey-operations staff to carry out randomized survey operations. This entry discusses properties and sources of random numbers.

For some randomization operations, the needed random numbers must be integers uniformly distributed between 1 and some maximum value. For other operations the needed random numbers must be uniformly distributed between 0 and 1. Statistical tests exist for testing the quality of random numbers. These include tests for goodness of fit to the uniform distribution, tests for the absence of trends in sequences of random numbers, and tests for the absence of nonzero correlations between pairs of random numbers at fixed lags. Random numbers obtained by using simple devices such as dice, slips of paper drawn from a hat, or numbered balls removed from an urn often fail one or more of these tests and should not be used in professional survey work.

Tables of random numbers appearing in textbooks about statistical methods or survey sampling procedures can be used as sources of small quantities of random numbers. Early tables of random numbers were created by using series of digits from an irrational number, such as e or π, or by using a special-purpose electronic "roulette wheel." A much easier way to create tables of random numbers and to produce large quantities of random numbers for automated operations is to have a computer program generate *pseudorandom numbers*. These are numbers that appear to be random but are actually deterministic. A computer program cannot generate true random numbers because a program's outputs are completely determined by its logic and inputs, so outputs from a computer program are known. Algorithms for generating pseudorandom numbers appear easy to program, but there are a number of machine-dependent considerations and choices of parameters associated with successful implementation, so it is usually better to use existing computer code that has been thoroughly evaluated.

Richard Sigman

See also Random Assignment; Random Order; Random Sampling; Random Start

Further Readings

Gentle, J. E. (2003). *Random number generation and Monte Carlo methods* (2nd ed.). New York: Springer.

RANDOM ASSIGNMENT

Random assignment is a term that is associated with true experiments (called controlled clinical trials in medical research) in which the effects of two or more "treatments" are compared with one another. Participants (respondents, subjects, etc.) are allocated to treatment conditions in such a way that each participant has the same chance of being a member of a particular treatment group. The groups so constituted are therefore as similar as possible at the beginning of the experiment before the treatments are introduced. If they differ at the end of the experiment, there will be a statistical basis for determining whether or not, or to what extent, it is the treatments that were the cause of the difference.

Traditionally, survey research and experimental research have not had much in common with one another. However, the following examples illustrate some of the many ways that survey researchers can benefit from random assignment and experimental design.

A survey researcher would like to determine whether it would be better to use answer sheets for a particular questionnaire in which the responses to individual items are given by blackening in small ovals (the "new" way) or by blackening in the spaces between pairs of vertical dotted lines (the "old" way). In a pilot study carried out prior to the main study, two versions of the answer sheets would be prepared and participants would be assigned to one version or the other in such a way that chance, and chance alone, determines which form they receive. This illustrates *simple* random assignment. (The effect of type of answer sheet might be operationalized by the difference between the percentages of omitted items for the two forms, since large numbers of omitted items are not desirable in survey research.)

For *stratified* random assignment, better designated as *blocking*, the participants are divided into two or more strata and then randomly assigned to treatments within strata (blocks). For the answer sheet example, if a researcher were carrying out the experiment to test the effect of the new way (the experimental treatment) versus the old way (the control treatment) for a sample that consisted of 10 males and 20 females and wanted to be sure that there were proper proportions of males and females in each of the treatments, he or she would randomly assign 5 of the males to the experimental treatment and the other 5 males to the control treatment, and would randomly assign 10 of the females to the experimental treatment and the other 10 females to the control treatment. That would permit testing for the "main effect" of treatment, the "main effect" of sex, and the sex-by-treatment "interaction effect."

There is occasional confusion in the literature between random *assignment* and random *sampling*. The purpose of the former, as noted earlier, is pre-experimental equivalence of treatment groups so that post-treatment differences can be attributed to the effects that are caused by the treatments themselves. Thus the objective is one of *internal validity*. The purpose of the latter, however, is to be able to generalize from a sample to the population from which the sample has been drawn. That objective is concerned with *external validity*.

Traditional approaches to sample-to-population inferences such as the *t*-test have often been incorrectly used to analyze the data for true experiments in which random assignment has been employed but random sampling has not; that is, the participants have been selected by some sort of convenience sampling procedure. The appropriate inferential statistical technique for such studies is a randomization test (sometimes called a permutation test). The actual difference between treatment groups is compared with all possible differences that could have been obtained under different randomizations.

Ideally, a study should possess both generalizability and causality; that is, researchers would like to be able to employ both random sampling and random assignment. For nonexperimental research, a researcher might have random sampling but not random assignment (e.g., because there are no "treatments" to "assign" subjects to), in which case there would be a statistical basis for generalizability to the population but an insufficient basis for assessing causality. Or a researcher may not have the luxury of either random sampling or random assignment. That does not necessarily mean that the researcher should not carry out the study and report its results. But it does mean that the researcher will be restricted to the use of descriptive statistics only, with any sort of generalizable or causal interpretation being necessarily subjective.

Although the objectives of random assignment and random sampling are different, researchers can use the same random-number "tables" for accomplishing both. There are computerized routines available on the Internet that provide, at no charge, a random sample of n numbers out of N numbers (where n is less than or equal to N) and/or a random assignment of N numbers into subsets of $n_1, n_2, \ldots, n_k$, where the sum of those subscripted n's is equal to N, and k is the number of treatments. For an example, see the Research Randomizer Web site, which offers a quick way to generate random numbers or assign participants to experimental conditions.

Thomas R. Knapp

See also Experimental Design; External Validity; Interaction Effect; Internal Validity; Main Effect; Random; Random Sampling

Further Readings

Campbell, D. T., & Stanley, J. C. (1966). *Experimental and quasi-experimental designs for research*. Chicago: Rand McNally.

Edgington, E. S., & Onghena, P. (2007). *Randomization tests* (4th ed.). London: Chapman & Hall/CRC.

Ludbrook, J., & Dudley, H. (1998). Why permutation tests are superior to t and F tests in biomedical research. *American Statistician, 52* (2), 127–132.

Orwin, R. G., & Boruch, R. F. (1982). RRT Meets RDD: Statistical strategies for assuring response privacy in telephone surveys. *Public Opinion Quarterly, 46* (4), 560–571.

RAND Corporation. (2001). *A million random digits with 100,000 normal deviates*. Glencoe, IL: Free Press. (Original work published 1955)

Research Randomizer: http:www.randomizer.org

RANDOM-DIGIT DIALING (RDD)

Random-digit dialing (RDD) refers to a set of techniques for drawing a sample of households from the frame or set of telephone numbers. The telephone number is the sampling unit that is the link to the household and its members. While the specific sampling techniques employed to draw RDD samples have changed over time, the three most influential RDD techniques are briefly described in this entry. RDD is distinguished from other telephone sampling methods because RDD selects the sample from the frame of telephone numbers, whereas the other methods select from lists of numbers in directories or commercial lists. The ability to sample all telephone households, not just those households on a list, is one reason for the popularity of RDD sampling. This entry ends by discussing two issues that often arise in RDD sampling: selecting RDD samples for local areas and selecting persons within the household to interview.

The basic RDD approach is simple. Using information on the structure of the telephone numbering scheme used in North America, the set of all numbers that could be assigned to households is identified. These numbers are randomly sampled, often with equal probability. The techniques for randomly selecting the numbers are defined by the specific RDD sampling scheme. The sampled numbers are dialed, and those that are residential are the sampled households. In many RDD surveys only members in a certain age range or of a specific sex are eligible to be interviewed. The data collected from the sample are used to make estimates or inferences. The estimates usually refer to all households, even though households without telephones are not covered.

RDD surveys became popular by the late 1970s, and the technique soon became the predominant method of sampling households in the United States. The popularity of RDD coincided with evidence that a large proportion of households lived in telephone households and could be sampled or covered in RDD surveys. By 1980, over 90% of adults lived in households with landline telephones and the percentage continued to grow slightly, to around 97% by 2000.

An important advantage of RDD sampling that helped to spur its acceptance is the relatively low cost of sampling and conducting surveys by telephone as compared to face-to-face surveys. An RDD sample is likely to cost less than 20% of the costs of an area probability sample that has the same precision. These great cost advantages fueled the early acceptance of RDD in commercial surveys. It also is the feature that makes it possible to conduct surveys of rare population groups with probability samples. For example, the Centers for Disease Control and Prevention conduct a survey to monitor childhood vaccinations in each state and large metropolitan area, even though they sample only households with children between 19 and 35 months old, that is, approximately 1 in 50 U.S. households. The cost of this type of survey by face-to-face methods would be astronomical.

Despite these advantages, the utility of RDD surveys has been questioned in recent years. One concern is the decrease in response rates in telephone surveys. Response rates in RDD surveys have always been lower than in face-to-face surveys but higher than in mail surveys conducted without extensive follow-up mailings. However, as response rates have continued to decline in RDD surveys, the potential for nonresponse bias in estimates has increased. An important reason for the lower response rates is that technological advances have made it easier for households to identify and avoid telephone calls from unrecognized telephone numbers.

Another challenge to RDD samples is the emergence of wireless or cell telephones as a major method of communication in the United States. As a larger proportion of households drop their landlines and subscribe only to wireless telephone service, the potential for noncoverage bias in estimates from RDD surveys increases because RDD surveys traditionally exclude wireless telephones. The percentage of U.S. households that have only wireless service has increased from less than 1% around 2000 to 20% by the end of 2007. A related problem for RDD samples is that even in some households that have retained a landline, household members may rely on their wireless telephones to such an extent that interviewers may not be able to contact the household members on their landlines. By the end of 2007,

approximately 10% of U.S. households fell into this category.

Other issues confronting RDD surveys include the introduction of Voice over Internet Protocol, number portability, and national do-not-call lists. The effects of most of these have not yet become clear. If RDD is to retain its role as a premier method for sampling households, these topics must be addressed. Fortunately, the history of RDD sampling suggests that survey researchers are innovative, and further developments in this tradition are possible. The key methods for selecting RDD samples (described next) exemplify this innovation.

RDD Sampling Methods

The three most important RDD sampling techniques are (a) the original RDD method, (b) Mitofsky-Waksberg RDD sampling, and (c) list-assisted RDD sampling. Because all three of these RDD methods depend on the structure of telephone numbers in the United States, a review of the U.S. telephone number plan is given before summarizing the sampling techniques.

Each telephone number in the United States has 10 digits; the first 3 are called the area code, the next 3 are the prefix, and the last 4 are the suffix. The first 8 digits are sometimes collectively called "100-banks" because they define sets of 100 possible telephone numbers with the same first 8 digits. Area codes have specific geographic boundaries, although these boundaries are not necessarily consistent with geopolitical boundaries other than state lines. In recent years, multiple area codes have been assigned that cover portions of the same geography in densely populated areas. Prefixes within an area code cannot be directly associated with a smaller geographic area, but households within a prefix traditionally have tended to be clustered spatially. Prefixes within an area code are assigned a designation that identifies the type of service (e.g., regular household service, paging, cellular) associated with these numbers. Although these designations are generally accurate, a small percentage of numbers may be for services not consistent with the designation for the prefix.

The Original RDD Sampling Method

The original RDD sampling technique was formally introduced in 1964. The approach involved identifying area code–prefix combinations assigned for regular household telephones, and then appending a random 4-digit number to create a sampled telephone number. This process was repeated until the desired sample size was achieved. In this scheme, each number has an equal probability of selection. Households, on the other hand, have unequal probabilities of selection because they may have more than one telephone line in the household; thus, the household could be sampled on any of these numbers. But this inequality is easily remedied by either weighting adjustments or further subsampling, as is often done in case-control RDD samples. In the early days, the area code–prefix combinations were identified from local telephone directories, but later eligible combinations became available nationally from computerized files. In this RDD method, all possible telephone numbers, not just those listed in telephone directories, could be sampled. Furthermore, by taking advantage of the area code–prefix combination, the efficiency of sampling (i.e., contacting a residence with the dialed number) increased from less than 1% to over 20%. Alternatives to further improve the efficiency of the calling were offered, such as the add-a-digit method, but most of these methods suffered from other problems that limited their acceptance.

Mitofsky-Waksberg (MW) RDD Sampling

The next major advance was named the Mitofsky-Waksberg (MW) RDD sampling technique after its two developers, Warren Mitofsky and Joseph Waksberg. The method was developed after it was observed that residential numbers tended to be clustered within 100-banks. More specifically, a large portion of the eligible 100-banks had no residential numbers assigned, whereas in those with any residential numbers, over 30% of the numbers were residential. This was due largely to the ways local telephone companies assigned the numbers to customers. The MW scheme takes advantage of this clustering to improve calling efficiency using an equal probability, two-stage sampling scheme. The first stage begins with the random selection of 100-banks from the frame of eligible area code–prefixes. Two random digits are appended to form 10-digit telephone numbers that are dialed. If a sampled number is not residential, then the 100-bank is not sampled in the first stage. If the number is residential, then the 100-bank is sampled, and a set of additional numbers within the 100-bank are sampled to achieve a fixed number of residences within the 100-bank that are sampled. This scheme is

very elegant theoretically because 100-banks are sampled with probability exactly proportional to the number of residential numbers in the bank even though the number of residential numbers is unknown at the time of sampling. All households have the same probability of selection, with the same caveat given previously concerning multiple lines within the household. The biggest advantage of the MW method is its efficiency: About 60% to 65% of the numbers sampled in the second stage are residential. This was a marked improvement over the original RDD sampling. Due to its efficiency, the MW technique became the main method of RDD sampling for nearly two decades.

List-Assisted Sampling

Despite the popularity of the MW sampling technique, many alternatives were suggested because the method had some implementation and operational difficulties and the sample was clustered (the 100-banks are the first-stage clusters). The clustering reduced the statistical efficiency of the sample. In the early 1990s alternative methods of stratified RDD sampling were being explored, and technological developments allowed easy and inexpensive access to data to support these schemes. The most recent method of RDD sampling, list-assisted RDD sampling, was spawned from this environment and was quickly adopted by practitioners. In list-assisted RDD sampling all 100-banks in eligible area code–prefix combinations are classified by the number of directory-listed telephone numbers in the bank. A sample of 100-banks with x or more listed telephone numbers is selected (when $x = 1$ this is called the listed stratum). The other stratum (called the zero-listed stratum when $x = 0$) may be sampled at a lower rate or may not be sampled at all because it contains so few residential telephone numbers. Commercial firms developed systems to implement this method of sampling inexpensively. When research showed that excluding the zero-listed stratum resulted in minimal noncoverage bias, list-assisted sampling from only the listed stratum became the standard approach.

The list-assisted method is an equal probability sampling method that avoids both the operational and statistical disadvantages of the MW method. The calling efficiency of the list-assisted technique is approximately equal to that of the MW method. The efficiency has decreased over time as there has been less clustering of residential numbers in 100-banks, but the reduced clustering also affects the MW method. The lower percentage of residential numbers is also less of a problem because many organizations use predictive dialing to lower the labor costs associated with nonresidential numbers. Even those organizations that do not use predictive dialing themselves often take advantage of telephone purging methods provided by sampling vendors. After purging, about 70% of the sample numbers remaining are residential. By the mid-1990s, list-assisted RDD sampling, excluding the zero-listed stratum, had displaced the MW method as the primary RDD sampling technique in the United States.

Sampling Issues With RDD

The methods for RDD sampling could be used to conduct a household survey in which any adult in the household reports for the entire household. However, typical RDD surveys require sampling one individual or more to be interviewed, such as any adult or persons with a particular characteristic (e.g., all women over 55 years). Many methods for sampling one adult from a household are in the literature, but techniques for other sampling requirements are less frequently discussed. Frequently, the household is screened to determine if any person in the household is eligible. If there are any eligible members, then all the eligible persons or a sample of them is selected.

Another issue arises when estimates are needed for a local area, such as a city or county, rather than the entire nation or state. In local areas, it may not be possible to cleanly identify area code–prefix combinations that serve the local area because the assignments do not follow political boundaries. Sampling for local areas became more difficult with the introduction of number portability, which often allows households to keep their telephone numbers when they move out of their local area. One sampling approach for local areas is to include only those combinations that are almost entirely within the area, accepting the loss in coverage from households outside these combinations and number portability. A more precise, but expensive, approach is to include all the combinations that serve the local area and screen out those households that are sampled but do not live in the area. Other choices are possible, but all result in some compromise between coverage of the target population and cost of data collection.

J. Michael Brick

See also Add-a-Digit Sampling; Cluster Sample; List-Assisted Sampling; Mitofsky-Waksberg Sampling; Number Portability; Telephone Surveys; Voice over Internet Protocol (VoIP) and the Virtual Computer-Assisted Telephone Interviewing (CATI) Facility

Further Readings

Blumberg, S., Luke, J., & Cynamon, M. (2006). Telephone coverage and health survey estimates: Evaluating the need for concern about wireless substitution. *American Journal of Public Health, 96*, 926–931.

Brick, J. M., Waksberg, J., Kulp, D., & Starer, A. (1995). Bias in list-assisted telephone samples. *Public Opinion Quarterly, 59*, 218–235.

Cooper, S. L. (1964). Random sampling by telephone: An improved method. *Journal of Marketing Research, 1*, 45–48.

Gaziano, C. (2005). Comparative analysis of within-household respondent selection techniques. *Public Opinion Quarterly, 69*, 124–157.

Nathan, G. (2001). Telesurvey methodologies for household surveys—a review and some thoughts for the future. *Survey Methodology, 27*(1), 7–31.

Tucker, C., Lepkowski, J. M., & Piekarski, L. (2002). The current efficiency of list-assisted telephone sampling designs. *Public Opinion Quarterly, 66*, 321–338.

Waksberg, J. (1978). Sampling methods for random digit dialing. *Journal of the American Statistical Association, 73*, 40–46.

RANDOM ERROR

Random error refers to the fact that any survey measure taken over and over again may well be different (by some small amount) upon each measure, merely due to chance measurement imprecision. Thus, compared to the true value of the measure for a given respondent, the observed value will be on the high side some of the time and on the low side other times. This deviation of the observed value from the true value often is signified by e in the following formula:

$$X = T + e,$$

where X is the observed value and T is the true value. In theory, over many similar measures of the same variable taken from the same respondent, the average of the observed values will equal the true value. That is, the random error in measuring the variable of interest will deviate from the true value so that the sum of those deviations is expected to be zero. Random error is not consistent error and thus, by definition, it is not a part of bias, which is consistent (i.e., directional) *nonrandom* error.

The concept of random error serves as the basis for statistical inference. By measuring the size of the random error, statistical tests can be applied to determine the confidence with which a statistical inference can be drawn. Every sample statistic will have its associated random error, which typically is expressed as its standard error. Researchers have some control over the magnitude of the size of random error by increasing the sample size or using a sampling design that is more precise. The trade-off is that these techniques raise survey costs.

Paul J. Lavrakas

See also Bias; Sample Size; Standard Error; Statistic; True Value; Variance

Further Readings

Agresti, A., & Finley, B. (1997). *Statistical methods for the social sciences.* Upper Saddle River, NJ: Prentice Hall.
Hays, W. L. (1994). *Statistics* (5th ed.). Belmont, CA: Wadsworth.

RANDOMIZED RESPONSE

Researchers who study sensitive topics are often confronted with a higher refusal rate and often obtain more socially desirable answers. To tackle these problems, Stanley L. Warner introduced the randomized response technique (RRT). This is an interview method that guarantees total privacy and therefore, in theory, can overcome the reluctance of respondents to reveal sensitive or probably harmful information. Warner's original method used a randomization device (usually colored beads, coins, or dice) to direct respondents to answer one out of two statements, such as:

A: *I am a communist.* (A: selected with probability p)

B: *I am not a communist.* (not-A: selected with probability $1 - p$)

Without revealing to the interviewer which statement was selected by the dice, the respondent answers true or not true according to whether or not he or she

is a communist. Elementary probability theory can be used to get a bias-free estimate ($\hat{\pi}$) of the population probability of A (being a communist).

Profits and Costs of Using Randomized Response Techniques

The advantage of randomized response is that more valid population estimates of sensitive behavior can be derived. The cost is that randomized response is less efficient than a direct question. The randomization procedure increases the sampling variance, which makes it necessary to use larger samples. For example, Warner's method typically needs as many as 10 times the number of respondents to be just as powerful as a direct question design.

Extra costs are also associated with the increased complexity of the randomized response question. When randomized response is used, respondents have to understand and follow the instructions, in addition to understanding and formulating a response to the question itself. This introduces a new source of error, namely, misunderstanding the RRT procedures, cheating on this procedure, or both.

The advantage of using a randomized response technique outweighs the extra costs only when the population estimates become significantly more valid than estimates obtained from direct question–answer designs. Meta-analysis has shown that the advantage of using randomized response outweighs the disadvantage of having to use a larger sample if the social sensitivity of a research topic is large.

Other Randomized Response Techniques

Since Warner's original idea, many adaptations and refinements have been developed. First, methods were developed to improve the power of the design. As previously noted, compared to a direct question, Warner's method typically needs much larger samples. Variations on Warner's original method have been developed that have a larger statistical power. These methods include the *unrelated question technique* and the *forced response technique*. In addition, randomized response methods have been developed that are easier for the respondent, such as *Kuk's card method* and the *item count technique*.

The Unrelated Question Technique

The unrelated question technique uses a randomization device to direct the respondent to one of two unrelated questions, the sensitive question and an innocuous question, for example:

Do you have (sensitive attribute A)?

Do you have (the nonsensitive attribute B)?

The unrelated question technique is most efficient if the prevalence of the nonsensitive attribute B is known. In that case only one sample is needed to compute the unbiased estimate for the sensitive attribute A. An example of such a nonsensitive question is for instance: *Is/was your mother's birthday in July?* In this case, a sample of about twice the normal sample size is needed for the question to be as efficient as a direct question.

A disadvantage of the unrelated question method is that it is difficult to find nonsensitive questions with known prevalence in the population. When the prevalence of the nonsensitive question is not known, a second sample is needed to estimate the prevalence, and the advantage of the unrelated question technique over Warner's original method is lost.

The Forced Response Technique

In the forced response technique, only the sensitive question is asked, and the randomization device specifies the direction of the answer. For example, a pair of dice could be used, and respondents are requested to answer the sensitive question truthfully with "Yes" or "No" if the total roll of these dice is between 5 and 10. When the roll of the dice is 2, 3, or 4, the respondent is forced to answer "Yes," independent of the true score on the sensitive question. When the dice roll 11 or 12, the respondent is forced to answer "No," regardless of the true score on the question. Again, the meaning of an individual respondent's "Yes" or "No" answer is nil (and unknown to the researcher), but knowledge of the proportion of forced responses allows the researcher to estimate the prevalence of sensitive attribute A in the population.

The forced response technique is as efficient as the unrelated question method with known prevalence of the nonsensitive question. As a result, the sample has to be only about twice as large compared to direct question samples.

Kuk's Card Method

Kuk developed a randomized response method that avoids requiring the respondent to give direct answers like "Yes" or "No." A respondent receives two decks of cards and a sensitive question. One pack of cards is named the Yes-pack, to be used when the respondent should respond with "Yes" on sensitive attribute A. The respondent picks a card from the Yes-pack and names the color of the card: red or black. When the respondent's true answer is "No," the card of the other pack is read. The major disadvantage of Kuk's method is that it is very inefficient; in fact, statistically it is equivalent to Warner's original method.

The Item Count Technique

The item count technique, also known as the *unmatched count technique* and the *list-experiment technique*, was developed to avoid the extra cognitive burden on the respondent and the distrust that sometimes is associated with the use of a randomizer. The method is compellingly simple. There are two lists with activities: One list contains only innocent activities, and the other list contains one additional activity, the sensitive activity of interest. Respondents are randomly assigned to one of the lists. Each respondent is asked to report the number of activities he or she has engaged in but not the name of the activities. The difference in mean activities between the first and the second list is an estimate for the prevalence of the sensitive attribute.

The advantages of this method are the absolute anonymity of the respondent, the lower cognitive burden for the respondents, and compared to the direct question method, the power does not decrease. However, if the sensitive activity is rare, its variance will be very small, compared to the total variance. This will lessen the reliability of the estimated prevalence of the sensitive activity.

Analysis of Randomized Response Data

For all randomized response techniques, straightforward analysis techniques exist to estimate the prevalence of the sensitive behavior and the corresponding sampling variance. For all techniques except the item count technique, it is also possible to use a modified logistic regression analysis to estimate the relationships of the sensitive behavior with respondent characteristics. Again, the cost of randomized response techniques is that the standard errors of the regression weights will be larger than with ordinary logistic regression of data obtained by direct questioning. In addition, special software is needed to carry out this analysis; standard statistical packages cannot be used.

Joop Hox and Gerty Lensvelt-Mulders

See also Disclosure Limitation; List-Experiment Technique; Privacy; Sensitive Topics; Social Desirability

Further Readings

Droitcour, J., Caspar, R. A., Hubbard, M. L., Parsley, T. L., Visscher, W., & Ezzati, T. M. (1991). The item count technique as a method of indirect questioning: A review of its development and a case study application. In P. P. Biemer, R. M. Groves, L. E. Lyberg, N. A. Mathiowetz, & S. Sudman (Eds.), *Measurement errors in surveys* (pp. 185–210). New York: Wiley.

Fox, J. A., & Tracy, P. E. (1986). *Randomized response: A method for sensitive surveys*. Beverly Hills, CA: Sage.

Hox, J. J., & Lensvelt-Mulders, G. (2004). Randomized response analysis in Mplus. *Structural Equation Modeling, 11*(4), 615–620.

Lensvelt-Mulders, G. J. L. M., Hox, J. J., van der Heijden, P. G. M., & Maas, C. J. M. (2005). Meta-analysis of randomized response research. *Sociological Methods & Research, 33*(3), 319–348.

Warner, S. L. (1965). Randomized response: A survey technique for eliminating evasive answer bias. *Journal of the American Statistical Association, 60*, 63–69.

RANDOM ORDER

Random order refers to the randomization of the order in which questions appear in a questionnaire. The purpose is to overcome a type of measurement error known as context effects. This randomization is most often done using a computer program that controls a computer-assisted interview (CAI) being conducted in person, over the phone, or self-administered. Prior to the common use of CAI in survey research, sets of questions were randomized using modified Kish tables that were generated prior to the beginning of the survey and printed on labels indicating to the interviewers what order the questions were to be asked. The order changed randomly for each label to be printed. The

labels were pasted next to the question sets in the paper version of the questionnaire. The questions in the set were asked in the random order of the numbers on the label.

There are many issues that impact the response process when a question is presented to a respondent. The items immediately preceding a specific question often have no consequence. Concrete questions addressing facts such as demographic characteristics or behaviors are less likely to be affected by the context effect of the previous questions. However, questions requiring an attitude or opinion can more readily be influenced by the issues addressed in previous questions. Questionnaires are often designed so that a series of topically related attitude questions are presented one after another. In this situation, the likelihood of earlier questions affecting the interpretation of, and responses to, latter questions increases. Presenting the questions in this type of set in a random order minimizes the likelihood of this type of measurement error.

A simple example of this is the set of questions regarding abortion that have been included for many years in the General Social Survey:

Please tell me whether or not you think it should be possible for a pregnant woman to obtain a legal abortion if:

1. *The woman's own health is seriously endangered by the pregnancy.*

2. *There is a strong chance of a serious defect in the baby.*

3. *She became pregnant as a result of rape.*

4. *The family has a very low income and cannot afford any more children.*

5. *She is not married and does not want to marry the man.*

6. *She is married and does not want any more children.*

7. *The woman wants it for any reason.*

Each of these questions is about abortion, but the scenarios elicit a variety of potential emotions, value judgments, and other unpredictable issues that might influence a person's response to successive questions. There is strong reason to believe that asking the last question (number 7) first each time is likely to result in different percentages of positive and negative responses to questions 1 through 6 than if it were always asked after all the other questions.

This problem is overcome by randomizing the order of the questions in the set for each interview. Current software used in personal (CAPI), self- (CASI), and telephone interviewing (CATI) or in Internet surveying makes implementation of this process quite easy by automatically randomizing question order at presentation but reordering the data for ease of analysis. The resulting aggregate results present a more balanced view than might otherwise be achieved if the questions were always asked in the same order.

James Wolf

See also Context Effect; Computer-Assisted Personal Interviewing (CAPI); Computer-Assisted Self-Interviewing (CASI); Computer-Assisted Telephone Interviewing (CATI); General Social Survey (GSS); Measurement Error; Questionnaire-Related Error

Further Readings

Davis, J. A., Smith, T. W., & Marsden, P. V. (Eds.). National Opinion Research Center (Producer). (2005). General Social Surveys, 1972–2004 [Cumulative data file] (Publication No. ICPSR04295-v2). Storrs: University of Connecticut, Roper Center for Public Opinion Research. Retrieved May 1, 2008, from http://www.ropercenter .uconn.edu/data_access/data/datasets/general_social_ survey.html

RANDOM SAMPLING

Random sampling refers to a variety of selection techniques in which sample members are selected by chance, but with a known probability of selection. Most social science, business, and agricultural surveys rely on random sampling techniques for the selection of survey participants or sample units, where the sample units may be persons, establishments, land points, or other units for analysis. Random sampling is a critical element to the overall survey research design.

This entry first addresses some terminological considerations. Second, it discusses two main components of random sampling: randomness and known probabilities of selection. Third, it briefly describes specific types of random samples, including simple random sampling (with and without replacement), systematic sampling, and stratification, with mention

of other complex designs. The final section touches on inference, which is the reason that random sampling is preferred in scientific surveys.

Terminological Considerations

Some authors, such as William G. Cochran, use the term *random sampling* to refer specifically to simple random sampling. Other texts use the term *random sampling* to describe the broader class of probability sampling. For this reason, authors such as Leslie Kish generally avoid the term *random sampling*. In this entry, random sampling is used in the latter context, referring to the broader class of probability sampling.

Critical Elements

The two critical elements of random sampling are randomness and known probabilities of selection.

Randomness

The first critical element in random sampling is the element of randomness. Ideally, all members in the survey's target population have a non-zero chance of selection.

In describing what random sampling is, it is helpful to highlight what it is not. The sample is not pre-determined. Nor is a random sample selected by expert judgment. Random sampling does not imply that the sampling is haphazard. Furthermore, random sampling is not convenience sampling, in which the interviewers take respondents that are easiest to obtain.

The element of randomness is applied to the process scientifically. That is, there is a method, usually mechanical, to the selection process that is rigorously followed. The precise method may rely on random number generators or tables of random numbers. By following the scientific process, the probabilities of selection are known and preserved.

Random number generators and tables of random numbers are not truly random, of course, but the process needs to be random enough. This is especially important in litigious contexts. Bruce D. McCullough and Wendy Rotz have tested the random number generators available in various data tools and statistical packages.

Known Probabilities of Selection

The probabilities of selection are important for the theory that enables researchers to estimate sampling error. Because a sample is a subset of the target population and not a census (complete enumeration), estimates derived from sample responses will rarely match the target population values exactly. The variable difference between the sample estimate and the population value is sampling error. (Nonsampling errors, such as inaccurate frames of the target population and imprecise measures of the questionnaire items, affect both surveys and censuses. Nonsampling errors are not covered in this entry.)

Having a randomly selected sample with known probabilities of selection enables the researcher to estimate the sampling error. That is, the researcher can use the sample to make inferences for the target population and to estimate the precision of the sample-based estimates.

The probabilities of selection may enter into the estimation process in another way, as well. Because the probabilities of selection for members of a random sample are known, the sample responses can be appropriately weighted (if the probabilities are different, as in complex sampling designs) to yield improved estimates for the target population. The weights are a function of the probabilities of selection, which are not known precisely for purposive, convenience, or other nonprobability samples.

Sample Designs

Simple Random Sampling

The most familiar type of random sampling is *simple random sampling*. Simple random sampling may be with or without replacement. The drawing of names out of a hat and the selection of official lotto numbers are examples of simple random sampling without replacement. In simple random sampling, all members of the population have the same probability of selection.

The selection is said to be *without replacement* if a member of the population cannot be selected more than once in the same sample. Usually the sample members are selected sequentially. Each selection is made from the population excluding those already selected. Therefore, the sample draws are not independent.

Simple random sampling is said to be *with replacement* if each selected sample member is replaced into the available population pool for subsequent draws. In practice, sampling with replacement is not as common as sampling without replacement.

An easy way of selecting a simple random sample of size *n* without replacement is to use a random number generator to assign a random number to each member of the population in the frame or population list, sort the frame by the random number, and select the first *n* units in the randomly ordered list.

Systematic Sampling

Another random sampling design is *systematic sampling*, in which the population is ordered, and every *k*th unit is selected. Once a random starting point is selected, the rest of the sample is determined; however, the randomness is in the selection of the starting point. In other words, a single sample is randomly selected from a set of *k* possible samples. (If *k* is not an integer, more samples are possible.)

Complex Designs

In practice, simple random sampling and systematic sampling are rarely used alone for large surveys, but are often used in combination with other design features that make for a more complex design. Complex random sampling designs tend to have smaller sampling error or lower cost, or both. The complex random sampling designs may incorporate elements that resemble purposive sampling, such as stratification. Double sampling, cluster sampling, multi-stage sampling, and sampling with probability proportional to size are other examples of complex probability or random sampling.

Stratified Sampling

Stratification involves dividing the target population into groupings, or strata, of relatively homogeneous members and selecting a random sample independently within each stratum. For example, a list of individuals may be divided into strata based on age and gender, or the population of businesses may be divided into strata based on geography, size, and industry. The variables for stratification need to be available for all population members and presumably related to the survey response variables or the propensity to respond. Because members within a stratum tend to be more alike, the emphasis is on selecting a broad sample across strata rather than extensively within each stratum. By selecting members from each stratum, the sample will capture much of the diversity in the population more efficiently than if the sample were selected purely randomly. Stratification also enables the researcher to sample from the strata at different rates if, for example, the researcher wants estimates for individual strata as well as for the population as a whole.

Inference

The survey design includes both the sampling technique and the corresponding estimators for inferences. With scientific random sampling and known probabilities, mathematical formulas exist for making inferences about the target population and for estimating the sampling error attributed to the inferences. Confidence intervals, tests of hypotheses, and other statistics are possible with random sampling and estimates of sampling error. While an expert may judiciously select a sample that is a good representation of the target population on some measure, a purposive sample of this sort cannot, by itself, be used to estimate the precision of the sample-based estimates because no such mathematical formulas are possible. Neither can the sampling error be estimated from a convenience sample.

Under simple random sampling, the distribution of the sample mean often approximates the normal distribution, where the variance decreases with sample size. That is, the sample mean is a good estimator for the population mean, and the error associated with the sample-based estimate is smaller for larger samples. This result is based on the central limit theorem.

Alternatively, in some circumstances, especially when sample sizes are small, the distribution of sample statistics may approximate Poisson, hypergeometric, or other distributions. The approximate distribution is what enables the researcher to make inferences about the population based on sample estimates.

Complex probability designs may have more complex mathematical forms for statistical inference and may require specialized software to properly handle the estimation. Some methods of variance estimation developed for complex designs may be less stable in some circumstances, an issue to be aware of as the field moves toward smaller samples and estimation using subsets of the sample. Nevertheless, inference is

possible because complex designs share the underlying concepts and theory of random selection with known probabilities.

Rachel Harter

See also Cluster Sample; Cochran, W. G.; Complex Sample Surveys; Convenience Sampling; Kish, Leslie; Multi-Stage Sampling; Nonprobability Sample; Nonsampling Error; Probability of Selection; Probability Proportional to Size (PPS) Sampling; Probability Sample; Purposive Sampling; Random; Sampling Error; Sampling Without Replacement; Simple Random Sample; Strata; Stratified Sampling; Systematic Sampling

Further Readings

Cochran, W. G. (1977). *Sampling techniques* (3rd ed.). New York: Wiley.

Kish, L. (1965). *Survey sampling*. New York: Wiley.

Liu, Y., Batcher, M., & Rotz, W. (2001, August). Application of the hypergeometric distribution in a special case of rare events. *Proceedings of the Section on Survey Research Methods* (pp. 941–954). Alexandria, VA: American Statistical Association.

Marsaglia, G. (1995). *The Marsaglia Random Number CDROM including the Diehard Battery of Tests of Randomness*. Retrieved May 1, 2008, from http://www.stat.fsu.edu/pub/diehard/

McCullough, B. D. (1998). Assessing the reliability of statistical software: Part I. *American Statistician, 52*(4), 358–366.

McCullough, B. D. (1998). Assessing the reliability of statistical software: Part II. *American Statistician, 53*(2), 149–159.

National Institute of Standards and Technology. (1980). *NMS Minimal BASIC Test Program for random generators* (Special Publication No. 500-70/1 and No. 500-70/2). Gaithersburg, MD: Author.

National Institute of Standards and Technology. (2001). *A statistical test suite for random and pseudorandom number generators for cryptographic applications* (Special Publication No. 800-22). Gaithersburg, MD: Author.

Rotz, W., Falk, E., & Joshee, A. (2004, August). A comparison of random number generators used in business—2004 update. *Proceedings of the Section on Business and Economic Statistics* (pp. 1316–1319). Alexandria, VA: American Statistical Association.

Rotz, W., Falk, E., Wood, D., & Mulrow, J. (2001, August). A comparison of random number generators used in business. *Proceedings of the Annual Meeting of the American Statistical Association, Section on Computational Statistics*. Alexandria, VA: American Statistical Association.

RANDOM START

The term *random start* has two separate meanings in survey research—one related to questionnaire item order and one related to sampling. This entry discusses both meanings.

Random Start in Questionnaire Construction

In terms of questionnaire item order, a random start means that a series of similar items (such as a set of agree–disagree questions) is administered in a way that the first question in the series that is asked of any one respondent is randomly chosen to "start" the series, and then the order of the subsequent questions is not randomized. For example, if Q23 through Q28 (six items in all) made up a set of attitude questions that use an agree–disagree response scale, by using a random start a researcher will have one sixth of the respondents asked Q23 first, one sixth asked Q24 first, one sixth Q25 first, and so on. All respondents are asked all the questions in the series, and each question follows its numerical predecessor, except when it is the first item asked in the series; for example, Q26 always follows Q25, except when Q26 is the first question asked (then Q25 is asked last as the random start order of the set would be Q26-Q27-Q28-Q23-Q24-Q25). The purpose of using a random start is to help control for possible item order effects, so that not all respondents will be asked the questions in the exact same order.

A random start set of questions differs from a random order set of questions in that the latter randomizes all questions within the set in all possible ways and then randomly assigns a respondent to one of the possible randomized orders. Random start questions are more readily analyzed and interpreted than random order questions, especially when there are more than a few questions in the set. Thus, for example, even with a set of 10 items using a random start deployment, a researcher with an overall sample size of 1,000 would have 100 respondents for each of the 10 random start orders in which the items would be asked. That would allow the researcher to investigate for order effects in how the random start series of questions were answered. In the case of a set of 10 items that were asked in a true random order, the permutations would be so great that the researcher could not investigate order effects with confidence unless the sample size were enormous (far greater than almost any survey would ever gather).

Random Start in Sampling

In terms of sampling, a random start refers to randomly selecting the first element in a systematic sampling procedure in order to avoid sampling error. Most forms of commonly used statistical analysis are based on the assumption that the data were selected using a procedure that allows for the calculation of a nonzero selection probability for each element in the sample frame. The least complex probability sampling procedure is simple random sampling, but this is not always an easy procedure to implement because it essentially requires that a separate random number be generated for each element to be selected for inclusion in the sample. Applied field work rarely presents the researcher with machine-readable lists of every eligible element of the population under study. Systematic sampling is often the preferred alternative.

A systematic sample procedure is a two-step process, and it uses a random start. The first step is to determine the sampling interval (k) by dividing the population size (N) by the desired sample size (n). The second step is to determine the random start by selecting a random number between 1 and k. Note that the selection probability is zero for elements that are not exact multiples of k unless a random start is used. Use of the random start and a properly calculated interval allows for a nonzero selection probability to be calculated for each element in the population. Like simple random sampling, the systematic sampling approach usually results in a sample that is generalizable to the population without the need for weights. Unlike simple random sampling, the systematic approach requires only one random number to be generated rather than one for each element selected.

The success of using a random start and set interval selection thereafter rests on a properly prepared sample frame. Care should be taken to ensure that the population sample frame to be used is either randomized or stratified sufficiently so that the interval selected via the random start will not match cycles in the sample frame order. For example, records reflecting daily aggregate data will have a 7-day cycle; thus, an interval that is a multiple of 7 will select only 1 day of the week. Similar cycles (months, semesters, seasons, etc.) must be considered in relation to the random start and interval in order to avoid sampling error through systematic exclusion.

Another issue to consider is when the population size (N) is not an integral multiple of the interval (k). In this case, the final interval has fewer elements than the rest. If the random start is greater than the size of the last interval, the target sample size (n) will not be achieved. This is not usually an issue in survey research, because of the larger sample sizes that surveys most often use ($n > 100$). However, there are several easily implemented solutions to this problem when smaller sample sizes are warranted.

James Wolf

See also Elements; Probability Sample; Question Order Effects; Random Order; Sampling Error; Sampling Frame; Simple Random Sample; Systematic Sampling

Further Readings

Kish, L. (1995). Systematic sampling: Stratification techniques. In *Survey sampling* (pp. 113–147). New York: Wiley.

RANKED-SET SAMPLING (RSS)

The most basic sampling technique to use, when collecting data from a population for a sample survey, is that of simple random sampling (SRS). Ranked-set sampling (RSS) is an alternative probability sampling technique to SRS. While the items in an simple random sample might or might not be mutually independent (depending on whether sampling is with or without replacement), it is always the case that such a sample is designed so that each measured observation can be viewed as "representative" of the underlying population. Even with this probabilistic guarantee, however, there is still the possibility that a given simple random sample, just by mere chance, might not represent the underlying population well. That has led statisticians to consider a variety of ways to guard against obtaining unrepresentative samples.

Approaches for Ensuring Representative Samples

One way to better ensure representative samples is to put additional structure on the sampling design. Some examples of this approach include *stratified element*

sampling and *stratified cluster sampling*. Sampling designs can become increasingly complex when the population of interest is large and diverse, such as when the goal is to collect data on a national sample. Although the primary goal is to select sampling units that are representative of the underlying population, a secondary, but often just as important, goal is to minimize the costs associated with collecting the data, that is, both the cost of measurement and that associated with obtaining the sample units.

An alternative cost-effective approach to obtaining more representative sample observations from a population is that of RSS. The RSS technique uses additional information about potential sample units as an aid in choosing which of the units should actually be measured on the variable(s) of interest. In this way information about all of the units selected for potential measurement is used to guide the selection of the specific units to be measured. It is this additional information that enables RSS techniques to generally outperform analogous SRS techniques when both involve the same number of measured observations.

Example of Ranked-Set Sampling

To provide a concrete illustration of how RSS is conducted, we consider the setting where our goal is to estimate the unknown population mean, $\bar{X}$, using the information in n measured observations. RSS takes advantage of available information from additional potential sample units to enable us to measure selected units that are, collectively, more representative of the population of interest. The net result of RSS is a set of measurements that are more likely to span the range of values in the population than can be guaranteed from SRS. Following is a more precise description of this process.

Suppose we wish to obtain a ranked-set sample of k measured observations. First, an initial simple random sample of k units from the population is selected and rank-ordered on the attribute of interest. This ranking can result from a variety of mechanisms, including expert opinion (called *judgment ranking*), visual comparisons, or the use of easy-to-obtain auxiliary variables; it cannot, however, involve actual measurements of the attribute of interest on the sample units. The unit that is judged to be the smallest in this ranking is included as the first item in the ranked-set sample, and the attribute of interest is formally measured on this unit.

Denote the measurement obtained from the smallest item in the rank ordered set of k units by $x^*_{(1)}$. The remaining $k - 1$ unmeasured units in the first random sample are not considered further in the selection of this ranked-set sample or eventual inference about the population. The sole purpose of these other $k - 1$ units is to help select an item for measurement that represents the smaller values in the population.

Next, a second independent random sample of size k is selected from the population and judgment ranked without formal measurement on the attribute of interest. This time we select the item judged to be the second smallest of the k units in this second random sample and include it in our ranked-set sample for measurement of the attribute of interest. This second measured observation is denoted by $x^*_{(2)}$.

From a third independent random sample we select the unit judgment ranked to be the third smallest, $x^*_{(3)}$, for measurement and inclusion in the ranked-set sample. This process is continued until we have selected the unit judgment ranked to be the largest of the k units in the kth random sample, denoted by $x^*_{(k)}$, for measurement and inclusion in the ranked-set sample.

The entire process described above is referred to as a *cycle*, and the number of observations in each random sample, k, is called the *set size*. Thus, to complete a single ranked set cycle, we judgment rank k independent random samples of size k each, involving a total of k^2 sample units to obtain k measured observations $x^*_{(1)}, x^*_{(2)}, \ldots, x^*_{(k)}$. These k observations represent a *balanced ranked-set sample* with set size k, where *balanced* refers to the fact that we have collected one judgment order statistic for each of the ranks $I = 1, \ldots, k$. To obtain a ranked-set sample with a desired total number of measured observations $n = km$, we repeat the entire cycle process m independent times, yielding the data $x^*_{(1)j}, \ldots, x^*_{(k)j}$, for $j = 1, \ldots, m$. The RSS estimator of the population mean $\bar{X}$ is

$$\bar{x}_{RSS} = \frac{1}{km} \sum_{j=1}^{m} \sum_{i=1}^{k} x^*_{(i)j}.$$

We illustrate the application of RSS methodology to a small sample of data from the National Health and Nutrition Examination Survey III (NHANES III). The NHANES III data set contains various body measurements and information on health-related variables for the respondents. For our example we consider the two variables body mass index (BMI) and thigh circumference (TC). We demonstrate how to use TC values to collect a structured ranked-set sample to estimate the mean BMI for the population of nonpregnant adults in the NHANES III data set.

We provide the details for estimating the mean BMI using a ranked-set sample of size $n = 6$ with a set size $m = 6$ and a single cycle ($k = 1$).

Step 1: Collect six independent random samples of size $m = 6$ potential sample units from the NHANES III data set. We obtain the following $n = 6$ subsets (random samples) of size $m = 6$ (BMI, TC) data pairs each. (For an actual ranked-set sample the BMI values would not be available until after the 6 subjects for the sample had been selected. Then we would only need to measure the BMI values for those 6 subjects, not for all 36 potential subjects. We include the BMI values for all 36 subjects here, however, for use in our comparison of the RSS estimates with competitors based on similar-sized simple random samples.)

Subset 1: (19.4, 43.7) (26.5, 52.1) (24.3, 48.3)
(34.0, 49.1) (23.9, 50.6) (25.8, 50.3)
Subset 2: (26.0, 49.0) (26.0, 46.3) (23.2, 50.7)
(32.6, 56.0) (24.3, 45.9) (22.9, 50.7)
Subset 3: (26.3, 49.5) (34.9, 56.4) (20.9, 46.2)
(32.3, 46.9) (28.3, 56.0) (25.0, 50.8)
Subset 4: (29.7, 53.5) (27.3, 50.8) (17.5, 42.9)
(27.6, 50.4) (24.9, 45.9) (22.5, 42.3)
Subset 5: (28.4, 52.1) (24.1, 49.1) (25.0, 52.5)
(28.1, 48.7) (24.6, 50.4) (23.7, 52.0)
Subset 6: (25.6, 42.5) (28.7, 55.6) (22.4, 46.4)
(21.4, 50.0) (23.3, 49.8) (22.9, 44.3)

Step 2: Rank order the pairs on the basis of their TC values (in bold) from smallest to largest, separately in each of the six subsets. The ranked pairs for our data are the following:

Subset 1: (19.4, **43.7**) (24.3, **48.3**) (34.0, **49.1**)
(25.8, **50.3**) (23.9, **50.6**) (26.5, **52.1**)
Subset 2: (24.3, **45.9**) (26.0, **46.3**) (26.0, **49.0**)
(23.2, **50.7**) (22.9, **50.7**) (32.6, **56.0**)
Subset 3: (20.9, **46.2**) (32.3, **46.9**) (26.3, **49.5**)
(25.0, **50.8**) (28.3, **56.0**) (34.9, **56.4**)
Subset 4: (22.5, **42.3**) (17.5, **42.9**) (24.9, **45.9**)
(27.6, **50.4**) (27.3, **50.8**) (29.7, **53.5**)
Subset 5: (28.1, **48.7**) (24.1, **49.1**) (24.6, **50.4**)
(23.7, **52.0**) (28.4, **52.1**) (25.0, **52.5**)
Subset 6: (25.6, **42.5**) (22.9, **44.3**) (22.4, **46.4**)
(23.3, **49.8**) (21.4, **50.0**) (28.7, **55.6**)

Step 3: For the ith subset, "measure" and record the BMI associated with the ith ordered TC value, $i = 1, \ldots, 6$. The resulting six recorded BMI values are 19.4, 26.0, 26.3, 27.6, 28.4, and 28.7.

Step 4: Compute the average for the six recorded BMI values obtained in Step 3. This is the RSS estimate of the population mean BMI. For our single cycle of ranked-set sample data, the estimate of the mean BMI is

$$\bar{x}_{BMI, RSS} = (19.4 + 26.0 + 26.3 + 27.6 + 28.4 + 28.7)/6$$
$$= 26.067.$$

Additional structure for RSS, compared to SRS, is achieved from the use of all 36 TC measurements to aid in the rankings and the eventual decision about which BMI measurements to obtain. It is this structure inherent in ranked-set sample data resulting from the use of additional concomitant information that leads to the improved properties of the RSS estimator.

Advantages of Random-Set Sampling

Statistical theory shows that the sample average from a ranked-set sample consisting of *n* measured observations is a more efficient estimator of the population mean than a simple random sample with the same number of measured observations. Both sample averages are unbiased estimators of the population mean, but the variance of the ranked-set sample average is never any greater than the variance of the simple random sample average. Thus the use of RSS leads to increased precision or, equivalently, to reduced sample sizes with the same precision relative to SRS.

This improvement from using an RSS approach to data collection as opposed to the standard SRS approach extends to many other settings. In particular, a ranked-set sample can be taken within strata, or a ranked-set sample of clusters could be selected. In fact, using RSS instead of SRS at the final stage in any sampling scheme will generally lead to estimators with smaller variances.

Douglas A. Wolfe and Elizabeth A. Stasny

See also Cluster Sample; National Health and Nutrition Examination Survey; Simple Random Sample; Stratified Sampling; Unbiased Statistic

Further Readings

Chen, Z., Bai, Z. D., & Sinha, B. K. (2004). *Ranked set sampling: Theory and applications.* New York: Springer.

Wolfe, D. A. (2004). Ranked set sampling: An approach to more efficient data collection. *Statistical Science, 19,* 636–643.

RANKING

There are a variety of formats that can be used in asking survey questions, from items that require a simple "yes" or "no" response to other types of forced-choice items, rating scales, and multi-part items in which respondents' opinions are determined through a series of questions. Ranking is a question response format used when a researcher is interested in establishing some type of priority among a set of objects, whether they be policies, attributes, organizations, individuals, or some other topic or property of interest.

For example, if city officials were interested in whether citizens thought it was most important to improve city services in the area of police protection, fire protection, garbage and trash collection, road maintenance and repair, or parks and recreation, one method they could use would be to use an open-ended question that asked respondents, *What service that the city provides do you think is most important to improve in the next 12 months?* The percentage of respondents that mentioned each of these services could then be used as a measure of priority for service improvement. Another method for determining this would be to ask a series of rating questions in which respondents were asked whether it was very important, somewhat important, not too important, or not at all important for the city to improve services in each of these five areas, and the option that received the highest percentage of "very important" responses or had the highest average rating would have priority for service improvement. A third way to accomplish this would be through a ranking question, for example: *The city provides a number of services, including police protection, fire protection, garbage and trash collection, road maintenance and repair, or parks and recreation. Of these, which do you think is most important for the city to improve in the next 12 months?* After respondents selected their "most important" service, they would then be asked, *And which service is next most important for the city to improve?* three times to identify their second, third, and fourth priority for service improvement, with the service not selected being ranked fifth by default.

Because ranking requires making choices from among a series of options, this format is generally thought to be more difficult (i.e., to create a greater cognitive burden) for respondents than other response formats. This is particularly true for telephone surveys in which the ranking of five items is considered to be the maximum number of objects that the average respondent accurately can rank. Rankings can be used more readily in face-to-face interviews or in a self-administered questionnaire when visual cues (e.g., show cards) can be used to assist respondents in remembering the options and making adjustments in their priority ordering, though there is a limit on the number of ranked items that should be displayed even with these methods of data collection.

When the research question requires a larger number of items to be ranked, several alternatives have been developed. One method is to have respondents rank only those items at each end of their preferences, leaving the middle preferences unranked. For example, if 15 items were to be ranked in terms of their perceived threat to the security of the United States, the three biggest threats could be selected (and these three ranked, if desired, to produce first, second, and third rankings of threat). Similarly, the three least threatening items could be selected (and ranked), producing differentiation at the "biggest" and "least" ends of the scale, but less differentiation in the middle.

Another method for obtaining rankings is through a series of paired comparisons. In using paired comparisons, a respondent considers each object in comparison with each of the other alternatives, one at a time. If there is an ordered quality to these objects (i.e., object A is preferred to B, B is preferred to C, and A is preferred to C), then paired comparisons provide a fairly robust method for ranking objects. In practice, however, respondents' choices are not always consistent, making the priority ranking of objects less clear. The number of paired comparisons that can be made is also limited to some extent, in that the number of comparisons that have to be made increases geometrically with the number of options that need ranking; for example, with 6 objects, 15 paired comparisons are required.

As with any decision about the format of the questions to be used in a survey, the determination of when to use rankings and the number of objects to be ranked should be guided by the research question of interest. In many research situations, the results produced by rankings, by a series of rating questions, or even by open-ended questions will produce similar results. Rankings have certain advantages, as well as disadvantages, relative to other formats; the substantive question being investigated should determine when their use is most appropriate.

Robert W. Oldendick

See also Forced Choice; Open-Ended Question; Paired Comparisons; Rating; Respondent Burden; Response Alternatives; Show Cards

Further Readings

Fowler, F. J., Jr. (1993). *Survey research methods* (2nd ed.). Newbury Park, CA: Sage.

Schuman, H., & Presser, S. (1996). *Questions and answers in attitude surveys*. Thousand Oaks, CA: Sage.

Sudman, S., & Bradburn, N. M. (1982). *Asking questions: A practical guide to questionnaire design*. San Francisco: Jossey-Bass.

Sudman, S., Bradburn, N. M., & Schwarz, N. (1996). *Thinking about answers: The application of cognitive processes to survey methodology*. San Francisco: Jossey-Bass.

RARE POPULATIONS

A rare population is generally defined as a small proportion of a total population that possesses one or more specific characteristics. Examples include billionaires; people with a certain illness, such as gall bladder cancer; or employees in a highly technical occupation. Although the literature offers no precise definition of *rare* or *small* in this context, researchers have proposed proportions of .10 or less to identify rare populations. (When this proportion is larger, standard sampling techniques can usually be used efficiently.) In addition, sampling frames are often nonexistent or incomplete for most rare populations. Although researchers can use convenience sampling (e.g., snowball samples) to study rare populations, most efforts in this area have focused on probability sampling of rare populations. The costs and benefits of the various approaches can be difficult to define a priori and depend on the type and size of the rare population.

Sampling Strategies

Generally, sampling frames for the total population do not contain information identifying members of the rare population; if they do, then the sampling process is trivial. If not, then screening must be used to identify members of the group. With screening, members of the rare population are identified at the beginning of the interview process. However, the costs of screening can often exceed the costs of interviewing, especially if the rare population is only a very small proportion of the sampling frame.

There are several ways in which screening costs can be reduced. Mail questionnaires can be used to identify members of the rare population if the sampling frame has correct address information; for in-person interviews, the use of telephone screening can reduce interviewer costs. If the rare population is geographically clustered, for example, in certain states or urban areas, screening based on clusters becomes less costly.

Besides cost, another potential drawback to the screening approach is response errors of commission and omission (i.e., false positives and false negatives, respectively) during the screening process, especially if many different questions must be correctly answered in order to identify a member of the rare population. Using less stringent criteria during screening to identify members is one approach to reducing response errors, because misclassified members (false positives) can be excluded after the full interview is complete. The main problem here is devising a screening process that avoids erroneously classifying members of the rare population as nonmembers (false negatives).

Whereas for many rare populations it is impossible to derive a complete sampling frame, one or more incomplete lists may be available. For example, hospital or pharmacy records may identify some, but not all, members of a population with a specific rare disease. A dual frame approach could then be used, in which the partial list is combined with screening of the total population to reduce screening costs. Alternatively, the partial list could be used with a cluster sampling approach to identify areas where members of the rare population are located.

In some situations multiplicity or network sampling can be used to locate and interview members of a rare population. Typically, a member of a household is interviewed and queried as to whether other members of the household or close relatives are members of a special population (although respondents also can be asked about neighbors or members of other social groups to which they belong). Occasionally, the researcher may need only an estimate of the size of the rare population; however, in most cases the researcher wishes to interview members of the rare population. If so, accurate contact information may be difficult to obtain from the respondent. In general, accuracy of reporting depends on the relationship between the respondent and the member of the rare population and the visibility of whatever characteristic(s) defines the rare population. For example, World War II veteran status is generally well known and thus visible to network members, whereas certain illnesses may not be. Researchers must use special weighting when deriving estimates from network samples, because the probability of selection can vary by the size of the network. Costs may be higher than with typical screening methods, especially if addresses are sought.

Special location samples are useful when the rare population is defined by an activity (e.g., spearfishing) or because the behavior that defines the rare population may not always be known by members of a network (e.g., married men who have sex with other men). With this approach, the researcher identifies specific locations where members of the rare population may congregate, usually through extensive field work, and potential members of the rare population are then approached at varying times throughout the day. Known as *time-space sampling* or *venue sampling*, this area of research has emphasized randomly selecting locations and times in an effort to yield a probability sample. Although costly, this approach can be used to study rare populations that might defy other sampling efforts.

Finally, adaptive sampling procedures have often been used to study rare populations, but their main drawback is the lack of a probability sample that can be used to make generalizations about the entire rare population. *Adaptive sampling* refers to a group of similar sampling procedures that "adapt" to the sampling situation based on information gathered during the sampling process. For example, members of a rare population may be asked to identify other members of a rare population; once identified, these new members are added to the sampling frame. *Snowball sampling* is one example of an adaptive sampling approach. Several scholars have developed estimation methods for adaptive samples that allow generalization. Generally, these methods depend on assumptions about the probability distribution generating the sample, although recent work has attempted to relax this restriction.

Stephen R. Porter

See also Adaptive Sampling; Cluster Sample; Convenience Sampling; Dual-Frame Sampling; Errors of Commission; Errors of Omission; Multiplicity Sampling; Network Sampling; Screening; Snowball Sampling

Further Readings

Kalton, G., & Anderson, D. W. (1986). Sampling rare populations. *Journal of the Royal Statistical Society, Series A (General), 149*(1), 65–82.

Kish, L. (1991). Taxonomy of elusive populations. *Journal of Official Statistics, 7*(3), 339–347.

Muhib, F. B., Lin, L. S., Stueve, A., Miller, R., Ford, W. L., Johnson, W. D., et al. (2001). A venue-based method for sampling hard-to-reach populations. *Public Health Reports, 116*(Suppl. 1), 216–222.

Sudman, S., & Kalton, G. (1986). New developments in the sampling of special populations. *Annual Review of Sociology, 12*, 401–429.

Sudman, S., Sirken, M., & Cowan, C. D. (1988). Sampling rare and elusive populations. *Science, 240*(4855), 991–996.

Thompson, S. K., & Collins, L. M. (2002). Adaptive sampling in research on risk-related behaviors. *Drug and Alcohol Dependence, 68*(Suppl. 1), S57–S67.

RATING

In constructing a survey questionnaire there are a number of response formats that can be used in asking respondents about their views on various topics. One of the most commonly used formats in survey questionnaires is the rating, or rating scale.

As the name implies, ratings are regularly used in surveys to evaluate an object along some dimension, such as performance or satisfaction. In a typical rating question, respondents are asked to make judgments along a scale varying between two extremes, such as from "very good" to "very poor," or "extremely positive" to "extremely negative," and the like. The following illustrates a common rating scale question: *How would you rate the job (PERSON's NAME) is doing as governor . . . Would you say she is doing an excellent job, a good job, a fair job, a poor job, or*

a very poor job? As another example, the item, *Some people don't pay much attention to political campaigns. How about you . . . would you say that you have been extremely interested, very interested, not too interested, or not at all interested in the political campaigns so far this year?* is a rating scale in which respondents are asked to assess their interest in campaigns among choices ranging from "extremely" to "not at all." A third example is the item, *Now I'd like to ask you to rate the city as a place to live and work on a scale of 0 to 10, with 10 being the highest rating you could give and 0 being the lowest.*

A rating question provides the topic to be evaluated, the dimension along which it is to be evaluated, and the scale of the evaluation. As the previously mentioned examples illustrate, rating questions vary widely in terms of the dimensions on which objects are evaluated (job performance, interest in political campaigns, place to live and work), the scales used ("excellent" to "very poor," "extremely interested" to "not at all interested," 0 to 10), and the number of response options (5, 4, and 11, respectively).

The various components of a rating question affect the results produced by such items. For example, in evaluating presidential performance, different— although very likely similar—results would be obtained if the item asked the respondents to assess such performance as *excellent, good, fair, poor,* or *very poor* than if it asked them whether they *strongly approved, somewhat approved, neither approved nor disapproved, somewhat disapproved,* or *strongly disapproved* of the president's performance. Even a seemingly minor change in the options provided— for example, changing "excellent" to "very good"—can yield different results and sometimes these differences are not negligible.

Another important factor in rating questions is the number of response options. It is generally considered that five options are the most respondents can understand without some type of visual aid, although some surveys use more, such as the "rate on a scale of 0 to 10" example described previously. Related to this is whether respondents should be provided with an odd or even number of response categories. Rating questions with an odd number of categories provide respondents with a true "middle" option, whereas items with an even number of categories force respondents who feel "in the middle" to lean in one direction or the other. The order in which the options are presented, from "most positive" to "least positive" or vice versa, can also make a difference in the results obtained. For any of these considerations, there are no technically right or wrong ways in which to ask a rating question. Each of the decisions made in developing an item should be guided by the research question of interest.

The mode used for survey data collection—face-to-face, telephone, mail, Web, or some other self-administered format—also can affect the types of rating questions that can be asked. Because visual aids cannot be presented over the telephone (at least not without a videophone), such surveys are more limited in the number of response options that can be provided. As a result, telephone surveys often employ "unfolding" questions. For example, in being asked their opinion on a particular policy, respondents may first be asked to rate whether they *favor, oppose,* or are *neutral.* Those who initially favor the option are then asked whether they favor it strongly or favor it only somewhat; those who initially oppose are asked to rate if they oppose it strongly or only somewhat; and initially neutral respondents are asked if they lean toward favoring or opposing it. The end result is a 7-point scale with the options *favor strongly*; *favor somewhat*; *lean toward favoring*; *neutral, lean toward neither*; *lean toward opposing*; *oppose somewhat*; and *oppose strongly.* Providing respondents with visual aids in face-to-face or self-administered surveys allows or more options in the number of response alternatives, such as a "feeling thermometer," which is based on the concept of a thermometer and typically asks respondents to rate some object from $0°$ (very cold or unfavorable) to $100°$ (very warm or favorable).

Robert W. Oldendick

See also Feeling Thermometer; Forced Choice; Likert Scale; Mode of Data Collection; Precoded Question; Ranking; Response Alternatives; Unfolding Question

Further Readings

Converse, J., & Presser, S. (1986). *Survey questions: Handcrafting the standardized questionnaire.* Newbury Park, CA: Sage.

Schuman, H., & Presser, S. (1996). *Questions and answers in attitude surveys.* Thousand Oaks, CA: Sage.

Sudman, S., & Bradburn, N. M. (1982). *Asking questions: A practical guide to questionnaire design.* San Francisco: Jossey-Bass.

RATIO MEASURE

Ratio measure refers to the highest (most complex) level of measurement that a variable can possess. The properties of a variable that is a ratio measure are the following: (a) Each value can be treated as a unique category (as in a nominal measure); (b) different values have order of magnitude, such as greater than or less than or equal to (as in an ordinal measure); (c) basic mathematical procedures can be conducted with the values, such as addition and division (as with an interval measure); and (d) the variable can take on the value of zero. An example of a ratio measure is someone's annual income.

A ratio measure may be expressed as either a fraction or percentage; in addition, a ratio measure may be written as two numbers separated by a colon. For example, if Susan earns $40 per hour and John earns $20 per hour, then the fraction of Susan's pay that John earns can be expressed as 2/4, the percentage of Susan's pay that John earns as 50%, and the ratio of John's pay to Susan's as 1:2.

There are many situations in which a ratio measure is more appropriate than a total or mean or other descriptive statistic when reporting the results of a survey. Ratio measures are utilized in the business world, in health care, in banking, and in government, as well as in other applications.

In the business world, there are a number of applications involving ratio measures. For example, suppose that one purpose of a survey of a sample of businesses is to assess liquidity. A commonly used measure of liquidity is the current ratio measure; this ratio measure is an important indicator of whether the company can pay its bills and remain in business. It is calculated by dividing a company's total current assets by total current liabilities for the most recently reported quarter. Thus, if a business has total current assets of $450,000 and total current liabilities of $200,000, then its liquidity ratio measure would be $450,000/$200,000 = 2.25. However, in the sample, a number of businesses are sampled and each reports its total current assets and total current liabilities. To determine the liquidity of the sample of businesses, one would calculate the total of the reported assets of all of the sampled businesses and divide by the total of the reported liabilities of the same businesses. That is, if the total assets of the sample equal $10 billion and the total liabilities equal $5 billion, then the cost ratio measure of the sample equals \$10,000,000,000/ \$5,000,000,000 = 2.0. One would then generalize to the population from which the sample of businesses was drawn.

Carla R. Scanlan

See also Interval Measure; Level of Measurement; Nominal Measure; Ordinal Measure

Further Readings

Babbie, E. (2006). *The practice of social research* (11th ed.). Belmont, CA: Wadsworth.

RAW DATA

The term *raw data* is used most commonly to refer to information that is gathered for a research study before that information has been transformed or analyzed in any way. The term can apply to the data as soon as they are gathered or after they have been cleaned, but not in any way further transformed or analyzed. The challenge for most researchers who collect and analyze data is to extract useful information from the raw data they start with.

First, it is important to note that *data* is a plural noun (*datum* is the singular noun). Second, all collections of raw data are, by definition, incomplete. Some data are uncollected because of a variety of constraints. Lack of time and money are common reasons researchers fail to collect all available raw data to answer a given research question. Increasingly, however, data collection has become easier and more efficient in many ways, and more and more of the data that are intended to be collected are collected. (Of note, a counter trend in survey research has led to a decrease in the amount of intended data that are able to be collected. This is the trend for sampled respondents to be more reluctant to cooperate with survey requests.) Absent the ability to process this additional raw data, merely having more data may not increase knowledge, but enhanced computing power has produced an ability to process more data at little or no additional cost.

Third, the expression *raw data* implies a level of processing that suggests that these data cannot provide useful information without further effort. *Raw* suggests the data have not yet been summarized or analyzed in a way so as to "release" the information for which it was collected.

Fourth, raw data may be collected in alternative representational schemes that affect how the researcher thinks about processing the data. Perhaps the easiest way to think about this is to consider the variety of symbolic formats used in computer processing of information. Data are commonly represented in binary, hexadecimal, or decimal number systems, or as ASCII (American Standard Code for Information Interchange) text. Data organization is also relevant: Information may be organized as bits, nibbles, bytes, words, or other such units.

In some cases, one researcher's processed data may be another's raw data. The methodology by which data are collected and the level of aggregation of collected data play important roles in defining information as raw data to be analyzed. Consider, for example, the collection of survey responses to a series of five questions designed to measure attitudes toward abortion. At one level, raw data are the individual responses to each of the five questions. These data might be used by a survey researcher to establish the consistency of each respondent's answers to the individual survey questions. Such efforts might produce a second level of data in which a "scale" is created to represent the responses to the series of questions, with one scale score assigned to each individual. A third level of data aggregation might be reached by summarizing the individual scale scores for subsamples or groups of the individuals interviewed. A fourth level of aggregation of these data would be to release data on what Benjamin Page and Robert Shapiro call "collective public opinion," by reporting the average scale score for the entire sample—usually in comparison to another sample taken from the same population at a different point in time or to a sample drawn from a different population at the same point in time.

Even more critical than the methodology used to collect data is the research question to be answered or the theory to be tested. Data must be identified and collected with a purpose. Research questions motivate the collection of some subset of all possible data and the exclusion of other information.

Raw data are not the exclusive bailiwick of quantitative (social) science. Scientists of many traditions collect data. The raw data of qualitative social scientists may include taped or transcribed interviews, impressions and judgments, and archival material of many types and varieties. Each of these pieces of information is combined with others to allow judgments and inferences.

Raw data are similarly collected and analyzed by businesses and governments for their own purposes. Corporations collect basic information down to the level of the individual transaction to assess the capacity and profitability of their company. Newspapers have common rules for translating raw data into news. Information is collected from multiple sources, and "facts" are cross-checked and verified to assure that accurate information has been collected and reasonable inferences drawn by the reporter. Similarly, analysts at the Central Intelligence Agency work with raw data, from mechanical telemetry to in-field human intelligence, to produce estimates of the capacities of foreign governments.

Calling data "raw" does not absolve its user of responsibility for assessing its quality. All data should be subject to a variety of assessments, including judgment as to the degree of error contained in the data relevant to the purpose for which the data were collected. Raw materials should be evaluated for accuracy and completeness. If raw materials are "sampled" from a larger universe, their representativeness should be considered. Assessments include establishing the reliability and validity of data as well as justifications for discarding some of the data and consideration of the problem of missing data.

John P. McIver

See also Missing Data; Quality Control; Reliability; Total Survey Error; Validity

Further Readings

Coombs, C. H. (1964). *A theory of data*. New York: Wiley.
Diesing, P. (1991). *How does social science work?* Pittsburgh, PA: University of Pittsburgh Press.
Hyde, R. (1996). *The art of assembly language*. San Francisco: No Starch Press.
Krippendorff, K. (2004). *Content analysis: An introduction to its methodology* (2nd ed.). Thousand Oaks, CA: Sage.
Page, B. I., & Shapiro, R. Y. (1992). *The rational public*. Chicago: University of Chicago Press.

REACTIVITY

Reactivity occurs when the subject of the study (e.g., survey respondent) is affected either by the instruments of the study or the individuals conducting the study in a way that changes whatever is being measured. In survey research, the term *reactivity* applies when the individual's response is influenced by some part of the survey instrument (e.g., an item on a questionnaire); the interviewer; the survey organization sponsor conducting the study, or both; or the environment where the survey is taking place. For example, the respondent may respond positively or negatively based on the interviewer's reactions to the answer. A smile, nod, frown, or laugh may alter how the subject chooses to respond to subsequent questions. Deliberate or accidental, the actions of the interviewer administering the survey instrument may affect the subject's response.

A second instance of reactivity is when the subject reacts to the instrument itself. An example of this is respondents who respond to questions based on how they wish to see themselves or the environment in which they are completing the survey, rather than answering accurately. The same subjects may answer the same questions differently depending on where the survey was completed—for instance, in a homeless shelter or a country club. Respondents especially may be sensitive to their sincere answers that are widely opposed or criticized. Whether deliberate or unintentional, the actions of the interviewer, the environment of the survey, or the survey instrument itself may affect the accuracy of the subject's response.

Reactivity is undesirable in social science research because it decreases the validity and veracity of the project's results. Unless the subject's response to the environment, the survey instrument, or the experimenter is the focus of the study, these stimuli may introduce nonreplicable and confusing effects into a research project. Loss of validity results from miscalculating the impact of parts of the project unrelated to the research question. The research project then drives the response from the subject, and the survey instrument reflects the faults of the study instead of the accurate answers of the respondent.

To avoid the problem of reactivity, a researcher begins with a sound research design. There are three ways to reduce reactivity in a survey. First, when designing the project, a researcher must be aware of how different individuals may react to different aspects of the research experience. Depending on the group under study, cultural, economic, and other social differences may yield unwanted results based on some parts of the questionnaire. Whenever possible, the research should also guard against environmental factors influencing the respondent. Second, a researcher needs to review the work of other analysts and investigate problems in other scholarly research projects. By taking note of the faults of other studies, researchers can avoid or remove similar difficulties in their own work. Finally, each interviewer must be well trained and monitored. The research design should include interviewer guidelines for behavior and demeanor when they are conducting the survey. Controlling these three areas of the study will reduce the likelihood of reactivity effects and thereby strengthen the external validity of the research project.

Ryan Gibb

See also External Validity; Interviewer Monitoring; Interviewer-Related Error; Interviewer Training; Measurement Error; Research Design

Further Readings

Berg, B. (1998). *Qualitative research methods for the social sciences.* Boston: Allyn & Bacon.

Manheim, J., Rich, R., Willnat, L., & Brians, C. (2006). *Empirical political analysis: Research methods in political science.* New York: Pearson Education.

Rosenthal, R. (1966). *Experimenter effects in behavioral research.* New York: Appleton-Century-Crofts.

RECENCY EFFECT

A recency effect is one type of response order effect, whereby the order in which response options are offered to respondents affects the distribution of responses. Recency effects occur when response options are more likely to be chosen when presented at the end of a list of response options than when presented at the beginning. In contrast, primacy effects occur when response options are more likely to be chosen when presented at the beginning of a list of response options than when presented at the end. Response order effects are typically measured by presenting response options in different orders to different groups of respondents. For example, if half of the respondents in a survey are asked, *Which of the following is the most important problem facing the country today: the economy or lack of morality?* and the other half are asked, *Which of the following is the most important problem facing the country today:*

lack of morality or the economy? a recency effect would be observed if a greater proportion of respondents chose the economy in response to the second question than in response to the first.

In the many studies of response order effects in questions with categorical response options, primacy effects were observed in some cases, recency effects were observed in others, and no significant response order effect was observed in others. One explanation for the mixture of findings comes from satisficing theory. Survey researchers hope respondents will answer questions carefully and thoughtfully, but respondents may not always be able or motivated to do so. Instead, they may shift their response strategies to minimize effort while providing a satisfactory response to the survey question (i.e., known as *satisficing*). One such strategy involves choosing the first response option that seems reasonable, and this strategy is believed to be responsible for response order effects.

When response options are presented visually, most respondents likely begin by considering the option presented first, then the second option, and so on. So if respondents choose the first reasonable response option they consider, primacy effects are likely to occur. But when response options are presented orally as happens in interviewer-administered surveys, respondents cannot think much about the first option they hear, because presentation of the second option interrupts this thinking. Similar interference occurs until after the last response option is heard, and at that point the last response option is likely to be the most salient and the focus of respondents' thoughts. People may also be most likely to remember the last response options in a long list of response options. So if respondents choose the first reasonable response option they consider, recency effects will occur. Consistent with this logic, mostly primacy effects have appeared in past studies that involved visual presentation, and mostly recency effects have occurred under oral presentation conditions.

In addition to mode of presentation, satisficing theory posits that response order effects depend on three factors: (1) the respondent's ability, (2) the respondent's motivation, and (3) the cognitive difficulty of optimizing inherent in the question. Respondents with greater ability and motivation are less likely to satisfice. Satisficing is also more likely when a question's stem or response choices are especially difficult to comprehend, when a question demands an especially difficult search of memory to retrieve needed information, when the integration of retrieved information into a summary judgment is especially difficult, or when translation of the summary judgment onto the response alternatives is especially difficult. Thus, recency effects in questions with orally presented, categorical response options are likely to be strongest among respondents low in ability and motivation, and for questions that are more difficult.

Allyson Holbrook

See also Primacy Effect; Response Alternatives; Response Order Effects; Satisficing

Further Readings

Bishop, G., & Smith, A. (2001). Response-order effects and the early Gallup split-ballots. *Public Opinion Quarterly, 65*, 479–505.

Krosnick, J. A. (1991). Response strategies for coping with the cognitive demands of attitude measures in surveys. *Applied Cognitive Psychology, 5*, 213–236.

Krosnick, J. A. (1999). Survey research. *Annual Review of Psychology, 50*, 537–567.

McClendon, M. J. (1986). Response-order effects for dichotomous questions. *Social Science Quarterly, 67*, 205–211.

McClendon, M. J. (1991). Acquiescence and recency response-order effects in interview surveys. *Sociological Methods and Research, 20*, 60–103.

Narayan, S., & Krosnick, J. A. (1996). Education moderates some response effects in attitude measurement. *Public Opinion Quarterly, 60*, 58–88.

Payne, S. L. (1949). Case study in question complexity. *Public Opinion Quarterly, 13*, 653–658.

Schuman, H., & Presser, S. (1996). *Questions and answers in attitude surveys: Experiments on question form, wording, and context.* Thousand Oaks, CA: Sage.

RECODED VARIABLE

Analysis with survey research data often first requires recoding of variables. Recode is a term used to describe the process of making changes to the values of a variable. Rarely can researchers proceed directly to data analysis after receiving or compiling a "raw" data set. The values of the variables to be used in the analysis usually have to be changed first. The reasons for recoding a variable are many. There may be errors in the original coding of the data that must be corrected. A frequency distribution run or descriptive

statistics on a variable can help the researcher identify possible errors that must be corrected with recodes. For example, if a variable measuring respondent's party identification has values of 1 for Democrat, 3 for Independent, 5 for Republican, and 7 for Other, and a frequency distribution shows values of either 2, 4, or 6, then these incorrect values can be recoded to their correct value by going back to the original survey instrument if it is available. More likely these incorrect values will have to be recoded to a "missing value" status. Computer-assisted data collection makes it impossible to check the correct value, as there is no paper trail, but makes it less likely that incorrect values will be entered in the first place.

Data are usually collected to get as much information as possible, but these data often must be recoded to yield more interpretable results. For example, respondents may be asked to report their date of birth in a survey. Recoding these values to age (in years) lets the researcher interpret the variable in a more intuitive and useful way. Furthermore, if the researcher wants to present the age variable in a frequency distribution table, then the interval measure of age can be recoded into an ordinal measure. For example, respondents between the ages of 18 and 24 can have their age value recoded to category 1, respondents between 25 and 34 can be recoded to category 2, respondents between 35 and 44 can be recoded to category 3, and so on. As interval- and ratio-level data can always be recoded into nominal- or ordinal-level data but nominal- and ordinal-level data cannot be recoded into interval-level data, it is always better to collect data at the interval or ratio level if possible.

Recoding is also necessary if some values of a variable are recorded inconveniently for analysis. For example, surveys typically code responses of "Don't know" and "Refused" as 8 and 9. The researcher needs to recode these values so they are recognized as missing values by the computer program being used for statistical analyses. Leaving these values unchanged will yield inaccurate and misleading results. Another reason to recode a variable is to transform the values of a variable (e.g., a log transformation) to tease out the true nature of the relationship between two variables. Also, if missing values are assigned a number in the original coding, the researcher needs to recode these values to missing before analyzing the data. As a final precaution, it is advisable to always run a frequency or descriptive statistics on the recoded variable to make certain that the desired recodes were achieved.

Charles Tien

See also Coding; Computer-Assisted Telephone Interviewing (CATI); Don't Knows (DKs); Frequency Distribution; Interval Measure; Nominal Measure; Ordinal Measure; Ratio Measure; Raw Data; Variable

Further Readings

Biemer, P. P., & Lyberg, L. E. (2003). *Introduction to survey quality*. Hoboken, NJ: Wiley.

Nagler, J. (1995). Coding style and good computing practices. *The Political Methodologist, 6*, 2–8.

Nardi, P. M. (2003). *Doing survey research: A guide to quantitative methods*. Boston: Allyn & Bacon.

RECONTACT

The term *recontact* has more than one meaning in survey research. It is used to refer to the multiple attempts that often must be made to make contact with a sampled element, such as a household or person, in order to gain cooperation and gather data and achieve good response rates. Recontacting hard-to-reach respondents is the most effective way to reduce survey nonresponse that is due to noncontact. This holds whether the mode of contact is via multiple mailings, multiple emails, multiple telephone calls, or multiple in-person visits.

The other meaning of *recontact* in survey research refers to the efforts that are made to validate completed interviews soon after they have been completed, by having a supervisory staff member recontact the respondent to validate that the interview was in fact completed and that it was completed accurately. These recontacts often are conducted via telephone even when the original interview was completed by an interviewer face-to-face with the respondent. Recontacts of this type are reasoned to reduce the likelihood of interviewer falsification, assuming that interviewers know that such quality assurance efforts are carried out by survey management.

Paul J. Lavrakas

See also Falsification; Noncontacts; Nonresponse; Quality Control; Response Rates; Validation

Further Readings

Groves, R. M., Fowler, F. J., Couper, M. P., Lepkowski, J. M., Singer, E., & Tourangeau, R. (2004). *Survey methodology*. Hoboken, NJ: Wiley.

RECORD CHECK

A record check study is one in which the validity of survey self-reports is assessed by comparing them to evidence in organizational records. Record check studies have been employed to evaluate the quality of data from existing surveys and also to test the relative quality of data from different prospective survey designs. Such investigations are often viewed as the gold standard for judging the validity of self-report information on behavior and experiences.

Record checks are infrequently conducted because of the limited availability of record information, as well as the cost and effort of obtaining and matching record and survey data for the same individuals. Although there are many potential sources of records, in practice it can be difficult to gain access to information that gives insight into the quality of survey data. The cooperation of record-holding organizations is required and, unfortunately, often hard to obtain. Records must be collected and preserved in a manner that permits investigators to use the information to make valid inferences. Organizations assemble records for their own aims, not for the purpose of validating survey data. Thus, information that survey investigators deem important may be missing or poorly maintained in records. Records may be organized in such a way that they require substantial transformation before they can be employed in a record check study. Finally, records are not kept on many things about which survey investigators are interested; record check studies are therefore confined to those matters in which human behavior comes in contact with bureaucratic systems. Other important behaviors, as well as attitudes, perceptions, and other mental constructs cannot be examined through the record check technique.

These points notwithstanding, it is clear that evidence from record check studies has been influential in understanding reporting errors and in designing important surveys. Record checks have been conducted in a number of contexts—for example, health, labor, voting, and victimization. In research done in connection with the National Health Interview Survey, medical records were employed to check the quality of reporting of doctor visits, hospitalizations, and morbidity. Records were obtained from physicians and hospitals detailing the date of medical encounters, along with the reasons for the visits. Respondents were then interviewed about their health experiences, and the survey reports were matched against the records. Comparisons revealed, for example, whether respondents reported a recorded medical contact or not. A result of one of these studies was that the reference period for the question on doctor visits was set at 2 weeks before the interview because comparison of survey reports with visit records showed that accuracy of recall was sharply lower for longer reference periods.

Another important series of record checks involved the American National Election Study. For several post-election waves of this biennial survey, respondent reports of voting were checked against public voting records. In this case, respondents were asked about their voting first and then interviewers attempted to verify the reports by examining voting records in county clerk offices. These comparisons suggested that there is an overreporting bias in self-reported voting. More people said that they voted than actually did. Since these studies were conducted, there have been many papers written on the possible causes and consequences of vote overreporting. In addition, the American National Election Study question used to measure voting was modified in an attempt to reduce the hypothesized "social desirability" bias attached to self-report of voting. Finally, there have been investigations of whether statistical models predicting voting differed in their predictive power if the analysis was confined to only "valid" votes—those reported that matched the official records—or also included the "invalid" votes. The findings suggest that the models performed equivalently in these cases.

In the development and the redesign of the National Crime Victimization Survey, police records were employed to validate reports of victimization. People who had reported crimes to the police were interviewed and asked if they had been victimized. The comparison of record information and self-reports suggested that victimization is underreported, particularly (as in the case of medical events) as the time between the police report and the survey interview increased and for less serious crimes. These findings influenced the designers of the National Crime Victimization Survey to set a 6-month reference period for asking questions about victimization and to employ a variety of

cues to assist respondents in recalling victimization experiences.

The research on the National Health Interview Survey, the American National Election Survey, and the National Crime Victimization Survey was preceded by a famous study conducted by Hugh Perry and Helen Crossley in Denver, Colorado, in the late 1940s. This study asked respondents about, for example, voting, library card ownership, and traffic offenses. The self-reports were matched against public records, and the results suggested that voting and library card ownership were overreported, whereas traffic offenses were underreported.

Combining the findings from all of these record check studies, general inferences have been made about factors affecting the validity of self-reports. First, social desirability is thought to affect the reporting of certain sorts of behavior: The more a behavior is thought to be meritorious (e.g., voting), the more it is likely to be overreported, whereas the more a behavior is thought to be undesirable (e.g., traffic offenses), the more it is apt to be underreported. Second, the elapsed time between an event and the survey is believed to affect the quality of self-reports: The longer the interval between the event (e.g., a doctor visit) and the interview, the less likely the event is to be recalled or reported accurately in time. Third, the importance or salience of an event is believed to affect the quality of reports. For example, more serious victimizations are more likely to be reported accurately than less serious ones, and hospitalizations that lasted a number of days are more likely to be reported accurately than overnight visits. Thus, record check studies have influenced greatly how survey practitioners think about possible reporting error and the means to reduce it.

Although these lessons are important, the picture presented by record check studies is not so clear that survey researchers can treat the inferences from them as "laws" of survey reporting. The basic assumption of record check research—that the records are generally free of error—is certainly questionable. For example, an investigation of police records in Chicago in the 1980s led to the suspicion that the records were being systematically altered to make it appear that crimes had been solved. Ironically, investigators in that case employed a survey of possible victims to see if what they said matched the records—but this time, they treated the victims' responses as "the truth." Further, voting records are not always correct. It may also happen that records and self-reports are both "true," even if they do not match. This is because official records capture human events differently from the way people experience them. For example, records of people receiving a governmental housing subsidy may not be reported by the recipients simply because they do not know that the rent they pay is subsidized. In sum, records, like self-reports, are fallible sources of information, and meticulous care must be taken in record check studies to see to it that proper inferences are drawn.

Peter V. Miller

See also National Election Studies (NES); National Health Interview Survey (NHIS); Reference Period; Respondent-Related Error; Reverse Record Check; Self-Reported Measure; Social Desirability; Telescoping

Further Readings

Cannell, C. F., Fisher, G., & Bakker, T. (1965). *Reporting of hospitalization in the Health Interview Survey*. Vital and Health Statistics, Series 2, No. 6. Hyattsville, MD: National Center for Health Statistics.

Cannell, C. F., Miller, P. V., & Oksenberg, L. (1981). Research on interviewing techniques. In S. Leinhardt (Ed.), *Sociological methodology* (pp. 389–437). San Francisco: Jossey-Bass.

Miller, P. V., & Groves, R. M. (1985). Matching survey responses to official records: An exploration of validity in victimization reporting. *Public Opinion Quarterly, 49*, 366–380.

Parry, H., & Crossley, H. (1950). Validity of responses to survey questions. *Public Opinion Quarterly, 14*, 61–80.

Traugott, M., & Katosh, J. (1981). The consequences of validated and self reported voting measures. *Public Opinion Quarterly, 45*, 519–535.

REFERENCE PERIOD

The reference period is the time frame for which survey respondents are asked to report activities or experiences of interest. Many surveys intend to measure frequencies of events or instances within a given period of time; for example, *How many times did you consult a medical practitioner during the last two months?* or *Think about the 2 weeks ending yesterday—have you cut down on any of the things you usually do about the house, at work, or in your free time because of illness or injury?* Most of the time, the reference period starts at some point in the past and ends

at the time of the survey. However, there are fixed reference periods as well—for example, a calendar year or a calendar quarter, depending on the design of the study. Whereas some ongoing surveys (rotating panels or ongoing cross-sectional surveys) aim to document change throughout the field period, others intend to measure the incidence or prevalence of certain events within a given period of time.

In addition to the relative position of the reference period in relation to the time of the interview, its length is of key interest for survey researchers. The length—for example, number of days, weeks, or months—affects the variance of the estimated frequency (prevalence) or the proportion of respondents who have experienced a certain event (incidence). The longer the reference period is, the more stable is the estimate in reducing the variance associated to the variable. Thus, considering a given level of precision, survey cost is reduced. However, the length of the reference period depends on the concept to be measured; in case of a high prevalence variable (e.g., number of restaurant visits) a relatively short reference period might be appropriate, whereas the same reference period would not be appropriate for events with a relatively low frequency of occurrence (e.g., crime victimization).

Whereas a lengthy reference period seems preferable in terms of the variance of the estimate, it has considerable drawbacks.

1. Measurements of past events are subject to recall error. Recall error consists of various components of which *recall loss* and *telescoping* are the predominant ones. Recall loss is due to respondents forgetting certain events or instances that actually happened within the reference period, which in turn reduces the estimate compared to the true value. By contrast, (forward) telescoping produces higher estimates because respondents accidentally place an event into the reference period although it actually happened before the starting point of the reference period. To compensate for recall loss, researchers make use of introductory questions that stimulate memory by asking for autobiographical events within the reference period or other landmark events. By contrast, telescoping may be dealt with by bounded recall. To reduce telescoping, respondents are asked in two or more consecutive interviews to report on the frequency of certain events. At the time of the second measurement, respondents are asked to report on the

number of events or instances since the last interview, which serves as the outer "bound" for recall. Thus, events or instances reported in the first interview can be excluded from the response at the time of the second interview. This expensive procedure addresses the problem of respondents' tendency to "telescope" too distant experiences into the reference period.

2. Besides recall loss and telescoping, lengthy reference periods have additional disadvantages because they increase the time until results can be reported. For example, in an ongoing panel study on crime victimization, a 12-month reference period requires a longer period of time between the first occurrence of a given victimization and the availability of the report.

3. When it comes to answering a frequency question, respondents make use of at least two different strategies to generate a reasonable response: They either recall every single event that has occurred in the reference period and count the number of instances, or they estimate the number of instances using various estimation strategies (rate-based estimation, guessing)—depending on the characteristic of the event in question (similar vs. dissimilar, regular vs. irregular). Generally speaking, "recall and count" is considered to be advantageous compared to "estimating" in terms of the validity of the response. Even though the literature offers a great variety of findings, it is safe to assume that with longer reference periods, the proportion of respondents who estimate the number of events increases.

Considering these implications, survey researchers must balance the size of the variance (and cost) against the biases and disadvantages associated with a lengthy reference period.

Marek Fuchs

See also Bounding; Respondent-Related Error; Telescoping

Further Readings

Cannell, C., Fisher, G., & Bakker, T. (1965). *A study of the reporting of visits to doctors in the National Health Interview Survey.* Vital and Health Statistics, Series 2, No. 6. Hyattsville, MD: National Center for Health Statistics.

Mathiowetz, N. (2000). *The effect of length of recall on the quality of survey data.* Paper presented at the fourth international conference on Methodological Issues in Official Statistics, Stockholm, Sweden. Retrieved February 23, 2007, from http://www.scb.se/Grupp/Omscb/_Dokument/Mathiowetz.pdf

Neter, J., & Waksberg, J. (1964). A study of response errors in expenditures data from household interviews. *Journal of the American Statistical Association, 59*(305), 18–55.

REFUSAL

In survey research, a refusal occurs when a request to participate in a survey is declined. In addition, some respondents who do participate can refuse to answer a particular question (sometimes called item nonresponse) or can refuse to finish the survey (sometimes called a partial or breakoff interview). The refusal rate is calculated as the proportion of contacted people who decline the survey request. Some researchers include partial interviews as refusals in the refusal rate calculation, others do not.

Refusals are important because they are a major type of nonresponse that can potentially introduce error in survey estimates. With refusal rates increasing both in the United States and worldwide, the reasons for refusals and how they are handled are important concerns for survey researchers.

In telephone surveys, the vast majority of refusals in surveys come shortly after the phone has been answered. As such, these nonresponders can be at the household level or at the respondent level. If the refusal occurs before the appropriate respondent within the household can be determined (either by random selection or other eligibility requirements), it is considered a household-level refusal. If the appropriate respondent has been determined and he or she is the person actually refusing the survey, it is considered a respondent-level refusal. A partial interview or breakoff is a respondent-level refusal.

For in-person and telephone surveys, interviewers may use a refusal report form to record any discernable details about the household or respondent, such as gender, age, and race. If the sample is from a client list or panel sampling frame, researchers may be able to estimate parameters related to nonresponse (e.g., demographics, past purchase behavior, or other list variables). These parameters from refusers can then be compared with the obtained sample to estimate the presence and impact of any potential nonresponse bias. Differences can be adjusted through survey weighting.

In self-administered surveys (e.g., mail survey, Internet survey), refusals make up some portion of those who do not return the questionnaire (nonresponders). For most self-administered studies, researchers know very little about why they did not participate because there is no interaction with an interviewer; for example, did they never receive the questionnaire or did they receive it but refuse? Depending on how the sample was obtained or constructed, researchers may or may not know which respondents did not participate or any other details about them. If parameters from nonresponders of self-administered surveys can be determined, again they can be used to determine potential nonresponse bias and used in survey weighting adjustments.

The reasons for refusal are varied. It is often difficult for researchers to ascertain the reasons for refusals because many do little more than hang up the phone ("immediate hang ups") or simply never respond in any way in the case of mail and Internet sampling. If there is an interaction with the interviewer, refusers usually do not communicate much aside from declining. Some may cite objections due to invasion of privacy, being reached at a bad time, length of interview, topic saliency, poor past survey experience, or a belief that the request is a telemarketing effort. Others may have a language barrier that prevents them from participating effectively. If the interviewer can determine (or at least suspect) a language barrier exists, this household can be recontacted by a bilingual interviewer.

Regardless of the reasons given, often the main reason for a refusal is that the interviewer has reached the household at an inconvenient time. In most mediated surveys, interviewers are initiating the contact with the household by proactively contacting it rather than a respondent returning an interviewer's call to take the interview, usually on a toll-free number. As such, the interviewer's request is often "interrupting" something at the household level. Unless specifically asked not to, researchers will typically recontact households that refused initially and will make a second request of the household to participate at a later date in the field period. Perhaps the interviewer will reach the household at a more convenient time or even talk to another household member than originally refused, possibly resulting in a completed interview. If a household refuses a second time, it is usually considered a "final" refusal and is not contacted again.

Although the Federal Trade Commission exempted survey and opinion research from the National Do Not Call Registry guidelines, most telephone survey organizations maintain internal do-not-call lists. Therefore, if a refuser asks to be placed on the do-not-call list, this information is recorded and this household will not be contacted again by that organization. Technically, if this household number is sampled in a subsequent survey by the same organization, it should be coded as a refusal even though it was not contacted.

In self-administered surveys, nonresponders are often sent reminders or additional requests to complete the survey. This could be a second copy of the questionnaire sent in the mail (the respondent could have misplaced the first one) or, in the case of an email invitation, a link to the online survey. Again, if respondents refuse and request not to be contacted further, they do not receive reminders or future survey requests. In fact, in most online surveys the invitation to participate includes simple instructions for how to opt out of any future requests or reminders.

Because handling refusers and potential refusers is a key part of an interviewer's job, training is especially important. A successful survey completion depends, in part, on the rapport established between the interviewer and the respondent. Poorly trained interviewers with nonneutral attitudes can hurt this relationship and lead to increased refusals. And given that the vast majority of refusals in telephone surveys occur in the first seconds of the interviewer–respondent interaction, the interviewer has very little time to develop rapport, anticipate potential barriers, and alleviate respondent objections. Refusal avoidance training focuses on how to avoid refusals by detecting respondent objections and proactively addressing them in an effort to persuade respondents to participate.

In most in-person surveys, interviewers have more time to develop rapport before the household member who opens the door refuses to cooperate. Furthermore, advance contact is more effective in in-person surveys as all sampled addresses can be mailed an advance letter. In telephone surveys of the U.S. general public only about half of the residences that are sampled can be matched to an accurate mailing address; but when this is possible sending an advance letter prior to placing the first call reduces the proportion of refusals appreciably.

In addition to learning how to disarm a potential refusal situation, interviewers can also be trained to "convert" initial refusals into completed interviews. This technique is called *refusal conversion*. Typically, sample households who have initially refused a survey request are called back by an experienced and trained interviewer. Some interviewers who are particularly adept at this type of respondent interaction may even be considered refusal conversion specialists. Converting refusals is important because it reduces nonresponse, saves costs, and may also reduce the potential bias it can introduce.

Sandra L. Bauman

See also Advance Contact; Advance Letter; Do-Not-Call Registries; Federal Trade Commission (FTC) Regulations; Household Refusal; Interviewer Training; Language Barrier; Missing Data; Nonresponse; Nonresponse Bias; Nonresponse Error; Nonresponse Rates; Partial Completion; Privacy; Refusal Avoidance; Refusal Avoidance Training (RAT); Refusal Conversation; Refusal Report Form (RRF); Respondent–Interviewer Rapport; Respondent Refusal; Response Rates

Further Readings

Brehm, J. (1993). *The phantom respondents: Opinion surveys and political representation*. Ann Arbor: University of Michigan Press.

Groves, R. M. (1989). *Survey errors and survey costs*. New York: Wiley.

Lavrakas, P. J. (1993). *Telephone survey methods: Sampling, selection, and supervision* (2nd ed.). Newbury Park, CA: Sage.

Stec, J. A., & Lavrakas, P. J. (2007, May). *The cost of a refusal in large national RDD studies*. Paper presented at the 62nd annual conference of the American Association for Public Opinion Research, Anaheim, CA.

REFUSAL AVOIDANCE

Because refusals make up a large portion of survey nonresponse, researchers want to minimize their occurrence as much as possible. Refusal avoidance is the researcher's awareness of, and efforts to eliminate or mitigate, factors that influence potential respondents toward refusing an invitation to participate in a survey. The relevance of concerted efforts to lower refusal rates is that the researcher is trying to reduce survey error through improvement in response rates,

thus ostensibly improving the overall quality of the research.

Although there are many factors that influence a potential respondent's decision to participate in research, it is logical and cost-effective for researchers to concentrate on those factors under the control of the researcher, such as survey design and administration. As an integral part of the survey design process, the researcher not only should provide positive influences to a respondent to encourage participation (e.g., persuasive introductory text or verbiage, visually appealing research material, use of noncontingent monetary incentives) but also should strive to reduce or eliminate negative influences. Once the survey has been designed, the administration of the survey can also be refined with refusal avoidance in mind (e.g., interviewer selection, training, survey procedures, timing).

Seeking to increase the positive aspects during survey design is a natural starting point to avoid refusals and thereby improve response rates. Crafting introductory verbiage and responses (i.e., persuaders and other fallback statements) to respondents for telephone or in-person recruitment and the textual and visual appeal of mail or Internet recruitment will help avoid refusals and thereby improve the likelihood of response. This may include pretesting and focus groups with potential respondents or effective interviewers. Additionally, increasing the visibility or positioning of other positives should be considered, such leveraging (a) the research topic or sponsor, (b) that the entire population or certain subpopulations will benefit from the research results, (c) that incentives being are being offered, and (d) that by cooperating one is representing one's community.

Decreasing negative elements to research requests also is important, though it may not receive as much attention as increasing the positives. Often researchers will review their research materials and survey design to eliminate obvious negatives, such as confusing language. However, the researcher should also concentrate on understanding the population of interest, their social environment, and social-psychological attributes. For example, surveys among the various segments of the Asian population must be sensitive to their cultural heritage, such as knowing that many Chinese respondents may consider the number "4" (e.g., a $4 incentive) bad luck whereas 8 is considered a good number, white color is less favorable than red, and a gift of a clock (i.e., as an incentive) is a bad omen.

A survey should be administered with the aim of preventing refusals; both the delivery mode of the survey request(s) and the rules for making requests should be devised with this aim in mind. The researcher may improve likelihood of participation by attending to interviewer selection, training, and appearance; materials and delivery method (email, U.S. Postal Service, UPS, FedEx, etc.); visual appeal (use of color, pictures, logos, etc.); and so forth. The study contact rules can also improve response and avoid refusals through using effective contact times (e.g., evenings and weekends), number of contact attempts, using multiple modes for making the survey request, and so on. Additionally, the researcher should evaluate the reasons for refusals through use of a refusal report form or other means during and after the field period to improve future research (e.g., debrief meetings or focus groups with interviewers to catalog specific objections, areas of concern, and breakoff points during request or survey).

Charles D. Shuttles

See also Fallback Statements; Interviewer Training; Nonresponse; Refusal; Refusal Avoidance Training (RAT); Refusal Rate; Refusal Report Form (RRF)

Further Readings

Groves, R. M., & Couper, M. P. (1998). *Nonresponse in household interview surveys*. New York: Wiley.

Groves, R. M., Dillman, D. A., Eltinge, J. L., & Little, R. J. A. (Eds.). (2002). *Survey nonresponse*. New York: Wiley.

Groves, R. M., & McGonagle, K. (2001). A theory-guided interviewer training protocol regarding survey participation. *Journal of Official Statistics*, *17*(2), 249–266.

Groves, R. M., Singer, E., & Corning, A. C. (2000). Leverage-saliency theory of survey participation: Description and an illustration. *Public Opinion Quarterly*, *64*, 299–308.

Lavrakas, P. J. (1993). *Telephone survey methods: Sampling, selection, and supervision* (2nd ed.). Newbury Park, CA: Sage.

Refusal Avoidance Training (RAT)

Research interviewers have the difficult task of obtaining the cooperation of respondents. Successful interviewers are able to achieve positive outcomes (completed interviews) while simultaneously avoiding negative outcomes (refusals). Researchers may employ several approaches to improving response rates through refusal avoidance, including the use of refusal avoidance training (RAT), which specifically concentrates on interviewers reducing the proportion of their survey requests that end as a refusal.

Experienced and successful interviewers tailor their approach to individual respondents, rather than using a "one size fits all" approach. To successfully tailor their approach, interviewers must have an extensive set of techniques, strategies, phrases, and so on, that have to be customized to the specific survey request. Interviewers must use *active listening skills* to pick up on the verbal and nonverbal cues of the respondent. These cues will assist the interviewer in selecting the appropriate response strategy most likely to elicit respondent cooperation.

Interviewers skilled at maintaining interaction (continuing their contact with the respondent) create more opportunity to tailor their approach. As the interaction between the interviewer and the respondent continues, and the time investment grows longer, it becomes more difficult, in theory, for the respondent to break off contact and refuse the survey request.

An innovative approach to the development and implementation of refusal avoidance training was first posited by Robert Groves and K. McGonagle. A three-step process is used to develop a customized (to the survey organization, topic, and sponsor) refusal avoidance training program. The steps are summarized as follows:

1. Focus groups of experienced interviewers are held to capture specific examples of the actual words used by reluctant respondents to describe their concerns about the survey request. Focus group moderators seek to maximize the number of different types of concerns recalled by the interviewers. Hundreds of utterances from respondents may be collected.

2. After assembly and elimination of duplicate concerns, senior interviewers and training staff classify the concerns into thematic sets (e.g., concerns about privacy, insufficient time), and then identify the desirable verbal behaviors of interviewers to address the concerns. There are often multiple alternative behaviors that may be used by the expert interviewers in response to a specific utterance; each, however, addresses the expressed concern(s) of the respondent.

3. A training curriculum can then be developed and concentrated on, imparting four refusal avoidance skills:

    a. Learning the themes of a potential respondent's concerns.

    b. Learning to classify a potential respondent's actual wording of a concern into those themes (the diagnosis step).

    c. Learning desirable verbal behaviors to address the concerns.

    d. Learning to deliver to the reluctant respondent, in words compatible with their own, a set of statements relevant to their concerns.

A major goal of the refusal avoidance training is to increase the speed of the interviewer's performance on points 3b through 3d.

Additional refusal avoidance skills go beyond quickly and effectively responding to respondent reluctance by concentrating on the opening 5 to 10 seconds of contact with the respondent. An effective introduction, and training to improve the introduction, focuses on interviewer alertness, prior knowledge, perceiving the nature of the respondent's "hello," and active listening. Effective interviewers are noted for being on high alert for their next survey request. Interviewers should specifically prepare themselves to react to the possible outcomes and reactions of requesting survey participation. Part of being prepared is to glean as much information as possible prior to the request, such as knowledge of the respondent's location (state, city, neighborhood, etc.), knowledge of prior attempts, and the like. Once the interviewer initiates a survey request, there are the verbal cues (and visual cues in the case of face-to-face interviewing) that result from the potential respondent's greeting (i.e., the hello). Does the respondent appear to be impatient? tired? curious? hostile? Interviewers should employ active listening for additional background cues to further tailor their introduction; for example, sounds of activity (kids, household guests, loud music, or television) could prompt the interviewer to use a briefer introduction.

Researchers can improve the effectiveness of their training techniques by incorporating large group, small group, paired, and individual exercises and role playing activities that concentrate on increasing interviewers' response speed and appropriate selection of effective responses to reluctant respondents. If effectively developed and administered, refusal avoidance training may substantially increase an interviewers' "toolbox" of possible effective responses to stated concerns from reluctant respondents and ingrain quick responses.

Charles D. Shuttles

See also Interviewer Training; Refusal; Refusal Avoidance; Tailoring

Further Readings

Groves, R. M., & McGonagle, K. (2001). A theory-guided interviewer training protocol regarding survey participation. *Journal of Official Statistics, 17*(2), 249–266.

Shuttles, C. D., Welch, J., Hoover, B., & Lavrakas, P. J. (2002, May). *The development and experimental testing of an innovative approach to training telephone interviewers to avoid refusals.* Paper presented at the 59th annual conference of the American Association for Public Opinion Research Conference, St. Petersburg, FL.

REFUSAL CONVERSION

Refusal conversions are the procedures that survey researchers use to gain cooperation from a sampled respondent who has refused an initial survey request. Refusal conversion may include different versions of the survey introductions and other written scripts or materials (e.g., cover letters), study contact rules, incentives, and interviewer characteristics and training. This is a common procedure for many surveys, but it requires careful consideration of the details of the refusal conversion efforts and the potential costs versus the potential benefits of the effort.

The goal of converting initial refusals is to raise the survey response rate, under the assumption that this may lower the potential for refusal-related unit nonresponse error. The research literature contains reports of successfully converting refusals in telephone surveys between 5% and 40% of the time. There is little reported in the research literature about whether refusal conversions efforts are effective in reducing nonresponse bias.

Gaining cooperation from a potential respondent during initial contacts is much more effective than attempts to "convert" that respondent after an initial refusal has been encountered. Thus, all researchers should pay attention to survey design and administration to effectively maximize cooperation and minimize refusals for initial contacts. However, despite researchers' best efforts to avoid refusals, they will still occur; thus, refusal conversion is an avenue to gain some amount of completed questionnaires from initial refusers. The basic procedures used to carry out the administration of the survey may need to be modified during refusal conversion attempts.

Refusal conversions often are attempted in surveys that are conducted via mail or the Internet. In these survey modes, refusal conversion essentially is part and parcel of the larger process of recontacting respondents who have not yet returned a completed questionnaire under the assumption that some portion of them initially have decided to refuse to do so. Procedures for doing these follow-up contacts of initial nonresponders in mail and Internet surveys are described elsewhere in this encyclopedia and will not be discussed here in any detail. Instead, the remainder of this entry focuses mostly on refusal conversion as applied in face-to-face and telephone interviewing.

Approaches

There are two basic ways to structure the refusal conversion process: (1) ignoring the fact that a respondent has refused an initial survey request and using the exact same survey request approach, or (2) implementing a revised or different approach when trying to convert the initial refusal. The first approach relies upon the hope that the timing will be more opportune or the respondent's inclination to participate will be more favorable when recontacted than at the time of the first contact. When using this approach, the researcher should modify survey procedures by designing recontact rules that use as much lag time (i.e., amount of time between the initial refusal attempt and the subsequent refusal conversion attempt) as possible. If the field period allows, lag time of 5 to 14 days has been found to increase the likelihood of encountering a different respondent (in household or organizational surveys) or reaching the original respondent at a more convenient or favorable time.

Many survey organizations use the second approach of doing a more extensive modification of survey procedures for subsequent contacts to a respondent after the initial refusal. For mail or Internet mode written survey requests, this may mean using different text in cover letters that acknowledges the previous attempt, addresses

the possible reason for refusing (e.g., privacy, survey sponsor, timing, legitimatizing research purpose[s]), and explaining the importance of participation (e.g., how a government program may benefit from higher research participation). For in-person or telephone surveys, this may mean using different introductory scripts that vary the appeal. Additionally, changing incentives, (e.g., increasing the incentives if lower amounts were initially offered) or offering different types of incentives (i.e., contingent vs. noncontingent) may be effective tactics to use during refusal conversion attempts. Another approach for researchers to consider is to offer a shortened questionnaire (containing only key questions) to reduce the burden on the respondent.

The contact or calling rules also can be varied to improve the likelihood of success during refusal conversion attempts, including mode of contact, interviewer assignment, advanced interviewer training, refusal conversion specialists, and gathering special information from the interviewer at the time of initial refusal, for example, through the use of a refusal report form.

Mode of Contact

If an initial refusal occurs in one mode (e.g., a mailed survey), the use of one or more other modes can be considered if cost and time permit. For example, a refusal to an initial mailed survey request could spur in-person or telephone refusal conversion attempts.

Interviewer Assignment

The attributes and skills of the original in-person or telephone interviewer may be related to why he or she did not gain the cooperation of the respondent during the initial survey request. By assigning a different "type" of interviewer in subsequent refusal conversion attempts, cooperation may be gained through different skills or a different approach of that interviewer. Some researchers believe it is wise to match demographic characteristics as closely as possible when deciding which interviewers will try to recontact an initial refuser. This, of course, can be done only if demographic information is available about the refuser, such as what can be captured in a refusal report form.

Refusal Report Form

The refusal report form contains information that can be collected at the time of the initial refusal in face-to-face and telephone surveys and can be extremely beneficial in assisting the subsequent refusal conversion attempt. Specifically, a refusal report form can be used to collect information such as (a) perceived respondent demographics (e.g., sex and age), (b) degree of interaction, (c) reasons and concerns given for refusing, (d) the strength of the refusal, (e) whether the refusal was at the household or respondent level, (f) when the refusal took place (e.g., immediate refusal, middle of introduction, after introduction, during data collection), and (g) other visual and audio cues (e.g., condition of household, neighborhood characteristics, presence of children). In this way, the interviewer performing the refusal conversion attempt can better prepare in advance of recontacting the initial refuser by using this information to tailor the approach during the conversion attempt to that particular refuser and his or her initial reasons for refusing.

Refusal Conversion Training

This type of advanced training concentrates on refusal conversion. The development of this training may be similar to, or combined with, refusal avoidance training.

Refusal Conversion Specialists

Evidence shows that some interviewers are better at refusal conversion than are others. Granted, researchers should concentrate on having interviewers who are all skilled at effectively gaining cooperation on the initial contact and thereby avoid refusals as often as possible. This notwithstanding, proper selection of effective refusal conversion specialists can maximize refusal conversions over what can be achieved by the general pool of interviewers. Attributes of successful refusal conversion specialists are (a) confidence, (b) perseverance in dealing with reluctant respondents, (c) appropriate assertiveness, (d) skill at tailoring and using multiple approaches, and (e) quick adaptation and response to whatever the reluctant respondent is saying. Refusal conversion can be assigned to supervisors or other interviewing specialists that often receive higher remuneration or incentives for taking on these especially difficult cases.

Recontact Determination

Deciding which initially refusing cases to try to convert is also an important part of the refusal conversation process. In almost all interviewer-administered surveys, the interviewer should never attempt to convert all initial refusers, because some of them will have refused so vehemently or pointedly as to make recontact wholly inappropriate. For example, it is generally agreed among survey professionals that any initial refuser who states something to the effect, "Don't ever contact me again!" should not be subjected to a refusal conversion attempt. The use of a refusal report form can be very helpful in determining which initial refusers to try to convert. This can be done manually by supervisory personnel reviewing the prior refusals, or if the data from the refusal report form are entered into a computer, an algorithm can be devised to select those initial refusers who should be tried again and select out those that should not be contacted again.

Costs Versus Benefits

Finally, the researcher should carefully consider the potential costs versus the benefits of trying to convert refusals. Refusal conversion efforts can span a wide spectrum of effort and contacts with a varied return on investment. For example, a possible outcome of too aggressive a refusal conversion process may be a decline in overall data quality. Thus, those initially refusing respondents who are extremely reluctant but who agree to be interviewed during the conversion contact may not be interested in the topic, the research sponsor, or in contributing to the outcome of the research and thus may provide low-quality data. By employing refusal conversion procedures, the researcher may motivate respondents just enough to participate but with increased item nonresponse or other types of low-quality responses (e.g., converted refusers may disproportionately employ satisficing, by giving answers that seem reasonable but without searching their memory or giving adequate cognitive consideration).

There has been little research on the costs of refusal conversions. But in 2007, Jeffrey A. Stec and Paul J. Lavrakas reported findings based on several very large random-digit dialing surveys that suggested that completed interviews gained from converted refusals are far less costly to obtain than a completed interview from a yet-to-be-attempted telephone number or address. If this finding holds up in other studies, it would indicate that refusal conversions not only increase survey response rates but also lead to cost savings compared to adding new samples to compensate for all the cases that were lost due to initial refusals.

Charles D. Shuttles, Paul J. Lavrakas,
and Jennie W. Lai

See also Calling Rules; Cover Letter; Nonresponse Bias; Nonresponse Error; Refusal; Refusal Avoidance; Refusal Avoidance Training; Refusal Report Form (RRF); Respondent Burden; Unit Nonresponse

Further Readings

Bauman, S. L., Lavrakas, P. J., & Merkle, D. M. (1994, May). *Data quality of reluctant respondents: Refusal conversions and item-nonresponse.* Paper presented at 49th annual conference of the American Association for Public Opinion Research, Danvers, MA.

Groves, R. M., & Couper, M. P. (1998). *Nonresponse in household interview surveys.* New York: Wiley.

Groves, R. M., Dillman, D. A., Eltinge, J. L., & Little, R. J. A. (Eds.). (2002). *Survey nonresponse.* New York: Wiley.

Lavrakas, P. J. (1993). *Telephone survey methods: Sampling, selection, and supervision* (2nd ed.). Newbury Park, CA: Sage.

Lavrakas, P. J., Bauman, S. L., & Merkle, D. M. (1992, May). *Refusal report forms, refusal conversions, and nonresponse bias.* Paper presented at the 47th annual conference of the American Association for Public Opinion Research, St. Petersburg, FL.

Stec, J. A., & Lavrakas, P. J. (2007, May). *The cost of a refusal in large national RDD studies.* Paper presented at the 62nd annual conference of the American Association for Public Opinion Research, Anaheim, CA.

REFUSAL RATE

The refusal rate is the proportion of all potentially eligible sample cases that declined the request to be interviewed. Before calculating the refusal rate, researchers must make some decisions about how to handle the types of nonresponse in the calculation.

There are two types of refusals that are generally included in the refusal rate calculation:

1. *Household-level refusals:* These refusals occur before the appropriate respondent within the household can be determined (either by random selection or other eligibility requirements). That is, the person refusing may or may not be the selected respondent within that household.

2. *Respondent-level refusals:* These are refusals that occur after the appropriate respondent has been determined. That is, the selected respondent has been identified and that individual is the one actually refusing.

Partial interviews ("partials"), or breakoffs, can be classified as another type of respondent-level refusal. Partials are when respondents begin an interview but do not finish it. They may be refusing to complete the questionnaire, or they may have other circumstances that interfere with finishing it (e.g., they initially ran out of time and were not recontacted to finish the interview during the field period). Depending on how many questions were answered, researchers may treat some breakoffs as completed interviews and others as respondent refusals or noncontacts as a final disposition.

There are three generally accepted refusal rate calculations that are included in the American Association for Public Opinion Research's 2006 Standard Definitions. In all three refusal rate calculations, the numerator is simply the total number of refusals (household- and respondent-level). But each of the calculations differs according to which dispositions or call outcomes are included in the denominator.

Refusal Rate 1. The denominator includes all possibly eligible cases still in the sample frame, regardless of whether or not the eligibility of the case could be determined. Thus, the denominator includes completed interviews, refusals, noncontacts (e.g., callbacks), and cases of unknown eligibility. This rate is the most conservative of the three refusal rate calculations.

Refusal Rate 2. The denominator is similar to Refusal Rate 1 except it uses only a proportion of the unknown cases, not all of them. This proportion is an estimate (e) of how many unknown cases would likely be eligible (e.g., is a household and meets other survey criteria). In estimating this proportion, researchers must be guided by the best available information on what share of eligible cases is likely among the unknown eligibility cases.

Refusal Rate 3. The denominator excludes all cases of unknown eligibility. In other words, this rate is the proportion of refusals among those sample cases known to be eligible sample units for the survey. Noncontact and other rates can be calculated in a manner similar to this rate so that, when summed, all will equal the total nonresponse rate.

The survey refusal rate has been increasing in the past 20 years in the United States and elsewhere in the world. This has happened despite the efforts of many survey researchers around the world. There is no easy or apparent solution to this decline other than to continue to investigate its causes and possible solutions.

Sandra L. Bauman

See also *e*; Household Refusal; Noncontacts; Nonresponse Bias; Partial Completion; Refusal; Respondent Refusal; Standard Definitions; Unknown Eligibility; Within-Unit Selection

Further Readings

The American Association for Public Opinion Research. (2006). *Standard definitions: Final dispositions of case codes and outcome rates for surveys* (4th ed.). Lenexa, KS: Author.

REFUSAL REPORT FORM (RRF)

A large proportion of nonresponse in surveys is due to refusals, which occur when a request to participate in a survey is declined. Researchers are concerned about the effect of refusals because of the potential error that they can introduce in survey estimates.

A refusal report form (RRF) is a structured form used by interviewers immediately after a refusal is encountered. The employment of an RRF process produces valuable paradata and has three main benefits:

1. It can provide estimates of relevant parameters (e.g., refuser gender, race, age) that can be compared with the obtained sample to help determine the presence and impact of potential nonresponse bias.

2. It can provide valuable information that can help interviewers in subsequent contact attempts to convert these refusals into completed interviews.

3. It can help researchers conduct investigations into the nature of refusals so as to plan better strategies on how to reduce their frequency of occurrence.

RRFs capture structured information about all individual refusals that most often is lost when interviewers are given only informal instructions to write down notes about the refusals if they think it is appropriate.

RRFs are used in mediated interviews—that is, those that are conducted by interviewers, either in person or on the phone. Information about the refusal is recorded based on estimates that interviewers make either visually (for in-person) or audibly (for telephone and in-person).

There is no standardized format for an RRF. (Paul J. Lavrakas appears to have been the first to describe the use and value of such a form and to show an example of it in a book on telephone survey methods.) Researchers develop RRFs with variables that are most relevant to the study and that are reasonable to be estimated by interviewers given the situation. For example, in an in-person survey, an interviewer may be able to provide information about the type of home, neighborhood setting, and so forth. Telephone interviewers could not begin to estimate those details from brief phone conversation but past research has shown that they can provide accurate estimates of certain demographic characteristics for the person being spoken to.

In any case, the RRF usually tries to capture two types of information, linked to the two benefits specified previously. Demographic information about the refuser (e.g., gender, age, race) and details about the context of the refusal (e.g., strength of the refusal, reasons given for refusal, perceived barriers to participating, etc.) may help interviewers, in future attempts, to convert that refuser into a cooperating respondent.

Given that the vast majority of refusals in telephone surveys typically occur in the first few seconds of the interviewer–respondent interaction, the interviewer has very little time to develop rapport, anticipate potential barriers, and alleviate respondent objections. Although there has been little published about the use of RRFs, research by Sandra L. Bauman, Daniel M. Merkle, and Paul J. Lavrakas suggests that telephone interviewers can accurately make estimates of gender, race, and age in a majority of cases, even when the interactions are brief. These estimates can be used to help determine the presence of nonresponse bias.

Interviewers are also able to provide details about the refusal that can help survey management determine which refusals to contact again and how best to approach that next interaction. For example, if an interviewer is recontacting a refusing household where the reason given was "We're just sitting down to dinner," they may start the next interaction with "I'm sorry we reached you at a bad time. Is this better?" Or, if the RRF indicates that a woman refused but during the conversion attempt a man answers, the interviewer can adjust the introduction accordingly.

When potential respondents refuse to cooperate, researchers know little about them and why they choose to not participate for the simple reason that they refuse to talk to the interviewer. In in-person surveys, more information about the refuser is at the interviewer's disposal because he or she actually saw the person who refused. The problem of gathering information on refusers is an especially challenging one for telephone survey researchers; often the best proxy is interviewer estimates (like those gathered via RRFs).

Sandra L. Bauman

See also Nonresponse Bias; Paradata; Refusal; Refusal Conversion; Refusal Rate; Respondent–Interviewer Rapport

Further Readings

Bauman, S. L., Merkle, D. M., & Lavrakas, P. J. (1992, November). *Interviewer estimates of refusers' gender, age, and race in telephone surveys.* Paper presented at the 16th annual conference of the Midwest Association for Public Opinion Research, Chicago, IL.

Lavrakas, P. J. (1993). *Telephone survey methods: Sampling, selection, and supervision* (2nd ed.). Newbury Park, CA: Sage.

Lavrakas, P. J., Bauman, S. L., & Merkle, D. M. (1992, May). *Refusal report forms, refusal conversions, and nonresponse bias.* Paper presented at the 47th annual conference of the American Association for Public Opinion Research, St. Petersburg, FL.

REGISTRATION-BASED SAMPLING (RBS)

Registration-based sampling (RBS) is a sampling frame and sampling technique that has been used, with growing frequency in the past two decades, for conducting election polls. RBS frames for a given geopolitical area can be built by researchers using public records for that political jurisdiction, or they can be purchased from vendors who already have done the legwork. Unlike the random-digit dialing (RDD) telephone sampling frame that has been used primary for election polling since the 1980s, the RBS frame is comprised of a list of names, addresses, and oftentimes telephone numbers of registered voters. An immediate advantage of RBS is that the name of the sampled voter is available for use in gaining that respondent's cooperation. Another major advantage of the RBS frame over the RDD frame is that RBS often comes with other valuable variables to help plan the sampling design that will be used for an election poll. These variables include information about the voter such as age, political party affiliation, and past voting frequency. A major disadvantage of the RBS frame compared to RDD is that the quality of RBS varies considerably across different jurisdictions, and coverage of the probable electorate can be so poor as to render the RBS frame invalid in some jurisdictions.

A major challenge faced by those who conduct polls to predict (forecast) an election outcome, and by those who study voters after an election, is to accurately identify who will vote or who has voted. Pre-election pollsters have created many approaches for use with RDD sampling to screen their samples for so-called likely voters who will make up the probable electorate. These approaches are imperfect and often do not work well, thereby contributing to inaccuracies in election outcome predictions. With RBS that uses an enhanced database that includes a registered voter's past voting frequency and party affiliation, a model can be devised not only to better predict the likelihood someone actually will vote but also to better predict for which candidate the person will vote, in the case of those who have declared a party affiliation. With such information appended to the RBS frame about each registered voter, an RBS researcher also can stratify the sample and make more cost-effective decisions about how many voters to interview who have declared a party affiliation versus those who have not (i.e., the independents).

When sampling from an RBS frame, the researcher will generally segment the frame into three strata: (1) those who voted in the past election(s), (2) those who were registered but did not vote in the past election(s), and (3) those who were not registered for the past election(s). Based on a number of auxiliary sources of information, the researcher then will estimate the proportion of registered voters in each of these groups who are expected to vote. Using all this information, the researcher will make decisions about how many voters to sample from each strata.

Because RBS frames have addresses, and often telephone numbers, for each registered voter, the mode of data collection can be mail, telephone, in-person, or any combination of these. Not enough methodological work has been done with RBS to conclude with confidence under what circumstances it should be used as opposed to RDD sampling, but as public records become more uniform in their quality, the field of election polling can expect to see an increasing use in RBS and a decreased use of RDD.

Paul J. Lavrakas

See also Coverage Error; Election Polls; Likely Voter; Probable Electorate; Random-Digit Dialing (RDD); Sampling Frame

Further Readings

Green, D. P., & Gerber, A. S. (2003, May). *Using registration-based sampling to improve pre-election polling*. Paper presented at the 58th annual conference of the American Association for Public Opinion Research, Nashville, TN. Retrieved April 10, 2008, from http://bbs.vcsnet.com/pdf/registrationbasedsampling_Smith-Richardson-Report_11_10_03.pdf

REGRESSION ANALYSIS

Regression analysis is the blanket name for a family of data analysis techniques that examine relationships between variables. The techniques allow survey researchers to answer questions about associations between different variables of interest. For example, how much do political party identification and Internet usage affect the likelihood of voting for a particular candidate? Or how much do education-related variables (e.g., grade point average, intrinsic motivation, classes taken, and school quality) and demographic variables (e.g., age, gender, race, and family income) affect standardized test performance? Regression allows surveyors to simultaneously look at the influence of several independent variables on a dependent variable. In other words, instead of having to calculate separate tables or tests to determine the effect of demographic and educational variables on test

scores, researchers can examine all of their effects in one comprehensive analysis.

Regression also allows researchers to statistically "control" for the effects of other variables and eliminate spurious relationships. In a more serious case, a case of noncausal covariation, two variables may be highly related but may not have a direct causal relationship. For example, in cities in the United States, murder rates are highly correlated with ice cream sales. This does not mean, however, that if the selling of ice cream is curtailed that the murder rate will go down. Both ice cream sales and murder rates are related to temperature. When it gets hot out, people buy more ice cream and commit more murders. In a regression equation, both ice cream sales and temperature can be included as predictors of murder rates, and the results would show that when temperature is controlled for, there is no relationship between ice cream sales and murder rates.

This ability to control for other variables makes arguments based on research results much stronger. For example, imagine that a test score regression showed that the more English classes a school required, the better their students did on standardized tests, controlling for median family income, school quality, and other important variables. Policy advocates can then propose increasing the required English courses without being as open to the criticism that the results were really due to other causes (such as socioeconomic status).

The regression approach can also simultaneously look at the influence of different important variables. For example, imagine that the head reference librarian and the head of acquisitions for a library disagree about whether it is customer service or having the most up-to-date bestsellers that influences patron satisfaction. A regression predicting patron satisfaction from both customer service ratings and percentage of recent bestsellers can answer the question of which one (or both or neither) of these factors influences customer service. Researchers can even look at interactions between the variables. In other words, they can determine if the effect of customer service on patron satisfaction is bigger or smaller at libraries with fewer bestsellers than those with more bestsellers.

At its base, the linear regression approach attempts to estimate the following equation:

$$y = b_1x_1 + b_2x_2 + \cdots b_nx_n + e,$$

where y is the dependent variable; $x_1, x_2 \ldots x_n$ are the independent variables; e is the error in prediction; and $b_1, b_2 \ldots b_n$ are the regression coefficients. The regression coefficients are estimated in the model by finding the regression lines that simultaneously best minimize the squared errors of prediction (i.e., the sums of squares). If a dependent variable, controlling for the effects of the other dependent variables, has a large enough relationship with the independent variable, then the regression coefficient will be significantly different from zero. Regression coefficients can be interpreted as partial slopes; in other words, the regression coefficient indicates that for each one-unit increase in the independent variable (and controlling for the effects of the other independent variables), the dependent variable increases or decreases by the amount of the regression coefficient.

Assumptions of Linear Regression

For a regression analysis to be valid, there are several assumptions that need to be satisfied. First, the errors must be independent and normally distributed. Nonindependent error terms often occur when there are relations between responses, such as responses from married couples or individuals from one household.

Somewhat obviously, it is important that the relationship between the independent variables and dependent variable are linear. Somewhat less obviously, it is important the errors of each independent variable have essentially the same variance (i.e., they do not exhibit heteroscedasticity).

Fortunately, regression is fairly robust to small violations of all of these assumptions. However, to be sure that a regression model is not affected by violating any of these assumptions, and therefore providing biased answers, researchers should ensure that they are using the correct technique and availing themselves of the regression diagnostic measures (primary among which include plotting both the data and the residuals) that any standard statistical software package provides.

Other Types of Regression

Many types of regression beyond linear regression have been developed to deal with special cases of analysis or for situations where using linear regression would result in a gross violation of its assumptions. While the description of all of the varieties of regression is beyond the scope of this entry, several common and useful methods are mentioned briefly.

Logistic regression is designed to handle categorical dependent variables (i.e., Yes–No questions or other cases without a continuum of answer options). Because categorical dependent variables do not have error distributions, logistic regression uses the logit function to transform the analysis into an examination of how independent variables affect the odds of the occurrence of a particular dependent variable response option choice. Because the results are expressed in odds and odds ratios, they can often be challenging to interpret.

Hierarchical linear models are a family of techniques designed to deal with data that have nonindependent errors. For example, if students from different classrooms from one school were sampled for a survey on preferred pedagogical techniques, responses from students from the same classroom would have similar answers because of their exposure to the same teacher. A hierarchical linear model would create a model where students (within classrooms) was the unit of analysis and another where classroom was the unit of analysis, looking at appropriate independent variables at each level.

Limits of Regression Analyses

Like any form of research, regression is not a panacea. In addition to the assumptions discussed previously, there are several limitations that researchers should be aware of, including (among others) the danger of the ecological fallacy, the issue of mis-specifying a model or not including all of the relevant predictors, or being led astray by an idiosyncratic sample. The foremost limitation is understanding that there is a difference between a relationship and a causal relationship. Even if there are statistically significant relationships between independent and dependent variables, that does not mean that there is necessarily a direct causal relationship between the variables. It is possible that there is a relationship but that the chain of causality is rather long or indirect. In the ice cream and murder example discussed earlier, high temperatures do not directly cause more murders. Higher temperatures likely cause more discomfort, which probably causes more frustration, which likely leads to lower thresholds for anger, which then probably leads to more violence, which leads to more murders. However, even in the absence of direct causality, regressions are a powerful tool that, with the selection of the proper control variables, can shed light on important relationships between variables and, with good statistical confidence, can examine the effects of one variable on another.

Geoffrey R. Urland and Kevin B. Raines

See also Alpha, Significance Level of Test; Analysis of Variance (ANOVA); Confidence Interval; Correlation; Dependent Variable; Ecological Fallacy; Independent Variable; Interaction Effect; Mean Square Error; Noncausal Covariation; Outliers; *p*-Value; Statistical Power; *t*-Test; Type I Error; Type II Error

Further Readings

Freedman, D. A. (1999). From association to causation: Some remarks on the history of statistics. *Statistical Science, 14*, 243–258.

Gelman, A., & Hill, J. (2007). *Data analysis using regression and multilevel/hierarchical models.* New York: Cambridge University Press.

Judd, C. M., & McClelland, G. H. (1989). *Data analysis: A model comparison approach.* San Diego, CA: Harcourt Brace.

REINTERVIEW

A reinterview occurs when an original respondent is recontacted by someone from a survey organization—usually not the original interviewer—and some or all of the original questions are asked again. Reinterviewing can serve more than one purpose in survey research, including (a) verifying that interviews were actually completed as the researchers intended with sampled respondents, (b) checking on the reliability of the data that respondents provided when they were originally interviewed, and (c) further studying the variance of survey responses.

As part of quality assurance efforts to monitor the quality of survey data collection when the questionnaire is interviewer-administered, some part of the recontacts made to selected respondents may include asking some of the original questions again, especially the questions that the researchers deem as key ones. Although there are many reasons why a respondent may not provide the exact same answer during the reinterview, including some legitimate reasons, the purpose of re-asking some of the questions is not to match answers exactly but rather to make sure there is no consistent pattern of deviation from the original data that could signal that the questionnaire was not administered properly by the interviewer, including the possibility that the interviewer falsified some or all of the data.

A reinterview also provides data that can be used by researchers to test the reliability of the original data. For example, demographic characteristics are unlikely to change if the reinterview is conducted within a few weeks or even a few months of the original data collection, although some might, such as someone turning one year older in age, or someone becoming a college graduate because of a recent graduation, or now becoming employed in a new occupation in the interim since first being interviewed. Other types of questions, such those concerning behaviors, experiences, perceptions, knowledge, attitudes, and opinions, also are unlikely to change much within a few weeks or even a few months, but they can be expected to be more likely to change than will demographics. Small changes in these types of variables do not necessarily mean the original data are unreliable, but large changes often signal problems with the quality of (1) the original interviewing, (2) the questionnaire wording, (3) the data collection performed during the reinterview, or all three of these factors. Data gathered from re-asking the same questions in the reinterview also provide researchers with additional ways to understand the variance that is associated with their questionnaire items.

Granted, reinterviewing is costly, but when survey budgets allow for it, there are many benefits that can be gained.

Paul J. Lavrakas

See also Falsification; Quality Control; Recontact; Reliability; Variance Estimation; Verification

Further Readings

Groves, R. M., Fowler, F. J., Couper, M. P., Lepkowski, J. M., Singer, E., & Tourangeau, R. (2004). *Survey methodology.* Hoboken, NJ: Wiley.

O'Muircheartaigh, C. (1991). Simple response variance: Estimation and Determinants. In P. Biemer, R. M. Groves, L. Lyberg, N. Mathiowetz, & S. Sudman (Eds.), *Measurement errors in surveys* (pp. 551–574). New York: Wiley.

RELATIVE FREQUENCY

Relative frequency refers to the percentage or proportion of times that a given value occurs within a set of numbers, such as in the data recorded for a variable in a survey data set. In the following example of a distribution of 10 values—1, 2, 2, 3, 5, 5, 7, 8, 8, 8—while the absolute frequency of the value, 8, is 3, the relative frequency is 30% as the value, 8, makes up 3 of the 10 values. In this example, if the source of the data has a wider range of possible scores than the observed values (such as a 0–10 survey scale), then it is permissible to report that some of possible values (e.g., 0, 4, 6, 9, and 10) were not observed in this set of data and that their respective relative frequencies were zero (i.e., 0%).

In survey research, the relative frequency is a much more meaningful number than is the absolute frequency. For example, in a news article using results from a poll of 800 citizens, it is more meaningful to know that approximately two thirds of them (67.5%) are dissatisfied with the job the president is doing than to know that 540 citizens who were polled think this way.

Relative frequency can be displayed in a frequency table—which displays each value in a distribution ordered from lowest to highest—along with the absolute and cumulative frequencies associated with each value. Relative frequency also can be displayed graphically in a bar graph (histogram) or pie chart.

Paul J. Lavrakas

See also Frequency Distribution; Percentage Frequency Distribution

RELIABILITY

The word *reliability* has at least four different meanings. The first of these is in an engineering context, where reliability refers to the likelihood that a piece of equipment will not break down within some specified period of time. The second meaning is synonymous with *dependability*, as in "She is a very reliable employee" (i.e., she is a good worker). The third has to do with the sampling variability of a statistic. A percentage, for example, is said to be reliable if it

does not vary by any nonnegligible amount from one sample to another of the same size and that are drawn in the same manner from the same population.

The fourth meaning is the one focused upon in this entry. A measuring instrument is said to be reliable if it yields consistent results, whether or not those results are valid (i.e., whether or not the results are relevant to the purpose for which the instrument is intended).

The social science literature is replete with discussions of different kinds of measurement reliability. There is test–retest consistency (agreement from time to time using the same instrument); parallel forms consistency (agreement between one instrument and another interchangeable instrument); internal consistency (agreement among the items within an instrument); interobserver consistency (or *intercoder reliability*; agreement between one rater and another); and intra-observer consistency (agreement within the same rater from one occasion to another).

The key concepts in the classical theory of reliability are "observed score" (the measurement actually obtained), "true score" (the measurement that, in some sense, should have been obtained), and "error score" (the difference between true score and observed score); the latter two are generally unknown. The reliability coefficient for an instrument in a given study is defined as the ratio of the variance of the true scores to the variance of the observed scores, and it is estimated by (a) the agreement between observed scores at Time 1 and observed scores at Time 2; (b) the agreement between observed scores on Form A and observed scores on Form B; (c) the agreement among the observed scores on the items that constitute the instrument; (d) the agreement between the ratings given by Judge A and the ratings given by Judge B; or (e) the agreement between the ratings given by Judge A on Occasion 1 and the ratings given by Judge A on Occasion 2.

Two Hypothetical Examples in Survey Research

1. In a pilot study preparatory to the main study in which a self-report questionnaire of cigarette smoking behavior (concerning the number of cigarettes smoked per day) is to be employed, a survey researcher might administer a trial version of the questionnaire to a sample of respondents at two different times, with perhaps a few days in between, and determine the extent to

which the responses given by the participants at Time 1 agree with (i.e., are reliable compared to) the responses given by those *same* participants at Time 2.

2. In an effort to study the reliability of people's self-reports of their ages, a survey researcher might send an initial mailing of a postcard to a sample of persons whose names and addresses have been randomly sampled from a telephone directory, asking them to record their birth date on the stamped return-addressed portion of the postcard and mail it back. At some subsequent point in time (perhaps a month or so later), the researcher might field a telephone survey of the same people including a question asking them to report their date of birth. The second set of birth dates could be compared with the first set, on a respondent-by-respondent basis, to see how well the two agree.

Relative Versus Absolute Agreement

Reliability is usually assessed by correlating the scores at Time 1 with the scores at Time 2, correlating the scores on Form A with the scores on Form B, and so forth. But correlation is concerned only with the relative relationship between two variables. Scores of 1, 2, 3, 4, and 5 correlate perfectly with scores of 1, 3, 5, 7, and 9, respectively, but there is perfect agreement only for the first pair (1,1). If a measure of absolute agreement is desired, the researcher should use something like the median absolute difference between paired scores.

Reliability of an Instrument Versus Reliability of Scores Obtained With an Instrument

It is somewhat controversial whether one should refer to the reliability of an instrument or the reliability of scores obtained with the instrument. (Scores need not be test scores as such; they could be heights, weights, temperature readings, etc.) If it is clear from the context what the reliability information is for a given instrument in a given study, no great harm is done by referring to the reliability of the instrument itself.

Other Approaches to Reliability in the Social Sciences

The preceding discussion has been concerned with so-called classical reliability. In recent years there has appeared a variety of other approaches to the reliability of measuring instruments. One of these is based upon generalizability theory; another is based upon item-response theory; a third is based upon structural equation modeling.

Thomas R. Knapp

See also Intercoder Reliability; Item Response Theory; Test–Retest Reliability; Validity

Further Readings

Bock, R. D. (1997). A brief history of item response theory. *Educational Measurement: Issues and Practice, 15*(4), 21–33.

Borsboom, D. (2005). *Measuring the mind: Conceptual issues in contemporary psychometrics.* Cambridge, UK: Cambridge University Press.

Brennan, R. L. (1997). A perspective on the history of generalizability theory. *Educational Measurement: Issues and Practice, 16*(4), 14–20.

Carmines, E. G., & Zeller, R. A. (1979). *Reliability and validity assessment.* Beverly Hills, CA: Sage.

Litwin, M. S. (1995). *The Survey Kit: Vol. 7. How to measure survey reliability and validity.* Thousand Oaks, CA: Sage.

Traub, R. E. (1997). Classical test theory in historical perspective. *Educational Measurement: Issues and Practice, 16*(4), 8–14.

REPEATED CROSS-SECTIONAL DESIGN

Many important cross-sectional surveys are repeated at regular or irregular intervals so that estimates of changes can be made at the aggregate or population level. Examples include monthly labor force surveys, retail trade surveys, television and radio ratings surveys, and political opinion polls. These surveys are designed to give good estimates for the current population and the changes or movements that have occurred since the last survey or previous surveys. Typically surveys are conducted on a monthly, quarterly, or annual basis, although other intervals are possible, such as daily or weekly in the case of TV ratings and opinion polls. Surveys may also be conducted at longer intervals, such as 3 years, or repeated on an irregular basis, but in all cases there will be interest in estimating and analyzing changes at the population level and also various subgroups of the population, which are often defined geographically or in terms of sociodemographic variables.

Repeated cross-sectional surveys differ from longitudinal surveys, which are designed specifically to permit analysis of change at the individual or micro level and usually involve following an initial sample over several waves even if respondents move location. The need to follow respondents contributes to the cost and complexity of a longitudinal survey. In a longitudinal survey, there may be no interest in ensuring good cross-sectional estimates for each wave of the survey, and it may be difficult to do so. Longitudinal surveys are subject to attrition bias and conditioning effects but are valuable when the main aim of the survey is to understand changes at the individual level. In a repeated cross-sectional design, there is a strong emphasis placed on maintaining good sample representation to produce unbiased estimates for each time period. This can be done without following respondents over time.

In a repeated survey, an independent sample may be selected on each occasion, and so there will be essentially no overlap in the samples between time periods. There is then no possibility of conditioning effects or respondent fatigue, although there are the costs involved in making the initial contact with respondents and obtaining their cooperation. Valid estimates of changes at the population level can be calculated from independent samples. If y_t is the estimate for the population for time t and y_{t-s} the estimate for the population for time $t-s$, then the change or movement between the two time periods can be estimated by $y_t - y_{t-s}$. With independent samples, there will be differences between estimates for different periods because they are based on different samples. The sampling variance of the estimate of change will be the sum of the sampling variance on each of the estimates, so $Var(y_t - y_{t-s}) = Var(y_t) + Var(y_{t-s})$. If the sampling variances of each of the estimates are approximately equal, then the sampling variance of the estimate of change will be twice that of the cross-sectional estimates, and hence the standard error will be about 40% higher. Reliable estimates of changes can be obtained provided the sample sizes at each period are large enough and an efficient sample design is used, which produces unbiased estimates for each period. There is no need for the same sample size or design to be used at each occasion although it is usually efficient to do so.

An alternative design is to use the same sample on each occasion with some small changes to allow for new units in the population and remove units that are known to have left the population, where this knowledge is based on information that is sample independent. This design reduces costs, as it often is cheaper to survey people at the second and subsequent occasions, and also reduces the sampling variance of estimates of change because the effect of new units in the sample is minimized. The sampling variance is still present because respondents' characteristics may change, and the correlation between the values for the same respondent will be an important factor in determining the sampling variance.

Such a design will lead to respondents being included in the survey for a long time, which may lead to respondent fatigue and a reduction in both response rate and quality of the information reported. For these reasons, designs that involve some replacement or rotation of selected units are often used. Such designs are called *rotating panel designs* and can be set up in various ways so that there is a specified overlap in the sample between different periods and respondents are released from the survey after a specified time. Having overlap in the sample between consecutive surveys usually reduces the variance of the estimates of changes between consecutive periods, or any periods for which there is sample overlap. This is because $Var(y_t - y_{t-s}) = Var(y_t) + Var(y_{t-s}) - 2 \sqrt{Var(y_t)Var(y_{t-s})} Corr(y_t, y_{t-s})$.

The correlation between the survey estimates, $Corr(y_t, y_{t-s})$, will be determined by the sample overlap, the sample design, and the correlation between individual-level values over the two time periods. It will have an appreciable beneficial effect if the sample overlap is high and the individual level correlation is also high and positive. If the individual-level correlation is low, then there is little benefit in having high sample overlap. Various rotation designs are possible and are chosen to balance cost, respondent burden, and impact on the important estimates of change.

In a rotating panel design, there is the opportunity to exploit the differences in the correlations between estimates that can be calculated from the overlapping and nonoverlapping samples to produce better estimates of level and change through composite estimation.

For a repeated survey, interest often will focus on the estimates of change between the most recent two periods, for example, between two consecutive months, $y_t - y_{t-1}$. However, to assess the general pattern of change, it is useful to estimate the changes over several periods to informally assess the trends in the time series of estimates. For a monthly survey, analysis may consider $y_t - y_{t-s}$ for $s = 1, 2, 3, 6, 12$. Formal methods of trend analysis can also be applied using filters or time series modeling. For monthly and quarterly surveys, seasonal adjustment also has to be considered.

In some applications the results from a repeated survey may be averaged. This may be done because the volatility of the estimates is too high, for example, for geographic areas. It may also be a deliberate part of the output strategy, for example, producing 3-month averages from a monthly survey. In this case, the positive correlation between estimates that is produced by having some sample overlap increases the sampling variances. For example, the average of 3 consecutive months would have variance

$$Var\left(\frac{y_{t+1} + y_t + y_{t-1}}{3}\right)$$
$$= \frac{1}{9}\left[\begin{array}{c} Var(y_{t+1}) + Var(y_t) + Var(y_{t-1}) \\ + 2Cov(y_{t+1}, y_t) + 2Cov(y_t, y_{t-1}) \\ + 2Cov(y_{t+2}, y_{t-1}) \end{array}\right].$$

In a repeated cross-sectional design with independent samples, at each occasion within the 3-month period the covariances are all zero. If there is sample overlap, the covariance usually become positive and therefore increases the sampling variance. Simple moving averages are crude filters, and this feature affects trend estimates calculated by using filters. It would be better to use independent samples if averages over time are the main estimates of interest.

David Steel

See also Attrition; Composite Estimation; Cross-Sectional Survey Design; Longitudinal Studies; Panel Conditioning; Panel Surveys; Respondent Burden; Rolling Averages; Rotating Panel Design; Sampling Variance; Trend Analysis; Wave

Further Readings

Duncan, G. J., & Kalton, G. (1987). Issues of design and analysis of surveys across time. *International Statistical Review, 55,* 97–117.

Kalton, G., & Citro, C. F. (1993). Panel surveys: Adding the fourth dimension. *Survey Methodology, 19,* 205–215.

Kasprzyk, D., Duncan, G., Kalton, G., & Singh, M. P. (Eds.). (1989). *Panel surveys.* New York: Wiley.

McLaren, C. H., & Steel, D. G. (2000). The impact of different rotation patterns on the sampling variance of seasonally adjusted and trend estimates. *Survey Methodology, 26,* 163–172.

Steel, D. G. (2004). Sampling in time. In *Encyclopedia of social measurement* (pp. 823–828). San Diego, CA: Academic Press.

Steel, D. G., & McLaren, C. H. (2008). Design and inference over time. In C. R. Rao & D. Pfeffermann (Ed.), *Handbook of statistics: Vol. 29. Sampling theory methods and inference* (chap. 32). Amsterdam: North Holland.

REPLACEMENT

Replacement is a term used in two different contexts in surveys. With-replacement sampling refers to methods of sampling in which the unit selected in a particular draw is returned to the finite population and can be selected in other draws. The other context refers to the substitution (replacement) of a sampled unit with another unit as a result of difficulties in contacting or obtaining cooperation. The entry discusses both with-replacement sampling and replacement substitution.

With-Replacement Sampling

One approach to selecting an equal probability sample of n units from a finite population of N units is to draw one unit randomly from the N and then independently draw subsequent units until all n are selected. If the selected unit can be sampled more than once, then the method is *sampling with replacement*. This particular form of sampling is called *multinomial sampling*. There are many other ways of drawing a sample with replacement. For example, suppose the multinomial sampling procedure is used, but each unit is assigned its own probability of selection. If all the assigned probabilities of selection are not the same, then this is a simple way to draw a with-replacement, unequal probability sample.

When sampling with replacement, theoretically the same unit should be interviewed independently the number of times it is selected. Because this is operationally infeasible in most cases, the unit is interviewed once and the sampling weights are adjusted to account for the number of times it was sampled.

In practice, with-replacement sampling is not used frequently. However, a with-replacement sample does have some very important advantages, especially in the estimation of the precision of estimates in multistage samples. When a small fraction of the population units is sampled, it is often convenient to assume with-replacement sampling has been used when estimating variances. The variances of with-replacement and without-replacement samples are nearly equal when this condition exists, so the computationally simpler with-replacement variance estimator can be used.

Substitution

When data cannot be collected for a sampled unit, some surveys replace or substitute other units for the sampled ones to achieve the desired sample size (e.g., in Nielsen's television meter panels). Often, the substitutes are done during the field data collection; this is called *field substitution*, and the substituted unit may be called a reserve unit.

There are many different ways of selecting substitutes. Almost all substitution methods try to select the substitute from a set of units that match the characteristics of the nonresponding unit in some way. Some methods use probability mechanisms; for example, the units in the population that match the nonresponding unit are sampled with equal probability. Other methods are not based on probability mechanisms; for example, the interviewer is allowed to choose another household in the same block of the nonresponding household.

Replacement substitution tries to deal with unit nonresponse by replacing the nonresponding unit with another unit. In this sense, it is the equivalent of an imputation method. Just like imputation, substitution makes it difficult to accurately assess the statistical properties of estimates, such as their bias and variance. Substitute responses are typically treated as if they were the responses of the originally sampled units, which is usually not completely appropriate.

J. Michael Brick

See also Imputation; Nonresponse; Sampling Without Replacement

Further Readings

Kalton, G. (1983). *Introduction to survey sampling*. Newbury Park, CA: Sage.

Lohr, S. (1999). *Sampling: Design and analysis*. Pacific Grove, CA: Brooks/Cole.

Vehovar, V. (1999). Field substitution and unit nonresponse. *Journal of Official Statistics, 15*, 335–350.

REPLICATE METHODS FOR VARIANCE ESTIMATION

Replicate methods for variance estimation are commonly used in large sample surveys with many variables. The procedure uses estimators computed on subsets of the sample, where subsets are selected in a way that reflects the sampling variability. Replication variance estimation is an appealing alternative to Taylor linearization variance estimation for nonlinear functions. Replicate methods have the advantage of transferring the complexity of variance estimation from data set end users to the statistician working on creating the output data set. By providing weights for each subset of the sample, called *replication weights*, end users can estimate the variance of a large variety of nonlinear estimators using standard weighted sums. Jackknife, balanced half-samples, and bootstrap methods are three main replication variance methods used in sample surveys. The basic procedure for constructing the replication variance estimator is the same for the three different methods. This entry describes the form of replication variance estimators, compares the three main approaches used in surveys, and ends with an illustration of the jackknife method.

Description

Replication variance methods involve selecting subsets from the original sample. Subsets can be created by removing units from the sample, as in the jackknife and balanced half-samples methods, or by resampling from the sample, as in the bootstrap method. A replicate of the estimator of interest is created for each subset. The replicate is typically constructed in the same way as the estimator of interest is constructed for the entire sample. Replication variance estimators are made by comparing the squared deviations of the replicates to the overall estimate. Thus, the replication variance estimator has the form $\sum_{k=1}^{L} c_k(\hat{\theta}^{(k)} - \hat{\theta})^2$, where k identifies the replicate, L is the number of replicates, $\hat{\theta}$ is the estimator of interest computed from the full survey, $\hat{\theta}^{(k)}$ is the kth replicate of the estimator constructed using the kth subset of the sample, and the c_k is the weight determined by the replication method and the survey design for the

k^{th} subset of the sample. The c_k's are often chosen so that the replication variance estimator is unbiased or nearly unbiased for the design variance of $\hat{\theta}$. The $\hat{\theta}$ in the replication variance estimator is often changed to the average of the replicates. Depending on the replication method, the number of replicates, L, may be large, but techniques for reducing L do exist.

Replication Method Comparison

For the jackknife method, subsets of the sample are constructed by removing elements systematically from the sample. The "delete-1" jackknife involves constructing n subsets where the ith subset is the sample with element i removed. The jackknife approach works well, much like a Taylor linearization variance estimator, for sufficiently smooth functions. To relax the smoothness requirement, a "delete-d" jackknife can be used, where subsets with d elements deleted form replicates. The delete-d and even delete-1 approaches can generate a large number of replicates when the sample size is large. A "delete-a-group" jackknife, where subsets are created by dividing the sample into G groups and deleting one group at a time, reduces the number of replicates from n to G at the cost of degrees of freedom in the variance estimator.

The *half-samples method* was originally developed for the special case where the sample design is such that two elements within each stratum are sampled. Subsets of the sample are formed by removing one element from each stratum, so that the each subset is half of the original sample. If there are H strata, 2^H replicates could be created. Typically, the number of half-samples selected is reduced through a technique that maintains the variance of the stratified mean for the replication variance. The reduced set of samples has a property referred to as being balanced. The balanced half-samples approach, also called balanced repeated replication, can be used to estimate the variance for the Horvitz-Thompson quantile estimator unlike the delete-1 jackknife. The balanced half-samples method has been extended to stratified sampling, where more than two elements are selected per stratum.

The bootstrap method is widely used outside of survey statistics but has been adapted for unequal probability designs. For many bootstrap subset selection procedures, replicate samples are selected by sampling with replacement from the original sample. A large number of with-replacement samples are required, as there is additional variability due to the randomness of

subset selection not present in the jackknife or balanced half-samples methods. The advantage of the bootstrap is that an estimate of the distribution of the estimator of interest is created by using the sampling distribution of the $\hat{\theta}^{(k)}$. Confidence intervals of size $1 - \alpha$ can be constructed by taking the range of $\hat{\theta}^{(k)}$ after removing the largest and smallest $\alpha/2$ fraction of values. The bootstrap can be used for a wider variety of estimators than the delete-1 jackknife, such as standard quantile estimators. However, the bootstrap procedure generally requires more replicates than the alternative replication methods, and creating the bootstrap estimator for unequal probability samples is often more difficult than forming the jackknife.

For many survey estimators, the jackknife performs comparably to the Taylor linearization variance in terms of mean squared error. In simulation studies by Jun Shao and Donsheng Tu, as well as other authors, the jackknife tended to outperform balanced half-sampling when the jackknife was applicable. Simulation studies show for many estimators that the bootstrap is worse than either the jackknife or balanced half-samples. However, the bootstrap confidence intervals may outperform the jackknife confidence intervals in terms of coverage rates because the bootstrap intervals are not constrained to be symmetric.

Replicate Weight Example

Table 1 shows how replicate weights can be made in the case of two strata and a simple random sample within each stratum. The replicate weights are created by reallocating the original weight of the deleted element equally to the remaining elements in the same stratum. Suppose one quantity of interest is the ratio of the total of y, T_y, to the total of x, T_x. We will use the ratio of the Horvitz-Thompson estimators, $\hat{T}_y$ and $\hat{T}_x$, as the ratio estimator $\hat{R}$.

Associated with the replicate weights in the example is the vector of c_k. Each c_k depends on the stratum for which the kth element belongs (see Table 2). Note that the average of the $\hat{T}_y^{(k)}$ (i.e., 4200/5) is equal to $\hat{T}_y$. The replication variance estimate of the Horvitz-Thompson estimator of T_y is 45150, which is the same as the Horvitz-Thompson stratified variance. The replicate variance for $\hat{R}$ is 0.0106. For comparison, the Taylor linearization variance for $\hat{R}$ is 0.0102.

The example illustrates how both the sample design and choice of using a delete-1 jackknife method impact the weights in the replication variance

Table 1   Example replication weights for a stratified sample

Stratum	Element	Original Weight	y	x	Replicate				
					1	2	3	4	5
1	1	21	9	10	0	42	21	21	21
	2	21	16	14	42	0	21	21	21
2	1	15	2	1	15	15	0	22.5	22.5
	2	15	14	13	15	15	22.5	0	22.5
	3	15	5	8	15	15	22.5	22.5	0

Table 2   Example jackknife weights and variance calculations

Replicate	c_k	$\hat{T}_y^{(k)}$	$\hat{T}_x^{(k)}$	$\bar{R}^{(k)}$	$c_k(\hat{T}_y^{(k)} - \hat{T}_y)^2$	$c_k(\hat{R}^{(k)} - \hat{R})^2$
1	20/42	987	918	1.08	10,290	0.0022
2	20/42	693	750	0.92	10,290	0.0033
3	28/45	952.5	976.5	0.98	7,875	0.0006
4	28/45	682.5	706.5	0.97	15,435	0.0011
5	28/45	885	819	1.08	1,260	0.0034
Sum		4,200	4,170		45,150	0.0106

estimator. In the case of multi-stage designs, care must be taken in selecting the subsets of the sample because of the correlation among elements in the same cluster. A common solution is to form replicate samples by selecting or deleting whole clusters; then estimated cluster totals are used in the variance estimator. Alternative replication procedures are available when the second-stage variance is important.

Jason C. Legg

See also Balanced Repeated Replication (BRR); Design-Based Estimation; Jackknife Variance Estimation; Taylor Series Linearization; Variance Estimation

Further Readings

Efron, B., & Tibshirani, R. J. (1998). *An introduction to the bootstrap*. Boca Raton, FL: CRC Press.

McCarthy, P. J. (1969) Pseudo-replication: Half samples. *Review of the International Statistical Institute, 37,* 239–264.

Shao, J., & Tu, D. (1995). *The jackknife and bootstrap*. New York: Springer.

Wolter, K. M. (1985). *Introduction to variance estimation*. New York: Springer.

REPLICATION

Replication is reanalysis of a study, building on a new data set that was constructed and statistically analyzed in the same way as the original work. Repeating the statistical analysis on the original data set is known as *verification* (or replication of the statistical analysis). Replicability should be maximized in both quantitative and qualitative works, as replication studies and verification of existing data sets may be extremely useful in evaluating the robustness of the original findings and in revealing new and interesting results.

Even if a given work will never actually be replicated, it still needs to be replicable, or else there is no possibility of refuting its findings; that is, it fails to hold the falsifiability criterion for scientific work. Because replicability is an underlying principle in science, most disciplines in social sciences hold some replication standards for publications, determining what information needs to be disclosed such that researchers may replicate the study without further guidance from the authors. In the case of survey research, the design and analysis of surveys call for many distinct decisions regarding the sampling, measurement, and methods used. As such, replication and verification of a survey is oftentimes extremely difficult to conduct, even by the original researchers. Thus, researchers should be sure to closely document their work process when gathering and analyzing their data.

To be able to replicate a given survey, researchers need to hold exact information on the sampling and the instruments used. First, decisions regarding the sample design and management need to be recorded, such as what list was used to sample from and how the sampling was conducted; who the interviewers (if any) were and how they were instructed and trained; what strata, quotas, or weights were used, if any; how many times people were recontacted; and how missing data was dealt with. Second, the exact instruments used should be recorded, including the question wording and order, split-half experimentation and any other randomizations (e.g., question order), counterbalancing or changes between questions, and whether the respondents were interviewed in their first language and what translations of the questionnaires were used, and so forth.

Another component of the work that needs to be replicable is the statistical analysis of the survey. In that vein, the researcher should document the construction of the variables, such as the coding of any open-ended questions (e.g., the list of categories, how many coders were employed, how they were instructed and trained, and what the intercoder reliability was), the construction of all variables used (e.g., the exact scales, techniques to deal with missing data, any rounding, mathematical transformations), as well as the exact software (statistical package and version) and statistical methods.

Even if replicable, studies in the social sciences usually cannot be entirely replicated when the measured phenomenon has changed between the original study and its replication attempt. This means that even if a researcher is able to retrieve the information from the real world and process and analyze it in the exact same way as did the original study, the results still may be different because the population under study had changed. Nevertheless, researchers should aim to maximize the replicability of their survey and analysis, and try to make certain that a full verification will be possible.

Pazit Ben-Nun

See also Coding; Missing Data; Sample Design; Sample Management

Further Readings

Herrnson, P. S. (1995). Replication, verification, secondary analysis, and data collection in political science. *PS: Political Science & Politics, 28*(3), 452–455.

King, G. (1995). Replication, replication. *PS: Political Science & Politics, 28*(3), 444–452.

King, G., Keohane, R. O., & Verba, S. (1994). *Designing social inquiry: Scientific inference in qualitative research.* Princeton, NJ: Princeton University Press.

REPRESENTATIVE SAMPLE

A representative sample is one that has strong external validity in relationship to the target population the sample is meant to represent. As such, the findings from the survey can be generalized with confidence to the population of interest. There are many factors that affect the representativeness of a sample, but traditionally attention has been paid mostly to issues related to sample design and coverage. More recently, concerns have extended to issues related to nonresponse.

Determining Representativeness

When using a sample survey to make inferences about the population from which the sampled elements were drawn, researchers must judge whether the sample is actually representative of the target population. The best way of ensuring a representative sample is to (a) have a complete list (i.e., sampling frame) of all elements in the population and know that each and every element (e.g., people or households) on the list has a nonzero chance (but not necessarily an equal chance) of being included in the sample; (b) use random selection to draw elements from the sampling frame into the sample; and (c) gather complete data from each and every sampled element. In most sample surveys, only the goal of random selection of elements is met. Complete and up-to-date lists of the populations of interest are rare. In addition, there are sometimes elements in the target population with a zero probability of selection. For example, in random-digit dialing telephone surveys, households without a telephone may belong to the population of interest, but if they do, then they have a zero chance of inclusion in the survey. Similarly, unless a cell phone frame is used in RDD sampling in addition to a landline frame, those with only cell phone service will have zero chance of inclusion. Thus, the random-digit dialing landline frame cannot fully represent the entire population of households. Researchers need to estimate sample coverage, which is an estimate of the proportion of elements in the population that are covered or included on the list or sample frame. To further complicate matters, almost all surveys have a significant number of sampled elements from which incomplete or no data are gathered because of unit nonresponse and item nonresponse.

Correcting for Biases

Given that two conditions of the criteria for a representative sample are rarely met in survey research, how is the likely representativeness of a sample determined? This is a crucial issue for sample surveys and one that is the subject of intense discussion and research. Representativeness is enhanced through one or more of the following. The first way is to rely on research conducted by other survey researchers on likely biases between the group of sampled elements (typically people) in a sample and the true characteristics of the population (i.e., population parameters, such as smoking prevalence or candidate preference). Much research has been conducted regarding the potential bias of working with an incomplete sampling frame of the population to draw the sample for the survey and into nonresponse of sampled elements (both item and unit survey nonresponse). Research regarding incomplete population coverage and nonresponse is often difficult to do because it is rare to have complete data on every element in a target population, as even censuses (such as the U.S. decennial census) have nonresponse and sample coverage problems. However, these data are the best available and are widely used as the "best guess" of the target population's characteristics. Most of the research on these two problems has found that nonresponse and sample frame noncoverage does bias the results of many sample surveys (thus lowering their external validity), as the responding sample often differs from characteristics of the entire population in nonnegligible ways. For example, for general population surveys in the United States and in many European countries, the responding sample is often better educated, more female, more likely to be home owners than renters,

more white, and less ethnic than the general population of interest.

To correct for these biases, survey researchers invoke a second way to deal with these problems, that is, post-stratification. Post-stratification is the process of weighting some of the respondents or households in the responding sample relative to others so that the characteristics of the responding sample are essentially equal to those of the target population for those characteristics that can be controlled to census data (e.g., age, race, ethnicity, sex, education, and geography). By invoking post-stratification adjustments, the bias due to sample noncoverage and differential nonresponse theoretically is reduced.

The final correction in which researchers should engage is to limit the inferential population of a survey to those elements on the sampling frame with nonzero probability of inclusion. For example, a careful and conservative researcher who conducts a traditional landline random-digit dialing survey of adults in Georgia, would limit inferences to "adults living in households with landline telephones, who respond to surveys, in the state of Georgia." In practice this is rarely done because research sponsors typically want the survey to be representative of all adults in a given geopolitical area (e.g., Georgia), and too often empirical reports are written assuming (and implying) this is the case.

Future Research

Striving for representative samples is key when conducting sample survey research. However, it is important that consumers of survey-based information recognize that the standards for true representativeness are rarely met, but the biases produced by failures often are not severe enough to threaten the ultimate value of the survey findings. Because of these challenges, it is critical that research continue into the problems of sample design flaws of popular techniques (e.g., Internet surveys) and into the impact of unit and item nonresponse on findings from the survey.

Michael Edward Davern

See also Coverage Error; External Validity; Inference; Nonprobability Sample; Nonresponse Error; Population of Inference; Post-Stratification; Probability Sample; Sampling Error; Sampling Frame; Target Population

Further Readings

Henry, G. T. (1990). *Practical sampling*. Newbury Park, CA: Sage.

Kish, L. (1965). *Survey sampling*. New York: Wiley.

Research Call Center

A research call center is the operational unit for survey data collection from which outbound telephone calls on a computer-assisted telephone interviewing survey are made. It can exist in many forms, including (a) a large single-site operation with many hundreds of booths; (b) several linked smaller sites; (c) a spare office with a few desks and phones; or (d) a virtual site, where the interviewers log into a Web application and do all the dialing from their homes.

Gathering data via the use of computer-assisted telephone interviewing is not the only research activity that might take place at the research call center, but this is the primary activity of such a set-up. Other research-related activities may include the following:

- Taking inbound calls, either as a support for an outbound survey (such as when a toll-free number is associated with a survey) or as part of data collection
- Editing and coding collected data
- Capturing (scanning or entering) data from hard-copy questionnaires
- Mailing out and receiving mail questionnaires
- Compiling the survey frame, including locating prior participants in a longitudinal study or recipients of a particular service being evaluated (i.e., by finding current addresses, telephone numbers, or both)
- Providing support services for other modes of data collection (e.g., providing a help desk function for respondents of a Web survey or collecting administrative data from field interviewers)

Research Versus Nonresearch Call Centers

Nonresearch call centers fall into two main groups: (1) predominantly outbound (such as a telemarketing or debt collection center) and (2) inbound (such as a customer assistance contact center for a bank or a catalogue sales support operation).

The common denominator among all call centers, including research call centers, is that there is a group of staff (interviewers or agents) sitting in booths either making or receiving calls. At this front stage of contact, there are rarely any formal educational requirements beyond high school reading ability; however, a clear voice is a necessity. Because calling volumes typically peak for only a small part of the day and often vary over the course of a year, most positions are part-time and often seasonal. As a result, many call centers in the same geographical locale tend to share the same labor pool, and the physical buildings in which they operate and the furniture needed tend to be very similar.

Technologically, there are a lot of similarities as well. All need a telephone system that can support many simultaneous calls and a computer system that will track and store the outcomes of the calls (such as completed questionnaires, completed applications for credit, or queries made and resolutions offered). However, an outbound center will require more sophisticated dialer equipment to place calls, whereas an inbound center will require a more sophisticated automatic call distributor and interactive voice response system to handle the queuing and directing of incoming calls to the most appropriate agent (not always an interviewer).

It is in the processes and procedures that the differences become more pronounced. For example, in comparing an outbound research survey operation and an outbound telemarketing operation, one of the main objectives of a research center is a high response rate, whereas for a telemarketing operation the overriding objective is to obtain a high volume of sales. Essentially, this is the difference between survey *quality* and telemarketing *quantity*, and this difference will play out in many ways. A research operation will make multiple calls to the same number following complex calling rules and will spend much more time on that one sample item. Shortcuts cannot be risked, the interviewers almost always will be paid by the hour rather than by the complete interview, in part on the assumption that this will help ensure they conduct the entire research task exactly as required (including gaining cooperation from as many respondents as possible and reading questions exactly as worded to minimize interviewer bias), and the dialer technology will be set to a slower rate to allow the interviewer time to read the call history notes from the previous call and to ensure that if the number answers, the interviewer is ready to take the call. The telemarketing operation will instead discard numbers very quickly and move onto fresh numbers, they will give their agents considerable latitude in the scripts and often pay commission rather than an hourly rate, and they will use high-volume predictive dialers to maximize the time their agents spend talking and selling as opposed to listening for answering machines or correctly classifying businesses.

Facilities

Research call centers are typically located in areas with a good supply of entry-level labor. Some are located near universities to take advantage of students looking for part-time work, while others are located in high immigrant areas if bilingual skills are needed. The long operating hours of call centers (usually 8:00 a.m. to 9:00 p.m. and often later if calls are being made across multiple Western time zones), combined with the usually low-income nature of the interviewing staff, often dictate the need for proximity to reliable and safe public transport.

Although a research call center can be constructed in any existing office, it usually consists of a large main floor where all the booths reside and has at least one training room and at least one break room, a secure insulated room to house the core technology, several offices to house administrative roles, and the usual amenities for any office building (bathrooms, storage, kitchenette, etc.).

The main floor is fitted out with both interviewer and supervisor booths. Because call centers usually operate for more than 80 hours a week, and the majority of staff will be working part-time, most booths are used by three or four interviewers each over the course of a working day or week. This limits the extent to which interviewers can personalize their booths.

The booths themselves usually are between 3 and 4 feet wide, with the trend being toward smaller ones matching the trend in the use of smaller hardware (flatscreen monitors, soft phones) and to maximize the use of the space available. Linear layouts (where there are straight rows of booths) offer the most efficient use of space and the best sight lines between interviewers and supervisors, but they might not be as attractive to work in as other configurations.

The more booths placed in an area, the more attention that needs to be paid to acoustics so that respondents cannot overhear other interviews taking place. Having good sound-absorbing surfaces (such as carpets, padded booth walls, and acoustic tiles on the ceiling) are essential, and if noise remains a problem, white noise generators can further assist.

Research Call Center Staffing

A typical research call center will have the following staff: interviewers, interview monitors, supervisors, and managers.

Interviewers

This is the entry level and most common position in a call center. Because the workload in most research call centers fluctuates considerably as projects come and go, and because of the predominance of household surveys where the most productive time to call is the relatively small window of weekday evenings, most if not all interviewing positions will be on a temporary and hourly or part-time basis. For a call center operating at full capacity, the number of interviewers on the payroll will need to be at least 2 to 3 times the number of interviewing booths available.

Few surveys require interviewers to have more than a high school education, although a clear speaking voice and the ability to persuade members of the public to take part in a survey also are essential. Most interviewers undergo approximately 40 hours of classroom training before they place their first call.

Interview Monitors

The key quality-control tool of a research call center is interview monitoring, where a trained member of the supervisory staff will listen in on interviews (either in real time while viewing simultaneously a copy of the interviewer's screen, or later to a recording of the interview along with a copy of the data collected) to check that the interviewer asked all questions in the prescribed way and faithfully recorded the answers given. Typically there will be one hour of monitoring for every 10 to 20 interviewer hours, so that 5% to 10% of all interviews are monitored.

Supervisors

Sometimes combined with the monitoring position, this position also acts as the first line of management and support for interviewers. Many supervisors are former interviewers. There will usually be at least one supervisor for every 10 to 20 interviewers. In larger operations, some supervisory positions are likely to be salaried, full-time positions. The supervisor level is usually the highest to which most interviewers can aspire without formal qualifications in survey methodology or a related field.

Managers

These positions usually carry both project management responsibility and day-to-day floor management. In larger operations these functions may be separated into specialist roles, but even where fewer than 50 booths are involved there will usually be two managers carrying both functions to provide redundancy. These are professional-level positions, requiring formal qualifications in survey methodology or a related field, along with substantial personnel management skills.

Large centers will also have specialized positions in technical support, human resource management, and training, whereas in smaller centers these functions will typically be spread among the supervisory and management staff.

Research Call Center Technology

The various technology components in a call center are, at the very minimum, the following:

- The telephone system, which includes the telephones on the interviewers' desks as well as the central PBX (private branch exchange) or call manager, which connects to the outside world
- The computer system, which runs the computer-assisted interviewing software and stores the collected data

Although research call centers often have a separate telephony infrastructure and computer infrastructure, as of 2007 these components are rapidly converging and there are already functions (such as dialing) that can reside in either. Many centers are also rapidly adopting the general call center trend toward Voice over Internet Protocol (VoIP) and other uses of Internet technology. VoIP allows the voice and data to be consolidated into a single network. This eliminates the need for parallel wiring systems (one for voice and another for data) within a center and reduces reliance on the more expensive telephone network.

Newer applications of computer-assisted interviewing are now written to be accessed via a Web browser, rather than residing on the interviewer's personal computer. This allows lower-specifications computers to be used in interviewing booths; saves the effort of individually configuring, testing, and managing all of the

interviewer booths; and, combined with VoIP, allows interviewer stations to be set up rapidly and cheaply wherever a high-speed Internet connection is available, including in interviewers' homes.

Jenny Kelly

See also Calling Rules; Coding; Computer-Assisted Telephone Interviewing (CATI); Inbound Calling; Interactive Voice Response (IVR); Interviewer; Interviewer Monitoring; Outbound Calling; Predictive Dialing; Research Management; Supervisor; Voice over Internet Protocol (VoIP) and the Virtual Computer-Assisted Telephone Interview (CATI) Facility

Further Readings

Hansen, S. E. (2008). CATI sample management. In J. Lepkowski, C. Tucker, M. Brick, E. de Leeuw, L. Japec, P. J. Lavrakas, et al. (Eds.), *Advances in telephone survey methodology* (pp. 340–358). New York: Wiley.

Kelly, J., Link, M., Petty, J., Hobson, K., & Cagney, P. (2008). Establishing a new survey research call center. In J. Lepkowski, C. Tucker, M. Brick, E. de Leeuw, L. Japec, P. J. Lavrakas, et al. (Eds.), *Advances in telephone survey methodology* (pp. 317–339). New York: Wiley.

Lavrakas, P. J. (1993). *Telephone survey methods: Sampling, selection, and supervision* (2nd ed.). Newbury Park, CA: Sage.

Steve, K., Burks, A. T., Lavrakas, P. J., Brown, K., & Hoover, B. (2008). The development of a comprehensive behavioral-based system to monitor telephone interviewer performance. In J. Lepkowski, C. Tucker, M. Brick, E. de Leeuw, L. Japec, P. J. Lavrakas, et al. (Eds.), *Advances in telephone survey methodology* (pp. 401–422). New York: Wiley.

RESEARCH DESIGN

A research design is a general plan or strategy for conducting a research study to examine specific testable research questions of interest. The nature of the research questions and hypotheses, the variables involved, the sample of participants, the research settings, the data collection methods, and the data analysis methods are factors that contribute to the selection of the appropriate research design. Thus, a research design is the structure, or the blueprint, of research that guides the process of research from the formulation of the research questions and hypotheses to reporting the research findings. In designing any research study, the researcher should be familiar with the basic steps of the research process that guide all types of research designs. Also, the researcher should be familiar with a wide range of research designs in order to choose the most appropriate design to answer the research questions and hypotheses of interest.

Generally, the research designs can be classified into one of three broad categories based on the nature of research, purpose of research, research questions, sample selection, data collection methods, and data analysis techniques: (1) quantitative research designs, (2) qualitative research designs, and (3) mixed-research designs.

Quantitative Research Designs

Quantitative research is a deductive theory-based research process that focuses primarily on testing theories and specific research hypotheses that consider finding differences and relationships using numeric data and statistical methods to make specific conclusions about the phenomena. Quantitative research designs can be classified into one of four broad research design categories based on the strength of the research design's experimental control: (1) true experimental research designs, (2) quasi-experimental research designs, (3) pre-experimental research designs, and (4) nonexperimental research designs.

Although each of the categories of research design is important and can provide useful research findings, they differ in the nature of the evidence they provide in establishing causal relations between variables and drawing causal inferences from the research findings. Experimental designs are the most rigorous, powerful, and the strongest of the design categories to establish a cause–effect relationship. Nonexperimental designs are the weakest in terms of establishing a cause–effect relationship between variables because of the lack of control over the variables, conditions, and settings of the study.

True Experimental Research Designs

The true experiment is a type of research design where the researcher deliberately manipulates one or more independent variables (also called experimental variable or treatment conditions), randomly assigns individuals or objects to the experimental conditions (e.g., experimental or control groups) and controls other environmental and extraneous variables, and measures the effect of the independent variable on one or more dependent variables (experimental outcome). The experimental group is the group that receives the treatment, and the control group is the group that receives no treatment or sometimes a *placebo* (alternative treatment that has nothing to do with the experimental treatment). Thus, in a typical experimental study, the researcher randomly selects the participants and randomly assigns them to the experimental conditions (e.g., experimental and control), controls the extraneous variables that might have an effect on the outcome (dependent) variable, and measures the effect of the experimental treatment on the outcome at the conclusion of the experimental study.

It is important to emphasize that the experimental research design, if well conducted, is the most conclusive and powerful of all the research designs and the only research design that tests research questions and hypotheses to establish cause–effect relationships. For this reason it is sometimes called the "Golden Design."

The simple randomized experimental designs with two groups can be conducted using one of the following four basic experimental designs:

Randomized Two-Group Posttest-Only Designs

The two-group randomized experimental design involves two groups of individuals or objects which, ideally, are randomly selected from the population and which are randomly assigned to the experimental and control (comparison) groups (a single independent variable with two levels: experimental and control groups). The effects of the experimental treatment on the dependent variable (experimental outcome) are measured at the conclusion of the experiment. It is represented as

$$\text{Experimental Group} : R \ E \ O$$
$$\text{Control Group} : R \ C \ O$$

where R is random assignment of individuals or objects, E represents the experimental treatment, C represents the control condition (no treatment or placebo treatment), and O represents the posttest observation (measurement).

An example of this design would be testing an alternative wording of the mail survey cover letter, compared to a standard cover letter, to determine whether the new cover letter raised cooperation. Households would be randomly assigned to either the standard or alternative cover letter. The resulting response rates between the two groups would represent the dependent variable used to test the hypothesis that the new wording raises cooperation.

Randomized Two-Group Pretest–Posttest Designs

This experimental design involves two groups of individuals or objects randomly selected from the population and randomly assigned to the experimental and control groups (a single independent variable with two levels: experimental and control groups). The two groups are pretested on the dependent variable before administering the experimental treatment and posttested on the same dependent variable at the conclusion of the experiment. This design is represented as

$$\text{Experimental Group}: R \ O_1 \ E \ O_2$$
$$\text{Control Group}: R \ O_1 \ C \ O_2$$

where R is random assignment of individuals or objects, E represents the experimental treatment, and C represents the control condition (no treatment or placebo treatment). The O_1 represents the pretest observation (measurement), and the O_2 represents the posttest observation (measurement).

An example of this design would be a telephone survey questionnaire that measures the effects of new information on approval versus disapproval of a proposed city bond to fund the building of a new bridge. All respondents would be asked whether they favor or oppose the new bridge funding early in the questionnaire. Later in the questionnaire they would be asked the same favor–oppose question again, but a random half of them would first be told some information about the value of the new bridge and the other half would not be told this information. Nothing else in the questionnaire would change. The difference in answers between the before- and after-questions about the funding for the two groups would serve as the dependent variable to test the hypothesis that the new information raises support for the bridge funding.

Solomon Four-Group Designs

This experimental design is a combination of the randomized two-group posttest-only design and the randomized two-group pretest–posttest designs. It involves randomly selecting a sample of subjects from

the targeted population and randomly assigning the random sample to one of four groups. Two of the groups are pretested (Experimental and Control Groups 1) and the other two are not (Experimental and Control Groups 2). One of the pretested groups and one of the not pretested groups receive the experimental treatment. All four groups are posttested on the dependent variable (experimental outcome). The design is represented as

$$\text{Experimental Group 1}: R \ O_1 \ E \ O_2$$
$$\text{Control Group 1}: R \ O_1 \ C \ O_2$$
$$\text{Experimental Group 2}: R \ E \ O_2$$
$$\text{Control Group 2}: R \ C \ O_2$$

Here, the researcher has two independent variables with two levels. One independent variable is the experimental conditions with two levels (experimental and control groups), and the other independent variable is the pretesting condition with two levels (pretested and not pretested groups). The value of this design is that it allows the researcher to determine if the pretest (O_1) has an effect on the resulting answer given in the posttest.

An example of this design would be one that builds on the previous example of the experiment to test the effect of the information about the value of the new bridge. However, in the Solomon four-group design, there would be two more randomly assigned groups of respondents, ones who were not asked whether they favored or opposed the bridge funding at the beginning of the questionnaire. Instead, one of these groups would be the second control group, asked only their opinions about the bridge funding later in the questionnaire. The other group would be the second experimental group, asked their opinions about the bridge funding only later in the questionnaire but after first being given the information about the value of the bridge. This design would allow the researchers to test not only the effects of the information but also whether the saliency of the bridge funding, by asking about it first before giving the new information, affected opinions given later about the funding.

Experimental Factorial Designs

Experimental factorial designs are extensions of single independent variable experimental designs to situations where there are two or more independent variables that are controlled by the researcher. Factorial designs allow the researcher to examine simultaneously the effects of one or more independent variables individually on the dependent variable (experimental outcome) as well as their interactions. These interactions cannot be examined by using single independent variable experimental designs.

The term *factorial* refers to experimental designs with more than one independent variable (factor). Many different experimental factorial designs can be formulated depending on the number of the independent variables. The Solomon four-group design is an example of a 2×2 factorial design with treatment conditions (treatment and control groups) crossed with pretesting conditions (pretested and not pretested groups).

Quasi-Experimental Research Designs

Quasi-experimental research is used in situations where it is not feasible or practical to use a true experimental design because the individual subjects are already in intact groups (e.g., organizations, departments, classrooms, schools, institutions). In these situations it is often impossible to randomly assign individual subjects to experimental and control groups. Thus, quasi-experimental designs are similar to experimental designs in terms of one or more independent (experimental) variables being manipulated, except for the lack of random assignment of individual subjects to the experimental conditions (i.e., experimental and control groups). Instead, the intact groups are assigned in a nonrandom fashion to the conditions. Types of quasi-experimental designs include nonequivalent control group designs, longitudinal research designs, and multi-level research designs.

Nonequivalent Control Group Design

The nonequivalent control group design involves assignment of intact nonequivalent groups (e.g., classrooms, schools, departments, and organizations) to experimental conditions (experimental and control groups). Thus, the intact groups are assigned to the treatment conditions and not the individual subjects, as was the case in the true experimental designs. For example, in a study of the effects of a new curriculum of students' knowledge of science and attitudes toward science, some classrooms would be assigned to receive the new curriculum and others would not. Toward the end of the school year, all students are measured on their science knowledge and attitudes toward science. Because the effects are being measured at the level of the individual student, but the students themselves were not randomly assigned to the control and treatment condition, this is a quasi-experiment, not a true experiment.

Longitudinal Research Designs

Longitudinal, repeated-measures, or time-series research designs involve repeated measurement or observation on the same individuals at several points over a period of time. It is an elaboration of the one-group pretest–posttest design and focuses primarily on change, growth, and developmental types of research questions across many different disciplines such as medicine, public health, business, and social and behavioral sciences. Longitudinal designs, if well designed and conducted, are usually more complex, time consuming, and expensive than the other types of research designs.

Multi-Level Research Designs

Multi-level or hierarchical research designs involve the nesting of individuals (micro-level units) within organizations (macro-level units) and having explanatory independent variables characterizing and describing both levels. For example, in a two-level design, the emphasis is on how to model the effects of explanatory variables (predictors) at one level on the relationships occurring at another level. These multi-level and hierarchical structured data present analytical challenges that cannot be handled by traditional linear regression methods because there is a regression model for each level of the hierarchy. Thus, hierarchical models explicitly model the micro and macro levels in the hierarchy by taking into consideration the interdependence of individuals within the groups.

Pre-Experimental Research Designs

Pre-experimental research designs are simple designs with no control groups. These designs are questionable because they lack control and thus should be used for exploratory or preliminary examination of research problems.

One-Group Posttest Experimental Design

The one-group experimental design, also called the one-shot experimental design, takes a single group of subjects or objects exposed to a treatment (X) and observes and measures its effects on the outcome (O). This simple design is represented as

$$X \rightarrow O$$

This is the most basic and simple design in experimental research. It is used as a starting point for preliminary examination of the precausal relationship of research problems for the purpose of developing better-controlled future experimental designs.

One-Group Pretest–Posttest Design

The one-group pretest–posttest design involves a single group of individuals or objects that are pretested or measured (O_1), exposed to an experimental treatment (X), and posttested or measured (O_2). This design is represented as

$$O_1 \rightarrow X \rightarrow O_2$$

Nonexperimental Research Designs

Nonexperimental or descriptive research designs aim to answer research questions about the current state of affairs, identify factors and relationships among them, and create a detailed quantitative description of phenomena. Thus, it provides a snapshot of the feelings, opinions, practices, thoughts, preferences, attitudes, or behaviors of a sample of people, as they exist at a given time and a given place. For example, measuring the attitudes of the employees in the organization toward adapting new technologies is an example of a research question that can be carried on using a nonexperimental descriptive survey research design. The following are short descriptions of some of these designs.

Nonexperimental Survey Research

Survey research is a systematic research method for collecting data from a representative sample of individuals using instruments composed of closed-ended and/or open-ended questions, observations, and interviews. It is one of the most widely used nonexperimental research designs across disciplines to collect large amounts of survey data from a representative sample of individuals sampled from the targeted population using a variety of modes such as face-to-face, telephone, mail, and electronic (Web-based and email). Each of these data collection modes has its own advantages and disadvantages in terms of cost, duration, and

response rate. Thus, the key goal of nonexperimental survey research is to collect data and describe the behaviors, thoughts, and attitudes of a representative sample of individuals at a given point in time and place.

Survey research is considered one of the most important research designs, and survey instruments and survey methods are frequently used to collect data for the other quantitative, qualitative, and mixed research designs. For example, it can be used to collect data for correlational research studies, experimental studies, and quasi-experimental studies.

Correlational Research

Correlational research is a type of descriptive nonexperimental research because it describes and assesses the magnitude and degree of an existing relationship between two or more continuous quantitative variables with interval or ratio types of measurements or discrete variables with ordinal or nominal type of measurements. Thus, correlational research involves collecting data from a sample of individuals or objects to determine the degree of the relationships between two or more variables for the possibility to make predictions based on these relationships. There are many different methods for calculating a correlation coefficient, which depends on the metric of data for each of the variables. The most common statistic that measures the degree of the relationship between a pair of continuous quantitative variables, having interval and ratio types of measurements, is the Pearson product–moment correlation coefficient, which is represented by the letter r.

Alternative correlation coefficients can be used when the pair of variables has nominal or ordinal types of measurement. If the pair of variables is dichotomous (a nominal type of measurement having only two categories), the Phi coefficient should be used. If the pair of variables has ordinal type of measurement, the Spearman rank order correlation coefficient should be used.

Another type of correlational research involves predicting one or more continuous quantitative dependent variables from one or more continuous quantitative independent variables. The most common statistical methods used for prediction purposes are simple and multiple regression analyses.

The significance of correlational research stems from the fact that many complex and sophisticated statistical analyses are based on correlational data. For example, logistic regression analysis and discriminant function analysis are quite similar to simple and multiple regression analyses with the exception that the dependent (criterion) variable is categorical and not continuous as in simple and multiple regression analyses. Canonical analysis is another statistical method that examines the relationship between a set of predictor (independent) variables and a set of criterion (dependent) variables. Path analysis and structural equation modeling are other complex statistical methods that are based on correlational data to examine the relationships among more than two variables and constructs.

Causal-Comparative Research

Causal-comparative or ex post facto research is a type of descriptive nonexperimental research because it describes the state of existing differences among groups of individuals or objects as they existed at a given time and place and attempts to determine the possible causes or reasons for the existing differences. Thus, the basic causal-comparative approach starts with selecting two or more groups with existing differences and comparing them on an outcome (dependent) variable. Also, it attempts to examine and explain the possible causes of the existing differences between the groups.

Some causal-comparative designs involve only two independent groups to be compared on a particular continuous dependent variable, for example, studying the differences between boys and girls on math achievement. In this causal-comparative study, the researcher needs to analyze the collected data using *t*-test for testing the research hypothesis that there are differences between the two independent sample means. Some other causal-comparative research designs involve more than two groups, for example, studying differences between white, black, and Hispanic students on math achievement. In this study, the researcher needs to use analysis of variance (ANOVA) to analyze the data.

Other causal-comparative designs involve studying differences between (among) two or more independent groups on two or more related dependent variables. In this case, multivariate analysis of variance (MANOVA) statistical procedure should be used to analyze the data to determine whether two or more independent groups differ on more than a single dependent variable.

It is important to note that the *t*-test, ANOVA, and MANOVA are parametric statistical procedures that require interval- or ratio-level data, a large sample size, and meeting the requirements of statistical assumptions (e.g., normality, independence of observations). The

nonparametric counterparts for these statistical methods should be used with nominal- or ordinal-level data and when one or more of the assumptions are violated in the research study and when the sample size is small. For example, a nonparametric statistical method such as Mann–Whitney U is an alternative to the parametric *t*-test.

Meta-Analysis Research

The meta-analysis design is used to quantitatively and systematically summarize and synthesize the research results and findings from a collection of primary studies that address and test the same research question. Meta-analytic research methods have established five major general stages that guide meta-analysts in their systematic quantitative review. These stages include (1) formulating research problems, (2) collecting primary research studies, (3) evaluating primary studies, (4) analyzing and modeling the meta-analytic data, and (5) interpreting and presenting the meta-analytic results.

Generally, the key goals of meta-analysis methods are to (a) produce quantitative summary measures of the effect sizes, (b) assess the heterogeneity (variation) among the effect sizes, and (c) model and explain the heterogeneity between the effect sizes using known study and sample characteristics as exploratory variables in the specified meta-analytic regression model.

Qualitative Research Designs

Qualitative research is inductive and context-specific research that focuses on observing and describing a specific phenomenon, behavior, opinions, and events that exist to generate new research hypotheses and theories. The goals of qualitative research are to provide a detailed narrative description and holistic interpretation that captures the richness and complexity of behaviors, experiences, and events in natural settings. Thus, qualitative research is an inductive research process, logically emerging from the specific phenomena to general conclusions and theories about the phenomena based on data collected by observations, documents, physical artifacts, interviews, and focus groups.

Case Study

Case study is an in-depth examination and intensive description of a single individual, group, and organization based on collected information from a variety of sources, such as observations, interviews, documents, participant observation, and archival records. The goal of the case study is to provide a detailed and comprehensive description, in narrative form, of the case being studied.

Ethnographic Research

Ethnographic research is a qualitative research design that is used for studying social groups, cultures, and human interactions in natural cultural and social settings. The goal of the ethnographic study is to provide a detailed, in-depth, and holistic narrative description of the group and the cultural setting being studied. The primary ethnographic data collection methods are in-depth interviews and participant observation to comprehensively describe a cultural and social setting.

Phenomenological Research

Phenomenological research, or phenomenology, is a qualitative research method in which the researcher attempts to understand and explain how an individual or a group of individuals experience a particular phenomenon from the individual's or individuals' own perspective(s). The primary method of data collection used in phenomenology is in-depth interviews of individuals who have experienced the phenomenon.

Action Research

Action research is a systematic research inquiry conducted by teachers, principals, school counselors, managers, or any other educational or organizational practitioners in the educational and organizational setting to collect information about educational and organizational practices and operations to resolve matters of concern or a problem in a particular setting such as classroom, playground, library, department, or company. Simply stated, action research is a study conducted by educational and organizational practitioners to help them to develop alternative reflective practices that lead to positive changes within their educational and organizational settings.

Historical Research

Historical research is a systematic process for searching, exploring, summarizing, and reporting past information and events using primary and secondary sources of historical data to gain understanding of historical events, issues, and policies. Primary sources of historical data are the original firsthand artifacts, documents, observations, oral presentations, diaries, photographs, and audio-visual recordings of past events. Secondary sources are secondhand nondirect oral and written documentations of past events that are summarized and documented by others and not the original primary sources.

Grounded Theory Research

Grounded theory research is an inductive qualitative research design that is used for generating and developing theories and explanations based on systematically collected qualitative data. The data collection process in grounded theory research is usually an ongoing iterative process that starts with collecting and analyzing qualitative data that leads to tentative theory development. Then, more qualitative data are collected and analyzed that lead to further clarification and development of the theory. The qualitative data collection and further theory development process continues until the particular theory is developed that is "grounded" in the data.

Mixed-Methods Research Designs

Mixed-methods research designs involve research studies that employ both quantitative and qualitative research methodologies to address the proposed research questions. Thus, mixed research methods combine the deductive and inductive inquiries of the scientific research methods as well as use a variety of data collection and analysis methods. The quantitative and qualitative methods can be conducted concurrently or sequentially to address a research question or questions. The mixed-methods research designs require from the researcher a considerable amount of time and energy as well as training in both quantitative and qualitative research designs. However, one of the significant advantages of the mixed-methods research design is that it provides a more comprehensive and enhanced image of the research problem that is under investigation than would either one of the designs (quantitative or qualitative) by itself. Specifically, the mixed-methods research designs can be classified into three types: exploratory, explanatory, and triangulation.

Exploratory Mixed-Methods Research Designs

Using this design, the researcher first conceptualizes a qualitative research study. Second, the researcher collects and analyzes the qualitative data. Third, the researcher uses the findings from the qualitative data analysis to conceptualize a quantitative research study. Finally, the researcher collects and analyzes the quantitative data to validate the qualitative findings.

Explanatory Mixed-Methods Research Designs

Using this design, the researcher first conceptualizes a quantitative research study. Second, the researcher collects and analyzes the quantitative data. Third, the researcher conceptualizes a qualitative research study. Finally, the researcher collects and analyzes the collected qualitative data to clarify and enhance the quantitative research findings.

Triangulation Mixed-Methods Designs

Using this design, the researcher simultaneously conceptualizes quantitative and qualitative research studies. Then, the researcher simultaneously collects and analyzes both quantitative and qualitative data. Finally, the researcher uses the results from the quantitative and qualitative studies to validate findings from both studies.

Sema A. Kalaian

See also Dependent Variable; Experimental Design; Factorial Design; Independent Variable; Longitudinal Studies; Random Assignment; Trend Analysis

Further Readings

Campbell, D. T., & Stanley, J. C. (1963). *Experimental and quasi-experimental designs for research*. Boston: Houghton Mifflin.

Frankel, J. R., & Wallen, N. E. (2006). *How to design and evaluate research in education* (6th ed.). New York: McGraw-Hill.

Marczyk, G., DeMatteo, D., & Festinger, D. (2005). *Essentials of research design and methodology*. Hoboken, NJ: Wiley.

Myers, J. L., & Well, A. D. (2003). *Research design and statistical analysis* (2nd ed.). Mahwah, NJ: Lawrence Erlbaum.

Shadish, W. R., Cook, T. D., & Campbell, D. T. (2002). *Experimental and quasi-experimental designs for generalized causal inference*. Boston: Houghton Mifflin.

RESEARCH HYPOTHESIS

A research hypothesis is a specific, clear, and testable proposition or predictive statement about the possible outcome of a scientific research study based on a particular property of a population, such as presumed differences between groups on a particular variable or relationships between variables. Specifying the research hypotheses is one of the most important steps in planning a scientific quantitative research study. A quantitative researcher usually states an a priori expectation about the results of the study in one or more research hypotheses before conducting the study, because the design of the research study and the planned research design often is determined by the stated hypotheses. Thus, one of the advantages of stating a research hypothesis is that it requires the researcher to fully think through what the research question implies, what measurements and variables are involved, and what statistical methods should be used to analyze the data. In other words, every step of the research process is guided by the stated research questions and hypotheses, including the sample of participants, research design, data collection methods, measuring instruments, data analysis methods, possible results, and possible conclusions.

The research hypotheses are usually derived from the stated research questions and the problems being investigated. After the research hypotheses are stated, inferential statistical methods are used to test these hypotheses to answer the research questions and make conclusions regarding the research problems. Generally, in quantitative research designs, hypothesis testing and the use of inferential statistical methods begin with the development of specific research hypotheses that are derived from the study research questions. Research hypotheses differ from research questions in that hypotheses are specific statements in terms of the anticipated differences and relationships, which are based on theory or other logical reasoning and which can be tested using statistical tests developed for testing the specific hypotheses.

The following are two examples of research questions and possible corresponding research hypotheses.

The first example is a nondirectional hypothesis, whereas the second is a directional hypothesis:

Research Question 1: What differences exist in attitudes toward statistics between male and female Ph.D. candidates in the technology program?

Research Hypothesis 1: There are statistically significant differences in attitudes toward statistics between male and female Ph.D. candidates in the technology program.

Research Question 2: Is rapport with graduate students different for professors using a student-centered teaching method than for those using a teacher-centered teaching method?

Research Hypothesis 2: Professors who use a student-centered teaching method will have a greater positive rapport with their graduate students than professors who use a teacher-centered teaching method.

It is important to note that in using some types of research designs, it is unnecessary and inappropriate to state research hypotheses because in these types of studies, it would be impossible to anticipate or predict the possible outcomes and findings of the study. For example, survey research that is designed to explore and describe the characteristics (e.g., attitudes, opinions) of a particular population often proceeds with no need to state research hypotheses. In addition, in qualitative research designs such as ethnographic, case studies, grounded theory, and phenomenological research, research hypotheses usually are not formulated at the beginning of the research. They are usually generated and emerged as qualitative data are collected and more understanding is gained about the phenomenon under investigation and may lead to follow-up quantitative studies to investigate the newly formed hypotheses.

There are three distinct properties that are shared by all types of research hypotheses. The first property is whether the hypothesis represents a difference between groups or a relationship hypothesis. The second property of research hypotheses is whether it is the null hypothesis or an alternative hypothesis. The third property is whether the hypothesis is directional or nondirectional.

Difference-Between-Groups Hypotheses Versus Relationship Hypotheses

Research hypotheses can take many different forms depending on the research design. Some hypotheses may describe and examine the relationship between two variables. Some hypotheses may examine the differences between two or more groups. Other hypotheses may examine the effect of particular explanatory independent variables on the dependent outcome variable.

Nevertheless, research hypotheses can be classified into two broad categories:

Difference hypotheses. This type of research hypothesis is used for group comparison purposes in randomized experimental designs, quasi-experimental designs, and causal-comparative research designs. Research hypotheses 1 and 2, presented in the previous section, are difference hypotheses.

Relationship hypotheses. This type of research hypothesis is used to examine the relationships between two or more variables in correlational research designs. The following is an example of a relationship research hypothesis: There is a positive (direct) relationship between Ph.D. students' attitudes toward statistics and their achievement in the research methods courses.

Null Versus Alternative Hypotheses

In hypothesis testing, there are two kinds of research hypotheses. One is the null hypothesis, symbolically stated as H_0, and the other is the alternative hypothesis, symbolically stated as H_1. The null hypothesis always states that there are no differences between groups on a particular variable being studied, no effects of particular independent variables on the dependent outcome variable, or no relationship between the variables being examined. In contrast, the alternative hypothesis states there are differences between two or more groups, there is an effect of an independent variable on the dependent variable, or there are relationships between pairs of variables.

It is important to note that the alternative hypothesis represents the researcher expectations about the range of the possible values that the hypothesized parameter might take in the population. For this reason it is impossible to test the alternative hypothesis directly for all the possible parameter values in that range. To confirm or disconfirm the research hypothesis, the researcher usually devises and tests the null hypothesis. The null hypothesis can be thought of as the complement of the alternative hypothesis where the hypothesized parameter is equated to a single value that can be directly tested by a statistical test. Rejecting the null hypothesis is an indirect way of "confirming" (supporting) the researcher's alternative hypothesis.

It is equally important to note that based on the results of the test statistic, the null hypothesis is either rejected or not rejected, but it can never be accepted. For example, if the premise that there is no difference between groups (i.e., the null hypothesis) is rejected, then the researcher concludes that there is a significant difference between the groups. On the other hand, if the same null hypothesis is not rejected, then the researcher concludes that there is no significant detectable difference between the groups of the study (at least not as measured in the current study).

Directional Versus Nondirectional Hypotheses

In hypothesis testing, it is important to distinguish between directional hypotheses and nondirectional hypotheses. The researcher should make the choice between stating and testing directional or nondirectional hypotheses depending on the amount of information or knowledge the researcher has about the groups and the variables under investigation. Generally, a directional hypothesis is based on more informed reasoning (e.g., past research) than when only a nondirectional hypothesis is ventured. Research Hypothesis 1 stated earlier is an example of a nondirectional research hypothesis. It can be represented along with its null hypothesis symbolically as

$$H_0 : \mu_1 = \mu_2$$
$$H_1 : \mu_1 \neq \mu_2.$$

μ_1 and μ_2 are the mean attitudes toward statistics held by the male and female Ph.D. students, respectively.

Research hypothesis 2 stated earlier is an example of a directional research hypothesis and it can be represented along with its null hypothesis symbolically as

$$H_0 : \mu_1 \leq \mu_2$$
$$H_1 : \mu_1 > \mu_2.$$

μ_1 and μ_2 are the mean levels of rapport with their students for professors who use a student-centered method and those who use a teacher-centered teaching method, respectively.

Sema A. Kalaian and Rafa M. Kasim

See also Alpha, Significance Level of Test; Alternative Hypothesis; Dependent Variable; Independent Variable; Null Hypothesis; Research Design; Research Question

Further Readings

Frankel, J. R., & Wallen, N. E. (2006). *How to design and evaluate research in education* (6th ed.). New York: McGraw-Hill.

Marczyk, G., DeMatteo, D., & Festinger, D. (2005). *Essentials of research design and methodology.* New York: Wiley.

RESEARCH MANAGEMENT

The function of research management is to coordinate disparate activities involved in planning and executing any research project. Ability to grasp the big picture, coupled with attention to detail, is required in this function. Regardless of research team size or the size of the project, the same management activities are required.

Research Plan

Research management begins at the initial phase of the research process. As survey research texts point out, identification of the research problem is the first step. From this, the research team develops testable hypotheses and the research plan. This research plan or process is the cornerstone of research management, and the more detailed the plan is, the more efficient the project implementation phase will be.

Identification of Sample

Once the research team has identified the population of interest, it is time to address sampling issues. Sample composition required to meet project goals, sample size (based on power calculations and tempered by monetary considerations), and source of the sample are specified in the research plan.

Timeline

Effective research management requires the development of a realistic timeline to ensure that the project proceeds in an organized and logical manner. Recognizing that the research process seldom proceeds on schedule, additional time is included in the timeline so that a delay does not compromise the entire project.

Funding

Research management requires an understanding of accounting, budgeting, and some basic contract management. An important research management function is to secure and manage funds necessary for the project's success. After the research plan is developed, the research budget is finalized. The budget must include all costs required to execute the project in accordance with the research plan. Survey administration modes impact the budget differently. Traditionally, mail has been the least expensive, followed by Internet, Web, computer-assisted self-interviewing (audio or not), and computer-assisted telephone interviewing (CATI). Face-to-face interviewing, including computer-assisted personal interviewing (CAPI), is the most expensive mode.

Often, a research proposal is submitted to federal, state, university, corporate, or other funding agencies to obtain adequate project funds. When working with a team of researchers, this activity can, and probably should, be shared. A first step in the proposal process is to identify an appropriate funding entity, that is, an agency where agency goals and those of the research project are similar. It also is important that the funding agency has the capacity to adequately fund the project. Conducting an expensive research project may require securing money from several funding agencies. Be aware that when obtaining funding, the funding agency often specifies question topics for the survey instrument and this may increase the questionnaire length and thus the cost.

Obtaining adequate funds impacts the timeline because of agency funding cycles and proposal requirements. It is not unusual to submit a proposal and revisions multiple times before funding is secured; thus, additional time should be included in the timeline for such a contingency. At the time funding is awarded, the research team and funding agency should have a shared understanding, in writing, about project deliverables.

Proposals submitted to organizations that are not federal, state, or university entities and do not receive funding from these sources are developed to address the client's requirements. Typically these proposals and the timeline for developing them are very short; therefore, it is prudent to have boilerplate proposal language developed to reduce proposal preparation response time. In most cases, the client will have specified the project budget. Research firms submitting successful proposals must either meet all proposal requirements within the specified budget or convince the client that the proposed activities cannot be performed with the budget specified.

Questionnaire Development

Research management's role in questionnaire development is to ensure that included survey questions answer the research questions and are appropriate for the selected survey mode. Competent research management occasionally requires interjecting realism into the questionnaire development process. Occasionally, those involved in writing survey questions assume that potential respondents have similar subject matter knowledge and language comprehension levels as themselves. When necessary, it is the responsibility of research management to disabuse them of this belief.

Unique challenges are encountered when sampling a multi-cultural, multi-lingual population because without interviewing in multiple languages, researchers cannot extrapolate their findings to the entire population. At the beginning of such projects, it is important to secure the services of an experienced translator or translation company. Researchers may be tempted to economize on the translation and discover, after the fact, that simply speaking and reading a language does not mean that the person is capable of translating a questionnaire. Specialized subject-matter knowledge greatly aids in the translation process. Cultural competencies and sensitivities also affect the translation. After the initial translation is completed, the questionnaire often is back-translated to ensure accuracy of the original translation.

Protection of Human Subjects

Once the research plan is completed, the sample defined, the questionnaire developed and translated, and federal, state, or university funding secured, the project must be submitted to a Committee for the Protection of Human Subjects. When only one funding agency is involved, the project is submitted to that agency's approved committee. In executing their mandate to protect research participants from harm, the committee may require any number of changes to a project. Mounting a large and expensive project involving multiple funding agencies requires submitting the project to multiple human subject committees. Adequate time should be included in the project timeline to account for differences in the frequency with which the committees meet and the necessity of coordinating changes required by each committee into a cohesive project approved by all.

Projects that do not involve federal, state, or university funds are subject to the review requirements of the client. Some commercial organizations have an institutional review board that performs the functions of the Committee for the Protection of Human Subjects, and projects must be approved through this committee. When working with clients whose organizations do not require the approval of an institutional review board, it is prudent to obtain approval, in writing, for all aspects of the project prior to data collection.

Data Collection

Activities involved in data collection are dependent upon the mode of administration and whether the research team is actively involved in data collection or is coordinating this activity with another entity. When collecting data in-house, research management's role is to ensure that the data collection team is large enough to complete the project on schedule and within budget and that the interviewers are adequately trained and supervised. If data collection is outsourced, research management involves identifying an organization capable of performing the required activities at the level of quality that is required. Active oversight of the contractor is another function of research management. Oversight involves ensuring that data are being collected according to the research plan; that, if required, the contractor adheres to the regulations of the Committee for Protection of Human Subjects; and that respondent confidentiality is not compromised.

When collected via the Internet, Web, CAPI, CATI, and other computer-assisted methods, data automatically are captured electronically, thus eliminating additional data entry costs. Projects conducted via mail or other paper-and-pencil modes require data entry; therefore, provisions should be made to test a proportion of the records for accuracy of data entry. For qualitative research, or when clients are uncertain about the appropriate response categories, open-ended text questions may be included on the survey instrument. While clients often see this as a way of obtaining the "best" data from respondents, question administration and coding present unique challenges. Frequently respondents have

not given much thought to issues addressed in open-ended questions and, therefore, may provide incomplete, somewhat incoherent, or other unusual responses. Prior to coding open-ended responses, it is suggested that clients be provided with the text responses and help develop a coding scheme for the research organization. In doing so, the client will gain the greatest benefit from the open-ended question responses. When clients are reluctant to do this, those coding the text responses should look for common response themes, receive client approval for the coding scheme, and code the data accordingly.

Data obtained using computer-assisted modes are relatively clean when the software programming is thoroughly checked for accuracy, response categories are appropriate, and when incomplete or out-of-range responses are not allowed. Paper-and-pencil administration often results in incomplete data because of item nonresponse, out-of-range responses, and illegible responses. Data cleaning becomes more onerous in this situation, and research management's role is to ensure that data quality is not compromised. Decisions regarding data cleaning, recoding, and acceptable data quality should be delineated in the data set documentation.

Data Analysis

Before data analysis and report writing, the audience for the report needs to be determined. The client should be asked about the degree of complexity desired and the type of report needed. While it may be tempting to "dazzle" a client by providing high-level statistical analysis in reports, if the client is unable to use the analysis, then the report may not be useful. All specifications of this deliverable should be delineated in writing prior to the start of analysis. A function of project management is to ensure that clients receive usable deliverables that meet their needs and, at the same time, enhance the survey organization's reputation.

Data Set and Documentation Development

The type of data set developed (e.g., SAS, SPSS) is dependent upon project deliverables. Documentation makes the data set useful to data users. In addition to a codebook, documentation usually includes a description of the sampling strategy used; source of the sample; information about the data collection process;

measures of data quality; and data weighting, if appropriate. Project complexity affects data set documentation development and can take weeks or months to complete. Just as with data collection, responsibility for overseeing this activity is a function of research management.

Project Success

A thorough understanding of the research process, coupled with a basic knowledge of fiscal management, is required for competent project management. Ability to communicate both orally and in written form with researchers, support staff, and interviewers is vital to project success. While not required, being personable and having some tact makes communication with the research team and others easier. Although a research team usually consists of many persons, ultimately research project success is dependent upon competent research management.

Bonnie D. Davis

See also Audio Computer-Assisted Self-Interviewing (ACASI); Codebook; Coding; Computer-Assisted Personal Interviewing (CAPI); Computer-Assisted Self-Interviewing (CASI); Computer-Assisted Telephone Interviewing (CATI); Interviewing; Protection of Human Subjects; Questionnaire; Research Design; Survey Costs

Further Readings

Alreck, P., & Settle, R. B. (1995). *The survey research handbook: Guidelines and strategies for conducting a survey.* Chicago: Irwin.

Buckingham, A., & Saunders, P. (2004). *The survey methods workbook: From design to analysis.* Cambridge, UK: Polity Press.

Couper, M. P., Baker, R. P., Bethlehem, J., Clark, C. Z. F., Martin, J., Nicholls, W. L., et al. (Eds.). (1998). *Computer assisted survey information collection.* New York: Wiley.

RESEARCH QUESTION

A research question is an operationalization of the purpose(s) to which a survey project aims. The research question(s) should state the research problem in a way that allow(s) for appropriate research methods to be applied to gathering and analyzing information to help answer the question(s) (i.e., solve the problem[s]). Ultimately it is the research questions that guide the entire design of a survey, including the population that is to be sampled, how it is sampled, what sample size will be used, what mode is used to gather data, what measures will be included in the survey instrument, and what analyses will be conducted.

Typically the research question is posed in terms of *What, Why,* or *How.* For example, *What are the major reasons that citizens disapprove of the President? Why do African Americans, on average, have lower levels of social-economic status than do whites? How are people affected by their criminal victimization experiences in the short and longer term?*

Research questions are much more likely to be identified formally (explicitly) in academic research and much less likely in commercial research. Once the research question is clearly articulated, and after a review of past research on the topic has been conducted, research hypotheses should logically follow. In many instances, however, survey researchers, such as pollsters, need not identify any hypotheses, and their research questions are not formalized and merely left implicit.

Paul J. Lavrakas

See also Research Design; Research Hypothesis

Further Readings

Babbie, E. (2006). *The practice of social research* (11th ed.). Belmont, CA: Wadsworth.

Blaikie, N. (2000). *Designing social research: The logic of anticipation.* Cambridge, UK: Polity.

RESIDENCE RULES

A design objective in many surveys is to measure characteristics of the population and housing in specified geographic areas. Some surveys, in addition, attempt to estimate counts of the population in these areas. A key component of the process needed to accomplish these goals is a clear set of *residence rules,* the rules that determine who should be included and who should be excluded from consideration as a member of a household.

It is important to recognize that the issue of defining residence applies to individuals rather than to households. In a given household, the residence of some members may be clear, whereas for others the rules discussed in this entry may need to be applied.

The question of "who belongs here" is self-evident in a large majority of households. The people residing there have no other place of residence, and there is no one missing who might be included in the household. People for whom determining residence is not so simple include college students, "snowbirds," commuter workers, live-in household help, military personnel, and migrant workers.

Usual Residence

The U.S. Bureau of the Census has traditionally used the concept of "usual residence." This is defined as the place where the person lives and sleeps most of the time and may be different from his or her legal address or voting address. As a general principle, people should be counted (i.e., included in a survey) at their usual place of residence. Some people have no usual place of residence; these people should be counted where they are staying at the time of the survey.

This gives rise to a set of rules that can be used to address most situations. They include the following:

- *People away on vacation and business* should be counted at their permanent residence.
- *Students*
  - Boarding school students should be counted at their parental homes. (This is the major exception to the usual rule.)
  - Students living away at college should be counted where they are living at college and therefore excluded from their parental homes.
  - Students living at home while attending college are counted at home.
- *Nonfamily members* in the home are included if this is where they live and sleep most of the time. Included here are live-in household help, foster children, roomers, and housemates or roommates.
- *Military personnel* are counted where they live or sleep most of the time, which generally means that they are not included in their permanent residence households. For example, personnel serving in Iraq, while absent, are not included in the household where they resided before they left and to which they will return.

- *Hospitals, prisons, and other institutions*
  - Persons staying temporarily at a general hospital, including newborn babies, are included in the household population, thus at their permanent residence.
  - Persons in chronic or long-term disease hospitals, such as a tuberculosis sanitarium or a mental hospital, are counted as living at the hospital, not at their previous permanent residence.
  - People in nursing or assisted-care homes are counted as living at the institution, not in the household from which they moved.
  - Inmates of prisons and jails, at any level, are counted at the penal institution and therefore not in their previous permanent residence household.

Some of the most difficult problems arise in the situations where a given person has more than one place of residence. This can happen because the person

- Has two (or more) homes,
- Has a permanent residence and another where he or she lives in order to commute to a job,
- Has a permanent residence and another where he or she lives in order to attend school, or
- Is a child living in joint custody, spending part of the time with one parent and the rest of the time with the other parent.

The general principle still applies in these situations: Where does the person live and sleep *most of the time*? This usually leads to counting the person at school (except for boarding school students), at the place where he or she lives to commute to the job, at the permanent residence rather than the vacation residence, and with the parent with whom the child spends the most time. When the question appears unanswerable, the general rule is to include the person where he or she is staying at the time of the interview.

These rules are derived from the standards set by the U.S. Bureau of the Census. However, there is a major case in which the bureau deviates from them: the American Community Survey (ACS). A 2-month residence rule applies for this survey. Its biggest effect is in situations where people have two residences and live in each part of the year. The ACS is a monthly survey conducted year-round. If the ACS sample finds the household in its second residence (e.g., in the state of Florida instead of the state of New York), and the household's total planned residence in the second home is at least 2 months, the residents are enumerated there. In parallel, if the sample hits the same household's permanent residence, it would be considered a "temporary vacancy." In the same situation in the decennial census, the household would be enumerated at its permanent residence, and the vacation home would be classified as a "vacant unit."

A place of residence is usually a *housing unit*, occupied by a *household* comprised of one or more persons, or vacant. It should be noted that not everyone lives in a household. Under current terminology, people who are not living in households are considered to be living in *group quarters* (unless they are literally homeless). Group quarters fall into two broad categories. *Institutional* facilities include prisons, nursing homes, mental hospitals, and other places where the residents are generally not free to come and go at will. *Noninstitutional* facilities include college dormitories, military barracks, and other places where the residents are free to move in, out, and about.

De Facto and De Jure Residence

The concepts of de facto and de jure residence are often used. The rules outlined here describe *de facto* residence, that is, the place where the person actually lives. *De jure* residence refers to the place where a person legally resides, for such purposes as estate taxes. The following are some classic cases where the two differ:

- College students usually maintain a de jure residence at their parental homes, which is the address used on their driver licenses and, often, on their voter's registration. In fact, the widespread implementation of motor–voter legislation has tied the two together.
- Senior citizens who spend most of their time in a warm climate, or even outside the United States, may maintain a de jure address for voting and estate purposes.
- Citizens living outside the United States often have a de jure voting address, from which they vote an absentee ballot.

In practice, survey research activities are rarely concerned with de jure residence. De facto residence, the place where people and households actually reside, is the relevant issue.

Patricia C. Becker

See also American Community Survey (ACS); U.S. Bureau of the Census

Further Readings

Panel on Residence Rules in the Decennial Census, Cork, D. L., & Voss, P. R. (Eds.), & National Research Council. (2006). *Once, only once, and in the right place: Residence rules in the decennial census*. Washington, DC: National Academies Press.

U.S. Census Bureau. (2003). *Plans and rules for taking the census: Residence rules*. Retrieved March 4, 2008, from http://www.census.gov/population/www/censusdata/resid_rules.html#resrules

RESPONDENT

A respondent is the person who is sampled to provide the data that are being gathered in a survey. (In some social science disciplines, such as psychology, the person from whom data are gathered is called the "subject.") A respondent can report data about himself or herself or can serve as a proxy in reporting data about others (e.g., other members of the household). Even when the respondent is serving as a proxy, he or she is directly generating the data and contributing to their accuracy, or lack thereof.

Some surveys sample respondents directly, whereas other surveys begin by sampling larger units, such as households, and then choose a respondent within the unit from whom to gather data. In interviewer-administered surveying, such as what is done face-to-face or via the telephone, rapport first must be developed by the interviewer with the respondent in order to gain cooperation and then gather accurate data. In self-administered surveys, such as those conducted via mail and the Internet, there is no one representing the researcher's interests who is available to mediate the respondent's behavior, and cooperation typically is gained from the respondent via printed materials, such as a cover letter, which are sent to the respondent to read.

Gaining cooperation from sampled respondents has become progressively more difficult in the past two decades as lifestyles have become more hectic. The quality of the data that a survey gathers will be no better than the quality of the effort the respondent makes and her or his ability to provide it. A respondent's willingness and ability to provide accurate data will vary considerably across respondents and also from time to time for the same respondent.

There are many factors that influence whether a respondent will agree to participate in a survey and whether a respondent will provide complete and accurate data after agreeing to participate. It remains the responsibility of the researcher to choose the best survey methods, within the limitations of the researcher's finite budget for conducting the survey, that make it most likely that a sampled respondent will agree to cooperate when contacted, and once the respondent agrees, that he or she will provide the highest possible quality of data when answering the questionnaire.

Paul J. Lavrakas

See also Cover Letter; Proxy Respondent; Respondent–Interviewer Rapport; Respondent-Related Error; Within-Unit Selection

RESPONDENT BURDEN

The degree to which a survey respondent perceives participation in a survey research project as difficult, time consuming, or emotionally stressful is known as respondent burden. Interview length, cognitive complexity of the task, required respondent effort, frequency of being interviewed, and the stress of psychologically invasive questions all can contribute to respondent burden in survey research. The researcher must consider the effects of respondent burden prior to administering a survey instrument, as too great an average burden will yield lower-quality data and is thereby counterproductive.

Mechanisms that researchers may use to minimize respondent burden include pretesting, time testing, cognitive interviewing, and provision of an incentive. With pretesting, cognitive interviewing, and debriefing of respondents (and sometimes of interviewers as well) after the completion of the pretest, a researcher may glean insights into how to reduce any especially onerous aspects of the survey task. For example, it may be possible to break up a long series of questions that uses the same response format into two or three shorter series and space them throughout the questionnaire so that they do not appear and are not experienced as overly repetitive and, thus, as burdensome to complete. With sensitive and otherwise emotionally stressful questions, special transition statements that an interviewer relates to the respondent prior to these being asked may lessen the burden. Using incentives, especially contingent (i.e., performance-based) incentives, as well as noncontingent ones, often will raise

the quality of the data that are gathered when the survey task is burdensome, as the respondents will strive to reach the level of data quality sought by the researcher, either because it will qualify him or her for an incentive or because he or she has a heightened feeling of obligation to the researcher to provide good quality data, or both.

Reduction of respondent burden may result in decreased nonresponse both at the unit level and the item level. When incentives are offered, data quality also should increase, as fewer respondents will turn to satisficing strategies to get them through the survey task as easily as possible regardless of how well they are complying with the task.

Ingrid Graf

See also Cognitive Interviewing; Debriefing; Incentives; Pilot Test; Respondent Fatigue; Response Rates; Satisficing

Further Readings

Krosnick, J. A. (1991). Response strategies for coping with the cognitive demands of attitude measures in surveys. *Applied Cognitive Psychology, 5,* 213–236.

Tourangeau, R., Rips, L. J., & Rasinski, K. (2000). *The psychology of survey response.* Cambridge, UK: Cambridge University Press.

RESPONDENT DEBRIEFING

Respondent debriefing is a procedure that sometimes is carried out at the end of a survey's data collection phase. That is, when an individual participant has completed all aspects of the survey, debriefing occurs for that person. Debriefing is usually provided in the same format as the survey itself, that is, paper and pencil, online, or verbally via telephone. There are two major reasons that a researcher may want to debrief respondents: (1) The researcher may want to gather feedback from the respondent about the respondent's experience participating in the study or about more details concerning the topic of the survey, and (2) the researcher may have used some form of deception as part of the study and will use the debriefing to inform the respondent of this and try to undo any harm the deception may have caused the respondent.

Typically, the debriefing begins with a statement of gratitude for the participation of the respondent. This is followed by a brief restatement of the objective of the survey that would have initially been provided to the participant at the time that informed consent was being sought. Third, an overview of the tasks completed during the survey is given. Fourth, a very general statement of what will be done with all participants' responses is provided. Fifth, the participant is given the chance to request a report of the results of the survey when data analysis is complete, and contact information must be collected so that the results of the survey can be provided the participant.

In addition, appropriate referrals relative to the nature of the survey should be provided. For example, in research into depression among college students, some researchers provide appropriate referrals, including the campus counseling center and the local county mental health agency. Finally, the name of the principal investigator is provided, as well as his or her contact information, in the event that the respondent would need to communicate a concern or ask questions about the survey; contact information should include office phone number, work email address, and office address.

After data analysis has been completed, either a report of the survey results is mailed to survey participants or the results of the survey are published on a Web site to which survey participants are provided the Web address, perhaps via postcard or email.

In the event that the research involved the use of deception, the debriefing phase must also attempt to undo the effect of the deception by acknowledging that false information was given to some survey participants. Those who were deceived must be told that fact, regardless of how slight the harm may be in the eyes of the researcher.

Carla R. Scanlan

See also Debriefing; Deception; Informed Consent

Further Readings

Campanelli, P. C., Martin, E. A., & Rothgeb, J. M. (1991). The use of respondent and interviewer debriefing studies as a way to study response error in survey data. *The Statistician, 40*(3), 253–264.

Hughes, K. A. (2003, November). *Comparing pretesting methods: Cognitive interviews, respondent debriefing and behavioral coding.* Paper presented at the annual meeting of the Federal Committee in Statistical Methodology, Arlington, VA. Retrieved May 18, 2008, from http://0-www.census.gov.mill1.sjlibrary.org/srd/papers/pdf/rsm2004-02.pdf

Toy, D., Wright, L., & Olsen, L. (2001). A conceptual framework for analyzing deception and debriefing effects in market research. *Psychology and Marketing, 18*(7), 691–719.

RESPONDENT-DRIVEN SAMPLING (RDS)

Respondent-driven sampling (RDS) is a method for drawing probability samples of "hidden," or alternatively, hard-to-reach, populations. Populations such as these are difficult to sample using standard survey research methods for two reasons: First, they lack a sampling frame, that is, an exhaustive list of population members from which the sample can be drawn. Second, constructing a sampling frame is not feasible because one or more of the following are true: (a) The population is such a small part of the general population that locating them through a general population survey would be prohibitively costly; (b) because the population has social networks that are difficult for outsiders to penetrate, access to the population requires personal contacts; and (c) membership in the population is stigmatized, so gaining access requires establishing trust. Populations with these characteristics are important to many research areas, including arts and culture (e.g., jazz musicians and aging artists), public policy (e.g., immigrants and the homeless), and public health (e.g., drug users and commercial sex workers).

These populations have sometimes been studied using institutional or location-based sampling, but such studies are limited by the incomplete sampling frame; for example, in New York City only 22% of jazz musicians are musician union members and they are on average 10 years older, with nearly double the income, of nonmembers who are not on any public list.

This entry examines the sampling method that RDS employs, provides insights gained from the mathematical model on which it is based, and describes the types of analyses in which RDS can be used.

Sampling Method

RDS accesses members of hidden populations through their social networks, employing a variant of a snowball (i.e., chain-referral) sampling. As in all such samples, the study begins with a set of initial respondents who serve as "seeds." These then recruit their acquaintances, friends, or relatives who qualify for inclusion in the study to form the first "wave." The first wave respondents then recruit the second wave, who in turn recruit the third wave, and so forth. The sample expands in this manner, growing wave by wave, in the manner of a snowball increasing in size as it rolls down a hill.

RDS then combines snowball sampling—a nonprobability sampling technique—with a mathematical model that weights the sample to compensate for the fact that it was not obtained in a simple random way. This procedure includes controls for four biases that are inherent in any snowball sample:

1. The seeds cannot be recruited randomly, because if that were possible, the population would not qualify as hidden in the first place. Generally, the seeds are respondents to whom researchers have easy access, a group that may not be representative of the full target population. Consequently, the seeds introduce an initial bias.

2. Respondents recruit their acquaintances, friends, and family members, whom they tend to resemble in income, education, race/ethnicity, religion, and other factors. This homophily principle was recognized by Francis Galton more than a century ago. Its implication is that by recruiting those whom they know, respondents do not recruit randomly. Instead, recruitments are shaped by the social network connecting the target population. Consequently, successive waves of recruitment introduce further bias into the sample.

3. Respondents who are well connected tend to be oversampled, because more recruitment paths lead to them. Therefore, higher-status respondents—those who have larger social networks—are oversampled.

4. Population subgroups vary in how effectively they can recruit, so the sample reflects, disproportionately, the recruitment patterns of the most effective recruiters. For example, in AIDS prevention research, HIV positives generally recruit more effectively and also tend to recruit other positives, so positives tend to be oversampled.

Mathematical Model

RDS is based on a mathematical model of the network-recruitment process, which functions somewhat like a corrective lens, controlling for the distorting effects of network structure on the sampling process to produce an unbiased estimate of population characteristics. Space here does not permit presentation of the mathematical model on which RDS is based, but two insights upon which it is based provide a sense for how the model operates. First, modeling the recruitment process as a regular Markov chain reveals that if referral chains are sufficiently long, that is, if the chain-referral process consists of enough waves, the composition of the final sample becomes independent of the seeds from which it began. The point at which the sample composition becomes stable is termed the *equilibrium*. Therefore, an important design element in RDS involves measures for increasing the length of referral chains. Means for creating long chains include that respondents be recruited by their peers rather than by researchers, providing rewards for peer recruiters, and setting recruitment quotas so a few cannot do all the recruiting. Through these means, a major concern is resolved regarding bias in chain-referral samples, that is, producing a population estimate that is independent of the seeds (initial subjects) with which the sampling began.

Second, gathering information about the network structures through which the sampling process expands provides the means for controlling for the biasing effects of those structures. This procedure entails a weighing process that quantifies the biasing effects of network structure, to compensate for oversampling groups with higher levels of homophily (i.e., network segmentation), groups having larger social networks, and those favored by the recruitment patterns of the most effective recruiting groups. These three potential sources of bias can operate in the same or opposite directions, and the model calculates the balance among them.

If the assumptions upon which RDS is based are satisfied, the sample is asymptotically unbiased, which means that bias is on the order of 1/(sample size), so bias is trivial in samples of meaningful size. The model is based on five assumptions. The first three specify the conditions under which RDS is an appropriate sampling method. First, respondents must know one another as members of the target population. Peer recruitment is a feasible sampling strategy only if this condition is satisfied. Consequently, RDS would not be suitable for sampling tax cheats, who can be friends and not know they share membership in that hidden population. On the other hand, it is suitable for sampling populations linked by a "contact pattern," such as musicians who perform together or drug users who purchase drugs together. Second, ties must be dense enough to sustain the chain-referral process. For populations linked by a contact pattern, this is rarely problematic, but it may be problematic for other groups. Third, sampling is assumed to occur with replacement, so recruitments do not deplete the set of respondents available for future recruitment. Consequently, the sampling fraction should be small enough for a sampling-with-replacement model to be appropriate.

The fourth assumption states that respondents can accurately report the number of relatives, friends, and acquaintances who are members of the target population. Studies of the reliability of network indicators suggest that this is one of the more reliable indicators; furthermore, the RDS population estimator depends not on absolute but on relative degree, so variations in name generators that inflate or deflate the reports in a linear manner have no effect on the estimates.

Finally, the fifth assumption specifies that respondents recruit as though they are choosing randomly from their networks. This is based on the expectation that respondents would lack an incentive or ability to coordinate to selectively recruit any particular group, and support for this expectation has been found. The plausibility of this assumption is determined, in part, by appropriate research design. For example, if a research site were located in a high-crime neighborhood, recruiting residents of the neighborhood might be easy, but recruiting peers from more comfortable neighborhoods might prove difficult, so sampling would be nonrandom because it excluded the latter group. However, if research identifies neutral turf in which all potential respondents feel safe, the random recruitment assumption is made more plausible. Similarly, if incentives are offered that are salient to respondents from all income groups (e.g., a choice between receiving a monetary reward and making a contribution to a charity of the respondent's choice), the random recruitment assumption is made more plausible.

Additional Analyses

RDS emerged as a member of a relatively new class of probability sampling methods termed *adaptive* or *link-tracing* designs, which show that network-based sampling methods can be probability sampling methods. RDS continues to evolve. Though originally limited to univariate analysis of nominal variables, it has

been extended to permit analysis of continuous variables and multivariate analysis. The significance of these methods is that they expand the range of populations from which statistically valid samples can be drawn, including populations of great importance to public policy and public health.

Douglas D. Heckathorn

See also Adaptive Sampling; Network Sampling; Nonprobability Sampling; Probability Sample; Sampling Frame; Snowball Sampling

Further Readings

Heckathorn, D. D. (1997). Respondent-driven sampling: A new approach to the study of hidden populations. *Social Problems, 44*(2), 174–199.

Heckathorn, D. D. (2007). Extensions of respondent-driven sampling: Analyzing continuous variables and controlling for differential recruitment. *Sociological Methodology, 37*, 151–207.

Salganik, M. J., & Heckathorn, D. D. (2004). Sampling and estimation in hidden populations using respondent-driven sampling. *Sociological Methodology, 35*, 193–238.

Thompson, S. K., & Frank, O. (2000). Model-based estimation with linktracing sampling designs. *Survey Methodology, 26*(1), 87–98.

Volz, E., & Heckathorn, D. D. (2008). Probability-based estimation theory for respondent-driven sampling. *Journal of Official Statistics, 24*(1), 79–97.

RESPONDENT FATIGUE

Respondent fatigue is a well-documented phenomenon that occurs when survey participants become tired of the survey task and the quality of the data they provide begins to deteriorate. It occurs when survey participants' attention and motivation drop toward later sections of a questionnaire. Tired or bored respondents may more often answer "don't know," engage in "straight-line" responding (i.e., choosing answers down the same column on a page), give more perfunctory answers, or give up answering the questionnaire altogether. Thus, the causes for, and consequences of, respondent fatigue, and possible ways of measuring and controlling for it, should be taken into account when deciding on the length of the questionnaire, question ordering, survey design, and interviewer training.

Participating in a survey requires time and effort; respondents often need to reflect on their behaviors, retrieve or construct opinions on issues, and evaluate candidates, policies, or products. As the time to complete the survey grows longer, the motivation and ability needed by respondents to accurately answer the questions may decline. The level of processing required to answer the questions may also induce fatigue, such that as the questions are more detailed, require recalling past events, comparing or choosing between many different options, motivation may wear thin. Another factor that can generate fatigue is the specific topic of the survey: how interesting or important it is to participants and the type of interaction they have with the interviewer about it. Generally speaking, as (a) the survey is more time consuming, (b) the questions are boring and complicated, (c) more open-ended questions are asked, (d) the interviewer does not motivate adequate answers, and (e) the issue of the survey is mundane or repetitive, respondents' motivation may decrease and fatigue effects may arise.

Fatigue effects may have several consequences for the later items of a questionnaire. Respondents in self-administered surveys may fail to read adequately the lists of response alternatives, skip questions more frequently, or be more likely to engage in satisficing by choosing answers such as "not applicable" or "don't know." Fatigue may also cause more stereotypical answers, known as straight-line (or response set) responding; these occur when a series of consecutive questions share the same answer choices that appear in the same order, such that an unmotivated person may answer with the same response on all items in the series.

There are several ways in which researchers try to measure and assess fatigue effects. First, the questionnaire may be split and the order of the questions may be randomized or counterbalanced in the different versions. The responses to items presented late on one version can be then compared to responses to the same items when presented earlier, in terms of percentage of nonresponses, don't knows, straight-line responding, and correlations with other variables. Another option to evaluate whether fatigue effects took place is by measuring the consistency of responses to repeated questions appearing early and late in the questionnaire, that is, including an alternative wording for some of the questions and measuring their reliability with the questions appearing earlier.

Perhaps the simplest and best way of dealing with fatigue effects is to avoid them. Although some research suggests that later items in a lengthy questionnaire may be systematically more vulnerable to poor response rates and to inadequate answers, it seems the fatigue effect may be avoided as long as respondent's motivation is maintained. Thus, a researcher should try to balance between collecting accurate and sufficient information and conducting a well-structured and not-too-long questionnaire.

Pazit Ben-Nun

See also Don't Knows (DKs); Nonresponse Bias; Nonsampling Error; Respondent Burden; Respondent-Related Error; Response Order Effects; Satisficing

Further Readings

Bradburn, N. M., & Mason, W. M. (1964). The·effect of question order on responses. *Journal of Marketing Research, 1,* 57–64.

Herzog, A. R., & Bachman, J. G. (1981). Effects of questionnaire length on response quality. *Public Opinion Quarterly, 45,* 549–559.

RESPONDENT–INTERVIEWER RAPPORT

Respondents and interviewers interact during the conduct of surveys, and this interaction, no matter how brief, is the basis for a social relationship between the two. Often this relationship begins when the interviewer calls or visits the respondent in an attempt to initiate and complete an interview. Other times, the respondent may call the interviewer in order to complete an interview. During the social interaction of conducting an interview, the respondent and interviewer will typically develop a rapport.

The establishment of rapport between the respondent and the interviewer, or lack thereof, is a key element in the interviewer gaining the respondent's cooperation to complete an interview. If a good rapport is not established, the likelihood of the interviewer completing an interview decreases. Further, good rapport will make the respondent comfortable with answering questions that could be considered personal or embarrassing. It is important for interviewers to convey a neutral, nonjudgmental attitude toward respondents regardless of the survey topic or the content of the respondents' answers in order to make the respondent as comfortable as possible. A respondent who is comfortable is more likely to provide accurate responses and take the survey request seriously.

The rapport between respondents and interviewers plays a large role in the interview process. Interviewers are largely initially responsible for developing and maintaining rapport with respondents. The respondent has to feel comfortable with the survey, and this can be influenced by how key information about what the survey requires is delivered by the interviewer. The respondent must also believe that the survey request is legitimate and the data they provide will be protected. Interviewers must explain the reason for the survey, set the tone for the interview, convey the importance of the survey, and set up the expectations for how the interview will proceed from the start of the interview. Further, a respondent's decision to participate, as well as his or her attitude about participating (e.g., the seriousness of the survey request) is impacted by his or her feelings about the interviewer and the rapport that has been established.

Rapport is usually established during the first few seconds of a call or visit; however, the rapport should continue to build throughout the interaction. Interviewers should be trained in ways to quickly establish a rapport with the respondents. Gaining cooperation to complete an interview through establishing rapport is the target outcome of each respondent–interviewer interaction, and this target outcome is the same for both in-person and telephone interviews. In both interview modes, it is important that interviewers convey a friendly, professional tone. Interviewers must also be sincere, confident, knowledgeable, and well prepared for their interactions with respondents. All of these interviewer characteristics taken together will impact the kind of rapport established with the respondent. However, the communication channels through which interviewers have to convey these key characteristics differ based on interview mode. For in-person interviews, respondents have all communication channels with which to establish rapport with the interviewer, including verbal and nonverbal. Conversely, for telephone interviews, the respondent has only verbal communication channels (which involves two things: the interviewers' voice characteristics and the words they say) on which to judge the interviewer. Because of these differences in communication channels, training

for in-person and field interviewers differs somewhat on how to convey the key interviewing characteristics.

Beyond the social rapport–building skills of interviewers, there are also ways to write a questionnaire to increase the likelihood that the rapport established during the gaining cooperation phase will continue throughout the survey administration. For example, asking interesting questions early on in the interview can increase the respondents' interest in the survey. Asking questions that are relatively simple to answer can increase the respondents' comfort with their role in the task and can influence their willingness to continue with the interview. Conversely, placing difficult-to-answer or sensitive questions too early in the interview can discourage respondents from continuing the interview. Although these questionnaire design techniques can prove effective in building or strengthening respondent–interviewer rapport, they are not utilized by all researchers.

Although in-person interviewers and telephone interviewers must use different channels of communication with respondents, many of the same techniques are taught to both types of interviewers. For example, trainers often use role playing, group or paired practice, and quizzes as ways to educate interviewers on building rapport.

No one interviewing style has been identified as being the best in establishing rapport and building relationships with respondents. While interviewers are trained on basic techniques that have been shown to have success in establishing rapport with the respondent and setting up the expectations for the interview, interviewers are often instructed to use these techniques in a way that is comfortable for them. The most important factors in establishing and maintaining a relationship with respondents are clearly communicating the role expectations for the relationship and setting up standards for the conduct of the interview early on in the interaction.

Lisa Carley-Baxter

See also Computer-Assisted Personal Interviewing (CAPI); Computer-Assisted Telephone Interviewing (CATI); Interviewer; Respondent

Further Readings

Fowler, F. J., Jr., & Mangione, T. W. (1990). *Standardized survey interviewing: Minimizing interviewer-related error.* Newbury Park, CA: Sage.

RESPONDENT REFUSAL

The respondent refusal disposition is used in telephone, in-person, mail, and Internet surveys to categorize a case in which contact has been made with the designated respondent, but he or she has refused a request by an interviewer to complete an interview (telephone or in-person survey) or a request to complete and return a questionnaire (mail or Internet survey). A case can be considered a respondent refusal only if the designated respondent has been selected and it is clear that he or she has stated he or she will not complete the interview or questionnaire. Respondent refusals are considered eligible cases in calculating response and cooperation rates.

In a telephone survey, a case is coded with the respondent refusal disposition when an interviewer dials a telephone number, reaches a person, begins his or her introductory script, and selects the designated respondent, and the respondent declines to complete the interview. In calls ending in a respondent refusal, the designated respondent may provide an explanation for the refusal such as, "I don't do surveys," "I don't have time," "I'm not interested," or "Please take me off your list." In other instances, the respondent contacted may simply hang up.

Respondent refusals in an in-person survey occur when an interviewer contacts a household, a household member answers the door, the interviewer begins his or her introductory script, and selects the designated respondent, and the designated respondent declines to complete the interview. Common explanations in in-person surveys for household refusals parallel those for telephone surveys.

Cases in a mail or Internet survey of specifically named persons are coded with the respondent refusal disposition when contact has been made with the sampled person and he or she declines to complete and return the questionnaire. Because little may be known in a mail survey about who in the household generated the refusal, it can be difficult to determine whether a household refusal or respondent refusal disposition is most appropriate. Different invitation methods for Internet surveys (such as contacting sampled respondents at their email addresses) make respondent refusals the most common type of refusal in an Internet survey.

Respondent refusals usually are considered a final disposition. Because refusal rates for all types of surveys have increased significantly in the past decade, many survey organizations review cases ending in respondent refusals and select cases in which the refusal is not extremely strong in nature to be contacted again in order to try to convert the case's disposition to a completed interview.

Matthew Courser

See also Final Dispositions; Household Refusal; Refusal Conversion; Refusal Report Form (RRF); Response Rates; Temporary Dispositions

Further Readings

American Association for Public Opinion Research. (2006). *Standard definitions: Final dispositions of case codes and outcome rates for surveys* (4th ed.). Lenexa, KS: Author.

Lavrakas, P. J. (1993). *Telephone survey methods: Sampling, selection, and supervision* (2nd ed.). Newbury Park, CA: Sage.

Weisberg, H. (2005). *The total survey error approach: A guide to the new science of survey research.* Chicago: University of Chicago Press.

RESPONDENT-RELATED ERROR

Respondent-related error refers to error in a survey measure that is directly or indirectly attributable to the behaviors or characteristics of respondents; it is distinguished from error resulting from other survey components, such as questionnaires, interviewers, or modes of administration. However, respondents may interact with these other components of survey design in producing errors. It is useful to dichotomize respondent-related errors into those that arise from nonobservation or nonresponse (e.g., during efforts to obtain interviews) and those that result from observation or measurement (e.g., during the administration of the survey).

Errors in survey measures have two components: bias and variable errors. Bias results when responses provided in the survey differ from their true values, which are typically unknown and unmeasured, in a systematic way across repeated measurements. For example, in contrast to the responses they enter onto self-administered questionnaires, respondents are more likely to underreport abortions they have had when data are collected by an interviewer. Variable errors result from differences across the source of the error.

For example, respondents sometimes provide different answers to interviewers who deviate from the rules of standardized interviewing. Survey methodologists also make a distinction between error associated with objective versus subjective questions. For objective questions about events and behaviors, error is expressed as the difference between the respondent's answer and what might have been observed if observation had been possible. For subjective questions about attitudes and opinions, error is conceptualized as sources of variation in the answers other than the concept the researcher is trying to measure.

Respondents and Nonresponse Error

Respondents may contribute to nonresponse bias when they refuse to participate in the study or cannot be located or contacted. Nonresponse bias varies as a function of the survey's response rate and the degree to which nonresponders differ from participants. Obtaining high response rates is generally considered an important protection from nonresponse bias. Nonetheless, nonresponse bias may be large, even with a high response rate, if those interviewed differ substantially from those who are sampled but are never contacted or those who refuse; conversely, bias may be small, even with a low response rate, if respondents are similar to noncontacts and refusers on the characteristics of interest. In longitudinal studies, nonresponse error also varies if respondents who drop out of the study systematically differ from respondents who are retained in the panel (i.e., so-called differential attrition).

Attempts to estimate the impact of different levels of response on survey estimates and nonresponse error suggest that improvements in response rates sometimes have a negligible impact on both estimates and error, but the results are unpredictable. At present there is little empirical or theoretical guidance to predict how much nonresponse or under what circumstances nonresponse will produce nonresponse error, but nonresponse can have a big impact on survey error, especially for some subgroups.

Even after they agree to participate in a survey, respondents may fail to provide data within the interview; they may do this intentionally, by refusing to answer questions or saying "don't know," or unintentionally, by skipping questions on self-administered questionnaires. Item nonresponse occurs more often for some types of questions than others. For example,

refusals are more common for questions about income and for questions that ask for sensitive or threatening information. Respondents may also provide responses that are incomplete, for instance, by not providing enough information to an open-ended question to allow their answers to be classified reliably.

Respondents and Measurement Error

Respondents contribute to measurement error in several ways, including the characteristics they bring to the interview, such as their cognitive skills or motivation; their behavior within the interview; and their interaction with the survey instrument and with interviewers. Certain demographic characteristics may be associated with errors. For example, some research indicates that older and male respondents may be more likely to misreport than younger and female respondents, respectively. Respondents' characteristics may interact with interviewers' characteristics and the topic of the survey to produce response effects. An oft-cited finding is that respondents report differently to interviewers of the same race or gender when the topic concerns attitudes about race or gender than they do to interviewers of a different race or gender. A respondent's level of motivation may be particularly important for questions about events and behaviors that require searching memory. Retrospective questions require respondents to remember information that may be difficult to retrieve or emotionally charged. Fatigue and boredom may also affect the data quality of survey reports and thereby lead the respondent to providing merely an "easy" answer (i.e., satisficing).

Roger Tourangeau and his colleagues have described the question–answer process using a model to describe the stages respondents go through when answering a survey question. The first stage, *encoding*, occurs before the survey when respondents store information about an event or experience into memory. The effectiveness of the initial encoding can have great bearing on the accuracy of a respondent's survey report. Errors due to encoding failures occur when respondents are asked to report about information they may not have encoded at all or only partially encoded, such as information about their children's immunizations, or when proxy respondents are used to report about others.

In the second stage of the response process, *comprehension*, respondents either hear or read the question and attempt to understand its words and phrases, general meaning, and the intent of the question writer. Respondent-related errors occur frequently at this stage. Experiments as well as research from cognitive interviewing demonstrate that the meaning of concepts within a question is frequently understood in unintended ways. For instance, context effects occur when respondents use information provided by previous questions or answers in interpreting meaning and formulating a response for the current question. Other errors at the comprehension stage can result if (a) questions contain vague terms or phrases that are too technical, (b) respondents lack an opinion on the topic, or (c) the questions are not understood as the researchers intended because the questions were poorly translated or because the respondent has vision or hearing problems. Respondents in interviewer-administered surveys may attempt to elicit the interviewer's help in resolving a comprehension problem. Traditionally, interviewers are trained to treat requests for clarification with the probe "whatever it means to you," which may not solve the comprehension problem. If, however, the interviewer responds to the respondent's request in a way that departs from the rules of standardized interviewing, the interviewer–respondent interaction may be another source of error.

Retrieval, the third stage in the question–answer process, involves accessing information from an inactive state in long-term memory and bringing it into working memory, a state of activation in which the information can be used. For objective questions that ask about events and behaviors, retrieval may involve recalling the number of times the respondent engaged in a particular action during a given time frame. For subjective questions, retrieval may involve recalling previously formulated opinions, attitudes, or feelings. For some types of questions, retrieval may also include consultation with external records, such as for reporting income, or consultation with others, such as for proxy reports.

Retrieval can influence response accuracy. For example, respondents engage in forward telescoping when they remember events or behaviors as having happened earlier than they actually took place; in backward telescoping, events are remembered as occurring later than they did. Errors due to omission also occur frequently, even for highly salient events such as hospitalizations. Events are best remembered when they are salient (i.e., unusual, costly, or enduring), infrequent, rare, and dissimilar from other events.

Several factors appear to be influential in increasing the effort expended by respondents during retrieval and in improving the accessibility of information stored in memory. Evidence suggests that the more time respondents are given to respond, the better their responses will be. This is probably attributable to the fact that recalling and counting events is an effortful process that can be discouraged both by the pace of the interview and by respondents themselves, who may want to finish quickly. Other methods that can increase respondent effort and accuracy are soliciting formal respondent commitment, limiting time frames to periods a respondent can reasonably access from memory, giving respondents multiple opportunities to answer a question (like in a "second guess"), and using longer questions that provide more time for respondents to process and retrieve answers. As an example, longer questions have been associated with better reporting for health events and higher reports of threatening behaviors like drinking and sexual activity.

In the fourth stage of the response process, *judgment* and *mapping*, respondents evaluate the information retrieved from memory and formulate a candidate response vis-à-vis the format of the survey question. Research suggests that the format of a question, such as whether it is open-ended or closed-ended, can influence respondent-related errors. Most survey questions are closed-ended and offer a set of predetermined response categories. A question on satisfaction might include the categories, "extremely satisfied/dissatisfied," "satisfied/dissatisfied," and "somewhat satisfied/dissatisfied." In assessing behavioral frequencies, however, closed-ended questions that offer response categories are associated with several undesirable outcomes. Categories may indicate to respondents the range of "acceptable" responses. The wording of response categories can decrease effort by indicating that an exact answer is not sought. The number and wording of verbal categories may decrease accessibility of memories by placing too great a load on cognitive processing, especially in a telephone survey where respondents cannot read and reread answer categories to ensure more thorough processing.

Many other kinds of response effects occur during retrieval, and these may interact with the mode of administration. For example, primacy effects, the tendency to select options at the beginning of a set of categories, are found in face-to-face interviews where questions with several options are often presented visually on show cards. In contrast, recency effects, the tendency to select options at the end of the scale, occur in telephone interviews in which questions are presented orally.

In the last stage of the response process, respondents report their answer. Respondents demonstrate many characteristic ways of "reporting" that are biasing. Some of the most common are providing answers that are socially desirable, satisficing, acquiescing, and intentionally misreporting in order to protect privacy (e.g., not reporting income for fear the results will be shared with the Internal Revenue Service). Social desirability bias refers to error resulting from respondents' tendencies to overreport attitudes or behaviors deemed socially desirable, such as voting, and underreport those judged undesirable, such as illegal drug use. Respondents may misreport for several reasons, possibly because they are used to doing so, or in order to present themselves positively to an interviewer or the researcher. Misreporting of answers has been documented for many diverse topics, including abortion, drug and alcohol use, sexual behaviors, voting and attention to politics, as well as attitudes about sensitive issues such as race. Many studies have explored the effect of data collection mode on reporting threatening questions. In comparison to reporting in self-administered interviews, respondents in interviewer-administered interviews are more likely to provide lower reports of these behaviors. Social desirability bias can be reduced and reporting accuracy can be enhanced by increasing respondents' trust in the legitimacy of the organization sponsoring the survey, by raising respondents' perceptions of the importance of the answers they are providing, and by heightening respondents' sense of privacy and confidentiality. For example, in face-to-face surveys, interviewers can provide respondents with a computer into which they can enter their responses directly, as is done with computerized self-administered questionnaires, rather than having respondents report sensitive or threatening information directly to the interviewer.

Acquiescing is the tendency of respondents to agree to or passively accept a proposition offered by the question. Satisficing is similar but somewhat broader. Satisficing occurs when respondents engage in the minimum amount of processing necessary to respond to a question, but without wholly investing in providing the most accurate answer possible. It is manifested when respondents choose an option such as "don't know" or when respondents repeatedly select the same or similar scale points in a battery of questions or in a scale. Both acquiescing and satisficing can reflect a lack of respondent motivation or ability or the difficulty of the survey task.

Methods for Studying Respondent-Related Error

What survey researchers know about respondent-related error comes from several paradigms for studying response errors. In record-check studies, survey reports are compared to external records (such as court records in a study of child support) to assess how accurately respondents report. Split-half experiments are conducted during interviews to test different wordings of questions and response categories. Qualitative methods such as focus groups, in-depth interviews, and cognitive interviews are conducted to determine how well respondents' understanding of survey concepts matches that of the question writers. Cognitive interviews are also used to understand retrieval and judgment processes. For interviewer-administered surveys, the interaction between the respondent and interviewer is recorded and analyzed. The methods for studying response errors are costly and complex and sometimes do not suggest a clear method for reducing error.

Jennifer Dykema, Steven Blixt,
and John Stevenson

See also Acquiescence Response Bias; Closed-Ended Questions; Cognitive Interviewing; Comprehension; Computerized Self-Administered Questionnaires (CSAQ); Context Effect; Differential Attrition; Encoding; Measurement Error; Nonresponse Error; Open-Ended Question; Primacy Effect; Proxy Respondent; Recency Effect; Record Check; Respondent Burden; Respondent Fatigue; Response Bias; Retrieval; Satisficing; Social Desirability; Split-Half; Telescoping

Further Readings

Biemer, P. P., Groves, R. M., Lyberg, L. E., Mathiowetz, N. A., & Sudman, S. (1991). *Measurement errors in surveys.* New York: Wiley.

Biemer, P. P., & Lyberg, L. (2003). *Introduction to survey quality.* Hoboken, NJ: Wiley.

Groves, R. M., Fowler, F. J., Jr., Couper, M. P., Lepkowski, J. M., Singer, E., & Tourangeau, R. (2004). *Survey methodology.* Hoboken, NJ: Wiley.

Tourangeau, R., Rips, L. J., & Rasinski, K. (2000). *The psychology of survey response.* New York: Cambridge University Press.

RESPONSE

In survey research, a response generally refers to the answer a respondent provides when asked a question. However, a response to a survey can also be considered to occur when a sampled respondent decides whether or not to participate in the survey. Both types of responses may affect data quality; thus, a well-trained researcher will pay close attention to each.

Response to the Request to Participate

At the time a person is notified of having been sampled to participate in a survey, he or she may decide to participate or not. This response, whether or not to participate, affects the response rate of the survey, which essentially is the proportion of eligible respondents who agree to participate. Response rates may vary as the result of a number of factors, including the population being studied, the procedures used for sampling, the mode of the survey (e.g., telephone, in person, mail, or Web), questionnaire length, field period length, number of contact attempts, the topic of the survey, and whether procedures such as advance letters, refusal conversions, and incentives are used.

Although no specific response rates are generally required for conducting a survey, researchers traditionally strive for high response rates. Low response rates may lead to nonresponse bias when certain groups of respondents are more likely to participate than others, which creates the phenomenon of under- or overrepresentation of the certain attributes that the survey is striving to measure. As such, it is in a researcher's interest to encourage an affirmative response to the request to participate from as many respondents as possible that are sampled.

Response to Survey Questions

When someone is asked a survey question, the effort that goes into determining and then providing an answer (the response) can vary considerably from respondent to respondent. Thus, respondent-related error is of considerable consequence to survey researchers. Such error may be introduced into survey responses to individual survey questions in a number of ways, such as when respondents answer survey questions based on what the survey designers expect.

This may occur because respondents want to please researchers or because of leading questions. Response error may also be introduced if respondents misinterpret or do not understand a question. The format of survey questions (e.g., whether they are open- or closed-ended, the number and specific response choices provided) influences respondents' comprehension of a survey question. Response error can be minimized if researchers consciously implement strategies while designing the instrument, such as avoiding leading questions and wording questions precisely. The order of questions in surveys can also contribute to response error, although there are also some general guidelines for minimizing error from this source (e.g., easy questions should be placed before hard ones).

Respondents themselves can also be a source of response error because respondents may not be willing or able to answer the questions with correct information. Thus, response error may be introduced if respondents satisfice or engage in socially desirable responding. These issues can also be somewhat alleviated through optimal questionnaire design.

Cary Stacy Smith and Li-Ching Hung

See also Questionnaire Design; Question Order Effects; Respondent; Respondent-Related Error; Response Rates; Satisficing; Social Desirability

Further Readings

de Leeuw, E. D. (1992). *Data quality in mail, telephone, and face to face surveys.* Amsterdam: TT Publications.

Fink, A. (2002). *The survey handbook* (2nd ed.). Thousand Oaks, CA: Sage.

RESPONSE ALTERNATIVES

Response alternatives are the choices that are provided to respondents in a survey when they are asked a question. Response alternatives are generally associated with closed-ended items, although open-ended items may provide a limited number of such choices.

Response alternatives can take a number of different forms, related to the type of question presented. In a Likert-type item, in which respondents are asked the extent to which they agree or disagree with a statement, the response alternatives might be *strongly approve, approve, neither approve nor disapprove,*

disapprove, and *strongly disapprove*. For a rating scale—for example, the rating of the job the president is doing—the response alternatives might be *excellent, good, fair, poor*, and *very poor*. Another example of a rating scale would be a "feeling thermometer" in which respondents would be asked to rate some individual or object on a scale from $0°$ to $100°$, in which the degrees would represent the response categories.

Types of response alternatives may vary depending on the method used for data collection. In face-to-face and self-administered surveys, respondents can be presented with visual materials displaying the response alternatives. For example, in a face-to-face survey, a respondent can be presented a show card describing the various alternatives, and a similar description of the response options can be provided in a mail or other self-administered survey and for surveys conducted via the Internet. As a result, a larger number of response alternatives can be presented in these modes of data collection than in telephone surveys. The number of response alternatives that an average respondent can remember over the telephone is generally limited to five. If a larger number of response alternatives is desired, the question is typically divided into a root item, which is then "unfolded" into this larger number of choices. For example, if researchers were interested in a person's ideology along a liberal–conservative scale, they might first ask, *In politics, do you generally consider yourself liberal, moderate, or conservative?* Those who said "liberal" would then be asked, *Would you say you are extremely liberal or somewhat liberal?* and, similarly, those who said "conservative" would be asked, *Would you say you are extremely conservative or somewhat conservative?* Respondents who answered "moderate" would be asked, *Do you lean toward the liberal side or lean toward the conservative side?* The result would be seven response alternatives: (1) extremely liberal, (2) somewhat liberal, (3) leans toward liberal, (4) moderate—leans toward neither, (5) leans toward conservative, (6) somewhat conservative, and (7) extremely conservative.

Another consideration in presenting response alternatives is whether to provide choices such as "don't know" and "refused" as explicit options to respondents. Typically such choices are not read to respondents in face-to-face or telephone interviews and are not included as options in self-administered or Internet surveys. There are situations, however, in which "don't know" or "no opinion" responses are important to the researcher; in such cases an explicit "no opinion"

response would be provided. For example, in the question, *Do you think state spending on roads and highways should be increased, kept about the same as it is now, decreased, or don't you have an opinion on this issue?* the response alternative *or don't you have an opinion on this issue* is an explicit "don't know" or "no opinion" option. When such options are provided as part of the question, the percentage of respondents who choose this alternative is higher than when it is not present, and respondents have to volunteer that they "don't know."

The fact that a larger percentage of respondents will choose a "don't know" response when offered explicitly applies more generally to all types of responses. For example, if survey respondents are presented with the question, *Do you think that federal government spending on national defense should be increased or decreased?* some percentage will volunteer that they believe it should be kept about the same as it is now. If the same group of respondents were asked the question, *Do you think federal government spending on national defense should be increased, decreased, or kept about the same as it is now?* a much higher percentage would select the "same as it is now" response alternative. Similarly, for items in which respondents are presented with some choices (generally the most likely options) but not an exhaustive list, researchers will often leave an "other" option. An example of such an "other" response is provide by the question, *Which television network do you watch most frequently, ABC, CBS, Fox, NBC, or some other network?* Although some respondents will provide other responses such as UPN or the CW, the percentage of such responses will typically be smaller than if these other networks had been mentioned specifically in the question.

An additional aspect of response alternatives is balance. In the design of most questions, researchers strive to provide balance in the response alternatives. If presenting a forced choice item, the strength of the arguments on one side of a question should be similar to the strength of the arguments on the other. Similarly, in asking an agree–disagree item, an interviewer would ask, *Do you agree or disagree that . . .*; asking only *Do you agree that . . .* would lead more respondents to choose this option. In asking about approval or disapproval of some individual or proposal, a question that asks, *Do you completely approve, approve a great deal, approve somewhat, or disapprove of . . .* is not balanced. Asking *Do you approve a great deal, approve somewhat, disapprove somewhat, or disapprove a great deal of . . .* provides a more balanced item.

Response alternatives are an important consideration in question design. The number of choices presented, how they are balanced, whether there is an explicit middle alternative, and an explicit "no opinion" option can all influence the results obtained by a survey question.

Robert W. Oldendick

See also Balanced Question; Closed-Ended Question; Feeling Thermometer; Forced Choice; Likert Scale; Open-Ended Question; Ranking; Rating; Response Order Effects; Show Card; Unfolding Question

Further Readings

Converse, J., & Presser, S. (1986). *Survey questions: Handcrafting the standardized questionnaire.* Beverly Hills, CA: Sage.

Schuman, H., & Presser, S. (1996). *Questions and answers in attitude surveys.* Thousand Oaks, CA: Sage.

Selltiz, C., Jahoda, M., Deutsch, M., & Cook, S. (1959). *Research methods in social relations.* New York: Holt, Rinehart & Winston.

RESPONSE BIAS

Response bias is a general term that refers to conditions or factors that take place during the process of responding to surveys, affecting the way responses are provided. Such circumstances lead to a nonrandom deviation of the answers from their true value. Because this deviation takes on average the same direction among respondents, it creates a systematic error of the measure, or bias. The effect is analogous to that of collecting height data with a ruler that consistently adds (or subtracts) an inch to the observed units. The final outcome is an overestimation (or underestimation) of the true population parameter. Unequivocally identifying whether a survey result is affected by response bias is not as straightforward as researchers would wish. Fortunately, research shows some conditions under which different forms of response bias can be found, and this information can be used to avoid introducing such biasing elements.

The concept of response bias is sometimes used incorrectly as a synonym of *nonresponse bias*. This use of the term may lead to misunderstanding. Nonresponse bias is related to the decision to participate in a study and the differences between those who decide to cooperate and those from whom data are not gathered. Response bias, on the other hand, takes place once a respondent has agreed to answer, and it may theoretically occur across the whole sample as well as to specific subgroups of the population.

Forms of Response Biases

Rather than being a direct function of respondents' own features per se, it is often the instrument (questionnaire item) characteristics that are responsible for this deviation, in the sense that there is something in the question or context that affects the way respondents undergo the cognitive process of responding, thereby distorting the true answer in some manner. This may occur consciously or not, and the resulting overreporting or underreporting may have different causes. A nonexhaustive list of different response biases is presented here to exemplify the kind of problems the researcher may encounter when conducting a survey.

1. Some effects are related to the length and type of the task. Aspects such as burdensomeness of the task may produce boredom or fatigue in the respondent, affecting the thoughtfulness of their answers.

2. The interaction between interviewer, respondent, and interviewing approach may also affect the way responses are produced. The most typical example of this is social desirability bias, but other effects might involve the interviewer's pace of speech, race, and gender. For example, fast-speaking interviewers may communicate to respondents that they are expected to give quick, off-the-top-of-their-heads answers. They may also affect how questions are understood.

3. The order of the questions and the order of response options may influence the likelihood of respondents to select a particular answer, eliciting context effects. The recency effect is an illustration of this type of bias; here, respondents are more likely to choose the last response options presented to them when the survey is conducted orally.

4. The wording of the question can tip the scale in one or another direction. Push polls are one example where the wording is intentionally manipulated with the intention to obtain a particular result, but unexpected or unintended wording effects are also possible.

5. Response styles are sometimes considered a type of response bias. When response options are presented, the way respondents use them may have a biasing effect. Some respondents seem to prefer a particular section of the scale as compared to others, irrespective of what their real attitude or behavior is.

6. Other forms of bias may appear as a result of lack of specificity in the definition of the task. Researchers need to be aware that conveying the need for high response accuracy is not a given. Discourse norms in everyday life dictate that precise estimates of certain quantities may be inadequate, unnecessary, or even undesirable. Spending several seconds trying to recall whether an activity lasted 13 or 14 days is usually not well received by the audience of a daily life conversation, where rough estimations are common. A similar phenomenon, the *rounding effect*, has been observed in surveys; researchers have identified that certain values (0, 25, 50, 75, and 100) are more likely to be chosen when using scales from 0 to 100.

7. People not only distort their answers because they want to create a positive impression on their audience, they may also edit (fake) their responses because they fear the consequences that the true answer might have and therefore do not wish to reveal the right information. Respondents, for instance, may lie about their legal status if they fear that confidentiality might be breached.

In essence, for any of the aforementioned examples, the reported information is not data the researcher is seeking. The distortion may set out at any stage of the cognitive processing: the comprehension of the question, the retrieval of the information, the judgment or the editing of the question. Question order effects, for example, can influence the way respondents understand the questions, while long reference periods can increase the likelihood of finding telescoping effects due to memory problems.

As with many other survey aspects, researchers can find that different cultures exhibit different patterns of response biases, which confound these with the actual substantive differences. Gender of interviewer bias, for example, may have a stronger presence in countries where the interaction of women with men outside their immediate family is rare or simply inappropriate.

Because of the widespread range of factors that can lead to response bias, all data collection methods are potentially at risk of being affected by response bias. Furthermore, different data collection modes may be more vulnerable to certain effects. Literature suggests, for instance, that self-administered modes reduce the impact of social desirability.

Similarly, different types of questions have also shown to be susceptible to response bias. Although attitude and behavioral questions receive perhaps more attention, demographic variables are also known to be sometimes biased. Household income, for example, is usually underreported among those with higher earnings and overreported by those with lower ones.

Avoidance Strategies

Researchers have proposed multiple ways to control and correct for response bias. Some of these strategies are broad ways to deal with the issue, whereas others depend on the specific type of effect. Conducting careful pretesting of the questions is a general way to detect possible biasing problems. An example of a specific strategy to detect acquiescence, for instance, is writing items that favor, as well as items that oppose, the object of the attitude the researcher wants to measure (e.g., abortion). Respondents that answer in an acquiescent way would tend to agree with statements in both directions.

If response bias is a function of how questions are worded, how they are ordered, and how they are presented to the respondent, then careful questionnaire design can help minimize this source of error. However, there are sources of error that cannot be predicted in advance and therefore are much more difficult to avoid. In that case, there are strategies that can be followed to identify response bias. If validation data are available, survey outcomes can be checked against them and response bias can be more precisely identified. Similarly, the use of split ballot experiments can provide insights about deviations across different conditions and point out biasing factors. Including interviewer characteristics and other external data to analyze survey outcomes can help reveal hidden effects. At any rate, the researcher should check for possible response biases in data, take bias into account when interpreting results, and try to identify the cause of the bias in order to improve future survey research.

Ana Villar

See also Acquiescence Response Bias; Context Effect; Interviewer-Related Error; Measurement Error; Primacy

Effect; Push Polls; Questionnaire Order Effects; Recency Effect; Record Check; Respondent Burden; Respondent Fatigue; Respondent-Related Error; Response Order Effects; Social Desirability; Split-Half; Telescoping; True Score

Further Readings

Belli, R. F., Traugott, M. W., Young, M., & McGonagle, K. A. (1999). Reducing vote overreporting in surveys: Social desirability, memory failure, and source monitoring. *Public Opinion Quarterly, 63,* 90–108.

Krosnick, J. A. (1991). Response strategies for coping with the cognitive demands of attitude measures in surveys. *Applied Cognitive Psychology, 5,* 213–236.

Tourangeau, R., Rips, L. J., & Rasinski, K. (2000). *The psychology of survey response.* Cambridge, UK: Cambridge University Press.

RESPONSE LATENCY

Response latency is the speed or ease with which a response to a survey question is given after a respondent is presented with the question. It is used as an indicator of attitude accessibility, which is the strength of the link between an attitude object and a respondent's evaluation of that object. While response latency has been used for some time in cognitive psychology lab experiments, its use in surveys came about more recently. In telephone surveys, response latency is measured in milliseconds as the elapsed time from when an interviewer finishes reading a question until a respondent begins to answer.

There are four stages that survey respondents use when answering questions: (1) question comprehension, (2) retrieval of information from memory, (3) integration of the information to form a judgment, and (4) selection of an appropriate response option. Response latency measures the time it takes to retrieve, form, and report an answer to a survey question. Response latency data can provide much useful information about attitude accessibility that can be incorporated into data analysis. For example, when attitudes are modeled to predict subsequent behavior, respondents with more accessible attitudes (indicated by shorter response times) often exhibit a stronger relationship between the attitude and the subsequent behavior. Attitude accessibility as measured by response latency is just one way of measuring the strength of an attitude, but it can be consequential

for attitude stability, a respondent's resistance to persuasion, as well as the influence of the attitude on behavior. Response latency has also been used as a method of pretesting survey questionnaires in order to identify problematic questions.

Response latency was first used in cognitive psychology lab experiments where the timer measuring the response latency is a function of the participants' own reaction time to a self-administered instrument. When adapted for use in telephone surveys, it is generally measured via a voice-activated or "automatic" timer (which requires special equipment) that senses when a response is given or through an interviewer-activated or "active" timer embedded into the programming of computer-assisted telephone interviewing (CATI) software. The active timer requires the interviewer to start and stop the timer at the appropriate time using the computer keyboard and then verify that the time measurement is valid. Response latencies are coded as invalid if the interviewer fails to apply the timer correctly or if the respondent asks for the question to be repeated. Response latency can also be measured using a "latent" or unobtrusive timer that is programmed into CATI software and is invisible to both interviewers and respondents. Latent timers simply measure the total duration of each question from the time the question appears on the interviewer's screen until the moment the respondent's answer is recorded. Such timers also can be used in computer-assisted personal interviewing (CAPI) and computerized self-administered questionnaires (CSAQ).

Regardless of how the response latency data are collected, the distribution of responses is frequently skewed, and the data require careful examination and cleaning before analysis. Invalid data and extreme outliers should be removed and the data transformed to eliminate the skew. Depending on how the data are collected, researchers using response latency data may also want to control for baseline differences among respondents in answering questions and interviewers in recording survey responses because some respondents are naturally faster in answering questions and some interviewers are naturally faster in recording responses.

J. Quin Monson

See also Attitudes; Attitude Strength; Comprehension; Computer-Assisted Personal Interviewing (CAPI); Computer-Assisted Telephone Interviewing (CATI); Computerized Self-Administered Questionnaires (CSAQ); Outliers; Retrieval

Further Readings

Bassili, J. N. (1996). The how and why of response latency measurement in telephone surveys. In N. Schwarz & S. Sudman (Eds.), *Answering questions* (pp. 319–346). San Francisco: Jossey Bass.

Huckfeldt, R., Levine, W., Morgan, W., & Sprague, J. (1999). Accessibility and the political utility of partisan and ideological orientations. *American Journal of Political Science, 43*(3), 888–911.

Mulligan, K., Grant, J. T., Mockabee, S. T., & Monson, J. Q. (2003). Response latency methodology for survey research: Measurement and modeling strategies. *Political Analysis, 11*(3), 289–301.

RESPONSE ORDER EFFECTS

A response order effect occurs when the distribution of responses to a closed-ended survey question is influenced by the order in which the response options are offered to respondents. Primacy and recency effects are two common types of response order effects. Primacy effects occur when response options are more likely to be chosen when presented at the beginning of a list of response options than when presented at the end. In contrast, recency effects occur when response options are more likely to be chosen when presented at the end of a list of response options than when presented at the beginning of the list. The research literature contains myriad examples of both types of effects.

Response order effects are typically measured by presenting different groups of respondents with a survey question with the response options in different orders and assessing the effects of order on the answer respondents give. For example, a random half of respondents in a survey might be asked, *Which do you think is more important for success in life: self-control or the ability to enjoy oneself?* The other random half of respondents would be asked, *Which do you think is more important for success in life: the ability to enjoy oneself or self-control?* A primacy effect would be observed if significantly more respondents answered "self-control" in response to the first question than in response to the second, but a recency effect would be observed if more respondents answered "self-control" in response to the second question than in response to the first. In questions with more than two categorical response options, the number of possible response option orders increases dramatically as the number of response options increases (e.g., there are 24 possible response option orders for a question with 4 response options). In questions with response options that fall along a scale (e.g., *How likely is it that you will watch the president's speech on television: extremely likely, very likely, somewhat likely, slightly likely, or not at all likely?*), the response options fall into a logical order. For these questions, response order effects can be assessed by providing half of respondents with the response options ordered in one direction (e.g., *extremely likely, very likely, somewhat likely, slightly likely, or not at all likely*) and providing the other half of respondents with the response options in the opposite direction (e.g., *not at all likely, slightly likely, somewhat likely, very likely, or extremely likely*).

A number of explanations have been provided for response order effects. For example, some researchers have argued that respondents have difficulty remembering all response options and that response order effects reflect the response options most memorable to respondents (those at the beginning and end of a list of response options). However, researchers have observed response order effects in very simple, short questions with only a few (e.g., two) response options. For these simple questions, it seems unlikely that respondents are unable to recall the question or the response options.

In a large body of evidence regarding response order effects in questions with categorical response options, recency effects have been observed in some cases, primacy effects have been observed in other cases, and in other cases, no significant response order effect was observed. Another theoretical account of response order effects provides an explanation for this mixture of findings. John Krosnick's satisficing theory suggests that although survey researchers hope respondents will answer questions by carefully and thoughtfully going through the four mental processes involved in answering survey questions (i.e., comprehending and interpreting the survey question, retrieving relevant information from memory, integrating that information into a judgment, and mapping their judgment onto the response format provided), respondents may not always be able or motivated to do so. Instead, they may shift their response strategies to minimize effort while providing a "satisfactory" response to the survey question (i.e., satisficing). In doing so, respondents are merely searching for strategies or cues in questions that they can use easily to find a satisfactory answer. One such strategy involves choosing the first response option that seems reasonable, and this strategy is believed to be responsible for response order effects.

Satisficing theory suggests that whether researchers observe primacy or recency effects in questions with categorical response options may depend on the mode in which response options are presented. When response options are presented visually, most respondents probably begin by considering the option presented first, then the second option, and so on. So if respondents choose the first reasonable response option they consider, primacy effects are likely to occur. But when response options are presented orally, respondents cannot think much about the first option they hear, because presentation of the second option interrupts this thinking. Similar interference occurs until after the last response option is heard, and at that point the last response option is likely to be the most salient and the focus of respondents' thoughts. People may also be most likely to remember the last response options in a long list of response options. So if respondents choose the first reasonable response option they consider, recency effects will occur. Consistent with this logic, mostly primacy effects have appeared in past studies that involved visual presentation of categorical response options, and mostly recency effects have occurred under oral presentation conditions.

In questions with response options that fall along a scale, however, mostly primacy effects have been observed, regardless of whether the response options are presented orally or visually. In questions with response options that fall along a scale, respondents who are reading or listening to the response options do not need to listen to the whole list of response options to form their answer to the question. Instead, they can infer the dimension on which they are being asked to make a judgment after just the first or second response option. For example, in the "likelihood" scale question described earlier, respondents are likely to know after just the first or second response option that they are being asked to report the likelihood of a particular behavior.

In addition to mode of presentation, satisficing theory posits that the strength of response order effects depend on three types of factors: (1) the respondent's ability, (2) the respondent's motivation, and (3) the cognitive difficulty of optimizing inherent in the question. Respondents with greater ability and motivation are less likely to satisfice. Satisficing is also more likely when (a) a question's stem or response choices are especially difficult to comprehend, (b) a question demands an especially difficult search of memory to

retrieve needed information, (c) the integration of retrieved information into a summary judgment is especially difficult, or (d) translation of the summary judgment onto the response alternatives is especially difficult. Thus, recency effects in questions with orally presented, categorical response options are likely to be strongest among respondents low in ability and motivation and for questions that are more difficult.

Although evidence on the prevalence of response order effects suggests that researchers may want to estimate and control for such effects, there may be some cases in which this is not appropriate. In some cases, there may be norms about the order in which response options should be presented. For example, in questions with positive and negative response options (e.g., approve or disapprove), it is conventional to offer the positive response option first. Violating this convention may distract and confuse respondents and introduce error into their responses, thereby causing other types of potential measurement errors. So although in most cases, researchers may want to routinely rotate response order effects across respondents so that they can estimate and control for response order effects, this is most appropriate for questions without conventions about the order in which response options should be offered.

Allyson Holbrook

See also Closed-Ended Question; Primacy Effect; Recency Effect; Response Alternatives; Satisficing

Further Readings

Bishop, G., & Smith, A. (2001). Response-order effects and the early Gallup split-ballots. *Public Opinion Quarterly, 65,* 479–505.

Holbrook, A. L., Krosnick, J. A., Carson, R. T., & Mitchell, R. C. (2000). Violating conversational conventions disrupts cognitive processing of attitude questions. *Journal of Experimental Social Psychology, 36,* 465–494.

Krosnick, J. A. (1991). Response strategies for coping with the cognitive demands of attitude measures in surveys. *Applied Cognitive Psychology, 5,* 213–236.

Krosnick, J. A. (1999). Survey research. *Annual Review of Psychology, 50,* 537–567.

McClendon, M. J. (1986). Response-order effects for dichotomous questions. *Social Science Quarterly, 67,* 205–211.

McClendon, M. J. (1991). Acquiescence and recency response-order effects in interview surveys. *Sociological Methods and Research, 20,* 60–103.

Narayan, S., & Krosnick, J. A. (1996). Education moderates some response effects in attitude measurement. *Public Opinion Quarterly, 60,* 58–88.

Payne, S. L. (1949). Case study in question complexity. *Public Opinion Quarterly, 13,* 653–658.

Schuman, H., & Presser, S. (1996). *Questions and answers in attitude surveys: Experiments on question form, wording, and context.* Thousand Oaks, CA: Sage.

RESPONSE PROPENSITY

Response propensity is the theoretical probability that a sampled person (or unit) will become a respondent in a specific survey. Sampled persons differ in their likelihood to become a respondent in a survey. These differences are a result of the fact that some persons are easier to get into contact with than are others, some persons are more willing and able to participate in a specific survey than others, or both. Response propensity is an important concept in survey research, as it shapes the amount and structure of unit nonresponse in a survey. The covariance between response propensity and the survey variable of interest determines the bias in survey estimates due to nonresponse. Theoretically, using response propensities, a researcher could entirely correct for nonresponse bias. However, such a correction requires that the researcher know the true value of this unobservable variable. In practice, researchers can use only estimates of response propensities, so-called propensity scores, using a logistic model that hopefully captures the concept well. The extent to which the nonresponse bias can be corrected using propensity scores depends on the quality of the propensity score model.

Determinants of Response Propensity

Response propensity is essentially a characteristic of the sampled person. Response propensities vary across persons according to their sociodemographic characteristics and various psychological predispositions. For example, persons in large households are easier to be contacted than those who live alone, whereas persons who are socially isolated are less likely to grant an interview than are people who are socially integrated. Response propensity can be regarded as a characteristic of the sampled person only, if defined as the probability that the sampled person will become a respondent in a random survey or, alternatively, as the probability

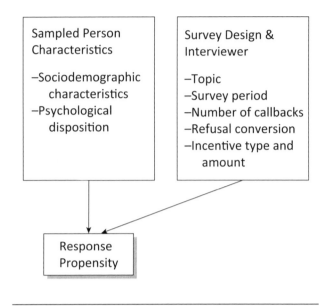

Figure 1 Determinants of response propensity

that the sampled person will become a respondent in a survey with "average characteristics." Considering a person's "baseline" response propensity within the characteristics of a certain survey then determines the probability that the person will be a respondent to that particular survey. So, in fact, response propensities are affected both by characteristics of the sampled person and by survey characteristics (see Figure 1).

Contactability and Cooperation

In the process of becoming a respondent, two important steps can be distinguished. The first step is that the respondent has to be contacted. The second step is that after being contacted, the respondent must be willing and able to cooperate with the surveyor's request. This observation suggests a straightforward decomposition of response propensity into two parts: contactability and cooperation.

The contactability $p_{contact,i,j}$ is the probability that individual i is contacted for survey j at any given moment in time. Typical characteristics of the sampled person that affect the contactability include factors such as (a) how often the person is at home, (b) whether there are physical impediments to contacting the person, and (c) to what extent the person is prepared to answer any incoming survey requests. Survey characteristics that affect contactability include (d) the number of contacts made by the interviewer, (e) the length of the survey period, and (f) the timing of the contacts.

For example, contact attempts in the evenings and on weekends are usually more successful than contact attempts at other times, thereby raising the response propensity.

The cooperation $p_{cooperation,i,j}$ is the probability that a contacted individual i will cooperate to survey j. Cooperation is in fact a conditional probability of cooperation on being contacted. From survey experience it is known that cooperation differs according to sociodemographic variables, such as gender, age, educational attainment, and the presence of children. The effects of sociodemographic variables are not believed to be causal. Theories on social isolation and authority have been developed to derive concepts that play a mediating role between these personal characteristics and cooperation. Many survey characteristics that affect cooperation, including the topic, the sponsor, incentives, perceived burden, and the interviewer, play a role in the decision of the contacted person to agree or refuse participation (see Table 1).

An interesting perspective on how the individual decision process of survey participation might work is provided by the leverage-saliency theory as articulated by Robert M. Groves and his colleagues. This theory acknowledges the threshold nature of survey participation. At the time of a survey request, a person will instantaneously evaluate different characteristics of the survey (e.g., topic, incentive, sponsor, burden) and will weight these characteristics on a personal scale. Depending on the "saliency" and "leverage" of the different characteristics of the survey, the scale will either tilt toward acceptance or toward refusal of the survey request.

Behind contactability and cooperation are two different processes that can have opposite effects. For example, in the case of a survey on cultural participation, culturally active persons may be harder to contact because of the fact that they are often away from home engaging in their cultural activities. At the same time, culturally active persons who are contacted may be very cooperative as their interest in the topic of the survey is above average.

For a given survey, contactability can be combined with cooperation to reveal the (overall) response propensity of sampled person i by multiplication of these probabilities:

$$p_{response,i} = p_{contact,i} \times p_{cooperation,i}$$

In survey research, next to contactability and cooperation, sometimes a third type of unit nonresponse is distinguished. It happens that persons who are contacted and who may even be willing to participate in the survey are not able to participate for reasons related to their physical health, literacy, or language problems. For surveys that deal with elderly and immigrants, this type of nonresponse can be serious and should not be ignored. Theoretically, it is possible to incorporate the inability to participate into a model for response propensity by extending the decomposition into three factors.

Using Response Propensity to Correct for Nonresponse Bias

In spite of surveyors' efforts to obtain high response rates (e.g., many callbacks, incentives, refusal conversion attempts), some sampled persons will become nonrespondents. It is common to apply post-survey adjustment techniques, such as post-stratification or raking methods, to reduce nonresponse bias. Alternatively, the concept of response propensity can be used to compensate for unit nonresponse, model it, and use estimated response propensities to correct for nonresponse bias.

Table 1	Survey characteristics that affect survey cooperation
Topic	Some survey topics are more popular than others.
Sponsor	Commercial organizations experience more refusals than official and academic research organizations.
Burden	Surveys with a high perceived burden (income and expenditure surveys, panel surveys) experience lower cooperation rates than surveys with low burden.
Incentives	Incentives offered to persons may stimulate cooperation.
Interviewers	Well-trained interviewers are more able to persuade persons to participate in the survey than are inexperienced interviewers. A persuasive counter to "I'm too busy" or "I'm not interested" is crucial to obtaining high cooperation rates.

The advantage of using the concept of response propensity over traditional methods is that this approach allows incorporating theoretical notions about survey participation into the procedure of bias reduction. From this perspective it makes sense to use a procedure that reflects the two-step process of survey participation and estimate multivariate logistic models for contactability and cooperation separately. The estimated models can then be used in a two-stage procedure to adjust the original sampling weight that corrects for unequal selection weights into weights to also correct for nonresponse bias. The quality of the procedure depends on the quality of the response propensity models. In practice, the quality of these models is still rather low. However, it is a challenge to find concepts that have strong relationships with contactability and cooperation, to obtain measures of these concepts on both respondents and nonrespondents, and to use these in estimating response propensity to correct for nonresponse bias.

Adriaan W. Hoogendoorn

See also Contactability; Contact Rate; Contacts; Cooperation; Cooperation Rate; Leverage-Saliency Theory; Nonresponse; Nonresponse Bias; Post-Stratification; Propensity Scores; Refusal Conversion; Response

Further Readings

Groves, R. M., & Couper, M. P. (1998). *Nonresponse in household interview surveys.* New York: Wiley.

Groves, R. M., Singer, E., & Corning, A. (2000). Leverage-saliency theory of survey participation: Description and illustration. *Public Opinion Quarterly, 64*(3), 299–208.

Singer, E. (2006). Nonresponse bias in household surveys [Special issue]. *Public Opinion Quarterly, 70*(5).

RESPONSE RATES

A response rate is a mathematical formula that is calculated by survey researchers and is used as a tool to understand the degree of success in obtaining completed interviews from a sample. In probability samples, where the intent of a survey is to project the results of the data onto a population (e.g., all adults in the United States), statistical theory rests on an assumption that data are collected from every unit, or person, selected. In practice, it is extremely rare for any survey to achieve this perfect level of cooperation from respondents. In turn, survey researchers may consider, examine, and when necessary, compensate for potential problems that this deficiency presents.

Response rates, sometime termed *outcome rates*, have traditionally been a topic of great interest because they describe the amount of nonresponse in a given survey. In doing so, they provide an indicator that can be used to better understand threats to the validity of survey data. Response rates inform researchers of the proportion of their sample that did not respond and also may lend insight into the reasons selected persons (or units) did not respond.

Background

Although nonresponse has been studied since the 1940s, serious efforts to standardize the measurement of nonresponse have arisen only within the last quarter of the 20th century. Furthermore, the common use of standardized response rate measurements has not yet been fully realized throughout the survey research profession.

Traditionally, there has been a great deal of overlap and inconsistency in both the definitions and formulas used to understand the concept of response rates. These discrepancies present a difficulty to the survey research profession because they often confuse consumers of survey information. Using consistent outcome rates is important because it allows the level of nonresponse to be compared more easily between different surveys. This provides researchers and clients or other end-users with a meaningful target when planning the design of research. Equally as important, standard outcome rates offer an important benchmark for understanding how well surveys performed.

For example, a lack of consistency prohibits the accurate comparison of nonresponse between two unique surveys, obscures agreement in target levels of nonresponse in research proposals, and hampers methodological research exploring nonresponse error.

In response to the historical differences among response rate calculations, the survey research profession has gradually worked toward a uniformly accepted set of formulas and definitions for nonresponse. These efforts are now spearheaded by the American Association for Public Opinion Research (AAPOR), which maintains a series of definitions, formulas, and dispositions that are continuously updated to reflect new technologies and changes in the survey research profession.

AAPOR Response Rates

AAPOR first published a series of response rates in 1998 for random-digit dialing and in-person surveys due to the concerted efforts of Tom. W. Smith and his colleagues. AAPOR based their development of the rates on the earlier work of the CASRO (Council of American Survey Research Organizations), which had published a set of formulas in 1982. Prior to that time, there had been numerous inquiries into the development of standards but no successful efforts put forth, at the association level, toward rate development.

Since the first release in 1998, AAPOR's volunteers have updated the response rates (and other outcome rates) three times (in 2000, 2004, and 2006). The most recent publication (2006) includes descriptions for calculating telephone, in-person, mail, and Internet survey response rates. AAPOR's development of response rates includes the formulas within a larger collection of "outcome rates."

Collectively, the four rates (response, cooperation, refusal, and contact) each help describe a different facet of survey nonresponse:

- *Response rates* describe the proportion of responders within a sample.
- *Cooperation rates* describe the proportion of responders who were contacted and who cooperated.
- *Refusal rates* describe the proportion of the sample who refused to take the survey.
- *Contact rates* describe the proportion of sample members who were contacted.

These rates also help describe the total nonresponse of a survey, as well as the type of nonresponse that a survey includes (e.g., refusal vs. noncontact).

Notably, AAPOR's set of outcome rates include numerous variations of each of the four types of formulas (response, cooperation, refusal, and contact). The six iterations that apply to response rates vary according to the type of information that is included in each part of the formula. For example, AAPOR Response Rate 1 (RR1) is calculated as follows:

AAPOR RR1:

$$\frac{\text{Completed Interviews}}{\begin{array}{l}(\text{Completed Interviews} + \text{Partial Interviews}) \\ + (\text{Refusals} + \text{Noncontacts} + \text{Other}) \\ + (\text{Unknown Eligibility})\end{array}}$$

AAPOR Response Rate 2 (RR2) is similar to RR1, except it considers partial interviews in the numerator of the formula. This potentially increases the response rate for a given survey.

AAPOR RR2:

$$\frac{(\text{Completed Interviews} + \text{Partial Interviews})}{\begin{array}{l}(\text{Completed Interviews} + \text{Partial Interviews}) \\ + (\text{Refusals} + \text{Noncontacts} + \text{Other}) \\ + (\text{Unknown Eligibility})\end{array}}$$

AAPOR's response rates are used widely within the survey research profession and academia. AAPOR maintains a policy of encouraging the use of their rates and definitions and has taken steps to see them proliferated throughout the survey research profession. Notably, at least two scholarly journals (*Public Opinion Quarterly* and *International Journal of Public Opinion Research*) have recognized the AAPOR formulas. Additionally, their use is endorsed by the CMOR (Council for Marketing and Opinion Research) for survey research conducted within the United States of America.

Survey response rates measure unit nonresponse. Unit nonresponse occurs when those who *have been selected* for participation in a survey *do not participate*. Nonresponders may not participate for numerous reasons ranging from circumstances where they plainly refuse to participate, to situations where they are never contacted and do not have the chance to participate. Survey nonresponse affects survey validity when nonresponders are different from those that do respond in ways that skew survey results. The following example illustrates a situation where nonresponders are absent from survey data in a way that affects survey validity:

A researcher interviewed a sample of college students from ABC University about extracurricular activities. Those students who were more engaged in university activities also tended to participate in the university survey in greater proportions than other students. Those "active" students skewed survey statistics because of their very distinct feelings about extracurricular activities. This led the university to believe that the student body held a more favorable opinion of extracurricular activities than was actually the case.

Declining Response Rates

For many years, response rates have been declining in the United States (as well as in many other countries).

There are multiple factors that are believed to have contributed to this phenomenon. This trend of declining response rates is attributed to survey refusals and noncontacts.

Survey refusals are cases where a respondent receives a contact to complete a survey but declines to participate. The increase in survey refusals has been attributed to both social changes and reactions to changes within the survey research profession. These factors include (a) a growing expectation for privacy among the public; (b) the use of *pseudosurveys* as a guise to sell, fund-raise, push-poll, create marketing databases, or engage in political telemarketing; (c) the commoditization of research and substantial increase in the number of surveys being conducted; and (d) a decrease in the perceived value of surveys by society.

Noncontacts are situations where researchers are unable to communicate with the selected respondent. The growing problem of survey noncontacts has also had a wide breadth of contributing factors. Many of the situations that are thought to add to noncontacts vary largely across survey modes. For example, telephone research has been particularly susceptible to technologies affecting noncontacts such as the advent of telephone screening devices and services, cellular phone only households and number portability. However, other modes of recruitment or data collection are also challenged by unique circumstances that may magnify survey noncontacts (e.g., spam filters blocking Internet survey invitations, doormen preventing interviewer access to respondents in in-person surveys).

Additionally, response rates in the United States are subject to a third growing category of nonresponse: language. Many survey research organizations may want to interview persons who do not speak English and yet do not have the mechanisms in place to translate into other languages than English. If not addressed, this problem is likely to continue growing in scope.

Direction of Research on Nonresponse

Numerous studies have been conducted on response rate trends and the factors that may influence response rates for individual surveys. In more recent times, researchers have turned to studying the circumstances where survey nonresponse may be likely to pose threats to survey validity.

Nonresponse tends to be a complex, sophisticated phenomenon in survey research. As such, the meaning of response rates is often misinterpreted. It is important to view survey response rates in the context of the survey design.

Recent research in survey methods lends support to the idea that response rates must be considered along with other information. This convention contrasts somewhat with previous notions of researchers who believed a certain minimum response rate would offer sufficient protection (or mitigation) against nonresponse error, which is recognized nowadays to not be the case.

Evaluating Response Rates

The body of literature on response rates and survey nonresponse nevertheless indicates that response rates remain an important indicator of survey quality and should be considered when performing survey research. For this reason, it is recommended that response rates be calculated and considered when conducting survey research that relies on probability samples. However, it is also important to analyze response rates (and other outcome rates) in the context of the design of the study.

All available sources of information should be considered when exploring the meaning of response rates on a particular study. Important considerations for evaluating response rates may include the survey variables of interest, the survey population of interest and sample, survey design choices (e.g., use of incentives, timing, and nature of information given to respondents throughout survey process), and the design and administration of the survey instrument.

Patrick Glaser

See also American Association for Public Opinion Research (AAPOR); Contact Rate; Cooperation Rate; Council for Marketing and Opinion Research (CMOR); Council of American Survey Research Organizations (CASRO); *International Journal of Public Opinion Research* (IJPOR); Noncontact; Pseudo Polls; *Public Opinion Quarterly* (POQ); Refusal; Refusal Rate; Standard Definitions; Unit Nonresponse

Further Readings

American Association for Public Opinion Research. (2006). *Standard definitions: Final dispositions of case codes and outcome rates for surveys* (4th ed.). Lenexa, KS: Author. Retrieved April 10, 2008, from http://www .aapor.org/pdfs/standarddefs_4.pdf

Smith, T. W. (2002, August). *Establishing standards for survey research: The case of nonresponse*. Paper presented at the International Conference on Improving Surveys, Copenhagen.

RETRIEVAL

Basic memory processes fundamentally affect the answers survey respondents give to survey questions, and retrieval is one of these memory processes. Retrieval refers to the active recovery of previously encoded information from long-term memory into conscious, working memory. Long-term memory that requires conscious retrieval is divided into (a) memory for facts and (b) memory for events. It is important for questionnaire designers to be aware of the limitations that retrieval processes place on the survey experience for the respondent.

The process of retrieving information and memories for events is closely related to the initial process of encoding, when a memory for the event is first stored by transferring information from active experience into long-term storage. The most difficult retrieval situation is unaided (free) recall, where there are no cues provided that relate to the desired information. However, questionnaires can avoid this situation by including cues in the survey questions that aid in recall. Retrieval is maximized when the cues present during encoding closely match the cues present in the questionnaire. If, for example, memory for a particular event is typically encoded in terms of time (i.e., filing your taxes), then survey questions that cue respondents to think about the event temporally will aid recall. The more cues there are, the more precise the retrieved information will be; for example, memory for a person's name may be aided by cueing specific events relating to that person, picturing their physical characteristics, thinking about the sound of her or his voice, or thinking about common acquaintances. Although the match between encoding and retrieval cues is important, it is also the case that, all other things being equal, some cues are generally better than others in aiding recall for events. Cues relating to the type of event work best; next best are cues relating to location and people and, finally, cues relating to time.

The depth of initial encoding is also important to later success in retrieving that information from memory; this phenomenon is referred to as the *levels-of-processing effect*. It is easier to remember information that was initially processed more deeply in comparison to information that was processed superficially. For example, information that is processed both visually (i.e., pictorially) and verbally is easier to remember than information processed in only one fashion.

Retrieval is greatly affected by the type of information that a survey question requires respondents to access. Memory access is first and foremost affected by how long ago the memory was initially encoded. Retrieval for older information and events is more difficult and error-prone, whereas memory for more recent information is easier to access. Certain kinds of information are also easier to retrieve from memory. For example, dates and names are forgotten easily. Information about a unique event is easier to remember, whereas memory for a specific event that is a repetitive and common experience of the respondent is more difficult to remember and more prone to errors. For example, it is easy to remember the details of meeting the president because this information is distinctive in comparison to other information in memory. In contrast, retrieving specific information about your last trip to the grocery store is more difficult to remember accurately because there are so many similar events in your past that the details for each event seem to blur into a general memory for "going to the grocery store." This difficulty leads to errors in identifying the source of a memory; that is, respondents are unable to accurately identify the specific originating event of the retrieved information.

It is important to note that the retrieval of information from long-term memory is a reconstructive process and fraught with possible error. When memory for an event or fact is accessed, this remembrance is not a perfect replica of that event or initially encoded fact. Retrieval errors affect survey responses in three common ways: (1) *Forgetting* occurs when respondents are simply unable to access information stored in memory, or the retrieved memory is partial, distorted, or simply false (false memories may occur even when respondents are quite confident in the accuracy and validity of the memory); (2) *estimation* occurs when respondents make a "best educated guess" that stands in for the retrieval of exact information, which often occurs because respondents satisfice; that is, they attempt to finish a survey by answering questions with as little effort as possible; and (3) *telescoping* occurs when respondents inaccurately include events that belong outside the reference period a survey question requires.

The constraints that retrieval processes impose on the ability of survey respondents to accurately recall information require special attention in the construction of survey questions. Questions should ask for information that is as recent as possible and provide cues that match the original encoding context. As noted earlier, cues relating to the type of event work best, followed by cues relating to location and people, and finally, cues relating to time. Cues that are distinctive and personally relevant to the respondent also aid retrieval. Lastly, questions that ask for information that is general or was initially superficially encoded are prone to greater error in comparison to questions with appropriate specific cues and therefore should be avoided if possible.

Gregory G. Holyk

See also Bias; Encoding; Questionnaire Design; Reference Period; Satisficing; Telescoping; Unaided Recall

Further Readings

Craik, F. I. M., & Lockhart, R. S. (1972). Levels of processing: A framework for memory research. *Journal of Verbal Learning and Verbal Behavior, 11,* 671–684.

Craik, F. I. M., & Tulving, E. (1975). Depth of processing and the retention of words in episodic memory. *Journal of Experimental Psychology: General, 104,* 268–294.

Tourangeau, R., Rips, L. J., & Rasinski, K. (2000). *The psychology of survey response.* New York: Cambridge University Press.

Tulving, E. (1983). *Elements of episodic memory.* New York: Oxford University Press.

REVERSE DIRECTORY

A reverse directory has two general definitions. The first is a residential telephone directory, which has been converted from a surname alphabetical ordered listing to a street name ordered listing. The second is a listing of addresses in a city, also known as a *city directory.*

A telephone directory covering a city or other geographic area consists of residential listed telephone numbers. The directory is in alphabetical order by surname. A first name or initials generally accompany the surname. The street address is then listed, although in some areas a household may decide to not have their address listed in the telephone directory. The telephone number follows the address. Because telephone directories are key-entered into a database by commercial firms, it is possible to manipulate the order of the listings.

In a reverse directory, the telephone directory database for a city is sorted into an alphabetical street order and then by address number within street name. In some cases the commercial firm will add additional information such as zip code, census tract, and census block number. This type of reverse directory makes it possible to sample households from very small geographic areas for a telephone survey or an in-person interview survey. However, there are several sampling issues that must be taken into account. One key issue is that the reverse directory is a listing of residential addresses with directory-listed landline telephone numbers, and therefore households with unlisted telephone numbers and households without landline telephone service are excluded. These types of households are likely to be demographically different from households that are listed in a reverse directory, thus leading to possible coverage error in a survey that is measuring the residential population in a local area.

The selection of a sample from a residential telephone directory, which has been converted from a surnamed alphabetically ordered listing to a street name ordered listing, involves the random selection of address listings. This can be accomplished by determining the number of pages in the directory and first selecting a systematic random sample of pages. For each selected page, one or more address listings can then be selected also through systematic random sampling. This approach assumes that the pages in the reverse directory contain approximately the same number of address listings. The survey researcher must keep in mind that such samples exclude telephone households with unlisted telephone numbers.

City directories, on the other hand, provide a listing of residential addresses in a city from which a sample can be drawn. RL Polk is the original commercial firm that sold city directories for many of the cities in the United States. The street guide section of the typical city directory provides a listing of streets in alphabetical order and addresses in numerical order. City directories are sometimes used to select dwelling units for area probability sampling of cities.

Sampling from city directories has its origins in area probability sampling, as discussed by Leslie Kish. Kish described sampling procedures for selecting an element sample of address listing from a city directory. For a large city, the selection of an element sample of address listings does not take advantage of two-stage sampling methods developed to reduce data collection costs for in-person surveys. This approach involves first selecting clusters of addresses and, for each sample cluster, drawing a sample of address listings.

Reverse directories are not used much anymore for sampling purposes. Today commercial sampling firms maintain computerized databases of residential directory-listed telephone numbers. Each listed telephone number is assigned to a county, census tract, block group and census block, as well as to a zip code. This makes it possible to sample residential directory–listed numbers from specific geographic areas, including small areas such as a single block group. For area probability sampling, the U.S. Postal Service (USPS) Delivery Sequence File (DSF) can be obtained for sample selection purposes. The DSF contains all delivery point addresses serviced by the USPS. Each delivery point is a separate record that conforms to all USPS addressing standards. Initial evaluations of the DSF as a means of reducing the costs associated with enumeration of urban households in area probability surveys have proven to be promising. Initial assessments of frame coverage found that the DSF covers approximately 97% of the households in the United States.

Michael P. Battaglia

See also Area Probability Sample; Directory Sampling; List Sampling; Probability Sample; Systematic Sampling; Reverse Directory Sampling; Unlisted Number; Unpublished Number

Further Readings

Iannacchione, V., Staab, J., & Redden, D. (2003). Evaluating the use of residential mailing addresses in a metropolitan household survey. *Public Opinion Quarterly, 76,* 202–210.

Kish, L. (1965). *Survey sampling.* New York: Wiley.

Schejbal, J. A., & Lavrakas, P. J. (1995). Coverage error and cost issues in small area telephone surveys. *American Statistical Association 1994 Proceedings: Section on Survey Research Method* (pp. 1287–1292). Alexandria, VA: American Statistical Association.

Sudman, S. (1976). *Applied sampling.* New York: Academic Press.

REVERSE DIRECTORY SAMPLING

A reverse directory is a residential telephone directory that has been converted from a surnamed alphabetically

ordered listing to a street name ordered listing. Reverse directory sampling refers to the selection of a sample of address listings—which may be residential, nonresidential, or both—from a reverse directory. The selection of a sample from a reverse directory involves the random selection of these address listings. This can be accomplished by determining the number of pages in the directory and first selecting a systematic random sample of pages. For each selected page, one or more address listings can then be selected also using systematic random sampling. This approach assumes that the pages in the reverse directory contain approximately the same number of address listings.

Today, such manual sampling procedures are rarely used. Telephone directories are key-entered so that computerized databases of telephone directories are available through various commercial sources. Geographic codes (such as county FIPS [Federal Information Processing Standard] code), census tract number, block group number, and zip code are assigned to each telephone number in the database. This makes it possible to draw a random sample of telephone numbers from a specific geographic area (e.g., a single zip code). The survey researcher must recognize that such samples exclude telephone households with unlisted telephone numbers and households without a landline and therefore may contain considerable coverage error.

Michael P. Battaglia

See also Reverse Directory; Unlisted Number; Unpublished Number

Further Readings

Kish, L. (1965). *Survey sampling.* New York: Wiley.

REVERSE RECORD CHECK

In survey research, a reverse record check is a method that can be used to verify the accuracy of data that a respondent provides against an information source that contains the "true" answer. Use of this method is not always feasible, even with ample funding, because external sources of information against which a survey response can be validated often do not exist.

The effect of human memory on the response to the survey questions has been the concern of survey methodology for many years. A survey respondent has to be in the position of providing accurate answers to survey questions involving memory. Naturally, this must depend on the nature of questions, but a number of empirical studies have demonstrated that fallibility of memory can be an important source of measurement error. In addition to memory failures, there are other reasons that the answers respondents sometimes provide are inaccurate, thus contributing to measurement error.

Perhaps the most common method of assessing measurement error is the use of a record check study or validation study. Such a study generally assumes that information contained in the external records is without error, that is, that the records contain the true values on the survey variables. In fact this may not be true, as the records may themselves be inaccurate, incomplete, or both. Furthermore, the matching and finding of records for survey individuals is often troublesome and expensive. Errors may occur in matching an individual's survey answer(s) and record data, and if no attempt is made to reconcile differences, such mismatches may indicate response errors where none exists. There are three kinds of record check study designs: (1) reverse record check study, (2) forward record check study, and (3) full design record check study. The reverse record check study is generally based on a retrospective design in which the entire sample is drawn from the record file for persons with a trait under study, interviews are conducted containing questions about information also contained on the records, and a comparison of survey data with record data is performed to estimate the extent and nature of any measurement error. The term *reverse record check* is used because after the survey is completed, the researcher goes back to the records to check the survey responses. The information can be gathered by using so-called retrospective questions, referring to a certain period of time preceding the date of the interview. In retrospective surveys, many types of recall errors, such as omission, telescoping (forward or backward), confusion, and reporting load effects, can occur.

Earlier studies involving reference period questions showed forward bias in reporting. When memory is inexact, forward bias will arise in answering such questions. Even if an upper bound is not imposed by the investigator, subjects may impose such a bound on their own reports. If subjects bound their reports, it leads to truncation of the distribution of reports just as when bounds are imposed in the question; it also leads to forward bias in reporting. It is important to note that reverse record check studies by themselves fail to measure errors of overreporting. Instead, reverse record checks can measure what portion of the records sampled correspond to events reported in the survey.

Record linkage and alternative matching procedures can be compared with the perfect matching situation. The expected *event location matching* is achieved by taking the record time as the base for the matching operation. Through this approach, reported events are matched with their expected location in the corresponding records. By this procedure, telescoping effects are replaced by omissions for given locations. One of the major drawbacks of this approach is the difficulty in placing the expected event location realistically. A second approach is nearest distance event matching, where the reported events are matched with their nearest counterpart in the recorded events in the ordered set for each respondent's individual records. This approach creates larger deviations between the reported and recorded values for each individual's record, because omission is replaced by telescoping effects in some locations. By this approach, omissions will not be eliminated and will still appear in the data set at a later location, when all the events are matched. Matching procedures conducted under different assumptions also can create different patterns in the matched data for the reverse record check study.

H. Öztas Ayhan

See also Errors of Omission; Event History Calendar; Measurement Error; Nonsampling Error; Overreporting; Record Check; Telescoping

Further Readings

Ayhan, H. Ö., & Isiksal, S. (2004). Memory recall errors in retrospective surveys: Reverse record check study. *Quality & Quantity 38*(5), 475–493.

Groves, R. M. (1989). *Survey errors and survey costs*. New York: Wiley.

Sudman, S., & Bradburn, N. M. (1973). Effects of time and memory factors on response in surveys. *Journal of the American Statistical Association, 68*, 805–815.

ρ (RHO)

A statistic that quantifies the extent to which population units within clusters are similar to one another (i.e., the degree of homogeneity within clusters) is called the *intraclass correlation coefficient* (ICC) and is often denoted by the Greek letter *rho* (ρ).

When population units are grouped or clustered into larger units, which are themselves easier to identify and sample (i.e., children grouped into classrooms or elderly citizens grouped into nursing homes), one- or two-stage cluster sampling becomes an appealing, cost-effective, and practical choice for a sampling strategy. These benefits are often counterbalanced by the usual expected loss in efficiency and precision in estimates derived from cluster samples that is, in large part, due to the fact that units within clusters tend to be more similar to each other compared to units in the general population for many outcomes of interest.

The computation of ρ essentially provides a rate of homogeneity for elements within a cluster relative to the overall population variance, as seen by the following equation:

$$ICC = \rho = \frac{\sum_{i=1}^{C} \sum_{j=1}^{M} \sum_{k \neq j}^{M} (y_{ij} - \bar{y}_{iU})(y_{ik} - \bar{y}_{iU})}{(CM - 1)(M - 1)S^2}, \qquad (1)$$

where C is the number of clusters in the population, M is the number of elements within each cluster, y_{ij} is the measurement for the jth element in the ith cluster, y_{ik} is the measurement for the jth element in cluster i, $\bar{y}_{iU}$ is the population mean for the ith cluster, and S^2 is the finite population variance defined by

$$S^2 = \sum_{i=1}^{C} \sum_{j=1}^{M} \frac{(y_{ij} - \bar{y}_U)^2}{CM - 1}, \qquad (2)$$

where $\bar{y}_U$ is the population mean.

Note that Equation 1 is equivalent to a simpler formula containing values easily obtained from an ANOVA table, accounting for clustering as follows:

$$ICC = \rho = 1 - \frac{M}{M-1} \frac{SSW}{SST}, \qquad (3)$$

where $SSW = \sum_{i=1}^{C} \sum_{j=1}^{M} (y_{ij} - \bar{y}_{iU})^2$ is the sum of squares within clusters and $SST = \sum_{i=1}^{C} \sum_{j=1}^{M} (y_{ij} - \bar{y}_U)^2$ is the total sum of squares about $\bar{y}_U$.

From Equation 3 and the fact that $0 \leq SSW/SST \leq 1$, it follows that $\frac{-1}{M-1} \leq \rho \leq 1$. If there is complete duplication within each cluster, then the ICC takes on the highest possible value of 1 to indicate complete homogeneity within clusters; on the other hand, if the heterogeneity within clusters is consistent with that of the overall population, then the ICC will assume its smallest value of $-1/(M-1)$. Cluster sampling will be more efficient than simple random sampling with the same overall sample size whenever $-1/M - 1 \leq \rho \leq 0$ and less efficient when the ICC values are positive and closer to 1.

Consider the following example to illustrate the computation of the ICC. Researchers are interested in determining the average fruit and vegetable intake of staff members of a nationally franchised health club in preparation for a campaign to promote exercise and diet among its members. The population consists of five franchised health clubs that each have eight staff members. The fruit and vegetable intake for each population member is provided in Table 1. In this scenario the number of clusters is five ($C = 5$), and the number of elements per cluster is eight ($M = 8$).

From the SSW and SST obtained with these results the ICC is computed using Equation 3 as follows:

$$ICC = \rho = 1 - \frac{8}{8 - 1} \times \frac{5.932}{114.690} = 0.941.$$

This large, positive ICC indicates that, on average, the staff members within each cluster tend to consume similar amounts of fruits and vegetables per day. In other words, the clusters are extremely homogeneous. The homogeneity within clusters also means that a one-stage cluster sample would be less efficient than a simple random sample of the same size (i.e., the design effect [*deff*] would be greater than 1).

It should be noted that in the example, population values were provided. In practice, estimated ICCs are obtained using comparable sample statistics, such as sample variance and within and total sums of squares derived from sample data.

Other applications of ρ include its use in the following: (a) determining the necessity of analyzing data using a multi-level modeling technique; (b) evaluating longitudinal data; (c) assessing intercoder reliability in research with complex coding schemes where the Kappa statistic would not suffice; and (d) studying interviewer-related measurement error due to the idiosyncratic effects that interviewers likely have on the subset of individual interviews each of them completes.

Trent D. Buskirk and Sarah Shelton

Table 1   Population values of fruit and vegetable intake for five health club franchises

Staff Member	Cluster	Average Daily Fruit and Vegetables	Cluster Average	$(y_{ij} - y_{iU})^2$	$(y_{ij} - y_U)^2$
1	1	2.05	2.35	0.090	2.250
2	1	2.20		0.023	1.823
3	1	2.15		0.040	1.960
4	1	2.30		0.003	1.563
5	1	2.45		0.010	1.210
6	1	2.50		0.023	1.103
7	1	3.05		0.490	0.250
8	1	2.10		0.063	2.103
1	2	4.00	4.03	0.001	0.203
2	2	3.75		0.078	0.040
3	2	4.10		0.005	0.303
4	2	4.35		0.102	0.640
5	2	4.05		0.000	0.250
6	2	3.90		0.017	0.123
7	2	4.00		0.001	0.203
8	2	4.05		0.000	0.250
1	3	3.35	3.38	0.001	0.040
2	3	3.50		0.014	0.002
3	3	3.65		0.073	0.010
4	3	3.20		0.032	0.123
5	3	3.10		0.078	0.203
6	3	3.40		0.000	0.023
7	3	3.45		0.005	0.010
8	3	3.40		0.000	0.023
1	4	6.10	6.40	0.090	6.503
2	4	7.10		0.490	12.603
3	4	6.25		0.023	7.290
4	4	5.95		0.203	5.760
5	4	7.05		0.422	12.250
6	4	6.40		0.000	8.123
7	4	6.05		0.123	6.250

Staff Member	Cluster	Average Daily Fruit and Vegetables	Cluster Average	$(y_{ij} - y_{iU})^2$	$(y_{ij} - y_U)^2$
8	4	6.30		0.010	7.563
1	5	0.50	1.61	1.232	9.303
2	5	0.75		0.740	7.840
3	5	1.25		0.130	5.290
4	5	1.65		0.002	3.610
5	5	2.30		0.476	1.563
6	5	2.25		0.410	1.690
7	5	2.05		0.194	2.250
8	5	2.10		0.240	2.103
		$\bar{y}_U = 3.553$	Total:	5.932	114.690
				SSW	SST

See also Analysis of Variance (ANOVA); Cluster Sample; Design Effects (*deff*); Interviewer-Related Error; Simple Random Sample

Further Readings

Fowler, F. J., Jr. (2002). *Survey research methods* (3rd ed.). Thousand Oaks, CA: Sage.

Groves, R. M. (1989). *Survey errors and survey costs.* New York: Wiley.

Kish, L. (1962). Studies of interviewer variance for attitudinal variables. *Journal of the American Statistical Association, 57,* 92–115.

Lohr, S. L. (1999). *Sampling: Design and analysis.* Pacific Grove, CA: Duxbury Press.

Luke, D. A. (2004). *Multilevel modeling.* Thousand Oaks, CA: Sage.

Singer, J. D., & Willett, J. B. (2003). *Applied longitudinal data analysis: Modeling change and event occurrences.* New York: Oxford University Press.

ROLE PLAYING

Role playing is an educational technique that is used in the training of survey interviewers. It involves face-to-face or telephone interviewers practicing the tailored use of the introduction of the survey in which an attempt is made to gain cooperation from a respondent, and practicing the proper way to administer the questions to respondents, or both. Role playing generally takes place toward the end of training, after the interviewers have been methodically exposed to the entire questionnaire by the trainer, on a question-by-question basis. The role playing part of training may last as long as 2 hours depending on the length and complexity of the questionnaire. Interviewers generally enjoy the role playing part of training, in part because it allows for their active participation in the training process.

Role playing typically takes two forms. One is where the supervisor or trainer takes on the persona of a respondent and interviewers in the training session go through the introduction or the questionnaire, or both, in a round-robin fashion asking the questions to the trainer and going on to the next appropriate question depending on the answer just given by the trainer. The trainer often varies his or her persona while this is happening—sometimes being cooperative and other times being uncooperative when the introduction is being practiced, and sometimes being an "easy" respondent and others times being a "difficult" respondent when questions are being asked. The second form of role playing is where interviewers are paired up and take turns interviewing each other with the questionnaire. As this is taking place, supervisory personnel typically move around the room observing the practice, making tactful suggestions for improvement where appropriate and being available to answer questions that might arise.

Role playing also is used in this "mock interviewing" fashion to help newly hired interviewers learn various basic interviewing skills. It also is used to help experienced or senior interviewers learn advanced interviewing techniques, such as with refusal avoidance training.

Paul J. Lavrakas

See also Interviewer-Related Error; Interviewer Training; Refusal Avoidance Training (RAT); Tailoring

Further Readings

Fowler, F. J., & Mangione, T. W. (1990). *Standardized survey interviewing.* Newbury Park, CA: Sage.

Stewart, C. J., & Cash, W. B. (2007). *Interviewing: Principles and practices* (12th ed.). New York: McGraw-Hill.

Tarnai, J., & Moore, D. L. (2008). Measuring and improving telephone interviewer performance and productivity. In J. Lepkowski, C. Tucker, M. Brick, E. de Leeuw, L. Japec, P. J. Lavrakas, et al. (Eds.), *Advances in telephone survey methodology* (pp. 359–384). New York: Wiley.

ROLLING AVERAGES

Rolling averages, also known as moving averages, are a type of chart analysis technique used to examine survey data collected over extended periods of time, for example, in political tracking polls. They are typically utilized to smooth out data series. The ultimate purpose of rolling averages is to identify long-term trends. They are calculated by averaging a group of observations of a variable of interest over a specific period of time. Such averaged number becomes representative of that period in a trend line. It is said that these period-based averages "roll," or "move," because when a new observation is gathered over time, the oldest observation of the pool being averaged is dropped out and the most recent observation is included into the average. The collection of rolling averages is plotted to represent a trend.

An example of how rolling averages are calculated is as follows. Imagine that a survey analyst is interested in computing 7-day rolling averages (i.e., a 1-week period) for a period of 52 weeks (364 days, approximately

1 year). Let us assume that the variable of interest was measured daily over a period of 52 weeks. The analyst would have to consider the simple average of Day 1 to Day 7 as the first rolling average, represented as $RA_1 = (d_1 + \cdots + d_7)/7$. The second 7-day rolling average would be the average of Day 2 to Day 8, represented as $RA_2 = (d_2 + \cdots + d_8)/7$. Subsequent rolling averages would be $RA_3 = (d_3 + \cdots + d_9)/7, \cdots,$ $RA_{358} = (d_{358} + \cdots + d_{364})/7$. The analyst then would have 358 points or rolling averages to plot a trend across the 364-day year.

In general, simple rolling averages are calculated as $RA_t = \sum_{i=1}^{k} d_i/(k-i) + 1$, where RA_t represents the set of rolling averages for specific time periods (t), d_i represents one unit in the rolling average, and $(k-i) + 1$ is the total number of time points in the rolling average (e.g., in the 7-day rolling averages example, $k = 7$). Overall, it is up to the analyst to decide the total number of time points, $(k-i) + 1$, to be averaged. For example, when variations are expected to occur within a 1-week period, the analyst can select 3-, 5-, or 7-day rolling averages, whereas in studies whose variations occurs monthly, 15-, 28-, or 30-day rolling averages could be selected. In studies with a larger scope, 1-, 2-, 3-year, or longer rolling averages would be needed.

Rolling averages reduce short-term effects; as a consequence, variations across time are decreased and the direction of the trend is more readily clarified. In that sense, variables subject to seasonality or periodic fluctuations in long-term studies are conveniently represented as rolling averages. For example, results of daily pre-election surveys conducted under the same methodology and by the same polling agency tend to fluctuate frequently because of campaigns, media-related effects, or any other aspect around elections; thus, a way to reduce variability and emphasize a voting-intention trend would be by means of rolling averages. Other variables subject to seasonality are, for instance, measures of donation behavior in fundraising studies or measures of exercise levels in health fitness surveys. These variables would be likely to display noticeable peaks or dips in winter and summer months.

Rolling averages do not have inherent predicting properties—they are mainly used to provide a more accurate idea of the construct being monitored over time by reducing variations due to temporary events.

Nevertheless, in situations where the long-term trend is relatively stable, and after careful examination of other indicators, rolling averages may allow the analyst to foresee upcoming observations. In addition to the already explained simple rolling averages, there are various types of rolling averages such as weighted, exponential, triangular, and variable rolling averages. While the simple version described in this entry assigns equal weight to all observations, weighted and exponential rolling averages tend to give greater weight to recent observations. Triangular rolling averages assign greater weight to observations in the middle of the group, and variable rolling averages assign weight depending on the level of variability to be reduced.

René Bautista

See also Tracking Polls

Further Readings

Nebraska Department of Environmental Quality. (2002). *How to calculate yearly and rolling totals and rolling averages.* Retrieved May 18, 2008, from http://www.deq .state.ne.us/Publica.nsf/c4afc76e4e077e11862568770059b73f/ 4cef88e8eab6bcf105256c55007535b7?OpenDocument

ROPER, ELMO (1900–1971)

Elmo Roper, born in 1900, was a leader in the fields of public opinion polling and market research for more than 30 years. He did not have formal academic training in these fields and, in fact, did not finish college. Rather, as the co-owner of a jewelry store in the 1920s, he became interested in customer opinions. He eventually left the jewelry business, and in 1933 he became a co-founder of one of the country's first market research firms, Cherington, Roper and Wood. Five years later Roper left that firm to found Roper Research Associates, Inc. He retired from the firm in 1966 but remained a senior consultant until his death in 1971.

Roper was deeply involved in popularizing market research and public opinion polling and increasing the influence of the fields in both private industry and within the U.S. government. From 1935 to 1950 he was the director of the "Fortune Survey" of public opinion, conducted for *Fortune* magazine. This was the first national opinion poll conducted using scientific sampling strategies.

In 1936 Roper solidified his reputation when the Fortune Survey very closely predicted the results of the presidential contest between Franklin Roosevelt and Alf Langdon. Roper bested the other major polls at the time, the Gallup Poll and the Crossley Poll. Gallup and Crossley predicted Roosevelt would win with 50% to 55% of the vote, while Roper predicted a Roosevelt win with more than 60% of the vote. Roosevelt won the election with 60.7% of the vote. This accuracy helped to establish scientific polling's position and importance on the political landscape. Roper maintained a high profile for the next 30 years. He accurately predicted the next two presidential elections, in 1940 and 1944, predicting results that were within 1% of the actual vote.

In 1948 he, like nearly all other pollsters at the time, incorrectly predicted that Thomas Dewey would defeat Harry Truman in the race for president. The field was badly shaken, but Roper's business survived, with some changes. Election polling in 1948 had stopped weeks before the election because pollsters believed the nation's voters would not change their minds close to the election. Election polling is now conducted up to the election itself and, in the case of exit polls, during it. Probability sampling also replaced quota sampling as the dominant methodology after 1948.

Roper Research Associates conducted polls for various government agencies and many private companies. Roper conducted polls for the New York Stock Exchange and the CBS television network. He was a deputy director of the Office of Strategic Services during World War II. He also wrote a syndicated newspaper column, had a radio show, and was editor at large for the *Saturday Review* magazine.

Outside the world of polling, Roper was a liberal democrat involved in many causes of the day. He sat on the board of Planned Parenthood. In 1955 he was elected president of the Atlantic Union Committee, succeeding Associate Justice Owen J. Roberts of the United States Supreme Court. The group sought to strengthen ties between Canada, England, Belgium, the Netherlands, and France as a counterbalance to the Soviet Union.

Roper believed that public opinion polls were important tools in a democracy and felt that good public opinion research could help scholars and government officials make more informed decisions. To this end, he believed that public opinion data from a variety of sources should be stored in a permanent collection, and in 1946 he created the Roper Center for

Public Opinion Research at Williams College. The center included data not only from Roper's work but also from the Gallup Poll and the Crossley Poll, among others. The Roper Center moved to the University of Connecticut in 1977 and remains the world's foremost archive of public opinion data.

Eric White

See also Probability Sample; Quota Sampling; Roper Center for Public Opinion Research

ROPER CENTER FOR PUBLIC OPINION RESEARCH

The Roper Center for Public Opinion Research, which now is located at the University of Connecticut, and is one of the world's largest collections of data on the social sciences, was founded at Williams College in 1946 by Elmo Roper, who anticipated the future value of the studies he and other survey research pioneers were conducting to better understand what was on the collective minds of the public. His vision was of the academic scholar in pursuit of the thoughts, opinions, and behaviors of the common person during the early days of polling. Shortly thereafter he was joined by George Gallup, Sr., who contributed his 17 years of data, followed by Archibald Crossley, the National Opinion Research Center, Opinion Research Corporation, and the earliest state polls from Minnesota, Texas, and Iowa. More than six decades later, the Roper Center archives are the largest archives of survey data in existence, including the work of more than 250 survey organizations, representing thousands of studies and hundreds of thousands of questions asked in the United States and abroad. A list of the center's data contributors reads like a "who's who" of the profession, including the major news media—paper and electronic—that sponsor and conduct surveys on a multitude of topics.

This comprehensive collection has fulfilled Elmo Roper's dream that the data be preserved for future generations. However, today the center's role of data steward goes beyond preservation measures and has expanded to include the provision of easy access tools to facilitate use of the collection. The center's membership includes nearly every major university in the United States and several in Europe and elsewhere.

The Tools

The iPOLL database contains a half-million questions and responses from surveys conducted in the United States since 1935. Using simple search terms, it is possible to identify hundreds of relevant questions on most public policy and social issues in a matter of seconds. Of these half-million questions, about 60% are from surveys where the entire data set has been archived with the Roper Center; the other 40% are from surveys that have yet to arrive, are only available in report form, or are archived elsewhere. Using the integrated RoperExpress service, it is possible to move directly from a question in the iPOLL database to the documentation and download the data set, as well. This service permits researchers to conduct secondary analyses (e.g., cross-tabulations that reveal more details about respondents answering in a particular way) on their desktop computers.

The drill-down functionality that permits this on-demand download of the documentation and data files is distinctive to the Roper Center's data archives. Although systems exist that permit searching at the question level, most of those organizations do not maintain the raw data set files. Conversely, there are institutions that offer direct download of data set files but have not developed a question-level retrieval system.

Contributions to the Field

To improve the understanding of the public in the aggregate, the Roper Center partners with those who conduct survey research. To achieve this, it has developed systems that permit broad access and utilization of the data entrusted to its care. Additionally, the Roper Center Web site offers educational modules to acquaint researchers with the fundamentals of opinion polling and to assist with interpreting results.

There are two important ways in which the archives serve the survey research profession. The first is educational. Sound secondary data analysis relies upon principles of triangulation—examining multiple sources of data and contextual variations in question wording, timing, or methodology for the purpose of building a firm base for understanding a complex phenomenon. This is more than gathering numerous data points;

it brings together different "views" into the topic by using an array of sources. The comprehensive iPOLL database decries the notion of cherry-picking data by providing broad, easy access to the data. Survey practitioners are further served by these resources when they observe the work generated by their contemporaries. Pointless "reinvention of the wheel" is avoided, and worthwhile research can be repeated.

The center also promotes the intelligent use of public opinion data by providing educational modules on survey practices and introductory views into different topics. Its Web site offers a glossary, online analysis tools, and training tutorials. Two teaching modules, dubbed Polling 101 and Polling 201, cover sources of error, sampling, reading data tables, and select criteria for assessing survey quality and strategies for analyzing data. The content is straightforward and presented clearly, inviting to both the novice and the professional seeking a refresher on survey research methods and terminology.

The second way in which the archives contribute to the profession is by providing a safe venue to ensure its data will exist in usable formats in perpetuity. Unlike Web sites that make data sets available only temporarily, the Roper Center carefully processes each data set and integrates the data into its permanent archives, migrating to current formats and creating finding-aids like iPOLL and RoperExpress to make such research less complicated.

Furthermore, this venue permits researchers from various sectors to scrutinize the surveys. Critics and supporters alike are provided the opportunity to test theories by easily accessing the individual-level data files to run secondary analyses and statistical tests, which makes the industry stronger as a whole. Disclosure has always been important in this field, and quality survey organizations have believed that depositing data with an institutional archive that permits such investigation can reveal ways to improve upon their work.

Lois E. Timms-Ferrara

See also Roper, Elmo

Further Readings

Rockwell, R. C. (2005). The role of the Roper Center in the polling industry. In S. J. Best & B. Radcliff (Eds.), *Polling America: An encyclopedia of public opinion*. Westport, CT: Greenwood Press.

Rockwell, R. C. (2001). Data archives, international. *International encyclopedia of the social and behavioral sciences*. Paris: Elsevier.

Roper Center for Public Opinion Research: http://www.ropercenter.uconn.edu

Smith, T., & Forstrom, M. (2001). In praise of data archives: Finding and recovering the 1963 Kennedy Assassination Study. *IASSIST Quarterly, 25*(4), 12–14.

Smith, T. W., & Weil, F. D. (1990). A report: Finding public opinion data: A guide to sources. *Public Opinion Quarterly, 54*(4), 609–626.

ROTATING PANEL DESIGN

A rotating panel design is a survey sampling strategy sometimes used when estimates are produced regularly over time. Under such a design, equally sized sets of sample units are brought in and out of the sample in some specified pattern. These sets, often called *rotation groups*, may be composed of households, business firms, or other units of interest to the survey. Rotating panel designs are used to reduce the variances of estimators of level or change and often to reduce the survey costs associated with introducing a new unit into the sample. The wide variety of such designs reflects (a) the types of data and the estimates to be produced by the survey, (b) the statistical relationships among the characteristics of interest, (c) the operational costs of the survey, (d) the burden on respondents, and (e) the effects of multiple contacts on data quality.

Examples of Rotating Panel Designs

Under one type of rotation scheme, during each time period, one rotation group is canvassed for the first time, while another is canvassed for the final time. As an example, in the Labour Force Survey conducted by Statistics Canada, the sample of households is divided into six rotation groups, with a new group entering each month. Thus, in any month, one group is canvassed for the first time, one for the second time, and so forth. After 6 months of responding, households are retired from the sample. The Labour Force Survey conducted by the Australian Bureau of Statistics uses a similar scheme, dividing the sample into eight rotation groups; households are in sample for 8 months.

The rotation pattern can be more complex. The Current Population Survey, jointly sponsored by the U.S. Bureau of Labor Statistics and the U.S. Census

Bureau to measure the U.S. labor force, uses eight rotation groups. A household is interviewed for 4 consecutive months, temporarily dropped from the sample for 8 months, brought back into sample for 4 more months, then retired. In any month one rotation group is interviewed for the first time, one for the second time, and so on, while one group is interviewed for the eighth and final time. For each of the surveys mentioned, the rotation pattern is said to be a "one-level" design because the respondents report for only the current period of time (1 month).

Other examples of surveys that use a rotating panel design are the National Crime Victimization Survey and the Consumer Expenditure Survey, each conducted by the U.S. federal government. In the Census Bureau's Survey of Income and Program Participation, although cross-sectional estimates are produced, the people in sample are contacted in a rotating pattern to obtain longitudinal estimates, that is, estimates of gross changes over time. These three surveys are examples of multi-level designs, as respondents report for several prior periods (months) during the same interview.

Under a different type of rotation scheme, groups cycle in and out of sample indefinitely or at least until the entire sample is retired. A good example is the former (before 1998) design of the monthly surveys of retail and wholesale trade in the United States, where the noncertainty sample was divided into three rotation groups. In each of 3 consecutive months, only one of the three groups was canvassed. This pattern was repeated, with each group reporting every third month, for the 5-year life of the sample.

Considerations in Selecting and Implementing the Design

In many ways, a rotating panel design is a compromise between taking a new, independent sample for each period and canvassing the same sample units repeatedly, that is, a complete sample overlap. Each of these extremes has its advantages statistically and in practice; a rotating panel design, sometimes thought of as a partial sample overlap, tries to reap the benefits of each.

Statistically, if the correlations in variables of interest are strong over time, estimates of change can usually be made more accurate by overlapping some or the entire sample across time. This is the case even without applying composite estimation, a statistical method that combines data from several sources, for example, different periods of time. However, composite estimation can reduce variances further in many cases, especially where estimates of means or totals are desired.

Many factors are considered before implementing a rotating panel design. Of primary concern are the types of data and estimates to be produced and how they rank in importance. The relative importance of estimates of level (totals, means, and proportions) at specific points in time, change across periods, and averages over time must be weighed. The variances and biases of these estimators will typically depend on the type of design, the amount of rotation, and the correlations among the rotation group estimates over time.

Operational aspects, such as survey costs, the mode of data collection, and respondent burden, are important considerations as well. For surveys that are conducted repeatedly, much of the cost may be incurred the first time a sample unit is contacted. For example, canvassing a region to devise an area sample can be very expensive, especially if the units are interviewed only once. Even with list sampling, the tasks may include (a) preparing introductory questionnaire materials, (b) finding the household or establishment (for a personal visit), (c) explaining the survey or special procedures to the respondent, (d) filing background information about the sample unit, and (e) preparing the database for each unit. Many of these steps need not be repeated if the same unit is canvassed a second or third time, as in a rotation design. For example, in some household surveys, the first contact is made in person because a telephone number is not available. When a rotating panel design is used, subsequent contacts can often be completed by telephone, reducing the cost per interview.

Issues of respondent burden and response are relevant in a rotating panel design. The burden on an individual household or establishment typically increases with the number of interviews and the length of the questionnaire. With increased burden might come decreased response rate or lower-quality data. For household surveys, how to handle people who move and what effect they have on the estimates can be a problem. These issues become more prominent as the time between contacts with the sample unit increases. For business surveys, various approaches have been proposed for continuous sample selection while controlling the overlap over time and the burden. The *permanent random numbers technique* has been implemented in several countries, whereby a unique random number is assigned to each sampling unit and stays assigned to that unit as long as the unit is in the sampling frame. This number is used to reduce the chances that any given unit will be selected for interviewing in two consecutive waves of the survey, thereby minimizing respondent burden over the entire panel study.

Other problems can arise with a rotating panel design. As the respondents in the sample grow accustomed to the repeated interviews, the values of their responses may be affected, a consequence known as panel conditioning. Specifically, time-in-sample bias refers to the deviation in the response for a rotation group that is interviewed for the first (or second, or third, etc.) time, due to the conditioning. The value of an estimator can be averaged over all the rotation groups for the same period. The differential bias—the value relative to the average—can then be computed for each individual group to illustrate the relative effect of panel conditioning on the estimator.

Maintaining rotation groups of nearly equal size can be difficult, especially with units in business surveys. At the start of the rotation design, the sample units are usually selected and assigned to groups so that each has approximately the same weighted total of some key characteristic. However, over time, as units grow in size or drop out of existence, the groups may become unbalanced. This phenomenon can add variability to the estimates if composite estimation is used.

Issues of recall can develop when respondents are asked to provide data for different periods of time during the same interview. The *seam effect*, observed in some household panel longitudinal surveys, is caused by difficulty recalling the timing of events as respondents think back further in time. The opposite problem—early reporting bias—can affect economic surveys. Respondents asked to provide very recent sales data often report low, perhaps because their business accounts are incomplete and they underestimate their recent sales. The same respondents may provide more accurate reports for earlier periods of time because more data are available and the respondents' accounts are more complete.

Patrick J. Cantwell

See also Bureau of Labor Statistics (BLS); Composite Estimation; Current Population Survey (CPS); Longitudinal Studies; Panel; Panel Conditioning; Respondent Burden; Respondent Fatigue; Response Bias; Seam Effect; Statistics Canada; Survey Costs; U.S. Bureau of the Census

Further Readings

Cantwell, P. (1990). Variance formulae for composite estimators in one- and multi-level rotation designs. *Survey Methodology, 16*(1), 153–163.

Cantwell, P., & Caldwell, C. (1998). Examining the revisions in monthly retail and wholesale trade surveys under a rotating panel design. *Journal of Official Statistics, 14*(1), 47–59.

Kasprzyk, D., Kalton, G., Duncan, G., & Singh, M. P. (Eds.). (1989). *Panel surveys.* New York: Wiley.

Ohlsson, E. (1995). Coordination of samples using permanent random numbers. In B. G. Cox, D. A. Binder, B. N. Chinnappa, A. Christianson, M. J. Colledge, & P. S. Kott (Eds.), *Business survey methods* (pp. 153–169). New York: Wiley.

U.S. Census Bureau. (2006, October). *Design and methodology* (Current Population Survey Tech. Paper 66). Retrieved March 4, 2008, from http://www.census.gov/prod/2006pubs/tp-66.pdf

Woodruff, R. S. (1963). The use of rotating samples in the Census Bureau's monthly surveys. *Journal of the American Statistical Association, 58*, 454–467.

S

SALIENCY

Saliency refers to the degree to which a topic or event resonates with a prospective respondent or sample member. The more a topic or event resonates with a sample member, the more salient or important that topic or event tends to be in that person's life. Conversely, topics or events that resonate little or hold little importance for the sample member are said to have little saliency.

What are the implications of saliency for survey researchers? Saliency actually operates at two levels: the question level and the survey level.

On the question level, saliency refers to the importance of an event or action in a person's life. More important events or actions are better remembered than actions or events of low saliency. Consequently, saliency can affect the accuracy with which an event is remembered, which, in turn, can affect the accuracy of the response. More important or unusual events are generally remembered with greater accuracy than are common or frequent events. For example, most people can tell you, with little effort, their date of birth, the highest degree they have completed, what major illnesses they have suffered, or how many children they have. Similarly, given the significance of the event, many can tell you where they were when they heard the news of 9/11 or when John F. Kennedy was shot. Items of lesser importance, on the other hand, have lower saliency and are thus more difficult to remember. For example, recalling the number of times you have visited the grocery store in the past month or the number of movies you have seen in the past year can be difficult. On the other hand, while remembering how many movies you have seen in the past year is probably difficult, remembering the number of movies you have seen in the past week is probably not difficult. This illustrates an important point, the lower the saliency of an item, the shorter the reference period should be.

On the survey level, the saliency of the survey topic refers to the degree to which the subject matter of the survey resonates for the population being surveyed. If the questions being asked are of great interest to the average sample member, the survey is said to highly salient, whereas surveys where the subject being investigated is of little interest are said to have low saliency. Gaining cooperation or attaining a high response rate is made more difficult when the saliency is low, because sample members have little motivation to respond. On the other hand, when the central topic of a survey is one of great interest to those being surveyed, sample members are more likely to respond. For them, the burden of responding is compensated for by their interest in the topic. Thus, saliency is an important factor when thinking about response rates and the level of effort required to attain a certain response rate. For example, a questionnaire with high saliency and low respondent burden (e.g., takes minimal time to complete, is easy and straightforward to understand) will require much less effort to attain a high response rate than will a survey that has both low saliency and high respondent burden (i.e., takes a long time to complete, requires a great deal of record checking, or asks difficult or complex questions that require a great deal of thought). Surveys where the burden is high and the saliency is low often require respondent incentives to improve response rates.

Geraldine Mooney

See also Leverage-Saliency Theory; Reference Period; Telescoping

Further Readings

Groves, R. M., Singer, E. & Corning, A. (2000). Leverage-salience theory of survey participation. *Public Opinion Quarterly, 64,* 299–308.

SAMPLE

In survey research, a sample is a subset of elements drawn from a larger population. If all elements from the larger population are "sampled" for measurement, then a census is being conducted, not a sample survey.

In a broad context, survey researchers are interested in obtaining some type of information for some population, or universe, of interest. A sampling frame, that is, a frame that represents the population of interest, must be defined. The sampling frame may be identical to the population, or it may be only part of the population and is therefore subject to some undercoverage, or it may have an indirect relationship to the population (e. g., the population is males and the frame is telephone numbers). It is sometimes possible to obtain the desired information from the entire population through a census. Usually, however, for reasons of cost and time, survey researchers will only obtain information for part of it, referred to as a sample of the population. There may be several different samples selected, one for each stage of a multi-stage sample. For example, there may be a sample of counties, a sample of blocks within sampled counties, a sample of addresses within sampled blocks, and a sample of persons from sampled addresses.

A sample can be obtained in many different ways, as defined by the sample design. Survey researchers usually will want to have a probability sample, which ensures that all units in the frame have a known nonzero probability of selection, rather than a convenience sample or nonprobability sample, which do not

sample respondents with known nonzero probabilities of selection.

Gary M. Shapiro

See also Census; Elements; Frame; Multi-Stage Sample; Nonprobability Sampling; Population; Population of Interest; Probability Sample; Representative Sample; Sample Design; Sampling; Sampling Frame; Undercoverage; Universe

Further Readings

Hansen, H. H., Hurwitz, W. N., & Madow, W. G. (1953). *Sample survey methods and theory.* New York: Wiley.
Särndal, C., Swensson, B., & Wretman, J. (1992). *Model assisted survey sampling.* New York: Springer.

SAMPLE DESIGN

A sample design is the framework, or road map, that serves as the basis for the selection of a survey sample and affects many other important aspects of a survey as well. In a broad context, survey researchers are interested in obtaining some type of information through a survey for some population, or universe, of interest. One must define a sampling frame that represents the population of interest, from which a sample is to be drawn. The sampling frame may be identical to the population, or it may be only part of it and is therefore subject to some undercoverage, or it may have an indirect relationship to the population (e. g., the population is preschool children and the frame is a listing of preschools). The sample design provides the basic plan and methodology for selecting the sample.

A sample design can be simple or complex. For example, if the sampling frame consists of a list of every unit, together with its address, in the population of interest, and if a mail survey is to be conducted, then a simple list sampling would be appropriate; for example, the sample design is to have a sampling interval of 10 (select every 10th unit) from the list. The sample design must vary according to the nature of the frame and the type of survey to be conducted (the survey design). For example, a researcher may want to interview males through a telephone survey. In this case, the sample design might be a relatively simple one-stage sample of telephone numbers using random-digit dialing. One aspect of the sample design in this case is to determine whether all males in a household are to be interviewed and, if not, how to select a second-stage sample of males from each sampled telephone number that reaches a household.

The simplest type of sample design is purposive sampling, or convenience sampling. Usually, however, the survey researcher wants every unit in the frame to have a known probability of selection, so a more complex sample design is needed. In many situations, for purposes of efficiency and reducing costs, a multi-stage sample is desirable. For example, suppose a researcher wants to do face-to-face interviewing for a population consisting of African American women. In this case, the survey researcher might select an area probability sample, with the first stage of selection being a sample of counties, or primary sampling units. The next stage of selection might be a sample of blocks within the sampled counties, followed by a sample of housing units from the sampled blocks. The appropriate sampling frame at the first stage of selection for such a survey would be all counties in the United States. However, the researcher might decide to restrict the frame to only those counties with more than a particular percentage or number of African Americans. In this case, the survey researcher is introducing undercoverage into the sample design, which will likely result in some degree of bias in survey estimates. In deciding on the preferred sample design, the researcher must weigh the bias concerns against cost issues. If the researcher has a fixed budget, then sampling from all counties will result in higher variances or standard errors, but in lower bias, than will sampling from a restricted frame of counties.

The decisions that survey researchers make about their sample designs are among the most important ones that must be made to ensure the research is adequate for the information needs for which the survey is being conducted. Too often inadequate consideration is given in selecting a sample design, which, in turn, yields data that do not adequately meet the goals of the research. Often this happens because of the additional costs associated with conducting a survey using a more robust (and thus more appropriate) sample design.

Gary M. Shapiro

See also Adaptive Sampling; Area Probability Sample; Cluster Sample; Complex Sample Surveys; Convenience Sampling; Cross-Sectional Survey Design; Cutoff Sampling; Directory Sampling; Dual-Frame Sampling; Equal Probability of Selection; List Sampling; Multiple-Frame Sampling; Multi-Stage Sample; Network Sampling; Nonprobability Sampling; Probability of Selection; Probability Proportional to Size (PPS) Sampling; Probability Sample; Purposive Sample; Quota Sampling; Random-Digit Dialing (RDD); Random Sampling; Representative Sample; Sampling; Sampling Without Replacement; Sequential Sampling; Simple Random Sample; Snowball Sampling; Stratified Sampling; Systematic Sampling

Further Readings

Cochran, W. G. (1977). *Sampling techniques*. New York: Wiley.

Hansen, H. H., Hurwitz, W. N., & Madow, W. G. (1953). *Sample survey methods and theory*. New York: Wiley.

Kish, L. (1995). *Survey sampling*. New York: Wiley.

Särndal, C., Swensson, B., & Wretman, J. (1992). *Model assisted survey sampling*. New York: Springer.

SAMPLE MANAGEMENT

In survey research, sample management refers to the efforts that must be made to coordinate the processing of sampled cases during a survey's field period so as to achieve the highest possible response rates within the finite budget that is allocated for data collection. This requires the coordination of whatever software is used to help manage the sample by the person(s) doing the managing.

The person or persons charged with sample management typically do this on a daily basis throughout the field period. For smaller surveys that involve a few hundred cases, this might be done by one person who may also have responsibility for other supervisory tasks. This person may manage the sample manually. In very large surveys with thousands of cases (including some large random-digit dialing surveys with millions of sampled telephone numbers), an entire team of supervisory personnel whose sole responsibility is sample management also will need to use specialized computer software to manage the sample.

Managing a survey sample differs greatly depending on whether or not the survey uses interviewers to gather the data. The following sections address sample management when the survey is interviewer-administered and when it is self-administered.

Sample Management in Interviewer-Administered Surveys

In interviewer-assisted surveying, both for in-person and telephone surveys, sample management can be viewed as being composed of two primary responsibilities that often are in direct conflict with each other. One of these responsibilities is to allocate enough sample cases to keep interviewers productive and, in turn, to employ the right number of interviewers to process the sample so as to achieve the number of completed interviews that are required for the survey within the field period. The other responsibility is to activate "just enough" cases so that the field period ends with the highest possible response rates at the lowest possible cost.

Based on past experience, the sample manager of an interviewer-administered survey will have an informed expectation of approximately how many sample cases will need to be activated from the available sample (i.e., the *sampling pool*) during the survey field period to achieve the required sample size of completed interviews. Oftentimes the sample will be divided into sample replicates, each containing random subsets of cases. Once a replicate of cases has been activated, the entire replicate must be fully processed to allow each case to reach its proper final outcome.

If cases are not worked enough during the field period, response rates will suffer. Thus, the sample managers need to activate the last replicate of cases, leaving enough time in the field period to allow those cases to be processed fully. If not enough time is left to process this final set of cases, the most hard-to-reach respondents within those cases will not be contacted and interviewed. In contrast, if cases are contacted too frequently during the field period, for example, by having an overabundance of interviewers constantly making contact attempts, response rates also will suffer because respondents will become annoyed if the survey organization contacts them too frequently. Thus, the challenge for the sample managers is to have the right number of sample cases active at any one time and the right number of interviewers scheduled to process these cases.

To this end, the sample manager likely will need to track the progress that interviewers are making on the sample on a daily basis. The metrics that the manager will consider include the hourly or daily productivity of interviewers. Are they gaining completions more slowly than anticipated, faster than anticipated, or at about the rate anticipated? If productivity is too low, then more sample, more interviewers, or both, will be needed, unless the field period can be extended. Neither of these is appealing because both add costs to the survey budget. If productivity is higher than anticipated, then fewer interviewers will need to be scheduled or less sample will need to be activated during the remainder of the field. Making the correct decisions on these matters is important because costs can be saved, and this is highly attractive to survey organizations and their clients.

The success of any refusal conversion process that the survey may deploy is another metric that the sample manager will consider in determining whether the correct amount of sample has been activated or the correct number of interviewers has been scheduled, or both. If refusals are being converted at a rate (higher or lower) different from what was anticipated, the sample manager will need to make adjustments in allocating fresh cases for the duration of the field period.

There also are myriad personnel issues that survey sample managers face given the temporary and part-time nature of the work done by many survey interviewers. As such, interviewer turnover (churn) often is a problem that must be anticipated throughout a field period, especially for field periods that last more than a few weeks. Ultimately, the sample manager must be confident that there will be enough qualified interviewers to work the amount of sample that must be processed each day of the field period.

Depending on the size of the sample that must be processed within the field period, managing it in an interviewer-administered survey can be an extremely demanding and nerve-racking experience. Assuming that the quality of the final sample is important to the survey organization (although this is not always the case), even when using sophisticated software to help control the sample, idiosyncratic cases constantly will arise that need decisions made by a human sample manager on a case-by-case basis if high-quality sampling is to be achieved.

Sample Management in Self-Administered Surveys

In mail, Internet, and Web surveys, in which interviewers play no part in the data collection, managing the sample is much less complex. This is especially true if no follow-up mailings or other types of contacts with the nonresponding cases are planned to increase the survey's response rates.

In self-administered mail and Internet surveys, the sample cases typically are contacted initially, via mail or email, to inform them that they have been selected to participate in a survey. This contact may include the survey questionnaire, or it may mention that the questionnaire will be arriving within a few days, or it may direct the sampled respondent to a Web site where the questionnaire may be completed online. If the mode of contact and the mode of returning a questionnaire are via a postal delivery service, it is not uncommon for completed questionnaires to begin arriving back to the survey organization 2 days following the day of the original mailing. If the mode of contact is via the Internet, it is not unusual for some questionnaires to be completed within hours after the first emails have been sent.

The sample manager(s) will need to track incoming mailed-back questionnaires or questionnaires completed on a Web site on a daily basis. In the case of questionnaires that are mailed back, there is a labor-intensive process that must be staffed to receive, open, screen for completeness, and log in the questionnaires. The managers will have expectations based on prior experience and the specific design features of the survey (e.g., the use of incentives to stimulate response) about what level of response is anticipated. The vast majority of replies to an initial mailing will come back within 2 weeks of the original mailing. If the survey has budgeted a follow-up mailing (or multiple follow-up mailings) to raise the response rate, then the sample managers will need to work with the staff that implements the follow-up mailing with enough lead time so that the second mailing can go out on a timely basis. In most survey designs, the researchers will know which specific cases already have responded prior to the second mailing and thus will be able to avoid the need to do a full follow-up mailing to all original sampled cases. However, it is impossible to avoid mailing a follow-up to some of the cases who already responded to the original mailing because (a) some of their returns will not arrive by the time of the follow-up mailing, and (b) some will never be received because of mail delivery or Internet problems.

Sample Management in Mixed-Mode Surveys

As response rates have dropped during the past two decades, the need for researchers to implement mixed-mode surveys, which often can achieve higher response rates at cost-favorable levels, has become more commonplace. For example, using an address-based sampling frame would allow a researcher to implement a design that begins the field period with a mail survey, as well as offering an Internet mode for completing the questionnaire and other survey task(s). Then, nonresponders for whom the researchers have a telephone number matched to their address would be followed up using telephone interviewers. Finally, in-person interviewers would be sent during the last stage of the field period to all addresses that have not responded to previous modes of contact. Managing a mixed-mode sample design such as this is much more complex than managing a sample for a survey that uses a single mode of data collection. In the case of the mixed-mode approach, with multiple channels allowed for data to be gathered and to be returned to the survey organization, it is paramount that the sample managers have the proper software systems in place to capture and safely store the incoming data and to accurately track the status of every case on a daily basis that remains active. If this does not happen, the response rates for the survey will suffer in ways that could have been avoided had a better sample management system been deployed.

Paul J. Lavrakas

See also Address-Based Sampling; Case; Case-Control Study; Contact Rate; Control Sheet; Face-to-Face Interviewing; Field Period; Hit Rate; Internet Surveys; Mail Survey; Mixed Mode; Refusal Conversion; Response Rates; Sample; Sample Replicates; Sampling Pool; Supervisor; Supervisor-to-Interviewer Ratio; Survey Costs; Telephone Surveys; Total Design Method (TDM); Web Survey

Further Readings

Couper, M. P., Baker, R. P., Bethlehem, J., Clark, C. Z., Martin, J., Nicholls, W. L., et al. (1998). *Computer assisted survey information collection.* New York: Wiley.

Hansen, S. E. (2007). CATI sample management. In J. Lepkowski, C. Tucker, M. Brick, E. de Leeuw,

L. Japec, P. J. Lavrakas, et al. (Eds.), *Advances in telephone survey methodology* (pp. 340–358). New York: Wiley.

Lavrakas, P. J. (1993). *Telephone survey methods: Sampling, selection, and supervision* (2nd ed.). Newbury Park, CA: Sage.

SAMPLE PRECINCT

Sample precinct refers to a sampling unit used in data collection and analysis on Election Day. The term is most commonly associated with media exit polling and election night projections. For voting purposes, jurisdictions such as counties or townships are divided into precincts based on geography. A precinct is the smallest voting unit in a jurisdiction. Voters are assigned to a precinct, which typically has one polling place where voters can go to cast their ballots. Data are collected from sample precincts, which are used to form estimates of the vote and voter opinions and characteristics.

For Election Day analysis, a sample of precincts is selected because it would be too costly and time consuming to collect data from all precincts in a jurisdiction (e.g., a state or city). Prior to the election, a representative sample of precincts is selected for a given jurisdiction. A listing of all precincts in the jurisdiction is compiled, and a probability sample of precincts is selected. Typically, stratified sampling is used to increase the precision of the estimates. Precincts can be stratified using such variables as historical voting patterns, geography, and race/ethnicity.

In practice, sample precincts are used for two purposes. The first is to provide data to project the outcome of the election using actual votes from the sample precincts. Workers, sometimes called *stringers*, are sent to the sample precincts on Election Day. As soon as possible after the polling place closes, the stringer's job is to get the actual vote totals from the polling place official and call these results into a central location where they are tabulated and fed into computerized statistical models for analysis. Sometimes it is also possible to get the sample precinct votes via the Internet or by phone. The sample precinct models can take various forms, including ratio and regression estimators. For statewide elections, a typical sample size for this purpose is about 80 precincts and usually varies from 15 to 100 depending on the characteristics of the state, the newsworthiness of the electoral contest, and how close the election is expected to be.

The second use of precinct samples is for conducting Election Day exit polls, such as those conducted for the National Election Pool by Edison Media Research each major election year since 2004. The exit poll precinct sample is usually a smaller subset of the sample used to collect the actual vote tallies. A typical statewide exit poll will have about 30 sample precincts and typically ranges from 15 to 60. Exit poll interviewers are sent to the sample precincts to interview voters as they exit the polling place. Data are collected on voters' demographics and opinions and how they voted. These data are called into a central location three times during the day and tabulated. The demographic and opinion data are cross-tabulated with the vote and are used to analyze why voters voted the way they did. These data help explain why candidates won or lost and what issues were important to voters. The data from the exit poll sample precincts are also used to help project the election outcomes.

Daniel M. Merkle

See also Election Night Projections; Election Polls; Exit Polls; National Election Pool (NEP); Stratified Sampling

Further Readings

Merkle, D. M., & Edelman, M. (2000). A review of the 1996 voter news service exit polls from a total survey error perspective. In P. J. Lavrakas & M. Traugott (Eds.), *Election polls, the news media, and democracy.* New York: Chatham House.

SAMPLE REPLICATES

A sample replicate is a random subset of the entire available sample (i.e., *sampling pool*) that has been drawn for a particular survey. Sample replicates help survey managers coordinate the progress that is made on data collection during the survey's field period. Sample replicates often are made up of a randomly assigned 1,000 of the sampled elements, although sometimes replicates may be as small in size as 100.

The value of structuring a survey sampling pool into replicates is that it is not possible to know in advance exactly how many of the telephone numbers, emails, or street addresses in a sampling pool actually will need to be released and processed in order to achieve the final sample size of completed interviews a given survey needs. Sometimes survey organizations make better progress than expected in processing their samples, whereas other times they make worse progress. Releasing the sample in these replicates prevents releasing more sampled elements than are needed, which in turn helps control survey costs.

A rule of thumb that is used by most survey organizations is that once a replicate has been released, all the elements in that replicate must be fully processed according to whatever contact rules are being applied. Doing otherwise would lead to a distortion of the final sample with the last-to-be-activated replicates having data collection take place only from the easiest-to-reach respondents in these replicates, whereas data collection would not be successful from the harder-to-reach respondents in the last-to-be-activated replicates. This would conflict with what will have taken place with replicates that were released earlier in the field period, where all possible completed interviews were attained regardless of how difficult it was to reach the respondents.

Organizing a sampling pool into replicates is straightforward and essentially occurs in one of two ways. First, a "large enough" sampling pool should be drawn from the sampling frame so that there are more elements drawn than would ever be expected to be needed to complete the survey. Then these elements are cleaned (e.g., duplicates are eliminated) and then randomly ordered and then divided (segmented) into replicates of whatever size is desired, for example, of size 1,000. This first approach works best when the sampling frame is not already in a random order. In cases where the sampling frame can be accessed randomly, then replicates can be created directly as elements are drawn from the frame. If the replicates are to be 1,000 in size, then under this second approach the first 1,000 elements drawn make up the first replicate, the second 1,000 drawn make up the second replicate, and so on. When using this second approach, safeguards must be used to make certain there will not be duplicate elements in different replicates.

Supervisory personnel who are responsible for controlling the data collection during the field period will generally start by releasing enough replicates to carry the interviewing staff through the first one third or one half of the field period. Based on the productivity that is observed in this early stage (e.g., looking at the

pattern of the final dispositions of the elements that have been processed to date), the sample managers will calculate whether the initial estimates of how much sample will be needed look to be on track, too low, or too high. If on track, nothing will be done about the amount of sample that will be processed. If too high, some of the replicates that were expected to be needed will be held back. If too low, more replicates will need to be released before the field period ends.

Managing the release and processing of sample replicates is very important for the end quality of a survey and its costs. Releasing too many replicates may lead to an erosion of the survey's response rates because there may not be enough staff or time to fully process the sample during the remainder of the field period. Releasing too few replicates will lead to staff not having enough sampled cases to work, and thus staff will not be able to operate at peak efficiency.

Paul J. Lavrakas

See also Calling Rules; Elements; Field Period; Final Dispositions; Sample; Sample Management; Sample Size; Sampling Frame; Sampling Pool; Survey Costs

Further Readings

Hansen, S. E. (2007). CATI sample management systems. In J. M. Lepkowski, C. Tucker, J. M. Brick, E. de Leeuw, L. Japec, P. J. Lavrakas, et al. (Eds.), *Advances in telephone survey methodology* (pp. 340–358). New York: Wiley.

Lavrakas, P. J. (1993). *Telephone survey methods: Sampling, selection, and supervision* (2nd ed.). Newbury Park, CA: Sage.

SAMPLE SIZE

The sample size of a survey most typically refers to the number of units that were chosen from which data were gathered. However, sample size can be defined in various ways. There is the *designated sample size*, which is the number of sample units selected for contact or data collection. There is also the *final sample size*, which is the number of completed interviews or units for which data are actually collected. The final sample size may be much smaller than the designated sample size if there is considerable nonresponse, ineligibility, or both. Not all the units in the designated sample may need to be processed if productivity in completing interviews is much higher than anticipated to achieve the final sample size. However, this assumes that units have been activated from the designated sample in a random fashion. Survey researchers may also be interested in the sample size for subgroups of the full sample.

In planning to conduct a survey, the survey researcher must decide on the sample design. Sample size is one aspect of the sample design. It is inversely related to the variance, or standard error of survey estimates, and is a determining factor in the cost of the survey. In the simplest situation, the variance is a direct function of the sample size. For example, if a researcher is taking a simple random sample and is interested in estimating a proportion p, then

$$\text{Variance} = (p)(1-p)/n,$$

where n is the sample size. More generally,

$$\text{Variance} = f(p)(1-p)/n,$$

where f is the design effect, which reflects the effect of the sample design and weighting on the variance.

In the planning effort for a more complex survey, it is preferable to not focus directly on sample size. It is best to either (a) set a budget and determine the sample size and sample design that minimize the variance for the available budget, or (b) set a desired variance or required reliability, possibly using statistical power analysis, and then determine the sample size and sample design that minimize costs while achieving the desired variance. Sample size does not solely determine either the variance or the cost of a survey and thus is not generally, by itself, a meaningful planning criterion. More useful is *effective sample size*, which adjusts the sample size for the sample design, weighting, and other aspects of the survey operation.

Even better than fixing the budget and minimizing the variance is to minimize the mean square error (MSE), the researcher can set a desired MSE and minimize the cost to obtain it. MSE is defined as the sum of the variance and the bias squared and thus accounts for more than just the variance. One sample design option may have a larger sample size and a lower variance than a second option but have a larger MSE, and thus it would be a poor choice.

A common misconception is that the needed sample size is a function of the size of the population of interest, or universe. For example, people often think that to achieve a given precision, a much larger sample size is required for a sample of the entire United States than of a large city. This is not generally true. However, if a survey researcher is considering a sample that is a substantial proportion of the population of interest, he or she might apply a finite population adjustment that reduces the variance. Thus, in the case of a sample that is large relative to the population, the needed sample size is reduced. When the researcher is interested in a superpopulation, which is much larger than the actual sampling frame, or is interested in an analytic survey, then the finite population adjustment should not be applied.

Frequently, the need is to determine the sample size for a given sample design that will produce "sufficiently reliable" estimates. There are a couple of ways to address this. One way is to estimate the standard error, or variance, that would be obtained for various sample size choices. The needed standard error, the needed *coefficient of variation*, or the needed confidence interval can be determined. The coefficient of variation is the standard error divided by the estimate and is sometimes more useful to consider than the standard error itself. A rule of thumb that is sometimes used for what is sufficiently reliable is that the coefficient of variation be no more than .10. Setting criteria on the desired size for a 90% or 95% confidence interval is often a useful method for determining what sample size is needed. Estimation of standard errors can be difficult with a complex sample design or if little is known about the population distribution for a characteristic of interest.

Another approach that often is used to determine sample size for a sufficiently reliable estimate is statistical power analysis. This considers both so-called Type I error or alpha (probability of rejecting a true null hypothesis) and Type II error (the probability of failing to reject a false null hypothesis) in determining the needed sample size. The researcher needs to specify a hypothesis test, an effect size, and an acceptable Type II error to be able to perform this calculation.

Gary M. Shapiro

See also Confidence Interval; Design Effects (*deff*); Effective Sample Size; Finite Population Correction (fpc) Factor; Mean Square Error; Population of Interest; *p*-Value; Sample Design; Sampling Pool; Statistical Power; Superpopulation; Type I Error; Type II Error; Variance

Further Readings

Bell, J. (1998). Big is not necessarily beautiful in survey design: Measurement error and the APU Science Survey. *Statistician, 40,* 291–300.

Cohen, J. (1988). *Statistical power analysis for the behavioral sciences.* Hillsdale, NJ: Lawrence Erlbaum.

Kraemer, H. C., & Thiemann, S. (1987). *How many subjects? Statistical power analysis in research.* Newbury Park, CA: Sage.

Lenth, R. V. (2001). Some practical guidelines for effective sample-size determination. *American Statistician, 55,* 187–193.

Milton, S. (1986). A sample size formula for multiple regression studies. *Public Opinion Quarterly, 50,* 112–118.

Rust, K., Graubard, B., Fuller, W. A., Stokes, S. L., & Kott, P. S. (2006). Finite population correction factors [Panel discussion]. *Proceedings of the Section on Survey Research Methods.* Alexandria, VA: American Statistical Association. Retrieved May 23, 2008, from http://www.cos.gmu.edu/~wss/wss070328paper.pdf

SAMPLING

Sampling is the selection of a given number of units of analysis (people, households, firms, etc.), called cases, from a population of interest. Generally, the sample size (*n*) is chosen in order to reproduce, on a small scale, some characteristics of the whole population (*N*).

Sampling is a key issue in social research designs. The advantages of sampling are evident: feasibility of the research, lower costs, economy of time, and better organization of the work. But there is an important problem to deal with: that is, sampling error, because a sample is a model of reality (like a map, a doll, or an MP3) and not the reality itself. The sampling error measures this inevitable distance of the model from reality. Obviously, the less it is, the more the estimates are close to reality. Unfortunately, in some cases, the sampling error is unknowable.

There are two main families of sampling methods: probability (random) sampling and nonprobability sampling, respectively typical of (but not exclusive to) quantitative and qualitative research.

Probability sampling, definitively codified in the 1930s by the Polish statistician Jerzy Neyman, is characterized by the condition that all units of the population have an (theoretically) equal, calculable (i.e., known), nonzero probability of being included in the sample.

Probabilistic samples are considered representative of reality: What can be said about the sample can be extended to the reality of what is sampled by statistical inference. Another advantage is that the sampling error, which is a crucial datum to assess the validity of the sample, is calculable: This is possible only for probability samples. The main problem, however, is that researchers need the complete list of the target population (i.e., the sample frame), though sometimes the exact number of the population is sufficient, to extract the sample, and often this is impossible to obtain (e.g., when a researcher wants to study the audience of a movie).

There are several types of probability sampling. The most common are simple, systematic, and stratified random sampling. Other types of probability samples are multi-stage, cluster, multi-phase, and spatial sampling.

In most cases, the size of a probability sample is determined by the following formula:

$$n = \frac{z^2 pqN}{E^2(N-1) + z^2 pq},$$

where *z* refers to the confidence level of the estimate (usually fixed at 1.96, corresponding to a 95% confidence level), *pq* is the variance (that is unknown and then fixed at its maximum value: 0.25), *N* is the size of the population, *E* is the sampling error (often ≤ 0.04).

Nonprobability samples are generally purposive or theory driven. This means they are gathered following a criterion the researcher believes to be satisfying to obtain typological representativeness. This latter is achieved, when the researcher has sufficient members of all the main categories of interest to be able to describe with confidence their patterned similarities and differences.

Being purposive, nonprobability samples are rather heterogeneous. Up to 16 different qualitative sampling strategies have been listed for choosing a nonprobability sample. It is almost impossible to give an exhaustive list, because they are continuously open to integrations and new solutions. However, quota, snowball, purposive, theoretical, and accidental sampling are among the most common types of nonprobability sampling techniques.

The main problem with nonprobability samples is that the researcher has only loose criteria for assessing their validity: The sampling error is unknowable, so the researchers cannot say whether the results are representative or not, and the risk of nonsampling errors is large.

The big issue with sampling remains representativeness (i.e., external validity). Are probability samples really representative? The answer to this question is not trivial. In fact, probability samples cannot guarantee representativeness, for at least four reasons:

1. Survey researchers cannot say whether a sample is indeed representative or not, because they generally sample precisely to find out something about an unknown reality. This is the so-called *sampling paradox*.

2. To prove or correct (in case of post-stratification) the representativeness of a sample, the estimates are often compared to census data. In this case, the researcher must take into account two further problems: (a) Census data may be too old, and (b) they could represent a benchmark only with respect to certain variables, so the best thing the researcher can obtain is a sample that is representative only with respect to those limited variables (mainly demographics).

3. The researcher must take into account nonsampling errors, trying to minimize them (e.g., through weighting). There are four major types of nonsampling errors: coverage errors (e.g., when the list of the population is incomplete), measurement errors (due to bad questionnaires); nonresponse errors (associated with refusals, noncontacts, movers, illiteracy, language barriers, and missing data); and processing errors (coding or inputting errors). These errors are often quite difficult to know and control.

4. Nonprobability samples may be representative by chance (e.g., many quota samples prove to be representative a posteriori).

These are the reasons why, on one hand, nonprobability samples are used even in important surveys, and, on the other, a hybrid direction is gradually getting a footing in the social research community, as the success of mixed strategies like respondent-driven sampling shows.

A recent frontier in sampling is the alliance with the new technologies. Though rather promising, however, Internet sampling, cell-phone sampling, and others still have to deal with many problems. For example, the number of Internet users is significantly lower among older people. For this reason,

some sort of adjustment or sampling mix often must be considered, and even then the results may not be representative.

Alberto Trobia

See also Case; Cluster Sample; Element; External Validity; Multi-Stage Sample; Nonprobability Sampling; Probability Sample; Purposive Sample; Quota Sampling; Representative Sample; Respondent-Driven Sampling (RDS); Sample Design; Sample Size; Sampling Error; Simple Random Sample; Snowball Sampling; Stratified Sampling; Systematic Sampling

Further Readings

Henry, G. T. (1990). *Practical sampling*. Newbury Park, CA: Sage.

Kish, L. (1965). *Survey sampling*. New York: Wiley.

Sudman, S., & Blair, E. (1999). Sampling in the twenty-first century. *Journal of the Academy of Marketing Science*, 27(2), 269–277.

SAMPLING BIAS

Sampling bias occurs when a sample statistic does not accurately reflect the true value of the parameter in the target population, for example, when the average age for the sample observations does not accurately reflect the true average of the members of the target population. Typically, sampling bias focuses on one of two types of statistics: averages and ratios. The sources of sampling bias for these two types of statistics derive from different sources; consequently, these will be treated separately in this entry.

Sampling Bias for Averages

For survey researchers, sampling biases for averages derive from three sources: (1) imperfect sampling frames, (2) nonresponse bias, and (3) measurement error. Mathematical statisticians may also consider biases due to sources such as using the sample size (n) instead of $n - 1$, or using a sample statistic (e.g., s^2) to estimate a population parameter (e.g., σ^2), but these tend to be of academic interest and of less interest to practical research concerns; therefore, these will not be considered in this entry.

Imperfect sampling frames occur frequently in research and can be classified into four general categories: (1) frames where elements are missing, (2) frames where elements cluster, (3) frames that include foreign elements, and (4) frames with duplicate listings of elements. For example, household telephone surveys using random-digit dialing samples for landline telephones exclude households that are cell phone only (missing elements), include telephone numbers in some dwelling units that include more than a single household (element cluster), include some telephone numbers that are dedicated solely to fax machines (foreign elements), and include some households with more than a single landline telephone number (duplicate listings). All of these can cause sampling bias if they are not taken into account in the analysis stage.

Sampling bias due to nonresponse results from missing elements that should have been included in the sample but were not; these can be classified as noncontact (missing), unable to answer, or refusal. Noncontacts are those elements that are selected into the sample but cannot be located or for which no contact can be made; whereas the unable-to-answer either do not have the necessary information or the required health or skills to provide the answer, refusals are elements that, once located, decline to participate. Each will contribute to sampling bias if the sampled nonresponding elements differ from the sampled elements from which data are gathered. This sampling bias for averages can be characterized as follows:

$$\bar{Y}_{responders} - \bar{Y}_{population} = \frac{n_{nonresponders}}{n_{sample}} \left(\bar{Y}_{responders} - \bar{Y}_{nonresponders} \right).$$

As can be seen, when the number of nonresponse represents a small proportion of the total sample, or when there is a small difference between those who respond and those who do not, the resulting sampling bias will be small or modest. If it is possible to place bounds on the averages (such as with probabilities and proportions), researchers can quantify the possible range of sampling bias.

The third source of sampling bias for averages results from measurement error—that is, when what is measured among the sample elements differs from what researchers actually wished to measure for the target population. Measurement error, however, can be divided into *random error* and *consistent bias*; only consistent bias results in sampling bias, as random error will appear as sampling variance. These components of measurement error can be represented as

$$y_{ij} = \mu_i + \beta_i + \varepsilon_{ij},$$

where y_{ij} represents the observed values of some variable y on j repeated observations of individual i, μ_i represents the true value of what the researchers wish to measure for individual i, β_i represents the consistent bias in individual i's response, and ε_{ij} represents the random error associated with observation j for individual i. In sample surveys, consistent measurement bias can occur for a number of reasons, such as the questions focus on issues that are subject to a social desirability bias (e.g., illegal drug use).

Sampling Bias for Ratios

Unlike the estimation of sample averages, ratio estimators computed from samples are biased. In the 1950s, Herman Hartley and A. Ross showed that the absolute amount of bias in a ratio estimator is small relative to its standard deviation if the coefficient of variation (i.e., the ratio of the standard deviation to the average) of the ratio's denominator variable is small. In general terms, the amount of bias in ratio estimates will be small if the sample size is large, the sampling fraction is large, the mean of the denominator variable is large, the variance of the denominator variable is small, or if the correlation between numerator and denominator variables in the ratio is close to positive 1.0.

Allan L. McCutcheon

See also Measurement Error; Nonresponse Bias; Parameter; Random Error; Sampling Frame; Social Desirability; Statistic; Target Population; True Value

Further Readings

Cochran, W. G. (1977). *Sampling techniques* (3rd ed.). New York: Wiley.

Hartley, H. O., & Ross, A. (1954). Unbiased ratio estimators. *Nature, 174*, 270–271.

Kish, L. (1965). *Survey sampling*. New York: Wiley.

Sampling Error

Sampling error consists of two components: *sampling variance* and *sampling bias*. Sometimes overall sampling error is referred to as *sampling mean squared error* (MSE), which can be decomposed as in the following formula:

$$MSE(p) = E(p - P)$$
$$= E[(p - p') + (p' - P)] \qquad (1)$$
$$= \text{Var}(y) + \text{Bias}^2,$$

where P is the true population value, p is the measured sample estimate, and p' is the hypothetical mean value of realizations of p averaged across all possible replications of the sampling process producing p.

Sampling variance is the part that can be controlled by sample design factors such as sample size, clustering strategies, stratification, and estimation procedures. It is the error that reflects the extent to which repeated replications of the sampling process result in different estimates. Sampling variance is the random component of sampling error since it results from "luck of the draw" and the specific population elements that are included in each sample. The presence of sampling bias, on the other hand, indicates that there is a systematic error that is present no matter how many times the sample is drawn.

Using an analogy with archery, when all the arrows are clustered tightly around the bull's-eye we say we have low variance and low bias. At the other extreme, if the arrows are widely scattered over the target and the midpoint of the arrows is off-center, we say we have high variance and high bias. In-between situations occur when the arrows are tightly clustered but far off-target, which is a situation of low variance and high bias. Finally, if the arrows are on-target but widely scattered, we have high variance coupled with low bias.

Efficient samples that result in estimates that are close to each other and to the corresponding population value are said to have low sampling variance, low sampling bias, and low overall sampling error. At the other extreme, samples that yield estimates that fluctuate widely and vary significantly from the corresponding population values are said to have high sampling variance, high sampling bias, and high overall sampling error. By the same token, samples can have average level sampling error by achieving high levels of sampling variance combined with low levels of sampling bias, or vice versa. (In this discussion it is assumed, for the sake of explanation, that the samples are drawn repeatedly and measurements are made for each drawn sample. In practice, of course, this is not feasible, but the repeated measurement scenario serves as a heuristic tool to help explain the concept of sampling variance.)

Sampling Variance

Sampling variance can be measured, and there exist extensive theory and software that allow for its calculation. All random samples are subject to sampling variance that is due to the fact that not all elements in the population are included in the sample and each random sample will consist of a different combination of population elements and thus will produce different estimates. The extent to which these estimates differ across all possible estimates is known as sampling variance. Inefficient designs that employ no or weak stratification will result in samples and estimates that fluctuate widely. On the other hand, if the design incorporates effective stratification strategies and minimal clustering, it is possible to have samples whose estimates are very similar, thereby generating low variance between estimates, thus achieving high levels of sampling precision.

The main design feature that influences sampling variance is sample size. This can be seen readily from the following formula for the sampling variance to estimate a proportion based on a simple random sample design:

$$var(p) = pq/n, \qquad (2)$$

where p is the sample estimate of the population proportion, $q = 1 - p$, and n is the sample size. (Formula 2 and subsequent formulae are relevant for proportions. Similar formulae are available for other statistics such as means, but they are more complicated.)

It can be easily seen from this formula that as n increases, the variance decreases in direct and inverse proportion. Because sampling variance is usually measured in terms of the confidence interval and standard error (which is the square root of the sampling variance), we usually refer to the impact of an increase in sample size in terms of the square root of that increase. Thus, to double the sampling precision, that is, reduce the sampling variance by 50%, we would have to increase the sample size by a factor of 4.

Sampling variance, or its inverse, sampling precision, is usually reported in terms of the standard error, confidence interval, or more popularly, the margin of error. Under a simple random sample design, the mathematical formula for the standard error (3) and the 95% confidence interval for a proportion p (4) are

$$se(p) = [\text{var}(p)]^2 \tag{3}$$

$$ci(p) = [p - 1.96se(p), p + 1.96se(p)]. \tag{4}$$

The margin of sampling error is equal to half the length of the confidence interval as defined in Formula 4. For example, a proportion of 50% from a sample size of 1,000 would have a margin of error of "plus or minus 3%," meaning that if we were to draw 100 simple random samples of approximate size of 1,000, for about 95 of the samples, the sample value would differ by no more than 3 percentage points in either direction from the true population value.

In general, the main drivers of sampling variance are stratification and clustering. Stratification usually results in a lower sampling variance because the number of possible samples is reduced in comparison with an unrestricted simple random sample. Not only is the number of possible samples reduced, but potential outliers are eliminated. For example, suppose we wanted to sample households in the United States. An unrestricted random sample might contain households that are all located in the Northeast—the probability is not high, but it is not zero. However, if we stratify by region, then we reduce the probability of such a skewed sample to zero. To the extent that the variable of interest is related to our stratification variables, in this case geography, stratification will reduce the overall sampling variance. In setting up the design, therefore, it is important to strive to define strata that are relatively homogeneous with respect to the variables of interest.

Clustering, on the other hand, works in a very different way. Clustering plays a role in sample designs that are used for surveys in which the data are collected in person, for example, via household visits. Clustering is used to control field costs, especially those related to travel, which often represent a significant portion of the overall survey budget. However, this results in fewer degrees of freedom in the sense that the sample now focuses on a smaller number of sampling units, that is, the first-stage clusters, often referred to as primary sampling units. For example, selecting an unclustered sample of 1,000 households throughout the United States would mean that the households could be located anywhere in the country and, of course, this would result in large travel costs.

Restricting the sample first to 100 clusters (e.g., counties), and then taking 10 households within each cluster, reduces the travel costs but reduces our ability to spread the sample effectively over the entire country. This reduction in efficiency is further exacerbated by the fact that within each cluster, usually a geographically contiguous area, households tend to be more alike than households across these units. This phenomenon, called *intraclass homogeneity*, tends to drive up the sampling variance because efficiency is lost and the original sample of 1,000 might, in effect, have only the impact of 100 if, in the extreme case, the clusters are perfectly homogeneous.

Thus, in summary, with respect to sample design optimization, stratification is beneficial in that it reduces sampling variance, whereas clustering is to be avoided when possible or at least minimized as its effect is to increase sampling variance. Usually the effect of clustering is more marked than that of stratification. In many situations, though, clustering is necessary for cost reasons; thus, the best clustered design strategy involves finding a compromise between the cost savings and the penalty to be paid in terms of lower precision.

Another important factor that influences sampling variance is weighting. Weighting refers to adjustment factors that account for design deviations such as unequal probabilities of selection, variable nonresponse rates, and the unavoidable introduction of bias at various steps in the survey process that are corrected for through a process called *post-stratification*. The effect of weighting is to increase the sampling variance, and the extent of this increase is proportional to the variance among the weights.

A useful concept that quantifies and summarizes the impact of stratification, clustering, and weighting on sampling variance is the *design effect*, usually abbreviated as *deff*. It is the ratio of the true sampling variance taking into account all the complexities of the design to the variance that would have been achieved if the sample had been drawn using a simple random sample, incorporating no stratification, clustering, or weighting. A value of 1.00 indicates that the complexity of the design had no measurable impact on the sampling variance. Values less than 1.00 are rare; values larger than 5.00 are generally considered to be high.

The design effect is closely related to *rho* (ρ), the intraclass correlation, mentioned previously. The following formula shows the relationship between the two:

$$deff = 1 + (b - 1)\rho, \qquad (5)$$

where *deff* is the design effect, ρ is the intraclass correlation, and *b* is the average cluster size.

The correct calculation of sampling variance, incorporating all the complexities of the design, is not straightforward. However, there is extensive software currently available that uses either the empirical bootstrap replication approach or the more theoretically based Taylor Series expansion. These systems typically allow for many types of stratification, clustering, and weighting although the onus is always on the user or the data producer to ensure that relevant information, such as the stratum identifier, cluster identifier, and weight, are present in the data set.

Sampling Bias

This component of sampling error results from a systematic source that causes the sampling estimates, averaged over all realizations of the sample, to differ consistently from their true target population values. Whereas sampling variance can be controlled through design features such as sample size, stratification, and clustering, we need to turn to other methods to control and reduce bias as much as possible.

Sampling bias can only be measured if we have access to corresponding population values. Of course, the skeptic will point out that if such information were available, there would be little point in drawing a sample and implementing a survey. However, there are situations in which we can approximate sampling bias by comparing underlying information such as basic demographics for the sample with corresponding data from another, more reliable, source (e.g., census or large national survey) to identify areas in the data space for which the sample might be underrepresented or overrepresented.

One major source of sampling bias is *frame coverage*; that is, the frame from which the sample is drawn is defective in that it fails to include all elements in the population. This is a serious error because it cannot be detected, and in some cases its impact cannot even be measured. This issue is referred to as *undercoverage* because the frame is missing elements that it should contain. The opposite phenomenon, *overcoverage*, is less serious. Overcoverage occurs when the frame includes foreign elements, that is, elements that do not belong to the target population. However, these elements, if sampled, can be identified during the field operation and excluded from further processing. A third potential source of frame bias is *duplication*. If certain elements appear several times on the frame, their probabilities of selection are higher and thus they might be overrepresented in the sample. Furthermore, it is not always known how many times the elements occur on the frame, in which case it is impossible to ascertain the extent of the problem and thus the size of the bias.

Sampling bias can also occur as a result of flaws in the sample selection process, errors in the sample implementation, and programming missteps during the sample processing stage. An example of bias occurring during sample selection would be a systematic sample of every fifth unit when, in fact, there is a repeating pattern in the list and every fifth unit belongs to a special group. An example of how sampling bias can occur during the sample implementation process is the method interviewers use to visit households in the field. Field instructions might indicate "every 10th household," and the interviewer might instead elect to visit households that appear more likely to generate an interview. This could, and often does, lead to sampling bias. Finally, sampling or estimation bias can occur during the sample processing stage, for example, by incorrect calculation of the weighting adjustment factors, giving excessive importance to certain subpopulations.

One severe challenge faced by all survey practitioners is how to measure bias. Whereas the estimation of sampling variance emanates from statistical theory (see Formula 2, presented earlier), the only way to measure sampling bias is to compare the resulting empirical value with the true target population value. Of course, this is problematic because we seldom possess the population value and thus must use indirect methods to estimate bias. One approach uses data from other sources, such as the census or large national samples, as surrogates for the population being sampled. The problem with this strategy is that even the census is subject to error, in terms of both variance and bias.

It was pointed out previously that weighting tends to increase sampling variance and reduce precision. The reason weighting is implemented in survey research, in spite of its negative effect on variance, is that in many cases it can be used to reduce bias by bringing the sampling distributions more in line with known population distributions. For example, it is often possible to weight to basic census distributions by gender and age, even for minor geographical subdivisions such as tracts. To take a hypothetical example, suppose the sample distribution by gender turns out to be 40% male, 60% female, a not uncommon result in a typical random-digit dialing telephone survey. Furthermore, assume that the corresponding census numbers are close to 50:50. Weighting would assign relative adjustment factors of 50/40 to males and 50/60 to females, thus removing the possible bias due to an overrepresentation of females in the sample.

Challenges

Overall sampling error needs to be viewed in terms of a combination of sampling variance and sample bias. The ultimate goal is to minimize the mean squared error. Survey researchers know how to measure sampling variance, and they have a good handle on how it can be reduced. Sampling bias represents more of a challenge as it is often difficult to measure and even if it is measurable, bias reduction is often expensive and problematic to achieve.

It is illustrative to discuss surveys that are based on nonprobability judgment, quota, or convenience samples—that is, samples that are not based on probability-based design. One currently prominent example is the Internet-based panel, which consists of members who choose (self-select) to belong to these panels. That is, the panel members are not selected randomly and then invited to join the panel, but rather, the members themselves decide to join the panels, hence the term *opt-in* populations. This means that the underlying frame suffers from undercoverage and many potential types of bias, only some of which are known. These samples might be appropriate for certain studies (e.g., focus groups), in which generalizing with confidence to the population is not an absolute prerequisite. But, in general, these surveys fall short of required methodological rigor on two counts. In the first place, the probabilities of selection are usually unknown and often unknowable, thus precluding any chance of calculating sampling variance. Second, these surveys suffer from coverage and selection bias issues that, in many cases, are not even measurable.

With the advent of relevant software, surveys now regularly produce large-scale sampling variance results showing not only standard errors and confidence intervals but also design effects and measures of intraclass correlation. The results typically are presented for the entire sample and also for important subpopulations that are relevant for data users. These are useful not only to shed light on the quality of the data but also to inform future sample designs. The choice of estimates and subpopulations for which to publish sampling errors is not simple, and some researchers have developed "generalized variance functions" that allow users to estimate their own sampling errors based on the type of variables in question, the sample size, and level of clustering. However, these results are usually limited to sampling variance, and much less is calculated, produced, and disseminated with respect to sampling bias. This is due largely to the difficulty of calculating these measures and to the challenge of separating sampling bias from other sources of bias, such as nonresponse bias and response bias.

Karol Krotki

See also Bootstrapping; Clustering; Coverage Error; Design Effects (*deff*); Duplication; Intracluster Homogeneity; Margin of Error (MOE); Mean Square Error; Nonprobability Sampling; Nonresponse Bias; Overcoverage; Post-Stratification; Probability of Selection; Response Bias; ρ (Rho); Sample Size; Sampling Bias; Sampling Frame; Sampling Variance; Self-Selection Bias; Simple Random Sample; Strata; Stratified Sampling; Systematic Sampling; Taylor Series Linearization; Undercoverage; Weighting

Further Readings

Kish, L. (1965). *Survey sampling*. New York: Wiley.
Lohr, S. L. (1999). *Sampling: Design and analysis*. Pacific Grove, CA: Duxbury Press.

SAMPLING FRACTION

A sampling fraction, denoted f, is the proportion of a universe that is selected for a sample. The sampling fraction is important for survey estimation because in sampling without replacement, the sample variance is reduced by a factor of $(1 - f)$, called the *finite population correction* or *adjustment*.

In a simple survey design, if a sample of n is selected with equal probability from a universe of N, then the sampling fraction is defined as $f = n/N$. In this case, the sampling fraction is equal to the probability of selection. In the case of systematic sampling, $f = 1/I$ where I is the sampling interval.

The sampling fraction can also be computed for stratified and multi-stage samples. In a stratified (single-stage) sample, the sampling fraction, f_h is computed separately for each of the h strata. For a stratified sample $f_h = n_h/N_h$, where n_h is the sample size for stratum h and N_h is number of units (in the universe of N) that belong to stratum h. Because many samples use stratification to facilitate oversampling, the probabilities of selection may differ among strata, in which case the f_h values will not be equal.

For multi-stage samples, the sampling fraction can be computed at each stage, assuming sampling is with equal probability within the stage. A two-stage sample could include selection of n_a primary sampling units from a universe of N_a, and within the ath primary sampling unit, selecting n_{ba} out of N_{ba} units (e.g., households or businesses). In this case, $f_a = (n_a/N_a)$ and $f_{ab} = (n_{ba}/N_{ba})$ and $f_b^* = (\bar{n}_{ba}/\bar{N}_{ba})$ where $\bar{n}_{ba}$ and $\bar{N}_{ba}$ are the mean values of n_{ba} and N_{ba}; the overall sampling fraction would then be $f = f_a(f_b^*)$.

However, many if not most multi-stage samples use selection with probability proportional to size, which makes computing sampling fractions at each stage problematic.

John Hall

See also Finite Population Correction (fpc) Factor; Primary Sampling Unit (PSU); Sampling Interval; Sampling Without Replacement; Strata; Universe

Further Readings

Hansen, M., Hurwitz, W., & Madow, W. (1953). *Sample survey methods and theory*. New York: Wiley.

Kish, L. (1965). *Survey sampling*. New York: Wiley.

Sampling Frame

A survey may be a census of the universe (the study population) or may be conducted with a sample that represents the universe. Either a census or a sample survey requires a sampling frame. For a census, the frame will consist of a list of all the known units in the universe, and each unit will need to be surveyed. For a sample survey, the frame represents a list of the target population from which the sample is selected. Ideally it should contain all elements in the population, but oftentimes these frames do not.

The quality of the sample and, to an extent, of the survey itself depends on the quality of the sampling frame. Selecting a sampling frame that is of high quality and appropriate both to the population being studied and to the data collection method is a key step in planning a survey. In selecting a sample frame, three questions can be asked: (1) Does it include members of the universe being studied? (2) Is it appropriate for the way the data will be collected? and (3) What is the quality of the frame in terms of coverage, completeness, and accuracy?

Types of Sampling Frames

Major categories of sampling frames are area frames for in-person interviews, random-digit dialing (RDD) frames for telephone survey samples, and a variety of lists used for all types of surveys. Few lists that are used as sampling frames were created specifically for that use. Exceptions are commercially available RDD frames.

The type of frame usually varies with the mode of interviewing, although many frames can be used for multiple modes. Some studies employ multiple frames, either because they use multiple modes of data collection, because no single frame has adequate coverage, or to facilitate oversampling of certain groups.

An in-person survey of households (or individuals living in households) may use multiple levels of frames: an area frame to select a sample of areas where interviews are conducted, and within the areas, lists of addresses compiled by field staff or obtained from commercial sources.

Telephone household surveys may employ RDD frames, directory-based frames, or a combination. Telephone surveys of businesses often use frames developed from telephone directories. Telephone surveys can also use as sampling frames lists from many sources, including government agencies, commercial vendors of lists, associations, and societies. Some of these lists are publicly available, and some can be used only when doing studies for the owner of the list. Examples of publicly available lists include lists of public school districts and schools maintained by the National Center for Education Statistics (there are also commercial frames of districts and schools) and lists of physicians maintained by the American Medical Association. Lists whose use is restricted include those of recipients of government assistance and customers of businesses.

Surveys conducted by regular mail or email often use as frames the same lists (mentioned in the previous paragraph) for telephone surveys. Web surveys could also use these lists as means to contact respondents via regular mail and request that they complete a questionnaire online. Another type of frame for Web surveys comprises one or more Web portals (Web sites that provide links to other Web sites).

Quality Issues

Ideally, the sampling frame will list every member of the study population once, and only once, and will include only members of the study population. The term *coverage* refers to the extent to which these criteria are met. In addition, the frame should be complete in terms of having information needed to select the sample and conduct the survey, and the information on the frame should be accurate.

Needless to say, almost no sampling frame is perfect. Examining the quality of a frame using the criteria discussed in this section may lead to looking for an alternative frame or to taking steps to deal with the frame's shortcomings.

Problems in frame coverage include both undercoverage and overcoverage. *Undercoverage* means that some members of the universe are neither on the frame nor represented on it. Some examples of undercoverage are the following:

1. All RDD landline frames exclude households with no telephone service, and those with only cellular phone service.

2. Frames drawn from telephone directories exclude those households (listed in #1 above) plus those with unpublished and recently published numbers.

3. New construction may be excluded from lists of addresses used as sampling frames for surveys conducted by mail or personal visit.

4. Commercial lists of business establishments exclude many new businesses and may underrepresent small ones.

Frames can also suffer from undercoverage introduced by self-selection bias, as in the case of "panels" recruited for Internet research, even if the panels were recruited from a survey that used a probability sample with a good frame.

Overcoverage means that some elements on the frame are not members of the universe. For example,

RDD frames contain nonworking and business telephone numbers, as well as household numbers. A frame may have both undercoverage and overcoverage. For example, to select a sample of students enrolled in a school, one might use a list provided by the school or the district; however, the list might include students who had dropped out or transferred and omit students who had enrolled after the list was compiled.

Frame undercoverage can lead to bias in estimates made from survey data. Overcoverage can lead to bias if ineligible units on the frame are not identified. However, the larger problem with overcoverage is usually one of cost, because ineligibles must be identified and screened out. If the ineligibles can be identified before selecting the sample, it is usually better to eliminate them at that time.

An issue related to coverage is that of duplicates on the frame, which can lead to units having unequal chances of selection. It is best to eliminate duplicates before selecting the sample. If this cannot be done, then the presence of duplicates should be determined for those units that are sampled, so the sample can be properly weighted.

In addition to issues of coverage, a sampling frame should have information that is complete and accurate. For a sampling frame to be complete, it must have enough information so that the sampled units can be identified and located. Further, this information should be accurate. Missing or inaccurate information on the frame can affect the survey's response rate and data collection costs.

John Hall

See also Area Frame; Coverage; Coverage Error; Ineligible; List-Assisted Sampling; Overcoverage; Random-Digit Dialing (RDD); Undercoverage; Universe

Further Readings

Kish, L. (1965). *Survey sampling*. New York: Wiley.

Levy, P., & Lemeshow, S. (1999). *Sampling of populations: Methods and applications* (3rd ed.). New York: Wiley.

Sampling Interval

When a probability sample is selected through use of a systematic random sampling design, a random start is chosen from a collection of consecutive integers that will ensure an adequate sample size is obtained. The *length* of the string of consecutive integers is commonly referred to as the *sampling interval*.

If the size of the population or universe is N and n is the size of the sample, then the integer that is at least as large as the number N/n is called the sampling interval (often denoted by k). Used in conjunction with systematic sampling, the sampling interval partitions the universe into n zones, or strata, each consisting of k units. In general, systematic sampling is operationalized by selecting a random start between 1 and the sampling interval. This random start, r, and every subsequent kth integer would then be included in the sample (i.e., r, $r+k$, $r+2k$, etc.), creating k possible cluster samples each containing n population units. The probability of selecting any one population unit and consequently, the probability of selecting any one of the k cluster samples is $1/k$. The sampling interval and its role in the systematic sample selection process are illustrated in Figure 1.

For example, suppose that 100 households are to be selected for interviews within a neighborhood containing 1,000 households (labeled 1, 2, 3,..., 1,000 for reference). Then the sampling interval, $k = 1,000/100 = 10$, partitions the population of 1,000 households into 100 strata, each having $k = 10$ households. The random start 1 would then refer to the cluster sample of households $\{1, 11, 21, 31, 41,..., 971, 981, 991\}$ under systematic random sampling.

In practice, the population size may not be an even integer multiple of the desired sample size, so the sampling interval will not be an integer. To determine an adequate sampling interval, one of the following adjustments may be useful.

1. Allow the sample size to be either $(n-1)$ or n. The sampling interval, k, is then chosen so that $(n-1) \times k$ is smaller than N and $n \times k$ is larger than N. Choosing a random start between 1 and k will imply a final sample size of either $(n-1)$ or n units. For example, if a sample of 15 houses is desired from a block containing 100, then $N/n = 100/15 = 6.67$. Choosing a sampling interval of $k = 7$ and allowing the sample size to be either 14 or 15 would then satisfy the requirement: $(15-1) \times 7 = 98 \leq 100$ and $15 \times 7 = 105 \geq 100$. In this case, the sampling interval would be $k = 7$; random starts 1 and 2 would yield samples of size 15 while random starts 3 through 7 would yield samples of size 14.

2. Allow circular references in the selection. In this case, the sampling interval is conveniently defined to be any integer no larger than N. A random start from 1, 2, ..., N is chosen and that unit along with every successive kth unit is selected—if the numbers being selected surpass N, simply continue counting from the beginning of the list as though the population identifications are arranged in a circular fashion. Continue selection until the desired sample size is reached. For example, suppose a sample of 5 households is to be selected from a block having 16 households; a sampling interval of 3 and a random start of 2 results in sampling households 2, 5, 8, 11, 14, 1 (identification number 17 exceeds the population size by 1, so the first element in the list is selected).

3. Use fractional intervals. This approach combines the last approach with a modified computation of sampling interval. For example, suppose there were 200 high school students within a particular graduating

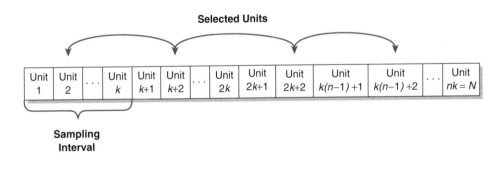

Selected Units

| Unit 1 | Unit 2 | ... | Unit k | Unit $k+1$ | Unit $k+2$ | ... | Unit $2k$ | Unit $2k+1$ | Unit $2k+2$ | Unit $k(n-1)+1$ | Unit $k(n-1)+2$ | ... | Unit $nk = N$ |

Sampling Interval

Figure 1   Illustration of sampling interval and its implication for systematic random sampling

Population units are ordered according to identification numbers: 1, 2, ...$nk = N$. The size of the sampling interval is k units from which a random start is selected. In this case, '2' is selected (circled) for the sample implying that every subsequent kth unit (i.e., 2, $k+2$, $2k+2$, ...), as shown by upper arrows, is selected for the sample.

class of which a sample of 16 was desired. The corresponding (fractional) sampling interval is $k = 200/16 = 12.5$.

Trent D. Buskirk

See also Cluster Sample; *n*; *N*; Random Start; Systematic Sampling; Weighting

Further Readings

Cochran, W. G. (1977). *Sampling techniques*. New York: Wiley.
Kish, L. (1995). *Survey sampling*. New York: Wiley.
Lohr, S. L. (1999). *Sampling: Design and analysis*. Pacific Grove, CA: Duxbury Press.

SAMPLING POOL

Sampling pool is a survey operations term, one that statisticians sometimes refer to as the *designated sample size*, which was proposed by Paul J. Lavrakas in the 1980s to refer to the set of elements selected from a sampling frame that may or may not all be used in completing data collection for a given survey project. The value of using this term is to be able to have a unique term to differentiate the sampling pool that a researcher *starts with* from the final sample (i.e., the *final sample size*) the researcher *finishes with*. Traditionally, survey researchers have used the word *sample* to refer to both the final number of completed interviewers a survey is striving to attain and the number of elements used to gain those completed interviews. Because noncontacts, nonresponse, and other reasons (e.g., ineligibility) cause many elements in a sampling pool to not end as completed interviews, the final sample is essentially always smaller in size than the sampling pool and, in many cases, is substantially smaller, for example, 1/10 or 1/20 the size of the sampling pool.

For example, if researchers have estimated that they will need 10,000 telephone numbers for a random-digit dialing (RDD) survey that has a goal of completing 800 interviews, the survey call center that does the interviewing may not need to activate all of those numbers during the data collection period. That is, their processing of the RDD numbers toward the goal of 800 completions may be more efficient than expected, and they may not need to activate all the

numbers that were selected for the sampling pool. To allow the sample coordinator the ability to closely manage the sampling, typically all the numbers in the sampling pool will be divided into *sample replicates*. If, for example, the sampling pool contained 10,000 RDD numbers made up of 100 replicates, then each replicate would contain a random subset of 100 of the 10,000 numbers. The sample coordinator may start data collection by releasing half of the replicates (thus a random half of the numbers in the sampling pool) on the first day of the survey's field period. Then the coordinator might observe for the next day or two how efficiently the interviewers are able to process the released numbers in achieving completed interviews. If the efficiency is better than the researchers anticipated, then the coordinator may only need to release another 30 replicates (another 3,000 numbers) to attain the final sample size goal of completed interviews for this survey. Thus, in this example, 2,000 numbers (i.e., 20 replicates) from the sampling pool would never be dialed by interviewers. Of further note, these unreleased numbers would not be considered in any response rate calculations the researchers performed after data collection was completed.

To estimate the size of the sampling pool a given telephone survey needs, Lavrakas advised use of the following formula:

$$Estimated\ Size\ of\ the\ Sampling\ Pool = (FSS)/((HR)(1 - REC)(1 - LE))$$

Here *FSS* stands for the final number of completed interviews the survey must attain; *HR* stands for the hit rate, or the estimated proportion of the sampling pool that will reach residences; *REC* stands for respondent exclusion criteria, or the estimated proportion of households that will be deemed ineligible for the particular survey; and *LE* stands for loss of eligibles, or the estimated proportion of eligibles that will end as nonresponders. For example, if in an RDD survey 1,000 completed interviews are desired and the HR is known to be about .65 (65% of the numbers will be households), REC is .05 (5% of households will not have an eligible adult in residence), and LE is .75 (75% of the eligible household will not complete an interview due primarily either to refusals or noncontacts), the estimated size of the sampling pool needed to complete this survey would be $(1000)/((.65)(1 - .05)(1 - .75))$ or 6,478 RDD numbers. Thus to be on the safe side, the researchers might decide to start with a sampling pool of 8,000 numbers.

Of note, although Lavrakas proposed the use of this term in reference to telephone surveys, the term can be applied to any survey sampling mode—in-person, mail, or Internet.

Paul J. Lavrakas

See also Elements; Nonresponse; Response Rates; Sample; Sample Replicates; Sample Management; Sample Size; Sampling Frame

Further Readings

Lavrakas, P. J. (1987). *Telephone survey methods: Sampling, selection, and supervision*. Newbury Park, CA: Sage.

SAMPLING VARIANCE

Sampling variance is the variance of the sampling distribution for a random variable. It measures the spread or variability of the sample estimate about its expected value in hypothetical repetitions of the sample. Sampling variance is one of the two components of sampling error associated with any sample survey that does not cover the entire population of interest. The other component of sampling error is coverage bias due to systematic nonobservation. The totality of sampling errors in all possible samples of the same size generates the sampling distribution for a given variable. Sampling variance arises because only a sample rather than the entire population is observed. The particular sample selected is one of a large number of possible samples of the same size that could have been selected using the same sample design. To the extent that different samples lead to different estimates for the population statistic of interest, the sample estimates derived from the different samples will differ from each other.

The positive square root of the sampling variance is called the *standard error*. For example, the square root of the variance of the sample mean is known as the *standard error of the mean*. The sample estimate and its standard error can be used to make inferences about the underlying population, for example, through constructing confidence intervals and conducting hypothesis testing. It is important to note, however, that sampling variance is measured about the expected value of the statistic under the sample design rather than the true population value. Therefore, inferences based on sampling variance do not reflect sampling biases or any possible nonsampling errors.

Under probability sampling, the sampling variance can be estimated using data collected from the sample. The estimation methodology for the sampling variance should take into account both the sample design and the estimation method. For standard sampling designs and estimators, standard variance estimation formulae are available. In his book *Introduction to Variance Estimation*, Kirk M. Wolter discussed nine basic sampling designs and their associated variance estimators.

In many samples, however, data are collected from individuals or organizations using complex sample designs that typically involve unequal selection probabilities, sample stratification, clustering, and multistage sampling. For such complex sample designs, although it is possible to produce unbiased point estimates by using proper sample weights, it is generally not possible to estimate appropriate sampling variances using standard estimation methods. In fact, for many complex sample designs and estimators, exact algebraic expressions of the sampling variances are not available, and hence there are no direct analytic methods for producing unbiased variance estimates.

One general approach to approximating the sampling variance of an estimator is to use sample replication methods such as jackknife and balanced repeated replication. An alternative approach is to approximate the estimator analytically using Taylor series expansion and then compute the variance of the linearized estimator. Statistical software packages that specialize in complex variance estimation include SUDAAN, WesVar, and STATA, among others.

Y. Michael Yang

See also Balanced Repeated Replication (BRR); Jackknife Variance Estimation; Nonsampling Error; Probability Sample; Sample Size; Sampling Bias; Sampling Error; Standard Error; Stata; SUDAAN; Taylor Series Linearization; Variance Estimation; WesVar

Further Readings

Cochran, W. G. (1977). *Sampling techniques* (3rd ed.). New York: Wiley.

Groves, R. M. (1989). *Survey errors and survey costs*. New York: Wiley.

Wolter, K. M. (1985). *Introduction to variance estimation*. New York: Springer.

SAMPLING WITHOUT REPLACEMENT

In sampling without replacement, each sample unit of the population has only one chance to be selected in the sample. For example, if one draws a simple random sample such that no unit occurs more than one time in the sample, the sample is drawn *without replacement*. If a unit can occur one or more times in the sample, then the sample is drawn *with replacement*. The same concept applies to other types of sample designs. For example, in multi-stage sampling the first-stage sampling units (primary sampling units) can be drawn from strata without replacement or with replacement.

In the case of simple random sampling, the estimator of the population mean is $\bar{y} = \frac{1}{n} \sum_{i=1}^{n} y_i$ where n is the sample size and y_i is the value of a study variable for the ith unit in the sample. The estimator of the variance of the sample mean is

$$s_{\bar{y}}^2 = \frac{(1-f)}{n} \sum_{i=1}^{n} \frac{(y_i - \bar{y})^2}{(n-1)}.$$

The term $(1-f)$ equals $(1 - \frac{n}{N})$ where N is the population size and is known as the *finite population correction* when sampling without replacement. Thus, if the sample size is large relative to the population size (e.g., 10% or higher), the finite population reduces the variance of the sample mean when compared to a simple random sample of the same size, n, drawn with replacement. The remainder of this entry provides a more detailed background for sampling without replacement.

A sample without replacement is usually defined as a subset of a finite population. A finite population of elements is represented by $U = \{1, \dots, N\}$. A *sample* is a vector $s = (s_1, \dots, s_N)^T$; T is used to denote matrix transposition, where $s_k \in \mathbb{N}$ ($\mathbb{N}$ is the set of natural numbers). If $s_k \in \{0, 1\}$ for all $k \in U$, then the sample s is without replacement. In other words, a sample without replacement is a vector of indicator variables. Furthermore, in a sample without replacement

$$s_k = \begin{cases} 1 & \text{if the element } k \text{ is in the sample,} \\ 0 & \text{if the element } k \text{ is not in the sample,} \end{cases}$$

for all $k \in U$. On the other hand, if s_k is any natural number, then s is a sample with replacement. The sample size of s is defined by

$$n(s) = \sum_{k \in U} s_k.$$

Let D be a set of samples. Moreover, let P be a probability mass function with support D. This probability mass function P is a *sampling design*. That means that P is a function from support D to $(0,1)$ such that $P(s) > 0$ for all $s \in D$ and $\sum_{s \in D} P(s) = 1$. If $D \subset \{0, 1\}^N$, then P is a *sampling design without replacement*. The term $D \subset \{0, 1\}^N$ means that any $s \in D$ is a vector of 0s and 1s; it is a sample without replacement. Furthermore, if $n(s) = n$, it is constant for all $s \in D \subset \{0, 1\}^N$, then P is a sampling design without replacement and with fixed sample size.

For clarifying concepts, the following example is provided. Let $U = \{1, 2, 3\}$ be a population of size three. Thus,

$$\{0, 1\}^3 = \{(0, 0, 0), (1, 0, 0), (0, 1, 0), (0, 0, 1),$$
$$(0, 1, 1), (1, 0, 1), (1, 1, 0), (1, 1, 1)\}$$

is the set of all possible samples without replacement. For example, the vector $(1,0,1)$ denotes that the first and third elements of the population U are in the sample. Moreover, $D_2 = \{(0, 1, 1), (1, 0, 1), (1, 1, 0)\}$ is the set of samples without replacement and with fixed sample size equal to 2. A possible sampling design P with support D_2 is

s	$(0, 1, 1)$	$(1, 0, 1)$	$(1, 1, 0)$
$P(s)$	$\frac{1}{4}$	$\frac{1}{4}$	$\frac{2}{4}$

Now, let P be a sampling design with support D and let $S = (S_1, \dots, S_N)^T$, $S_k \in \mathbb{N}$ for all $k \in U$, be a random vector such that $\Pr(S = s) = P(s)$ for all $s \in D$. Sometimes, D is also referred to as the support of this random vector S; it is the set of possible values of S. Consequently, the expectation of the random vector S is $\pi = E(S) = \sum_{s \in D} P(s)s$. Observe that π is a vector of the same dimension of S. Furthermore, if the sampling design P is a sampling design without replacement, then π is the vector of the first inclusion probabilities. Observe that, in the case of sampling without replacement, the kth component S_k of S only takes values in $\{0, 1\}$. Hereby, the kth component of the vector of expected values π can be expressed as $\pi_k = E(S_k) = \sum_{s \in D} P(s)s_k = \sum_{\{s \in D : s_k = 1\}} P(s)$, the known definition of the first inclusion probability of the sample unit $k \in U$. Now, the matrix of second moments of

S is $\Pi = E(SS^T) = \sum_{s \in D} P(s)ss^T$. Once more, if the sampling design P is without replacement, then Π is the matrix of second inclusion probabilities, with $\pi_{kk} = \pi_k$ for all sample unit $k \in U$.

The best-known sampling without replacement designs are the Bernoulli sampling, simple random sampling without replacement, and Poisson sampling. In the Bernoulli sampling, the support is $D = \{0,1\}^N$; the set of the all possible subsets of U. Moreover, its sampling design is $P(s) = \theta^{n(s)}(1-\theta)^{N-n(s)}$, where the $S_1, \ldots, S_N$ are independent and identically distributed Bernoulli random variables with parameter $\theta \in (0,1)$. In the case of Poisson sampling, the support also is $D = \{0,1\}^N$ and its sampling design can be expressed by $P(s) = \prod_{k \in U} \pi_k^{s_k}(1-\pi_k)^{1-s_k}$ for all $s \in D$, where the $S_1, \ldots, S_N$ are independent, distributed Bernoulli random variables with parameters $\pi_1, \ldots, \pi_N \in (0,1)$ respectively.

Bernoulli sampling and Poisson sampling are designs that produce variable size samples. If the support D is restricted to samples of fixed size, say n, then the Bernoulli sampling turns into the simple random sampling without replacement. In this case the support is $D_n \subset \{0,1\}^N$; the set of all the possible subsets of U but with fixed sample size n. The sampling design for simple random sampling without replacement is

$$P(s) = \frac{1}{\binom{N}{n}}.$$

However, the $S_1, \ldots, S_N$ are not independent; the correlation between S_i and S_j is

$$-\frac{1}{N-1}, \ i \neq j \in U.$$

On the other hand, if Poisson sampling also is restricted to a support with samples of fixed size, then the conditional Poisson sampling is obtained.

José Elías Rodríguez

See also Finite Population Correction (fpc) Factor; Probability Proportional to Size Sampling (PPS); Sample; Sample Design; Sampling With Replacement; Simple Random Sample

Further Readings

Cochran, W. G. (1977). *Sampling techniques* (3rd ed.). New York: Wiley.

Kish, L. (1965). *Survey sampling*. New York: Wiley.

Lohr, S. L. (1999). *Sampling: Design and analysis*. Pacific Grove, CA: Duxbury Press.

Särndal, C. E., Swensson, B., & Wretman, J. (1992). *Model assisted survey sampling*. New York: Springer.

Tillé, Y. (2006). *Sampling algorithms*. New York: Springer.

SAS

SAS (pronounced "sass") is the name of one of the world's largest software development corporations. Originally an acronym for "statistical analysis software," SAS was created by Jim Goodnight, John Sall, and other researchers at North Carolina State University in the early 1970s. What began as a locally developed set of programs for agricultural research quickly became so popular that in 1976 the SAS Institute was formed in Raleigh, North Carolina, to meet the growing demand. The company immediately formed an alliance with IBM and created the first SAS Users Group International (SUGI), which continues to provide assistance to SAS users, distribute newsletters, maintain a popular Web site and hold conferences throughout the world.

Within 5 years, SAS outgrew its original site and moved to its current campus in Cary, North Carolina. By this time, it was installed in thousands of sites around the world. Within 10 years, not only was SAS installed on 65% of all mainframe sites, but partnerships had been established with Microsoft and Apple as the personal computer revolution began. Throughout the 1990s and early 2000s, SAS has been the recipient of many prestigious awards for its technical accomplishments. Annual revenues in 1976 were $138,000; by 2006 they were $1.9 billion.

The features of SAS software cover a large family of products with applications in the government, academic, and private sectors. The characteristics most used by survey research professionals are common to most data analysis software, although the implementation can be very different from one software package to another. First, SAS has the ability to read electronically stored data in almost any format from almost any medium. Second, it has an enormous array of data transformation options with which to recode existing variables and create new ones. Third, SAS has an unlimited number of data analysis procedures from commonly used procedures to the most exotic analysis and the capability of creating user-developed applications that can be implemented from within existing SAS applications. Fourth, output can be in tabular or graphical form. Finally, SAS has a full-featured macro language with which to control data processing and output.

James Wolf

Further Readings

SAS: http://www.sas.com

SATISFICING

The notion of satisficing is consistent with cognitive theory articulated by Roger Tourangeau, Lance Rips, and Kenneth Rasinski that survey respondents must execute four stages of cognitive processing to answer survey questions optimally. Respondents must (1) interpret the intended meaning of the question, (2) retrieve relevant information from memory, (3) integrate the information into a summary judgment, and (4) map the judgment onto the response options offered. When respondents diligently perform each of these four steps, they are said to be *optimizing*. However, instead of seeking to optimize, respondents may choose to perform one or more of the steps in a cursory fashion, or they may skip one or more steps altogether. Borrowing Herbert Simon's terminology, Jon Krosnick has referred to this behavior as *satisficing* in his seminal paper published in 1991.

Whereas some people may begin answering a questionnaire without ever intending to devote the effort needed to optimize, others might begin to answer a questionnaire with the intention to optimize, but their enthusiasm may fade when they face a long questionnaire or questions that are difficult to understand or answer. As they proceed through the questionnaire, these respondents may become increasingly fatigued, distracted, and uninterested. But even after motivation begins to fade, the fatigued and unmotivated respondent is nevertheless expected to continue to provide answers to questions with the implicit expectation that he or she will answer each one carefully. At this point, a respondent may continue to expend the effort necessary to provide optimal responses or may choose instead to answer questions more superficially, expending less mental energy and short-cutting the steps necessary for optimal answering; in other words, they might satisfice.

Forms of Satisficing

Respondents who devote less-than-optimal effort to the task of answering questions can engage in weak or strong satisficing. Weak satisficing occurs when a respondent performs all four cognitive steps but performs one or more of these less carefully or attentively than is needed to optimize. A respondent implementing weak satisficing may be less thoughtful in inferring the intended meaning of a question, less thorough in searching memory for all relevant information, less balanced in integrating the retrieved information into a summary judgment, and more haphazard in selecting the appropriate response option from the list offered. Strong satisficing occurs when a respondent skips the retrieval and judgment steps altogether and seeks merely to identify a plausible answer based on cues provided by the question, without reference to any internal psychological cues directly relevant to the attitude, belief, or event of interest to the researcher. If no cues pointing to such an answer are immediately evident in a question, a satisficing respondent may choose a response at random. Strong satisficing allows a respondent to provide a reasonable and seemingly defensible answer while applying very little effort. Rather than making a sharp distinction between weak and strong satisficing, Krosnick proposes that an individual's response to any given question can fall somewhere along a continuum ranging from optimizing at one end to strong satisficing at the other.

Conditions Under Which Satisficing Is Likely

Krosnick has hypothesized that the likelihood a survey respondent will satisfice is a function of the respondent's ability to perform the cognitive tasks of optimizing, the respondent's motivation to perform the tasks, and the difficulty of the tasks. Satisficing should be more common when the respondent has less ability to optimize, when the respondent is less motivated to optimize, and when the tasks are more difficult.

Ability

A key aspect of ability is the respondents' level of cognitive skills to perform the complex mental operations required by optimizing. Satisficing theory defines cognitive skills as the ensemble of abilities needed to interpret questions, retrieve information from memory, integrate that information into a summary judgment, and express it verbally. People with limited skills at language interpretation, knowledge retrieval, retention and manipulation of information in working memory, judgment, and verbal expression are presumably least able to optimize and are therefore especially likely to satisfice instead. In contrast, people with strong skills in these areas should find it easy to execute the steps of optimizing and may therefore be especially likely to do so. Thus, differences between respondents in levels of cognitive skills should differentiate satisficers from optimizers.

Motivation

There are many potential sources of motivation to optimize when answering questionnaires, including the respondent's need for cognition, the extent to which the question topic is personally important to the respondent, the degree to which the respondent is held accountable for the answers he or she provides, the number of previous questions he or she has answered in a questionnaire, and more. More motivation presumably enhances the likelihood of optimizing.

Task Difficulty

Task difficulty is a feature of a question and depends on how much mental work is required to accomplish the task set out by the question. For example, interpreting the meaning of a question can be especially challenging if the words in it have multiple meanings, so respondents are forced to use linguistic context to infer the intended meanings of the words. Likewise, extraneous events occurring during questionnaire completion may distract a respondent from thinking about a question, making the task more difficult. These and other sources of difficulty may decrease the likelihood that respondents will perform all four steps of optimizing fully.

In his original formulation, Krosnick raised the possibility that ability, motivation, and task difficulty may interact to regulate satisficing. The interaction could manifest in one of two ways: (1) Optimizing might be the default approach that respondents take to answering questionnaires, so satisficing may be more likely when low levels of ability co-occur with low level of motivation, high task difficulty, or both, or (2) satisficing might be the default approach that respondents take to answering questionnaires, so optimizing might occur only when high levels of ability co-occur with high motivation, low task difficulty, or both.

Satisficing has been posited to at least partly explain several response effects, including acquiescence effects, response order effects, no opinion option effects, and nondifferentiation in answering batteries of rating scale items. Respondents inclined to satisfice may employ a number of different strategies to select seemingly legitimate answers while expending minimal cognitive effort. If offered a closed-ended question with categorical response options (e.g., *Which of the following experiences frustrates you most often: waiting in long lines, accidentally dropping things, or forgetting things you need to remember?*), a respondent may choose the first response option that seems reasonable, rather than reading the entire list of choices and thinking carefully about each option individually; this situation yields response order effects. When questions ask whether a set of statements are true or false or whether respondents agree or disagree with specific statements, a confirmatory bias in retrieval and reasoning would lead satisficing respondents to agree with assertions rather than disagreeing with them (acquiescence bias). And when offered a question with an explicit "don't know" response option, respondents might pick it to avoid answering the question substantively. All of these strategies allow respondents to appear to answer questions legitimately without having to think about their topics at all.

A good amount of evidence has accumulated that is consistent with satisficing theory's contention that response order, acquiescence, and Don't Know response option effects are more common under the three conditions described earlier. For example, these effects tend to be stronger among respondents with limited cognitive skills, when questions are more difficult to comprehend, among respondents who are not motivated to think, when questions are placed later in a long questionnaire, and under many more such conditions.

Questionnaire design features that minimize cognitive burden for the respondent (e.g., using commonly used words and avoiding jargon, keeping the questionnaire to a reasonable length, and more) can help to increase the likelihood of optimal responding to survey questions.

Sowmya Anand

See also Acquiescence Response Bias; Cognitive Aspects of Survey Methodology (CASM); Nondifferentiation; Questionnaire Length; Respondent Burden; Respondent Fatigue; Response Bias; Response Order Effects

Further Readings

Krosnick, J. A. (1991). Response strategies for coping with the cognitive demands of attitude measures in surveys. *Applied Cognitive Psychology, 5,* 213–236.

Krosnick, J. A. (1999). Survey research. *Annual Review of Psychology, 50,* 537–567.

Tourangeau, R., Rips, L. J., & Rasinski, K. (2000). *The psychology of survey response.* Cambridge, UK: Cambridge University Press.

SCREENING

Screening is the process by which elements sampled from a sampling frame are evaluated to determine whether they are eligible for a survey. Ideally, all members of the sampling frame would be eligible, but eligibility information is often not available prior to constructing the frame. In this case, the sampling frame must be narrowed to include only eligible sample members by subsectioning the frame, matching it against an external administrative data source, or collecting eligibility information directly from a sampled respondent or a proxy for that respondent.

Screening Types

When the sample frame is subsectioned or matched against an external administrative data source, this is referred to as *passive screening* because a respondent is not directly involved in the process. Passive screening uses existing data to determine who, from a sampling frame of individuals, establishments, or other, is likely eligible for a survey. For instance, a survey of pediatric specialty hospitals in the western United States may begin with a list of all hospitals across the United States. Based on the original list itself, or another that has been merged with the original, the is

can be narrowed down to those hospitals located in western states. The list could be further screened to include only those with a pre-designated classification of being a pediatric hospital.

When eligibility information is obtained directly from a respondent or proxy, this is referred to as *active screening.* Active screening involves direct contact with potentially eligible respondents and is typically undertaken when the eligibility criteria are not available from the sample frame. In this scenario, potentially eligible respondents are contacted in person, by phone, by Web, or by mail to determine their eligibility through a short screening interview (or "screener"). A variety of eligibility criteria may be evaluated by actively screening respondents. Considerations may include age, race, education, income, or geographic location, among others, depending on the purpose of the survey. Active screening is also often done to identify rare or difficult-to-locate populations. For example, a household survey of Hispanic single mothers may include an active screening component to determine the age, ethnicity, and relationships among all household members to make a determination as to whether anyone in that household is eligible as "Hispanic single mother." Households would be contacted and asked questions related to these demographic characteristics, and only those meeting the eligibility criteria would be retained for possible participation in the survey.

Active screening can be completed using several different modes and at a time different from data collection for the main survey. Often, but not always, the screening takes place in the same mode as the main survey interview. For instance, in a general population household survey, an interviewer may visit the household in person to administer the screener to the person answering the door. The screener may be designed to identify household members with a certain characteristic or within a certain age range. From the screener results, the main interview respondent or respondents can be selected as specified by the sampling criteria from the pool of eligible household members, and the interview can then be conducted in person with the selected respondent or respondents. Screening can also take place over the phone, Web, or by mail, which are often more cost-effective techniques compared to in-person screening, though each has associated sources of potential error.

In random digit dialing surveys, active versus passive screening for geographic location is becoming increasingly necessary. The portability of telephone numbers and the growth rate of cell phone only households who can take their cell phone number with them when they move have made it more difficult to determine with which geographic area a phone number is associated. Active screening for geographic eligibility is often difficult because there is some degree of error associated with respondents' ability and willingness to report their location, even when detailed descriptions of the study geography are provided.

Other sources of error are associated with both passive and active screening. In passive screening, false positive eligibles may be retained in the frame if the data related to eligibility indicate eligibility when the case is truly ineligible. Conversely, false negatives might be erroneously excluded if the sample frame incorrectly suggests the case is ineligible or eligibility information is missing. Active tracing is subject to error from false positives and false negatives as well. If a respondent advertently or inadvertently provides incorrect eligibility information about himself or herself, the family, or the establishment, the pool of eligible respondents may be incorrect. To the extent this error is correlated with some attribute important to the study purpose, bias may be introduced that could negatively affect the quality of the final survey estimates.

Screening Techniques

Because screening is often conducted very early in the interview process, it is vital that screening techniques are designed to foster, rather than discourage, participation. Screening questions and interviews should be as brief and to the point as possible. The screener language should not be written in a way that might bias the response decision process. For instance, a survey on charitable donations among wealthy people may include a screener that simply obtains the respondent's basic demographic information and general income range rather than collecting a great deal of information about the respondent's sources of wealth and charitable behaviors. Such detailed questions can be administered in the main survey once the correct respondents have been identified and the specifics of the survey topic and benefits have been explained. A brief and persuasive screening approach can help limit the potential for nonresponse bias by maximizing the rate of successful

screening. However, it is paramount that those being screened remain unaware of which responses will screen them "in" or "out." Were this not to happen, some respondents purposely would provide incorrect answers in order to lead to a screening result they preferred, which likely would bias the screening process.

In many cases, it may be difficult even to conduct screenings. Respondents may be unavailable or unwilling to complete a screener. When eligibility for these screening nonrespondents is not obtained, they are referred to as being of "unknown eligibility." When computing outcome rates, there are many methods for treating cases of unknown eligibility, but it is always the goal of a screening to end the survey's field period with the number in this group minimized.

Screening and Response Rates

In multi-stage sample designs, the ability to successfully screen potential households or respondents is calculated as a *screening rate*. The screening rate is often multiplied by the main interview response rate to obtain an overall response rate for a survey. Multiplying the rates assumes that the distribution of eligible persons in nonrespondent sample households is the same as in the respondent sample households. The American Association for Public Opinion Research recommends that some investigation of this assumption be conducted if this overall response rate computation is utilized.

Joe Murphy

See also Elements; Eligibility; Geographic Screening; List-Assisted Sampling; Multi-Stage Sample; Number Portability; Proxy Respondent; Rare Populations; Response Rates; Sampling Frame; Unknown Eligibility

Further Readings

American Association for Public Opinion Research. (2006). *Standard definitions: Final dispositions of case codes and outcome rates for surveys* (4th ed.). Lenexa, KS: Author. Retrieved April 17, 2008, from http://www.aapor.org/uploads/standarddefs_4.pdf

Ezzati-Rice, T., Coronado, V., Frankel, M., Hoaglin, D., Loft, J., & Wright, R. (1999). *Estimating response rates in random-digit-dialing surveys that screen for eligible subpopulations.* Paper presented at the International Conference on Survey Nonresponse, Portland, OR.

Retrieved December 21, 2006, from http://www.jpsm
.umd.edu/icsn/papers/EzzatiRiceCoronado.htm

Massey, J. T. (1995). Estimating the response rate in
a telephone survey with screening. *Proceedings of the
Section on Survey Research Methods* (Vol. 2, pp. 673–676).
Alexandria, VA: American Statistical Association.

Meegama, N., & Blair, J. (1999). The effects of telephone
introductions on cooperation: An experimental
comparison. *Proceedings of the Section on Survey
Research Methods* (pp. 1029–1031). Alexandria,
VA: American Statistical Association.

Smith, T. W. (2003). *A review of methods to estimate the
status of cases with unknown eligibility.* Retrieved April
17, 2008, from http://www.aapor.org/uploads/erate.pdf

Snyder, D. C., Sloane, R., Lobach, D., Lipkus, I., Clipp, E.,
Kraus, W., et al. (2004, October). Agreement between
a brief mailed screener and an in-depth telephone survey:
Observations from the Fresh Start Study. *Journal of the
American Dietetic Association, 104*, 1593–1596.

Seam Effect

The seam effect, also called the *seam bias*, a phenomenon specific to longitudinal panel surveys, refers to the tendency for estimates of change, as measured across the "seam" between two successive survey administrations (or "waves"), to far exceed change estimates that are measured within a single survey wave—often by a factor of 10 or more. Seam effects have been found in virtually every panel survey examined, regardless of the characteristics under study, the data collection methods, or the length of the recall period. Seam bias almost always signals the presence of serious measurement error, which can severely compromise the statistical utility of estimates of change. A considerable amount of research over the past two decades has documented the existence of seam effects in longitudinal surveys and also has shed light on their essential nature—too little change is observed within the reference period of a single interview wave, and too much is observed at the seam.

Figure 1 presents a typical seam bias profile. It shows month-to-month transitions in reported receipt of Food Stamps and Social Security retirement benefits from the first three interview waves of the 1984 panel of the U.S. Census Bureau's Survey of Income and Program Participation (SIPP). SIPP waves occur at 4-month intervals and collect data about the preceding 4-month period; thus Months 4 and 5, and

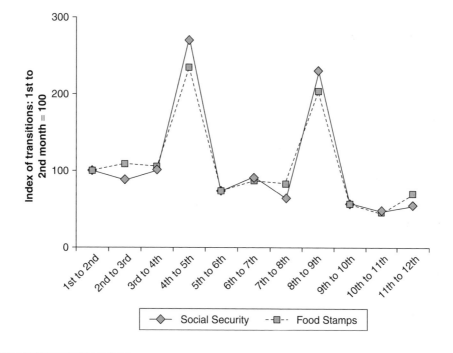

Figure 1   Survey of income and program participation month-to-month transition rates for receipt of social security benefits and food stamps

Source: Adapted from Burkhead and Coder, 1985, pp. 355–356.

Months 8 and 9, comprise the "seams" between Waves 1 and 2 and Waves 2 and 3, respectively, which are reflected by the large spikes in Figure 1.

Many factors have been cited as potential contributors to seam effect phenomena, including the following:

- *Data processing actions*—for example, strategies for assigning missing values and errors in linking cases across interview waves can create spurious transitions at the seam.
- *Interviewer, coder, or respondent inconsistencies*—any kind of interviewer error or inconsistency across successive survey waves is a possible cause of seam bias, as are coder inconsistencies in classifying open-ended questions and respondent inconsistencies in applying labels to phenomena of interest.
- *Self or proxy response status*—spurious change at the seam may result from the fact that respondents can change across successive waves of panel surveys; questionnaire design—unlike most response errors, seam effects characterize phenomena (i.e., month-to-month changes) that generally are not measured directly from respondents' reports but rather are derived in the analysis stage from those data.
- *Memory issues*—memories for more recent portions of the response period of one wave are likely to be of different quality and to result from different recall strategies (e.g., direct recall vs. estimation), as compared to memories for the most remote portion of the response period of the subsequent wave.
- *Satisficing*—in response to a difficult or burdensome recall task, respondents may adopt short-cut strategies such as constant wave responding, in which the same answer is reported for all months of an interview wave's reporting period.

Most evidence, however, discounts the relative importance of the initial, more "extrinsic" factors in the preceding list and suggests instead that questionnaire design, respondent memory issues, and recall strategies play the predominant roles in producing seam effects.

One approach to the amelioration of seam effects is through statistical adjustment after the data have been collected. However, different data collection methods have also been shown to produce different seam effects. In particular, use of *dependent interviewing* has been shown to substantially reduce, although not eliminate, seam bias.

Mario Callegaro and Jeffrey C. Moore

See also Aided Recall; Coding; Dependent Interviewing; Interviewer-Related Error; Longitudinal Studies; Measurement Error; Panel; Questionnaire Design; Record Check; Respondent-Related Error; Satisficing; Unaided Recall; Wave

Further Readings

Burkhead, D., & Coder, J. (1985). Gross changes in income recipiency from the Survey of Income and Program Participation. In *Proceedings of the Social Statistics Section* (pp. 351–356). Washington, DC: American Statistical Association.

Callegaro, M. (2008). Changes in seam effects magnitude due to changes in question wording and data collection strategies. An analysis of labor force transitions in the PSID. In American Statistical Association (Ed.), *Proceedings of the 62nd annual conference of the American Association for Public Opinion Research*, Anaheim, CA.

Moore, J. C., Bates, N., Pascale, J., & Okon, A. (2008). Tackling seam bias through questionnaire design. In P. Lynn (Ed.), *Methodology of longitudinal surveys*. Hoboken, NJ: Wiley.

SEGMENTS

Segments is a term for sample units in area probability sampling (a specific kind of cluster sampling). Most often, segments are sample units in the second stage of area probability sampling and are more formally referred to as *secondary sampling units* (SSUs).

As second stage sample units, segments are neighborhoods or blocks (either census-defined or practically defined by field workers) within the selected *primary sampling units*, which are often counties or whole metropolitan areas). Occasionally, segments can refer to the first-stage sample units or to larger areas than neighborhoods or blocks, such as entire census tracts or even counties, but this entry describes them in their more common usage as second-stage sample units.

Individual units (often housing units, or sometimes clusters of housing units) within the selected segments are selected for inclusion in the sample. Traditionally, field workers are sent out to the selected segments to list every housing unit. New lists are becoming available for segments in urban areas built from postal address lists. These lists are not yet available in rural areas, but as rural addresses in the United States get converted to city-style addresses for 911 reasons, the postal address lists available commercially will continue to increase their coverage.

Segments are usually defined only within primary sampling units that have been selected in the first stage of sample selection. Segments are designed to be as contiguous as possible because this reduces interviewer travel between selected units, but if selected using census data, consecutive-numbered blocks may not be strictly contiguous. There are two key decisions to be made in defining segments. The first is how large to make the segments, and the second is how many segments to select within each primary sampling unit.

Deciding how large to make the segments involves a trade-off of survey cost versus variance. Under traditional listing, larger segments will cost more to list every housing unit. Larger segments will also necessitate more travel between individually selected sample units, which increases survey costs. However, smaller segments result in a more homogenous sample, as measured by larger intraclass correlations, often represented by the Greek letter *rho* (ρ). Larger rho values reduce the *effective sample size*, which results in more variance. The rho differs for each variable, depending on how similar people who live near each other are on any particular characteristic. As a general rule, socioeconomic characteristics (e.g., income) tend to have higher rho values than do behavioral variables. This is because people who live near each other tend to have similar financial situations, but even people in similar financial situations tend to have different opinions and behaviors.

Morris H. Hansen, William N. Hurwitz, and William G. Madow suggested a logarithmic relationship between the average cluster size and rho:

$$\rho = a(\bar{N})^m,$$

where a and m are different parameters for different variables, and $\bar{N}$ represents the average segment size. The assumption in the formula is that $m < 0$ so that as the average cluster size increases, the value of rho will decrease. This is explained by the fact that smaller areas tend to be more similar than larger areas (e.g., one neighborhood vs. an entire city).

Deciding how many segments to select within each primary sampling unit also involves a trade-off of survey cost versus variance. Selecting more segments will reduce the average number of selected third-stage units per segment and, therefore, the average number of cases per segment. Having more cases per segment allows the rho value to affect the sample estimates more.

The variability of sample estimates depends on the number of cases per segment and the value of rho. In fact, there is a well-known approximation to the relationship of the rho value given here:

$$n(eff) \approx \frac{n}{[1 + \rho(\bar{b} - 1)]},$$

where $\bar{b} = n/(\#SSUs)$ is the average number of cases per segment. Note that if ρ is 0 or $\bar{b} = 1$ (simple random sampling has no clustering), the effective sample size is the same as the total sample size g. However, the value of rho is generally positive, so the effective sample size is generally less than the total sample size.

Steven Pedlow

See also Area Probability Sample; Case; Clustering; Cluster Sample; Effective Sample Size; Multi-Stage Sample; Primary Sampling Unit (PSU); ρ (Rho); Survey Costs; Simple Random Sample; Unit; Variance

Further Readings

Hansen, M. H., Hurwitz, W. N., & Madow, W. G. (1953). *Sample survey methods and theory*. New York: Wiley.

SELF-ADMINISTERED QUESTIONNAIRE

A self-administered questionnaire (SAQ) refers to a questionnaire that has been designed specifically to be completed by a respondent without intervention of the researchers (e.g., an interviewer) collecting the data. An SAQ is usually a stand-alone questionnaire though it can also be used in conjunction with other data collection modalities directed by a trained interviewer. Traditionally the SAQ has been distributed by mail or in person to large groups, but now SAQs are being used extensively for Web surveys. Because the SAQ is completed without ongoing feedback from a trained interviewer, special care must be taken in how the questions are worded as well as how the questionnaire is formatted in order to avoid measurement error.

A major criterion for a well-designed SAQ is proper wording and formatting of the instructions, the questions, and the answer categories. Don Dillman has succinctly stated that the goal of writing a survey question for self-administration is to develop a query that every potential respondent will interpret in the same way, be able to respond to accurately, and be willing to answer. Dillman also describes a variety of conditions that need to be considered when writing questions for an SAQ. Because respondents usually will have no one to ask for clarification, the SAQ must be completely self-explanatory. However, experience shows that respondent creativity knows no bounds for misunderstanding an SAQ. Thus, all types of alternative interpretations must be considered for each question in order to avoid item nonresponse due to confusion or, a more insidious problem, an improper response based on a misunderstanding of the instructions or question. The structure of the questions is also critical to collecting appropriate data. Closed-ended versus open-ended question structures, ordered versus unordered answer categories, and the anticipated respondent characteristics need to be assessed for their utility for each question.

Another critical criterion for high-quality SAQs is appropriate formatting of the questionnaire, including the size of the font, spacing, navigational aids, use of color, and other aspects. Regardless of how well the questions are worded, a poorly formatted SAQ will result in a variety of problems. A questionnaire should progress in a manner that makes sense to the respondents, not the researcher. Following general principles of conversation is recommended. Questions on similar issues are usually grouped together with topics most relevant to the respondent appearing before others. When topics change, the visual layout should reinforce the switch to a new subject. Consistent use of symbols and other graphics (text boxes, navigational arrows, etc.) can be very useful in helping the respondent follow skip patterns and other deviations from sequential administration. Even for computer-assisted interviewing, the layout of each screen can be as important as that of the printed page. Respondents often begin answering questions without reading instructions unless the layout makes reading those sentences seem particularly important.

The most common form of SAQ is the printed questionnaire delivered to the respondent, usually with a postage-paid envelope for returning the completed questionnaire. As the general public has become more familiar with using personal computers, the SAQ is increasingly being administered using computer programs running either on a stand-alone personal computer or on a Web site designed to present the questions and have respondents enter their answers directly into the database. Research has shown that respondents are more likely to report sensitive or illegal behavior when they are allowed to use a SAQ format rather than during a personal interview on the phone or in person. For this reason SAQs are commonly used to supplement face-to-face interviews when researchers are concerned about social desirability issues.

James Wolf

See also Closed-Ended Question; Computer-Assisted Self-Interviewing (CASI); Computerized Self-Administered Questionnaires (CSAQ); Gestalt Psychology; Internet Surveys; Mail Survey; Open-Ended Question; Questionnaire Design; Question Order Effects; Respondent-Related Error; Sensitive Topics; Social Desirability; Total Design Method; Web Survey; Visual Communication

Further Readings

Dillman, D. A. (2000). *Mail and internet surveys: The tailored design method* (2nd ed.). New York: Wiley.

SELF-REPORTED MEASURE

Self-reported measures are measures in which respondents are asked to report directly on their own behaviors, beliefs, attitudes, or intentions. For example, many common measures of attitudes such as Thurstone scales, Likert scales, and semantic differentials are self-report. Similarly, other constructs of interest to survey researchers, such as behavioral intentions, beliefs, and retrospective reports of behaviors, are often measured via self-reports.

Self-reported measures can be contrasted to other types of measures that do not rely on respondents' reports. For example, behavioral measures involve observing respondents' behaviors, sometimes in a constrained or controlled environment. Similarly, physiological measures like galvanic skin response, pupillary response, and subtle movements of facial muscles rely on biological responses rather than self-report. Measures of other variables, such as weight, height, or cholesterol level could also be assessed without self-report by weighing or measuring respondents or by taking specimens like blood or urine samples, as often is done in health surveys. Finally, implicit measures such as the Implicit Association Test (IAT) and Russell H. Fazio's priming paradigm involve tasks that are not under conscious control and that do not make respondents overtly aware that their attitudes are being measured.

Historically, surveys have almost exclusively made use of self-report measures, but technological advances have made other types of measures more plausible. For example, response latencies can be measured in survey questions either by having interviewers record the length of time respondents take to answer a question. They also can be measured in computer-assisted self-administered and Internet surveys. Biological specimens or measurements can be taken in in-person interviews. Implicit measures like the IAT or priming tasks can be implemented in computer-assisted self-interviewing surveys or Internet surveys.

Although self-report measures are widely used, survey researchers using these measures should be aware that their use is based on the assumptions that respondents are able to answer the questions posed to them and that they are willing to do so, and that these assumptions may not be true. For example, people have limited and often imperfect access to many of their own internal mental processes, and they may therefore not be able to give accurate responses to questions about these processes. However, when asked about internal mental processes, respondents may construct a logical response based on their theories about their mental processes, rather than on actual knowledge of these processes. Thus, respondents will answer questions about these processes, but those answers may not be accurate reflections of the processes themselves. For example, respondents in a survey may willingly answer questions about why they voted for one presidential candidate over another, but those answers may not reflect their actual decision processes. Respondents' self-reports may also be inaccurate because they can be influenced by context, which is demonstrated by research exploring the effect of question order on survey responses. Furthermore, respondents' answers to survey questions may also be inaccurate because of limits to memory or errors in memory.

The use of self-report measures also assumes that respondents are willing to answer researchers' questions. Because being viewed favorably by others is more likely to bring rewards and minimize punishments than being viewed unfavorably, people may sometimes be motivated to construct favorable images of themselves for other people (e.g., for interviewers), sometimes via deceit. Such systematic and intentional misrepresentation by respondents when answering questionnaires has been well documented. For example, people are more willing to report socially embarrassing attitudes, beliefs, and behaviors when their reports are anonymous and when respondents believe researchers have other access to information about the truth of their thoughts and actions. Thus, some people sometimes distort their answers to questions in order to present themselves as having more socially desirable attitudes, beliefs, or behavioral histories, and people's reports may therefore be distorted by social desirability bias.

Allyson Holbrook

See also Behavioral Question; Cognitive Aspects of Survey Methodology (CASM); Computer-Assisted Self-Interviewing (CASI); Likert Scale; Question Order Effects; Response Latency; Semantic Differential Technique; Social Desirability

Further Readings

Bargh, J. A., Chen, M., & Burrows, L. (1996). Automaticity of social behavior: Direct effects of trait construct and stereotype activation on action. *Journal of Personality and Social Psychology, 71,* 230–244.

Cacioppo, J. T., & Petty, R. E. (1979). Attitudes and cognitive response: An electrophysiological approach. *Journal of Personality and Social Psychology, 37,* 2181–2199.

Fazio, R. H. (1995). Attitudes as object-evaluation associations: Determinants, consequences, and correlates of attitude accessibility. In R. E. Petty & J. A. Krosnick (Eds.), *Attitude strength: Antecedents and consequences* (pp. 247–282). Mahwah, NJ: Lawrence Erlbaum.

Greenwald, A. G., Banaji, M. R., Rudman, L. A., Farnham, S. D., Nosek, B. A., & Mellott, D. S. (2002). A unified theory of implicit attitudes, stereotypes, self-esteem, and self-concept. *Psychological Review, 109,* 3–25.

Hess, E. H. (1965). Attitude and pupil size. *Scientific American, 212,* 46–54.

Likert, R. (1932). A technique for the measurement of attitudes. *Archives of Psychology, 140,* 5–53.

McClendon, M. J., & O'Brien, D. J. (1988). Question-order effects on the determinants of subjective well-being. *Public Opinion Quarterly, 52,* 351–364.

Nisbett, R. E., & Wilson, T. D. (1977). Telling more than we can know: Verbal report on mental processes. *Psychological Review, 84,* 231–259.

Osgood, C. E., Suci, G. J., & Tanenbaum, P. H. (1957). *The measurement of meaning.* Urbana: University of Illinois.

Paulhus, D. L. (1984). Two-component models of socially desirable responding. *Journal of Personality and Social Psychology, 46,* 598–609.

Porier, G. W., & Lott, A. J. (1976). Galvanic skin responses and prejudice. *Journal of Personality and Social Psychology, 33,* 317–326.

Thurstone, L. L. (1927). A law of comparative judgment. *Psychological Review, 34,* 273–286.

Thurstone, L. L. (1927). Psychophysical analysis. *American Journal of Psychology, 38,* 368–389.

SELF-SELECTED LISTENER OPINION POLL (SLOP)

A self-selected listener opinion poll, also called SLOP, is an unscientific poll that is conducted by broadcast media (television stations and radio stations) to engage their audiences by providing them an opportunity to register their opinion about some topic that the station believes has current news value. Typically two local telephone numbers are broadcast for listeners to call to register their opinion on a topic. One number might be for those who agree with the issue, and the other might be for those who disagree. For example, a question might be to indicate whether a listener agrees or disagrees that *"the mayor should fire the police commissioner."*

Because the people who choose to call in do not represent a known target population, the findings from such polls have no external validity as they cannot be generalized to any particular population and therefore are not valid as measures of public opinion. Although these polls may provide some entertainment value for the station and its audience, especially for those who call in, they are not scientifically valid measures of news or public opinion.

Paul J. Lavrakas

See also Call-In Polls; Computerized-Response Audience Polling (CRAP); 800 Poll; External Validity; 900 Poll; Pseudo-Polls

Further Readings

Traugott, M. W., & Lavrakas, P. J. (2008). *The voter's guide to election polls* (4th ed.). Lanham, MD: Rowman & Littlefield.

SELF-SELECTED SAMPLE

A sample is self-selected when the inclusion or exclusion of sampling units is determined by whether the units themselves agree or decline to participate in the sample, either explicitly or implicitly.

How Does Self-Selection Enter Into a Sampling Design?

There are three main routes through which self-selection enters into a sampling design. The first is nearly ubiquitous, and the latter two are more preventable.

Refusals

When survey units are chosen by surveyors, but these units nonetheless elect not to participate (also called refusal-related nonresponse), self-selection occurs. Nonresponse can occur in probability or nonprobability sampling designs. If many such units elect not to participate, the representativeness of the resultant observed sample can be called into serious question as it may result in nonnegligible nonresponse bias. Self-selection can occur at the interview level (i.e., missing data due to a refusal to be interviewed) or at the item/question level (i.e., a refusal to answer a specific question or questions during the interview). For example, in a survey administered to a probability sample of adults in a particular city with the goal of estimating the city's mean income level, some persons will refuse to be interviewed, and of those who agree to be interviewed, some will refuse to report their income.

Volunteers

When survey units volunteer to be included in the sample, this introduces self-selection. Volunteer samples are one type of nonprobability sampling design. They are most common when rare, difficult-to-locate, demographic subpopulations are sampled, or when surveyors seek to obtain information from many people, quickly, at relatively low cost. For example, in an Internet survey of the prevalence of student drug use, students could be recruited by first asking school principals to volunteer their schools for participation, then asking teachers within schools to volunteer their classrooms to participate, and third asking students to volunteer to participate by going to a Web site to fill out the questionnaire.

Incidental Truncation

When units are sampled if, and only if, they engage in some behavior, then the distribution of the outcome variable is truncated at an unknown point. This is *incidental truncation*. For example, consider a survey in which researchers are interested in estimating the mean Scholastic Aptitude Test (SAT) score in each of the 50 United States. However, students' SAT scores can be sampled only if they choose to take the SAT, which results in incidental truncation because it is very likely that among those who do not take the SAT, there will be scores even lower (were they to take the test) than the lowest score among those taking the SAT.

What Is the Self-Selected Sample Problem?

The underlying statistical problem is that if the reasons for a sampling unit's selection into or out of the sample relate to the outcome variable of interest, then *self-selection bias* occurs. Quite simply, this bias occurs when self-selection is either a function of the survey unit's score on the outcome variable or is codetermined with the outcome variable. In this event, point estimates and standard errors will be biased, and statistical inference about population parameters from sample statistics may be invalid.

Returning to the first example given, this problem would occur if low-income persons refuse to report their income because they are too embarrassed. Returning to the second example, this problem would occur if the propensities for self-selection at each stage are (a) related to each other, and (b) based on unmeasured characteristics, such as motivation and obedience, which are, in turn, related to the outcome variable. Returning to the third example, one way this problem would occur is if students who are intending to go to college and have higher grades are more

likely to take the SAT and also more likely to get higher SAT scores than would those who are not college bound were they to have taken the SAT. Should these biases be present, their severity would be positively related to the magnitude of the difference between those who participated and those who did not and also positively related to the proportion that elects not to participate.

There is one misconception involving self-selected samples that is worth noting. Researchers often assume that even if selection bias is present, estimates of the outcome of interest will be unbiased for the part of the outcome distribution not truncated by the self-selection process. That is, they assume they will be able to make valid inferences about the subpopulation of self-selecters but unable to generalize results to the larger population, which includes the noncompliers, nonresponders, and nonvolunteers. In fact, if selection bias is present, regression coefficients estimated for the subsample of self-selecters will be biased as well.

Solutions

Essentially, for unbiased point estimates and standard errors, researchers need to be able to assume that selection into or out of the sample is either random (i.e., a sampled unit is an independent draw from the marginal population distribution of the outcome variable) or conditionally random (i.e., a sampled unit is an independent draw from the conditional population distribution of the outcome variable, conditioning on measured covariates). In most instances, it is highly unlikely that sampling units self-select into or out of a sample for reasons completely independent of the outcome of interest. More often, sampling units can be thought of as self-selecting into or out of a sample for reasons that are conditionally independent from the outcome variable. If this assumption is met, several solutions are possible.

One solution that is available when dealing with a probability sample with nonresponse is to identify those units who opted not to participate, identify variables measured on both responders and nonresponders that are also related to the outcome variable, and stratify the sample on these measured variables. This amounts to constructing weighting classes. The surveyor can then adjust raw sampling weight for each unit by the inverse of their response propensity in the weighting class (i.e., weighting class adjustment).

Returning to the first example, final estimates could be re-weighted to give more weight to persons from strata with low probabilities of responding to the income question.

Another solution is to identify observable reasons why some sampling units chose not to participate and statistically control for these in a model-based analysis. This will yield a conditional estimate of the outcome of interest. Depending on the relations among the outcome, predictors, and selection variables, as well as the model employed, this can reduce bias. Returning to the third example, the survey researcher could conceivably measure—and covary out—potential selection variables such as high school grade point average and whether or not the student's school requires the SAT to be taken from a regression equation predicting SAT score from socioeconomic status. These selection covariates would be expected to relate to the outcome of interest, SAT score, as well as to other observed predictors in the model, such as socioeconomic status.

Many times, however, researchers simply are not able to find measured selection variables that explain the self-selection process, nor do they have a probability sampling design such that they can adjust sampling weights for nonresponse. This problem would occur if self-selection were based on the outcome variable itself or on unobservable variables correlated with the outcome. This situation is considerably more complicated.

One possible approach is to model the joint distribution of the outcome of interest, along with the distribution of the self-selection process. In a typical model-based analysis, the mechanism by which the outcome variable in the sampled population is generated is modeled in a hypothetical superpopulation. In this more complicated circumstance, however, the researcher also has to simultaneously model the self-selection mechanism by which the outcome variable in the sample is selected from the sampled population. Estimates from such joint models depend heavily on the plausibility of the underlying model assumptions for the sample selection model. If these are severely violated, estimates of the outcome of interest can be as biased as or more biased than ignoring the self-selection mechanism altogether.

Overall, it is of paramount importance for any presence of self-selection to be made transparent in the reporting of survey results so that the consumers of the research can be aware of hidden biases that may have affected results.

Sonya K. Sterba and E. Michael Foster

See also Convenience Sampling; Missing Data; Model-Based Estimation; Nonprobability Sampling; Nonresponse; Nonresponse Bias; Purposive Sample; Refusal; Representative Sample; Response Propensity; Self-Selection Bias; Superpopulation

Further Readings

Berk, R. A. (1983). An introduction to sample selection bias in sociological data. *American Sociological Review*, 48, 386–398.

Davidson, R., & MacKinnon, J. G. (2004). *Econometric theory and methods*. New York: Oxford University Press.

Wainer, H. (1986). *Drawing inferences from self-selected samples*. New York: Springer.

SELF-SELECTION BIAS

Self-selection bias is the problem that very often results when survey respondents are allowed to decide entirely for themselves whether or not they want to participate in a survey. To the extent that respondents' propensity for participating in the study is correlated with the substantive topic the researchers are trying to study, there will be self-selection bias in the resulting data. In most instances, self-selection will lead to biased data, as the respondents who choose to participate will not well represent the entire target population.

A key objective of doing surveys is to measure empirical regularities in a population by sampling a much smaller number of entities that represent the whole target population. Modern sampling theory is predicated on the notion that whether an entity is eligible for interview should be determined by a random mechanism as implemented by the researcher that ensures that, for defined subpopulations formed by a partition of the entire population, the probability of selection is either proportional to the number in the subpopulation or, after weighting, weighted sample size is proportional to the number in the subpopulation. Further, the notion that sampling is random rules out selection based on behaviors or attributes about which the researchers are attempting to learn. For example, if researchers seek to learn about political affiliation, the sample will be compromised if the probability of inclusion varies by the respondent's political affiliation. Unfortunately, virtually all survey samples of human beings are self-selected to some degree due to refusal-related nonresponse among the sampled elements. In some cases this merely contributes negligible bias, whereas in others the bias is considerable.

The problem with self-selected samples comes when a respondent chooses to do a survey for reasons that are systematically related to the behaviors or attributes under study. The starting point for the literature on *selectivity bias* dates back more than 30 years to the work of labor economists. Central to the selectivity bias literature is that the seriousness and intractability of the problem increase when selection into the sample is driven not by exogenous or predetermined variables (under the researcher's control) but by unmeasured effects that also influence the behaviors and other variables the survey researchers want to learn about. In the latter case, the threat to validity is large when the rate of nonresponse is also large. An all-volunteer sample is the worst case of nonresponse bias when no one is selected based upon a scientific sampling rule. Consequently, threats to validity peak with self-selected samples—a category into which, for example, far too many Internet polls fall. The goal of sampling is to reduce the scope for people to opt into a study based upon the measures under study. Thus, respondents should be chosen for a survey sample based upon some mechanism that is well understood and statistically independent of the researchers' measurement protocol.

When the respondent chooses the study rather than the study choosing the respondent, the respondent may opt into a study based upon predetermined, observable characteristics, such as age, race, sex, or region of origin or, more dangerously, based upon some characteristic that is respondent determined (or at least heavily influenced), such as political ideology, hours worked, religiosity, or other attitudes. When respondents choose a survey for reasons related only to their demographic characteristics, such as age, race, or sex, the damage to randomness often can be "undone" by judicious post-stratification weighting, so long as researchers know the correct universe estimates for these characteristics. However, when omitted variables affect both the propensity to

volunteer and the measures under study, the situation becomes difficult, requiring substantial structure to undo the damage of a self-selected sample.

With political polling that aims to measure the population's ideology, the risk that some respondents might step forward to do the poll based on their ideology is a problem that cannot be undone by weighting, for if researchers already knew the breakdown of ideology in the population, why would they be conducting the survey in the first place? Thus, for example, there is a good reason organizations doing exit polls select every *n*th voter as opposed to all voters with particular bumper stickers.

Unfortunately, when it comes to sampling, the statistician proposes and the respondents dispose. Self-selection creeps in when a respondent's propensity to cooperate is related to the survey's measurement objectives. As cooperation rates fall for scientifically designed samples, the scope for self-selection increases. Consider an exit poll being done for a newspaper or television network that respondents broadly perceive as having a particular ideological predisposition (i.e., an organization that is viewed as very conservative or very liberal). If the interviewer reveals the name of the newspaper or network, respondents having the same worldview may be predisposed to cooperate, and others without that worldview may not.

Ironically, while academic survey organizations are frequently seen as more dispassionate collectors of data, they are frequently subject to regulation by institutional review boards that often circumscribe the ability of interviewers to secure cooperation from all respondents. With less latitude to convert reluctant respondents, completion rates decline, magnifying the impact of self-selection via differential cooperation.

Randall Olsen

See also Bias; Differential Nonresponse; External Validity; Institutional Review Board (IRB); Nonprobability Sample; Nonresponse Bias; Probability Sample; Response Propensity; Sampling Bias; Self-Selected Sample; Weighting

Further Readings

Gronau, R. (1974). Wage comparisons—a selectivity bias. *Journal of Political Economy, 82*, 1119–1143.

Heckman, J. (1976). The common structure of statistical models of truncation, sample selection, and limited dependent variables and a simple estimator for such models. *Annals of Economic and Social Measurement*, 5, 475–492.

Olsen, R. (1977). *An econometric model of family labor supply*. Unpublished doctoral dissertation, University of Chicago.

Olsen, R. (1980). A least squares correction for selectivity bias. *Econometrica*, 48, 1815–1820.

SEMANTIC DIFFERENTIAL TECHNIQUE

The semantic differential measurement technique is a form of rating scale that is designed to identify the connotative meaning of objects, words, and concepts. The technique was created in the 1950s by psychologist Charles E. Osgood. The semantic differential technique measures an individual's unique, perceived meaning of an object, a word, or an individual.

The semantic differential can be thought of as a sequence of attitude scales. Using a 7-point bipolar rating scale, respondents are expected to rate an object. The 0 position typically means "neutral," 1 means "slightly," the 2 position means "quite," and 3 is "extremely." The scales are designed such that the left side is generally positive and the right is generally negative. This allows the semantic differential to measure intensity and directionality.

The rating scale consists of a list of bipolar responses. These responses are simply opposing adjectives. For example, the semantic differential might use the terms *rough* and *smooth* as its bipolar responses. Using an adapted Likert scale, the respondent chooses a point on the continuum to indicate to which term the object is most closely related. Once this has been completed, the researcher can "map" the respondent's connotations for the object. An example of a semantic differential is provided in Figure 1.

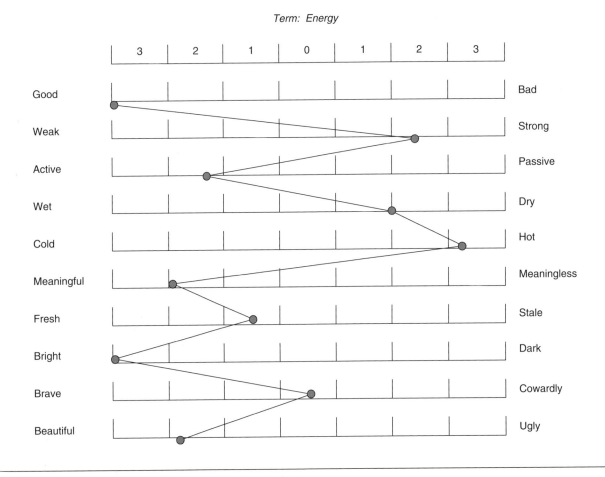

Figure 1   Example of the semantic differential technique

The Logic of the Semantic Differential Technique

The semantic differential is based on the following hypotheses:

1. The process of description or judgment can be conceived as the allocation of a concept to an experiential continuum, definable by a pair of polar terms.

2. Many different experiential continua, or ways in which meanings vary, are essentially equivalent and hence may be represented by a single dimension.

3. A limited number of such continua can be used to define a semantic space within which the meaning of any concept can be specified.

The first hypothesis assumes that discriminations in meaning cannot be finer or involve any more variables than are made possible by the sensory nervous system. The second assumes that the terms used are unique and independent of one another, which is why measurement is possible. The third hypothesis identifies a factor analysis form of methodology, and it allows for the opportunity of measuring meaning-in-general objectively.

Semantic Space

Factor analysis of the semantic differential data allows the researcher to explore a respondent's "semantic space." The semantic space represents the three underlying attitudinal dimensions that humans are hypothesized to use to evaluate everything. Research has demonstrated that these dimensions are present regardless of the social environment, language, or culture of the respondent. The three dimensions are *evaluation*, *power*, and *activity*.

The evaluation factor can be thought of as the good/bad factor. Common bipolar responses are "good/bad," "fresh/stale," "friendly/unfriendly," or "interesting/uninteresting." The power factor, which is sometimes called the potency factor, is the strong/weak factor. Common semantic differential responses for the power factor include "strong/weak," "powerful/powerless," "large/small," or "brave/cowardly." The activity factor is characterized as the active/passive factor. A number of bipolar responses can measure this, including "active/passive," "tense/relaxed," and "fast/slow."

Using these scales, the researcher can attain a reliable measure of a respondent's overall reaction to something. Researchers can obtain a subject's dimensional average by dividing the scales into their appropriate dimensions and averaging their response scores. Once completed, these measurements are thought of as the concept's profile.

Critique

Although the semantic differential technique has been widely used since its inception, there are some concerns about it. Theoretically, using the scale rests on the assumption that humans' connotations of a word are not the same, which is why this technique is needed. Paradoxically, the scale assumes that the chosen adjectives mean the same to everyone. For the scale to work, it must be assumed that humans share the same connotations for some words (i.e., the bipolar adjectives). This is a fairly strong assumption. For instance, looking at Table 1, the bipolar pairs of adjectives generally are set out with "positive" adjectives on the left. However, for the cold/hot dyad it is not clear that "cold" is always associated with positive thoughts. Indeed, depending upon the respondent's past, "cold" could easily evoke negative thoughts.

Another concern is that attitudes do not always match up with behavior. As such, attitudes can be poor predictors of action or behavior. The semantic differential ought to be able to overcome these concerns simply by design, but that does not mean that it can do so on its own. If respondents give socially desirable answers, it will negatively impact the reliability of the measure. Also, if a respondent begins to consistently answer in the same way (i.e., all neutral or always agreeing), the reliability must be questioned. Yet another critique is that the semantic differential does not actually identify individual emotions. Because of its design, the semantic differential technique cannot distinguish beyond the one continuum, but then it never was intended to do so in the first place.

James W. Stoutenborough

See also Attitudes; Bipolar Scale; Likert Scale; Rating; Respondent; Social Desirability

Further Readings

Osgood, C. E., Suci, G. J., & Tannenbaum, P. (1957). *The measurement of meaning*. Urbana: University of Illinois Press.

Osgood, C. E., & Tzeng, O. (Eds.). (1990). *Language, meaning, and culture: The selected papers of C. E. Osgood*. Westport, CT: Praeger.

Snider, J. G., & Osgood, C. E. (Ed.). (1969). *Semantic differential technique: A sourcebook*. Chicago: Aldine.

SENSITIVE TOPICS

There is no widely accepted definition of the term *sensitive topics*, even though most survey researchers would probably agree that certain subjects, such as income, sex, and religion, are definitely examples of the concept. In their classic text *Asking Questions: A Practical Guide to Questionnaire Design*, Seymour Sudman and Norman Bradburn avoided the term altogether and instead talked about "threatening" questions.

Part of the problem is that topics or questions can be sensitive in at least three different, though related, senses. The first sense is that of *intrusiveness*. Some questions are inherently offensive to some (or most) respondents; some topics are seen as inappropriate for a survey. Respondents may find it offensive to be asked about their religion in a government survey or about their income in a study done by market researchers. Sudman and Bradburn used the phrase "taboo topics," and some topics are clearly out of bounds in certain contexts. It would be odd (and impolite) to ask a new coworker intimate details about his or her sexual life or medical history; in the same way, respondents may regard some survey topics or questions as none of the researcher's business. A second sense of "sensitivity" involves the risk that the information may fall into the wrong hands. Teenagers in a survey on smoking may worry that their parents will overhear their answers; respondents to the American Community Survey may worry that the Internal Revenue Service will be able to access their answers to the income questions on the survey. Questions are sensitive in this second sense when they raise concerns that some third party (whether another household member or some agency or business other than the survey firm) will learn what the respondents have reported. For example, in business surveys, responding firms may worry that their competitors will gain proprietary information about them. The final sense of sensitivity involves the social desirability of the behavior or attitude that is the subject of the question.

A question is sensitive in this sense when it asks respondents to admit that their behavior has not lived up to some widely held standard or norm; such questions place the respondents at risk of embarrassing themselves. The embarrassing admission may involve perceived sins of commission (using illicit drugs or having had an abortion), or perceived sins of omission (not exercising enough or failing to vote in a recent election). Perhaps because the concept of sensitivity has multiple senses, there is no generally accepted method for measuring the sensitivity of a question or topic. Instead, most researchers rely on their professional judgment (including their intuitions) about which questions are likely to be sensitive.

These different senses of the term have somewhat different implications for surveys. For example, what makes a question intrusive appears to be the combination of the topic and sponsor of the survey. For example, although it would appear reasonable to most people for the Council of American Catholic Bishops to do a survey on religion, it may not appear reasonable to many for the U.S. Census Bureau to do so. Similarly, people worry more about disclosure risk or embarrassment when they have something they do not want others to find out and they fear the consequences of its becoming known. The consequences may, in turn, depend on who finds out. For a teenage girl, it is one thing for a classmate to learn that she occasionally smokes a cigarette but it may be quite a different thing for her parents to find out.

Consequences of Sensitivity

Despite respondents' potential objections to such topics, surveys often include questions about sensitive topics. To cite one example, since 1971 the federal government has sponsored a series of studies (most recently, the National Survey on Drug Use and Health) to estimate the prevalence and correlates of illicit drug use in the United States. Because surveys cannot always avoid asking about sensitive subjects, it is important to know how people react to them and how those reactions may affect the statistics derived from the surveys.

Asking about sensitive topics in surveys is thought to have three negative consequences for survey statistics. First, sensitive items may produce higher-than-normal levels of item nonresponse (missing data), reducing the number of cases available for analysis and possibly biasing the results. Often, the income question in a survey has the highest level of missing data of any item. The Current Population Survey imputes 20% or more of the responses to the income questions in that survey. These results suggest that one way respondents cope with sensitive questions is not to answer them.

A second way for respondents to avoid answering sensitive questions is not to take part in the survey at all. If the topic of the survey is known beforehand or if the respondent is worried that the survey information may be disclosed to third parties, he or she can refuse to participate. Like item nonresponse, unit nonresponse reduces sample sizes and can bias the results (e.g., if those with the most to hide are also the least likely to take part). Partly to counter such concerns, many federal surveys provide assurances that the data will not be disclosed to outsiders in an identifiable form. Research by Eleanor Singer and her colleagues suggests that these confidentiality assurances have a small but reliable positive effect on response rates.

Relatively little methodological work has explored the effects of question sensitivity on item and unit nonresponse, but a good deal has examined the third possible consequence of question sensitivity—respondents deliberately giving inaccurate answers to the questions, or misreporting. Methodological studies have examined overreports of socially desirable behaviors ranging from voting to attending church to exercising regularly. Similarly, they have explored underreporting of various undesirable behaviors, including having undergone an abortion, consuming too much fat in one's diet, and using illicit drugs. Still other studies have examined reports about sexual behaviors and attempted to explain why men report so many more sexual partners than do women. These studies tend to show high levels of systematic error (bias) in survey reports about sensitive behaviors. For example, more than 20% of nonvoters claim that they voted; similarly, surveys underestimate the number of abortions in the United States by 50% or more, presumably because the respondents underreport their abortions.

Coping With Sensitivity

Methodological textbooks recommend many tactics to reduce the effects of asking sensitive questions in surveys. Some of them attempt to address specific concerns about disclosure of the information to third parties. For example, as already noted, many surveys promise the respondents that the information they provide will remain confidential, partly to blunt any effects of sensitivity on unit nonresponse. Most of these recommended tactics attempt to improve the amount and accuracy of reporting. They include (a) increasing privacy, (b) asking indirect questions, (c) using "forgiving wording," and (d) other special question strategies and methods.

Increasing Privacy

Some methods used in surveys with sensitive questions increase the privacy of the data collection process in an attempt to reduce the motivation to misreport. For example, the data may be collected in a private setting, either away from anyone else in the respondent's home or in a setting outside the home. Evidence shows that interviews are often conducted in the presence of bystanders and, at least in some cases (e.g., when the bystander is the respondent's parent), this inhibits truthful reporting. Because of the threat that other family members may learn sensitive information, other settings, such as schools, may be better for collecting sensitive information from teenagers.

Another method that may increase the respondent's sense of privacy is self-administration of the questions. Both paper questionnaires and computerized self-administration (such as audio computer-assisted self-interviewing) increase reporting of sensitive information, and some studies indicate that computerized self-administration is even more effective than the self-administration via paper questionnaires. Collecting the data anonymously (with no identifying information that links the respondents to their answers) may produce further gains in reporting. However, having respondents put their completed questionnaires in a sealed ballot box does not appear to enhance the basic effect of self-administration, although there is little firm evidence on this point.

Indirect Question Strategies

A variation on the anonymity strategy is to use indirect (i.e., masked) questions that do not directly reveal the sensitive information to the interviewers or the researchers. One such set of methods is the *randomized response technique* (RRT), in which respondents use a randomizing device (a spinner or the flip of a coin) to determine the question they are supposed to answer. In one version of the technique, the respondent answers either the sensitive question (*Have you used cocaine in the last 30 days?*) or an unrelated innocuous question with a known probability of a "yes" answer (*Were you born in April?*). In another approach, the randomizing device determines whether the respondent is instructed to say "yes," say "no," or even answer the sensitive question. Although the randomized response technique seems to be effective (yielding more accurate answers), these gains come at a price. The estimates based on the RRT are more variable than estimates based on direct questions (because fewer respondents actually answer the sensitive question), and it is harder to determine the correlates of the sensitive behavior (because the researchers cannot be sure which individuals answered the sensitive question).

A strategy related to RRT is the *item count technique* (also called the *unmatched count technique* and the *list experiment technique*). This procedure involves asking respondents to say how many behaviors they have done on a list of behaviors; they are not asked to report which behaviors they did, just how many. Some respondents get a list that includes the sensitive item; the rest get the same list without that item. For example, the question might ask one group of respondents, *How many of the following have you done in the past 30 days: Bought new shoes, read a newspaper, donated blood, smoked marijuana, and visited a foreign country?* A second group gets the same list without the item on smoking marijuana. The evidence is mixed about how well the item count technique actually works and, like RRT, it has rarely been used in general population surveys.

Forgiving Wording and Other Wording Approaches

Survey textbooks often recommend "loading" sensitive questions to invite a socially undesirable answer. The question might presuppose the behavior (*How often have you smoked marijuana in the last month?*) or suggest that a particular "bad" behavior is very common (*We often find a lot of people were not able to vote because they weren't registered, they were sick, or they just didn't have the time.*). There is surprisingly little evidence one way or the other on the effectiveness of *forgiving wording*. Familiar wording (asking about *having sex* rather than *sexual*

intercourse) does seem to increase reporting of sensitive information.

One other method has been used to reduce item nonresponse for sensitive questions. In collecting income or other financial information, researchers sometimes use an approach called *unfolding brackets*. For example, respondents who will not (or cannot) report an exact income figure get bracketing questions (*Was the amount more or less than $25,000? More or less than $100,000?*) that allow the respondents to be placed into a broad category. Some respondents are willing to answer the bracketing questions but not those calling for exact information; still, some refuse to provide either type of information.

Bogus Pipeline and Other Methods

Many studies show that an effective method for improving reports about sensitive topics is the *bogus pipeline*. This method involves leading respondents to believe that the interviewer or researcher can determine whether the respondent is telling the truth. Researchers have used a variety of means to convince the respondents that they can detect false reports, ranging from (bogus) polygraph-like devices to (real) biological assays that actually can detect false reports (such as urinalyses that can detect recent drug use). The bogus (or real) pipeline presumably reduces the respondent's motivation to misreport, since the truth will come out anyway. The bogus pipeline is not always very practical in a survey setting (how does one get the equipment to the respondent?) and, when the pipeline is bogus, researchers may be unwilling to engage in the requisite deception.

One other tactic is sometimes recommended—that of matching interviewers and respondents on background characteristics (such as sex). This seems to be based on the idea that respondents are more likely to confide in interviewers who are similar to them than to ones who are dissimilar, but there is little evidence on the effectiveness or ineffectiveness of interviewer–respondent matching. For example, a 1992 study by Paul J. Lavrakas found that men were twice as likely to report having sexually harassed someone when they were interviewed by a male interviewer than when they were interviewed by a female interviewer, and that women were three times as likely to report having sexually harassed someone when they were interviewed by a female interviewer than by a male interviewer.

Conclusion

Surveys that ask people sensitive questions are here to stay. Unfortunately, people come to surveys armed with a lifetime of experience of fending off unwelcome questions. They can avoid the questions by avoiding the survey entirely, by refusing to answer specific sensitive questions, or by deliberately misreporting. Many surveys have adopted self-administration to improve reporting; this and the randomized response technique both seem to be effective. The key to both procedures is that the interviewer is not aware of the embarrassing information being revealed. Unfortunately, none of the survey techniques for dealing with sensitive questions eliminates misreporting entirely. Research methodologists still have a lot to learn about how best to collect sensitive information in surveys.

Roger Tourangeau

See also Anonymity; Audio Computer-Assisted Self-Interviewing (ACASI); Confidentiality; List Experiment Technique; Misreporting; Missing Data; Mode of Data Collection; Overreporting; Privacy; Randomized Response; Refusal; Response Bias; Social Desirability; Underreporting; Unfolding Question; Unit Nonresponse

Further Readings

Barton, A. J. (1958). Asking the embarrassing question. *Public Opinion Quarterly*, 22, 67–68.

Lavrakas, P. J. (1992, November). *Attitudes toward and experience with sexual harassment in the workplace.* Paper presented at the 14th annual conference of the Midwest Association for Public Opinion Research, Chicago.

Singer, E., von Thurn, D., & Miller, E. (1995). Confidentiality assurances and response: A quantitative review of the experimental literature. *Public Opinion Quarterly*, 59, 66–77.

Sudman, S., & Bradburn, N. (1982). *Asking questions: A practical guide to questionnaire design.* San Francisco: Jossey-Bass.

SEQUENTIAL SAMPLING

For survey sampling applications, the term *sequential sampling* describes any method of sampling that reads an ordered frame of N sampling units and selects the sample with specified probabilities or specified expectations. Sequential sampling methods are particularly well suited when applied with computers. They can also be applied for selecting samples of a population resulting from some other process: for example, cars coming off an assembly line, patients arriving at a clinic, or voters exiting the polls. Examples of sequential sampling schemes discussed in this entry include simple random sampling, systematic sampling, and probability proportional to size (PPS) sequential sampling.

Simple Random Sampling (Without Replacement)

Simple random sampling without replacement is defined as selecting one of the possible distinct samples of size n from a population of size N. There are $\binom{N}{n}$ such possible samples, and each has an equal probability of being selected. Other methods generally involve selecting random numbers between 1 and N, discarding any repeats, and retaining the first n distinct units selected. Random ordering before selecting a pre-specified chunk is often used in computerized selection of simple random samples. The sequential procedure requires selecting a random number, R_i, for each population element and comparing it to a conditional probability based on what has occurred up to this point. Select Unit 1 if $R_1 \leq n/N$. If Unit 1 is selected, select Unit 2 if $R_2 \leq (n-1)/(N-1)$; if Unit 1 is not selected, select Unit 2 if $R_2 \leq n/(N-1)$. Proceed through the list decreasing the denominator for each new unit but decreasing the numerator only when a selection occurs.

Systematic Sampling

For the simplest case, where sampling is with equal probabilities and $k = N/n$ is an integer, a random integer, I, between 1 and k is drawn and when the Ith element is encountered it is included in the sample. I is then incremented by k, and the $(I + k)$th element is included in the sample when encountered. The process continues until n units have been designated for the sample.

A more general form of systematic sampling can be applied where sampling is with unequal probabilities and/or $k \neq N/n$. Define the desired probabilities of selection for each unit as π_i for $i - 1, 2, \ldots, N$. For an equal probability design, $\pi_i = n/N$. For unequal probability designs, it is only necessary that $0 < \pi_i$

≤ 1 and $\sum_{i=1}^{N} \pi_i = n$. To select the sample sequentially, it is necessary to draw a uniform $(0,1)$ random number, R. For Unit 1, define $S = \pi_1$. If $R \leq S$, then select Unit 1 and increment R by 1. For subsequent Unit i increase S by π_i and if $R \leq S$, then select Unit i and increment R by 1.

PPS Sequential

PPS sequential sampling is defined for probability minimum replacement (PMR) sampling. Sampling without replacement is then shown as a special case. Rather than working with the probability of selection, PMR selection schemes work with the expected number of hits or selections for each unit designated by $E(n_i)$, where n_i is the number of times unit i is selected for a particular sample. When a size measure X_i is used, the expected number of selections per unit i is set as

$$E(n_i) = \frac{nX_i}{\sum_{i=1}^{N} X_i}.$$

Note that this formulation allows $E(n_i)$ to be greater than 1. The defining PMR principle is that for every sample, the actual value of n_i will be either the integer portion of $E(n_i)$ or one greater.

Application of PPS sequential sampling requires keeping track of the two sums during the process:

$$S_i = \sum_{j=1}^{i} E(n_j) \quad \text{and} \quad T_i = \sum_{j=1}^{i} n_j.$$

The first sum is partitioned into integer component, I_i, and a fractional component, F_i, with $0 \leq F_i < 1$. S_0 and T_0 are set to 0 to start the process. The sequential selection process proceeds as follows:

- If $T_{i-1} = I_{i-1}$ and $F_i = 0$ or $F_{i-1} \geq F_i > 0$, then $T_i = I_i + 1$ with probability 0.
- If $T_{i-1} = I_{i-1}$ and $F_i > F_{i-1} \geq 0$, then $T_i = I_i + 1$ with probability $\frac{F_i - F_{i-1}}{1 - F_{i-1}}$.
- If $T_{i-1} = I_{i-1} + 1$ and $F_i = 0$, then $T_i = I_i + 1$ with probability 0.
- If $T_{i-1} = I_{i-1} + 1$ and $F_i > F_{i-1} \geq 0$, then $T_i = I_i + 1$ with probability 1.

- If $T_{i-1} = I_{i-1} + 1$ and $F_{i-1} \geq F_i > 0$, then $T_i = I_i + 1$ with probability $\frac{F_i}{F_{i-1}}$.

The number of times a unit is selected is then computed as $n_i = T_i - T_{i-1}$.

An estimate of a population total is analogous to Horvitz-Thompson estimator for PPS without replacement sampling except selection probabilities, π_i, are replaced with expected sample sizes. In the variance formula and in the variance estimator, the pairwise probabilities π_{ij} are replaced by expectation of the product of achieved sample sizes for the two units, $E(n_i n_j)$. To allow for unbiased variance estimation, $E(n_i n_j)$ must be positive for all pairs of units. This can be achieved by first ordering the list along some meaningful stratification dimension and considering the ordering as a closed loop. Then a random starting unit is selected, and the process is applied for the complete ordered list. As an example, the sampling units on the frame (or within a single stratum) may be ordered along some continuation (such as income levels) within a geographic area. With two areas, the order of sorting on income may be specified as increasing in one area and decreasing in the other. Any two neighboring elements on the closed loop will have at least one characteristic in common: same area, similar income, or both. Similar sorting schemes can be set up for more ordering variables.

Note that if the expected sample sizes are all less than 1, the selection procedure produces a probability without replacement sample. If all expected sample sizes are equal and less than 1, then it produces an equal probability sample.

James R. Chromy

See also Probability Proportional to Size (PPS) Sampling; Sampling Without Replacement; Simple Random Sample; Systematic Sampling

Further Readings

Chromy, J. R. (1981). Variance estimators for a sequential selection procedure. In D. Krewski, R. Platek, & J. N. K. Rao (Eds.), *Current topics in survey sampling* (pp. 329–347). New York: Academic Press.

Fan, C. T., Muller, M. E., & Rezucha, I. (1962). Development of sampling plans by using sequential (item by item) selection techniques and digital computers. *Journal of the American Statistical Association, 57,* 387–402.

SHEATSLEY, PAUL (1916–1989)

Paul B. Sheatsley was an early leader in the new field of survey research. He was born in New York City in 1916 and received a bachelor's degree from Princeton University in 1936. While following a career in journalism and public relations as editor of the *Boonton Tribune* in New Jersey (1937–1939) and public relations director for the Yankees' farm team, the Newark International Baseball Club (1939), Sheatsley started working as a part-time interviewer for George Gallup. Gallup then hired him to be field director of the Audience Research Institute (1940–1942). In early 1942, Harry Field, the founder of the recently organized National Opinion Research Center (NORC) at the University of Denver, approached his friend and former colleague, Gallup, and asked to "borrow" Sheatsley to head NORC's New York office and direct the important series of studies that NORC was to do for the Office of War Information (1942–1944). Once he had gone to NORC, Sheatsley never left. He headed the New York office until 1963 and directed many major studies, such as the foreign policy series for the U.S. State Department (1945–1957). Then he moved to NORC's headquarters at the University of Chicago to direct its new Survey Research Service. He led that department until 1976 and served as NORC's acting director in 1970–1971. From 1976 until his retirement in 1986, Sheatsley was a senior survey director heading such large-scale projects as the National Ambulatory Medical Care Survey. From 1986 until his death in 1989, he continued as a consultant to NORC.

Sheatsley made major contributions in the areas of survey professionalization, methodology, and substantive analysis. He attended the first conference of survey researchers ever held that was organized by Field in Central City, Colorado, in 1946. This conference led to a second conference in Williamstown, Massachusetts, in 1947 where the American Association for Public Opinion Research (AAPOR) was organized. Sheatsley became a leader of AAPOR. He served on its council longer than any other person, holding offices in each decade from the 1940s to the 1980s. He was AAPOR president in 1967–1968 and was awarded AAPOR's Exceptionally Distinguished Achievement Award in 1982. He was coeditor with Warren J. Mitofsky of *A Meeting Place: The History of the American Association for Public Opinion Research* (1992).

While directing many seminal surveys for NORC, Sheatsley conducted a long series of methodological studies to improve data quality. He published articles on such topics as interviewer training, question wording, the use of incentives, validation, and open- versus closed-ended items.

Substantively, Sheatsley did pioneering work in the area of intergroup relations. He was coauthor of a series of four articles published in *Scientific American* between 1956 and 1978 that has been recognized as the first trend studies on intergroup relations, and he studied the race riots in the 1960s. Another seminal study that he analyzed was the Kennedy Assassination Study in 1963 that measured the public response to the president's murder and served as the baseline for NORC's National Tragedy Study, conducted in the aftermath of the 9/11 terrorist attacks in 2001.

Sheatsley's liberal arts education and journalistic training served him well in the field of survey research. Besides mastering the complex task of managing large-scale, national surveys and the quantitative skill of data analysis, he was able to both write clear and precise questions easily understandable by both respondents and interviewers and then present results that were insightful, true to the data, and comprehensible to the reader.

Tom W. Smith

See also American Association for Public Opinion Research (AAPOR); George Gallup; National Opinion Research Center (NORC)

SHOW CARD

Within the context of survey research, a show card or *show sheet* is a visual aid used predominantly during in-person surveys. It is a card, a piece of paper, or an electronic screen containing answer categories to a question, from which the respondent chooses the answer to the survey question. The respondent may either look at the answer categories listed on the show card when providing the answer or mark the answer directly on the show card. The answers listed on the show card can be in the form of words, numbers, scales, pictures, or other graphical representations.

Telephone interviews may also employ show cards, although mailing the show cards or setting up Internet sites with the digital equivalents of show cards can be logistically and financially impractical.

Show cards are used by survey organizations internationally. In the United States, the use of show cards is somewhat wide-scale, including the federal government and private sector organizations. However, because they usually require in-person administration, show cards are not as well known or as well researched as other survey tools. The primary purpose for using show cards is to reduce survey measurement error. Show cards reduce error by (a) encouraging respondents to provide more accurate answers by increasing the perceived confidentiality of the answers, and (b) making it easier for respondents to provide a more accurate answer, for example, through presenting the entire answer category set in one visual field.

Providing More Accurate Answers on Sensitive Issues

Respondents may be uncomfortable providing accurate responses to some questions. Sensitive information can be easier for respondents to provide if they can do so under an additional veil of confidentiality, even from the interviewer. Sensitive information can range from health information (anything from weight to sexual history) to demographic information (anything from age to income). Accepted thinking is that granting the respondent maximum privacy during data collection is conducive to obtaining accurate answers.

In some cases, the respondent himself or herself marks the correct answer on the show card without verbally stating to the interviewer what that answer is. A different approach is to precede the answer categories with letters or other abstract identifiers, as in Figure 1. This allows the respondent to provide abstract answers, such as letters or other abstract identifiers, instead of verbalizing the specifics of the answer (e.g., "less than $25,000").

Making It Easier for Respondents to Provide More Accurate Answers

Some questions may be difficult to answer because of the complexity of the response choices. Questions that

SHOWCARD A

Please provide the letter (a, b, c, d, e, or f) next to the line that best matches your household's total income from last year. Your household's total income should include the money earned by all members of your household before taxes.

a) less than $25,000
b) $25,000 to $49,999
c) $50,000 to $74,999
d) $75,000 to $99,999
e) $100,000 to $150,000
f) more than $150,000

Figure 1   Income show card

contain lengthy or complex answer choices may use show cards so that the respondent can visualize and review the full field of possible answer categories before choosing the most accurate answer.

There is no standard for answer complexity level that benefits from the use of a show card. Some research organizations employ show cards for questions with as few as four or five answer categories.

Best Practices for the Use of Show Cards

Research on show cards is scarce at present. Thus, best practices for their use are experientially based rather than experimentally based. Some organizations appear to have their own idiosyncratic preferences for the frequency and appropriateness of show card use. A few general best practice principles detail commonalities shared by the majority of show cards.

As with other survey materials, researchers should aim for answer categories that are mutually exclusive and comprehensive. Because show cards offer visual representations of answer categories, the researchers need to consider the appearance of the card during its creation. There is some concern that show cards may be conducive to primacy effects (respondents choosing answers that disproportionately fall within the first few answer categories on the card), which should factor into the card design and pretesting considerations.

Show cards generally do not include "Refuse" or "Don't Know" as answer categories. The additional level of confidentiality afforded by the show card aims to reduce the need for someone to refuse, and the in-person nature of the data collection allows for follow-up probes by the interviewer in instances of "Don't Know" answers.

Agnieszka Flizik

See also Face-to-Face Interviewing; Field Survey; Graphical Language; Measurement Error; Primacy Effect; Privacy; Probing; Sensitive Topics

Further Readings

Davis, W., Wellens, T. R., & DeMaio, T. J. (1996). *Designing response scales in an applied setting.* Washington, DC: U.S. Census Bureau. Retrieved April 17, 2008, from http://www.census.gov/srd/papers/pdf/wd9601.pdf

Dillman, D. A. (2006). *Mail and internet surveys: The tailored method, 2007 update with new internet, visual, and mixed-mode guide.* Indianapolis, IN: Wiley.

General Registrar Office for Scotland. (2006). *Census test follow up survey: Information about Scotland's people.* Retrieved April 17, 2008, from http://www.gro-scotland.gov.uk/files1/the-census/2006-census-test-evaluation/j8566b.pdf

Research Triangle Institute. (2007). *2007 National Survey on Drug Use and Health—Showcard booklet.* Retrieved April 17, 2008, from http://www.oas.samhsa.gov/nsduh/2k7MRB/2k7Showcards.pdf

U.K. Data Archive. (2003). *Family Resources Survey: Show cards.* Retrieved April 17, 2008, from http://www.data-archive.ac.uk/doc/4803%5Cmrdoc%5Cpdf%5C4803userguide9.pdf

SIGNIFICANCE LEVEL

The significance level (also called Type I error rate or the level of statistical significance) refers to the probability of rejecting a null hypothesis that is in fact true. This quantity ranges from zero (0.0) to one (1.0) and is typically denoted by the Greek letter alpha (α). The significance level is sometimes referred to as the probability of obtaining a result by chance alone. As this quantity represents an "error rate," lower values are generally preferred. In the literature, nominal values of α generally range from 0.05 to 0.10. The significance level is also referred to as the "size of the test" in that the magnitude of the significance level determines the end points of the critical or rejection region for hypothesis tests. As such, in hypothesis testing, the *p*-value is often compared to the significance level in order to determine if a test result is "statistically significant." As a general rule, if the *p*-value is no larger than the significance level, the null hypothesis is rejected and the result is deemed statistically significant, thus supporting the alternative hypothesis.

The level of significance can refer to the Type I error for a single hypothesis test or for a family of simultaneous tests. In the latter case, the "experiment-wise" or "family-wise" significance level refers to the probability of making at least one Type I error over the collection of hypothesis tests that are contained in the family. So for example, a survey may contain questions to solicit data to be used to compare the average expenditures, household ownership percentage, and education levels across two possible geographic sectors of a particular county. Because there are three main variables of interest that are to be compared across the two geographical regions, the family-wise level of significance will refer to the probability of making a Type I error rate on at least one of the three hypothesis tests that are performed for this family of tests.

In another example of multiple comparisons, comparisons of the average length of unemployment were made across four racial post-strata after an omnibus analysis of variance (ANOVA) revealed that the average unemployment periods are not equal across the four race groups. One possible set of post-hoc multiple comparisons consists of all pairwise tests for differences in the average unemployment period for two race groups at a time (i.e., six pairwise tests).

A Bonferroni adjustment or other multiple comparisons adjustment is typically made to the overall nominal Type I error rate to ensure the proper significance level is achieved for the family of tests. For example, to ensure that the overall significance level for a family of three hypothesis tests, the nominal significance level, α, would be divided by 3, and the adjusted significance level, $\alpha/3$, would be used as the Type I error rate for each of the three hypothesis tests in the family. In the second scenario, six comparisons would be made, so the Bonferroni adjustment for multiple comparisons equates to using $\alpha/6$ as the Type I error rate for each of the pairwise comparisons.

Large values of α generally imply more powerful tests but also introduce a higher likelihood for rejecting a null hypothesis that is in fact true. Conversely, smaller α values imply less tolerance for making a Type I error; values of α that are too small make rejection of the null hypothesis virtually impossible, thereby reducing the statistical power of the test (i.e., increase Type II error). Thus, values for the significance level are generally fixed by the researcher prior to data collection (often at .05) to ensure proper protection against making a Type I error while allowing for a reasonable level of statistical power to be achieved for the particular hypothesis test or family of tests at hand.

Trent D. Buskirk

See also Alternative Hypothesis; Analysis of Variance (ANOVA); Null Hypothesis; *p*-Value; Statistical Power; Type I Error; Type II Error

Further Readings

Yates, D., Moore, D., & McCabe, G. (1999).*The practice of statistics*. New York: W. H. Freeman.

Simple Random Sample

There are two varieties of simple random samples: (1) with replacement and (2) without replacement. To draw a simple random sample, one must have a frame drawn up for the population of interest prior to sampling or at least know the size of the frame in advance. For a simple random sample without replacement, all $\binom{N}{n}$ possible subsets of *n* units have equal probability of selection. For a simple random sample with replacement, all N^n *n*-tuples of units have equal probability of selection. Although simple random samples are rarely used in sample surveys, they have played an important role in the development of the epistemological theory for survey research, and they continue to be useful in pedagogy, as an efficiency benchmark, and as a proving ground for demonstrating the properties of complex estimation strategies.

In most cases, a researcher who chooses a simple random sample design would be doing two things contrary to good judgment by ignoring all cost considerations and ignoring all prior knowledge about the population. Quite to the contrary, information about heteroscedasticity (i.e., differences in variances among variables) in the variable of interest or about its relationship to variables known for the entire population should be used to improve the efficiency of the sample through stratification, systematic selection, or differential probabilities of selection. Similarly, analysis of the components of cost often leads to the decision to draw a multistage sample. Usually, stratification, systematic selection, unequal probabilities of selection, and clustering are all employed in sample surveys. In fact, historians of survey methodology have dug hard to find examples where simple random samples were actually employed. Those, of course, could have been improved.

Regarding epistemology, simple random samples played an important role in Jerzy Neyman's communication of his theory of confidence intervals in his landmark 1934 paper. More recently, those in favor of likelihood-based inference (frequentist or Bayesian) have sometimes argued their points under the assumption that the design-based statistician would use a simple random sample. This is not exactly fair, perhaps, but the simplicity of the design does make it easier to grasp the fundamental differences in approaches. That same simplicity makes these designs useful in the teaching of survey methodology, as well as in demonstrating the asymptotic properties of complex estimation techniques (e.g., ratio-estimation and regression estimation, raking, and imputation). The "design effect" is a useful tool for comparing the efficiency of alternate designs and is defined with reference to the variance arising from a hypothetical simple random sample of the same size.

There are scattered earlier references to "simple random sampling," but the first formal use of the phrase appears to be Harald Cramer's 1946 text on mathematical statistics. The first sampling textbooks by Frank Yates in 1949 and by W. Edwards Deming in 1950 did not use the phrase at all. The next appearances were in the 1953 textbooks of William Cochran and of Morris Hansen, William Hurwitz, and William Madow. Cramer reserved it for sampling with replacement, whereas the others reserved it for sampling without replacement. Leslie Kish in his 1965 text used the term *simple random sampling* if without replacement and *unrestricted sampling* if with replacement, a term which Arthur Bowley and Jerzy Neyman used for both variants some 30 years earlier. Current usage is ambiguous with respect to replacement.

David Ross Judkins

See also Design Effects (*deff*); Frame; Multi-Stage Sample; Nonprobability Sampling; Random Sampling; Sampling Without Replacement; Stratified Sampling; Survey Costs

Further Readings

Kish, L. (2003). The hundred years' war of survey sampling. In S. Heeringa & G. Kalton (Eds.), *Selected papers*. Hoboken, NJ: Wiley-Interscience. (Reprinted from *Statistics in Transition*, 1995, 2[5], 813–830)

Neyman, J. (1967). On the two different aspects of the representative method: The method of stratified sampling and the method of purposive selection. In *A selection of early statistical papers of J. Neyman*. Berkeley: University of California Press. (Reprinted from *Journal of the Royal Statistical Society*, 1934, 97[4], 558–625)

Smith, T. M. F. (1994). Sample surveys 1975–1990; An age of reconciliation? *International Statistical Review*, 62(1), 3–34.

SMALL AREA ESTIMATION

Survey data have been effectively used to provide suitable statistics for the target population and for many subpopulations, often called *domains* or *areas*. Domains may be geographical regions (e.g., states or counties), sociodemographic groups (e.g., nonwhite Hispanic women between 18 and 65 years) or other subpopulations. A domain or an area is considered "large" or "major" if the domain sample is sufficiently large so that it can provide a *direct estimate* of the domain parameter, for example, the mean, with adequate precision. A domain or an area is regarded as "small" if the domain-specific sample is not large enough to produce an estimate with reliable precision. Areas or domains with small samples are called *small areas, small domains, local areas, subdomains,* or *substates*.

Beginning in 1996, the U.S. Congress began to require that the Secretary of Commerce publish, at least biennially, current data related to incidence of poverty for states, counties, and local jurisdictions of government and school districts "to the extent feasible." State and county estimates of the number of 5- to 17-year-old children in poverty and those among 65 and older are required. Poverty estimates for children are used to allocate federal and state funds, federal funds nearly $100 billion annually in recent

years. As such, small area estimation is very important for the well-being of many citizens.

A Brief Primer on Important Terms in Small Area Estimation

For m small areas, suppose $Y_{ij}, j = 1, N_i$ denote values of a response variable (Y) for the N_i units in the ith small area. Imagine one would like to estimate $\gamma_i = N_i - 1 \sum_{j=1}^{N_i} Y_{ij}$, the finite population mean. Suppose X is a vector of explanatory variables. If explanatory variables are available for all the sampled units in the ith small area, to be denoted for simplicity by $1, \ldots, n_i$, then a *unit-level model* is used. But if only direct estimates Y_i for γ_i and summary data x_i for explanatory variables are available at the small area level, then an *area-level model* is used. If indirect small area estimates are produced by fitting a model relating the response variable and explanatory variables, and prediction of a small area mean is obtained by substituting explanatory variables into the estimated model, one gets a *synthetic estimate*, denoted by $\hat{\gamma}$. Synthetic estimates are much too model dependent, susceptible to model failure, and not design-consistent. A composite estimate, which is a convex combination of Y_i and $\hat{\gamma}_{is}$, rectifies these deficiencies.

This entry considers only some of the basic aspects of small area estimation. For example, neither the time series and cross-sectional approach to small area estimation nor the interval estimation problem is considered here. For this and many other important topics, the advanced reader should consult J. N. K. Rao's *Small Area Estimation*.

Two Popular Small Area Models

Both linear and nonlinear models and both Bayesian and frequentist approaches are popular in small area estimation. While the *estimated best linear unbiased prediction (EBLUP)* approach is key to developing composite estimates based on mixed linear models, the empirical Bayes (EB) and the hierarchical Bayes (HB) approaches can be used for both linear and nonlinear models. Many model-based developments in small area estimation use normality assumptions. For normal linear models, the EBLUP and EB predictors of the small area means are identical.

The nested error regression model is a popular unit-level model given by

$$Y_{ij} = X_{ij}^T \beta + v_i + e_{ij}, j = 1, \ldots, N_j, I = 1, \ldots, m, \quad (1)$$

where X_{ij} is a p-component vector of auxiliary variables, v_i and e_{ij} are independently distributed with $v_i \overset{iid}{\sim} N(0, \sigma_v^2)$ and $e_{ij} \overset{iid}{\sim} N(0, \sigma_e^2)$, $j = 1, N_j$, $i = 1, \ldots, m$. G. E. Battese and colleagues proposed this model to estimate areas under corn and soybeans for 12 counties in Iowa based on unit-level auxiliary data obtained from the LANDSAT satellite readings and unit-level response variable available from farm survey data.

An early application of the area-level model is by Robert E. Fay and R. A. Herriot in order to improve the direct estimator Y_i for estimating the per capita income of small places, denoted by μ_i. They assumed for their problem that a p-vector of auxiliary variables x_i was available for each area i given by county values, housing data from the census, and tax returns from the Internal Revenue Service. They assumed

$$Y_i = \mu_i + e_i, \quad \mu_i = x_i^T \beta + v_i, \quad i = 1, \ldots, m, \quad (2)$$

where $e_i \overset{ind}{\sim} N(0, D_i)$ and $v_i \overset{ind}{\sim} N(0, \sigma_v^2)$. Sampling variances D_is are assumed to be known.

For brevity, this discussion is confined to unit-level models under the normality assumption. The next two sections discuss, respectively, the EBLUP (or EB) and HB approaches to small area estimation.

EBLUP and Mean Squared Error

This section focuses on the nested error regression model. Rao discusses general mixed linear models. For large values of N_i, γ_i can be approximated by $\mu_i = \bar{X}_i^T \beta + v_i$, where $\bar{X}_i = N_i^{-1} \sum_{j=1}^{N_i} X_{ij}$, and we use EBLUP of μ_i to predict γ_i. Let $Y^{(1)} = (Y_{11}, \ldots, Y_{1n_1}, \ldots, Y_{m_1}, \ldots, Y_{mn_m})^T$, $X^{(1)} = (X_{11}, X_{1n_1}, \ldots, X_{m1}, \ldots, X_{mn_m})^T$, $\Sigma_{11} = Diag(\sigma_e^2 I_{n_1} + \sigma_v^2 11^T, \ldots, \sigma_e^2 I_{n_m} + \sigma_v^2 11^T)$, I_p is a $p \times p$ identity matrix and 1 is a vector of ones. For known variance components $\psi = (\sigma_v^2, \sigma_\epsilon^2)^T$, the best linear unbiased prediction (BLUP) of μ_i is

$$\tilde{\mu}_i(\psi) = \bar{X}_i^T \tilde{\beta}(\psi) + \delta_i(\bar{Y}_{is} - \bar{x}_{is}^T \tilde{\beta}(\psi)), \quad (3)$$

where $\bar{Y}_{is}$ is the ith area sample mean. Similarly, $\bar{x}_{is}$ is defined. Also, $\tilde{\beta}(\psi)$ is the weighted least squares estimator of β based on Equation 1 corresponding to the sampled units, and $\delta_i = \sigma_v^2 (\sigma_v^2 + \sigma_\epsilon^2 n_i^{-1})^{-1}$. For unknown variance components ψ, the BLUP cannot

be calculated. Let $\hat{\psi}$ denote an estimator of ψ, estimated by ANOVA methods or maximum likelihood or residual maximum likelihood methods. For subsequent discussion, let us assume ANOVA estimates of the variance components are used. Then $\tilde{\mu}_i(\hat{\psi})$ is an EBLUP of μ_i.

The mean squared error (MSE) of an EBLUP of μ_i, given by $E[\tilde{\mu}_i(\hat{\psi}) - \mu_i]^2$, usually has no closed-form expression. A second-order approximation to this MSE ignoring all terms of order lower than $1/m$ is studied by Prasad and Rao and others. Indeed the approximation

$$MSE = E[\tilde{\mu}_i(\hat{\psi}) - \mu_i]^2 = g_{1i}(\psi) + g_{2i}(\psi) + g_{3i}(\psi),$$

where $g_{1i}(\psi) = (1 - \delta_i)\sigma_v^2$, and

$$g_2 i(\psi) = (\bar{X}_i - \delta_i \bar{x}_{is})^T (\bar{X}^{(1)T} \Sigma_{11}^{-1}(\psi) X^{(1)})^{-1}$$
$$(\bar{X}_i - \delta_i \bar{x}_{is}), g_{3i}(\psi)$$
$$= \frac{var(\sigma_v^2 \hat{\sigma}_\epsilon^2 - \sigma_\epsilon^2 \hat{\sigma}_v^2)}{n_i^2(\sigma_v^2 + \sigma_\epsilon^2/n_i)^3}. \quad (4)$$

Note that $g_{1i}(\psi) = 0(1)$ but $g_{2i}(\psi), g_{3i}(\psi)$ are $0(m^{-1})$. An estimator MSE is second-order unbiased if $E[mse] = MSE + 0(m^{-1})$. According to N. G. N. Prasad and Rao, $mse = g_{1i}(\hat{\psi}) + g_{2i}(\hat{\psi}) + 2g_{3i}(\hat{\psi})$ is second-order unbiased.

Hierarchical Bayes Approach to Small Area Estimation

For the nested error regression model, Gauri Datta and Malay Ghosh considered the HB model

1. $Y_{ij}|\beta, v_1, \ldots, v_m, \sigma_v^2, \sigma_\epsilon^2 \sim N(X_{ij}^T \beta + v_i, \sigma_\epsilon^2)$ independently $j = 1, \ldots, N_i, I = 1, \ldots, m$;

2. $v_i|\beta, \sigma_v^2, \sigma_\epsilon^2 \sim N(0, \sigma_v^2)$, independently $I = 1, \ldots, m$;

3. Independent prior on the second-stage parameters: β an improper uniform prior on R^p, σ_v^2 and $\sigma_\epsilon^2 \sim$ inverse gamma prior (possibly improper).

The HB predictor for γ_i is obtained from the predictive distribution of the unsampled units $Y_{ij}, j = n_i + 1, \ldots, N_i, i = 1, \ldots, m$ given the sampled units. Datta and Ghosh gave the predictive distribution in two steps. In Step 1, the predictive distribution is given for fixed hyperparameters σ_v^2 and σ_ϵ^2. In Step 2, the posterior distribution of the hyperparameters is given. Under squared error loss, for known hyperparameters, the Bayes predictor is also the BLUP. The HB predictor, typically with no closed-form, is obtained by integrating the above Bayes predictor with respect to the posterior distribution of the hyperparameters. Instead of assigning priors to the hyperparameters, if one estimates them from the marginal distribution of the data and replaces the variance components by their estimates in the Bayes predictor of γ_i, the result is the EB predictor. In fact, the EB predictor is identical to the EBLUP of γ_i. The HB predictor and associated measure of uncertainty given by the posterior variance can be computed by numerical integration or *Gibbs sampling*.

While the EBLUP is applicable to mixed linear models, the HB and the EB approaches can be applied even to generalized linear models, thereby making a unified analysis of both discrete and continuous data feasible.

Gauri Sankar Datta and Malay Ghosh

See also Composite Estimation; Parameter

Further Readings

Battese, G. E., Harter, R. M., & Fuller, W. A. (1988). An error components model for prediction of county crop area using survey and satellite data. *Journal of the American Statistical Association, 83*, 28–36.

Datta, G. S., & Ghosh, M. (1991). Bayesian prediction in linear models: Applications to small area estimation. *Annals of Statistics, 19*, 1748–1770.

Datta, G. S., & Lahiri, P. (2000). A unified measure of uncertainty of estimated best linear unbiased predictors in small area estimation problems. *Statistica Sinica, 10*, 613–627.

Datta, G. S., Rao, J. N. K., & Smith, D. D. (2005). On measuring the variability of small area estimators under a basic area level model. *Biometrika, 92*, 183–196.

Fay, R. E., & Herriot, R. A. (1979). Estimates of income for small places: An application of James-Stein procedure to census data. *Journal of the American Statistical Association, 74*, 269–277.

Gelfand, A. E., & Smith, A. F. M. (1990). Sampling-based approaches to calculating marginal densities. *Journal of the American Statistical Association, 85*, 398–409.

Ghosh, M., & Rao, J. N. K. (1994). Small area estimation: An appraisal. *Statistical Science, 9*, 55–93 (with discussion).

Lahiri, P., & Rao, J. N. K. (1995). Robust estimation of mean squared error of small area estimators. *Journal of the American Statistical Association, 90*, 758–766.

Prasad, N. G. N., & Rao, J. N. K. (1990). The estimation of mean squared error of small area estimators. *Journal of the American Statistical Association, 85*, 163–171.

Rao, J. N. K. (2003). *Small area estimation*. Hoboken: NJ: Wiley.

SNOWBALL SAMPLING

Snowball sampling is a technique that can be applied in two survey contexts. The first context involves surveying members of a rare population. The second involves studying mutual relationships among population members. In both cases, respondents are expected to know about the identity of other members of the same population group.

Studying Rare Populations

In this context, snowball sampling is a nonprobability sampling technique. The general objective is to identify members of the rare population. It involves identifying one or more members of a rare population and asking them to name other members of the same population. These additional persons are then contacted and asked to name additional persons in the rare population; and so forth. The process continues until an adequate sample size has been obtained or until no new names are elicited from the process.

If terminated when adequate sample size is obtained, the method yields a sample, but not a probability sample.

If the population can be restricted in some way, say to a limited geographic area such as a county, snowball sampling may be successful as a rare population frame-building technique. To be successful, several rounds of the process must be conducted, and the initial sample should be large and adequately distributed among the rare population members. Within this restricted population, the identified rare population members can then be sampled using probability sampling techniques, or a complete enumeration (census) may be conducted. If the limited geographic areas are first-stage units in a multi-stage probability sample design, the approach can yield an estimate for a larger target population.

If some members of the targeted rare population are isolated from the remainder of the population, they are not likely to be named even after several rounds of enumeration. Serious coverage problems may remain even if the process is carried out diligently.

Studying Relationships

In the early 1960s, sociologist Leo Goodman proposed a probability sample–based method for studying relationships among individuals in a population. An initial zero-stage (Stage 0) probability sample is drawn. Each person in the sample is asked to name k persons with some particular relationship; example relationships are best friends, most frequent business associate, persons with most valued opinions, and so on. At Stage 1 these k persons are contacted and asked to name k persons with the same relationship. The Stage 2 sample consists of new persons named at Stage 1, that is, persons not in the original sample. At each subsequent stage, only newly identified persons are sampled at the next stage. The process may be continued for any number of stages, designated by s.

The simplest relationships involve two persons where each names the other. If the initial sample is a probability sample, an unbiased estimate of the number of pairs in the population that would name each other can be obtained. More complex relationships such as "closed rings" can be studied with more stages of sampling. For example, person A identifies person B; person B identifies person C; and person C identifies person A.

If the initial sample is drawn using binomial sampling so that each person has probability p of being in the sample and $s = k = 1$, an unbiased estimate of the number of mutual relationships in the population designated by M_{11} is

$$\hat{M}_{11} = \frac{y}{2p},$$

where y is the number of persons in the Stage 0 sample who named a person who also names them when questioned either in the initial sample or in Stage 1.

The theory for estimating the population size for various types of interpersonal relationships has been, or can be, developed assuming binomial sampling and may apply, at least approximately, when using other initial sample designs more commonly applied in practice, for example, simple random sampling (without replacement).

James R. Chromy

See also Coverage Error; Multi-Stage Sample; Nonprobability Sampling; Probability Sample; Rare Populations; Respondent-Driven Sampling (RDS); Sampling Frame; Sampling Without Replacement

Further Readings

Goodman, L. A. (1961). Snowball sampling. *Annals of Mathematical Statistics, 32,* 148–170.

Kalton, G., & Anderson, D. W. (1986). Sampling rare populations. *Journal of the Royal Statistical Society, Series A, 149,* 65–82.

Social Capital

Building on the work of sociologist James Coleman, political scientist Robert Putnam popularized the term *social capital* to describe how basic features of civic life, such as trust in others and membership in groups, provides the basis for people to engage in collective action. Even though social capital is not explicitly political, it structures various types of activities that are essential to maintaining civil and democratic institutions. Thus, *social capital* is defined as the resources of information, norms, and social relations embedded in communities that enable people to coordinate collective action and to achieve common goals.

It is important to recognize that social capital involves both psychological (e.g., trusting attitudes) and sociological (e.g., group membership) factors and, as such, is a multi-level construct. At the macro level, it is manifested in terms of connections between local organizations, both public and private. At the meso level, it is observed in the sets of interpersonal networks of social affiliation and communication in which individuals are embedded. And at the micro level, it can be seen in the individual characteristics that make citizens more likely to participate in community life, such as norms of reciprocity and feelings of trust in fellow citizens and social institutions.

Research on social capital, despite its multi-level conception, has focused on the micro level with individuals as the unit of analysis, typically using cross-sectional surveys to measure citizens' motivation, attitudes, resources, and knowledge that contribute to the observable manifestation of social capital: civic participation. The meso-network level is represented through individuals' reports of their egocentric networks in terms of size and heterogeneity as well as frequency of communication within these networks. Examinations of individuals' connections to community institutions and the connections among them are rare. These studies have been restricted to examining individuals' perceptions and attitudes regarding specific local institutions and the community generally (e.g., community attachment) as they relate to participation.

Most prominent among these institutional assessments has been political trust or trust in government, again measured mainly through individual-level survey assessments. Trust developed in interactions with social groups and government institutions is thought to function as a heuristic that is applied to decisions to participate in collective action efforts and is seen as foundational to the decision to become involved in civic life. The experience of participating in community projects, volunteering, and engaging in other membership activities reinforces feelings of trust and norms of cooperation, encouraging future civic involvement.

Survey measurement of civic participation, discussion networks, and social trust have often centered on the relationship between these indicators of social capital and patterns of media use. Survey evidence largely confirms that participation and trust have slipped in tandem, contributing to the erosion of community life. Changes in media adoption and use—for example, rising rates of television usage and declines in newspaper readership—across generational cohorts is thought to explain this decline, with television use both privatizing leisure time and presenting an increasingly harsh picture of the social world in televised representations of social reality. The combination was theorized to explain the correspondence between the rise in television use and the decline in social capital. Recent survey evidence from Dhavan Shah and his colleagues, from both cross-sectional assessments and panel survey designs, calls these assumptions into question. Instead, this research finds viewing news, documentary, and dramatic content can have pro-civic effects. This logic has been extended to the Internet, which has also been found to sustain social capital when used to gather information and strengthen social linkages.

Dhavan V. Shah and
Homero Gil de Zuniga

See also Trust in Government

Further Readings

Brehm, J., & Rahn, W. M. (1997). Individual level evidence for the causes and consequences of social capital. *American Journal of Political Science, 41,* 999–1023.

Coleman, J. (1990). *Foundations of social theory.* Cambridge, MA: Harvard University Press.

Ostrom, E. (1990). *Governing the commons: The evolution of institutions for collective action.* New York: Cambridge University Press.

Putnam, R. D. (1993). *Making democracy work: Civic traditions in modern Italy.* Princeton, NJ: Princeton University Press.

Putnam, R. D. (1995). Bowling alone: America's declining social capital. *Journal of Democracy, 6,* 65–78.

Putnam, R. D. (2000). *Bowling alone: The collapse and revival of American community.* New York: Simon & Schuster.

Shah, D. V., Cho, J., Eveland, W. P., Jr., & Kwak, N. (2005). Information and expression in a digital age: Modeling Internet effects on civic participation. *Communication Research, 32*(5), 531–565.

Shah, D. V., McLeod, J. M., & Yoon, S. H. (2001). Communication, context and community: An exploration of print, broadcast and Internet influences. *Communication Research, 28,* 464–506.

SOCIAL DESIRABILITY

Social desirability is the tendency of some respondents to report an answer in a way they deem to be more socially acceptable than would be their "true" answer. They do this to project a favorable image of themselves and to avoid receiving negative evaluations. The outcome of the strategy is overreporting of socially desirable behaviors or attitudes and underreporting of socially undesirable behaviors or attitudes. Social desirability is classified as one of the respondent-related sources of error (bias).

Social desirability bias intervenes in the last stage of the response process when the response is communicated to the researcher. In this step, a more or less deliberate editing of the response shifts the answer in the direction the respondent feels is more socially acceptable. Since the beginning of survey research, there have been many examples of socially desirable answers: for example, overreporting of having a library card, having voted, and attending church and underreporting of bankruptcy, drunken driving, illegal drug use, and negative racial attitudes.

The concept of social desirability has four nested characteristics: (1) The highest layer is a cultural characteristic, followed by (2) a personality characteristic, (3) mode of data collection, and (4) an item characteristic. The cultural characteristic is determined by the norms of that particular group or culture. For example, social desirability differs in conformist and individualist societies. Members of individualist societies tend to reveal more information about themselves to out-group representatives (the interviewer/researcher) than members of collectivist societies where the distinction between in-group and out-group is sharper. Within a society, specific cultural groups differ in level of social desirability. For example, studies conducted in the United States have shown higher scores of social desirability for minority groups when compared to majority groups.

The second characteristic is tied to a personality trait. Researchers describe it as the need to conform to social standards and ultimately as a response style. Some scales have been developed to measure the tendency of respondents to portray themselves in a favorable light, for example, the Marlowe-Crowne scale, the Edwards Social Desirability scale, and the Eysenck Lie scale.

The third characteristic is at the mode of data collection level. Social desirability has been found to interact with some attributes of the interviewer and the respondent, such as race/ethnicity, gender, social class, and age. One of the most consistent findings in the literature is that self-administered methods of data collection, such as mail surveys and Internet surveys, decrease the prevalence of social desirability bias. The general explanation is that the absence of the interviewer reduces the fear of receiving a negative evaluation, and responses are, therefore, more accurate. The item characteristic is the question wording. For items that have shown social desirability bias or that are expected to show it, some question wording techniques successfully reduce it. Methods include loading the question with reasonable excuses, using forgiving words, and assuming that respondents have engaged in the behavior instead of asking if they have. Another strategy is the randomized response method.

From a practical point of view, the researcher should be aware of potential social desirability effects—especially in cross-cultural research. Although the researcher has no control over the cultural and personal characteristics, question wording and mode of data collection can be used to decrease potentially socially desirable responses. Particular care should be taken when mixing modes of data collection.

Mario Callegaro

See also Cognitive Aspects of Survey Methodology (CASM); Interviewer Effects; Mode Effects; Mode of Data Collection; Randomized Response; Respondent-Related Error; Sensitive Topics

Further Readings

De Maio, T. J. (1984). Social desirability in survey measurement: A review. In C. F. Turner & E. Martin (Eds.), *Surveying subjective phenomena* (Vol. 2, pp. 257–282). New York: Russell Sage.

Johnson, T. P., & Van de Vijver, F. J. R. (2003). Social desirability in cross-cultural research. In J. A. Harkness, F. J. Van de Vijver, & P. P. Mohler (Eds.), *Cross-cultural survey methods* (pp. 195–204). Hoboken, NJ: Wiley.

Krysan, M., & Couper, M. P. (2003). Race in the live and the virtual interview: Racial deference, social desirability, and activation effects in attitude surveys. *Social Psychology Quarterly, 66,* 364–383.

Social Exchange Theory

Social exchange is the theoretical approach most frequently invoked by survey methodologists when interpreting the decisions people make about whether or not to participate in surveys. In essence, social exchange theory holds that many interactions proceed from the assessment of costs versus benefits. Exchanges occur in purest form in economic transactions, in which it is fully realized that the exchange of goods or services for money or for barter is rational and voluntary, with the respective values for each party understood. Because money is so liquid, little social relationship is required for economic exchanges, and the individual is as often exchanging with the market as with other individuals. Social exchange theory widens the focus to a broad social realm, which includes intangibles such as maintenance of tradition, conformity to group norms, and self-esteem. The nature of the relationship between those exchanging then becomes important.

Examples of a social exchange explanation of seemingly irrational behavior appear in print within long-ago anthropological accounts of tribal life, for example, Bronislaw Malinowski's 1920s analysis of Kula exchange (the circulation of necklaces and armlets among Trobriand Islanders). Social exchange became a more widely known school of thought in work in the United States with the late 1950s and 1960s contributions by figures such as George C. Homans, J. W. Thibault and Harold H. Kelly, and Peter Blau.

By the mid-1970s, explicit applications were appearing of social exchange ideas to the understanding of nonresponse on surveys. An important statement was in *Mail and Telephone Surveys: The Total Design Method for Surveys* by sociologist Don Dillman in the late 1970s. Part of the total design was attending to several details of survey fieldwork likely to lower the cost and raise the rewards of participation for any sampled person. A stamped and addressed return envelope, for example, would lower the cost of responding to a mailed questionnaire, not just financially to a slight degree, but with a saving in time. Hand-signed cover letters on a questionnaire were a reward that acknowledged the importance of each individual drawn for the sample. Printing questionnaires in booklet form (in the pre–desktop publishing days of Gestetner machines) reduced the eyestrain costs of filling in a questionnaire while underscoring the importance of the research topic. Cash incentives drew their effectiveness primarily from social rather than economic exchange theory, when presented in prepaid form in small denominations. The money was symbolic, with high cultural resonance as a gift. Each item within the total design might seem slight, but the cumulative effect led to some highly respectable response rates on mailed surveys.

There is, however, a danger of overapplying social exchange theory as the explanation for why people do or do not respond to survey requests. Robert M. Groves and his colleagues have raised awareness of other factors not fitting so centrally into the social exchange framework. Especially on a telephone survey using unannounced calls, time does not exist for social exchange calculations to take place. Social exchange notions are most clearly valid where some degree of relationship exists between people, even if the relationship arises simply from the sequence of postal contacts in a mailed survey. When the telephone rings unexpectedly, and especially in a world of frequent beseeching telephone contacts from telemarketers and charities, most of the mental effort goes into making an instantaneous decision of whether and/or how to say "No." The decision making becomes heuristic, based on previous mental associations and rules of thumb. A "sing-song" voice, for example, instantly telegraphs that a call is not from a personal acquaintance.

Social exchange theory is a broad perspective that can embrace a wide conceptual territory. It is not so much that a cognitive heuristic interpretation of survey response decisions is diametrically in opposition to an exchange perspective as that heuristics are a particularly behaviorist version of exchange. The depth of decision making is much shallower on a cold telephone call than a decision, for example, about whether to continue participation in a panel study in which several household interviews have already taken place.

Thinking about the kind of social exchange that takes place around response decisions sensitizes the survey researcher to the kinds of people who are being included and excluded from their survey net. At the level of aggregates, exchange theory can guide researchers toward effective techniques, as Dillman's work demonstrated. For those seeking exact propositions about who among the public will and will not consent to a particular survey, social exchange theory is bound to disappoint. For unlike more behaviorist approaches, a prediction from social exchange theory requires full knowledge of a person's attitude toward survey research, the topic being examined, and whether the field contacts create a sense of benefit or at least minimize cost. If such information were already in hand from a sampling frame, a survey would hardly be necessary. It is no coincidence that modern empirical work on social exchange theory within social psychology involves laboratory settings where full background information indeed can be assembled.

John Goyder and Luc Boyer

See also Economic Exchange Theory; Nonresponse; Total Design Method (TDM)

Further Readings

Cropanzano, R., & Mitchell, M. S. (2005). Social exchange theory: An interdisciplinary review. *Journal of Management, 31,* 874–900.

Dillman, D. A. (1978). *Mail and telephone surveys: The total design method for surveys.* New York: Wiley.

Goyder, J., Boyer, L., & Martinelli, G. (2006). Integrating exchange and heuristic theories of survey nonresponse. *Bulletin de Méthodologie Sociologique, 92,* 28–44.

Homans, G. C. (1958). Social behavior as exchange. *American Journal of Sociology, 62,* 597–606.

SOCIAL ISOLATION

Theories of social isolation (or "social location") have been used to explain lower cooperation in responding to surveys among certain subgroups in society, such as the elderly, minority racial and ethnic groups, and lower socioeconomic status groups. The social isolation theory of unit nonresponse states that subgroups in a society that are less connected to the dominant culture of the society—that is, those who do not feel part of the larger society or bound by its norms—will be less likely to cooperate with a survey request that represents the interests of the dominant society. According to the leverage-saliency theory, respondents decide to participate in a survey depending on survey attributes such as how long the interview might take, the presence of an incentive, and what the data might be used for. They may also make this decision depending on who is sponsoring the survey and what the topic of the survey is. The hypothesis of social isolation comes into play in these last two aspects.

Survey researchers have noted that sometimes sentiments of "civic duty" prompt survey participation and that these feelings of civic duty are associated with survey participation, especially when a properly constituted authority is requesting the participation of the sampled respondent. In theory, organizations with greater legitimacy, for example, those representing federal government agencies, are more likely to positively influence a respondent's decision to participate in a survey than, for example, a commercial survey research firm with less authority. However, according to some researchers, individuals who are alienated or isolated from the broader society feel less attachment to that society and thus have a lower sense of civic duty, which in turn will lead to a higher refusal rate in surveys conducted by and for those perceived as being in authority. Similar reasoning is often advanced regarding interest in and knowledge of the survey topic, in particular when focusing on political and election surveys. There are a number of studies that link political participation with survey participation. Results from these studies indicate that individuals who feel more isolated from the dominant society may also lack interest in politics and may feel less willing to respond to a political poll. In addition, nonresponse among members of socially isolated groups may be due to *self-disqualification.* That is, socially isolated individuals may feel they are not qualified to give an opinion on the topic or that their opinion is not valued.

Aspects of social isolation are both structural and social-psychological. For this reason, multiple indicators of social isolation should be used to study its relationship with survey cooperation. With demographic indicators (e.g., age) as a proxy for social isolation, some studies have found that elderly people are less likely to cooperate than are other subgroups. Elderly people often have fewer ongoing relationships with the larger society and thus are more isolated from the larger society. However, the effect of older age also has been found to be mitigated by living conditions and household composition. Single-person households tend to be less cooperative, whereas households with young children tend to be more cooperative. It is hypothesized that parents of young children are more likely to interact with strangers in the community on a daily basis, thereby increasing the level of connection with the society and thus also their likelihood of cooperating in surveys when a stranger (the interviewer) contacts them to seek cooperation with the survey.

If a survey is conducted using a sample that previously responded to an earlier wave of the survey, the data collected from the previous wave can be used to compare respondents and nonrespondents to the subsequent survey in terms of more direct indicators of social isolation, including variables such as time spent on voluntary work or contacts with neighbors, if those types of variable were measured in the previous wave. Studies of nonrespondents have found, for example, that people who spend more time on voluntary work tend to be more cooperative with survey requests, while those who have no close relatives or have no contact with neighbors are less likely to cooperate.

Mario Callegaro and Femke De Keulenaer

See also Cooperation; Leverage-Saliency Theory; Nonresponse; Refusal; Unit Nonresponse

Further Readings

Groves, R. M., & Couper, M. P. (1998). *Nonresponse in household interview surveys*. New York: Wiley.

Groves, R. M., Singer, E. & Corning, A. (2000). Leverage-salience theory of survey participation. *Public Opinion Quarterly, 64*, 299–308.

Loosveldt, G., & Carton, A. (2002). Utilitarian individualism and panel nonresponse. *International Journal of Public Opinion Research, 14*, 428–438.

Voogt, R. J. J., & Saris, W. E. (2003). To participate or not to participate: The link between survey participation, electoral participation, and political interest. *Political Analysis, 11*, 164–179.

Solomon Four-Group Design

The Solomon four-group design is an experimental design that assesses the plausibility of *pretest sensitization effects*, that is, whether the mere act of taking a pretest influences scores on subsequent administrations of the test. For example, if respondents complete a questionnaire measuring their knowledge of science as a pretest, they might then decide to subsequently seek answers to a few unfamiliar equations. At the posttest they might then score better on the science test compared to how they would have scored without taking the pretest. Meta-analytic results suggest that pretest sensitization does occur, although it is more prevalent for some measures than others, and the more time passes between pretest and posttest, the less likely a testing effect will occur.

In the Solomon four-group design, the researcher randomly assigns respondents to one of four cells constructed from two fully crossed factors: *treatment* (e.g., treatment and control) and *pretest administration* (present or not). Therefore, the four cells are (1) treatment with pretest, (2) control with pretest, (3) treatment without pretest, and (4) control without pretest. The analysis tests whether treatment effects are found, whether the groups who received the pretest performed better than those who did not, and whether taking a pretest interacts with treatment effects. If X (or its absence) is treatment (or its absence), and O_1 is pretest and O_2 is posttest, the design is diagrammed as follows:

Experimental Group	O_1	X	O_2
Control Group I	O_1	O_2	
Control Group II		X	O_2
Control Group III			O_2

History of the Design

Richard Solomon first proposed a three-group design that consisted of an Experimental Group that was exposed to the pretest and the treatment; Control Group I that was exposed to the pretest, but not the treatment; and Control Group II that was not exposed to the pretest but received the treatment. The three-group design served the same purpose as the four-group design, but the two designs used slightly different statistical analyses. While Solomon believed that the three-group design was sufficient for laboratory experiments, a four-group design would be better suited for field studies, including those that use sample surveys to gather data. Therefore, he added Control Group III, in which units were not exposed to either the pretest or the treatment. He originally saw the fourth group as a way to estimate effects of threats to validity other than testing, such as maturation or history, but this four-group design has become the preferred method for examining testing effects.

Analysis and Interpretation

Using this design, pretest sensitization is determined by conducting a two-factor analysis of variance (ANOVA), in which treatment and presence of pretest are the factors and posttest scores are the dependent variable. It is not necessary to include the pretest scores in the analysis because random assignment ensures that pretest scores should be the same for each group on expectation. A significant interaction between treatment and pretest suggests that exposure to the pretest may influence the treatment effect. If there is no interaction, a significant main effect for treatment indicates that the treatment had an effect, and a significant main effect for the pretest indicates that pretest may influence posttest.

Improving Validity

The Solomon four-group design provides information relevant to both internal and external validity. Regarding internal validity, for example, many single-group quasi-experiments use both pretests and posttests. If a pretest sensitization occurs, it could be mistaken for a treatment effect, so that scores could change from pretest to posttest even if the treatment had no effect at all. In randomized experiments, pretest sensitization effects do not affect internal validity because they are randomized over conditions, but those effects affect external validity if the size of the effect depends on whether a pretest is administered.

Examples

John Spence and Chris Blanchard used a Solomon four-group design to assess pretest sensitization on feeling states and self-efficacy and treatment effects when using an aerobic fitness intervention to influence feeling states and self-efficacy. The pretest and posttest questionnaires were (a) the Subjective Exercise Experience Scale, a 12-item questionnaire that measures psychological responses to stimulus properties of exercise, and (b) a self-efficacy questionnaire, which asked respondents about their ability to exercise at a high level for various time lengths. The intervention required respondents to pedal on a cycle ergometer at 60 rotations per minute for 12 minutes at three different target heart rates. There was no main effect for pretest sensitization for feeling states, nor was there an interaction between pretest administration and the treatment. However, the aerobic intervention did affect feeling states: Treated respondents reported a better sense of well-being and decreased psychological distress. There were no significant main effects or interactions for self-efficacy.

Bente Traeen used a Solomon four-group design as part of a group randomized trial, in which schools were randomly assigned to the four conditions. The intervention consisted of a sexual education course to increase contraceptive use; the pretests and posttests were self-report questionnaires asking about sexual activity. The researcher found an interaction between the pretest and intervention, indicating that the pretest may have affected the size of the treatment effect.

M. H. Clark and William R. Shadish

See also Experimental Design; External Validity; Factorial Design; Interaction Effect; Internal Validity; Main Effect; Random Assignment

Further Readings

Campbell, D. T., & Stanley, J. C. (1963). *Experimental and quasi-experimental designs*. Chicago: Rand McNally.

Solomon, R. L. (1949). An extension of control group design. *Psychological Bulletin, 46*, 137–150.

Spence, J. C., & Blanchard, C. (2001). Effect of pretesting on feeling states and self-efficacy in acute exercise.

Research Quarterly for Exercise and Sport, 72(3), 310–314.

Traeen, B. (2003). An effect of an intervention to prevent unwanted pregnancy in adolescents. A randomized, prospective study from Nordland County, Norway, 1999–2001. *Journal of Community and Applied Social Psychology, 13*, 207–223.

Willson, V. L., & Putnam, R. R. (1982). A meta-analysis of pretest sensitization effects in experimental design. *American Educational Research Journal, 19*, 249–258.

SPIRAL OF SILENCE

Originally developed in the early 1970s by German political scientist and pollster Elisabeth Noelle-Neumann, the spiral of silence remains one of the few theoretical approaches that attempts to understand public opinion from a process-oriented perspective. The general conceptual premise of this theory is that there are different styles of communicative behavior for those who are in the majority versus those in the minority for a given issue.

According to the theory, those who are in the majority are more likely to feel confident in expressing their opinions, while those in the minority fear that expressing their views will result in social ostracism, and therefore they remain silent. These perceptions can lead to a spiraling process, in which majority viewpoints are publicly overrepresented, while minority viewpoints are increasingly withheld and therefore underrepresented. This spiral results in escalating social pressure to align with the majority viewpoint, which in turn can lead to declining expressions of minority viewpoints. As the apparent "majority" position gains strength (i.e., is expressed more and more confidently in public), those who perceive themselves as being in the minority will be more likely to withhold their opinion.

In responding to those who have attempted to explain public opinion as a rational, informed process, Noelle-Neumann has argued repeatedly that public opinion is a method of social control, akin to the latest fashion trends, which exert pressure to conform and comply. At the heart of the spiral of silence theory is the notion that people are highly motivated to fit in and get along with others. Noelle-Neumann refers to this motivation to avoid group exclusion as the "fear of isolation." Noelle-Neumann's argument for the existence of the fear of isolation is based primarily on the conformity research conducted by Solomon Asch in the 1950s. Asch found that subjects who were asked to judge the length of clearly different-sized lines were surprisingly willing to offer an obviously incorrect answer when other subjects—all of whom were confederates instructed by the experimenter to offer an incorrect judgment—had also offered incorrect judgments.

Noelle-Neumann, citing the influence of Alexis de Tocqueville, posits that most people would rather go along with an incorrect majority than strike out on their own and risk social isolation from the majority group. Exceptions are noted, however, in the form of the "hardcore," who seem to pay little mind to social isolation and are willing to hold onto and express unpopular opinions. These "avant-garde" are noted for their willingness to express viewpoints that are not popular, yet their opinions are often predictive of future trends that will later be accepted as the majority view.

In noting that individuals are constantly scanning their environments for clues regarding what others think, the spiral of silence accounts for the iterative and dynamic nature of public opinion. Through interpersonal interaction and exposure to media, people are able to gauge public opinion (referred to as a "quasi-statistical sense" by Noelle-Neumann) and use that information as a means of predicting how others will react if they decide to express or withhold certain opinions. The media comprise the second key theoretical element of the spiral of silence theory. Noelle-Neumann posited that the media are consonant and ubiquitous in their presentation of issues, resulting in a media-driven opinion context. By linking this media force with interpersonal interactions, the theory incorporates two key elements of communication research: media effects and interpersonal/group dynamics.

Measurement

Early research on the spiral of silence was almost exclusively limited to survey and interview contexts. In most survey-based studies, the key dependent variable is generally conceptualized as the respondent's willingness to express his or her opinion. Yet the operationalization of this expression has varied widely. Noelle-Neumann's original research focused on West Germans' views of East Germany. Specifically, her research sought to determine whether West Germans were for or against recognizing East Germany as a second German state, what their impressions were of the

views of other West Germans, and what their perceptions were of how other West Germans would view this issue in one year's time. As Noelle-Neumann's research program expanded, survey questions were created with the goal of simulating a typical public situation in which an individual would have the choice to express or withhold his or her own opinion on a variety of political and social issues. The public situations included riding in a train compartment with a stranger and conversing at a social gathering where the respondent did not know all of the guests. By varying the opinion of the hypothetical conversation partner or group, Noelle-Neumann and colleagues were able to gauge the effect of respondents' perceptions that they were either in the minority or the majority on a given issue. Results from this initial wave of research were mixed, with some combinations of issue and setting producing a silencing effect while others produced no such effect.

In addition to replicating Noelle-Neumann's research by asking survey respondents about hypothetical opinion expression situations involving strangers, scholars have expanded on this line of work by gauging respondents' willingness to speak out by measuring voting intention, evaluating willingness to discuss issues with family and friends, assessing financial contributions to candidates, and determining respondents' willingness to express their views on camera for news broadcasts. Several of these methods have been criticized for various methodological weaknesses. For example, some scholars have noted that voting is a private act that differs significantly in its social context from expressing an opinion to another person or in a group. Expressing an opinion to family and friends introduces a variety of social-psychological considerations, including interpersonal dynamics, as well as knowledge about the opinions of other group members, as knowledge about the opinions of close friends and family members is likely to be much greater than knowledge about the opinions of other groups. Whereas financial contributions can be associated with individuals through public finance records, writing and mailing a check is certainly a behavior distinct from publicly voicing support for a candidate. Asking respondents about a hypothetical chance to express their opinion on a news broadcast evokes a social setting in which they could face recriminations for their views, but it also lacks the immediacy of reaction in comparison to an interpersonal exchange.

To assess the opinion climate in which respondents are basing their intention to express their views, survey approaches to the spiral of silence must also include some type of contextual measure in which respondents are asked about their perceptions of the opinions of those around them or in whatever specific social environment the researcher is interested. Social scientists typically take one of two approaches in assessing the climate of opinion: (1) asking respondents whether they feel most people are in agreement with them or are opposed to their personal view, or (2) asking respondents to specifically estimate what percentage or proportion of others (voters, people in your neighborhood, etc.) are in favor of or opposed to this issue or candidate. With this information, dichotomous comparisons are possible between those who feel they are in the majority versus those who feel they are in the minority on a given issue. When respondents are asked to offer specific percentages in estimating perceptions of opinion climates, researchers are also afforded the opportunity to correlate the size of majorities and minorities with respondents' willingness to express an opinion (especially if opinion expression is gauged on a continuum rather than as a dichotomous variable). Additionally, a willingness to express one's opinion also can be used in conjunction with extant opinion polls for a given issue. This approach avoids perceptual errors in individual perceptions of the opinion climate, such as the *looking glass perception* and *pluralistic ignorance*.

Inconsistent Results

In the late 1990s, Carroll Glynn and colleagues conducted a meta-analysis of spiral of silence research. Results indicated that there was a statistically significant relationship between individual perceptions that others hold similar opinions and individual willingness to express an opinion, but the relationship was quite weak across 9,500 respondents from 17 published and unpublished studies. Suggesting that hypothetical opinion expression situations might not evoke the psychological response to contextual pressures, this study called for experimentally created opinion environments in future spiral of silence work. With experimental research, respondents could be presented with the opportunity to express an opinion or to keep silent in the face of experimentally controlled majorities and minorities through the use of confederates or deliberately constructed groups. The meta-analysis also tested the impact of moderators on willingness to

express an opinion; no significant relationships were found among the moderating factors that were tested.

Though no significant moderators were found in the meta-analytic review, other research has found that key variables can impact the relationship between the perceived opinion climate and respondents' willingness to express their opinions. Demographic variables such as gender, age, education, and income have been found to account for significant differences in willingness to speak out, even when controlling for the climate of opinion. Other possible moderators include political interest and knowledge, self-efficacy, the extent to which an opinion is based on moral considerations, and perceived personal "correctness" with respect to one's opinion. Contextual moderators include characteristics of the reference group in question (i.e., whose opinions constitute the opinion climate?) as well as specific characteristics about the setting in which an opinion can be expressed or withheld.

Future Applications

The spiral of silence has remained a viable approach in social science research perhaps because it addresses the inherent multi-level nature of public opinion processes. At the macro or contextual level, whether media outlets tend toward consonance or present a multi-faceted representation of events, these outlets create a mediated context in which opinions are formed and shaped. It is also within these mediated contexts that the interpersonal exchange of opinions occurs. In other words, media outlets create the backdrop for interpersonal exchanges of opinion, and these opinion exchanges can further influence the process of opinion formation—spiraling or otherwise.

With this in mind, studying the spiral of silence within a given context requires careful planning in terms of the following:

- The unit of analysis—How will opinion expression be operationalized?
- Contextual parameters—Within what context will opinion expression occur?
- Contextual characteristics—How will the opinion climate be measured?
- Individual factors—What can moderate this relationship?
- Issue contexts—What types of issues are most susceptible to the spiral of silence?

With the increasing use of multi-level modeling in the social sciences, scholars are afforded the opportunity to capture both contextual-level and individual-level variables as they impact opinion expression. After determining the contextual parameters of the opinion environment in question (e.g., small group, metropolitan area, state, or nation), it should then be possible to establish what media channels and sources are likely to produce opinion-influencing content (e.g., newspapers, television news or ads, Web sites, blogs). By content-analyzing these outlets, researchers are able to measure exactly how consonant media outlets are in presenting issue stances. This information can then be used as a contextual- or group-level variable in predicting opinion expression within a survey or experimental environment. The hierarchical structure of multi-level modeling also allows the inclusion of possible moderators that may impact the relationship between the context and opinion expression.

Recent research concerned with the spiral of silence process has focused on cultural characteristics as moderating variables in terms of contextual impacts upon willingness to express an opinion. Results have been less than consistent, but some findings indicate that collectivist cultures, which focus on face-saving techniques in the name of group harmony, are more susceptible to pressure to conform to a majority opinion (or withhold a minority opinion). This group-level result contrasts with individualistic cultures, which tend to favor personal ideas over the views of others.

Another underdeveloped area of spiral of silence research is investigation of the concept of fear of isolation. Noelle-Neumann's theory has been repeatedly criticized for assuming that all individuals—with the exception of the avant-garde and hardcore—are equally averse to social isolation and therefore will react to majority pressure in a similar way. If certain individuals are willing to express an opinion in the face of a hostile majority (e.g., the hardcore), it stands to reason that fear of isolation is a continuous concept rather than a dichotomous one.

Though some spiral of silence research has employed lagged design or panel studies in which changes in opinion can be documented, time is yet another important variable that is often overlooked when studying opinion contexts. If a true spiraling effect is to be found, opinions must be measured at multiple time points in order to gauge the effect of the pressure exerted by the climate of opinion.

Michael Huge and Carroll J. Glynn

See also Opinion Norms; Panel Survey; Public Opinion; Social Isolation

Further Readings

Glynn, C. J., Hayes, A. F., & Shanahan, J. (1997). Spiral of silence: A meta-analysis. *Public Opinion Quarterly*, *61*, 452–463.

Noelle-Neumann, E. (1993). *The spiral of silence*. Chicago: University of Chicago Press.

Price, C., & Allen, S. (1990). Opinion spirals, silence and otherwise: Applying small-group research to public opinion phenomena. *Communication Research*, *17*, 369–392.

Salmon, C. T., & Kline, F. G. (1985). The spiral of silence ten years later: An examination and evaluation. In K. R. Sanders, L. L. Kaid, & D. Nimmo (Eds.), *Political communication yearbook 1984* (pp. 3–30). Carbondale: Southern Illinois University Press.

Scheufele, D. A., & Moy, P. (2000). Twenty-five years of the spiral of silence: A conceptual review and empirical outlook. *International Journal of Public Opinion Research*, *12*(1), 3–28.

SPLIT-HALF

Split-half designs are commonly used in survey research to experimentally determine the difference between two variations of survey protocol characteristics, such as the data collection mode, the survey recruitment protocol, or the survey instrument. Other common names for such experiments are *split-sample*, *split-ballot*, or *randomized experiments*. Researchers using split-half experiments are usually interested in determining the difference on outcomes such as survey statistics or other evaluative characteristics between the two groups.

In this type of experimental design, the sample is randomly divided into two halves, and each half receives a different treatment. Random assignment of sample members to the different treatments is crucial to ensure the internal validity of the experiment by guaranteeing that, on average, any observed differences between the two groups can be attributed to treatment effects rather than to differences in subsample composition. Split-half experiments have been successfully used in various survey settings to study measurement error bias as well as differences in survey nonresponse rates.

This experimental design has been used by questionnaire designers to examine the effects of questionnaire characteristics on answers provided by survey respondents. Current knowledge of question order effects, open- versus closed-response options, scale effects, response order effects, and inclusion versus exclusion of response options such as "Don't Know" is based on split-half experiments. These experiments have been conducted both in field surveys and in laboratory settings. Researchers usually assume that the experimental treatment in questionnaire split-half designs that produces the better result induces less measurement bias in the survey statistic of interest. However, these researchers often conduct such experiments because they do not have a gold standard or true value against which to compare the results of the study. Thus, the difference in the statistic of interest between the two experimental groups is an indicator of the difference in measurement error bias. Without a gold standard, it does not, however, indicate the amount of measurement error bias that remains in the statistic of interest.

Split-half experiments have also proven useful for studying survey nonresponse. Experimenters interested in how variations in field recruitment procedures—such as interviewer training techniques, amounts or types of incentive, advance and refusal letter characteristics, survey topic, and the use of new technologies such as computer-assisted self-interviewing—affect unit response, contact, and refusal rates have used split-half designs. These experiments often state that the design feature that had the higher response rate is the better outcome. Nonresponse bias is less frequently evaluated using a split-half design. Such designs have also been used to study item nonresponse as a function of both questionnaire characteristics and survey recruitment protocol characteristics.

Split-half experiments are an important experimental design when examining the effect of different survey protocol features on survey statistics. However, they do not automatically reveal which protocol or instrument choice is better. In general, to determine the "better" treatment, the researcher fielding a split-half experiment should use theory to predict the desirable outcome. For example, the type of advance letter that produces a higher response rate will often be considered superior, under the hypothesis that higher response rates lead to more representative samples. Alternatively, the mode of data collection that increases the number of reports of sensitive behaviors is considered better under the assumption that respondents underreport sensitive behaviors. Although split-half experiments are a powerful experimental design that isolate, on average, the effects that different treatments, survey protocols, or other procedures have on various types of outcomes, they are made practically useful when the survey researcher has a theory on which outcome should be preferred.

A final point of interest, despite the name split "half," survey researchers are not obligated from a statistical standpoint or methodological standpoint to actually split their samples exactly in half (i.e., 50/50). For example, a news organization may be conducting a survey on attitudes towards the Iraq war and want to determine whether alternative wording for the primary support/opposition attitude question will elicit different levels of support/opposition to the president's policies. However, the news organization may not want to "dilute" their measurement of this key attitude, for news purposes, by assigning half of their sample to the alternative wording and may choose to assign far less than 50% of respondents to the alternative wording.

Sonja Ziniel

See also Experimental Design; Internal Validity; Measurement Error; Missing Data; Nonresponse; Nonresponse Bias; True Value

Further Readings

Fowler, F. J. (2004). The case for more split-sample experiments in developing survey instruments. In S. Presser, J. M. Rothgeb, M. P. Couper, J. T. Lessler, E. Martin, J. Martin, et al. (Eds.), *Methods for testing and evaluating survey questionnaires* (pp. 173–188). New York: Wiley.

Groves, R. M. (1989). *Survey errors and survey costs.* New York: Wiley.

STANDARD DEFINITIONS

Broadly, the term *standard definitions* refers to the generally accepted nomenclature, procedures, and formulas that enable survey researchers to calculate outcome rates for certain kinds of sample surveys and censuses. Specifically, *Standard Definitions* is the shorthand name for a booklet published by the American Association for Public Opinion

Research (AAPOR) titled *Standard Definitions: Final Dispositions of Case Codes and Outcome Rates for Surveys*. Much of this entry is gleaned from that booklet.

At least two major survey organizations have formal definitions for outcome rates: AAPOR and the Council of American Survey Research Organizations (CASRO). Both organizations' formal definitions are easily accessible on the Internet. However, AAPOR provides an Excel spreadsheet response-rate calculator that makes it easy to calculate and track different outcome rates for different surveys and quickly compare rates across surveys.

Response rates—more properly known as *case outcome rates*—are survey research measures that indicate the proportion of a sample or census that do or do not responded to a survey. They are one of a number of indicators that can point to the quality of the survey. Generally, outcome rates can be broken down into four categories: cooperation rates, refusal rates, incidence rates, and overall response rates. Their calculation is based on the classification of the final disposition of attempts to reach each case in a sample, such as a household or an individual respondent.

Importance of Outcome Rates

Outcome rates of sample surveys and censuses are important to understand because they are indicators of potential nonresponse effects. Nonresponse and its effects are one of several types of potential nonrandom errors in surveys (others include coverage error and measurement error). Nonresponse bias is the extent to which the representativeness of a sample is compromised if there are nonnegligible differences between nonresponders (i.e., those who were in the originally drawn sample but who did not complete an interview) and respondents (those who did complete an interview).

A sample is a set of elements, or cases—in social science research, they usually are people or households—drawn from some population. The population may be adults in the United States, likely voters in an election, newspaper readers in a metropolitan area, college students on a campus, or some other identifiable group. The researcher measures the characteristics of these cases, usually with an instrument called a questionnaire, and in the subsequent statistical analysis infers the statistics from the sample to the

population. Error bias in the sample can hamper the ability of the researcher to infer accurately the sample statistics to the population.

Just as doctors can get indicators of a patient's health by checking key components of blood chemistry, researchers can get hints at sample validity by carefully performing certain checks on the sample. One, for example, is comparing sample statistics to known population parameters: the sample's percentage of men and women, say, to U.S. Census percentages. A second is to compare the sample's findings to other, similar samples done with similar populations at about the same time. Outcome rates also can be indicators of sample validity, but they should never be used as the sole judge of a sample's quality.

Categorization of Outcomes

Just as doctors have to prepare equipment (and even the patient) before testing blood, the researcher also has to carefully categorize the outcome of each attempt to reach respondents in the sample and use that information to determine final outcome codes for each case. All this has to be done before the researcher can calculate final outcome rates. Classifying final dispositions can come at any time during the data collection period for some clear-cut cases: completed interviews, refusals, or, in random-digit dialing (RDD) samples, telephone numbers that are not working or have been disconnected.

However, during the data collection period, many attempts to reach respondents must be assigned temporary outcome codes for cases where the final disposition may not be known until the field work is over. An example for mail surveys is when the first attempt at mailing a respondent a questionnaire results in a returned envelope with no questionnaire, in which case the researcher could mail a second questionnaire with a letter asking the respondent to complete it. An example for a phone survey is one in which a respondent agreed to complete the interview but asked the interviewer to call back at a more convenient time. In both examples, the researcher likely would be using temporary outcome codes (i.e., part of what has come to be considered *paradata*) that would be useful in keeping track of the respondent sampled and would be useful in guiding the researcher later when it came time to assign final outcome codes.

Generally, final outcome categories for survey cases can be divided into (1) interviews, (2) cases that were eligible to be included but were not (nonrespondents), (3) cases that were not really eligible to be in the sample and therefore excluded from the outcome rate classifications, and (4) cases of unknown eligibility. Examples of the first two are relatively easy to understand: completed and partial interviews; and noncontacts, refusals, and language or other barriers to participation. In the third case, especially for RDD telephone samples of the general population, some of the elements clearly do not belong in the sample and are discarded: business or government telephone numbers in a sample of adults in residential households, for example.

Calculation of Outcome Rates

In many samples, it is unclear whether particular cases (e.g., household addresses, specific people, or phone numbers) really should be a part of the sample. In RDD phone samples researchers may never resolve the disposition of many telephone numbers originally included in the designated sample to which many call attempts were made but no one ever answered the phone, or those for which the researcher continually reached answering machines on which the message was unclear about the classification of the phone numbers, that is, whether they were households, businesses, or government offices.

A system of measurement needed to be developed to help researchers classify the outcomes of their attempts to reach the phone numbers, or people in mail surveys, or voters in exit polls so that they can calculate their response rates and understand if they may have issues with nonresponse bias. One of the early attempts to do this was in the 1980s by a team of researchers who developed a rudimentary way of calculating the overall response rate for CASRO. That approach was deployed by CASRO and the Market Research Association for many years. However, it provided little diagnostic information for researchers to understand the quality of their samples. One reason was because it did not allow researchers to understand the components of overall response rate, such as cooperation or contact rates. The other was because there were few standard definitions of final outcomes classifications for researchers to use when they input their outcomes into the calculator.

In the 1990s, a team of researchers working under the auspices of the American Association for Public Opinion Research, and led by Tom W. Smith, Paul J. Lavrakas, and Rob P. Daves, developed standard definitions of outcomes and used those definitions to develop a number of outcome rate formulas for RDD telephone surveys, mail surveys of individual persons, and in-home face-to-face surveys of individual persons.

The AAPOR method of calculating outcome rates allowed researchers for the first time to use standard definitions for outcomes of interviewing attempts. It also, for the first time, allowed researchers to examine the major components of nonresponse: incidence rates, cooperation rates, refusal rates, and proportions of unidentified cases. Additionally, it allowed researchers to compare response rates for one mode, such as an RDD phone survey, to another mode, such as a mail survey.

Classification Problems

One of the problems that plague survey researchers is when case outcomes are not clear-cut. For example, in face-to-face interviews with people in their own households, a researcher may never find any eligible respondent at home during the field period. There may clearly be an eligible respondent, but the interviewer is never able to talk to him or her because he or she is unavailable during the data collection period. This is a case of nonresponse, but it cannot be classified as a respondent's refusal.

Some telephone survey case outcomes are even harder to classify. If the researcher uses an RDD sample of landline telephone numbers, many will be business, government, disconnected, fax or computer lines, or not working; these clearly are not considered to be part of the eligible telephone numbers for a residential sample and are excluded from outcome rate calculations. But what happens, for example, when during the data collection period, interviewers call a dozen times and it always rings but no one answers? This example falls into a group of outcomes that force the researcher to make assumptions about the proportion that might be truly eligible. There are many ways to deal with this. One is to assume that the group of phone numbers with an unknown eligibility split in the same proportion of eligible-to-ineligible phone numbers in the group with known eligibility in the sample. This may not be always accurate, but it may be the best that the researcher can do. The AAPOR standard definitions and formulas take this into account. Certain AAPOR formulas use this assumption as the default.

Outcome Rate Categories

Outcome rates generally fall into four categories. They are as follows:

1. *Contact rates*—the proportion of all cases in the sample (or census) in which some responsible housing unit member was reached

2. *Refusal rates*—the proportion of all cases in which there is a refusal to be interviewed

3. *Cooperation rates*—the proportion of all eligible units reached in which there was a completed interview

4. *Response rates*—The number of complete interviews divided by the number of eligible units in the sample

In 2001, AAPOR researchers put the *Standard Definitions* guide on AAPOR's Web site; it was updated in 2006. They also developed an Excel spreadsheet that allows other researchers to quickly and accurately enter their final case dispositions and calculate the various outcome rates. (This spreadsheet is downloadable free at the AAPOR Web site.)

Sample Validity

Because using standard definitions of case outcomes is relatively recent and their adoption has not been universal, AAPOR outcome rates appear to be used more among academic researchers and those who do media polls and less among commercial market researchers. Researchers have only just begun exploring how differences in outcome rates affect sample validity. Some early research suggests that extremely high outcome rates in samples of likely voters actually can hinder the ability of public opinion researchers to be as accurate as they need to be in pre-election polls. Other research for general population samples suggests that validity of samples for some types of measures response rates between 40% and 70% does not hamper validity. In fact, a team at the University of Michigan, the University of Maryland, and the Pew Center for the People and the Press found that for

many measures of political attitudes, there were few differences between a survey conducted with a short data collection period (and thus a low response rate) and one in which the data collection period was greatly extended with the use of many extraordinary techniques to increase response rates. However, it is crucial to understand that researchers are continuing to investigate the effect of nonresponse on sample surveys, and as yet there is no conclusive evidence.

Robert P. Daves

See also American Association for Public Opinion Research (AAPOR); Council of American Survey Research Organizations (CASRO); Dispositions; Elements; Nonresponse; Paradata; Response Rates; Sample

Further Readings

American Association for Public Opinion Research: http://www.aapor.org

American Association for Public Opinion Research. (2006). *Standard definitions: Final dispositions of case codes and outcome rates for surveys.* Ann Arbor, MI: Author. Retrieved April 19, 2008, from http://www.aapor.org/uploads/standarddefs_4.pdf

Frankel, L. R. (1982). *On the definition of response rates: A special report of the CASRO Task Force on Response Rates.* Retrieved April 19, 2008, from http://www.casro.org/resprates.cfm

STANDARD ERROR

Statistics are derived from sample data, and because they are not taken from complete data, they inevitably vary from one sample to another. The standard error is a measure of the expected dispersion of sample estimates around the true population parameter. It is used to gauge the accuracy of a sample estimate: A larger standard error suggests less confidence in the sample statistic as an accurate measure of the population characteristic. Standard errors can be calculated for a range of survey statistics including means, percentages, totals, and differences in percentages. The discussion that follows focuses on sample means and proportions.

In a survey of families, let X represent family income, and let $\bar{X}$ denote the mean family income, which is an example of a statistic resulting from the data. Although the survey may be designed to provide an estimate of the mean in the entire population of interest, it is highly unlikely that the estimate from the survey, $\bar{X}$, will be equal to μ, the mean income of all families in the targeted population.

Assuming that each family in the population has an equal chance of being selected for the survey, the true standard error of $\bar{X}$ could be derived, hypothetically, by conducting an infinite number of identical surveys of independent samples of the same size from the same population. The distribution of the values of $\bar{X}$ comprises the sampling distribution of $\bar{X}$. The mean of this sampling distribution is the true value of the parameter, that is, μ, that the statistic is meant to estimate, and the standard deviation of the sampling distribution is the true standard error associated with the statistic. It can be denoted by $\sigma_{\bar{x}}$.

In practice, however, the true population mean μ and the true standard error $\sigma_{\bar{x}}$ of $\bar{X}$ are not derived from repeated surveys. In fact, they are rarely known. Instead, they are estimated from a single sample, and it is this estimate of the standard error that has become synonymous with the term *standard error* in survey research. With this understanding, the standard error of $\bar{X}$, denoted $s_{\bar{x}}$, is defined in the following section.

The Standard Error of a Sample Mean

If s is the standard deviation of the family income variable X, and n is the number of households surveyed, the standard error of $\bar{X}$, the mean family income, is estimated as $s_{\bar{x}} = s/\sqrt{n}$. For example, if the sample size is 100, and the standard deviation of family income is \$15,280, then the standard error is equal to \$1,528 because $15,280/\sqrt{100} = 15,280/10 = 1,528$.

The standard error, by itself, is not easily interpreted, and that is why confidence intervals and margins of error are more often reported with a survey statistic. These measures are closely related to the standard error, but, perhaps, offer a more intuitive interpretation of the uncertainty of a survey result. Recall the true standard error of $\bar{X}$ is the standard deviation of sample means around the true mean in the population. When the sample size is large, the sampling distribution of $\bar{X}$ is normally distributed, which means approximately 68% of all values will lie within one standard deviation of the true mean μ. Therefore 68% of all sample estimates of μ will lie within the interval $\bar{X} +/- s_{\bar{x}}$, which is the usual estimate for the 68% confidence interval for μ. If the

mean family income resulting from the survey is $\bar{X} = 37,500$, and its standard error is $s_{\bar{x}} = 1,528$, then the 68% confidence interval for μ is \$37,500 +/- \$1,528 or the interval, \$35,972 − \$39,028.

Given $\bar{X}$ and $s_{\bar{x}}$, any confidence interval can be calculated, but it is conventional in survey research to report the 95% confidence interval. If 68% of the values in a normal distribution fall within one standard deviation of the mean, then 95% of the values lie within 1.96 standard deviations of the mean. The 95% confidence interval is expressed, then, as $\bar{X} +/- 1.96 * s_{\bar{x}}$. The margin of error is usually defined as the radius of the 95% confidence interval, or $1.96 * s_{\bar{x}}$. In the example of family income, where $\bar{X} = $ \$37,500 and $s_{\bar{x}} = $ \$1,528, the 95% confidence interval is \$37,500 +/- \$2,994.88 and the margin of error is \$2,994.88.

The Standard Error of a Sample Proportion

In surveys and polls the result of interest is often the proportion of sample elements that belongs to a class or possesses an attribute, denoted $\hat{p}$. For example, in a survey of families, it might be important to estimate the proportion of families with two parents in residence. If $\hat{p}$ is the sample proportion possessing the attribute, then $\hat{q}$ is the proportion not possessing the attribute. The standard error of $\hat{p}$ is defined as $s_{\hat{p}} = \sqrt{\frac{\hat{p}\hat{q}}{n}}$. If the survey found that 80 of the 100 families had two parents present, then $\hat{p} = 80/100 = 4/5$ and $\hat{q} = 20/100 = 1/5$. The standard error of $\hat{p}$ would be

$$s_{\hat{p}} = \sqrt{\frac{\frac{4}{5} * \frac{1}{5}}{100}} = \sqrt{\frac{\frac{4}{25}}{100}} = .04.$$

Confidence intervals could be constructed for p in the same way as for μ (shown in the previous section). The 95% confidence interval for p is estimated as $\hat{p} +/- 1.96 * s_{\hat{p}}$ and the margin of error is $1.96 * s_{\hat{p}}$. The 95% confidence interval for the proportion of families with two parents is then $.8 +/- 1.96 * .04$, which is $.8 +/- .0784$. The margin of error is .0784.

The Standard Error and Sample Size

In the calculations presented previously, the standard errors for the sample means and proportions would decrease in magnitude if sample sizes were larger; that is, the n in each formula is a denominator, and as it grows larger, the standard error grows smaller. In general, larger samples have less random sampling error and provide more accurate estimates of the unknown population parameter. Sample size also affects the accuracy of confidence intervals and margins of error estimates. These are usually approximated by assuming that the distribution of sample estimates is a normal distribution. This assumption is warranted for the distributions of $\bar{X}$ and $\hat{p}$ when the sample size is large—generally greater than 30. However, when the sample size is small, the normality assumption is a stronger assumption, and estimates of confidence intervals and margins of error based on the assumption of normality are more questionable.

The Standard Error, Sampling Strategy, and Survey Methods

Sampling design and survey methods influence the accuracy of sample estimates and therefore affect the magnitude of the standard error. The methods described here for calculating standard errors assume a simple random sample, in which every element in the targeted population has an equal probability of being selected. When the sample is not a simple random sample but rather a more complicated probability sample, standard errors and confidence intervals must be estimated through more advanced techniques. In any case, standard errors are measures of sampling error. They do not take into account other sources of error such as a nonrepresentative sampling, poorly phrased questions, untruthful responses, missing data due to "don't know" or "undecided" responses, and overall response rates.

Jani S. Little

See also Confidence Interval; Equal Probability of Selection; Margin of Error (MOE); Population Parameter; Probability Sample; Sampling Error; Simple Random Sample; Standard Error of the Mean; Statistic; Variance

Further Readings

American Statistical Association, Survey Research Methods Section: http://www.amstat.org/sections/srms/

Devore, J. L. (1991). *Probability and statistics for engineering and the sciences* (3rd ed.). Pacific Grove, CA: Brooks/Cole.

Kish, L. (1995). *Survey sampling* (Reprinted ed.). New York: Wiley. (Original work published 1965)

Section on Survey Research Methods. (1998). *What is a survey? What is a margin of error?* Alexandria, VA: American Statistical Association. Retrieved on May 29, 2008, from http://www.whatisasurvey.info

Standard Error of the Mean

The standard error of the mean refers to the standard deviation of the sampling distribution of the sample mean. This distribution represents all possible sample means that could be computed from samples selected according to a specified sample size and sampling design. The standard error of the mean quantifies how much variation is expected to be present in the sample means that would be computed from each and every possible sample, of a given size, taken from the population. The standard error of the mean is measured in the same units as the original data and is often denoted by $SE(\bar{X})$ or simply as SE. Larger SE values imply more variation in sample means across possible samples of the same size; smaller SE values imply that the sample mean is more precise, or varies less from one sample to another.

The SE is typically estimated by dividing the estimate of the population standard deviation by the square root of the sample size: $SE(\bar{X}) = \frac{\hat{\sigma}}{\sqrt{n}}$. Generally, increases in sample size imply decreases in the SE. Additionally, the SE is usually much smaller than the sample standard deviation with the degree of the difference being inversely proportional to the square root of the sample size.

In the context of a simple random sample of size n, selected without replacement from a finite population of size N with a population standard deviation σ, the standard error of the mean is given by

$$SE(\bar{X}) = \frac{\sigma}{\sqrt{n}} \times \sqrt{1 - \frac{n}{N}},$$

where the last part of the formula represents the "finite population correction." If the population is much larger compared to the actual size of the sample, then the two SE formulas will be approximately equal. If σ is unknown, it can be estimated using information from the latest version of the survey (i.e., estimate from previous cycle) or from the sample (i.e., sample standard deviation).

Uses of the Standard Error of the Mean in Survey Research

The design effect for the mean for a given survey sampling design is the square of the quotient of the standard error of the mean, based on the particular design, to the standard error of the mean based on simple random sampling without replacement.

Confidence intervals for the population mean are also computed using the sample mean estimate along with an estimate of the standard error of the mean. Typically formulas for a $(1 - \alpha) \times 100\%$ confidence interval for the population mean are presented in the form

$$\bar{X} \pm Critical\ Value \times SE(\bar{X}),$$

where the "critical value" is computed according to some statistical reference distribution such as the standard normal or t-distribution.

The coefficient of variation is simply the quotient of the standard error of the mean to the sample mean. Because the standard error of the mean is influenced by the units of the data, the coefficient of variation allows researchers to compare variability in the sample means across different samples using the same variables that are perhaps measured on different scales, such as income ranging in the thousands of dollars compared to income measured in millions of dollars.

For example, suppose that there is an interest in estimating the mean number of days in the past year that teenagers living in a rural community consumed at least one alcoholic beverage, and data from a probability sample, such as that provided by the National Survey on Drug Use and Health, are used to make this estimate. Assuming that a simple random sample of 100 teenagers from the rural community of 1,000 teenagers produces a sample mean of 25.75 and a sample standard deviation of 30.0 days, then the estimated SE is $SE(\bar{X}) = 30/\sqrt{100} = 3$. Using the finite population version, the estimated SE becomes

$$SE(\bar{X}) = \frac{30}{\sqrt{100}} \times \sqrt{1 - \frac{100}{1000}} = 2.846.$$

Trent D. Buskirk

See also Confidence Interval; Design Effects (*deff*); Finite Population Correction (fpc) Factor

Further Readings

van Belle, G. (2002). *Statistical rules of thumb*. New York: Wiley.

Yates, D., Moore, D., & McCabe, G. (1999). *The practice of statistics*. New York: W. H. Freeman.

STANDARDIZED SURVEY INTERVIEWING

In a standardized survey interview, the interview proceeds according to a script (the introduction and the questionnaire) that is intended to minimize any potential impact of individual interviewers' behavior on respondents' answers and the resulting data. Standardized interviewing procedures for sample surveys were developed over several decades of the 20th century as evidence accrued that even seemingly minor differences in how interviewers behaved in interviews sometimes affected answers and data quality. Interviewers' biases or assumptions about particular types of respondents could creep into the interview through subtle changes in wording or tone that could lead respondents to interpret questions or the situation differently than they would have with a different interviewer. Even without intending to influence answers, interviewers who attempted to increase rapport by rephrasing a question the second time they asked it, or politely did not present all the response alternatives to a question because they judged that some alternatives would not fit a particular respondent's circumstances, could harm the quality of the data. It also became clear that interviewers could, in all innocence and with good intentions, introduce bias through how they reacted when a respondent expressed reservations or uncertainty about an answer; interviewers could subtly encourage respondents to give answers that fit the interviewers' preconceptions rather than the respondent's actual circumstances or opinions.

Standardized survey interviewing procedures are designed to circumvent these problems and to ensure that the data from all respondents are fully comparable because all respondents have answered the same questions under the same procedures. Standardizing the interviewing procedures is intended to address the measurement error due to interviewers, which is assumed to be independent of measurement error due to question wording (which can be addressed through better question pretesting) and measurement error due to respondents (which cannot easily be addressed by survey researchers).

Ideally, interviewers adhering to standardized procedures read (either from paper or from a computer screen) survey questions and all response alternatives precisely as worded by the designers of the survey, and they repeat the full question and all response alternatives when asked to repeat the question. In the strictest forms of standardized survey interviewing, interviewers also leave the interpretation of questions entirely up to respondents and only respond to any requests for clarification with neutral probes like "whatever it means to you" and "let me repeat the question." The logic is that if only some respondents receive clarification or help with answering, then the stimulus (the question wording and response alternatives) is different for a different respondent, and thus there is no guarantee that the data are comparable.

The broad consensus is that standardized interviewing procedures are the most desirable for sample surveys and that more idiosyncratic or ethnographic forms of interviewing that are useful for other more qualitative research purposes are risky or undesirable in surveys. But this consensus can manifest itself somewhat differently in different survey organizations, where the precise procedures that count as "standardized" in one center can differ from those in other organizations. For example, organizations differ on whether providing clarification to a respondent counts as nonstandardized or standardized and on whether repeating only the most appropriate response alternatives is better than repeating them all. Survey organizations can also vary in how extensively they train and monitor their interviewers for adherence to the standardized procedures they advocate, which means that in practice some standardized surveys turn out to be less standardized than others.

Controversies

Starting in the 1990s, methodological researchers who closely examine interview recordings began documenting that strictly standardized procedures sometimes can create uncomfortable interactions that not only frustrate respondents but also lead to demonstrably poorer data quality. When interviewers "force" respondents into answers that do not reflect their circumstances, when they repeat information that the respondent already knows, when they ask for information the respondent has already provided, or when they refuse to clarify what their questions mean, respondents can become alienated and recalcitrant,

and they can provide incorrect answers. When viewed through this lens, the practical results of strict standardization can, on occasion, run counter to the intended effects. Perhaps, in the attempt to standardize wording in the interview, survey researchers are failing to standardize what really ought to be standardized: the "meaning" of the questions. Within this view, to serve the goal of making sure that respondents' answers are truly comparable, interviewers should instead work to make sure that respondents are interpreting questions in the same way—even if this means deviating from a script and tailoring clarification and probes to individual respondents.

The jury is still out on the implications of this work and what it will mean for the future of standardized interviewing. There are a number of important considerations. First, much is unknown about how often problematic interactions occur and how often respondents' interpretations of questions differ from interpretations of the survey designers in different domains of questioning; if problems and misinterpretations are too frequent, then alternate ways of implementing standardized interviews are worth investigating, but if they are quite rare then revamping procedures on a large scale is clearly not worthwhile. Second, the survey enterprise currently relies on a particular model of hiring and training interviewers, and it is not yet clear how training and monitoring interviewers who implement a less scripted version of standardization would work. Based on some reports, some interviewers would prefer to implement less strictly standardized interviews, but whether a different kind of interviewer (e.g., those with higher levels of education or subject matter expertise) and different levels of compensation would be needed to do this is unknown.

The larger question about the best way to achieve the goals of standardization remains: Should survey researchers standardize the stimulus (question) and the subsequent interaction? Or should survey researchers standardize the respondent's interpretation of the question and experience of the interaction?

This question is put into sharp relief by comparing standardized interviewing with self-administered surveys. In a sense, a self-administered survey (whether administered via paper and pencil, via clicking on a textual Web survey, or via listening to a recorded voice on a laptop computer) is the ultimate in standardization: All respondents are presented with precisely the same stimulus, with no variation in what the "interviewer" (words on the page, audio recording) does. One could argue that the future of standardized interviewing is to migrate human interviews into automated self-administered interviews, because, in essence, this creates one interviewing agent for the entire survey sample, and so the differential impact of different interviewers disappears. (The less-quantified aspects of human contact and rapport building would also, of course, disappear.)

But the larger question about what it takes to make survey responses comparable and minimize the effects of the interviewer or interviewing agent would still not be addressed, even with full self-administration. For example, in a paper-and-pencil survey, the interpretation of the questions is left entirely up to the respondent, but should it be? Would the data be more comparable if respondents were all assisted in interpreting the questions in the same way (e.g., via clarification dialogue in a Web survey)? In an audio self-administered survey, will different respondents interpret the recorded interviewer's vocal tone differently in ways that affect their answers? Would the data be more comparable if the interviewer's voice were variably tailored so as to be experienced as more similar across respondents?

Theories and practices of standardization—and thus questions about standardization—are thus expanding rapidly with new interviewing technologies. Not only will debates about, and data from, studies of human interviews inform those new technologies, but also the careful manipulation of features of human interaction that will come from new technologies will inform ongoing debates about standardization in human interviewing.

Michael F. Schober

See also Audio Computer-Assisted Self-Interviewing (ACASI); Conversational Interviewing; Dependent Interviewing; Interviewer Monitoring; Interviewer-Related Error; Interviewer Training; Introduction; Measurement Error; Probing; Questionnaire; Respondent–Interviewer Rapport; Tailoring; Verbatim Responses

Further Readings

Beatty, P. (1995). Understanding the standardized/non-standardized interviewing controversy. *Journal of Official Statistics*, *11*, 147–160.

Conrad, F. G., & Schober, M. F. (2000). Clarifying question meaning in a household telephone survey. *Public Opinion Quarterly*, *64*, 1–28.

Fowler, F. J., & Mangione, T. W. (1990). *Standardized survey interviewing: Minimizing interviewer-related error*. Newbury Park, CA: Sage.

Houtkoop-Steenstra, H. (2000). *Interaction and the standardized survey interview: The living questionnaire*. Cambridge, UK: Cambridge University Press.

Maynard, D., Houtkoop-Steenstra, H., Schaeffer, N. C., & van der Zouwen, J. (Eds.). (2002). *Standardization and tacit knowledge: Interaction and practice in the survey interview*. New York: Wiley.

Suchman, L., & Jordan, B. (1990.) Interactional troubles in face-to-face survey interviews. *Journal of the American Statistical Association*, *85*, 232–253.

STATA

STATA is a general-purpose interactive statistical software package available in major platforms such as Windows, Unix, and Macintosh. In part due to its up-to-date coverage of statistical methodology and flexibility in implementing user-defined modules, STATA has gained considerable popularity among social and behavioral scientists, including survey researchers, in recent years despite its initial learning curve for the uninitiated.

STATA comes in four versions: (1) small STATA, a student version; (2) intercooled STATA, the "standard" version; (3) STATA/SE, a version for large data sets; and (4) STATA/MP, a parallel-processing-capable version of STATA/SE. Depending on size of data and number of variables as well as computer capacity, most survey researchers will likely choose Intercooled STATA and STATA/SE, in that order of preference.

With a fairly developed graphics capacity, STATA offers a vast array of commands for all kinds of statistical analysis, from analysis of variance to logistic regression to quantile regression to zero-inflated Poisson regression. Although not an object-oriented language like C, R, or S, STATA is fairly programmable, and that is why there is a huge collection of user-written macros, known as *ado-files*, supplementing the main program of STATA and which are typically well documented and regularly maintained. These ado-files satisfy a spectrum of needs among common users. Two examples provide a sense of the range: *SPost*, which is a set of ado-files for the post-estimation interpretation of regression models for categorical outcomes, and *svylorenz*, which is a module for computing distribution-free variance estimates for quantile group share of a total, cumulative quantile group shares (and the Gini index) when estimated from complex survey data.

STATA already has good capacity for analyzing survey data in its main program. For example, the *svyset* command declares the data to be complex survey type, specifies variables containing survey design information, and designates the default method for variance estimation. Many regression-type commands work with the cluster option, which gives cluster-correlated robust estimate of variance. Adjustment for survey design effects can also be achieved by using the *svy* prefix command (e.g., *svy: logit*) before a command for a specific operation. STATA supports three major types of weight: frequency weight (*fweight*) denoting the number of duplicated cases, probability or sampling weight (*pweight*) for indicating the inverse of the probability that the observation is included due to sampling design, and analytic weight (*aweight*) being inversely proportional to the variance of an observation. (Another weight, importance weight, can be used by a programmer for a particular computation.)

The *xt* series of commands are designed for analyzing panel (or time-series cross-sectional) data. These, coupled with the reshape command for changing the data from the wide to the long form (or vice versa) when survey data from multiple panels are combined into one file, are very attractive features of STATA for the survey data analyst.

Tim F. Liao

See also SAS; Statistical Package for the Social Sciences (SPSS)

Further Readings

Hamilton, L. C. (2006). *Statistics with STATA*. Belmont, CA: Duxbury.

STATISTIC

A statistic is a numerical summary of observed values for a random variable (or variables) in a sample. The term *random* indicates that the variable's value, and thus its statistic, may differ across samples that are drawn from the same sample population. A statistic is used to estimate a parameter, a numerical summary of a given variable (or variables) in the population.

A statistic is commonly represented with the common alphabet rather than with Greek letters, as is typically the case with a parameter. For example, a statistic such as a standard deviation is represented by *s*, whereas the corresponding population parameter is represented by σ.

Describing characteristics of a sample variable (or variables) is often called *descriptive statistics*. Examples include computing the sample's mean or standard deviation on a variable such as age or weight or describing proportions for categorical variables such as race or marital status. The process of using the sample's descriptive data to generate population estimates is typically referred to as *inferential statistics*.

It should be recognized that if data are available for the entire population of interest, inference is unnecessary as the parameter can be calculated directly.

Kirsten Barrett

See also Inference; Parameter; Population; Random; Sample

Further Readings

Agresti, A., & Finlay, B. (1997). *Statistical methods for the social sciences*. Upper Saddle River, NJ: Prentice Hall.

STATISTICAL PACKAGE FOR THE SOCIAL SCIENCES (SPSS)

In 1968, Normal Nie and Dale Bent, Stanford doctoral candidates, and Hadlai Hull, a Stanford graduate with a master's in business administration, developed a software system that allowed for the transformation of raw data into information using statistical applications. Their creation, the *Statistical Package for the Social Sciences (SPSS)*, was not developed with the intent of mass distribution. However, its appeal quickly caught on and, soon after its development, it was in high demand in universities across the United States. This demand further increased after McGraw-Hill published the first SPSS user's manual in 1970. SPSS incorporated in 1975.

SPSS, Inc., offered the first mainframe statistical package to appear on a personal computer (in the mid-1980s) and, in 1992, was the first organization to release a statistical package for use with the Microsoft

Windows operating system. In the 21st century, SPSS, Inc., now offers a broad array of products and services to meet the diverse needs of its customers, both in the United States and abroad. The flagship product for SPSS, Inc., is SPSS Base, available for both Windows and Apple platforms. This product provides survey researchers with a powerful and user-friendly data management and statistical analysis package. SPSS Base allows the researcher to generate both descriptive and bivariate statistics. Further, with SPSS Base, the survey analyst can run predictive analytics such as factor and regression analyses.

A number of add-on modules and stand-alone products further enhance the capabilities of SPSS Base. Add-on modules allow for advanced multivariate analysis of survey data, including data derived from surveys with complex sample designs. Included are modules that allow for generalized linear models, hierarchical linear models, survival analysis, and categorical regression. SPSS, Inc., stand-alone products serve to add power to the data management and analysis system provided in SPSS Base. Stand-alone products are available to help with all phases of the survey process, including sample selection and data collection, data management and cleaning, data analysis, and data dissemination.

Kirsten Barrett

See also SAS; STATA; SUDAAN

Further Readings

SPSS, Inc. (2008). *About SPSS, Inc.—Corporate history.* Retrieved February 5, 2007, from http://www.spss.com/corpinfo/history.htm

STATISTICAL POWER

The probability of correctly rejecting a null hypothesis that is false is called the statistical power (or simply, power) of the test. A related quantity is the Type II error rate (β) of the test, defined as the probability of *not* rejecting a false null hypothesis. Because power is based on the assumption that the null hypothesis is actually false, the computations of statistical power are conditional probabilities based on specific alternative values of the parameter(s) being tested. As a probability, power will range from 0 to 1

with larger values being more desirable; numerically, power is equal to $1 - \beta$.

The statistical power is also related implicitly to the Type I error rate (α), or significance level, of a hypothesis test. If α is small, then it will be more difficult to reject the null hypotheses, implying that the power will also be low. Conversely, if α is larger, then the null hypotheses will have a larger rejection region, and consequently the power will be larger. While power and Type I error rates do covary as these extremes suggest, the exact relationship between power and α is more complex than might be ascertained by interpolating from these extreme cases.

Statistical power is usually computed during the design phase of a survey research study; typical values desired for such studies range from 0.70 to 0.90. Generally many survey items are to be compared across multiple strata or against some prior census value(s). For example, researchers may use data from the Current Population Survey to determine if the unemployment rate for California is lower than the national average. Power calculations can be computed for each questionnaire item, and the *maximum sample size required* to achieve a specified power level for any given question becomes the overall sample size. Generally, in practice, one or two key items of interest are identified for testing, or a statistical model relating several of the items as predictors and others as key independent variables is specified. Power calculations to determine the adequacy of target sample sizes are then derived for these specific questionnaire items or particular statistical tests of model parameters.

Consider a scenario involving a random-digit dialing sample of households selected to estimate the average food replacement costs after an extended power outage for the residents within a midwestern U.S. county. The average food loss cost per household based on data from previous storms was $500.00 ($\mu_0$). Because this particular storm was slightly more severe than a previous storm, officials believe that in actuality, the average food loss cost for households for the current storm is somewhere closer to $550.00 ($\mu_1$). The standard deviation of the distribution of food loss costs was assumed to be $100.00. The statistical power for the one-tailed hypothesis test based on a sample of 25 houses using a Type I error rate of 5% is to be computed. In this case, the particular *effect size* used in the computation of statistical power is Effect Size $= \frac{|500 - 550|}{100} = 0.50$. The statistical power for this test is 80.51%, which represents the probability of rejecting the null hypothesis of average food loss of $500.00 given that the actual average food loss costs is $550.00 using an estimated standard deviation of 100, a sample size of 25, and $\alpha = 0.05$. Thus, there is roughly an 81% chance for detecting a positive difference in the average food loss costs of $50.00 using this hypothesis test. This power calculation is depicted graphically in Figure 1.

Notice that the Type I error rate (darker gray area) is computed with respect to the distribution defined by the null hypothesis (the curve on the left). Specifically, the Type I error rate is the area under the curve defined by the *null* hypothesis to the right of the critical value that defines the null hypothesis rejection region. On the other hand, the statistical power (light gray region) is computed as the area to the right of the null hypothesis rejection region under the curve that is defined by parameters that are given in the *alternative* hypothesis (gray/dashed curve line).

No matter what the form of the comparison (i.e., one/two sample or advanced statistical model), the power of the test is generally a function of three key values:

1. Level of significance/Type I error rate of the particular statistical test

2. The effect size—defined as the standardized difference between the null and alternative values for the parameter (which assumes some knowledge or estimate of the population standard deviation)

3. The sample size

Several Web applets are available for computing power for simple designs (e.g., http://davidmlane.com/ hyperstat/power.html). Typically, these computations ignore the finite population correction. In addition to computing power values for a specific sample or effect size, statistical calculators can generate "power curves" that graphically plot the power of a statistical test (y-axis) as a function of either the effect or sample size (x-axis), for a fixed significance level. An example of a series of power curves

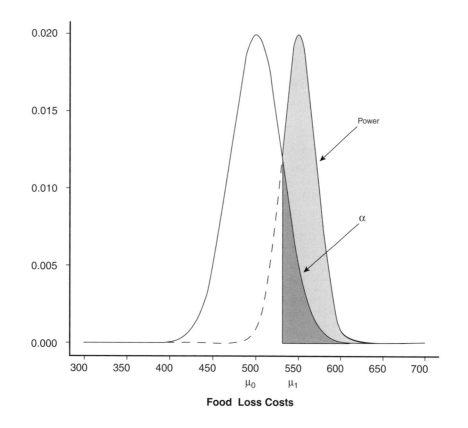

Figure 1   Illustration of the statistical power computation for a one-tailed hypothesis test for a single population mean assuming the Type I error rate is .05

computed for three different effect sizes for one-sided hypothesis tests involving a single mean is depicted in Figure 2. Notice from the figure that the statistical power increases as the sample size increases. Also notice that for any given possible sample size, the power increases as the effect size increases. Finally, note that the height of the solid curve in Figure 2 (corresponding to an effect size of .50) at the possible sample size of 25 is approximately .81, consistent with previous calculations.

Statistical power computations are to hypothesis testing of parameters as precision is to interval estimation of parameters. For example, if the goal of a survey sample is to produce reliable statewide estimates of obesity, average consumer spending per month, or other variables of interest, then precision is the defining computation that drives estimates of sample size. However, if interest is given to making comparisons for average obesity rates across several strata or post-strata, or in comparing average unemployment rates from one year to another within a state, then statistical power computations can be useful in understanding how likely one is to detect a given effect with a particular sample size. Of course, these quantities are closely intertwined statistically, but typically they imply different uses of the data at hand.

Trent D. Buskirk

See also Alternative Hypothesis; Finite Population Correction (fpc) Factor; Null Hypothesis; Sample Size; Type I Error; Type II Error

Further Readings

D'Agostino, R. B., Sullivan, L. M., & Beiser, A. S. (2006). *Introductory applied biostatistics*. Belmont, CA: Thomson.

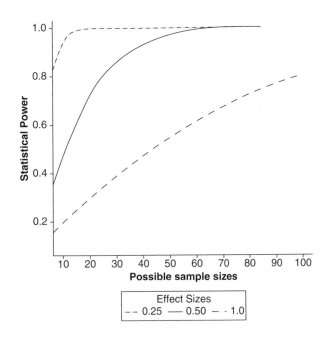

Figure 2   Statistical power curves illustrating how statistical power can be influenced by both possible sample size as well as effect size assuming a fixed Type I error rate of .05

STATISTICS CANADA

Statistics Canada is Canada's national statistical agency. Prior to 1971, Statistics Canada was known as the Dominion Bureau of Statistics. The bureau was created in 1918 as a permanent home for the national census and to develop a standardized form and database for the collection of vital statistics. In addition to the census and collection of vital statistics, Statistics Canada administers more than 400 surveys and compiles a number of different administrative data sources. Some examples of their cross-sectional surveys include the Labour Force Survey, Survey of Household Spending, and the General Social Survey. Statistics Canada also completes several longitudinal surveys, such as National Population Health Survey—Household Component, National Graduates Survey, National Longitudinal Survey of Children and Youth, and the Survey of Labour and Income Dynamics. These surveys about employment, income, education, health, and social conditions are a handful of the many Statistics Canada surveys.

Many census data reports are free to the public through Statistics Canada's online data source Community Profiles. CANSIM, another online data source, includes summary tables from many of Statistics Canada's surveys and administrative data sources. Some of these summary tables are free, and other tables have a nominal fee. Government officials, academics, the media, and members of the general public receive daily updates about these data sources through *The Daily*, Statistics Canada's official release bulletin.

Census

The first national census was in 1871, a few years after Confederation (1867). The census included the four original provinces and expanded as additional provinces joined Confederation. When the prairie provinces joined Confederation, an Agricultural Census was initiated (1906) and repeated every 5 years to help monitor the growth of the west. Since 1956, these two censuses have been administered together every 5 years. Agricultural producers across the country received a copy of the Census of Population questionnaire as well as a copy of the Census of Agriculture questionnaire. Participation in the census is required by law.

The intent of the first national census was to determine population estimates to ensure representation by population in Parliament, a purpose still relevant today. In Canada, the census is also used to calculate transfer payments between the different government jurisdictions (federal government to the provinces and territories; provinces and territories to municipalities). The transfer payments fund schools, hospitals, and other public services.

Prior to the 1950s, the census involved multiple questionnaires and ranged from 200 to 500 questions. To reduce response burden and administration costs, sample surveys were initiated to gather certain data and the census questionnaires were reduced in size. Two versions of the census questionnaire were introduced. The short version is administered to all Canadian households, except every fifth household, which receives a long version of the questionnaire. The short version gathers information about names of household members, relationship to the head of household, sex, age, marital status, and language. The long version includes these questions as well as additional questions about education, ethnicity, mobility, income, and employment. The content of the long version is more apt to change across time, with the short version staying more consistent in content.

In 1971, several innovations were introduced to the census. First, one in three households received the long questionnaire, but this innovation was abandoned in subsequent years in favor of the one in five sampling approach. Second, the census moved from being interviewer-administered to being self-administered for most of the population. The latter innovation has continued, and in 2006, this self-administered mode included the option of completing the questionnaire online. In 2006, almost 20% of Canadian households opted to complete the survey online. The Census 2006 also contained an additional innovation: As part of ensuring more ethical standards in data collection, the Census 2006 included a question requesting permission to release census responses to the public in 92 years.

Shelley Boulianne

See also Census; *Survey Methodology*

Further Readings

Statistics Canada. (1993). *75 Years and counting: A history of Statistics Canada*. Ottawa, ON: Minister Responsible for Statistics Canada. (Statistics Canada Catalogue no. 11-531).

Statistics Canada. (2007, March). *History of the census of Canada*. Retrieved May 28, 2007, from http://www.statcan.ca/english/census96/history.htm

STEP-LADDER QUESTION

A step-ladder question refers to a type of question sequence that yields more complete and accurate data than would a single question on the same topic. Step-ladder questions are used by survey researchers in an attempt to reduce item nonresponse (missing data), measurement error, or both, although they add slightly to the cost of gathering the data since more than one question needs to be asked.

For example, asking someone into which of the following income categories his or her 2007 total household income fell—less than $20,000; $20,000–$39,999; $40,000–$59,999; $60,000–$79,999; $80,000–$99,999; $100,000 or more—will lead to a good deal of "Don't Know" or "Refused" answers. Researchers have found that a step-ladder question about income will substantially reduce item nonresponse and thus the need to impute those missing values.

A step-ladder question sequence for the income variable referenced in the previous paragraph, that was programmed to be asked in a computer-assisted interview, would be as follows:

Q1. *Was your total household income from all sources in 2007 more than $19,999?*
    < 1 > YES (GO TO Q2)
    < 2 > NO (GO TO Q6)

< 8 > REFUSED (GO TO Q6)
< 9 > UNCERTAIN (GO TO Q6)
Q2. *And was it more than $39,999?*
< 1 > YES (GO TO Q3)
< 2 > NO (GO TO Q6)
< 8 > REFUSED (GO TO Q6)
< 9 > UNCERTAIN (GO TO Q6)
Q3. *And was it more than $59,999?*
< 1 > YES (GO TO Q4)
< 2 > NO (GO TO Q6)
< 8 > REFUSED (GO TO Q6)
< 9 > UNCERTAIN (GO TO Q6)
Q4. *And was it more than $79,999?*
< 1 > YES (GO TO Q5)
< 2 > NO (GO TO Q6)
< 8 > REFUSED (GO TO Q6)
< 9 > UNCERTAIN (GO TO Q6)
Q5. *And was it more than $99,999?*
< 1 > YES (GO TO Q6)
< 2 > NO (GO TO Q6)
< 8 > REFUSED (GO TO Q6)
< 9 > UNCERTAIN (GO TO Q6)

In this example, after the income sequence has been administered all respondents are taken to Q6 (i.e., whatever is the next logical question in the questionnaire after the income sequence). Of note, even though the entire step-ladder sequence comprises five questions, any one respondent would be asked more questions in the sequence only up until he or she said "No." As such, proportionally few respondents would be asked four or five of the questions (i.e., only a minority will have incomes exceeding $80,000). The majority would only be asked one, two, or three of the questions in this step-ladder sequence. This step-ladder sequence will lead to far fewer missing income values than a single income question that presents to the respondent essentially the same income categories all at once. It also will yield data that the researchers can combine to form a single income variable with the desired six categories in the original one-question income example.

Step-ladder questions can be used for other constructs that are measured on some form of numerically ordered scale. They are particularly useful when there are many response choices on the response scale and the cognitive burden on many respondents is too great to present all the choices at once. If all choices were presented at once, primacy, recency, and/or other satisficing effects would likely lead to errors in the data.

Paul J. Lavrakas

See also Imputation; Measurement Error; Missing Data; Primacy Effect; Recency Effect; Respondent Burden; Satisficing

STRATA

Strata in stratified sampling are distinct subsets of all entries on a sampling frame. These subsets are strategically defined by one or more stratification variables to improve the statistical quality of findings for the population as a whole or for important population subgroups. Once strata are formed and the sample is allocated among strata, stratified sampling is accomplished by randomly selecting a sample within *each* stratum.

Sampling strata may be formed explicitly from a list of population members or as a part of the selection process in individual stages of a cluster sample. Strata may also be considered "implicit" when the frame is sorted by variables that could otherwise define strata, and sampling is done in each of a set of groups of neighboring entries throughout the frame (e.g., as in systematic sampling). For simplicity, this entry focuses largely on explicit stratification of individual population members, although the same principles of stratum formation apply to other forms of stratified sampling as well.

Stratification Variables

The final set of strata used for sampling is usually some type of cross-classification of the stratification variables. For example, stratification of individuals by two gender categories (i.e., male or female) and four educational attainment categories (i.e., less than a high school diploma, high school diploma, some college, or college degree and beyond) would imply $2 \times 4 = 8$ fully cross-classified strata. If the number of males in the population with some college or a college degree and beyond were considered to be too small, a partially collapsed set of seven strata might be formed from these two stratification variables by using all four female strata and by considering all males with some college or a college degree and beyond to comprise one stratum.

The choice of stratification variables depends on how sample stratification is to be used. When the purpose of stratification is to reduce the variance of the estimate of a characteristic of the population as a whole, it is best for the stratification variables to be statistically correlated with key outcome variables (i.e., member measurements that define the characteristics of interest). Thus, for example, if the outcome variable, annual income, is correlated with educational attainment among population members, then stratification by educational attainment would be a good choice when the population characteristic to be estimated is the average annual income of all population members.

Stratification may also be used to improve the quality of estimates for population subgroups. For instance, when stratification is used to disproportionately sample the subgroup, it is preferable to define strata by whatever characteristics define the subgroup. For instance, educational attainment, as defined earlier, should be a stratification variable when disproportionately sampling persons with less than a high school diploma. Note however, that equally valid though slightly less precise estimates can be obtained for subgroups, even if the categorical variables that would isolate the subgroup are not used to form the strata.

Defining Useful Strata

The ultimate goal in forming strata to improve the quality of estimates for the population as a whole is to define strata that are as internally homogeneous as possible with respect to the survey's key outcome variables. Thus, for example, if the main purpose of a sample of persons is to estimate their average annual income, then one hopes to sample from strata where members of each stratum have relatively similar income levels. This would mean that some strata have low-income earners, others have high-income earners, and the rest separately include those with various intermediate income levels.

In addition to using variables that are highly correlated with key study variables, there are two other considerations in forming strata that will lead to more precise overall population estimates. One is to define "optimum" stratum boundaries when stratification variables are continuous (i.e., numerical, such as age

in years or annual income in dollars). The most common approach for doing this is the "$cum\sqrt{f(x)}$ rule," where $f(x)$ is the frequency of the value (x) of a continuous stratification variable among all population members. Optimum boundaries for H strata under this rule are located at points of equal increment in the cumulative of $\sqrt{f(x)}$ (i.e., the $cum\sqrt{f(x)}$) among all values of x.

Another consideration is the number of strata. The general guidance here is that while increasing the number of strata will never diminish the quality of estimates, having too many strata may be impractical or of limited additional benefit. Because a sample size of at least two is needed for unbiased variance estimates, the maximum practical number of strata is the sample size divided by two, as seen in stratified sampling with "paired selection" (i.e., sample size of two in each stratum). Six to 10 well-formed strata are often sufficient to stratify individual population members, while paired selection from equal-sized strata is commonly used to choose clusters in the first stage of multi-stage samples.

William D. Kalsbeek

See also Correlation; Disproportionate Allocation to Strata; Multi-Stage Sample; Stratified Sampling; Subgroup Analysis; Systematic Sampling; Variance Estimation

Further Readings

Cochran, W. G. (1977). *Sampling techniques* (3rd ed.). New York: Wiley.

Kish, L. (1965). *Survey sampling*. New York: Wiley.

Levy, P. S., & Lemeshow, S. (1999). *Sampling of populations: Methods and applications*. New York: Wiley.

Lohr, S. (1999). *Sampling: Design and analysis*. Pacific Grove, CA: Duxbury.

Stratified Sampling

Sample selection is said to be stratified if some form of random sampling is separately applied in each of a set of distinct groups formed from all of the entries on the sampling frame from which the sample is to be drawn. By strategically forming these groups, called "strata," stratification becomes a feature of sample designs that can improve the statistical quality of survey estimates. Procedurally, stratum formation and sample allocation to strata are important preliminary steps to sample selection. After the sample has been selected, data are gathered from its members, and analysis accommodating the use of stratification is conducted.

Stratification and sampling clusters are sometimes confused, as both involve groups of one form or another. These two design features are distinguishable by how sampling is applied to the groups. Whereas sampling is done within each of the groups (strata) in stratified samples, only some of the groups (clusters) are randomly selected in cluster samples.

Stratified sampling is statistically beneficial in two ways. First, it may be used to enable the sample to better represent the measurements that define the mean, total, or other population characteristics to be estimated from the sample. A sample also may be stratified to promote adequate sample sizes for analysis of important subgroups of the populations, such as racial/ethnic minority groups.

Forming Strata

Strata are formed by deciding on one or more stratification variables and then defining the actual strata in terms of those variables. Improving the statistical quality of sample estimates through stratification implies that the stratification variables should (a) be statistically correlated with the measurements that define the main population characteristics to be estimated, (b) effectively isolate members of important analysis subgroups, or both. Indeed, the first goal implies that useful strata will be internally homogeneous with respect to the main study measurements, while the second goal suggests that key subgroups should be identifiable by one or more strata. Although the number of formed strata need not be large, it should be large enough to meet the needs of later analysis.

There are two common misconceptions about stratum formation. One is that subgroup analysis will be valid only if the subgroups are defined by those comprising one or more sampling strata. In fact, valid estimates can be produced for subgroups defined by portions of one or more strata, although their precision will be slightly less than if complete strata define the subgroup. Another myth is that incorrect stratum assignment (e.g., due to measurement error in the values of the stratification variables) will invalidate

sample estimates. In reality, bias does not result from stratum assignment errors provided random selection is done in each stratum, although the precision that is gained from strata with assignment errors may be compromised by these errors.

Sample Allocation to Strata

Deciding how a stratified sample will be distributed among all strata is called "stratum allocation." The most appropriate allocation approach depends on how stratification is being used. If, for example, the main purpose of stratification is to control sample sizes for important population subgroups, stratum sample sizes should be sufficient to meet precision requirements for subgroup analysis. A special case of this occurs when the subgroups of interest are explicitly defined by individual strata (e.g., stratification by geographic region) and an important part of analysis is to produce comparisons among all subgroup strata. In this instance, equal allocation (i.e., equal sample sizes) among subgroups would be appropriate. Meeting sample size needs for subgroups usually makes the allocation disproportionate, wherein sampling rates differ among strata.

Proportionate allocation is often a prudent choice when the main focus of analysis is characteristics of several subgroups or the population as a whole and where the appropriate allocations for these analyses are discrepant. Proportionate allocation involves applying the same sampling rate to all strata, thus implying that the percent distribution of the selected sample among strata is identical to the corresponding distribution for the population. This allocation is "safe" under these circumstances because, if well-formed strata are used, the precision of resulting estimates from the stratified sample will be at least as good as those from an unstratified sample of the same size.

"Optimum" stratum allocation, in which the most cost-efficient stratum sample sizes are sought, can lead to estimates of overall population characteristics that are statistically superior to those from a proportionately allocated sample. When all stratum unit costs are the same, the stratum sampling rates that yield the most precise sample estimates are directly proportional to the stratum-specific standard deviations of the stratum measurements that define the population characteristic to be estimated. This is called "Neyman allocation." When unit costs vary among strata, the optimum sampling rate for a stratum is also inversely related to the square root of the average cost of adding another sample member to the stratum. A practical limitation of optimum allocation is that its statistical utility is tied to the existence of good measures of stratum standard deviations and unit costs, which may be hard to find.

Sample Selection in Each Stratum

Most stratified samples use the same random selection method (e.g., simple random sampling) in each stratum. Because these selection methods need not be the same in each stratum, stratification offers flexibility that may lead to solutions to certain practical problems facing the survey designer. For instance, using a 5-year-old frame to sample hospitals directly for a national study of patient visits may lead to coverage bias in estimates if a large percentage of new hospitals are left off the list. To solve this problem, a separate stratum of recently opened hospitals might be sampled by first selecting counties and then searching for newly opened hospitals in the selected counties.

Analysis of Stratified Samples

Sample stratification is accommodated in two ways during analysis. First, separate stratum estimates are combined to produce the final estimates. This requires that the analyst be able to identify each respondent by stratum of selection. Second, the approach to stratum allocation is addressed through the use of sample weights that account for any sample disproportionality. These weights may also be calibrated through post-stratification and adjusted to account for other sources of imbalance in sample composition due to nonsampling error.

Failure to properly account for stratification in analysis of stratified samples can seriously invalidate estimated variances of survey estimates and thus compromise analysis findings that rely on them (e.g., confidence intervals and hypothesis tests). More specifically, if variance estimation ignores stratification, the variance estimates will generally be positively biased, thus causing confidence intervals to be too wide and tests of hypothesis to be too conservative.

William D. Kalsbeek

See also Clustering; Confidence Interval; Multi-Stage Sample; Neyman Allocation; Post-Stratification; Random Sampling; Sample Design; Sample Size; Sampling Frame; Simple Random Sample; Strata; Subgroup Analysis; Weighting

Further Readings

Cochran, W. G. (1977). *Sampling techniques* (3rd ed.). New York: Wiley.

Hansen, M. H., Hurwitz, W. N., & Madow, W. G. (1953). *Sample survey methods and theory; Vol. 1. Concepts and discussion.* New York: Wiley.

Kish, L. (1965). *Survey sampling.* New York: Wiley.

Levy, P. S., & Lemeshow, S. (1999). *Sampling of populations—Methods and applications.* New York: Wiley.

Lohr, S. (1999). *Sampling: Design and analysis.* Pacific Grove, CA: Duxbury.

Scheaffer, R. L., Mendenhall, W., & Ott, L. (2006). *Elementary survey sampling* (6th ed.). Belmont, CA: Duxbury.

STRAW POLLS

Straw polls originated as small, informal public opinion "surveys" that later evolved into large-scale, random sample surveys used primarily to determine the viability of potential political candidates. Nowadays, pollsters offer a litany of straw polls before nearly every national election and several state elections.

The phrase *straw poll* has its origins in the idea of "straws in the wind," which were used to determine which way the wind is blowing. The earliest use of a straw poll was by a newspaper, *The Harrisburg Pennsylvanian*, during the 1824 presidential election. Historically, straw polls were not scientific, and often they were conducted haphazardly. They relied on relatively large and sometimes massive samples to achieve some semblance of accuracy. Early on this included going to public places such as bars, political rallies, train stations and such, where groups of people were gathered and asking them their voting preferences. There was no sampling science at work at all.

However, as straw polling moved into the 20th century, this situation began to change. Yet, even with more than 2 million potential voters surveyed, straw polls were often quite biased, as demonstrated in the often-cited example of the *Literary Digest*'s 1936 declaration that, by a landslide, Alf Landon was going to beat Franklin Delano Roosevelt. (It should be noted that the *Literary Digest* accurately predicted each presidential election from 1920 through 1932.) Recognizing the folly of the *Literary Digest*'s approach, George Gallup, Elmo Roper, and Archibald Crossley each began using a more scientific approach. Specifically, with the help of demographers, they used quota sampling to build their list of poll respondents. Gallup's mistake in 1948 caused the major polling organizations to reconsider that approach. Recognizing the downfalls of a quota sample, subsequent polling adopted much more strict probability methods. These probability methods have been modified to fit specific needs, but they have all held true to one standard: that of random samples.

Straw polls have become commonplace in the news today. They have helped to create the horse race approach to reporting on elections. For example, a Gallup straw poll, conducted December 11–14, 2006, of Republicans and Republican leaders nationwide asked the following: *Next, I'm going to read a list of people who may be running in the Republican primary for president in the next election. After I read all the names, please tell me which of those candidates you would be most likely to support for the Republican nomination for the president in the year 2008, or if you would support someone else?* With an *n* of 425 and a margin of error of ± 6, Gallup found that 28% would support both John McCain and Rudy Giuliani. Another 12% would support Condoleezza Rice, and 8% supported Newt Gingrich.

Although the 2008 Republican nomination process would not formally begin for more than a year after this poll was conducted, the results indicated relatively little support for a number of other potential Republican presidential candidates which might well have caused one or more of them to reconsider actually running. A poll like this also may influence potential funders for particular candidates. It also may help the potential candidates themselves refine their campaign to try to capture support among the population that was not supporting them.

With the availability of the Internet, unscientific straw polls have expanded well beyond the realm of politics. They have been used to vote for favorite contestants on reality television shows, possible actors and actresses for television shows and movies, and even ranking of teams in college sports.

James W. Stoutenborough

See also Gallup, George; Gallup Poll; Horse Race Journalism; Margin of Error (MOE); *n*; Poll; Pollster; Probability Sample; Quota Sampling; Random Sampling; Trial Heat Question

Further Readings

Herbst, S. (1995). *Numbered voices: How opinion polling has shaped American Politics*. Chicago: University of Chicago Press.
Warren, K. F. (2001). *In defense of public opinion polling*. Boulder, CO: Westview Press.
Young, M. L. (Ed.). (1990). *The classics of polling*. Metuchen, NJ: Scarecrow Press.

SUBGROUP ANALYSIS

Subgroup analysis involves subdividing respondents in a survey into groups on the basis of demographic characteristics (e.g., race, ethnicity, age, education, or gender) or other variables (e.g., party identification, health insurance status, or attitudes toward the death penalty). Analyses of subgroups can be done for a number of reasons. A researcher might analyze differences in variable means or distributions across subgroups to identify disparities or other differences. For example, a researcher studying health care insurance may want to test whether there are differences in the proportion of respondents in different income, education, or race subgroups who are covered by private health care insurance.

Researchers may also want to compare bivariate relationships or multivariate analyses across subgroups to test whether relationships between variables are moderated by subgroup membership. Alternatively, these subgroup comparisons may be conducted to test or establish the generalizability of a relationship or model across subgroups of respondents. For example, a researcher may want to compare the extent to which respondents' pre-election reports of their presidential candidate preferences correspond to their post-election reports of vote choice for respondents who are strong partisans versus those who are weak partisans.

In research involving experimentally manipulated variables, researchers may compare the characteristics of respondents assigned to experimental groups to test whether random assignment has been successful. Researchers also may compare the effect of an experimental manipulation across subgroups to determine if characteristics of respondents moderate the effect of the experimental manipulation or to test or establish the generalizability of the effect across subgroups. For example, survey researchers studying the effects of question order on survey responses could compare the effect of question order for respondents with different levels of education.

For research involving data collected at multiple times (either from the same or different samples of respondents as in longitudinal and panel surveys), subgroup analysis can be used to test whether variable changes over time are the same or different across subgroups. For example, researchers using a panel design to examine changes in math skills in children between the ages of 6 and 10 might compare changes across these ages separately for male and female children.

Subgroup analysis is often used to better understand survey data. However, researchers who intend to use subgroup analysis should keep in mind a number of statistical cautions when using the approach. First, researchers should plan to conduct subgroup analysis in advance (i.e., a priori) rather than deciding to do so after the fact (i.e., post hoc). This helps to address possible concerns with sample size and power. If one or more subgroups are very small, the power to detect effects may be very small, and Type II errors (i.e., concluding there is no difference between groups when there actually is) may be likely. In addition, researchers should be concerned when they are making many subgroup comparisons. Conducting multiple statistical comparisons with the same data increases the chance of Type I error (i.e., concluding there is a difference between groups when the difference is likely due to chance) and researchers conducting subgroup analyses should utilize *familywise error* in estimating the significance of their statistical tests to adjust for this possibility.

Allyson Holbrook

See also Demographic Measure; *n*; Sample Size; Type I Error; Type II Error

Further Readings

Chambers, R. L., & Skinner, C. J. (2003). *Analysis of survey data*. Hoboken, NJ: Wiley.

Davis, J. A., & Smith, T. W. (1991). *The NORC General Social Survey: A user's guide*. Newbury Park, CA: Sage.

Narayan, S., & Krosnick, J. A. (1996). Education moderates some response effects in attitude measurement. *Public Opinion Quarterly, 60*, 58–88.

Pahkinen, E. (2004). *Practical methods for design and analysis of complex surveys*. Hoboken, NJ: Wiley.

SUDAAN

SUDAAN is a statistical software package for the analysis of correlated data, including but not limited to the analysis of correlated data encountered in complex sample surveys. Correlation between observations may exist, for example, in multi-stage studies where units such as geographic areas, schools, telephone area codes, or hospitals are sampled at the first stage of selection. A correlation may exist between observations due to the increased similarity of the observations located in the same cluster compared to observations between clusters. During any statistical analysis with survey data, the complex design features of the study, including clustering, unequal weighting, stratification, and selection with or without replacement, should be accounted for during the analysis. Standard software packages that do not account for the complex design features can produce biased results. In fact, in most instances the precision of statistics will likely be underestimated if one were to use a standard software package that does not account for the complex design features of a study. Software packages, such as SUDAAN, that are specifically designed for the analysis of data from survey studies will properly account for many of the complex design features of the study during an analysis.

SUDAAN originated in 1972 at Research Triangle Institute (RTI) and, over the years, has evolved into an internationally recognized, leading software package for analyzing correlated and complex survey data. SUDAAN 9.0, which was launched in August 2004, offers several additions and enhancements to prior releases. RTI statisticians are currently working on the next major release of SUDAAN and plan to have that available in 2008. SUDAAN can be run on any DOS or Windows platform and is also available for the SUN/Solaris and LINUX operating systems (32- and 64-bit operating systems). SUDAAN is available as a stand-alone software package or can be used in SAS-callable format. The SAS-callable format is of particular value to SAS users because it allows SUDAAN to be run directly within any existing SAS job. SUDAAN's syntax is very similar to SAS (e.g., a semicolon must appear at the end of every statement), and SUDAAN has the ability to read data files in various formats such as SAS, SAS XPORT, SPSS, and ASCII.

As noted earlier in this entry, SUDAAN provides estimates that correctly account for complex design features of a survey. These features include the following:

- Unequally weighted or unweighted data
- Stratification
- With- or without-replacement designs
- Multi-stage and cluster designs
- Repeated measures
- General cluster-correlation (e.g., correlation due to multiple measures taken from patients)
- Multiply imputed analysis variables

Currently, SUDAAN is a single program that offers nine analytic procedures. SUDAAN is one of the few software packages that offers three of the most commonly used robust variance estimation methods, including Taylor series linearization (generalized estimating equations for regression models), jackknife (with or without user-specified replicate weights), and balanced repeated replication.

All three variance estimation methods are available in all of SUDAAN's procedures. The nine procedures consist of three descriptive procedures, four regression procedures, and two survival procedures.

Michael B. Witt

See also Balanced Repeated Replication (BRR); Clustering; Complex Sample Surveys; Jackknife Variance Estimation; Multi-Stage Sample; Sampling Without Replacement; SAS; Taylor Series Linearization

Further Readings

SUDAAN: http://www.rti.org/sudaan

Suffix Banks

Telephone numbers in the United States, Canada, and the Caribbean consist of 10 digits divided into three components: The first three digits are the area code; the next three digits are the prefix or exchange; and the final four digits are the suffix, or local number.

For each area code-prefix combination, the 10,000 possible numbers for a suffix can be subdivided into banks or blocks of consecutive numbers: 1000-banks (Nnnn), 100-banks (NNnn), or 10-banks (NNNn).

As the sampling method of random-digit dialing (RDD) evolved, the underlying assumption was that residential telephone numbers tended to cluster. Based on this assumption, one of the earliest methodologies consisted of simply adding one to a directory-listed number or randomizing the last digit of a directory-listed number. Both methodologies proved to introduce bias. At the other end of the spectrum, randomizing all four digits of suffixes in residential exchanges eliminated bias but proved to be too inefficient and expensive to field.

Since the early mechanical switches came in banks of 1,000 numbers, telephone companies avoided purchasing unnecessary equipment by assigning numbers in suffix blocks of 1,000 numbers (or "1000-banks"). Later research showed that this clustering of numbers extended to 100-banks as well, primarily to accommodate businesses.

Two classes of RDD methodologies were developed to take advantage of this clustering effect: two-stage designs (such as Mitofsky-Waksberg) and single-stage, list-assigned designs that use a database of listed numbers to qualify banks (1000-banks or 100-banks) for inclusion in the telephone frame, based on the presence of directory-listed numbers. Although not all countries have fixed-length telephone numbers, these designs have been successfully adapted for use around the world.

Linda Piekarski

See also Cell Phone Sampling; Mitofsky-Waksberg Sampling; Prefix; Random-Digit Dialing (RDD)

Further Readings

Lepkowski, J. M. (1988). Telephone sampling methods in the United States. In R. M. Groves, P. P. Biemer, L. E. Lyberg, J. T. Massey, W. L. Nicholls II, & J. Waksberg (Eds.), *Telephone survey methodology* (pp. 73–98). New York: Wiley.

Piekarski, L. (1996). *A brief history of telephone sampling*. Fairfield, CT: Survey Sampling, Inc.

Tucker, C., Lepkowski, J. M., & Piekarski, L. (2002). The current efficiency of list-assisted telephone sampling designs. *Public Opinion Quarterly, 66,* 321–338.

SUGING

SUGing, or Selling Under the Guise of research (also known as "sugging"), is the act of telemarketing or pre-qualifying customers while pretending to conduct a legitimate survey. Because it is, by definition, a practice that seeks to deceive the respondent, it is an unethical business and research practice. In addition, there is essentially no interest in the "data" being gathered other than to help make the sales pitch more effective.

It also has the side effect of increasing the victim's suspicion of subsequent legitimate survey contacts, thereby reducing the population of individuals readily willing to answer survey questions. In short, SUGing not only represents illegitimate and thus unethical research in itself, but it also has a long-term negative impact on legitimate research projects. SUGing is proscribed by numerous public opinion, market research, and direct marketing trade associations.

In SUGing, the respondent's answers to the purported survey questions serve as a means of setting up a sales pitch. This is in contrast with legitimate survey research, in which obtaining the respondent's answers is the desired goal. Questions used in SUGing, therefore, are often superficial or biased to create a favorable disposition toward the sales solicitation. In some cases, however, SUGing solicitations can be extremely detailed in order to develop a detailed profile of the respondent to facilitate a custom tailored sales pitch that arrives later (e.g., via mail), which itself may represent another violation of ethical obligations to protect respondent confidentiality. Regardless of the nature of the questions, a key feature of a SUGing solicitation is its deceptiveness. There is no indication of the true nature of the interview until the sales pitch is given.

SUGing is illegal in several jurisdictions, including the United States, Canada, and the European Union. As a complicating factor, though, there is some international disagreement about the exact meaning of *SUGing*. Although public opinion and market research organizations in the United States, the United Kingdom, and continental Europe all define *SUGing* as selling under the guise of research, in Canada the *S* also stands for "soliciting" (giving the term a similar meaning to *FRUGing*, which is fund-raising under the guise of research), and deceptive survey-like sales pitches are known as *MUGing* (marketing under the guise of research).

One area where legitimate survey research may seem like SUGing is the practice of "sales waves." A sales wave attempts to determine the sales potential of a new product by offering to sell the new product to a respondent immediately at, or soon after, the conclusion of a legitimate market research interview about the product. Although the intent of a sales wave is to understand product demand and not to sell the product, the structure of a sales wave is similar enough to SUGing as to potentially create misunderstanding and resentment among many respondents.

The extent of SUGing is difficult to estimate, although empirical research on nonresponse in North America has indicated that up to 50% of individuals have received a SUGing call or mailing.

Geoffrey R. Urland and Kevin B. Raines

See also Deception; Ethical Principles; FRUGing; Nonresponse; Pseudo-Polls; Survey Ethics; Telemarketing

Further Readings

Kimmel, A. J. (2007). *Ethical issues in behavioral research: Basic and applied perspectives.* Malden, MA: Blackwell.

Market Research Association. (2007). *Research resources: For the consumer—Research abuse (sugging and frugging).* Retrieved February 15, 2007, from http://www.mra-net.org/resources/abuse.cfm

SUPERPOPULATION

When data for a variable are gathered from a finite population and that variable is regarded to be a random variable, then the finite population is referred to as being "a realization from a superpopulation." A superpopulation is the infinite population that elementary statistical textbooks often describe as part of the enumeration of a finite population. It is because sampling theory is based on making inference for a well-defined finite population that the concept of superpopulation is needed to differentiate between a finite population and an infinite superpopulation.

This distinction is important for two reasons: (1) Sampling theory estimation and inference can be based entirely on a finite population (in the absence of nonsampling errors), with no recourse to a superpopulation; and (2) even when a superpopulation is of primary interest (such as parameter estimation of the superpopulation model), the finite population may have been sampled in a way that distorts the original distribution of the finite population.

The superpopulation and the finite population concepts are compatible if one views the finite population labels (which are needed to allow specific units to be sampled) to be part of the superpopulation model. Doing so, the final sample can be thought of as the result of a two-step process. First, the finite population is selected from a superpopulation according to the superpopulation model. Then, after each unit is identified with a label and related information, a sample design is formed and the final sample of units is selected. The measured characteristics are known only for the final sample. However, other information, such as the information used as part of the sample design, will be known for the entire finite population.

The superpopulation approach allows the use of additional model assumptions by specifying either a frequency distribution for the finite population characteristics or by specifying a prior distribution directly for them. Including this extra information as part of the inference often increases precision. A potential danger is that inference may be either biased, due to model misspecification, or inappropriate if prior information used is not shared by others.

A different but related concept is that of a nested sequence of populations that increases to an arbitrary large total. This has been used to demonstrate asymptotic properties of finite population estimates.

Donald J. Malec

See also Finite Population; Inference

Further Readings

Cassel, C.-M., Särndal, C.-E., & Wretman, J, H. (1977). *Foundations of inference in survey sampling.* New York: Wiley.

Madow, W. G. (1948). On the limiting distributions of estimates based on samples from finite universes. *Annals of Mathematical Statistics, 19*(4), 535–545.

Skinner, C. J., Holt, D., & Smith, T. M. F. (Eds.). (1989). *Analysis of complex surveys.* New York: Wiley.

SUPERVISOR

Survey research supervisors are tasked with two main responsibilities: managerial or administrative duties and research-specific duties. It is the supervisors who are responsible for ensuring projects are proceeding on schedule and are within budget, the research process is carried out with due regard for ethical obligations, and all research goals are satisfied. To do this, supervisors must have a firm grasp on the operations of their research firm, knowledge of the entire research process, and an understanding of business policies and practices. A comprehensive knowledge of the science of survey research is also very helpful to supervisors. In addition, direct experience with various survey tasks is an inherent necessity for survey research supervisors.

Administrative Duties

Research operation supervisors typically oversee a staff of department or area supervisors, administrative personnel, interviewers, and other research assistants. Department supervisors are often responsible for specific tasks, such as data collection, computer-assisted data collection programming, or data coding and editing. These supervisors are responsible for the day-to-day supervisory activities.

Proposals

Research supervisors are often tasked with the responsibility of helping to submit proposals. This can become an arduous activity with little promise of success. Typically for large contracts, multiple proposals for different projects must be submitted before a project is approved. It is beneficial for the supervisor to have a full-time staff member assisting with proposal submissions.

Budgetary

Budget is a primary concern for all organizations. Supervisors must have a clear picture of all operational costs affecting their department, including facility costs, payroll, and supply expenditures. Research supervisors may be responsible for estimating project costs and then ensuring actual costs fall within those projections.

Hiring

Supervisors are engaged in various aspects of the hiring process. This may include advertisement, application review, interviews with candidates, and often acting as the liaison between human resources and their data collection staff.

Staff Performance Evaluation

Performance evaluations are critical to the growth of an organization. Evaluations outline goals for individuals which, if carried out, can improve the organization's performance. It is imperative supervisors have in place an equitable and regular evaluation system.

Research Duties

Project Development

Research supervisors are often tasked with developing the operational features of projects from the ground up. They may work in cooperation with their client or with topical experts, as necessary, to develop the operationalization of the research design, questionnaire, and data processing stages. Of course, this varies greatly depending on the specific research firm or project. At times, research supervisors may be fulfilling only specific research requests such as data collection. This is often the case when research firms conduct data collection for government agencies.

Survey Design

Clear research objectives need to be set in advance of creating any research design. The target population and points of interest must be outlined. Question design is both a science and an art form and should be handled by the most experienced and knowledgeable people. Objectivity should be the goal of every question. This can be difficult when researching heated or political topics. Supervisors have the responsibility to make certain all these aspects of the survey design have been addressed and resolved before a project can begin data collection.

Sampling and Sample Size

Supervisors are responsible for the successful processing of the sample. This includes issuing new cases to interviewers on a timely basis, overseeing the system that sets callbacks and recontacts, sending out follow-up mailings; and making certain that the final sample size of completed interviews is accomplished within the needed time frame and, ideally, on budget. If problems arise during the field period, especially ones that were unanticipated by the researchers, it is the responsibility of supervisors to bring these problems immediately to the attention of their superiors and seek their immediate resolution. They must ensure that the solution is implemented properly, and they must monitor the effectiveness of the solution and provide continuous feedback to their superiors.

Timelines

Supervisors must ensure a realistic schedule is set at the beginning of the project and that this schedule is followed. Regular meetings with department supervisors provide up-to-date information on a project's progress. The research process seems to always have its share of troubles which inherently affects the calendar. When available, a buffer window should be built into the schedule to protect against unforeseen difficulties, and it is the supervisors' responsibility to see that this happens.

Interviewer Training and Monitoring

Developing, implementing, and maintaining a comprehensive interviewer training and monitoring system is a central task of research supervisors. Training and monitoring systems build flexibility into an organization in case unexpected absences or needs arise. Often it is the task of department supervisors to develop training materials for their respective research areas.

Jeff Toor

See also Interviewer Monitoring; Interviewer Training; Mode of Data Collection; Questionnaire Design; Research Design; Research Management; Sample Design; Sample Size; Supervisor-to-Interviewer Ratio; Survey Costs; Survey Ethics

Further Readings

Lavrakas, P. J. (1993). *Telephone survey methods: Sampling, selection, and supervision* (2nd ed.). Newbury Park, CA: Sage.

Rea, L., & Parker, L. (2005). *Designing and conducting survey research: A comprehensive guide.* San Francisco: Jossey-Bass.

Stouthamer-Loeber, M., & Bok van Kammen, W. (1995). *Data collection and management: A practical guide.* Thousand Oaks, CA: Sage.

Supervisor-to-Interviewer Ratio

This entry addresses the issue of how the average number of interviewers that are assigned to a survey supervisor affects data quality. There are many factors that affect survey interviewer performance and success. Individual skill set, training, experience, and questionnaire design all influence the ability of interviewers to gain cooperation and gather accurate data. The one ongoing factor that has a significant impact on data quality in surveys that are interviewer-administered is the interaction of the supervisor with the telephone interviewer. Sometimes called a monitor, coach, team lead, or project/section/floor supervisor, this staff position gives management the greatest leverage to influence the human aspect of such survey projects.

The supervisors of survey interviewers may fulfill many roles in a survey project, including any or all of the following:

- Monitor the quality of the data being collected.
- Motivate the interviewers to handle a very difficult job.
- Provide insight into how a study is going and what the problem areas are.
- Provide training to improve the interviewing skills of the interviewers.
- Supply input for the interviewer performance evaluation.

It is the supervisor who is in daily contact with the interviewers and who knows each interviewer's strengths and skills to be developed, maintained, or enhanced. The supervisor answers questions, guides interviewers through new or difficult processes, and sets the mood, pace, and outlook of the whole team. A supervisor who is positive, uplifting, professional, and supportive will increase retention of interviewers, improve data quality, and lower costs of the project. There have been many human resource studies that show employees are most influenced by their immediate supervisor to be happy in their jobs or to leave a job. To ensure the best results on survey projects, research management must not only select the right people to be motivating, inspiring supervisors but also determine the right ratio of interviewer to supervisor.

The right ratio for a project is the one that provides enough supervisory coverage to meet the above goals: retain interviewers, ensure good quality, and provide cost efficiencies. A ratio that is too high (e.g., $> 1:20$) for a project's needs will lead to too little interaction with interviewers, lower-quality data, and increased turnover. A ratio that is too low (e.g., 1:5 or less) for a project's needs will increase costs and may lower supervisory motivation due to boredom. To meet the challenge of determining the correct ratio for a project, research management can use a checklist of criteria questions.

Some suggested questions to help develop the right ratio include the following:

1. Is the study a new type of survey in its content, group to be sampled, procedures, or client/industry? If the interviewers are not experienced with the type of study being done, the supervisor-to-interviewer ratio should be lower than the normal benchmark (e.g., $< 1:10$).

2. Is the study an ongoing survey that will change very little, or will the questions, procedure, shifts, and sample change frequently? An ongoing study with few changes will need a lower ratio of supervisor to interviewer, but a survey with constantly changing requirements needs proportionally more supervision.

3. Does the study have very stringent or complex requirements, such as complicated sample quotas, sensitive or difficult selection criteria, or comprehensive validation? If there are other measurements besides real-time monitoring of interviewers' work and answering questions that must be tracked hourly, daily, or frequently within a shift by the supervisors, such as in the case of centralized telephone surveys, then a lower ratio is demanded.

4. Is the project a business-to-business study, or a social/political study that requires respondents who are professionals or executives, like doctors, lawyers, chief executive officers, and so forth? Interviewers will have to possess more professional skills on these projects and may need more guidance from supervisors on getting through gatekeepers and other obstacles. Surveys conducted with professionals or highly

affluent households or households with high-security access challenges often require a lower ratio than general consumer surveys.

5. Does an ongoing project typically have a high percentage of new or inexperienced interviewers? If a survey organization experiences a steady, high level of turnover and an influx of raw interviewers, the supervisor-to-interviewer ratio will need to be lower to support the development of this staff.

6. Is the study or project one that is audited by an independent group, or is there a third party that has oversight on the survey procedures and requirements, such as a government agency or industry watchdog committee? The project may need proportionally more supervisors to ensure compliance with the audit or oversight.

7. Does the client funding the project represent a major portion of the survey organization's business or is otherwise a high-profile client with heavy impact on the organization's success? If so, then management may allocate more supervision to make sure all aspects of the work are going well and according to client expectations.

8. What is the budget for the project? How was the bid costed out when the work was contracted? How much supervisory costs were built in? The manager may be restricted in what he or she can work with on the ratio by the cost expectations already set up by the company or the client.

Once all of these questions have been answered, the project management can derive the supervisory ratio best suited for that project. There has to be a beginning point, or benchmark, that the manager uses to develop the specific ratio. Although there is no one benchmark used by all survey research data collection centers, a common range of ratios for supervisor to interviewer in many commercial organizations that do interviewing is in the range of 1:15 to 1:20 of supervisor per interviewers. Starting with that range, the manager can work up or down in setting the ratio against the sample questions listed previously. In contrast, since the 1980s, Paul J. Lavrakas has advised that for high-quality supervision, this ratio for supervising telephone interviews should be more in the 1:8 to 1:10 range.

As an example, imagine an ongoing general consumer survey that changes only every 6 months and uses 60% or more experienced interviewers. This survey will probably be fine with a ratio of one supervisor to 15 interviewers (or more). In contrast, a new study on a complex technical issue, where all the interviewers are new and the respondent pool is sensitive, might require a ratio of one supervisor to 8 interviewers in the very beginning or if the study has short duration. Or, for example, an ongoing study that adds or changes questions every 3 or 4 days, that has complex sample quotas, and that has 40% experienced interviewer levels may well require a ratio of one supervisor to 10 to 12 interviewers.

The data collection manager can experiment with the ratio at the beginning of the project, observing the interaction of supervisors with interviewers, checking the data quality, and watching for problems and issues at first, to decide if the ratio is too high, too low, or just right. It is better to start out with a lower ratio (thus a more conservative, but also more expensive, ratio) if the manager has no experience with a particular set of survey conditions, and then raise the ratio (i.e., more interviewers per supervisor) if appropriate as the project progresses.

If still unsure after using the previously listed criteria questions, a research manager can consult other managers in the organization, seek out peers in the industry through association contact, or look for information in research industry association publications, guidelines, or training material. There are also courses on project management and field director management that a research manager can participate in for better understanding.

In the end, the research manager should rely on his or her own experiences, instincts about the project, and "eyeball" observations of the daily activity when the study first starts. Valuable information also can be obtained by asking both the supervisors and interviewers on the study for their thoughts on how the supervision is working. Every study will have its own dynamics as far as the supervisor-to-interviewer ratio is concerned; the wise manager will learn from past experience and from peer input what works best on various kinds of studies.

Kathy Pilhuj

See also Interviewer; Interviewer Monitoring; Supervisor; Validation

Further Readings

Lavrakas, P. J. (1993). *Telephone survey methods: Sampling, selection, and supervision* (2nd ed.). Newbury Park, CA: Sage.

SURVEY

Survey is a ubiquitous term that is used and understood differently depending on the context. Its definition is further complicated because it is used interchangeably as a synonym for other topics and activities listed under the broad classification of survey research or survey methods. There are multiple uses of the term *survey* that are relevant to particular linguistic applications. Survey is used as a noun when it refers to a document (e.g., fill out this survey) or a process (e.g., to conduct a survey); as an adjective (e.g., to use survey methods); or as a verb (e.g., to survey a group of people). *Survey* is used interchangeably with and strongly associated with the terms *poll* and *public opinion polling*, and survey methods are used to conduct a census—an enumeration of the total population. In addition to being used to identify a type of research tool, survey research is a subject that can be studied in an educational course or workshop, and it is an academic discipline for undergraduate and graduate degrees. This entry focuses on the basic definition from which these other uses of the term *survey* have evolved by outlining the essential elements of this term as it relates to the scientific study of people.

A survey is a research method used by social scientists (e.g., economists, political scientists, psychologists, and sociologists) to empirically and scientifically study and provide information about people and social phenomena. A survey is scientific because there is an established process that can be followed, documented, and replicated. This process is rigorous and systematic. The typical steps in the survey process are (a) problem formation, (b) hypothesis development, (c) research design, (d) sample design and selection, (e) questionnaire development, (f) data collection, (g) data analysis, (h) reporting and dissemination, and (i) application of information. Underscoring the complexity of a survey, each of these steps in the process also has a set of essential and accepted practices that is followed, documented, and replicated, and specific professional training is required to learn these practices. The documentation that accompanies a survey provides the information necessary to evaluate the survey results and to expand the understanding and analysis of the information provided from the survey. Sampling error and nonsampling error are two dimensions of survey error. Most scientific surveys could more accurately be called "sample surveys" because probability theory is used to scientifically select subgroups of the population to study, and there is a body of knowledge on acceptable statistical procedures for sampling and for calculating sampling error. Quantifying the nonsampling error associated with other steps in the survey process (e.g., question wording, interviewer effects, and item and unit nonresponse) is more challenging. Total survey error incorporates the error possible in any of the steps in the survey process. When the results of a survey are reported and, particularly, when people use survey results to make decisions, it is very important to review the documentation that describes how the survey was conducted so the quality of the data can be assessed.

A survey can be used to find out the opinions, attitudes, and behaviors of persons who are contacted to participate in the survey and to obtain other factual information about members of this population. (Surveys also can be conducted to study animals other than humans, such as buffalo in a game preserve; crops in a field; or inanimate objects, such as books in a library collection.) The information from individuals is then aggregated to provide a statistical profile of the survey population. Surveys are conducted by many types of organizations and researchers. Federal, state, and local government surveys are conducted to obtain information to guide public policy decisions, and some surveys are legislatively mandated to evaluate social programs. A well-known government survey is the U.S. Census, which attempts to collect information about every person in the United States. More typically, the government conducts sample surveys to learn about and monitor topics such as employment trends (Bureau of Labor Statistics) and health issues (Centers for Disease Control and Prevention and the National Center for Health Statistics). Surveys are used by academic researchers to test hypotheses such as those related to social behaviors (e.g., marriage and families, alcohol and drug consumption, preparation for retirement) and to conduct social experiments (e.g., cost-effectiveness of different interventions to prevent obesity). Corporations use surveys to make decisions about the products they invest in and bring into the marketplace and to determine customer satisfaction with these products after they have been purchased. Familiar to many households is the Nielsen TV Ratings survey, which monitors the public's use of television. The Gallup Poll and the Pew Research Center, as well as electronic and print news organizations (e.g., *New York Times/ CBS News* poll; *ABC News/Washington Post* poll) use surveys to provide timely profiles and to track public opinion about current issues. A prominent use of surveys is the pre-election polls that inform candidates and the public about important campaign issues.

Janice Ballou

See also Complex Sample Surveys; Poll; Research Design; Response Rates; Standard Definitions; Total Survey Error (TSE)

Further Readings

American Statistical Association. (n.d.). *What is a survey?* Retrieved April 19, 2008, from http://www.whatisa survey.info

Converse, J. M. (1987). *Survey research in the United States: Roots and emergence 1890–1960.* Berkeley: University of California Press.

Turner, C. F., & Martin, E. (Eds.). (1984). *Survey subjective phenomena* (Vol. 1). New York: Russell Sage Foundation.

Survey Costs

Survey costing is a complex process that balances a survey organization's financial objectives against the expenses associated with achieving or maintaining the scientific standards that govern validity and reliability, or quality, of the final product. Achieving optimum balance between budgetary and scientific goals requires that researchers first understand how survey operational components are related to costs and how changing each influences both data quality and budgetary outcomes.

It is important to separate survey costs (direct and indirect, variable and fixed) from survey price, as price includes costs plus profit, for those organizations that are for-profit. Profit does not necessarily have any relationship to cost other than being added to it to create total price. As a result, profit and price are not discussed in this entry.

Managerial Accounting

Managerial accounting defines the principles used to develop costs. It differs from financial accounting in that it is intended to provide insight for better organizational decision making. As such, managerial accounting has no standards, and its formulas and data are often unique to an organization. To learn more about managerial accounting, see the Institute of Management Accountants' Web site (www.imanet.org).

Much of what goes into managerial accounting is built on an organization's operations and is often proprietary and confidential. However, there are some basic concepts that are universal to costing in all survey operations. These concepts, and the costing principles derived from them, provide the foundation for any organization to understand and build its own managerial accounting system for survey costing and budget management. Understanding them helps researchers understand how their budget and costs are related to survey quality.

Managerial accounting uses six basic concepts to define costs:

1. Cost object: The thing managers want to know how to cost

2. Cost driver: Any factor that affects costs

3. Variable cost: A cost that changes in proportion to a *cost driver*

4. Fixed cost: A cost that does not change in total

5. Direct cost: Those costs traced to a cost object. These are usually, but not always, variable costs.

6. Indirect cost: Those costs allocated to a cost object. These are often, but not always, fixed costs.

What constitutes a fixed or variable cost changes by survey mode. What constitutes a direct or indirect cost can also change by mode of data collection, but usually less often. What is important to remember is that the determination is made by the cost drivers and object(s).

Some cost drivers are generally constant across all survey modes. General cost drivers that cross survey modes include the following:

- Number of completed interviews (*n* size)
- Topic
- Survey length
- Time in field
- Data manipulation
- Validation requirements
- Net effective incidence
- Desired response rate

- Analytical labor
- Travel to client

For example, if the cost object is a computer-assisted telephone interviewing (CATI) survey, cost drivers might include the following list of items:

- Length and complexity of CATI programming
- Number of open-ended questions and associated coding
- Desired data outputs and associated reporting

Once the cost drivers have been identified for a particular cost object, a list of direct and indirect costs associated with those cost drivers can be constructed. These cost categories will also usually be constant across organizations, although the actual costs associated with each can be highly variable. Using the CATI example, an organization might see the following direct and indirect costs:

Direct Costs:
- Interviewer labor
- Telephone long distance
- Production floor management
- CATI programming
- Cost of sample
- Data manipulation
- Manual reports

Indirect Costs:
- Telephone line charges
- Management
- Rent
- Insurance
- Technical infrastructure

For many organizations some costs tend to remain fixed regardless of survey size. These could include upper management, rent, insurance, technical infrastructure, manual reports, and data manipulation.

A closer look at the CATI example will demonstrate that the majority of direct and indirect costs for this mode are variable costs, meaning that their amount goes up or down based on the size of the survey sample. This is due primarily to the fluctuations in interviewer labor required. Interviewer and floor management labor, telephone long distance, and power are just a few of the variable costs tied to labor. Other variable costs, including cost of sample and CATI programming, are tied to survey length and sample size.

In contrast, consider an Internet survey. In addition to the general cost drivers outlined earlier, cost drivers for an Internet survey might include:

- Concurrency/bandwidth
- Data manipulation
- Manual reports
- Length and complexity of programming

It is important to remember that in some cases, whether a cost is variable or fixed depends on the organization's managerial accounting approach. Similarly, whether a cost is considered direct or indirect is a function of the accounting approach.

Rate Calculations

Because of the dominance of variable costs in survey data collection modes which rely on interviewing labor (in-person and telephone), formulas to assist in calculating production accuracy have been developed to predict costs for these modes. This is true particularly of survey modes that are applied to difficult-to-reach populations and those with large sample sizes. In these cases, variable direct costs can fluctuate tremendously with the slightest change in specification.

There are three fundamental formulas used to predict cost for surveys that include interviewing labor. These are (1) net effective incidence rate, (2) respondent cooperation rate, and (3) production rate.

These three rates often have different names, depending on the country or even which professional association's standards are being employed within an organization. It is not the intent here to suggest that any one association's or organization's labels are preferred.

Fortunately, the research industry in the United States has reached a point where the mathematical formulas for calculating net effective incidence and respondent cooperation rate are generally agreed upon. Production rates are derived using incidence and respondent cooperation calculations. They are managerial accounting equations and, as such, are proprietary and confidential. However, a universal standard for CATI surveys is offered here as an example and as a baseline for any organization or researcher building an accurate production rate.

Incidence is another way of saying frequency of a desired characteristic occurring in some group of people. It is sometimes expressed as eligibility. There are as many names for incidence as there are types of research. The term *incidence* is business language used primarily in commercial research, though the concept and mathematics involved are universal to all forms of survey research.

What is important to remember from a costing perspective is that there may be a difference between incidence of a desired characteristic within the universe versus among the selected population from which the sample frame is drawn. If the sample frame is poorly drawn, there may yet be another difference between the selected population and the sample frame.

Net effective incidence is one industry term used to mean the percentage of respondents known to be eligible for the survey in the sample frame, meaning that they have been qualified through contact. *Net effective incidence* is the term used by companies whose business language is influenced primarily by the standards of Marketing Research Association (MRA) and the Council of American Survey Research Organizations (CASRO), among others. Eligibility calculations are the equivalent for those organizations whose business language is driven by the American Association for Public Opinion Research (AAPOR) formulas.

Net effective incidence is a critical variable in the production rate equation. It is therefore important to accurately estimate what the net effective incidence rate will be when estimating costs. The calculation for actual net effective incidence is effectively a function of multiplying the percentage of the sample frame eligible for each desired criterion by the percentages for other desired criteria. This can be expressed as

$$Q_1 * Q_2 * Q_3 * Q_4 = Net\ Effective\ Incidence.$$

It is important to note that for costing purposes net effective incidence is based on actual eligibility rates of screened respondents only. Initial estimates must be based on the estimated or projected eligibility rate of screened respondents. This difference makes knowing in advance the eligibility differences of the desired universe, population, and sample frame design used important to survey costing.

Net effective incidence also can be used to make estimates of screenings that will be required to achieve minimum sample sizes by multiplying incidence by minimum sample size desired. This is sometimes referred to as *net incidence*. It is a useful calculation to survey costing in predicting sample and labor requirements, for example. It is important to note, however, that achieved cooperation rate (discussed later in this entry) also influences how much sample and labor are required. The formula for the net incidence calculation, using a prediction of cooperation rate, would be

$$(Q_1 * Q_2 * Q_3 * Q_4) * Cooperation\ Rate$$
$$= Net\ Incidence.$$

For those organizations that have response rates as a cost driver, total projected interviewing labor effort to meet a response rate goal can also be derived from this calculation by building on net incidence.

Cooperation rate is a term used widely throughout the research industry and has various definitions based upon which association standards are being used. The use of different definitions will yield different rates from the same formula, so it is important to note which definition is being applied in any production formula.

The MRA defines cooperation rate as the percentage of all qualified respondents who agree to complete an interview. The AAPOR has four definitions, all derived from a definition that the rate is the proportion of all cases interviewed of all eligible units ever contacted. CASRO, the Advertising Research Foundation, and the CMOR (Council on Marketing and Opinion Research) all use the AAPOR definition. The definition used here is that of the proportion of all cases interviewed of all eligible units ever contacted, or the AAPOR COOP1 formula expressed as

$$COOP1 =$$
$$\frac{Interviews}{(Interviews + Partial\ Interviews + Refusals + Other)}.$$

Where live interviewing is involved, cooperation rates are influenced by the skill of the interviewing staff, the topic of the survey, the length of the study, and the population being interviewed. As a result, the rates themselves are unique to the operation conducting the work and often proprietary. Cost estimates must be built using cooperation rate data from past performance inside the same operational unit on previous, similar surveys with similar populations. Once a survey is under way, more accurate projections can be made from the survey's own performance for cost control purposes.

Benchmarks are available for some types of general population research. CMOR publishes average industry cooperation rates annually for CATI research.

With cooperation rate and net effective incidence in hand, a researcher or organization can accurately estimate production rate: the holy grail of labor-intensive, variable-cost survey modes. The values for variables in production rate formulas are unique to individual production operations. They are based on management effectiveness, labor quality, operational standards, quality control standards, and even weather. They are also closely guarded to maintain competitiveness.

However, the variables themselves in the production rate formula are universal. A CATI production rate formula is given here as an example.

$$\frac{(60 \ minutes - B)}{L + S((1/I) - 1) + W/(C * I) + X}$$

B = break, brief, coach time in minutes (any idle time)

L = length of one survey in minutes (including screener)

S = average time to screen per survey in minutes

W = wait time between contacts in minutes

C = cooperation rate as %

I = net effective incidence as %

X = wrap time per interview in minutes

The nature of the variable labels makes clear the degree to which operational and management factors influence survey costing as much as survey design in projects using live interviewers. Break and coaching time are functions of operations management. Wait time is driven by technology. Survey length is a function of design.

Production rates are designed to derive a number of completed surveys per hour (or in some cases, a number of hours per completed survey). Having a solid estimate or mid-term projection of this figure allows for accurate cost estimating for variable data collection costs. Even in cases where live interviewing labor is not required, one or more rates are often an appropriate method for estimating some variable, direct costs (e.g., cooperation rates for self-administered surveys via mail or Internet to project mail-out rate to receive sufficient returns on schedule).

There are live interviewing environments where these formulas need be modified or even eliminated. Some countries of the world pay CATI or face-to-face interviews by the piece rather than per hour. In these cases, net effective incidence and cooperation rate may become less important cost drivers, affecting direct variable cost of management labor and sample acquisition, for example, but not interviewing labor.

The use of these formulas, as with all other costing calculations, is dependent on the cost drivers involved.

Estimating and Controlling Costs

Derived production rates per hour allow organizations and researchers to project estimated or actual variable, direct costs for surveys. To turn those hours into a budget requires the application of costs per hour. How those costs per hour are derived is as variable as there are managerial accounting systems.

Fixed and indirect costs are added as line items to variable and direct costs to build an entire budget. In others they are allocated by the hour. In some cases, these costs are estimated at their actual usage by a specific project. In some cases, they are allocated proportionally to entire labor hours. In yet other cases, they are derived from estimated company expenses which are included in a markup ratio to project expense.

Researchers need to understand how their organizations' accounting rules affect the way their costing is designed in order to control and modify their budgets most effectively. As a study progresses, estimated rates and the budget built on them can be replaced with actual rates to project final costs. When a budget shortfall is projected, researchers can then dig into all the cost drivers that go into the costing equation to find ways to realign costs while balancing quality considerations.

Some common approaches to budget realignment include the following:

- Increase field time, which can boost cooperation rates and boost production.
- Decrease total sample size, screening criteria, or response rate goals to reduce labor and sample required.
- Change the proportionality of samples that are not reflective of the population's natural characteristics, thereby increasing net effective incidence.
- Reduce production quality control standards, thereby reducing floor management labor costs.
- Move work to an operation with less expensive costs.
- Incentivize labor to produce at a more rapid rate.
- Renegotiate price with operations supplier.

Net effective incidence deserves special note here. The relationship between incidence and production rate is not linear, but rather curved. Low incidences have much lower rate of completion per hour than high incidences. As a result, the most effective way to increase production rates in low incidence studies is to eliminate screener questions.

Of course, eliminating screeners, as well as most of the other options listed here has direct and significant impacts on survey validity and reliability. Researchers must use their best judgment and understanding of how costs are derived and controlled to design and manage cost-effective yet scientifically useful research.

Karl G. Feld

See also American Association for Public Opinion Research (AAPOR); Coding; Computer-Assisted Telephone Interviewing (CATI); Cooperation Rate; Council for Marketing and Opinion Research (CMOR); Council of American Survey Research Organizations (CASRO); Eligibility; Interviewer Productivity; Mode of Data Collection; Quality Control; Research Management; Total Design Method (TDM)

Further Readings

American Association for Public Opinion Research: http://www.aapor.org

American Association for Public Opinion Research. (2004). *Standard definitions: Final dispositions of case codes and outcomes rates for surveys.* Lenexa, KS: Author.

Council of American Survey Research Organizations: http://www.casro.org

Council of American Survey Research Organizations/ Marketing Research Association (1995). *Incidence guidelines.* Port Jefferson, NY, & Rocky Hull, CT: MRA-CASRO.

Dawson, K. (2004). *The call center handbook.* San Francisco: CMP Books.

Feld, K., & Haynes, D. (2004, October). *Costing quantitative live interview and Web data collection.* Short course taught for the Marketing Research Association, Richmond, VA.

Institute of Management Accountants: http://www.imanet.org

Marketing Research Association: http://www.mra-net.org

SURVEY ETHICS

Survey ethics encompasses a set of ethical procedures that are intended to guide all survey researchers. These procedures are essential to the research process so that explicit care is taken that (a) no harm is done to any survey respondent, and (b) no survey respondent is unduly pressured or made to feel obligated to participate in a survey. This entry discusses informed consent, the rights of respondents, and the social responsibility of researchers.

Informed Consent

The ethics of survey research and its importance often are not covered thoroughly in research methods textbooks and courses. However, the acquisition of knowledge through survey research requires public trust and, therefore, researchers must adhere to ethical practices and principles involving human subjects. Most governmental bodies throughout the industrialized world have established ethical guidelines for conducting survey research. Research proposals often are subject to regulatory review by one or more ethics boards (e.g., an institutional review board) that have been established to ensure that the ethical guidelines set forth by the governing body will be followed. In addition to regulatory bodies overseeing research activities involving human subjects, most professional organizations and associations also have established guidelines and standards of conduct for conducting research that are expected to be maintained by organizational members. The primary tenet among these governing bodies and organizations, as it relates to carrying out research on human subjects in an ethical manner, is that the researcher be cognizant of research participants' rights and minimize the possibility of risk (i.e., avoid exposing research participants to the possibility of physical or psychological harm, discomfort, or danger).

To that end, central to all research ethics policy is that research participants must give their informed consent voluntarily. The purpose of informed consent is to reasonably ensure that survey respondents understand the nature and the purpose of the survey, what is expected of them if they participate, the expected length of time necessary for them to complete the survey (and, if a longitudinal study, the frequency with which their participation will be requested), how the data will be utilized, and their rights as research participants, including their right to confidentiality. Based on the information provided by the researcher, potential respondents can then make an informed determination as to whether they are willing to participate in a given study (i.e., give their consent). In addition to the willingness to participate, it is fundamental that potential respondents have the competence to understand why the study is being conducted and what their rights and responsibilities are as respondents in order to participate.

Survey research among children and adolescents under the age of 18 requires parental or guardian consent before the researcher can even speak with the juvenile. Frequently parental consent must be given in writing through use of either an active or passive consent form. Also, some ethics boards may require, in addition to parental consent, the assent of juvenile participants. If assent is required of juvenile participants, they must also have the capacity to comprehend the purpose of the study and their rights and responsibilities as participants.

Respondents' Rights

Respondents' rights are paramount to any ethical survey research project and an integral part of informed consent. Researchers have an obligation to their subjects to minimize the possibility of risk. Granted, respondents participating in the bulk of survey research are not generally at a high risk of physical or psychological harm. However, some survey research topics are very sensitive in nature and may cause a considerable amount of discomfort for some respondents. In addition, researchers are ethically bound to report any child abuse that is suspected. Therefore, it is essential to minimize risk through a thorough advance disclosure of any possible harm or discomfort that may result from survey participation. If there are compelling scientific reasons that respondents must be kept "blind" to, or entirely deceived about, some of the aspects of a study before they give their consent, and while the study is being conducted (e.g., an experimental design would be compromised if the respondents knew it was being conducted), then it is the responsibility of the researcher to debrief the respondents about any deception they may have experienced, even if it can be argued that the deception was trivial in nature. It also is the responsibility of the researcher to "undo any harm" he or she may have caused associated with any deception or other withholding of information.

Furthermore, respondents are afforded additional rights that also minimize any risks associated with their participation, including the right that their responses will be kept confidential and the right to privacy. Confidentiality protects respondents' identities so that their participation in a given study cannot be determined and, likewise, ensures that their responses are not linked to them personally. The importance of maintaining confidentiality is closely related to minimizing risk. For example, survey data on a study of criminal behavior could be subject to subpoena, but if identifier data are never collected or are destroyed, the individuals and their responses cannot be identified. Thus, the data collected through the survey research process should not contain identifying information about individual respondents, and data records should be securely stored and destroyed as soon as is appropriate.

Survey research is intrusive in nature: Respondents are asked to reveal personal information about themselves, their behaviors, and their beliefs. Thus, researchers must consider respondents' right to privacy when administering surveys. The right to privacy does not suggest that personal questions should not be asked of respondents (as long as they are relevant to the study being conducted), but it protects respondents from disclosing such information if they choose not to respond. In other words, respondents' right to privacy is the freedom afforded survey respondents to control the personal information that is disclosed, under what circumstances they will do so, and with whom such information is shared. Subjects must be informed that their participation is voluntary, that their refusal to participate will not involve any penalty, and that they may skip any question they do not feel comfortable answering or discontinue their participation at any time.

In some instances, respondents are provided incentives for their participation in a given study; however, this does not negate their right to skip certain questions or end their involvement in the study at their will. Furthermore, incentives should never be used to "coerce" (even subtly) a respondent to participate in a study or to answer a specific question if he or she really does not want to do so. Ethical researchers do not force, coerce, "seduce," trick, or otherwise threaten potential subjects when attempting to gain cooperation or administer a survey.

Social Responsibility

Social responsibility is key to survey ethics. Research findings contribute to the larger body of knowledge for purposes of better understanding social behavior and improving the quality of life among members of society. Thus, researchers have an obligation of being forthright not only with research participants but also with society in general. Deception in research practices and principles can lead to public distrust and bring even the best research under public and professional scrutiny. Ethics boards ensure, in principle, that a given study meets ethical guidelines. However, there is little ethical oversight once data collection has begun. As such, regulation and oversight through audits of individual researchers' or research firms' ethics policies and practices regarding survey research could potentially decrease public deception and potential harm.

Researchers have an obligation to protect and respect not only the rights of research participants, but to society as a whole as well. Informed consent outlines the information necessary for respondents to make voluntary informed decisions about participating in a given study based on their understanding of what the study is about, how the data will be used, and what their rights and responsibilities are as participants. Research participants' rights are paramount when conducting survey research. If the study cannot be designed ethically, then it should not be conducted. The continuation of survey research as an invaluable tool for gathering information is contingent upon maintaining public confidence which can only be accomplished through upholding ethical practices and principles.

Lisa M. Gilman

See also Confidentiality; Consent Form; Debriefing; Deception; Ethical Principles; Incentives; Informed Consent; Institutional Review Board (IRB); Privacy; Voluntary Participation

Further Readings

Areen, J. (1991). Legal constraints on research on children. In B. Stanley & J. E. Sieber (Eds.), *The ethics of research on children and adolescents*. Newbury Park, CA: Sage.

Israel, M., & Hay, I. (2006). *Research ethics for social scientists*. Thousand Oaks, CA: Sage.

Sales, B. D., & Folkman, S. (Eds.). (2000). *Ethics in research with human participants*. Washington, DC: American Psychological Association.

Sieber, J. E. (1992). *Planning ethically responsible research: A guide for students and internal review boards*. Newbury Park, CA: Sage.

SURVEY METHODOLOGY

Survey Methodology is a peer-reviewed journal published twice yearly by Statistics Canada. The journal publishes articles dealing with various aspects of statistical development relevant to a statistical agency, such as design issues in the context of practical constraints, use of different data sources and collection techniques, total survey error, survey evaluation, research in survey methodology, time-series analysis, seasonal adjustment, demographic methods, data integration, estimation and data analysis methods, and general survey systems development. Emphasis is placed on development and evaluation of specific methodologies as applied to data collection, data processing, estimation, or analysis.

The journal was established in 1975, as a Statistics Canada in-house journal intended primarily to "provide a forum in a Canadian context for publication of articles on the practical applications of the many aspects of survey methodology." Its basic objectives and policy remained unchanged for about 10 years. During this period, however, the journal grew to the point that pressing demands and interests could not be met within the framework established at its inception.

In 1984 several major changes were introduced, which included broadening the scope of the editorial policy and expansion of the editorial board. A separate management board was also established. The editorial board now consists of the editor, a deputy editor, approximately 30 associate editors, and six assistant editors. M. P. Singh was the editor of the journal from the beginning until his death in 2005. The current editor is John Kovar. The associate editors are all leading researchers in survey methods and come from academic institutions, government statistical agencies, and private-sector firms around the world.

Since its December 1981 issue, one unique feature of the journal is that it is fully bilingual, with submissions being accepted in either English or French and all published papers being fully translated. The French name of the journal is *Techniques d'Enquête*.

From time to time the journal has included special sections containing a number of papers on a common theme. Topics of these special sections have included, among others, census coverage error, small area estimation, composite estimation in surveys, and longitudinal surveys and analyses. The June 2002 issue of the journal included a special section in honor of Leslie Kish.

In December 1999 and June 2000, *Survey Methodology* celebrated its 25th anniversary with two special issues containing invited papers from several prominent statisticians. The lead paper in the December issue (volume 25, number 2) by Richard Platek, founding chairman of the management board, gives an overview of the gradual evolution of the journal from its humble beginnings to a well-known international publication.

In 2000 the *Survey Methodology* journal, in cooperation with the American Statistical Association and Westat, established an annual invited paper series in honor of Joseph Waksberg. Each year a prominent survey researcher is chosen by a committee to write a paper reviewing the development and current state of a significant topic in the field of survey methodology. Winners of the Waksberg Award to date are Gad Nathan, Wayne Fuller, Tim Holt, Norman Bradburn, J. N. K. Rao, Alastair Scott, and Carl-Erik Särndal.

The journal is available on the Statistics Canada Web site, starting with the year 2000 issue up to the most current issue. Prior issues are available on request. Printed copies of the journal can be obtained by paid subscription.

John Kovar

See also Statistics Canada

Further Readings

Statistics Canada: http://www.statcan.ca

Survey Sponsor

The sponsor of a survey is responsible for funding part or all of the sampling and data collection activities and typically has first or exclusive rights to the data. Often, survey sponsors do not have the in-house capacity (i.e., facilities or interviewing staff) to administer a survey and, as a result, contract these data collection activities to a third party. These third-party organizations focus on survey administration, such as selecting the sample, interviewing and distributing questionnaires, and data entry and analyses. Sometimes these third parties (i.e., survey research

firms) are asked to provide expertise in questionnaire design and data analysis and asked to draft an analytic report. These contracted services do not negate the survey sponsor's exclusive (or first) rights to the survey data. Typically, a respondent is informed of both parties involved in conducting the survey—the data collection body and the survey sponsor. Identifying these different parties may impact response patterns.

Effects of Survey Sponsorship on Survey Accuracy

Several theories explain why survey sponsorship may affect response patterns, including the response rate, data quality, and responses. Government-sponsored research may produce higher response rates, because people think their responses are required by law and think that the government can compel a response to the survey, such as in population censuses. (In general, survey participation tends to be voluntary, but in some instances, survey participation is required by federal law in the United States and elsewhere.) These perceptions could impact responses and data quality. Perceptions that responses are required may lead to less-motivated respondents completing the survey, which may impact data quality, leading to more skipped questions or less-thoughtful responses. In addition, respondents may respond to these surveys differently when the government sponsor is identified or made salient because they fear that their responses may affect their access to government services. Alternatively, other people may be more likely to respond to government-sponsored surveys and provide more complete responses because they believe these survey findings are more likely to have a direct effect on them through policy changes.

Government and university-sponsored surveys may produce higher response rates merely because these institutions have higher prestige, are a moral authority, or are more "official" than other types of sponsors, such as private-sector firms. People may also be more willing to participate in government or university-sponsored surveys because they recognize that these types of surveys are not disguised sales calls. Furthermore, university-sponsored surveys may produce higher response rates, as well as more complete and thoughtful responses, because people believe they are contributing to the advancement of science and knowledge.

Private-sector companies and politicians, for example, share concerns about response bias and response quality, but they also have concerns around disclosing their sponsorship of a survey. These types of sponsors may be reluctant to disclose themselves as a sponsor to a sampled respondent—at least prior to the survey being completed—fearing that this information may bias survey responses, with respondents conveying their opinions about the sponsor rather than the survey questions. In addition, private-sector companies and politicians may be reluctant to identify their sponsorship out of fear that their competitors may learn about their proprietary market research.

Prior to the 1990s, several experiments were conducted related to the effects of the survey sponsor on response rates, data quality, and response bias. In general, the studies found that government or university sponsorship yielded higher response rates compared to sponsorship by a commercial organization. This body of research is not consistent about whether university sponsorship or government sponsorship produces a higher response rate. A well-cited British study by Christopher Scott suggested that government sponsorship yielded a slightly higher response rate over the London School of Economics or British Market Research Bureau (a commercial agency). Thomas A. Heberlein and Robert Baumgartner's meta-analysis in the 1970s found that government-sponsored research produced higher initial response rates, but controlling for topic saliency and other factors, sponsorship had no significant effect on the final response rate. John Goyder's test of the Heberlein and Baumgartner model of predicting response rates, using a more expansive database of research, found that government-sponsored surveys have significantly higher response rates.

Although many studies document differences in response rates depending on sponsorship, many researchers remain unconvinced that survey sponsor has a significant effect on response patterns. The advantage of noncommercial sponsorship (university, government) may diminish if the survey sponsor is identified as the survey organization conducting the survey (rather than a separate entity that is paying for the study). Commercial survey research firms (when no additional sponsor is identified) may produce slightly lower response rates than university-administered surveys, but these differences may not be statistically significant.

Although research tends to suggest an effect of sponsorship on response rates, the effects of sponsorship on data quality is more evenly split between finding no significant differences and finding that university sponsorship improved data quality by reducing item nonresponse. Several studies have compared survey responses under different sponsorship conditions to determine whether the responses differ, depending on the sponsor. This body of research suggests some small differences in responses to specific questions, but overall, responses to the survey tend to not differ, depending on sponsorship condition. In sum, sponsorship effects on response patterns may be more pronounced in participants' decisions whether to participate in a survey rather than in their responses to survey questions.

Shelley Boulianne

See also Bias; Missing Data; Response Rates

Further Readings

Goyder, J. C. (1982). Further evidence on factors affecting response rates to mailed questionnaires. *American Sociological Review, 47*(4), 550–553.

Heberlein, T. A., & Baumgartner, R. (1978). Factors affecting response rates to mailed questionnaires: A quantitative analysis of the published literature. *American Sociological Review, 43*(4), 447–462.

Scott, C. (1969). Research on mail surveys. *Journal of the Royal Statistical Society, 124 Series A, Part 2*, 143–191.

SYSTEMATIC ERROR

Systematic errors result from bias in measurement or estimation strategies and are evident in the consistent over- or underestimation of key parameters. Good survey research methodology seeks to minimize systematic error through probability-based sample selection and the planning and execution of conscientious survey design. There are two key sources of systematic error in survey research: sample selection and response bias.

In the context of survey research, systematic errors may be best understood through a comparison of samples in which respondents are randomly selected (i.e., a probability sample) and samples in which respondents are selected because they are easily accessible (i.e., a convenience sample). Consider, for example, a research project in which the analysts wish to assess attitudes about a town's public library. One way to proceed might be to post students in front of the main entrance to the library and to have them survey individuals as they enter and leave the library. Another strategy would be to randomly assign households to participate in the survey, in such a way that every household in the town has a nonzero probability of participating, and to send students to the households to conduct the interview.

How would the results of the survey differ as a consequence of these differences in sample selection? One might reasonably expect that the first research design, in which the sample is composed entirely of current library patrons, yields a sample that uses the library more frequently and, as a consequence, has more favorable views about the library and its importance to the community than does the larger, more representative sample of the entire town. In this case, the selection bias inherent in the convenience sample of library patrons would lead the researchers to systematically overestimate the use of, and support for, the town's public library.

Although in the library example, systematic error resulted from the selection bias in the sampling mechanism, William G. Cochran, Frederick G. Mosteller, and John Tukey state that systematic errors more often result from bias in measurement. In the context of the physical sciences, it is easy to imagine a scale that consistently overestimates the weight of whatever it measures by five units. There are analogies to this scale in survey research: In election surveys, for example, researchers often want to identify the issues or problems most important to voters and assess their effect on voting decisions. Typically, survey items about the most important issue are asked as the open-ended question, *What do you think is the most important problem facing this country today?* An alternative format uses a closed-ended question, in which respondents are presented with a list of issues and asked how important they perceive each issue to be. The proportion of the sample that reports that they consider an issue to be "very important" in the closed-ended format is typically much larger than the proportion of the sample who identify the issue when asked the open-ended question. Social desirability, priming, and frame effects also shift responses in predictable ways and complicate the measurement of attitudes and opinions. Similarly, question structure and order effects can generate spurious patterns in survey responses that undermine the ability to evaluate public opinion.

Good survey research methodology strives to minimize both the selection bias and response bias that induce systematic error.

Systematic Error and Bias

The concept of systematic error is closely related to the more general statistical understanding of bias. To illustrate this relationship more concretely, suppose one is interested in estimating the population mean of the distribution of opinion on an issue that can be measured in a continuous way (e.g., the amount of funding to be devoted to a particular policy). After drawing a random sample of respondents and soliciting their opinion, a researcher estimates the sample mean and its variance. Under what conditions can the population mean be inferred from the sample mean, when considering the distribution of opinion on the issue the researcher cares about? The sample mean will be a misleading representation of the population mean if systematic error is incorporated in the sample selection mechanism—if the sample over- or underrepresents a subset of the population—or if the questions are constructed in a way that shifts responses away from the respondents' true opinions. Under these conditions, even if the researchers repeated the exercise of sampling and interviewing an infinite number of times, the sample means will never equal the population mean in expectation. Thus, as this example illustrates, bias can be attributed to systematic error in the measurement or estimation of key parameters.

Karen Long Jusko

See also Bias; Convenience Sampling; Probability Sample; Random Error; Response Bias; Self-Selection Bias

Further Readings

Cochran, W. G., Mosteller, F., & Tukey, J. W. (1954). Principles of sampling. *Journal of the American Statistical Association, 49*(265), 13–35.

Green, D. P., & Citrin, J. (1994). Measurement error and the structure of attitudes: Are positive and negative judgments opposites? *American Journal of Political Science, 38*(1), 256–281.

Schuman, H., Ludwig, J., & Krosnick, J. A. (1986). The perceived threat of nuclear war, salience, and open questions. *Public Opinion Quarterly, 50,* 519–536.

Systematic Sampling

Systematic sampling is a random method of sampling that applies a constant interval to choosing a sample of elements from the sampling frame. It is in common use in part because little training is needed to select one. Suppose a sample of size n is desired from a population of size $N = nk$. Systematic sampling uses a random number r between 1 and k to determine the first selection. The remaining selections are obtained by taking every kth listing thereafter from the ordered list to yield the sample of size n. Because it designates the number of records to skip to get to the next selection, k is referred to as the *skip interval.*

Systematic sampling is particularly desirable when on-site staff, rather than a data collection vendor, select the sample. For example, one-page sampling instructions can be developed for a survey of mine employees that explain how the mine operator is to order the employees and then make the first and subsequent sample selections using a pre-supplied random starting point. Systematic sampling is also useful in sampling on a flow basis, such as sampling clients entering a facility to obtain services such as emergency food assistance or health care. In this situation, the facility manager is approached to determine how many clients might visit in the specified time period. This population estimate $\hat{N}$ is used to determine the skip interval k based upon the desired sample n of clients from the facility. At the end of specified time period, the actual population N of clients is recorded.

Frequently, the population size N, together with the desired sample size n, results in a skip interval k that is a real number as opposed to an integer value. In this case, the simplest solution is to round k down to create a skip interval that is an integer. This approach results in a variable sample size (n or $n + 1$), but it is preferable for use by nontechnical staff. Alternately, the list can be regarded as circular, with a random number between 1 and N selected and then a systematic sample of size n selected using the integer value of k obtained by rounding down. An easily programmable option is to select a real number between 1 and k as the random starting point and then continue adding the real number k to the random starting point to get n real numbers, which are rounded down to integers to determine the records selected for the sample.

Systematic sampling can be viewed as a form of implicit stratification. Conceptually, the frame is split into n zones each of size k and one selection made from each zone. When the frame is sorted by key analysis domains prior to selection, this implicit stratification results in a sample that is close to the results of stratification with proportional allocation. Care must be taken in ordering the sample and in using a pre-ordered frame when systematic sampling is planned. A frame sorted by age, for instance, could produce samples that skew young or skew old, depending on the random start. The worst case scenario is a list that has an underlying periodicity to the observations, and this periodicity corresponds to the skip interval.

Unlike stratified sampling, systematic sampling is not independently executed across the zones or implicit strata. The initial selection from the first zone determines the selections made from the remaining $n - 1$ zones. Hence, systematic sampling can also be viewed as a form of cluster sampling, where the random start identifies a cluster of size n from the total of k possible clusters. The precision of survey estimates can be improved by sorting the frame prior to sample selection to get the benefits of implicit stratification and to create systematic clusters whose units are representative of the entire population of units.

Direct calculation of the variance requires that the systematic sampling process be replicated, so that it can be treated as a clustered design where each replicate is a cluster. Without replication, the variances of estimates derived from systematic samples are not estimable. Analysts typically approximate the variance by making assumptions about the ordered frame from which the systematic sample was selected. A common practice is to treat the systematic sample as if it were a simple random sample. Random ordering of the frame prior to systematic selection would have produced a simple random sample, for instance. This simple random sample assumption may over- or underestimate the variance of survey estimates depending on the intracluster correlation induced by the frame ordering. This approach is likely to produce conservative estimates (overestimates) of the variance for well-designed systematic samples with judiciously chosen sort variables that induce beneficial implicit stratification.

Sometimes, it may be appropriate to regard the systematically sampled units as being derived from a stratified sample with two units per strata. The systematic ordering of the population is used to define these pseudo-strata. This technique is most commonly used when systematic sampling has been used to select a probability-proportional-to-size sample, such as primary sampling units for an area household survey. Here, the skip interval and random starting point for the systematic sample are based upon the units' size measures, which are accumulated across units to yield the aggregated total M.

Brenda G. Cox

See also Cluster Sample; n; N; Probability Proportional to Size (PPS) Sampling; Proportional Allocation to Strata; Sampling Frame; Simple Random Sample; Stratified Sampling

Further Readings

Buckland, W. R. (1951). A review of the literature on systematic sampling. *Journal of the Royal Statistical Society B 13*, 208–215.

Iachan, I. (1982). Systematic sampling: A critical review. *International Statistical Review*, *50*, 293–303.

T

TAILORING

Tailoring is a term that is used in different ways in social behavioral research. It often is used to describe health behavior and health education messages that have been crafted to appeal to and influence the individual, with the intent of modifying the individual's attitudes and behavior such that he or she engages in healthier endeavors. A message that is tailored is a personalized message that attempts to speak to the individual *as an individual* and not as a member of any group or stratum. Additionally, a tailored message attempts to create a customized, personally meaningful communication—based on knowledge (data and information) about individuals. A more formal definition comes from M. W. Kreuter and C. S. Skinner and indicates that a tailored message is any combination of information or change strategies intended to reach one specific person, based on characteristics that are unique to that person, related to the outcome of interest, and have been derived from an individual assessment. This definition highlights the two features of a tailored health promotion intervention that distinguish it from other commonly used approaches: (a) Its collection of messages or strategies is intended for a particular person rather than a group of people, and (b) these messages or strategies are based on individual-level factors that are related to the behavioral outcome of interest. Tailoring techniques are utilized also by marketing practitioners but with the marketing goal of selling consumer goods and services.

Tailored messages can be based on age, sex, educational attainment, and other sociodemographics, as well as cognitive, motivational, and behavioral attributes. These messages usually refer to interventions created specifically for individuals with characteristics unique to them, and they are usually based on data collected from them as well.

Tailoring Versus Targeting

A closely related term that is often used interchangeably with tailoring is *targeting*. Although controversy and debate over definitions continue, the two strategies are clearly distinguishable. Targeting involves identifying a specific population, such as a group with a high rate of smoking prevalence, and designing a program, intervention, or marketing campaign that includes specific messages or materials intended for that group of smokers. For example, a targeted health message might attempt to influence these people to stop smoking. So, this kind of message can be thought of as focusing on the group attribute of smoking behavior, at least in terms of how the intervention could be focused. Tailoring, on the other hand, could be an approach to health messaging that could also be utilized, but one that focuses on more individual attributes. If health organizations were able to discern people's ages, their sex, or educational attainment, then health messaging might be made more "personalized" and thus more "meaningful" to the individual by creating more focused messages. The point where a group attribute becomes an individual attribute is when the message begins to be segmented or subdivided by individual attributes. While the point where that occurs still may be debated, targeted interventions can be thought of as strategies based on group-level variables and tailored interventions as strategies and messages that are customized based on individual-level variables.

Theoretical Approach

Tailored communications are not theory-specific, in that many different kinds of theory might be used to anchor an approach to attitudinal or behavioral modification. The important point is that a theoretical approach is utilized, as a systematic means to achieve a desired end, and different theories are best used as a basis for tailoring in relation to different behaviors and audiences. The parameters of a message—the quality, appearance, literacy level, and packaging of tailored communications—can vary widely. In the ideal, tailored materials eliminate all superfluous information and just transmit the right message to the right individual, through the right channel at the right time. Of course, reality is far from that ideal, as few behaviors have been subject to enough rigorous theory-based research. It is the utilization of theory that guides a reasoned and grounded approach that clearly delineates what is superfluous and what part of the message contains the "active ingredients," that is, the parts that get people to think, act, buy, cooperate with a survey request, and so forth. Moreover, tailored materials can be designed well or poorly. So, just because tailoring is used as a messaging technique does not mean that other elements of creative design become meaningless. In fact, those other elements are likely to become more important. Tailoring holds great promise and great challenges as well. For example, tailoring population-level interventions so that they also are personalized at the individual level could have a wide-scale impact on public health outcomes.

Application to Public Health

Using tailored health messages is an emerging strategic area for health communications, which attempts to maximize overall effects by striking an effective balance between personalization and cost. Multiple messages can be delivered over time, and because communication does not require one-on-one interpersonal interaction, costs may be greatly reduced. Information on the individual may be gathered through a survey or through a brief, personal interview with a professional. The results of these questions are entered into a computer, which draws from a "library" of possible messages to create materials that directly address the individual's needs, interests, or concerns. Once a program has been developed for a certain health issue, it can be used to produce tailored materials with the potential to reach large populations. Thus, tailored communications are an ideal tool to address a variety of public health issues.

Although the field of tailoring is still in its infancy, empirical research shows that tailored print materials are more effective than nontailored ones in helping people change health-related behaviors such as smoking, diet, and physical activity. According to Skinner and colleagues, who published the first scientific review of tailored research, not only are tailored (print) communications more effective than nontailored ones, but also they can be an important adjunct to other intervention components.

There are many exciting future directions and huge potential for tailorized approaches. Constantly evolving personal technology, such as Internet Web sites, email, instant messaging, personal desktop assistants, cell phones, and computerized kiosks, to name just a few, will make it easier to administer behavioral interventions on a wide scale, changing the landscape of public health in a dramatic fashion.

Special Application Within Survey Research

Survey researchers have developed an innovative method that utilizes tailoring to improve response rates. Following from leverage-saliency theory, an interviewer will be most likely to gain cooperation from a reluctant respondent if the interviewer "tailors" his or her introductory spiel to the specific concerns that the respondent expresses (or appears to be expressing). Linked to this, refusal avoidance training (also called *interviewer refusal aversion training*) curricula are ones that build on an understanding of this interviewer–respondent interaction to help interviewers deal effectively with respondent reluctance and avoid refusals by tailoring persuasive strategies to answer the callers' specific questions and keeping them talking. What is theorized to occur with inexperienced or unskilled interviewers is that they either press the respondent to make a decision too quickly, or they do not give an effective response to specific respondent concerns or questions, thus, leading to a refusal. Because experienced and skilled interviewers are more adept at tailoring their answers to the specific household they are calling, while maintaining continued conversation with the caller, they are more successful in getting respondents to complete the survey. Robert M. Groves and Mick P. Cooper have described a training protocol that can be grounded in this theory. In their model, the following components are necessary for tailoring to be successful: (a) The interviewer must have a repertoire of techniques, strategies, phrases, and so forth, related to the particular survey request; (b) the interviewer must be adept at reading the verbal and nonverbal cues from the respondent; (c) the interviewer must be able to apply the appropriate strategy according to the cues received from the respondent; and (d) the interaction between the interviewer and respondent must be long enough so that tailoring can be applied.

Joseph E. Bauer

See also Interviewer Training; Leverage-Saliency Theory; Refusal Avoidance Training (RAT)

Further Readings

Glanz, K., Rimer, B. K., & Lewis, M. (Eds.). (2002). *Health behavior and health education: theory, research, and practice* (3rd ed.). New York: Wiley.

Groves, R. M., Cialdini, R. B., & Couper, M. P. (1992). Understanding the decision to participate in a survey. *Public Opinion Quarterly, 56,* 475–495.

Groves, R. M., & Couper, M. P. (1998). *Nonresponse in household interview surveys.* New York: Wiley.

Kreuter, M., Farrell, D., Olevitch, L., & Brennan, L. (2000). *Tailored health messages: Customizing communication with computer technology.* Mahwah, NJ: Lawrence Erlbaum.

Kreuter, M. W., & Skinner, C. S. (2000). Tailoring, what's in a name? *Health Education Research, 15,* 1–4.

Noar, S. M., Benac, C. N., & Harris, M. S. (2007). Does tailoring matter? Meta-analytic review of tailored print health behavior change interventions. *Psychological Bulletin, 133*(4), 673–693.

Skinner, C. S., Campbell, M. K., Rimer, B. K., Curry, S., & Prochaska, J. O. (1999). How effective is tailored print communications? *Annals of Behavioral Medicine, 21*(4), 290–298.

TARGET POPULATION

The target population for a survey is the entire set of units for which the survey data are to be used to make inferences. Thus, the target population defines those units for which the findings of the survey are meant to generalize. Establishing study objectives is the first step in designing a survey. Defining the target population should be the second step.

Target populations must be specifically defined, as the definition determines whether sampled cases are eligible or ineligible for the survey. The geographic and temporal characteristics of the target population need to be delineated, as well as types of units being included. In some instances, the target population is restricted to exclude population members that are difficult or impossible to interview. For instance, area household surveys tend to define their target populations in terms of the civilian, noninstitutionalized population of the United States. Any exclusion made to the target population must also be reflected in the inferences made using the data and the associated presentations of findings. Undercoverage of the target population occurs when some population units are not linked or associated with the sampling frame and hence have no chance of inclusion in the survey. The subset of the target population that has a chance of survey inclusion because of their membership in, or linkage to, the sampling frame is referred to as the *survey population*. Traditional telephone surveys have a survey population of households with landline telephone service but typically are used to make inferences to target populations of all households, regardless of telephone service. In some instances, surveys have more than one target population because analysis is planned at multiple levels. For instance, a health care practices survey might have a target population defined in terms of households, another defined in terms of adults, and another defined in terms of children. Such a survey might sample households, collect household-level data, and then sample an adult and a child for interviews at those levels.

For business surveys, the target population definition must also specify the level of the business that comprises the units of the target population. Surveys of business finances typically define their target populations in terms of the enterprise—the organizational level that has ownership and ultimate responsibility for making decisions for the entire business. Labor force surveys define their target populations in terms of the establishment, that is, at the organizational level, where employment activities are conducted at or from a particular geographic location.

Brenda G. Cox

See also Establishment Survey; External Validity; Sampling Frame; Undercoverage

Further Readings

Lessler, J. T., & Kalsbeek, W. D. (1992). *Nonsampling error in surveys.* New York: Wiley.

Nijhowne, S. (1995). Defining and classifying statistical units. In B. G. Cox, D. A. Binder, B. N. Chinnappa, A. Christianson, M. J. Colledge, & P. S. Kott (Eds.), *Business survey methods* (pp. 49–64). New York: Wiley.

TAYLOR SERIES LINEARIZATION (TSL)

The Taylor series linearization (TSL) method is used with variance estimation for statistics that are vastly more complex than mere additions of sample values.

Two factors that complicate variance estimation are complex sample design features and the nonlinearity of many common statistical estimators from complex sample surveys. Complex design features include stratification, clustering, multi-stage sampling, unequal probability sampling, and without replacement sampling. Nonlinear statistical estimators for complex sample surveys include means, proportions, and regression coefficients. For example, consider the estimator of a subgroup total, $\hat{y}_d = \sum_i w_i d_i y_i$, where w_i is the sampling weight, y_i is the observed value, and d_i is a zero/one subgroup membership indicator for the ith sampling unit. This is a linear estimator because the estimate is a linear combination of the observed values y_i and d_i. On the other hand, the domain mean, $\hat{\bar{y}}_d = \sum_i w_i d_i y_i / \sum_i w_i d_i$, is a nonlinear estimator as it is the ratio of two random variables and is not a linear combination of the observed data.

Unbiased variance estimation formulae for linear estimators are available for most complex sample designs. However, for nonlinear estimators, unbiased variance estimation formulae are often not available, and approximate methods must be used. The most common approximate methods are replication methods, such as the *jackknife method* or *balanced repeated replication*, and the TSL method.

The TSL method uses the linear terms of a Taylor series expansion to approximate the estimator by a linear function of the observed data. The variance estimation formulae for a linear estimator corresponding to the specific sampling design can then be applied to the linear approximation. This generally leads to a statistical consistent estimator of the variance of a nonlinear estimator.

To illustrate the TSL method, let $\hat{\theta} = F(\hat{y}, \hat{x})$ be an estimate of the parameter θ where $\hat{y}$ and $\hat{x}$ are two linear sample statistics. For example, $\hat{\theta} = \hat{\bar{y}}_d$. Also define μ_y and μ_x to be the expected values of $\hat{y}$ and $\hat{x}$, respectively. θ can be expanded in a Taylor series expansion about μ_y and μ_x so that

$$\hat{\theta} = F(\mu_y, \mu_x) + (\partial F_y)(\hat{y} - \mu_y) + (\partial F_x)(\hat{x} - \mu_x) + \text{higher-order terms},$$

where ∂F_y and ∂F_x are the first-order partial derivatives of F with respect to $\hat{y}$ and $\hat{x}$ evaluated at their respective expectations, μ_y and μ_x. If the higher-order terms are negligible, then variance of $\hat{\theta}$ can be approximated by

$$\begin{aligned} \text{Var}(\hat{\theta}) &\cong E[\hat{\theta} - F(\mu_y, \mu_x)]^2 \\ &= (\partial F_y)^2 E(\hat{y} - \mu_y)^2 + (\partial F_x)^2 E(\hat{x} - \mu_x)^2 \\ &\quad + 2(\partial F_y)(\partial F_x) E[(\hat{y} - \mu_y)(\hat{x} - \mu_x)] \\ &= (\partial F_y)^2 \text{Var}(\hat{y}) + (\partial F_x)^2 \text{Var}(\hat{x}) \\ &\quad + 2(\partial F_y)(\partial F_x) \text{Cov}(\hat{y}, \hat{x}). \end{aligned}$$

This approximation can easily be extended to functions of more than two linear sample statistics. An approximate estimate of the variance of $\hat{\theta}$ is then obtained by substituting sample-based estimates of μ_y, μ_x, $\text{Var}(\hat{y})$ and $\text{Var}(\hat{x})$ in the previous formula.

An equivalent computational procedure is formed by recognizing that the variable portion of the Taylor series approximation is $\hat{z} = (\partial F_y)\hat{y} + (\partial F_x)\hat{x}$ so that

$$\text{Var}(\hat{\theta}) \cong \text{Var}[(\partial F_y)\hat{y} + (\partial F_x)\hat{x}] = \text{Var}(\hat{z}).$$

Because $\hat{y}$ and $\hat{x}$ are linear estimators, the Taylor series variance approximation can be computed using the linearized values $z_i = w_i[(\partial F_y)y_i + (\partial F_x)x_i]$ so that

$\hat{z} = \sum_i z_i$. As before, substituting sample-based estimates of μ_y and μ_x, namely, $\hat{y}$ and $\hat{x}$, in the formula for z_i and then using the variance formula of a linear estimator for the sample design in question to estimate the variance of $\hat{z}$ yields an approximate estimate of the variance of $\hat{\theta}$. This reduces the problem of estimating the variance of a nonlinear statistics to that of estimating the variance of the sum of the linearized values. As an example, the linearized values for the mean $\hat{\bar{y}}_d$ are $z_i = w_i d_i (y_i - \hat{\bar{y}}_d) / \sum_i w_i d_i$.

This illustration of the TSL method was for an estimator that is an explicit function of the observed data such as a mean, proportion, or linear regression coefficient. There are extensions of the TSL method to estimators that are implicitly defined through estimating equations, such as the regression coefficients of logistic, log-link, or Cox proportional hazards models.

Rick L. Williams

See also Balanced Repeated Replication (BRR); Clustering; Complex Sample Surveys; Jackknife Variance Estimation; Multi-Stage Sample; Probability of Selection; Replicate Methods for Variance Estimation; Sampling Without Replacement; Stratified Sampling; SUDAAN

Further Readings

Binder, D. A. (1983). On the variances of asymptotically normal estimators from complex surveys. *International Statistical Review, 51,* 279–292.

Groves, R. M., Fowler, F. J., Couper, M. P., Lepkowski, J. M., Singer, E., & Tourangeau, R. (2004). *Survey methodology.* New York: Wiley.

Wolter, K. M. (2007). *Introduction to variance estimation.* New York: Springer.

Woodruff, D. (1971). A simple method for approximating the variance of a complicated estimate. *Journal of the American Statistical Association, 66,* 411–414.

TECHNOLOGY-BASED TRAINING

Technology-based training uses computer-based tools to enhance the training process, typically by involving trainees actively rather than passively. For survey research, technology-based training is usually used to build and sharpen interviewer skills, particularly skills required for successfully interacting with survey respondents. Traditionally, interaction-skills training relied on peer-to-peer role playing or passive learning through videos. Technology-based training, in contrast, facilitates self-directed learning with rich media sources and abundant learner-assessment and remediation options. The benefits of technology-based training for survey research include (a) reduced learning time; (b) reduced or eliminated travel time and expense; (c) improved consistency by capturing and replicating best practices and expert knowledge; (d) increased availability of training (with just-in-time access on personal computers in any location); (e) enhanced productivity by decreasing on-the-job error rates and reducing reliance on on-the-job learning; and (f) increased ability to adapt to interviewers' knowledge, experience, learning style, and motivation.

Some technology-based training programs are based on a programmed learning model: Information is delivered through multimedia (text, graphics, video, and narration), and trainees' understanding of the material is tested through multiple-choice questions and other basic evaluation methods. This approach usually involves breaking large blocks of training content into discrete modules that can be searched electronically and then studied by the trainee in a short time. Breaking down a skill into many component parts allows users to gain competency quickly. Learning objectives also help users who need to brush up on a skill when they are back on the job. Trainees can skim through the list of topics in a course module and find the answer they need immediately without wading through many pages of text.

In contrast, an experiential learning model emphasizes trainees' actual experiences as the starting point of the training process. The mental processes used to analyze these experiences are also stressed. New technologies also allow trainees' skills to be developed and practiced in realistic settings with realistic spoken interaction. For example, *virtual reality* is a realistic, three-dimensional, interactive simulation of the trainees' work environment, and *natural language processing* allows trainees to speak into a microphone and have the computer application recognize their words, interpret them in context, determine their meaning, and generate an appropriate response. Such approaches increase the time trainees spend acquiring and practicing critical skills, increase active learning (which allows trainees to retain skills better than does passive learning), improve the realism of practice sessions, and facilitate intelligent tutoring. A training session in virtual reality typically includes (a) instruction on the scope of the task; (b) a definition of the goals and objectives; (c) a representation of an environment through visual, auditory, and at times kinesthetic information; (d) control systems to determine how the learner interacts with the simulation; (e) embedded instruction about content and process; and (f) coaching assistance.

Flexibility and responsiveness are critical for developing effective interaction skills and for performing well under difficult conditions, such as in a limited time or with limited information. To acquire flexible and effective skills at gaining respondents' cooperation, new and experienced interviewers require a learning environment that realistically simulates the environment they face in an interviewing situation. The consistency that is gained by repetitive practice in virtual and constructive learning environments leads directly to effective decisions in the production environment. Practice also leads to increased confidence before the first on-the-job experience, minimizing the amount of on-the-job learning necessary.

In the survey world, on-the-job-learning can translate into numerous unsuccessful interview attempts by a new interviewer at the start of a study, leading to lower response rates, lower-quality data, delayed schedules, and increased costs. This is exactly the scenario that *virtual training environments* can be most effective at preventing. Generally, interviewing skills are taught through a combination of lecture, mock practice sessions with other interviewer trainees, and audiotapes of real or mock exchanges between interviewers and survey respondents. Virtual environments, however, facilitate skill building at a higher level, by providing a simulated but realistic environment in which interviewers can practice and hone their skills.

Use of virtual environments for skill building also has disadvantages. Most importantly, current technology does not produce fully realistic conversational partners. Advances in natural language dialogue features and behavior models will add tremendously to the realism as this technology evolves. In addition, technology for training works best when the technology is used to enhance, rather than replace, well-prepared training materials. If the training program itself is badly conceived, sophisticated technology will not rescue it. Conversely, inappropriate use of technology can make a good training program less effective.

Michael Link

See also Interviewer Training

Further Readings

Link, M., Armsby, P., Hubal, R., & Guinn, C. (2006). Accessibility and acceptance of responsive virtual human technology as a telephone interviewer training tool. *Computers in Human Behavior*, 22, 412–426.

TELEMARKETING

Organizations engage in various forms of direct marketing to sell their products and services, solicit money, or nurture client relationships. Telemarketing is one such direct marketing technique that can target either individual consumers or other organizations. Groups that engage in telemarketing include nonprofit organizations, institutions, and political interest groups. A telemarketing call could come from a charity soliciting a small donation, an alumni group from a university, or a political party seeking support for a candidate. However, the prototypical use of telemarketing is for purposes of private enterprise. For businesses, telemarketing is a common form of direct selling, which originated with the advent of the telecommunications industry. Though it had been used with varying degrees of success for decades, it was not until the 1970s that the telephone became a standard tool of mass marketing. *Cold calling*, the unsolicited calling of large groups of people, is just one form of profit-seeking telemarketing. It should be recognized that although many firms do engage in cold calling, the two primary technological advances that popularized telemarketing practice are not closely tied to this practice.

By the late 1970s, AT&T widely disseminated toll-free numbers, which allowed for customers to call *into* a business to gather more product information, receive specific services, and place long-distance orders free of a telephone line usage fee. The second technology that can be credited with the rise of telemarketing is the electronic management of database information. As computers increased in capability and declined in price, businesses capitalized on the ability to marry customer information and phone numbers, with their own product catalogs. Consequently, while cold calling is a "shot in the dark" for businesses, the use of the phone can take on more strategically focused forms. For example, telemarketers can manage customer accounts or screen the person on the phone for characteristics that would qualify him or her for different sales techniques. Product information, such as marketable innovations, can be relayed to past customers. Further, market surveys are completed over the telephone. For instance, at the point of sale a retail consumer can be provided with a toll-free number and a unique identification code that he or she can use to access an automated phone survey system using interactive voice response software.

Telemarketing is not without its faults and criticisms, and it is often perceived to carry a worse reputation with the public than mail- or Internet-based contact methods. Because of its personal yet faceless nature, telemarketing has been used fraudulently and unethically. One example of this is with unscrupulous magazine selling, which can trap consumers into sales agreements that stretch on for years at above-market prices. This happens, in part, because laws in a number of states require nothing more than verbal consent for a consumer to be legally bound to paying for a magazine subscription. Another pitfall in magazine sales, and otherwise, is the intentional incomplete disclosure of sales terms and prices over the telephone while the salesperson continues to seek a commitment from the possible buyer. However, it is the claimed invasion of privacy into the household that most frequently draws the ire of the phone-owning masses. In response to this, the Federal Trade Commission manages the National Do Not Call Registry, which allows people to submit their phone number for exclusion from most types of unsolicited sales calls.

Many believe that survey research response rates have been seriously harmed by the effects of telemarketing. As public annoyance with unsolicited telemarketing has grown, more and more citizens are refusing legitimate telephone survey contacts, in part because they do not differentiate the two types of call. Survey research professional organizations, such as CMOR(Council for Marketing and Opinion Research) and CASRO (Council of American Survey Research Organizations), strive to educate the public so that legitimate surveys are not confused with telemarketing. These efforts have not yet been very successful.

Matthew Beverlin

See also Council for Marketing and Opinion Research (CMOR); Council of American Survey Research Organizations (CASRO); Do-Not-Call Registries; FCC Regulations; FRUGing; FTC Regulations; Interactive Voice Response (IVR); SUGing

Further Readings

Federal Trade Commission: http://www.ftc.gov

National Do Not Call Registry: https://www.donotcall.gov/default.aspx

National Fraud Information Center: http://www.fraud.org/telemarketing/teleinfo.htm

Osborne, G. S. (1984). *Electronic direct marketing*. Englewood Cliffs, NJ: Prentice Hall.

TELEPHONE CONSUMER PROTECTION ACT OF 1991

In 1991, the U.S. Congress, in response to concerns and complaints about the increasing number of unsolicited telemarketing calls to consumers, passed the Telephone Consumer Protection Act (TCPA). The TCPA (Public Law 102–243) updated the Communications Act of 1934 and is the primary law governing telemarketing. The TCPA mandated that the Federal Communications Commission (FCC) amend its rules and regulations to implement methods for protecting the privacy rights of citizens by restricting the use of the telephone network for unsolicited advertising as stated in the TCPA. Although the TCPA was specifically directed at telemarketing activities and abuses, some of its prohibitions and some of the subsequent FCC "Rules and Regulations Implementing the Telephone Consumer Protection Act of 1991" are not specific to telemarketing. Rather they are aimed at protecting individual privacy in general and, as such, can impact telephone survey research.

TCPA

The TCPA specifically restricted the use of automatic telephone dialing systems, prerecorded voice messages and unsolicited fax advertisements:

It shall be unlawful for any person within the United States to (A) make any call (other than a call made for emergency purposes or made with the prior express consent of the called party) using any automatic telephone dialing system or an artificial or prerecorded voice to any emergency telephone line (including any "911"), to the telephone line of any guest room or patient room of a hospital, health care facility, elderly home, or similar establishment; or to any telephone number assigned to a paging service, cellular telephone service, specialized mobile radio service, or other radio common carrier service, or any service for which the called party is charged for the call; (B) to initiate any telephone call to any residential telephone line using an artificial or prerecorded voice to deliver a message without the prior express consent of the called party, unless the call is initiated for emergency purposes or is exempted by rule or order by the Commission under paragraph (2)(B); (C) to use any telephone facsimile machine, computer, or other device to send an unsolicited advertisement to a telephone facsimile machine; or (D) to use an automatic telephone dialing system in such a way that two or more telephone lines of a multi-line business are engaged simultaneously.

The TCPA and the FCC granted individuals and states the right to sue for damages in state court for individual violations of its rules and regulations and granted states the right to take civil action in federal district court against telemarketers "who engage in a pattern or practice of violation." The TCPA also allowed the FCC to define exemptions to some of the rules. Finally, the TCPA required the FCC to develop regulations to implement methods and procedures for protecting the "residential telephone subscribers' privacy rights to avoid receiving telephone solicitations to which they object."

FCC Reports and Orders

On September 16, 1992, the FCC adopted its first report and order (FCC 92-443), which established rules and regulations implementing the Telephone Consumer Protection Act of 1991. With the exception of the rule prohibiting the use of automatic telephone dialing systems, the FCC rules specifically refer to "telephone solicitation" and "unsolicited advertisement," more commonly known as telemarketing. Some exemptions were made to these rules for "tax-exempt nonprofit organizations" and "established business relationships." Of note, the Federal Trade Commission (FTC) has defined research as "informational" and not "telemarketing" and as such cannot be granted, nor does it need, exemption status.

In this first order the FCC opted for "the most effective and efficient" solution for complying with the TCPA requirement that they define procedures allowing subscribers to avoid unwanted solicitations—company-specific *do-not-call lists*. This first order also required telephone solicitors to have a written policy for maintaining a do-not-call list for the purpose of eliminating from their future solicitations any person who requested they not be called again by this organization. Do-not-call lists were to be maintained indefinitely. In 1995, responding to complaints from the telemarketing industry, the FCC modified its do-not-call rules. The new order required that do-not-call requests had to be honored for 10 years instead of indefinitely as originally ruled. In June of 2003, following the establishment of the National Do Not Call Registry, the FCC adopted another report and order (FCC 03-153), which established call abandonment rules, caller ID rules, and national do-not-call rules.

Automatic Telephone Dialing Systems

Initially the TCPA rules regulating the use of automatic telephone dialing systems had little or no impact on random-digit dialing telephone surveys. Most emergency numbers, hospital numbers, and wireless numbers were either in dedicated prefixes or blocks (not in a list-assisted frame) or removed as out-of-scope business numbers during sample generation. All this changed with the implementation of local number portability. In 1996 the U.S. Congress amended the Telecommunications Act of 1934 to establish a national framework that would promote competition for telephone service. One of the major barriers to competition had been the inability of customers to switch from one telephone service provider to another while retaining the same phone number. Local number portability is the ability of users of telecommunications services to keep their existing telephone number when changing from one service provider to another.

Local number portability was implemented in stages. By 2004 full portability had been implemented, allowing porting between all types of service: wireline to wireline, wireless to wireless, wireless to wireline, and wireline to wireless. At this point telephone survey research was affected because a wireline or landline telephone number appearing in a telephone directory or in a random-digit dialing sample might have been ported to a wireless phone, and dialing such numbers using automated telephone equipment in the United States would violate TCPA regulations. Given the significant financial penalty for such a violation, telemarketers and the research industry lobbied the FCC to provide a method for identifying these numbers. *NeuStar*, the designated administrator of the national database of ported numbers, and the FCC agreed to license wireless porting information for an annual fee. Licensees have access to two files of ported numbers, which are updated daily: a file of wireless-to-wireline telephone numbers and a file of wireline-to-wireless. These files are used by sample providers, research firms, and telemarketing firms to comply with TCPA regulations.

This TCPA prohibition has impacted telephone survey research in another emerging arena: cell phone sampling. As the number of households that have only a cell phone increases (approximately 20% by the end of 2007, with another 10% of households using their cell phones almost exclusively to receive calls even though they also have a landline), researchers will need to develop sampling methodologies that will include cell phone only and "cell phone mostly" households. The requirement that cell phone numbers must be hand-dialed in the United States will clearly add to survey costs and complexity.

Do-Not-Call Legislation

The TCPA had required the FCC to "compare and evaluate alternative methods and procedures (including the use of electronic databases, telephone network technologies, special directory markings, industry-based or company-specific 'do-not-call' systems, and any other alternatives, individually or in combination) for their effectiveness in protecting such privacy rights, and in terms of their cost and other advantages and disadvantages." Originally the FCC had opted for company-specific do-not-call lists. In the absence of a national database, many states enacted their own do-not-call legislation and lists. Some states also implemented special directory markings. Consumers still were not satisfied.

Responding to ongoing consumer complaints, the Do-Not-Call Implementation Act of 2003 (Public Law No. 108-10) was signed into law on March 11, 2003. This law established the FTC's National Do Not Call (DNC) Registry in order to facilitate compliance with

the Telephone Consumer Protection Act of 1991. The FTC is responsible for the enforcement of the Telemarketing Sales Rule, which was mandated by Congress through the Telemarketing and Consumer Fraud and Abuse Prevention Act of 1994 and had been in effect since December 31, 1995. The Telemarketing Sales Rule was enacted to protect consumers from deceptive and abusive telemarketing practices. This legislation gives the FTC and state attorneys general law-enforcement tools to combat telemarketing fraud and levy penalties for violations and abuses.

The FTC's National Do Not Call Registry went into effect on October 1, 2003. Because the FCC and FTC regulate different components of the telecommunications industry (interstate and intrastate respectively), the FCC redefined its do-not-call rules in its 2003 report and order to implement the Do-Not-Call Implementation Act of 2003. FCC rules related to company-specific do-not-call lists remained in place. The National Do Not Call Registry is, as the name implies, national in scope and applies only to telemarketing calls. Telemarketers are required to download and "scrub" their lists against the national registry at least every 31 days. Exemptions have been made in the legislation for political organizations, charities, organizations with an established business relationship with the consumer or prior consent to call. It is important to remember that survey research is not formally exempted; it is simply not covered by this legislation. In other words telephone survey research is implicitly, not explicitly, exempt.

Access to the National Do Not Call Registry is limited to a "seller" of goods and services, a "telemarketer," a "service provider" (defined as a person or business that provides assistance to sellers or telemarketers) or an "exempt organization" (defined in the previous paragraph). In order to access the registry, an organization must pay the appropriate fee and agree to the certification requirements to receive a subscription account number with the National Do Not Call Registry. Certification stipulates that the registrant can use the list only to remove, or "scrub," a number from their lists. FCC rules specifically prohibit any person (not just a telemarketer) from using any do-not-call list for any purpose other than deleting such numbers from their call lists or sample. Violations are considered an abusive act by the Telemarketing Sales Rule and subject to penalties.

Research industry organizations such as AAPOR (American Association for Public Opinion Research),

CASRO (Council of American Survey Research Organizations), CMOR (Council for Marketing and Opinion Research), and the MRA (Marketing Research Association) continue their lobbying efforts in Washington to ensure that telephone survey research remains outside the scope of do-not-call legislation and distinct from telemarketers. In the interest of preserving this distinction, survey organizations are encouraged to define their own written do-not-call policies. By the end of 2006, the Do-Not-Call Registry contained over 132 million landline and wireless residential telephone numbers, according to the FTC's 2007 annual report to Congress. This is over half of the U.S. adult population at the time. Even allowing for multiple numbers per person, household, or both, excluding DNC numbers would necessarily introduce significant coverage bias to telephone surveys and flagging them for special treatment is potentially a violation of FCC and FTC rules.

Linda Piekarski

See also Caller ID; Cell Phone Only Household; Cell Phone Sampling; Do-Not-Call Registries; Number Portability; Predictive Dialing; Telemarketing; Telephone Surveys

Further Readings

Direct Marketing Association. (n.d.). *Telephone Consumer Protection Act*. Retrieved March 5, 2008, from http://www.the-dma.org/guidelines/tcpa.shtml

Federal Communications Commission. (2007). *Unwanted telephone marketing calls*. Retrieved March 5, 2008, from http://www.fcc.gov/cgb/consumerfacts/tcpa.html

Lavrakas, P. J. (2004, May). *Will a perfect storm of cellular forces sink RDD sampling?* Paper presented at the 59th annual American Association for Public Opinion Conference, Phoenix, AZ.

TELEPHONE HOUSEHOLDS

A telephone household is one that has some type of telephone service on which members of the household, in theory, can be reached by an external party, assuming they are called at a time they will answer their telephone. By definition, a telephone survey of the public can include only telephone households in its sampling frame.

In the United States, in 2007, approximately 97% of all households had landline (wired) telephone service, cell (wireless) telephone service, or both. The approximately 3% without service at a given point in time—the nontelephone households—are households that may have service a few months of the year but cannot afford it consistently. These households are disproportionately low-income renters, who live in very rural areas or inner-city poverty areas. Telephone surveys cannot reach (cover) households without any telephone service, and if the topic of the survey is correlated with whether or not a household has telephone service, the telephone survey may suffer from nonnegligible coverage error.

It was not until the 1970s in the United States that telephone service existed in at least 90% of households, although at that time in certain regions of the country less than 80% of households had telephone service. Nowadays the vast majority of households in the United States have both landline and cell telephone service, although reliable and up-to-date statistics on the exact proportions of landline only, cell phone only, and those that have both types of telephone service are not routinely available, especially not at the nonnational level. However, as of late 2007, a federal government study determined that 20% of U.S. households had only cell phone service and approximately 77% had landline service (with most of these also having a cell phone). Survey researchers who choose to sample the public via telephone must pay close attention to the prevalence of telephone households in the geographic areas that are to be sampled. Many challenges exist for telephone survey researchers as of 2008 due in part to (a) the rapid growth of the cell phone only phenomenon, especially among certain demographic segments of the population (e.g., renters and adults under the age of 30), (b) number portability, (c) difficulties in knowing how to properly sample from both the landline and cell frame, especially at the state and local level, and (d) difficulties in knowing how to weight the resulting data that come from both frames.

Paul J. Lavrakas

See also Cell Phone Only Household; Coverage Error; Nontelephone Household; Number Portability; Telephone Penetration; Telephone Surveys

Further Readings

Blumberg, S. J., & Luke, J. V. (2007). *Wireless substitution: Early release of estimates based on data from the National Health Interview Survey, July–December 2006.*

Hyattsville, MD: National Center for Health Statistics. Retrieved April 21, 2008, from http://www.cdc.gov/nchs/data/nhis/earlyrelease/wireless200705.pdf

Frankel, M. R., Srinath, K. P., Hoaglin, D. C., Battaglia, M. P., Smith, P. J., Wright, R. A., et al. (2003). Adjustments for non-telephone bias in random-digit-dialing surveys. *Statistics in Medicine, 22,* 1611–1626.

Lepkowski, J., Tucker, C., Brick, M., de Leeuw, E., Japec, L., Lavrakas, P. J., et al. (2008). *Advances in telephone survey methodology.* New York: Wiley.

TELEPHONE PENETRATION

The term *telephone penetration* refers to the number of households in a given survey area with one or more telephones. Traditionally, this has meant one or more landline or wired telephones, not including cell phones. A major challenge for drawing proper survey samples is ensuring that the sample represents a very high proportion of the population of interest. Traditionally, bias as a result of undercoverage in telephone surveys was credited to households without phones. As time has gone on, the rate of households without phones has been declining, leading to a decline of said bias. In its infancy, telephone interviewing was used only as a method of support for other interviewing techniques, such as face-to-face interviewing. However, by the 1970s the penetration of telephones in U.S. households had exceeded 90%, and this higher telephone penetration resulted in the evolution of telephone interviewing as it has become a centralized and exact data collection method, evolved further through the use of networked computers and computer-assisted telephone interviewing (CATI).

Telephone penetration in the United States has been on the rise ever since the invention of the telephone in 1861. The percentage of households in the United States with telephones increased from less than 40% in 1940, to above 95% as of 2008. Because of coverage issues, telephone surveys, while often regarded as cheaper than face-to-face interviews, lacked respectability for much of the early 20th century. In the first half of the 20th century, telephone ownership was a privilege for those who could afford it. Its use was not common, and ownership was limited to a select group of citizens. For this very reason, telephone directories and telephone surveys were limited to surveys of special populations.

Perhaps one of the most famous examples of the effect of undercoverage on the results of a survey came in 1936, when the *Literary Digest* incorrectly predicted a victory for presidential candidate Alf Landon. Although the survey was conducted by mail, its sample was built from telephone directory listings. In the end, Franklin D. Roosevelt handily defeated Landon, and the general consensus was that poor coverage by the telephone directories used to draw the survey's sample was the cause.

As the number of households equipped with telephones increased, other changes to the survey landscape were also occurring. The increasing costs of face-to-face interviewing and a growing resistance to face-to-face data collection led to the need for researchers to find an alternative that was both affordable and adequate in terms of coverage. Increasing telephone penetration, over 90% by 1970, made telephone surveys a more practical alternative to face-to-face interviewing for obtaining information from a representative sample. As telephone interviewing has become more centralized, interviewing has evolved further through the use of networked computers and CATI.

Although telephone penetration has increased enough over time to make telephone interviewing a viable option for survey research, issues surrounding the potential undercoverage of subgroups in the United States still exist. Research has shown that undercoverage exists in certain demographic subgroups (e.g., Native Americans in the Southwest). Because of this, there is still great concern that the exclusion of non-telephone households from research efforts can lead to the underrepresentation of specific subgroups.

In general, telephone penetration, as it applies to survey research, has focused largely on households with traditional landline telephones. However, increased cell phone usage over time, especially by households who are discontinuing landline service and becoming cell-only, has again threatened the validity of telephone surveys that exclude cell phones from their sampling frames. The increase of cell-only and no-phone households has created a need for researchers to look more closely at the potential biases introduced by excluding cell phone numbers from telephone frames and to develop research strategies that include these numbers.

Excluding cell-only households from random-digit dialing (RDD) sampling frames has become more problematic as the percentage of cell-only households in the United States has risen. As researchers begin to track closely the number of households in the United

States that have become cell-only, the increase in these types of households becomes clearer. By the second half of 2005, the estimated percentage of households in the United States with only a cell phone had reached almost 8%. By early 2008, approximately 20% of Americans could be reached only by cell phone, with an even greater percentage of renters and young adults being cell phone only. Thus, telephone surveys that rely exclusively on landline numbers will have significant undercoverage of these and other portions of the population.

As this trend continues, researchers must attend to the possibility that this growing group, usually eliminated from traditional RDD samples, may display a homogeneity, demographically speaking, that could bias the results of landline RDD surveys. Recent data suggest that those who are cell-only are more likely to be young, nonwhite, and unmarried, with age and marital status subject to the largest undercoverage biases. Further, recent research points to differences between cell-only households and landline households in terms of health and health behavior. Some have dismissed these differences as small and of no threat to the validity of national surveys, but as more people and households convert from landline to cell-only, these biases are likely to increase. Researchers planning to use the traditional landline RDD frame for their telephone surveys will need to attend very closely to the changing penetration of landlines in the population.

David James Roe

See also Bias; Computer-Assisted Telephone Interviewing (CATI); Coverage Error; Cell Phone Only Household; Cell Phone Sampling; Random-Digit Dialing (RDD); Undercoverage

Further Readings

Lavrakas, P. J. (1993). *Telephone survey methods: Sampling, selection, and supervision* (2nd ed.). Newbury Park, CA: Sage.

Lepkowski, J., Tucker, C., Brick, M., de Leeuw, E. Japec, L., Lavrakas, P. J., et al. (2008). *Advances in telephone survey methodology*. New York: Wiley.

TELEPHONE SURVEYS

Surveys for which data collection is conducted via a telephone interview represent a major source of all current survey data. Even as Internet surveys have gained greatly in popularity in the past several years, telephone surveys remain a major source of the data gathered for media, marketing, academic, and other types of research. Since the 1970s, the prevalence of telephone interviewing has steadily increased and has surpassed face-to-face interviewing, which had previously been the most commonly used method of conducting survey research. Currently the use of other data collection modes of survey research, particularly Internet surveys, has been increasing, but telephone interviewing still remains a widely used method. This entry discusses systems and techniques used to conduct telephone surveys, the evolution and length of telephone surveys, and the advantages and challenges of such surveys.

Systems and Techniques

Most professional telephone surveys are conducted using a computer-assisted telephone interviewing (CATI) system, which allows, among other things, interviewers to enter respondent information directly into the computer. Questions in CATI can be designed to appear for telephone interviewers one at a time or in blocks of similar questions. This helps to promote a similar interviewing experience for all respondents and limits possible confusion among telephone interviewers. CATI systems also allow *skip patterns*, in which one or more questions are skipped depending on the answers given to previous questions, and other programming such as randomly rotating the order of response options in order to help counterbalance the effect on respondent answers based on the order in which they hear the answer choices.

To further reduce survey error, CATI systems allow for intensive monitoring of interviewers. Interviewers can be monitored for productivity, data quality, and data falsification, among other things. Supervisors are able to monitor interviewers in real time from remote locations. CATI can also improve interviewer productivity by allowing for automatic scheduling of callbacks. This allows interviewers to set up specific times to call back a respondent (often based on a specific respondent request), which helps to increase response rates and productivity.

One of the major benefits of using a CATI system is the ability to easily implement random-digit dialing. This technique is used often in telephone surveys to access a random selection of households within a target population. Random-digit dialing works by allowing area codes and telephone prefixes to be selected in a representative fashion and the remaining digits to be randomly generated by computer. By purposely selecting specific area codes, it is possible to geographically target the geopolitical areas of interest (although the accuracy with which this can be accomplished has decreased considerably due to the effects of number portability and cell phone only households that no longer live in the geopolitical area in which their cell phone was purchased). By specifying telephone prefixes in addition to area codes, many ineligible numbers can be eliminated from the sample even before they are called. Such banks of telephone numbers often include businesses, which many times have different prefixes than do residential numbers. Eliminating these numbers from a sample allows for an increase in overall productivity, as interviewers do not need to spend time calling them.

Evolution

Advances in computer and software technology have allowed the practice of telephone interviewing to evolve over the past few decades. Currently the majority of survey organizations rely on a paperless system that assigns a specific identification number to each telephone number that is part of the sample, that is, to each potential respondent. This allows a record to be kept of every time that number is called and what the outcome of each call was (such as no one was home, a busy signal was received, an interview was completed, etc.). It also enables a record to be kept of the date and time that each call to a number was placed, which helps to ensure that numbers in the unresolved sample are called back at the appropriate time (such as calling back a respondent who is available only in the afternoons).

Length

Telephone surveys vary greatly in length. Many news and election-related polls can be on the shorter side: approximately 2 to 5 minutes. Surveys employed for academic research can range up to 45 minutes or more, and market research surveys are often somewhere in between. Longer surveys tend to elicit a lower participation rate due to respondent fatigue. However, many media polls and marketing surveys, for example, are not as concerned with the response

rate of surveys and instead focus on obtaining a specific number of completed interviews without regard for the number of telephone numbers at which no person was reached or for which the person at the number refused to participate. Other surveys, in particular government and academic surveys, are more concerned with these aspects because they need to obtain results that are more certain to be representative of the population of interest.

Advantages

Telephone surveys have many advantages over face-to-face interviewing, mail surveys, and Internet surveys. When compared to face-to-face and mail surveys, telephone surveys can be completed much more quickly and cheaply, which is almost always a major consideration in the field of survey research. Although telephone surveys are still more expensive than Internet surveys, they have the advantage that they are much better able to represent the general population, despite the challenges posed by cell phone only households in the United States. Even though Internet access and use have been on the rise over the past several years, the percentage of U.S. households that have such access is still not as high as the percentage that can be reached by telephone (97% in 2008). Therefore, in surveys that attempt to contact members of a large or diverse population, the representativeness of the data is questionable when Internet surveys are employed instead of telephone surveys. Furthermore, surveys that use interviewers, such as telephone surveys, will almost always elicit higher response rates, all other factors being equal, than surveys that do not use interviewers, such as Internet surveys.

Challenges

The telephone survey represents a major way that a large population can be accurately surveyed, but it still possesses many challenges to survey accuracy. Response rates have been declining as the use of caller ID and cellular telephones has been on the rise, which represents a major problem for the industry. As response rates decline, the accuracy of the data becomes more questionable. For example, if only a small portion of the selected sample participates in a survey, it could mean that those people who were sampled but did not participate are, in some way, inherently different from those who do participate and would therefore give different responses to the interview questions. The end result would be that the data would be skewed toward a certain set of opinions due to nonresponse bias. Coverage rates in landline telephone surveys also have decreased to below 80% as of 2008.

Innovations such as caller ID and privacy manager allow potential respondents to screen out calls before they even find out the purpose of the call. Telemarketers are generally thought to be a compounding factor because so many households receive a large number of telephone solicitations from telemarketers, and potential respondents begin to assume that any telephone number appearing on caller ID that is not recognizable is likely to be a telemarketer. Another contributor to the decline in telephone survey response rates are the popular do-not-call lists. Created to reduce the number of unwanted telemarketing calls, many people assume that if they are on such a list, they should not be called by anyone whom they do not personally know. Even though such lists do not apply to legitimate survey research organizations, many potential respondents do not make such distinctions. Additionally, the increased use of the telephone to conduct surveys over the past few decades has contributed to the decline in response rates. As people become used to receiving solicitations for their opinions, it becomes easier to refuse those requests.

Finally, the use of SUGing and FRUGing has also contributed to the decline in response rates for telephone surveys. SUGing (Soliciting Under the Guise of survey research) and FRUGing (Fund-Raising Under the Guise of survey research) is done by organizations that attempt to give the purpose of the calls greater legitimacy by claiming to only be interested in surveying opinions. This tactic quickly degenerates into a sales or fund-raising call but leaves the lasting impression on the respondent that telephone surveys often are merely a disguised way of selling products or raising money.

Mary Outwater

See also Caller ID; Cell Phone Only Household; Cell Phone Sampling; Computer-Assisted Telephone Interviewing (CATI); Do-Not-Call Registries; FRUGing; Interviewer Monitoring; List-Assisted Sampling; Nonresponse Bias; Number Portability; Random-Digit Dialing (RDD); Response Rates; SUGing

Further Readings

Groves, R. M., Biemer, P. P., Lyberg, L.E., Massey, J. T., Nicholls, W. L., II, Waksberg, J. (Eds.). (1988). *Telephone survey methodology*. New York: Wiley.

Groves, R. M., Fowler, F. J., Jr., Couper, M. P., Lepkowski, J. M., Singer, E., & Tourangeau, R. (Eds.). (2004). *Survey methodology*. New York: Wiley.

Lavrakas, P. J. (1993). *Telephone survey methods: Sampling, selection, and supervision*. Newbury Park, CA: Sage.

Lepkowski, J., Tucker, C., Brick, M., de Leeuw, E., Japec, L., Lavrakas, P. J., et al. (2008). *Advances in telephone survey methodology*. New York: Wiley.

Weisberg, H. F., Krosnick, J. A., & Bowen, B. D. (1996). *An introduction to survey research, polling and data analysis* (3rd ed.). Thousand Oaks, CA: Sage.

TELESCOPING

Telescoping describes a phenomenon that threatens the validity of self-reported dates, durations, and frequencies of events. Respondents often are asked in surveys to retrospectively report when something occurred, how long something lasted, or how often something happened within a certain time period. For example, health surveys often ask respondents the date of the last time, how often, or how many days they were hospitalized during the last calendar year. Answering this type of question requires the respondent to remember exact dates and temporal sequences and to determine whether an event happened within a certain time period. At this stage of the response process, dates or events can be forgotten entirely or "telescoped" forward or backward. While forgetting describes not remembering an event at all, telescoping focuses on errors made by incorrectly dating events that were recalled.

Survey researchers distinguish between two types of telescoping: *forward* and *backward*. Forward telescoping occurs when an event is erroneously remembered as having occurred more recently than it actually did. A backward telescoped event is erroneously remembered as having occurred earlier than its actual date. In general, empirical data show that forward telescoping is more likely to occur than backward telescoping.

Why telescoping occurs is not fully understood. Two main theories have emerged in the literature: the time compression and variance theories. However, these theories explain only parts of the phenomenon. The *time compression theory* focuses only on explaining forward telescoping, arguing that telescoping occurs because of a subjective distortion of the time line. Time is compressed when respondents perceive that events happened more recently than they actually did or a time period seems shorter than the true length of time. This theory also hypothesizes that forward telescoping decreases as the length of the reference period increases. Empirical findings testing this hypothesis, however, have been mixed. Variance theory uses the uncertainty in one's memory about the time of an event as an explanation for telescoping. The theory argues that uncertainty about the timing of an event increases as the elapsed time from the event to when the question is asked expands, explaining both forward and backward telescoping.

Several methods are used to reduce the amount of telescoping. First, "landmark events" can be used to clearly mark the beginning of the reference period. Landmark events are defined as personal or public events that are meaningful and highly salient to the respondent and can therefore provide a temporal structure of events; for example, something happened before or after a car accident. Personally meaningful events are better encoded in autobiographical memory than public events and therefore appear to be better landmark events. These events limit the reference period, provide a temporal structure to the events, and increase accuracy of reports. Bounded interviews are also used to reduce the incidence of telescoping. Used most frequently in panel surveys, bounded interviews permit the interviewer to remind the respondent of his or her reports in the previous interview or to check for overlaps between the current report of events and previously reported events. This technique improves report accuracy by eliminating forward telescoping of previously reported events. Finally, decomposition of a question into several more specific questions has been used. Research has shown that decomposition improves reporting only if the behavior is irregular and dissimilar. Otherwise, decomposing the question can lead to less accurate reports. Thus, the effectiveness of this technique varies over the population, and the use of this strategy should be carefully assessed.

Sonja Ziniel

See also Behavioral Question; Bounding; Measurement Error; Overreporting

Further Readings

Tourangeau, R., Rips, L. J., & Rasinski, K. (2000). *The psychology of survey response*. Cambridge, UK: Cambridge University Press.

Temporary Dispositions

Temporary disposition codes are used to record the outcomes of specific contact attempts during a survey that are not final dispositions, and provide survey researchers with the status of each unit or case within the sampling pool at any given point in the field period. Temporary disposition codes provide a record of what happened during each contact attempt prior to the case ending in some final disposition and, as such, provide survey researchers with the "history" of each active case in a survey sample. Temporary dispositions function as an important quality assurance component in a survey—regardless of the mode in which the survey is conducted. They also serve as "paradata" in some methodological research studies. However, the primary purpose of temporary dispositions is to assist researchers in controlling the sampling pool during the field period.

Temporary dispositions usually are tracked through the use of an extensive system of numeric codes or categories that are assigned to each element in the sampling pool once the field period of the survey has begun. Common temporary sample dispositions include the following:

- No one at home/answering
- Busy signal (telephone survey only)
- Fast busy (telephone survey only)
- Callback
- Privacy manager (telephone survey only)
- Unable to participate
- Unavailable respondent
- Household refusal (a temporary disposition if refusal conversions are planned)
- Respondent refusal (a temporary disposition if refusal conversions are planned)

Temporary disposition codes may also be matched with "action codes" that take into consideration the *status* of a case at any given point in the field period and lead logically to what the next action on the case should be. Examples of these types of action codes include *maximum number of call attempts* and *supervisor review.* Although these action codes are important in managing a survey sample, they should not be used as temporary disposition codes.

Temporary dispositions may change often during the field period of a survey—usually as often as the status of each case in the sample changes or as interviewers work cases in the sample. For example, the temporary disposition code of each telephone number in the sample for a telephone survey is updated after every call that is made to the number by an interviewer. In the case of a mail survey, sample dispositions may be updated as completed survey questionnaires are returned to researchers by respondents or as the postal service brings questionnaires "returned to sender" or "post office return" in the case of incorrect addresses or respondents who have moved. In an Internet survey, sample dispositions may be updated as email invitations are sent to individuals in the sampling pool, as email messages are returned to the sender after not being able to be delivered (in the case of an incorrect email address), as respondents log in to complete the Web survey, and as respondents complete the questionnaires.

Currently there is no standardized set of temporary disposition codes, and many survey firms develop their own systems. Although this is not a problem, it is important that the system of temporary codes used by an organization be compatible with the standard definitions of final case disposition codes that have been developed by survey-related professional organizations such as AAPOR (American Association for Public Opinion Research).

Matthew Courser

See also Dispositions; Final Dispositions; Paradata; Standard Definitions

Further Readings

American Association for Public Opinion Research. (2006). *Standard definitions: Final dispositions of case codes and outcome rates for surveys* (4th ed.). Lenexa, KS: Author.

Lavrakas, P. J. (1993). *Telephone survey methods: Sampling, selection, and supervision* (2nd ed.). Newbury Park, CA: Sage.

TEST–RETEST RELIABILITY

Test–retest reliability is a statistical technique used to estimate components of measurement error by repeating the measurement process on the same subjects, under conditions as similar as possible, and comparing the observations. The term *reliability* in this context refers to the precision of the measurement (i.e., small variability in the observations that would be made on the same subject on different occasions) but is not concerned with the potential existence of bias.

In the context of surveys, test–retest is usually in the form of an interview–reinterview procedure, where the survey instrument is administered on multiple occasions (usually twice), and the responses on these occasions are compared.

Ideally the reinterview (henceforth referred to as T_2) should exactly reproduce the conditions at the original interview (T_1). Unfortunately, learning, recall bias, and true changes may have occurred since the original interview, all leading to T_2 not matching T_1 answers.

Which measurement error components are of interest may affect certain decisions, such as whether to use raw data (if the focus is on response error alone) or edited data and imputed data (if editing and imputation errors are of interest). Oftentimes raw responses need to undergo light editing for practical reasons. Reliability measures (discussed later in this entry) may be calculated for individual questions to identify ones that may be poorly worded or others that may need to be followed by probing. Also, reliability measures may be calculated for population subgroups or by type of interviewer (e.g., experienced vs. novice) to detect problems and improve precision.

Further considerations in the design of a test–retest study include considering whether the interview–reinterview sample should be embedded in the main survey sample or exist as an additional, separate sample. An embedded sample is obviously cheaper, but sometimes a separate sample may be more advantageous. Another issue to consider is using the same interviewer at T_2 or not. Using the same interviewer in part of the sample and assigning different interviewers to the rest may help in assessing interviewer effects. The duration of time between T_1 and T_2 (the test–retest "lag") often has an effect on the consistency between the interviews. Thus, limiting to a certain time range may be an important consideration.

Furthermore, it is important to properly inform the respondents of the need for the reinterview, because respondents' perceptions of its necessity may affect the quality of the data they provide. After the reinterview is completed, additional special questions may be asked of respondents, such as how much they remembered from the original interview and what effect it may have had on the responses. The interviewers themselves may be debriefed on what they observed in the reinterview.

Considerations in the Analysis of Test–Retest Studies

The analyses may use information gathered at T_1 on T_2 nonrespondents for the purpose of making nonresponse adjustments, particularly if refusal to T_2 was related to questions asked at T_1. Reliability may depend on the interviewer and on interactions between interviewers and respondents (e.g., dependence on interviewer and respondent being of same gender or background may affect reliability). Further, if some of the respondents were interviewed by the same interviewer at T_1 as they were at T_2, whereas others were not, relationships between this factor and reliability can be analyzed. Because the time lag between T_1 and T_2 may have an effect on recall and learning effects, analysis of the dependence of the agreement between the two interviews on the lag may be warranted. The relative duration of the T_2 interview to that of T_1 may be related to learning (e.g., shortening of duration) and also should be explored.

Measures of Test–Retest Reliability

There are a number of reliability measures proposed in the literature for nominal, ordinal, and continuous (interval and ratio) responses. Although some of these measures are widely used, there is no general consensus which ones are best.

A raw measure of reliability of any single item is the proportion (%) of agreement. Consider the case of a binary variable having levels Y and N as shown in Table 1.

The proportion of agreement is $p_0 = p_{yy} + p_{nn}$. Because part of this agreement could be by chance alone, a chance-corrected measure called kappa (κ), as proposed by J. Cohen in 1960, is defined by $\kappa = (p_0 - p_e)/(1 - p_e)$ where p_e is the probability of chance agreement: $p_e = p_{y+} p_{+y} + p_{n+} p_{+n}$. Extension to the general nominal variable case is straightforward. For categorical responses, Cohen's kappa is the most commonly used measure in reliability studies. Nevertheless, there has been criticism of some of

Table 1 Test–retest proportion of agreement with a binary variable

		T_1		
		Y	N	Row total
T_2	Y	p_{yy}	p_{yn}	p_{y+}
	N	p_{ny}	p_{nn}	p_{n+}
Column total		p_{+y}	p_{+n}	1

kappa's undesirable properties (e.g., when the marginal distributions of the prevalence are asymmetric). Weighted kappa is a version of Cohen's kappa for ordinal responses, where differences between the levels of the response variable are weighted, based on judgment of the magnitude of the discrepancy. For continuous responses, a measure called the concordance correlation coefficient was proposed by L. Lin in 1989.

L. Pritzker and R. Hansen proposed another measure called the index of inconsistency (IOI). Its complement, $1 - \text{IOI}$, is referred to as the index of reliability. The IOI is defined as the ratio of the measurement variance to the total variance, and thus can be viewed as an intracluster correlation. (Of note: Some measures defined for continuous responses can also be used for dichotomous or ordinal data.) Finally, various types of models have also been used to make inference on reliability. While modeling involves making certain distributional assumptions, it allows for adjusting for covariates.

Moshe Feder

See also Measurement Error; Probing; Raw Data; Reinterview; Reliability

Further Readings

Barlow, W. (1996). Measurement of interrater agreement with adjustment for covariates. *Biometrics, 52,* 695–702.

Blair, J., & Sudman, S. (1996). The survey reinterview: Respondent perceptions and response strategies. *Journal of Official Statistics, 12,* 421–426.

Cohen, J. (1960). A coefficient of agreement for nominal scales. *Educational and Psychological Measurement, 20,* 37–46.

Falorsi, P. D., Pallara, A., & Russo, A. (2003, November 17–19). *Measuring response errors in censuses and surveys through reinterview data having a different measurement error variance.* Paper presented at the

Federal Committee on Statistical Methodology Research conference, Arlington, VA. Retrieved April 21, 2008, from http://www.fcsm.gov/03papers/falorsi_pallara_russo.pdf

Fleiss, J. L. (Ed.). (1981). The measurement of interrater agreement. In *Statistical methods for rates and proportions* (pp. 212–236). New York: Wiley.

Forsman, G., & Schreiner, I. (1991). The design and analysis of reinterview: An overview. In P. P. Biemer, R. M. Groves, L. E. Lyberg, N. A. Mathiowetz, & S. Sudman (Eds.), *Measurement error in surveys* (pp. 279–301). New York: Wiley.

Landis, J. R., & Koch, G. G. (1977). The measurement of observer agreement for categorical data. *Biometrics, 33*, 159–174.

Lin, L. I.-K. (1989). A concordance correlation coefficient to evaluate reproducibility *Biometrics, 45*, 255–268.

Pritzker, L., & Hanson, R. (1962). Measurement errors in the 1960 census of population. In *Proceedings of the Section on Social Statistics* (pp. 80–89). Washington, DC: American Statistical Association.

Yawn, B. P., & Wollan, P. (2005). Interrater reliability: Completing the methods description in medical records review studies. *American Journal of Epidemiology, 161*, 974–977.

THIRD-PERSON EFFECT

The *third-person effect* is a term that refers to the documented belief held by many people that mass communication has different and greater effects on others than on themselves, and because of this perception, some of these people will support certain policies and actions based upon the presumed effect on others. The phenomenon has been linked to public opinion research, and it often is studied through survey research methods.

Background and Theoretical Origins

What began as an eclectic litany of recollections and ruminations accumulated over nearly a lifetime of one scholar's experience—supplemented by little formal data or analysis—blossomed into a fertile site of rigorous interdisciplinary scholarship.

In his seminal work in the early 1980s, W. Phillips Davison relayed several anecdotes of how different people in different circumstances estimated different presumed impacts of the same messages. Davison later reported that he "didn't really want to write the article," in part because he thought the phenomenon

was of "minor theoretical significance" and his observations were based on sketchy data. Nevertheless, his observations were considered intriguing by many others who read and elaborated on his work, and in 2004 the third-person effect was named one of the most popular communication-theory frameworks of the early 21st century.

Davison explained the third-person effect in the following terms:

- People will tend to overestimate the influence that mass communications have on the attitudes and behaviors of others.
- People will expect the communication to have a greater effect on others than on themselves.
- Whether or not these individuals are among the *ostensible* audience for the message, the impact that they expect this communication to have on others may lead them to take some action.

Davison went on to explain that there are two ways in which the notion of a "third person" can be interpreted. First, individuals often believe that people like "me" or "you" will not be impacted by communications as much as "them," that is, the third persons. Second, some individuals who themselves are not members of the ostensible (or intended) audience nonetheless are concerned about the presumed effects of messages on the ostensible audience. These third persons, especially if in positions of authority, are driven by this presumption of effects to make what could be characterized as paternalistic decisions about the fate of the messages and the rights of members of the ostensible audience to be exposed to the messages.

Research on the Third-Person Effect

Since Davison's original articulation of the third-person effect, considerable scholarly effort has been invested in attempts to provide a suitable theoretical context and explanation for Davison's observations and insights. Other efforts have focused on methodological issues relating to study and instrument design. For example, Richard Perloff has written several broad and cogent analyses of theoretical and methodological conundrums associated with formal empirical tests of Davison's propositions.

Over the past 25 years, the third-person effect has been explained by, and linked to, a variety of established social psychological theories and models, including attribution, social comparison, social desirability, social distance, unrealistic optimism, symbolic interactionism, and self-categorization, among others. The third-person effect has also been connected to the larger scholarly body of public opinion theory and research, including such phenomena as spiral of silence and pluralistic ignorance. Additional theoretical attention has been paid to the role that message variables may play in contributing to the third-person effect. Evidence is mixed across studies, but there is some indication that the desirability of a message, that is, whether it is pro- or anti-social, can influence the nature and magnitude of the third-person effect. In addition, some studies have found that certain messages can elicit a "reverse" third-person effect, that is, a situation in which individuals report a greater effect of the message on one's self than on others. Another key consideration in third-person research has to do with the nature of the "other" and his or her relation to, and psychological distance from, the self.

Turning to issues more methodological in nature, early formal tests of third-person propositions tended to employ lab-based experimental designs, but the phenomenon has been studied extensively with survey research methodology as well. Results across studies indicate that the third-person effect occurs independently of the methodological approach used to study it. Several studies have investigated whether the phenomenon is simply a methodological artifact relating to question wording, question order, or study design (e.g., whether a between- or within-subjects design is employed). Results of these studies indicate that the third-person effect is more than a mere methodological quirk.

What originally appeared to be an assortment of observations of seemingly minor theoretical significance subsequently has achieved the status of a vibrant media-effects approach that has important implications for survey research and public opinion theory.

Charles T. Salmon

See also Experimental Design; Public Opinion; Public Opinion Research; Question Order Effects; Social Desirability; Spiral of Silence

Further Readings

Andsager, J. L., & White, H. A. (2007). *Self versus others: Media, messages, and the third-person effect.* Mahwah, NJ: Lawrence Erlbaum.

Davison, W. P. (1983). The third-person effect in communication. *Public Opinion Quarterly, 47*(1), 1–15.

Gunther, A. C., Perloff, R. M., & Tsfati, Y. (2008). Public opinion and the third-person effect. In W. Donsbach & M. Traugott (Eds.), *Handbook of public opinion.* Thousand Oaks, CA: Sage.

Perloff, R. M. (in press). Mass media, social perception and the third-person effect. In J. Bryant & M. B. Oliver (Eds.), *Media effects: Advances in theory and research* (3rd ed.). New York: Taylor & Francis.

Sun, Y., Pan, Z., & Shen, L. (in press). Understanding the third-person perception: Evidence from a meta-analysis. *Journal of Communication.*

TOPIC SALIENCY

The saliency of a topic—that is, its importance or relevance to potential respondents—can affect response patterns to surveys. There are several explanations as to how and why topic saliency affects response rates. First, if a potential respondent believes the topic to be important, he or she may be more likely to rationalize incurring the costs of responding to the survey. Second, responding to a survey topic that is of personal interest may have intrinsic rewards, such as providing an opportunity to exhibit one's knowledge or share one's opinion. Third, responding to a survey about a salient topic may be motivated by perceived direct benefits. Survey participation may be viewed as an opportunity to advance one's own needs, interests, or agenda. All of these explanations may apply to explain why a single respondent or respondents are more apt to complete a survey about a salient topic.

Research suggests that people are more likely to respond to a survey if the topic is of interest to them. For example, teachers are more likely than nonteachers to respond to, and cooperate with, a survey about education and schools; senior citizens are more likely than younger adults to respond to a survey about Medicare and health.

In addition to its impact on survey participation, topic saliency is important for attitude formation and response retrieval. Theories about the representation of attitudes in memory suggest that attitudes reported by the respondent as being more important or as being more strongly held are also more stable over time. Attitudes about salient topics require less cognitive effort to recall, resulting in attitude responses that are more stable over time, more stable when presented with counterarguments, and more consistent with other attitudes and considerations.

There is great debate about whether attitudes are saved in memory and retrieved when the situation or the survey question arises (the online model of attitude formation), or whether attitudes are continually constructed from multiple considerations that are sampled each time they are needed (the memory model). The online model implies a continuum ranging from nonattitudes to "true" attitudes, where attitude stability and consistency are partly determined by topic saliency. The memory model implies that attitude formation is a stochastic process subject to some variability where the respondent samples considerations off the "top-of-the-head" when asked a survey question. In this model, more salient topics result in a response distribution for each individual that is more tightly clustered and therefore also more stable.

Whether the attitude is "true" or constructed on the spot, attitudes about salient topics are often considered to be more resistant to differences in questionnaire form. However, the evidence is mixed and depends highly on how topic saliency is measured. Self-reports of attitude importance, certainty, or strength are more resistant to certain questionnaire design features. When salience is measured by interest in politics or by the cognitive accessibility of those attitudes, evidence is tenuous on whether topic salience is related to questionnaire form or other survey response patterns.

Topic saliency has implications for survey operations, countering survey nonresponse, questionnaire design, and analysis. People are more likely to cooperate with, and respond more quickly to, a survey if the survey topic is of interest to them, suggesting a need to compensate for the potential bias this effect may cause by using a multiple contact strategy. Questionnaire designers and analysts need to consider the implications of their question form for their response distribution and thus for the interpretation of the results.

Shelley Boulianne and Danna Basson

See also Attitudes; Leverage-Saliency Theory; Nonattitude; Nonresponse; Questionnaire Design; Response Rates; Saliency

Further Readings

Bassili, J. N., & Krosnick, J. A. (2000). Do strength-related attitude properties determine susceptibility to response effects? New evidence using response latency, attitude extremity, and aggregate indices. *Political Psychology*, *21*(1), 107–134.

Groves, R. M., Presser, S., & Dipko, S. (2004). The role of topic interest in survey participation decisions. *Public Opinion Quarterly*, *68*(1), 2–31.

TOTAL DESIGN METHOD (TDM)

The total design method (TDM) is an approach to obtaining response to surveys. Under this approach, social exchange theory is used to identify ways to improve the quantity and quality of survey response by organizing the data collection process in a way that increases trust that the *rewards* of responding will be seen by the respondents as outweighing the *costs* of doing so. The TDM was developed by Don A. Dillman, in 1978, as a general framework for designing both mail and telephone surveys, but it is most identified with developing and implementing surveys by mail. In recent years, it has been recast as the tailored design method and applied to the design of Internet and mixed-mode surveys as well as postal surveys.

Elements of the Total Design Method

The original TDM consisted of two parts. The first was to identify each aspect of the survey process likely to affect either the quality or quantity of responses and to shape them in ways that would improve response. The second part was aimed at organizing the survey efforts so that the design intentions were carried out in complete detail.

The problem that the TDM was designed to solve was that much of the research literature on mail survey design emphasized the individual influence of single techniques—from sending multiple contacts to placing real stamps on return envelopes—without focusing on combined overall effects aimed at achieving the best possible response from respondents. Combining techniques into an overall approach to data collection, focusing on both elements and their temporal interconnections, raised issues of compatibility and of how the use of some techniques might need to be reshaped to be compatible with other response-inducing techniques.

To make decisions on how to combine multiple techniques, social exchange theory was utilized as a conceptual framework. The behavioral assumption implied by this framework is that people's actions are typically motivated by their expectations that in the long run, the rewards for taking action will outweigh the costs of doing so. The process of sending a questionnaire to sampled individuals, persuading them to complete it in an accurate manner, and return it were viewed as a special case of social exchange.

Social exchange differs in significant ways from economic exchange. Social exchange involves diffuse obligations, whereby one person does something in anticipation of the likelihood that the other person will do something in response that will benefit the respondent or others. In addition, the reciprocal obligation is not something that can be bargained with. With respect to social exchange in survey research, it is left up to the potential respondent to take action based upon what the sender of the questionnaire has already done. Social exchange contrasts in significant ways with economic exchange, for which people involved in a transaction typically agree on a price before the transaction occurs and may bargain on that price prior to deciding whether to participate in it. Social exchange does not generally involve explicit bargaining.

Obtaining a Positive Response From Respondents

In the design of mail surveys, three different factors are subject to design actions aimed toward obtaining a positive response from respondents: (1) rewards, (2) costs to the respondent, and (3) the trust of the respondent that, in the long run, the rewards for completing the survey will outweigh its costs.

Rewards

Normally, rewards for completing a questionnaire are small. Social factors that have reward value may include explaining why completing a questionnaire is helpful to solving a problem that the respondent considers important. Writing something supportive of the values held by the survey respondent may also have positive reward value. In addition, developing and ordering questions in ways that make them interesting to the respondent and easier to understand may have

reward value, as does expressing appreciation for the respondent's help.

Costs

The second factor important in social exchange is the costs to the respondent. Social costs can be lowered. One way to do this is by making sure that letters are worded so that they do not subordinate the respondent, psychologically, to the study sponsor (e.g., "I'm doing this study to help people like yourself improve your eating habits"). Embarrassing the respondents by creating questions that are difficult, require knowledge the respondent does not have, or create anxiety for other reasons may incur social costs to respondents. Costs that flow from consideration of how the respondent is treated go far beyond factors normally thought of as having economic cost.

Trust

The third important aspect of the social exchange equation is trust on the part of the respondent that, in the long run, rewards for completing a questionnaire are likely to exceed the costs incurred by that action. Respondents need to feel that promises made by the survey sponsor (e.g., "to make public officials aware of the results of the survey") will be carried out. Sponsorship by an organization that is viewed as legitimate by the person asked to respond is an important feature that may create trust that research findings from a survey will be helpful to someone. This helps to explain why surveys sent by the government typically get higher response rates than those sent by market research organizations. The sending of token cash incentives of a few dollars with a request, which has been found to be quite effective for improving survey response rates, may stem from the creation of trust that a survey is important. Inclusion of token noncontingent incentives ahead of time conveys both the idea that the survey is important and trust that the respondent will consider the request. Research has shown that contingent cash payments, even sizable ones, offered in return for returning a completed questionnaire are far less effective than token cash incentives sent ahead of time. This difference provides strong evidence of the social, as opposed to economic, nature of the questionnaire completion process.

Based on the social exchange framework, a series of specific recommendations for designing mail surveys was developed. Features included (a) ordering questions in a particular manner from being of greater to lesser interest to respondents, (b) printing questionnaires as booklets small enough to fit in regular business mail envelopes when folded, (c) particular sizes of envelopes, (d) letters with specified content, (e) personalization of those letters through individually typed names and addresses, (f) a timed sequence of four contacts (questionnaire, postcard reminder, replacement questionnaire, another replacement questionnaire), and (g) stamped return envelopes. Application of these procedures in concert produced mail survey response rates averaging more than 70% in the 1970s from a wide variety of survey populations.

Uses of the TDM

Although the TDM is also applied to telephone surveys, the window of opportunity for applying social exchange principles, except for the use of advance letters, is narrow. In addition, differences in response rates between telephone surveys that use the TDM approach and those that do not is much less than for mail surveys. Thus, the TDM has been identified primarily as a mail survey methodology.

TDM principles have been applied successfully to the design of thousands of mail surveys from the 1970s through the 1990s. Surveys acknowledging use of the total design framework have been conducted throughout the United States by government, education, and private organizations. Published surveys have also been conducted in many countries throughout the world, such as New Zealand, Japan, China, Australia, the Netherlands, Spain, the United Kingdom, Israel, and Germany.

Critiques

One of the effects of publication of the TDM was to shift the emphasis away from looking for a magic bullet that might improve response rates toward providing a template, which, if followed carefully, was likely to produce high response rates. Its use also has shown that mail response rates of the public can often rival or even surpass those obtained in telephone surveys; this was true especially for surveys conducted in the 1980s and 1990s. Thus, the overall effect was to give legitimacy to mail surveys as a way of undertaking serious research.

It also became apparent that the TDM was not an adequate design for mail surveys in certain respects.

First, the TDM, as originally conceived, was focused heavily on improving response rates. Although response rates are important, they remain one step removed from nonresponse error (e.g., differences between respondents and nonrespondents that are relevant to the study objectives). Although detailed attention was given to survey measurement and the writing of unbiased questions in the original TDM, comparable interest was focused on organizing questions in a way that would entice recipients of questionnaires to respond. Coverage error was, and remains, the major barrier to the effective use of mail surveys for general public populations because of the lack of adequate sampling frames for drawing samples. In addition, satisfactory selection procedures for randomly choosing particular respondents within households to represent the general public remain more of a concern for self-administered mail surveys than for either personal or telephone surveys.

Second, the TDM also had a one-size-fits-all character (e.g., the same procedures were advocated for use in all survey situations). The need to modify specific procedures for special situations and populations was mostly ignored. Such challenges range from the completion of time-sensitive diaries (e.g., Nielsen's 7-day TV ratings diary), in which it makes no sense to use the 2-month implementation cycle described as a standard TDM procedure, to business surveys that have to be passed from person to person to be completed and thus require a far longer time frame.

Third, concerns about encouraging response selectivity were raised by the strong focus on ordering questions from most to least interesting and on giving corresponding attention to the use of letters explaining the survey topic and why it was of importance. That is, appeal to respondent interests in the survey topic might discourage those with less interest in the survey content. Thus, concern was raised as to whether use of the TDM would increase nonresponse error rather than decrease it.

In addition, the TDM was bound by the technology of the times. Advocating the insertion of individual names and addresses into the salutation space of preprinted letters represented a significant advance forward in personalization in the 1970s. However, it was a typewriter-based technology that is as quaint today as it was innovative and time-consuming at that time.

The TDM also exhibited a bias toward university-sponsored studies and rural as well as state population surveys associated with the location of the university where the TDM was initially developed. Evidence was lacking that it would work for national surveys, particularly those of residents in large cities. Although such studies were eventually done, response tended to be lower and perhaps less subject to some of the exchange principles advocated in the original TDM.

Replacement of the TDM With Tailored Design

In 2000, some 20 years after its original development and publication, Dillman replaced the total design method with the tailored design method. The revised approach retained the social exchange framework for design, but it began with the recognition that the full application of social exchange would suggest using different procedures to obtain response from different populations, on different topics and in different survey situations, as well as sponsorship, which is consistent with leverage-saliency theory. Thus, an attempt was made to more specifically identify issues that may increase rewards, decrease costs, or encourage trust with specific populations or even portions of a particular population (e.g., small as opposed to large business owners).

In addition, tailored design was connected explicitly to the four cornerstones of total survey error: sampling error, coverage error, measurement error, and nonresponse error. For example, relatively less emphasis was placed on response rates and more on finding ways to ensure results did not exhibit nonresponse error, by methods such as using token cash incentives in advance, which are more effective with younger people (who are less likely to respond to surveys) than they are with older respondents (who have a greater propensity to answer questionnaires). In addition, more emphasis was placed on mixed-mode surveys, which provide a way of getting respondents who cannot or will not respond by one mode to respond via another one.

The tailored design recognizes that methods inappropriate or less effective with some populations may be acceptable or effective with others. For example, while six or seven contacts made within a 2- or 3-week period would be appropriate when trying to obtain television or radio listening for a specific set of days, that number of contacts in such a short period of time would not be appropriate for a lengthy business survey that required involving several people in

order to get a complete response. Also, whereas government surveys carry great legitimacy and obtain relatively high response rates without the use of cash incentives, private-sector surveys make the use of such incentives more appropriate. The variety of situations calling for design variations is quite large, ranging from employee surveys sent through internal company mail (for which there is strong employer encouragement to respond) to election surveys that use voter registration lists and require focusing contacts on a deadline date.

The development of the tailored design, or the "new TDM" as it is sometimes called, also reflected a rapidly growing science based on factors that influence responses to survey questions. Research that began in the 1990s made it clear that people who respond to mail surveys are influenced by the graphical layout of questionnaires as well as the use of symbols and numbers, and that their reactions to these features of construction are influenced by behavioral principles such as the gestalt laws of psychology. Whereas the original TDM included a focus on visual layout, the scientific underpinnings of those principles had not yet been demonstrated or methodically tested. Another aspect of the science base that provided a basis for tailored design was nearly two decades of research on question order and context affects. Thus, measurement principles developed for tailored design gave much greater importance to what questions were to be asked and the order in which they needed to be asked as well as how they were to be displayed on pages, while giving somewhat less interest to what questions would appeal most to respondents.

Development of a tailored design perspective was facilitated by the development of information technologies that make it possible to treat different sample units in different ways, efficiently and accurately. Active monitoring of response and the timely tailoring of specific follow-up letters to different types of respondents were not feasible in the 1970s.

Internet surveys have now been encompassed within the tailored design perspective. Because mail and Web surveys are both self-administered as well as visual, they share many commonalities. Whereas the technological interface between respondent and response mechanisms clearly distinguishes Web from mail, its similar exchange processes appear to occur between respondent and the questionnaire and its sponsor. Both mail and the Internet face the challenge of not having an interviewer who can provide additional explanations for what questions mean and ask probing follow-up questions that are responsive to answers and comments just offered by the respondent.

During the past decade, evidence has accumulated that fundamentally different communication processes occur in visual (Web and mail) versus aural (telephone) surveys. Telephone surveys rely mostly on words for communication, which are given a limited amount of additional meaning by interviewer characteristics that permeate the delivery of those words. However, mail and Web surveys depend not only on words to communicate question meaning but also on symbols, numbers, and graphics that may give meaning to verbal language, quite apart from words themselves. Experimental research published since 2000 makes it quite evident that answers to survey questions and the completion process are influenced by how scales are visually displayed. Identification of these differences in respondent answers now raises important questions about which visual formats translate most effectively between aural and visual modes of conducting surveys.

The original TDM was developed at a time when mail was by far the least expensive survey mode, costing far less to implement than the alternatives of telephone or face-to-face interviews. The attention to detail encouraged by the TDM raised mail costs significantly, but they remained low compared to the face-to-face and telephone alternatives. In the new TDM era, mail surveys are now considered a high-cost methodology, fairly equivalent in cost to telephone interviews but far more expensive than Internet surveys once the fixed costs of creating Internet surveys have been met. In addition, declining response rates to the telephone and low response to and the limited coverage of Web surveys have provided strong encouragement for mixing modes. Thus, in the early 21st century a new feature of tailored design receiving much attention is how to use it to obtain as many responses as possible by Web and to supplement those responses with surveys by mail or telephone of respondents who lack access to, or will not respond over, the Internet.

One of the practical outcomes of development of the original TDM and now tailored design is that the attention of surveyors is drawn to the fact that responding to surveys involves communicating effectively with potential respondents through all aspects of the survey design process and not just survey questions. It is a process in which both the surveyors and the respondent take into account the expectations of the other. Its effectiveness as a guide for designing surveys has gained importance, as surveyors have recognized the explicitly voluntary nature of surveys, and seems likely to continue to influence survey design throughout the world.

Don A. Dillman

See also Advance Letter; Contingent Incentives; Coverage Error; Economic Exchange Theory; Gestalt Psychology; Incentives; Internet Surveys; Leverage-Saliency Theory; Mail Questionnaire; Mail Survey; Noncontingent Incentives; Nonresponse Error; Response Rates; Social Exchange Theory; Total Survey Error (TSE); Visual Communication; Within-Unit Coverage

Further Readings

Dillman, D. A. (1978). *Mail and telephone surveys: The total design method.* New York: Wiley.

Dillman, D. A. (1991). The design and administration of mail surveys. *Annual Review of Sociology, 17,* 225–249.

Dillman, D. A. (2000). *Mail and internet surveys: The tailored design method.* New York: Wiley.

Dillman, D. A. (2007). *Mail and internet surveys* (2nd ed.). New York: Wiley.

TOTAL SURVEY ERROR (TSE)

Total survey error (TSE) is a term that is used to refer to all sources of bias (systematic error) and variance (random error) that may affect the validity (accuracy) of survey data. Total error in surveys can be conceptualized and categorized in many ways. One traditional approach is dividing total error into sources of sampling error and sources of nonsampling error. Another categorization is dividing it between coverage error, sampling error, nonresponse error, and measurement error. A more modern approach is to group various sources of error into the classes of *representation* and *measurement*. This entry provides a big picture perspective on all of the major types of error that occur in surveys and thus comprise total survey error.

Unfortunately, there is no such thing as a survey without error. Nevertheless, survey methodologists and survey practitioners aim for the most accurate surveys that can be conducted given the finite budget available to fund them. The quality of a survey statistic such as a mean, a percentage, or a correlation coefficient is assessed by multiple criteria: the timeliness of reporting, the relevance of the findings, the credibility of researchers and results, and the accuracy of the estimates—just to mention a few. Among those criteria the accuracy of the estimate is not necessarily the most important one. However, the accuracy is a dimension of the overall survey quality for which survey methodology offers a wide range of guidelines and instructions. Also, standard measures for the magnitude of the accuracy are available. The accuracy of a survey statistic is determined by its distance to or deviation from the true population parameter. If, for example, a survey aims to determine the average household income in a certain population, any deviation of the sample estimate from the true value—that is, what would have been determined if all members of the target population were asked their income and they all answered accurately—would decrease accuracy.

Representation and Measurement

There are two types of survey error that harm the accuracy of a survey estimate: random error and systematic error. Whereas random errors are assumed to cancel out each other—that is, negative deviations of the measurement from the true value are compensated by an "equal" amount of positive deviations—systematic errors shift the sample estimate systematically away from the true value; for example, because of certain question wording, respondents in a survey may tend to report a higher number of doctor visits than actually occurred in a given reference period. For linear estimates (such as means, percentages, and population totals), an increase in the random error leads to an increase in variance, whereas a rise in any systematic error results in an ascended bias of the survey estimate. The accuracy of a survey estimate is affected by either an increase of the bias or by a rise of the variance.

In a traditional view, the driving factors or sources of those survey errors are differentiated into two groups: sampling error and nonsampling error. Nonsampling error would then be further differentiated into coverage error, nonresponse error, and measurement error—some older textbooks mention processing error as well. However, a more modern theory-driven approach differentiates *observational errors* and *nonobservational errors*. While observational errors are related to the measurement of a particular variable for a particular sample unit, nonobservational errors occur when a net sample is established that is supposed to represent the target population. Following this path, Robert M. Groves and his colleagues have grouped the sources of error into two primary classes: *representation* and *measurement*:

1. The first class of error sources applies to the representation of the target population by the weighted net sample (representation).

2. The second class of error components adds to the total error by affecting the edited survey responses obtained from a respondent (measurement).

This extension of the traditional total survey error concept provides room for a detailed analysis of the mechanisms by considering several sources of error at the same time, including possible interaction effects between the sources.

Total Survey Error Components Affecting Representation

Coverage Error

For a sample to be drawn, a sampling frame is necessary in order to provide the researcher with access to the members of the population from whom data are to be gathered. The incompleteness of this frame and the possible bias of its composition cause misrepresentations of the population by the sample. If a group is underrepresented in the frame—for example, individuals who own mobile phones as their only telecommunications device are missing from traditional random-digit dialing (RDD) sampling frames because they do not have a landline telephone number—the sociodemographic or substantive characteristics of this group cannot be considered when computing the survey statistic. This causes a lack of accuracy of the survey estimate since some groups might be underrepresented in the frame and subsequently in any sample that is selected from the frame, resulting in coverage bias.

Sampling Error

Once a frame is available, a random sample needs to drawn: for example, a simple random sample, a stratified sample, a cluster sample, or a more complex sample design. Based on this sample, the standard error is computed by taking the square root of the division of the variance in the sample and the number of cases in the sample. The standard error is then used to compute the confidence limits and the margin of error—both are indicators for the precision of the estimate. Accordingly, the magnitude of the sampling error is one key component of the total survey error. It depends heavily on the design of the sample. For a fixed number of sample cases, the standard error usually decreases if stratification is applied. By contrast, a clustered sample is generally characterized by a larger variance which, in turn, raises the sampling error for a particular estimate. However, within a fixed budget, clustering usually increases precision, because the effective sample size can be increased even though the variance suffers from the inflationary design effect (i.e., *deff*) caused by clustering.

Nonresponse Error

Unit nonresponse error is the facet that is the best studied among all bias components within the TSE framework. Since the early days of survey methodology, researchers have been aware of the fact that some portions of the gross sample cannot be reached in the field phase of a survey or are not willing to comply with the survey request for cooperation. Because the responses of those groups may differ considerably from the responses of those members of the gross sample who can be reached and who are willing to cooperate, unit nonresponse is considered a serious source of systematic error that generates nonresponse bias. The literature provides comprehensive theoretical approaches to explain the various stages of respondent cooperation and also findings that can be generalized beyond particular surveys. In part, this is due to the fact that a potential nonresponse bias can be assessed for variables where parameters are available from official statistics (e.g., household income). Compared to other sources of error, this leaves survey researchers in a comfortable situation, as a possible bias can be observed more easily and taken into consideration when survey findings are interpreted.

Adjustment Error

Finally, the net sample needs to be adjusted for design effects introduced by the sample design. If the sample design, for example, would require a disproportional stratified sample, an appropriate weighting procedure would have to be devised to compensate for the unequal selection probabilities when estimating the population parameter. In addition, and as noted earlier in this entry, the net sample may need to be adjusted for possible nonresponse bias. Both procedures require complex computations that take into account information from the gross sample, official statistics, or both. Whereas the first approach may potentially increase the random error of the estimate, the second approach may introduce systematic errors into the sample and thus bias the estimate.

Total Survey Error Components Affecting Measurement

The four sources of error discussed so far were related to the representation of the target population by the weighted net sample. Coverage error, sampling error, nonresponse error, and adjustment error all potentially contributed to the random error or systematic error of the survey estimate. The next three sources of error—specification error, measurement error, and processing error—are concerned with the measurement process.

Specification Error

Most concepts of interest in surveys cannot be observed directly. Instead, the measurement process requires researchers to operationalize and translate the construct into questionnaire items that can be asked by interviewers and answered by respondents. For example, the general public's attitudes about illegal immigration ideally should be decomposed into several questionnaire items about the various dimensions of illegal immigration. Respondents then would be asked to report attitudes on each of these items. The combined score of all items would then be treated as a scaled measurement of the attitudes toward illegal immigration. If an important aspect of this construct were omitted from the scale, then the validity of the operationalization of the construct would be harmed, because the scale would not measure the construct completely and a specification error would occur. This can result in a serious bias, because the estimates based on an incomplete scale often would not mirror the complete true attitudes of the members of the target population on illegal immigration.

Measurement Error

Measurement error is a complex component of total survey error. It consists of various elements that individually and jointly may cause systematic survey error as well as random survey error. Accordingly, measurement error potentially contributes to an increase of the estimate's variance as well as to its bias. Measurement error arises from the mode of survey administration, from the questionnaire or survey instrument and from the setting in which the instrument is administered, from the interviewers (if present), and also from the respondents.

Survey Mode

A traditional trichotomy of data collection modes differentiates face-to-face surveys, telephone surveys, and self-administered (mail and Internet) surveys. They differ with respect to (a) the presence or absence of an interviewer—which allows for various degrees of standardization of the measurement process, for different types of motivational support to the respondent, as well as explanation and help for the respondent—and (b) the dominant communicative channel (audiovisual, audio-only, visual-only). In recent years, many new survey modes have evolved with the introduction of modern information and communication technologies. Some of these modes transfer an established methodology into a computer-assisted mode (e.g., the shift from paper-and-pencil personal interviewing [PAPI] to computer-assisted personal interviewing [CAPI] or computer-assisted telephone interviewing [CATI]), other new modes evolve as a consequence of merging survey modes (e.g., mobile Web surveys that use messenger systems or agents or avatars). Each of these survey modes has its particular strengths and weaknesses for specific survey topics and survey designs. Whereas a Web survey might increase the variance of an estimate because respondents tend to answer a frequency question superficially compared to a face-to-face interview, the response to a face-to-face version of the very same questions might be prone to a higher degree of systematic social desirability distortion because of the presence of an interviewer, which in turn contributes to measurement bias.

Questionnaire

During the past 25 years, questionnaire design has been seriously developed from an art of asking questions to the science of asking questions. This line of research has demonstrated on innumerable occasions that slight modifications in the wording of a question and/or the response categories, or of the order of the questions and/or response categories, or in the visual design of the whole questionnaire, as well as of single questions, can affect the answers obtained from the respondents. Since the early days of the Cognitive Aspects of Survey Measurement (CASM) movement, numerous research papers and textbooks have contributed to a coherent theoretical approach that helps explain and predict random measurement error and systematic measurement error related to the questionnaire.

Respondent

Also within the CASM framework, a detailed theoretical approach on how respondents consider and answer survey questions has been developed. As a result, the question–answer process has been described psychologically in great detail. Using this framework, several systematic and random respondent errors have been identified related to what may happen when respondents answer survey questions. For example, satisficing behavior—as opposed to optimizing response behavior—as well as mood effects have been demonstrated to occur by methodological research.

Interviewer

Finally, it has been demonstrated that the personal and social characteristics of interviewers, if they are present, as well as their task-related and non-task-related behaviors may have a considerable influence on the answers obtained from the respondents. Accordingly, a great deal has been learned in the past 30 years about how to train and monitor interviewers to reduce the likelihood that their behavior will negatively impact respondents' answers. However, it should be recognized that it is impossible to eliminate all of the effects of individual respondent reactions to the personal and social characteristics of an interviewer, as interviewer-administered surveys require a personal encounter of respondents and interviewers.

Processing Error

In addition to lack of specification validity and to measurement error, the errors that may occur when editing and processing survey responses obtained from the respondents are part of the TSE framework. Poor handwriting with open-ended questions, the treatment of answers that were initially not codable, and the classification of occupations are just a few examples of possible errors that may occur at the data-editing stage of a survey. Also, scanning paper forms using OCR (optical character recognition) technology or keying the answers from a paper questionnaire into a database are prone to errors. In addition, crucial responses may need to be imputed as a result of item nonresponse (i.e., missing data), and this is susceptible to random error and to systematic error. Accordingly, these survey steps and the errors associated with them might either increase the variance of a variable—which in turn inflates the standard error and the margin of error—or compromise the accuracy of a response because a bias is introduced.

TSE and a Simplified Formula for Mean Square Error

Statistically speaking, TSE is the difference of a sample estimate and the respective parameter in the target population. This difference is measured by the mean square error (MSE), which in turn consists of two components: (a) the squared sum of the bias components plus (b) the sum of the variance components. For the mean square error, one needs to combine both bias and variance from all sources to obtain an estimate of the TSE. However, although most sources of possible error contribute to bias and to variance simultaneously, some error sources are predominantly responsible for an increase of either variance or bias. Thus, a simplified formula for the mean square error is as follows:

$$MSE = (B_{spec} + B_{meas} + B_{proc} + B_{cov} + B_{nr})^2 + VAR_{meas} + VAR_{samp} + VAR_{adj},$$

where the terms have the following meaning:

B_{spec} = Specification bias (reduced construct validity)

B_{meas} = Measurement bias

B_{proc} = Processing bias

B_{cov} = Coverage bias

B_{nr} = Nonresponse bias

VAR_{meas} = Measurement variance

VAR_{samp} = Sampling variance

VAR_{adj} = Adjustment variance

Even though it is easy to estimate sampling variance, as explained in every introductory statistics textbook, it is less than trivial to estimate the other types of variance and especially the biases. Thus, the MSE as a measure for the TSE is often only of heuristic value, because the exact value of a particular variance or bias component cannot be computed reliably.

The MSE offers the opportunity to evaluate survey designs and the estimates computed based on a survey design. Thus, when reporting the results of a survey, end-users of the particular survey data can assess the quality of the estimate not only based on sampling error and the margin of error but also based on other error components. This is especially important because the bias component of the MSE generally is assumed to exceed the size of the variable error. Thus, the sample estimate of the population parameter often departs more from the true value than what is assumed based on the sampling error alone.

Also, the MSE allows an assessment of various survey designs to facilitate the decision of which design likely would produce data of the highest quality in a given time frame and for a fixed amount of money. However, in practice, survey designs are not only evaluated in terms of their MSE. Instead, survey design A may be preferred even though it produces data of lower quality in terms of the MSE compared to survey design B. For example, if the estimated cost for survey design B is considerably higher that design A's costs, the person responsible for the survey may have no choice but to go with survey design A. Thus, the TSE framework also relates to survey costs and requires survey designers to consider the accuracy in relation to cost and the timeliness of reporting.

Ultimately, the researcher's goal is to reduce the TSE by balancing various trade-offs in design decisions. Most of the time, design decisions—like choosing a certain mode of administration or choosing a special interviewer training procedure—affects not only one source of error but rather multiple sources. Thus, each desirable reduction in terms of a particular error source may be accompanied by an undesirable increase of some other error. Therefore, survey designers need to be able to compromise and balance several sources of error simultaneously.

Limitations of the TSE Framework

Even though TSE offers a convincing framework for the accuracy of a survey estimate, it also suffers from a serious drawback. Currently, the effort necessary to compute a reasonable quantitative estimate of the magnitude for a particular error component usually exceeds the available resources. The estimation of the MSE requires multiple repetitions of the survey design, which is usually too costly and also not feasible because the target population does not remain unchanged in between the repetitions. Also, for many survey designs some error components are not accessible because of the field procedures applied or legal constraints (e.g., privacy laws prohibit extensive nonresponse follow-up studies in many countries). Also, it should be noted that for the exact computation of the MSE, the population parameter needs to be readily available. Because this is usually not the case, the MSE is seldom explicitly determined in practice. More often only a few key components are estimated, or a survey design is rated along the various components of bias and variance on a scale from "low" to "high." The decision for a particular survey design then is made on the basis of a detailed computation of some of the error of the components and a rough assessment of the magnitude of some of the other error components. This leaves the researcher, as well as the end-user of a survey statistic, in a situation where a qualitative assessment of the magnitude of the total survey error is the best available assessment.

Strengths and Benefits of the TSE Framework

Nevertheless, survey research and survey methodology have benefited greatly from the emerging TSE approach. The TSE framework has helped to make researchers more aware of possible errors in their survey statistics and the implications of these likely errors. For example, if the response rate and the size of the net sample are the only noticeable indicators for a given survey, many likely biases remain undetermined. Thus, the TSE framework motivates a systematic reflection on possible impairments of survey quality. In doing so, it stimulates a professional evaluation of ongoing surveys in terms of data quality and provides a common language and terminology for a critical discussion.

In addition, the framework provides a theoretical explanation for the various types of possible errors (variance and bias) and also for the underlying mechanisms (random error vs. systematic error). Also, it names a wide range of possible sources of threats to data quality. Hence the TSE framework suggests a theoretical approach for further developments of the survey methods beyond traditional approaches (ones that are not working well enough). In addition, it provides measurable indicators in order to evaluate the improvements of these new survey methods.

The TSE framework also has provided a basis for heightened interdisciplinary discourse across the boundaries of traditional disciplines. Surveys have been used for a long time in sociology, psychology, economics, and educational research, but until relatively recently, professionals in these disciplines have not been in close communication with each other. Even though it is too early to state a true integration of the field-specific methodologies, one can say that the survey branches of the subject-specific methodologies have merged, or at least are in the process of integration, based on the TSE framework and the methodological advances it has stimulated.

In an international perspective, the integrated concept of a TSE has contributed to the dissemination of "standardized" quality criteria and a set of methods to meet those criteria. International survey endeavors like the Programme for International Student Assessment, the International Social Survey Program, and the European Social Survey would not be feasible if researchers of diverse cultural and disciplinary backgrounds had not begun to interact and cooperate within a common framework. Even though there are still many national specifics in the design and the administrations of a survey, a minimum degree of concordance in the assessment of the data quality is provided by the TSE framework.

From a constructivist perspective, the TSE framework seems to be naive in one of its fundamental assumptions: Is there really something like a true value? Although one could argue that it is a reporting error if a respondent omits a certain portion of his or her income when asked for the monthly gross income of the household (e.g., the portion that comes from child support/alimony), one might also argue that this survey's definition of income also contributes to a social construction of "income." More traceable, surveys contribute to the shape and guise of public opinion when results of attitude surveys are repeatedly reported by the media and thus function as a reference point for the general public while they form their opinions on various public issues. Even from a less fundamental perspective, it remains questionable whether there is a perfect, faultless way of designing and conducting a survey. Accordingly, the true value is rather a chimera that cannot be measured without intervening with instruments and procedures that are, by themselves, selective and incomprehensive in principle.

However, from an analytic point of view, it definitely makes sense to assume fixed and constant true values at a given point in time. And it remains the principal goal of survey methods that they measure and mirror these parameters in the target population. With the aid of the TSE framework, survey researchers and survey practitioners have the instruments at hand to assess, discuss, and improve the quality of the respective estimates.

Marek Fuchs

See also Bias; Cognitive Aspects of Survey Methodology (CASM); Construct Validity; Coverage Error; Design Effect (*deff*); Interviewer-Related Error; Mean Square Error; Measurement Error; Missing Data; Mode-Related Error; Nonresponse Error; Nonsampling Error; Questionnaire-Related Error; Random Error; Respondent-Related Error; Sampling Error; Sampling Frame; Survey Costs; Systematic Error; True Value; Unit Nonresponse; Variance

Further Readings

Biemer, P. P., & Lyberg, L. E. (2003). *Introduction to survey quality*. New York: Wiley.

Groves, R. M. (1989). *Survey error and survey cost*. New York: Wiley.

Groves, R. M., Fowler, F. J., Couper, M. P., Lepkowski, J. M., Singer, E., & Tourangeau, R. (2004). *Survey methodology*. New York: Wiley.

Lessler, J. T., & Kalsbeek, W. D. (1992). *Nonsampling errors in surveys*. New York: Wiley.

Weisberg, H. F. (2005). *The total survey error approach: A guide to the new science of survey research*. Chicago: University of Chicago Press.

Touchtone Data Entry

Touchtone data entry (TDE) is a method used with telephone surveys to enable the respondent to directly enter information using the keypad on his or her phone rather than speaking the information to an interviewer. The technology is the same as that used extensively by financial institutions and customer service contact centers. The applications of TDE for survey research include the following:

- As a cost-saving method where the interviewer is replaced by pre-recorded questions delivered by the computer. This is called IVR/TDE, where IVR refers to interactive voice response, and differs from IVR/ASR (automatic speech recognition) in that the latter uses speech recognition in place of TDE.
- To reduce respondent burden when only a small amount of information is needed. For example, respondents to a quarterly business survey might have the option of returning a short paper form, entering the information via a Web site, or dialing in the information using TDE.
- To increase respondent convenience. TDE systems are usually operational 24 hours a day, 7 days a week.
- To provide additional privacy for sensitive questions within an interviewer-administered survey, as the response will not be overheard by someone else in the same room as the respondent (e.g., a parent overhearing a teenager), and the system can be configured to prevent the interviewer from seeing the information entered.

Because of the limitations of most telephone keypads (only 12 keys, including # and *), TDE is best used only for binary responses (e.g., "enter 1 for Yes, 2 for No"), limited choice sets (e.g., "1 for Yes, 2 for No, 3 for Undecided), and simple numeric entry (e.g., "Please enter your year of birth in four digits").

Other numeric information can be collected via TDE, but additional read-back checks (e.g., "You entered 10 thousand and 43 dollars, is that correct? Press 1 for Yes, 2 for No") are necessary because many phones do not have a visual display whereby the respondent can readily see if he or she made an error.

Drawbacks of TDE include the following:

- The need for the respondent to have a touchtone phone
- The increasing tendency of phones to have the keypad embedded in the handset (such as with cordless and mobile phones), making TDE physically awkward as the respondent juggles trying to listen with trying to respond

- Very limited options regarding text, as opposed to numeric, entry due to the many-to-one relationship between alpha characters to numeric keys on keypads
- The need to keep the TDE component of a survey very short and simple (Few people can recall more than four menu items, and if that is combined with a lengthy question administered by a mechanical voice that cannot respond to respondent queries, the respondent may become frustrated and give up.)
- The risk of lower response rates, if a live interviewer who can keep the respondent engaged and motivated is not present

Jenny Kelly

See also Interactive Voice Response (IVR); Telephone Surveys

TRACKING POLLS

A tracking poll is a series of individual surveys repeated continuously over time to measure attitudinal and behavioral changes in a target population. While most commonly associated with election campaigns, tracking polls also are used for a variety of other research needs, from measurement of consumer sentiment to ad tracking in marketing research.

The term *tracking* often mistakenly is used to describe any trend data obtained over time. In fact it correctly applies only to continuous measurements in stand-alone samples. In all applications, the aim of a tracking poll is to produce an ongoing, rather than a one-time or episodic, assessment of evolving attitudes.

Tracking polls provide substantial flexibility in data analysis. The consistent methodology produces useful time trends. Tracking data can be segregated before and after an event of interest—a major policy address, a campaign gaffe, or an advertising launch—to assess that event's impact on attitudes or behavior. These same data can be aggregated to maximize sample sizes for greater analytical power. And tracking surveys can be reported in *rolling averages*, adding new waves of data while dropping old ones to smooth short-term or trendless variability or sampling noise.

The most publicized use of tracking polls is in election campaigns, particularly in the often-frenzied closing days of a contest when campaign advertising spikes, candidates voice their final appeals, voter interest peaks, and tentative preferences become final choices. Campaigns conduct their own private tracking polls to find their best prospects, target their message, and gauge their progress. The news media use tracking polls to understand and report the sentiments behind these crystallizing choices and to evaluate preferences among population groups, as well as to track those preferences themselves.

Election tracking surveys customarily are composed of a series of stand-alone, 1-night surveys, combined and reported in 3- or 4-day rolling averages. In well-designed election tracking polls, the limitations of 1-night sampling on dialing and callback regimens are mitigated by sample adjustments, such as a mix of new and previously dialed sample and the integration of scheduled callbacks into fieldwork protocols.

Election tracking polls have acquired a negative reputation in some quarters because of their reputed volatility. Thoughtful analysis by Robert Erikson and his colleagues, however, has established that volatility in pre-election polls, where it exists, is introduced by idiosyncratic likely voter modeling rather than by tracking poll methodology.

Humphrey Taylor, chairman of the *Harris Poll*, is credited with creating the first daily political tracking polls, a series of twice-daily, face-to-face surveys done for the Conservative Party in the last 4 weeks of the 1970 British general election: One survey tracked media exposure, while the other tracked issue priorities and party preferences on the issues. Taylor (personal communication, January 29, 2007) relates that his tracking data picked up "a collapse in confidence in the Labor government's ability to manage the economy following bad economic news three days before the election. And this was the reason why almost all the polls which stopped polling too soon failed to pick up a last-minute swing to the Conservatives." The Tories won by two points.

Given such sensitivity, tracking polls have developed into an election fixture. In the largest media-sponsored tracking poll in the 2004 election cycle, ABC News and *The Washington Post* conducted 21,265 interviews over the final 32 days of the presidential campaign. In a variation on the election tracking theme, an academic poll that focused on political issues, the National Annenberg Election Survey, interviewed 81,422 respondents in continuous interviewing from October 2003 through Election Day 2004.

In another use of tracking, ABC, with the *Post* (and previously with an earlier partner, *Money* magazine), adapted election tracking methodology in creating the ongoing consumer confidence survey it has conducted weekly since late 1985. Rather than daily sampling, 250 respondents are interviewed each week, with results combined in 4-week rolling averages. By its 21st anniversary in December 2006, the survey comprised more than 280,000 individual interviews.

Despite the attention focused on election tracking polls, by far the heaviest use of tracking surveys is in market and other commercial research, where tracking polls are used to measure consumer behavior or brand attitudes across time—often to gauge customer satisfaction and loyalty, measure advertising exposure and effectiveness, and direct and assess brand image and crisis management efforts.

Gary Langer

See also Election Polls; Media Polls; Pre-Election Polls; Rolling Averages

Further Readings

Erikson, R. S., Panagopoulos, C., & Wlezien, C. (2004). Likely (and unlikely) voters and the assessment of campaign dynamics. *Public Opinion Quarterly, 68,* 588–601.

TRAINING PACKET

A training packet contains the materials that are used to train survey interviewers, either in general interviewing skills or for a specific survey project. The interviewer training packet is an important part of interviewer training and quality data collection. Interviewers often will use the training packet they receive throughout a study to review procedures, and thus it serves an important role in continuous, on-the-job training.

The entire research process relies upon well-trained, knowledgeable interviewers to ensure the success of a project and the integrity of the data. Managers who are tasked with training interviewers must prepare a thorough training curriculum and system to provide the interviewers with the necessary tools to carry out their duties in an ethical and quality-minded manner. Trainers must always keep in mind that many interviewers do not have formal academic experience with the research process. Thus, it is important that interviewer training not only discusses the techniques

of interviewing but also the scientific objectives and ethical obligations of researchers. It should be the goal of every interviewing facility and field staff to standardize the interviewing process, which can be quite difficult considering the complexities of social interaction.

The following sections discuss the basic principles necessary for a thorough interviewer training packet and the content that is used to accomplish this.

Administrative

Typically, general training begins with an overview of the research organization and applicable administrative tasks. Administrative information includes time reporting, assignment logging, and work hour scheduling. The addition of an overview of the research firm provides interviewers with the "big picture" by showing them how they fit into the organization as well as the research process.

The Science of Social Research

The science of social research has come a long way in the past half century. It is imperative that interviewers have an understanding of research ethics and the scientific approach. Most interviewers will not be well versed in these ideas.

The research process begins with project development—that is, what and who are the researchers studying. Depending on the research firm, this could come from an outside client or from within the research organization. The second phase includes the development of the sampling methodology and the instrument (questionnaire) design. The third phase is data collection, which could be computer-assisted telephone interviewing (CATI), computer-assisted personal interviewing (CAPI), Web, or some other collection method. Data entry may also be included in this phase depending on the chosen data collection method. The final phase includes data reduction and analysis as well as reporting.

Interviewing

The following outlines important interviewing training topics that should be addressed in the training packet. It is important to note, some of these topics may only be relevant to certain types of interviewing modes, such as CATI or face-to-face (field) interviewing, but most are universally applicable.

Interviewer Bias

It is important to begin interviewer training with a discussion of interviewer bias. Interviewer bias is the altering of respondent answers due to interviewer actions. Interviewers should keep in mind that everything they say or do can affect respondents. They can lead respondents to answer a certain way or be less truthful. Interviewers should never give respondents any inclination as to what their own opinions may be; instead, they should maintain neutrality at all times.

Approach

The approach an interviewer uses to successfully interview a respondent includes the concepts of rapport, interviewer neutrality, and reading questions exactly as they are written. In addition the interviewer training packet should contain contact information and instructions about each of these matters.

Developing rapport is a great asset to an interviewer. It can help prevent a respondent from terminating before finishing the questionnaire, smooth out the interviewing process, and leave the respondent feeling good about participating in a survey. Building rapport begins with the use of a professional but pleasant demeanor and tone. Interviewers must balance being too happy and enthused, which appears very sales-like or "false," with being too scientific, which comes across as cold.

At the same time, interviewers must always take a neutral demeanor when it comes to anything that could distort the answers given by a respondent. They cannot impart any of their own opinions, as this may bias the respondent. There will be times when interviewers will undoubtedly come across respondents with radically different views from their own; however, they must not show surprise or disagreement with the respondent or judge the respondent in any way. Instead, interviewers must always remember that they are there to collect accurate information, not to impart their own judgments upon respondents.

Interviewers are to read the questions exactly as they are written. Interviewers should be informed that the researchers deliberately, and with great effort, analyze each and every word during the development of the questionnaire. Interviewers are not to provide definitions or clarifications for questions unless instructional materials allow for such actions.

Initial Interaction

The first few seconds of contact between interviewer and respondent often set the tone for all that follows. Within the first few seconds, respondents often will have made up their mind whether they will continue speaking with an interviewer or will terminate the contact. Interviewers must build rapport quickly, deliver their introduction, and screen for eligible respondents within this initial interaction.

The training packet should include instructions and examples about how the interviewer can deliver the introduction of the interview with confidence. Interviewers may have some input into the development of the introductory text, but once it is set they cannot alter it beyond their own ability to properly tailor it to each individual respondent.

The introduction is typically followed by a screening section. This should be explained in the training packet and may be complex with multiple questions, or it may be simple with only a single question. Interviewers must be trained to take extra precaution when asking screening questions. All too often, a respondent will automatically answer in agreement with an interviewer only to have the interviewer discover later that the respondent actually did not qualify to participate. Interviewers should be trained to always encourage respondents to think before they respond. This can be done through the instructions about the use of an appropriate pace and thought-provoking tone of voice.

Techniques for Question Delivery

The training packet also should include information about the following techniques used by interviewers to properly administer the questionnaire.

When a respondent gives an ambiguous answer, an interviewer must probe respondents for clarification. Probing is the use of a nonleading phrase to encourage a respondent to provide a more precise response. Probing should be described in the training packet, and examples of appropriate and inappropriate probes should be included. Interviewers must be comfortable with this technique, as it is needed in a variety of situations. It can be used when respondents do not adhere to a closed-ended question or when an unclear open-ended response is given.

Respondents will sometimes stray from the questions. Interviewers must know how to refocus respondents' attention to the task. Focusing is necessary when a respondent becomes irritated by a particular question and proceeds to rant about the failures of the questionnaire or when a respondent gives open-ended responses to closed-end questions. Interviewers can use reassuring phrases demonstrating that they are listening to the respondent but that they must proceed with the interview. The training packet also should include instructions on how to accomplish this.

Jeff Toor

See also Computer-Assisted Personal Interviewing (CAPI); Computer-Assisted Telephone Interviewing (CATI); Ethical Principles; Face-to-Face Interviewing; Interviewer-Related Error; Interviewer Training; Interviewer Neutrality; Mode of Data Collection; Probing; Respondent-Interviewer Rapport; Tailoring

Further Readings

Barber, A. (1997). Essential interviewing techniques. *National Network of State Polls Newsletter, 27,* 1–5.

Fowler, F., & Mangione, T. (1990). *Standardized survey interviewing: Minimizing interviewer-related error.* Newbury Park, CA: Sage.

Gwartney, P. (2007). *The handbook of training and practice in infant and preschool mental health.* San Francisco: Jossey-Bass.

TREND ANALYSIS

Trend analysis is a statistical procedure performed to evaluate hypothesized linear and nonlinear relationships between two *quantitative* variables. Typically, it is implemented either as an analysis of variance (ANOVA) for quantitative variables or as a regression analysis. It is commonly used in situations when data have been collected over time or at different levels of a variable; especially when a single independent variable, or *factor*, has been manipulated to observe its effects on a dependent variable, or *response variable* (such as in experimental studies). In particular, the means of a dependent variable are observed across conditions, levels, or points of the manipulated independent variable to statistically determine the form, shape, or *trend* of such relationship.

Examples of a quantitative variable that a survey researcher may be interested in manipulating to measure its effects on another quantitative variable are amount of incentives provided in a survey (e.g., 0, 2, 4, and 6 dollars), interviewer training time (e.g., 0, 1, 2, 3 hours), number of interviews assigned to interviewers, time allowed to perform a memory task, distance of exit polling interviewers from the voting booth, number of callbacks in a telephone survey, time elapsed between the first occasion on which participants were sent questionnaires and follow-up surveys, among others.

Using trend analysis, the researcher evaluates statistically whether the relationship between the dependent and independent variable is linear, quadratic, cubic, or other high-order function. The number of *bends* to be tested in a polynomial function is determined by the number of *conditions*, or *levels*, of the independent variable. For instance, if there are two conditions in an experiment, only a linear trend can be tested; if there are three conditions, only a quadratic trend is testable; if there are four conditions, a cubic trend is possible, and so on.

To implement this analysis, it is common practice to have an ordered and equally spaced metric for levels of the independent variable and an equal number of subjects allocated exclusively to each condition of such variable. In cases where the number of subjects allocated into each condition varies, weighting procedures may be used; however, there may be limitations associated with weighted trend analysis that the researcher should further identify. Additionally, interpretation of trend analysis results requires attention to surrounding aspects such as statistical power and effect size.

If implemented as regression analysis, the independent variable (X) is entered into the equation and followed sequentially by increasing powers of the same variable. Consequently, regression equations for trend analysis may be specified as $Y = a_1X + b$ (linear), $Y = a_1X + a_2X^2 + b$ (quadratic), $Y = a_1X + a_2X^2 + a_3X^3 + b$ (cubic), and so forth, where Y represents the dependent variable, b the intercept, and $a_1 \ldots a_k$ regression coefficients. The highest-order regression coefficient in the equation being statistically significant settles the shape of the relationship. p-values help determine whether the observed trend is due to a systematic influence of the manipulated variable or by chance alone.

Under ANOVA, trend analysis is conducted using *contrast coefficients*, also known as *polynomial contrasts*. These coefficients are numbers usually taken from either available tables or user-designed tables. They help represent a hypothesized trend. For example, contrast coefficients for testing a linear trend would be -1.5, -0.5, 0.5, and 1.5, if the independent variable had four levels. For a quadratic trend they would be 1, -1, -1, 1; for a cubic, -1, 3, -3, 1. Contrast coefficients can be plotted over the *y*-axis across levels of the independent variable to visualize the hypothesized trend, for example, a straight line, a u-shape line, an s-shape line, or higher-order trends. Departures of the actual trend (plot of actual means) from the hypothesized trend (plot of contrast coefficients) are analyzed in terms of *p*-values to determine the type of relationship. Currently, commercial statistical packages can perform trend analysis, but they require user-entered contrast coefficients.

René Bautista

See also Analysis of Variance (ANOVA); Dependent Variable; Experimental Design; Independent Variable; *p*-Value; Regression Analysis; Sample Size; Statistical Power

TRIAL HEAT QUESTION

Nearly all pre-election polls include some type of measure of voter choice in one or more candidate races. Unlike many other kinds of survey measures, voter choice is one of the few in which a definitive and highly visible external validation exists. Polls conducted near the time of an election can be compared with the actual election results.

The key measure used in election polling is the *trial heat question:* the question that asks a respondent how he or she is going to vote in a given race. Although such questions might appear to be very straightforward, there are numerous choices in deciding exactly how the question should be worded and where it should be placed in the questionnaire.

Wording of Trial Heat Questions

Among the choices to be made are (a) whether to include the names of all candidates who are on the ballot or just the major candidates, (b) whether to mention the party affiliation of each candidate named, (c) whether to probe respondents for a choice if they say they are undecided, and (d) whether to obtain some measure of strength of support or certainty of the choice.

Nearly all trial heat questions ask respondents to react as if "*the election were held today.*" Most do mention the party affiliation of candidates, though party labels are not on the ballot in all states. There are many ways to probe certainty of choice or strength of support. Most pose a binary choice: strong supporter or not strong, certain or not. One question used by some organizations asks about the candidate not chosen: *Do you think there is a chance that you might vote for _____ in November, or have you definitely decided not to vote for (her)(him)?*

The decision regarding whether or not to include third-party and minor-party candidates is often not a straightforward one. In 2000 and in 2004, Ralph Nader had no realistic chance of winning the presidency, but his candidacy did attract enough support to have arguably affected the outcome of the race in one or more states. All major polling organizations in both years included Nader and his running mate in poll questions conducted in states where Nader was on the ballot. Other third-party candidates were qualified for the ballots in some states, but most polls did not include their names in the question wording asked of respondents, although respondents could volunteer their names.

One practice common to nearly all election pollsters is the rotation of the order of presentation of candidates in the question. Experiments have shown that the order can create small biases in response, and rotation is designed to prevent this. An alternative view is that candidates should be presented in the order they will appear on the ballot (which is itself often determined by chance but then fixed for all ballots in a given jurisdiction). It is not clear whether preserving the ballot order in a telephone survey, for example, re-creates the same cognitive experience a voter will have when encountering the printed ballot or a voting machine on Election Day. In any event, it is almost never feasible for national surveys to implement a state-by-state ballot order.

Pollsters face a somewhat more difficult decision in primary elections, where the number of candidates may be large and no simple criterion, such as the likelihood of winning, can be used to exclude some of the candidates. In presidential campaigns where there is no incumbent, it is not unusual for the field of serious contenders (at least as assessed by political position or experience) to include 10 or more candidates. Until the primary and caucus process gets under way and the field begins to be winnowed, it may be difficult to find grounds for excluding candidates. Thus, pre-primary telephone polls in such instances may require that respondents be read lengthy lists of candidates.

Generic Ballot Questions

A different type of trial heat question does not match the candidates against one another by name but rather asks about voter intention to vote for one party or the other in the election. So-called *generic ballot questions* are commonly used by national polling organizations trying to gauge voter sentiment in elections for the U.S. House of Representatives, where it is not feasible to substitute the names of actual candidates in all of the districts covered by a typical national telephone survey. Generic ballot questions in U.S. House elections have been generally accurate in forecasting the party division of the national House vote in nonpresidential years, despite the fact that only a small percentage of House races are truly competitive in any given election.

Placement of Trial Heat Questions

There is a consensus that trial heat questions should be placed near the front of pre-election polls, with few if any politically substantive questions coming before them. The reason for this is that questions about issues or candidate qualities or traits can raise particular considerations that could affect the choice expressed by respondents, especially among those who are undecided or only weakly committed to a candidate. Voters on Election Day get no such "warm-up" before casting a ballot.

Dealing With Undecided Voters

In any election poll, some respondents will decline to express a choice in response to a trial heat question. It is standard practice to ask these respondents if they "lean" toward one of the candidates. Most polls include the "leaners" in the percentage supporting each candidate.

Even after being asked which way they lean, a small percentage of undecided voters will remain undecided (noncommittal). Pollsters have different ways of dealing with this group. A default assumption is that undecided voters will split in the same proportions as

decided voters. Simply omitting the undecided voters achieves the same result. Others split the undecided half-and-half. But most attempt to make some type of *allocation of undecided voters*, based on other responses they have given in the survey. This allocation may be based on party affiliation, images of the candidates, or even responses to a further probe for a candidate preference (known as the "whiny leaner" question because the interviewer typically tells the respondent that "my supervisor insists that I put down something for your preference so could you please help me out?"). Nonetheless, many of those who decline to state a preference after the standard leaner question has been asked may be unlikely to vote, lacking a strong commitment to one of the candidates.

Other questions ask for the certainty of support, strength of support, and even whether the respondent would ever be willing or unwilling to vote for the candidate.

Scott Keeter

See also Election Polls; Horse Race Journalism; Leaning Voters; Undecided Voters

Further Readings

Daves, R. P. (2000). Who will vote? Allocating likelihood to vote and modeling a probable electorate in preelection polls. In P. J. Lavrakas & M. W. Traugott (Eds.), *Election polls, the news media, and democracy* (pp. 206–223). Washington, DC: CQ Press.

Daves, R. P., & Warden, S. P. (1995). Methods of allocating undecided respondents to candidate choices in pre-election polls. In P. J. Lavrakas, M. W. Traugott, & P. V. Miller (Eds.), *Presidential polls and the news media* (pp. 101–123). Boulder, CO: Westview Press.

Visser, P., Krosnick, J., Marquette, J., & Curtin, M. (2000). Improving election forecasting: Allocation of undecided respondents, identification of likely voters, and response order effects. In P. J. Lavrakas & M. W. Traugott (Eds.), *Election polls, the news media, and democracy* (pp. 224–262). Washington, DC: CQ Press.

TROLDAHL-CARTER-BRYANT RESPONDENT SELECTION METHOD

Researchers often desire a probability method of selecting respondents within households after drawing a probability sample of households. Ideally, they wish to simultaneously maximize response rates (by gaining the respondent's cooperation) and within-unit coverage (by obtaining an accurate listing of all eligible persons in a household). However, they need to balance these two goals because no selection technique is perfect at accomplishing both. In the early history of telephone surveys, one procedure that was considered easy, quick, and likely to improve respondent cooperation was known as the Troldahl-Carter method, to which Barbara Bryant later suggested some modifications. Face-to-face surveys commonly used the Kish technique, which asks for a listing of all men and all women in the household, ranked by age.

Verling Troldahl and Roy Carter feared that informants (those who answer the phone) in a telephone survey would become suspicious of questions that try to obtain a listing of all eligible household members and refuse to participate. So they suggested a brief procedure, building on Kish's work but requiring only two questions: (1) *How many persons (18 years or older) live in your household . . . counting yourself?* and (2) *How many of them are men?* Once interviewers knew the basic household composition by sex and age, according to responses to the two questions, they requested the appropriate respondent after consulting one of four versions of simplified selection tables assigned to households randomly. Because this selection method specified that the respondent be the youngest or oldest male or female, it involved a small violation of random sampling and full coverage because some adults in households of three or more adults of the same sex had no opportunity to be chosen. The amount of bias depends on the proportion of persons in the population barred from the sample and the degree to which they differ from the respondents in the variables studied. In addition, in three-adult households, one of the adults would have the chance of selection into the sample twice. Troldahl and Carter thought these biases were minimal. (Kish's plan also contained a small violation of random sampling, although it is considered to be an almost pure probability method.) In subsequent testing of the Troldahl-Carter method, other modifications to it were suggested, such as changing the second question to *How many of them are women?*

Troldahl and Carter provided an example of an interviewer's selection sheet. The potential numbers of adults in the household were shown at the top (1, 2, 3, or 4 or more). Interviewers circled the correct number and drew a line down the column under that number to the number of men in the household, ranging from 0 to

4 or more. For example, if there were three adults in the household and two were men, one version of the tables showed that the column at which those items intersected designated the respondent as "youngest man." The interviewers' instructions were to say, *I have to ask some questions of the* [PERSON SELECTED] *in your household.* If the informant was of the correct gender, the interviewer asked, *Would that be you?* If the desired respondent was of the opposite sex, the interviewer asked for the chosen person and implemented follow-up procedures if he or she was unavailable.

By the mid-1970s, the distribution of women and men within households had changed, although the proportion of men to women had not. Young males were less likely to be at home than they had been in the 1960s. Thus, Bryant suggested a solution to the problem of obtaining better representation of males and females, though she had no suggestions about the problem of unavailable young males. She proposed using the fourth Troldahl-Carter table just half as often as the other three. The sequence of tables used was 1, 2, 3, 4, 1, 2, 3. Many researchers adopted this idea, and this modification became known as the Troldahl-Carter-Bryant (T-C-B) respondent selection method. Ron Czaja, Johnnie Blair, and Jutta Sebestik compared the T-C-B method with a further modification of T-C-B asking for women instead of men, as well as with the Kish procedure. In T-C-B/women, the order of tables is 1, 2, 3, 4, 2, 3, 4. They concluded that the T-C-B/men sample had the highest proportion of males, followed by the T-C-B/women sample. The T-C-B/women version had the best completion rate. The T-C-B/men adaptation produced the highest proportion of married-person households, as well as a lower proportion of one-adult households, possibly linked to sex differences and a lower cooperation rate. Later work has attempted to simplify the T-C-B method, such as the Hagan and Collier technique or the "youngest male/oldest female" method.

Cecilie Gaziano

See also Hagan and Collier Selection Method; Kish Selection Method; Within-Unit Coverage; Within-Unit Selection

Further Readings

Bryant, B. E. (1975). Respondent selection in a time of changing household composition. *Journal of Marketing Research, 12,* 129–135.

Czaja, R., Blair, J., & Sebestik, J. P. (1982). Respondent selection in a telephone survey: A comparison of three techniques. *Journal of Marketing Research, 19*, 381–385.

Gaziano, C. (2005). Comparative analysis of within-household respondent selection techniques. *Public Opinion Quarterly, 69*, 124–157.

Hagan, D. E., & Collier, C. M. (1983). Must respondent selection procedures for telephone surveys be invasive? *Public Opinion Quarterly, 47*, 547–556.

Keeter, S., & Fisher, K. (1997–1998). Comparison of two respondent selection methods. *National Network of State Polls (NNSP) Newsletter, 31*(Winter), 1–3.

Kish, L. (1949). A procedure for objective respondent selection within the household. *Journal of the American Statistical Association, 44*, 380–387.

Troldahl, V., & Carter, R. E., Jr. (1964). Random selection of respondents within households in phone surveys. *Journal of Marketing Research, 1*, 71–76.

TRUE VALUE

A true value, also called a *true score*, is a psychometric concept that refers to the measure that would have been observed on a construct were there not any error involved in its measurement. Symbolically, this often is represented by $X = T + e$, where T is the (error-free) true value, e is the error in measurement, and X is the observed score. For example, a survey respondent's true value (T) on a measure (e.g., a 5-item Likert scale measuring attitudes toward her ancestor's native land) might be 13, but her observed score (X) on a given day may be 15 or 17 or 10. There are many reasons why the observed score may deviate from the true value, but the researcher will rarely know exactly why or exactly by how much. In theory, if the error on the observed score is truly random, then a researcher could take the same measure from the same respondent over and over again, and assuming the true value on that measure for that respondent did not actually change over the time the various measures were being taken, then the mean (average) score of the various observed scores would be the true value. The concept of a true value relates to the concepts of reliability and validity.

For survey researchers, the true value has some very practical applications. First, it reminds researchers that random error is always to be assumed and that any one measurement should never be regarded as error-free. Second, if the researcher has the test–retest reliability on a given variable (x), then the researcher can apply a *correction for attenuation* to adjust any correlations that are calculated between x and some other variable of interest. The correction of attenuation recognizes that any observed correlation between two variables will be suppressed (i.e., lower than their true correlation) by a function linked to the amount of unreliability in the observed scores for the variables. That is, only when there is no error in the observed variables, and thus the observed scores are in fact the true values, will the observed correlation be the true correlation value.

Paul J. Lavrakas

See also Construct Validity; Measurement Error; Random Error; Reliability; Test–Retest Reliability; Validity

Further Readings

Guilford, J. P. (1954). *Psychometric methods* (2nd ed.). New York: McGraw-Hill.

TRUST IN GOVERNMENT

Trust in government has multiple meanings, many sources, and numerous consequences. David Easton distinguished between *diffuse support*—that is, trust in the institutions and mechanisms of government—and *specific support*, trust in current officeholders. Researchers also can ask about trust in specific institutions within government (legislative, judicial, executive, law enforcement), at all levels (federal, state, and local).

Political life, even at a routine and mundane level, entails risk. When we vote for a candidate, pay our taxes, or obey the law, we hope that our efforts will not be wasted or exploited. Civic life, in a nutshell, demands that we trust our government to uphold its end of the democratic bargain. Survey research has tracked the rise and fall in political trust over the decades and has tried to identify the factors that sustain this tenuous but critical component of civilization.

Many surveys use a single item that simply asks respondents how much they "trust the government." By far the most frequently used item is Question 1 from the biennial National Elections Study (NES): *How much of the time do you think you can trust the government in Washington to do what is right—just about always, most of the time, or only some of the time?*

But what exactly is being measured? Many scholars criticize the NES scale (consisting of four items) for tapping predominantly short-term feelings about current office-holders, rather than long-term beliefs about the institutions and mechanisms of government. Because continuity is everything in the study of political trends, however, the NES instrument is likely to remain.

Survey results indicate that trust in government has declined substantially since the 1960s. A majority of the American public these days trusts the government "only some of the time." This has caused great concern for the survival of government and civic life in general. Several scholars have proposed a reciprocal relationship between trust in government and *social capital*, which can be thought of as trust in one's fellow human beings. To investigate this hypothesis, scholars have used data from the General Social Survey, which asks participants to report on the *confidence* they hold in various institutions, including the Executive Branch, the Supreme Court, and Congress. Congress, it turns out, is the institution Americans love to hate more than any other.

Fluctuations in trust follow recent government performance as well as political scandal, but a dislike for today's politicians does not necessarily mean rejection of our way of government. Standard trust measures perhaps exaggerate public disregard for government, for they lump together *skeptical* respondents with the truly *cynical*. When the scale is extended on the less trusting end, only about a quarter of the population place themselves below the midpoint. Still, trust in government has never approached the high point it reached in the 1960s, even after the economic boom of the late 1990s. The accumulation of political scandal, beginning with Watergate and Vietnam, seems to have soured a whole generation on politicians, if not the basic foundation of democratic government.

Polls taken in the months following the September 11 attacks showed an extraordinary jump in trust. This was commonly seen as a "rally round the flag" effect, wherein the attacks inspired extraordinary national unity. A closer look revealed that the attacks merely temporarily shifted respondents' focus to international affairs, where the government has always enjoyed greater public confidence.

Thomas E. Nelson

See also General Social Survey (GSS); National Election Studies (NES); Public Opinion; Social Capital; Trend Analysis; Validity

Further Readings

Hibbing, J. R., & Theiss-Morse, E. (Eds.). (2001). *What is it about government that Americans dislike?* New York: Cambridge University Press.

Langer, G. (2002). Trust in government . . . to do what? *Public Perspective*, (July/August), 7–10.

Levi, M., & Stoker, L. (2000). Political trust and trustworthiness. *Annual Review of Political Science, 3*, 475–508.

Putnam, R. D. (1995). Bowling alone: America's declining social capital. *Journal of Democracy, 6*(1), 65–78.

t-Test

A *t*-test is a statistical process to assess the probability that a particular characteristic (the mean) of two populations is different. It is particularly useful when data are available for only a portion of one or both populations (known as a *sample*). In such a case, a *t*-test will enable an estimate of whether any differences in means between the two groups are reflective of differences in the respective populations or are simply due to chance. This statistical process is called a *t*-test because it uses a *t*-distribution to generate the relevant probabilities, typically summarized in a *t*-table.

There are many types of *t*-tests, each of which is appropriate for a particular context and nature of the data to be analyzed. Each *t*-test has its own set of assumptions that should be checked prior to its use. For instance, comparing the average value of a characteristic for independent samples (i.e., when individuals in each sample have no systematic relationship to one another) and for dependent samples (such as when related pairs are divided into two groups) requires different kinds of *t*-tests.

Frequently, a *t*-test will involve assessing whether a sample comes from a specific population or whether average values between two samples indicate differences in the respective populations. In the latter case, three factors determine the results of a *t*-test: the size of the difference in average value between the two groups; the number of data points, or observations, in each group; and the amount of variation in values within each group.

A *t*-test is conducted by calculating a *t*-statistic and by using a *t*-table to interpret its value. The equation for the *t*-statistic depends on the context and nature of data. For instance, when comparing the likelihood that a sample belongs to a particular population, the equation for the *t*-test is $t = (x - \mu)/(s/\sqrt{n})$ where x is the mean for the sample, μ is the known value for the population, s is the standard deviation of the sample, and n is the number of data points in the sample.

As an example, in a study that examines the effectiveness of a new math curriculum, researchers might ask whether the curriculum is related to students' state standardized math test scores. A survey might be used to collect state test score data for students who participate in the new curriculum and for those who use a different curriculum. The researchers would want to make generalizations for all students who use and do not use the curriculum. However, because gathering the test score data for every student might be difficult and expensive, the researchers might send the questionnaire to only a sample of students in each group.

After calculating the average test score of each sample, the researchers could use a *t*-test to estimate the likelihood that the difference between the two samples' average test scores was really reflective of different test scores between the populations and not simply due to chance. If, for instance, the averages of the two samples were very similar, data were only available for a handful of students in each sample, and students' test scores in each sample varied greatly, then a *t*-test would likely show that the two populations did not necessarily have different average test scores and that the differences in the samples were simply due to chance. This would be shown by a very low value of the *t*-statistic. If, on the other hand, the difference in average test scores between the samples was great, there were many students in each sample, and students' scores within each sample did not vary greatly, a *t*-test would support the conclusion that the populations' average test scores were truly different from one another. This would be evidenced by a very high value of the *t*-statistic.

Joel K. Shapiro

See also *F*-Test; Mean; *n*; *p*-Value; Regression Analysis; Research Hypothesis; Statistic; Type I Error

Further Readings

Kvanli, A. H., Guynes, C. S., & Pavur, R. J. (1986). *Introduction to business statistics*. St. Paul, MN: West Publishing.

Wonnacott, T. H., & Wonnacott, R. J. (1990). *Introductory statistics* (5th ed.). New York: Wiley.

TYPE I ERROR

Type I error refers to one of two kinds of error of inference that could be made during statistical hypothesis testing. The concept was introduced by J. Newman and E. Pearson in 1928 and formalized in 1933. A Type I error occurs when the null hypothesis (H_0), that there is no effect or association, is rejected when it is actually true. A Type I error is often referred to as a *false positive*, which means that the hypothesis test showed an effect or association, when in fact there was none.

In contrast, a Type II error occurs when the null hypothesis fails to be rejected when it is actually false. The relation between the Type I error and Type II error is summarized in Table 1.

The probability of a Type I error is usually denoted by the Greek letter alpha (α) and is often called the *significance level* or the *Type I error rate*. In the table, the Greek letter beta (β) is the probability of a Type II error. In most studies the probability of a Type I error is chosen to be small—for example, 0.1, 0.05, 0.01—or expressed in a percentage (10%, 5%, or 1%) or as odds (1 time in 10, 1 time in 20, or 1 time in 100). Selecting the alpha level of 0.05, for example, means that if the test were to be conducted many times where the null hypothesis is true, one can expect that 5% of the tests will produce an erroneously positive result. A Type I error is an error due to chance and not because of a systematic error such as model misspecification or confounding.

A Type I error could be illustrated with an example of a disease diagnostic test. The null hypothesis is that a person is healthy and does not have a particular disease. If the result of a blood test to screen for the disease is positive, the probability that the person has the disease is high; however, because of the test used, a healthy person may also show a positive test result by chance. Such a false positive result is a Type I error for the disease diagnostic test. Note that a Type

Table 1   Type I and Type II errors in hypothesis testing

Statistical Decision	True State of the Null Hypothesis (H_0)	
	H_0 True	H_0 False
Reject H_0	Type I error (i.e., wrong decision) Probability $= \alpha$	Correct decision Probability $= 1 - \alpha$
Do not reject H_0	Correct decision Probability $= 1 - \beta$	Type II error (i.e., wrong decision) probability $= \beta$

I error depends on the way the hypothesis test is formulated, that is, whether "healthy" or "sick" is taken as the null condition. In survey research, an example of a Type I error would occur when a pollster finds a statistically significant association between age and attitudes toward normalization of U.S. relations with Cuba, if in fact no such relationship exists apart from the particular polling data set.

When testing multiple hypotheses simultaneously (e.g., conducting post-hoc testing or data mining), one needs to consider that the probability of observing a false positive result increases with the number of tests. In particular, a *family-wise* Type I error is making one or more false discoveries, or Type I errors, among all the hypotheses when performing multiple pairwise tests. In this situation, an adjustment for multiple comparison, such as Bonferroni, Tukey, or Scheffe adjustments, is needed. When the number of tests is large, such conservative adjustments would often require prohibitively small individual significance levels. Y. Benjamini and Y. Hochberg proposed that, in such situations, other statistics such as false discovery rates are more appropriate when deciding to reject or accept a particular hypothesis.

Georgiy Bobashev

See also Alternative Hypothesis; Errors of Commission; Null Hypothesis; Statistical Power; Type II Error

Further Readings

Benjamini, Y., & Hochberg, Y. (1995). Controlling the false discovery rate—a practical and powerful approach to multiple testing. *Journal of the Royal Statistical Society: Series B (Statistical Methodology) 57,* 289–300.

Neyman, J., & Pearson, E. S. (1967). On the use and interpretation of certain test criteria for purposes of statistical inference, Part I. In J. Neyman & E. S. Pearson

(Eds.), *Joint statistical papers of J. Neyman and E. S. Pearson* (pp. 1–66). London: Cambridge University Press.

Neyman, J., & Pearson, E. S. (1967). The testing of statistical hypotheses in relation to probabilities a priori. In J. Neyman & E. S. Pearson (Eds.), *Joint statistical papers of J. Neyman and E. S. Pearson* (pp. 186–202). London: Cambridge University Press.

TYPE II ERROR

Type II error refers to one of two errors that could be made during hypothesis testing. The concept was introduced by J. Newman and E. Pearson in 1928 and formalized in 1933. A Type II error occurs when the null hypothesis (H_0), that there is no effect or association, fails to be rejected when it is actually false. A Type II error is often referred to as a *false negative* because the hypothesis test led to the erroneous conclusion that no effect or association exists, when in fact an effect or association does exist. In contrast to Type II errors, a Type I error occurs when the null hypothesis is rejected when it is actually true. The features of Type II and Type I errors are summarized in Table 1, above.

In the table, the maximum probability of a Type II error is denoted by the Greek letter beta (β), and $1 - \beta$ is often referred to as the *statistical power of the test*. It is intuitive to require that the probability of a Type II error be small; however, a decrease of β causes an increase in the Type I error, denoted by Greek letter alpha (α), for the same sample size.

In many statistical tasks, data collection is limited by expense or feasibility. Thus, the usual strategy is to fix the Type I error rate and collect sufficient data to give adequate power for appropriate alternative hypotheses. Although power considerations vary depending on the purpose of the study, a typical requirement for the power is 0.8, which corresponds to a 20% Type II error rate. However, when data exist in abundance, this strategy will lead to rejecting the null hypothesis in favor of even tiny effects that might have little practical value. For practical use, it is important to have a clear and measurable statement of the alternative hypothesis. For example, if H_0 for a continuous effect x states that there is no effect (e.g., $x = 0$) and the alternative hypothesis (H_1) states that there is some effect (e.g., $x \neq 0$), the concept of Type II error is not practical because H_1 covers all possible outcomes except a single value (that for H_0). Commonly, an alternative hypothesis is given in terms of the measurable effect size, based on the scientific relevance.

For example, the use of mammography to screen for breast cancer provides an illustration of how Type II error operates. The null hypothesis is that a subject is healthy. A positive test result does not necessarily mean that a woman has breast cancer. The main purpose of the mammogram is to not miss the cancer if it is present, that is, to minimize the Type II error. However, tests like mammograms have to be designed to balance the risk of unneeded anxiety caused by a false positive result (Type I error) and the consequences of failing to detect the cancer (Type II error). In survey research, an example of a Type II error would occur when a pollster fails to find a statistically significant association between age and attitudes toward normalization of U.S. relations with Cuba, if in fact such a relationship exists apart from the particular polling data set.

If a number of studies have been conducted on the same topic, it is possible sometimes to pool the data or the results and conduct a meta-analysis to reduce type II error. Because of the relationship between the two types of error, many considerations regarding the Type I error—such as multiple tests and rejecting (H_0) by chance—also apply to the Type II error.

Georgiy Bobashev

See also Alternative Hypothesis; Errors of Omission; Null Hypothesis; Statistical Power; Type I Error

Further Readings

Neyman, J., & Pearson, E. S. (1967). On the use and interpretation of certain test criteria for purposes of statistical inference, Part I. In J. Neyman & E. S. Pearson (Eds.), *Joint statistical papers of J. Neyman and E. S. Pearson* (pp. 1–66). London: Cambridge University Press.

Neyman, J., & Pearson, E. S. (1967). The testing of statistical hypotheses in relation to probabilities a priori. In J. Neyman & E. S. Pearson (Eds.), *Joint statistical papers of J. Neyman and E. S. Pearson* (pp. 186–202). London: Cambridge University Press.

U

UNABLE TO PARTICIPATE

The *unable to participate* survey disposition is used in all types of surveys, regardless of mode. It occurs when the selected respondent for a survey is incapable of completing the telephone or in-person interview or of completing and returning the Web-based or mail questionnaire. Cases coded with the unable to participate disposition often are considered eligible cases in calculating survey response rates.

A variety of permanent and temporary reasons may cause respondents to be unable to participate in a survey. Permanent reasons for being unable to participate in a survey include language barriers, physical or mental disabilities, and chronic severe illnesses. The sampled respondent in a telephone or in-person survey may not speak English (or another target language) well enough to complete the interview. Respondents with a mental disability may not have the cognitive capacity to complete the survey questionnaire or the interview. Being hospitalized beyond the survey's field period would also be considered a permanent reason for being unable to participate in the survey. In the case of a mail or Internet survey, being illiterate would constitute a permanent reason for being unable to participate. The unable to participate survey disposition usually is considered a final disposition in cases where there is a permanent or long-term reason for the respondent not being capable of participating in the survey.

In other cases, the reason for a respondent being unable to participate in a survey may be temporary in nature. For example, the sampled respondent might be intoxicated or might be ill or in the hospital for a brief period. In these cases, the unable to participate disposition should be considered a temporary disposition although the interviewer should do his or her best to determine how long this situation will last (even if just an estimated number of days) and note this in the case history file; then the case should be recontacted after an appropriate amount of time has passed.

It is important to note that cases in which the respondent indicates that he or she is unable to participate in the survey may be a tactic by the respondent to avoid completing the interview or the questionnaire. Although these instances are not common, cases in which it is detected should be considered indirect respondent refusals.

Matthew Courser

See also Final Dispositions; Language Barrier; Respondent Refusal; Response Rates; Temporary Dispositions; Unavailable Respondent

Further Readings

American Association for Public Opinion Research. (2006). *Standard definitions: Final dispositions of case codes and outcome rates for surveys* (4th ed.). Lenexa, KS: Author.
Lavrakas, P. J. (1993). *Telephone survey methods: Sampling, selection, and supervision* (2nd ed.). Newbury Park, CA: Sage.

UNAIDED RECALL

One of the first decisions a designer of a questionnaire must make is whether the information sought can best and most appropriately be gathered from respondents by asking questions with or without clues to the possible or most appropriate answers. A question-asking strategy that relies on as few cues as possible, or even none whatsoever, in order to encourage the respondent to spontaneously mention items of interest is known as *unaided recall*. Such question tools are commonly used in marketing research and other situations in which it is desirable to know the respondent's reaction to questions unprompted by previous questions or topics mentioned in previous questions. In social science surveys, it is often desirable to elicit answers unstructured by other specific political or social questions. These types of subtle cues and reminders have a way of prompting, structuring, and defining the range of suitable ideas and events to be recalled.

Unaided recall questions typically ask respondents to mention specific instances of more general phenomena that are typically construed rather broadly. For example, an unaided recall question might ask respondents to describe all television news programs they watched in a given day or week. Such a question design places the cognitive burden on the respondent to remember, name, and categorize his or her answer. The strength of such a question is that it allows the respondent to respond naturally, that is, unprompted by various cues as to what kind of specific information is sought. However, this question format can be subject to a variety of errors, including accuracy and omission. On occasion, for certain question topics, accuracy can be assessed by comparing the respondents' unaided responses to various types of records. Omission of useful information is likely when questions are unaided because particular information might easily be forgotten or considered irrelevant by the respondent. Cues, as in *aided recall*, can improve memory for suitable events and ideas by providing examples, but they can also introduce error by suggesting inappropriate ideas to the respondent. Most importantly, however, cues can affect and even structure the kinds of ideas and events that the respondent mentions.

People's memory for particular things may fail for many reasons, including that they may have never really known the information, have honestly forgotten it, or they are unwilling to spend the required time and mental effort to recall completely and make sure their answers are as accurate as can be. People might remember the information incompletely, recall it incorrectly, or express it poorly so that it is misunderstood by the researcher.

However, sometimes researchers want to know exactly whether a respondent can instantaneously remember (recall) something without being prompted with any clues, such as when branding studies are done and respondents are asked on the spur of the moment to come up with a name of a company (e.g., *Please name a company that makes digital video recorders*). In these cases, it is informative to the survey sponsors (e.g., the client company) to know what portion of the sample is able to spontaneously generate their name and their competitors' names without any prompting. In such a case, unaided recall would be the preferred research strategy. This does not preclude use of additional aided recall questions later in the survey.

Certain types of unaided recall question characteristics can affect memory. In designing a survey question to ask people about certain events, the survey designer could allow the respondent to list the relevant events in any order. When faced with particular tasks, however, such as biographical information, it may be most effective to ask in reverse chronological order, depending perhaps on the topic domain. The survey designer would also want to make certain that respondents have sufficient time to think the issue through carefully before responding and not be hurried along by the interviewer. Survey designers can also aid respondent recall by including separate questions about smaller, less inclusive categories of events. A question requiring respondents to recall interactions with a physician might inquire separately about office visits and email or telephone consultations.

Another significant problem of the unaided recall question strategy relates to the covered time frame. One problem is *telescoping*, which is a type of mental bias such that a respondent may recall a specific event but misremember the time frame in which it occurred. As Seymour Sudman and Norman Bradburn have noted, telescoping can be forward, in which people recall events as occurring more recently than they really did, or backward, in which people recall events as happening longer ago than they really did. Telescoping poses significant problems for estimation, as this type of bias may increase as the time period becomes shorter. This can cause large problems of overestimation.

Bounded recall is one question-asking procedure that reduces telescoping bias by repeating interviews with the same respondents over periods of time. The first round of questions is typically unstructured, with repeated rounds involving various structured questions in which the answers to previous unstructured questions are incorporated as reminders. At the same time, new behaviors are checked with previous ones to avoid duplications. In this way, the first round of unaided questions can be said to bound the responses and provide a kind of baseline for subsequent rounds of questions and answers. Bounding can reduce telescoping but does not improve the problem of omissions. Bounding, in its full implementation, requires expensive panel data in which the same respondents are repeatedly interviewed. But modified bounding questions can be implemented in a single interview by asking first about an earlier time period and then referring back to that period when asking about subsequent time frames.

The mode by which the question is administered is also important to consider, that is, face-to-face, telephone, or self-administered interview, such as in a mail or Internet survey. If the questionnaire is self-administered, presumably the respondent could take as much time to think about the answer as needed. A person might feel under more time pressure if an interviewer is waiting for the answer on the telephone than in person. In self-administered online questionnaires, the designer might want to control cueing effects of question context or order by requiring people to answer questions in a fixed order and present them one at a time, thus limiting people's ability to scroll ahead to learn more about the question context. If the question is being posed to a respondent by an in-person interviewer, it also places some burden on the interviewer to gather verbatim answers on the fly as the respondent provides the information. To ensure this information is gathered completely and accurately, the interviewer must be carefully instructed to reproduce the respondent's comments with precision.

Accuracy and completeness can be enhanced by training interviewers to use procedures such as asking the respondent to slow down, to repeat, and to review the answer with the respondent more than once to make sure the answer accurately reflects what the respondent intended. Such interviewers might also be equipped with voice recording technology or be specifically trained to write down material rapidly and accurately. Interviewers must also be given specific and uniform instructions regarding the appropriate probing that they are to do to make certain that the respondent has told all they need to in order to answer the questions completely. Standard probing protocols are important to minimize the likelihood that a respondent's

ability to provide answers is not confounded with loquaciousness and perhaps general social skills.

Commonly anticipated answers to unaided recall questions can be precoded and be available for selection by the interviewer, but they are not to be read to the respondent. This strategy requires judgment on the part of the interviewer to recognize and categorize the answer properly. Unaided recall is an important tool in the design of questionnaires.

Gerald M. Kosicki

See also Aided Recall; Aided Recognition; Bounding; Cognitive Aspects of Survey Methodology (CASM); Errors of Omission; Interviewer Training; Mode of Data Collection; Precoded Question; Probing; Satisficing; Telescoping; Verbatim Responses

Further Readings

Sudman, S., & Bradburn, N. M. (1982). *Asking questions: A practical guide to questionnaire design.* San Francisco: Jossey-Bass.

Tanur, J. M. (Ed.). (1992). *Questions about questions: Inquiries into the cognitive biases of surveys.* New York: Russell Sage Foundation.

Tourangeau, R., Rips, L. J., & Rasinski, K. (2000). *The psychology of survey response.* New York: Cambridge University Press.

Weisberg, H. F. (2005). *The total survey error approach: A guide to the new science of survey research.* Chicago: University of Chicago Press.

UNAVAILABLE RESPONDENT

The *unavailable respondent* survey disposition is used in all types of surveys, regardless of mode. It occurs when the selected respondent for a survey is not available (a) at the time of interview, (b) for some portion of the survey field period (temporarily unavailable), or (c) until after the field period of the survey has ended (permanently unavailable). Cases in which the respondent is unavailable, regardless of the duration, are considered eligible cases in calculating survey response rates.

In most surveys, less than half of the completed interviews result after the first contact with the respondent, regardless of whether that contact occurs in person, by telephone, by mail, or by Internet. Many respondents simply are not available at the time of an interviewer's telephone call or visit to the respondent's residence. Respondents may also be away from their residence, may not have retrieved or processed their postal mail or their electronic mail, or may be too busy to complete the survey immediately after it is received. In these situations, it is important to make additional contacts with the selected respondent. For example, in-person and telephone interviewers may ask questions to determine a good day or time for another call or visit to the respondent; survey firms may send a reminder postcard or email message to the respondent asking him or her again to complete and return the survey questionnaire.

In other situations, respondents might be unavailable for several days or longer (not just at the time of contact by an interviewer or at the time a survey is delivered). Respondents may be on vacation or away on a business trip. As long as these temporary periods of unavailability do not extend beyond the field period of a survey, most survey firms hold these cases for an appropriate amount of time and then make additional attempts to contact these respondents and to obtain their cooperation.

There also are instances when the respondent is unavailable during the entire field period of a survey. These instances can include, for example, extended vacations and business travel to other countries. Unless the field period of the survey is extended, these cases usually are coded as permanently unavailable and are not processed further or contacted again.

Matthew Courser

See also Callbacks; Final Dispositions; Response Rates; Temporary Dispositions

Further Readings

American Association for Public Opinion Research. (2006). *Standard definitions: Final dispositions of case codes and outcome rates for surveys* (4th ed.). Lenexa, KS: Author.

Lavrakas, P. J. (1993). *Telephone survey methods: Sampling, selection, and supervision* (2nd ed.). Newbury Park, CA: Sage.

Unbalanced Question

An unbalanced question is one that has a question stem that does not present the respondent with all reasonably plausible sides of an issue. The issue of balance in a survey question also can apply to the response alternatives that are presented to respondents. Unbalanced questions generally are closed-ended questions, but it is possible to use open-ended questions in which the question stem is unbalanced. An unbalanced question will not always lead to biased data, but that is the concern in most instances.

For example, the following closed-ended question is unbalanced for several reasons and will lead to invalid (biased) data:

Many people believe that American troops should be withdrawn from Iraq as soon as possible. Do you Strongly Agree, Agree, Somewhat Agree, or Strongly Disagree?

First, the question stem is unbalanced because it presents only one side of the issue in noting only one position taken by some in the general public. Second, the response alternatives are not balanced (symmetrical) as there are three "agree" choices and only one "disagree" choice. Third, the three response alternatives have no true midpoint; this is another aspect of the asymmetrical (unbalanced) nature of the response alternatives.

In contrast, a balanced version of this question would be as follows:

Some people believe that American troops should be withdrawn from Iraq as soon as possible, whereas other people believe that they should remain in Iraq until the country is more stable. What is your opinion on whether the troops should be withdrawn as soon as possible? Do you Strongly Agree, Somewhat Agree, Somewhat Disagree, or Strongly Disagree?

This wording is balanced because it poses both sides of the issue. It also has a symmetrical set of response alternatives with two choices for "agree" and two similarly worded choices for "disagree." Furthermore, it has a true midpoint even though that midpoint does not have an explicit response alternative associated with it. If the researchers wanted to add a fifth choice representing the midpoint they could have added, "Neither Agree nor Disagree" in the middle.

In writing survey questions, it is easy for a researcher to avoid using unbalanced questions, unless there is a specific purpose to use such a question. A legitimate use would be the methodological testing of such question wording to study how such wording affects the answers given by respondents. In some other cases, an unethical or unscrupulous researcher may purposely use unbalanced questions to bias data in the directions that favor his or her client's interests. For example, a client with a particular political agenda can have a researcher word questions in an unbalanced fashion to make it more likely the answers respondents give are in a direction favored by the client. The unbalanced question—*Many people believe that American troops should be withdrawn from Iraq as soon as possible. Do you Strongly Agree, Agree, Somewhat Agree, or Strongly Disagree?*—makes it more likely that respondents will agree than if they were presented with a balanced version of this question. If the client wanted data to show that a larger proportion of the public wants troops to be withdrawn, then using an unbalanced question such as this would accomplish that end. Because too few reporters, editors, and producers in the news media ask to see the exact question wording that underlies survey data, they are not in a position to know whether the data are likely to be biased. As a result, data from unbalanced questions are easily disseminated without the news organization or the public knowing better.

Paul J. Lavrakas

See also Balanced Question; Closed-Ended Question; Open-Ended Question; Question Stem; Random Assignment; Response Alternatives

Further Readings

American Association for Public Opinion Research. (2007). *Question wording*. Retrieved March 6, 2008, from http://www.aapor.org/questionwording

Shaeffer, E. M., Krosnick, J. A., Langer, G. E., & Merkle, D. M. (2005). Comparing the quality of data obtained by minimally balanced and fully balanced attitude questions. *Public Opinion Quarterly, 69*(3), 417–428.

UNBIASED STATISTIC

An unbiased statistic is a sample estimate of a population parameter whose sampling distribution has a mean that is equal to the parameter being estimated. Some traditional statistics are unbiased estimates of their corresponding parameters, and some are not. The simplest case of an unbiased statistic is the sample mean. Under the usual assumptions of population normality and simple random sampling, the sample mean is itself normally distributed with a mean equal to the population mean (and with a standard deviation equal to the population standard deviation divided by the square root of the sample size). A sample proportion is also an unbiased estimate of a population proportion. That is not surprising, as a proportion is a special kind of mean where all of the observations are 0s or 1s.

The matter is more complicated with regard to the sample variance. If the sum of the squared differences of the sample observations from the sample mean is divided by the sample size n, that statistic is *not* unbiased for estimating the population variance. To get an unbiased estimate of the population variance, the researcher needs to divide that sum of squared deviations by one less than the sample size.

The situation is even more complicated for the sample standard deviation. Although the sample variance obtained by dividing the sum of squares by $n - 1$ provides an unbiased estimate of the population variance, the square root of that statistic is *not* an unbiased estimator of the square root of the population variance (i.e., the population standard deviation), despite some claims made in certain statistics textbooks. (In mathematical statistical jargon, the expected value [mean] of the square root of a statistic is not, in general, equal to the square root of the expected value of the original statistic.)

For bivariate normal distributions for which the Pearson product–moment correlation coefficient (r) is a measure of the direction and the degree of linear relationship between the two variables, the sample r does not have a normal sampling distribution and is not an unbiased estimate of its population counterpart. The principal reason for this is that r is "boxed in" between -1 and $+1$. Fisher's z-transformation of r can be employed to partially remove the bias, and it is used frequently in testing hypotheses about population correlations and in establishing confidence intervals around sample correlations. The r is transformed to z (Fisher's z, not standardized variable z), and the test is carried out in that metric. For the confidence interval, r is transformed to z, the interval is obtained for z, and the end points of the interval are transformed back to the r scale.

In the survey sampling context, a well-known statistic for estimating the population total or mean in the presence of additional auxiliary information is the ratio estimator. Although this estimator is not unbiased for the corresponding population parameter, its bias is in part a decreasing function of the sample size.

It perhaps should go without saying, but an unbiased statistic computed from a given sample is not always equal to the corresponding parameter. Unbiasedness is strictly a "long run" concept. Thus, although not necessarily equal to the population parameter for any given sample, the expected value of the statistic across repeated samples is, in fact, the parameter itself. On any given occasion, a biased statistic might actually be closer to the parameter than would an unbiased statistic. When estimating a population variance, for example, division of the sum of squares by n rather than $n-1$ might provide a "better" estimate. That statistic is the "maximum likelihood" estimator of a population variance. So care should be taken when choosing a statistic based on its bias and precision; that is, variability.

Thomas R. Knapp

See also Bias; Design-Based Estimation; Model-Based Estimation; Population Parameter; Precision; Variance

Further Readings

Knapp, T. R. (1971). N vs. N-1. *American Educational Research Journal, 7*, 625–626.
Lohr, S. (1999). *Sampling: Design and analysis*. Pacific Grove, CA: Duxbury.

UNDECIDED VOTERS

Undecideds, in election campaign lingo, are voters who have yet to decide which candidate—or side of an issue or referendum—they will support on Election Day. In pre-election polls, there are several ways of measuring support for a candidate or issue and, concomitantly, the number of undecided voters. A few researchers argue for an open-ended question format, in which the respondent volunteers the name of his or her preferred candidate. Answering such open-ended questions requires respondents to recall candidate names on their own, which means that these questions generally have larger percentages of "don't know" responses than closed-ended questions in which respondents hear or read candidates' names.

More frequently, however, researchers use a closed-ended "trial heat" question because the closed-ended measure has proven over time to be most accurate if comparison to Election Day results is the yardstick. These "read-list" questions in a telephone survey typically list all the candidates—or at least the major party candidates in a race—and ask whom the respondent would vote for "*if the election were held today.*" Some research suggests that, especially in state and local races, it is important to list all candidates and their parties, rather than asking only about major-party candidates or about major-party candidates and the nonspecific ideal candidate, "someone else." For those who were initially undecided or refused to express a candidate preference, the question would attempt to ascertain whom the respondent leaned toward supporting. By combining these "leaners" with the original "choosers," the question determines overall support.

At least three other types of respondents are interviewed in pre-election polls: (1) those who say they will vote in the election but won't cast a vote in one race or another, (2) those who refuse to say whom they will support, and (3) those who are truly undecided. Often election pollsters combine the three types for reporting and analysis purposes into a category called "no opinion."

Proportions of Undecided Voters

Generally, the percentage of undecided voters in pre-election polls dwindles the closer to the election that the polls are taken. This certainly is the case in presidential elections. In local elections, however, the proportion of undecided voters often is quite large right up until Election Day. Any number of factors could explain the relatively large or changing size of undecided voters: low candidate name recognition, low salience of the election or issue, or events that cause a dramatic shift in support late in the campaign.

One such event is the death of the incumbent candidate during the campaign, especially when the death occurs late in the campaign, such as the 2002 plane crash that killed U.S. Senator Paul Wellstone (D-Minn.). Another such event would be the withdrawal of a candidate from the race because of ethical revelations late in the campaign. Some researchers also suggest that a large proportion of undecided voters late in the campaign may indicate a faulty likely voter model.

Examining demographic, geographic, political, and attitudinal profiles of undecided voters can provide useful information to campaign and party pollsters, who want to know what it might take to persuade undecided voters to support their candidate. Pollsters for news organizations do similar analyses because understanding undecided voters is an important part of the news story, particularly close to Election Day.

These analyses often reveal that undecided voters have lower socioeconomic status and are less connected to the political process than are decided voters. Politically, they are less likely than decided voters to be partisans, and they are often more likely to be moderates than liberals or conservatives. Demographically, they tend to have less education and lower incomes than decided voters.

Allocating Undecided Voters

Part of the analysis of undecided voters is the examination of several "what if" scenarios that ask the question, "How will undecided voters split on Election Day?" There are several methods of allocating undecided voters to candidates or to one side or the other of ballot issues such as constitutional amendments or referenda.

Proportional allocation of undecided voters simply means allocating them in the same proportion as overall candidate support. For example, suppose that Candidate A has 50% of the support in a pre-election poll and Candidate B has 40%, with 10% undecided. Dividing 50% by 90% (the total "decided" pool) gives Candidate A 56% of the support; dividing 40% by 90% gives Candidate B the remaining 4%, thus 44% overall.

Equal allocation means dividing the undecided vote evenly between or among the candidates. In the previous example, 5% of the undecided voters would be allocated to each of the two candidates, with Candidate A predicted to receive 55% of the vote and Candidate B 45%. Many researchers would be cautious about using this method in races where there are two major-party candidates and many minor-party candidates, simply because large numbers of undecided voters rarely break toward minor-party candidates.

More sophisticated *statistical modeling allocation*, such as discriminant analysis, can also be used.

Discriminant analysis and other multivariate techniques first look at candidates' supporter profiles using researcher-specified variables such as party identification or gender. Then the technique allocates undecided voters to candidates based on how similar they are to the candidates' supporters on these variables. The technique usually involves using a random half of the sample to generate the statistical formula or model that will classify undecided respondents and using the other half to test the accuracy of the formula.

A fourth method of allocation, which some campaign researchers favor, has two steps. First, because party identification is so closely correlated with candidate choice, undecided partisan voters are allocated to their party's candidate—undecided Democrats would be allocated to the Democratic candidate and undecided Republicans, to the Republican candidate. Next, the remaining undecided voters without a party affiliation are allocated proportionally.

There are other less-empirical ways of allocating undecided voters. One is called the "incumbent rule," as advocated by pollster Nick Panagakis. Although popular references call it a "rule," it is less a formula than it is a conventional wisdom guideline adopted by some pollsters over the past two decades. The rule, which has received very little attention from political scientists, suggests that in an election where there is a well-known incumbent with less than 50% of the support and a well-known challenger, the majority of the undecided voters ultimately will vote for the challenger and against the incumbent. The rule assumes that the election is a referendum on the incumbent, and if voters do not back the incumbent after a term in office, they probably are not supporters. The rule appears to hold better in state and local elections than in presidential elections. Recently there has been some evidence that the incumbent rule may be weakening.

Robert P. Daves

See also Leaning Voters; Likely Voter; Pre-Election Polls; Trial Heat Question

Further Readings

Blumenthal, M. (2006, August 14). *Incumbent rule redux.* Retrieved December 26, 2006, from http://www.pollster.com/incumbent_rule/incumbent_rule_redux_1.php

Daves, R. P., & Warden, S. (1995). Methods of allocating undecided respondents to candidate choices in pre-election polls. In P. J. Lavrakas, M. W. Traugott,

P. V. Miller (Eds.), *Presidential polls and the news media* (pp. 101–122). Boulder, CO: Westview Press.

Panagakis, N. (1989, February 27). Incumbent races: Closer than they appear. *The Polling Report, 5*, 1–3.

Vanishing Voter Project. (2006). *One in seven likely voters still undecided on a presidential candidate.* Retrieved March 8, 2008, from http://www.ksg.harvard.edu/presspol/ vanishvoter/VV2000/Press_Releases/10-18-00.shtml

UNDERCOVERAGE

Undercoverage occurs when an element of the target population is not represented on the survey frame and therefore not given any chance of selection in the survey sample; that is, the element has zero probability of selection into the sample. Undercoverage is the most serious type of coverage error because it can be difficult to detect and even more difficult to solve. Therefore, preventing undercoverage is often a priority during survey design. Large survey operations often plan and budget for extensive coverage evaluations. For example, a large sample survey called the Accuracy and Coverage Evaluation was conducted by the U.S. Census Bureau during Census 2000, with separate staff and separate physical office space. Its primary purpose was to evaluate the coverage of the census.

In household surveys of the general population, there are generally two levels at which undercoverage is a concern. First, households may be missing from the frame. For example, in a random-digit dialing telephone survey, households without telephone service will be missed. In addition, while landline telephone coverage of most U.S. populations had been increasing, the recent popularity of cell phones has begun to jeopardize coverage of traditional landline telephone frames because of the rapidly growing cell phone only population—more than 20% of all U.S. households as of 2008. In surveys that use an area frame, households can be missed during the listing operation for a variety of reasons; for example, difficult to visually spot, misclassified as vacant or business, incorrectly assigned to across a boundary into an unsampled geographic area.

Second, even when a household is on the frame, some people within the household may not be covered. Unfortunately, this type of undercoverage cannot be prevented by good frame construction. There are two major theories on why people fail to identify

with the household. Roger Tourangeau found that the initial contact person at the household underreported the number of household members when he or she was asked for a list with several pieces of information on each person. In contrast, when asked for only each person's initials, more household members were reported. The authors theorized that this was because of privacy concerns. Elizabeth Martin found that in many cases the initial contact person at the household lacked enough knowledge about other household members to accurately include or exclude them according to the survey's residency rules. Both studies found issues tended to arise under complicated living arrangements (multiple roommates, group housing, recent changes, etc.).

There are several ways to prevent undercoverage. The survey should use a frame that provides the necessary unit coverage. That is, a survey that is estimating mobile phone use should not use a traditional landline telephone frame. For surveys that use lists for frame construction, the lists should be as recent as possible. In business surveys, lists of establishments or enterprises can quickly become out of date due to mergers, acquisitions, and new openings or closings. For surveys that use an area frame, quality checks can be performed on the address listing operation (i.e., "re-listing") using a subsample of areas or more expert staff.

There are both simple checks for undercoverage and extensive studies of undercoverage. Simple checks include comparing simple survey estimates (e.g., demographics) to other sources, such as recent prior surveys or census data. Using external data, post-survey adjustments to the analysis weights can be made if necessary.

Some surveys budget for extensive undercoverage evaluations, but this is not practical for all surveys. Dual-frame estimation can be used if there is an independent data collection and survey elements can be matched. Other data outside the survey can be analyzed for verification. For example, J. Gregory Robinson evaluated the coverage of the 1990 U.S. census using birth, death, immigration, and emigration records. This type of analysis can give useful coverage estimates in different demographic categories.

Jeffrey M. Pearson

See also Address-Based Sampling; Area Frame; Cell Phone Only Household; Coverage Error; Elements; Frame; Target Population; Unit Coverage; Within-Unit Coverage

Further Readings

Groves, R. M. (1989). *Survey errors and survey costs.* New York: Wiley.

Kish, L. (1965). *Survey sampling.* New York: Wiley.

Lessler, J. T., & Kalsbeek, W. D. (1992). *Nonsampling error in surveys.* New York: Wiley.

Martin, E. (1999). Who knows who lives here? Within-household disagreements as a source of survey coverage error. *Public Opinion Quarterly, 63*(2), 220–236.

Pearson, J. M. (2005). Quality and coverage of listings for area sampling. *2005 Proceedings of the American Statistical Association, Section on Government Statistics* [CD-ROM]. Alexandria, VA: American Statistical Association.

Robinson, J. G., Ahmed, B., Gupta, P. D., & Woodrow, K. A. (1993). Estimation of population coverage in the 1990 United States Census based on demographic analysis. *Journal of the American Statistical Association, 88*(423), 1061–1071.

Tourangeau, R., Shapiro, G., Kearney, A., & Ernst, L. (1997). Who lives here? Survey undercoverage and household roster questions. *Journal of Official Statistics, 13*(1), 1–18.

U.S. Census Bureau. (2004). *Accuracy and coverage evaluation of Census 2000: Design and methodology.* Washington, DC: Author.

UNDERREPORTING

When answering questions on sensitive behaviors, many respondents show a specific variant of response error: They tend to report fewer instances of undesired behaviors compared to what they have actually experienced. This is called *underreporting*. It is assumed that respondents avoid reporting unfavorable conduct because they do not want to admit socially undesirable behaviors, which in turn leads to this type of misreporting. Similar effects are known for responses to survey questions about unpopular attitudes.

Currently, it is not known whether underreporting is the result of a deliberate manipulation of the true answer or whether it occurs subconsciously. Nevertheless, for the most part it is assumed to be a response error that is associated to the cognitive editing stage of the question–answer process. Misreporting due to forgetting or other memory restrictions is considered to be a minor source of underreporting.

Several validation studies use records of the true answers to provide evidence for underreporting. For example, studies on abortion or illegal drug use show that fewer respondents admit those behaviors, or if they admit them, they report fewer instances of the presumed undesired behavior.

Since underreporting is related to social desirability bias it occurs more often in interviewer administered settings compared to self-administered surveys. Accordingly, audio, audiovisual, and telephone audio computer-assisted self-interviewing methods have been used extensively when collecting responses on socially undesirable behaviors or attitudes. These modes reduce the response burden of answering sensitive questions, which in turn is assumed to reduce underreporting of undesirable behaviors or attitudes.

Also, several question techniques have been developed to reduce underreporting. Besides forgiving question wording, the "everybody approach," and indirect questioning, the sealed ballot method has proven to effectively reduce underreporting. In addition, several variants of the randomized response technique are available. However, because the instructions necessary for those question types are rather complicated and not always understood by the respondent, they are practically seen as less effective in reducing underreporting.

Marek Fuchs

See also Audio Computer-Assisted Self-Interviewing (ACASI); Overreporting; Randomized Response; Response Error; Self-Administered Questionnaire; Sensitive Topics; Social Desirability

Further Readings

Magura, S., & Kang, S.-Y. (1996). Validity of self-reported drug use in high risk populations: A meta-analytical review. *Substance Use and Misuse, 31*(9), 1131–1153.

Tourangeau, R., Rips, L. J., & Rasinski, K. (2000). *The psychology of survey response.* Cambridge, UK: Cambridge University Press.

UNFOLDING QUESTION

An unfolding question refers to a type of question sequence that yields more complete and accurate data than would a single question on the same topic. Unfolding questions are used by survey researchers in an attempt to reduce item nonresponse (i.e., missing data) and measurement error.

For example, asking someone into which of the following income categories her 2007 total household income fell—less than $20,000; $20,000–$39,999; $40,000–$59,999; $60,000–$79,999; $80,000–$99,999; $100,000 or more—will lead to a good deal of "Don't Know" or "Refused" answers. Researchers have found that an unfolding question about income will substantially reduce item nonresponse and thus the need to impute those missing values.

An unfolding income question sequence for the income variable referenced in the preceding paragraph, that was programmed to be asked in a computer-assisted interview, would be as follows:

Q1. Was your total household income from all sources in 2007 more or less than $60,000?
    < 1 > MORE (GO TO Q4)
    < 2 > LESS (GO TO Q2)
    < 3 > $60,000 (GO TO Q6)
    < 8 > REFUSED (GO TO Q6)
    < 9 > UNCERTAIN (GO TO Q6)
Q2. And was it more or less than $40,000?
    < 1 > MORE (GO TO Q6)
    < 2 > LESS (GO TO Q3)
    < 3 > $40,000 (GO TO Q6)
    < 8 > REFUSED (GO TO Q6)
    < 9 > UNCERTAIN (GO TO Q6)
Q3. And was it more or less than $20,000?
    < 1 > MORE (GO TO Q6)
    < 2 > LESS (GO TO Q6)
    < 3 > $20,000 (GO TO Q6)
    < 8 > REFUSED (GO TO Q6)
    < 9 > UNCERTAIN (GO TO Q6)
Q4. And was it more or less than $80,000?
    < 1 > MORE (GO TO Q5)
    < 2 > LESS (GO TO Q6)
    < 3 > $80,000 (GO TO Q6)
    < 8 > REFUSED (GO TO Q6)
    < 9 > UNCERTAIN (GO TO Q6)
Q5. And was it more or less than $100,000?
    < 1 > MORE (GO TO Q6)
    < 2 > LESS (GO TO Q6)
    < 3 > $100,000 (GO TO Q6)
    < 8 > REFUSED (GO TO Q6)
    < 9 > UNCERTAIN (GO TO Q6)

In this example, after the income sequence has been administered, all respondents are taken to Q6 (the next logical question topic). Of note, even though the entire unfolding sequence comprises five questions, any one respondent would only be asked one, two, or three of the questions, not all five of them and

the majority would only be asked one or two. This five-question unfolding sequence will lead to far fewer missing income values than a single income question that presents essentially the same income categories all at once. It also will yield data that the researchers can combine to form a single income variable with the desired six categories in the original one-question income example.

Unfolding questions can be asked for other topics that are measured on some form of ordered scale. They are particularly useful when there are many response choices on the scale and when the cognitive burden on many respondents is too great to present all the choices at once. If all choices were presented at once, primacy, recency, and other satisficing effects would likely lead to errors in the data. For example, a scale measuring political orientation that uses the eight response options (e.g., Extremely Conservative, Very Conservative, Conservative, Somewhat Conservative, Neither Conservative Nor Liberal, Somewhat Liberal, Liberal, Very Liberal, Extremely Liberal) would gather more accurate data if it were presented as an unfolding question sequence starting with a question asking, *"In terms of politics, are you liberal or conservative?"*

Paul J. Lavrakas

See also Imputation; Measurement Error; Missing Data; Primacy Effect; Recency Effect; Respondent Burden; Satisficing

Further Readings

Duncan, G. J., & Petersen, E. (2001). The long and short of asking questions about income, wealth, and labor supply. *Social Science Research*, *30*(2), 248–263.

Unit

Sampling, variance, analysis, reporting, and dissemination units cover most of the unit types of interest in survey methodology. *Sampling units* can be primary, secondary, tertiary, and beyond—also known as first-stage, second-stage, and so on. These refer to a hierarchy of smaller and smaller geographic or organizational structures that have been exploited in the sample design to improve efficiency. In face-to-face surveys of the general population, the stages are typically county (or count group), block (or cluster of neighboring blocks), housing unit (or other quarters), and person. In student surveys, the stages are typically school district, school, classroom, and student. In random-digit dialing surveys, the stages are typically just household and person, although sometimes a 100-bank is also a stage.

Variance units are often the same as primary sampling units (PSUs) but can be different. Sometimes PSUs are collapsed into super PSUs to reduce the number of replicate weights that need to be created for variance estimation via resampling methods such as the bootstrap or jackknife. Other times, PSUs are split into pseudo PSUs to improve the stability of variance estimates even if it means a downward bias in the variance estimates. Both operations can also be done to make it harder for data snoopers to discover anything about known sample members from public use files.

Analysis units are often people but can be households or families. However, these other constructs usually are well-defined only at a particular point in time. Efforts to define stable interpersonal groupings over time have been largely unsuccessful, in the United States at least. Even the concept of "parent" is hard to keep stable over time, as varying constellations of adults can provide parenting services to children during their minor years. Where family structures and parents have been of interest over time, the most successful approach has been to follow the persons of interest and report the characteristics of their families or parents as attributes of themselves.

Reporting units are generally the same as ultimate stage sample units, but in surveys of businesses and other larger social constructs such as governmental bodies, a "large" sample unit may need to be split into multiple reporting units. For example, in a survey of energy usage in commercial buildings, the individual tenants might be the reporting units for a multitenant building with separately metered utilities.

Dissemination units are the smallest geographic or organizational structures for which formal estimates are published. Typical examples in the United States include the four census regions, the states, and counties, depending on the size of the survey. Sometimes, there is interest in the primary sampling units as analysis or dissemination units. Metropolitan areas constitute one example where attempts have been made to use them both as sampling units and as dissemination units. These attempts are not, however, very satisfying.

Sample sizes are generally too small within individual PSUs to satisfy user expectations for the precision of formally published estimates. Also, it is hard to explain why, if such estimates are important or useful, they are only available for a few dozen of them.

David Ross Judkins

See also Level of Analysis; Level of Measurement; Primary Sampling Unit (PSU)

Further Readings

Sukhatme, P. V., Sukhatme, B. V., Sukhatme, S., & Asok, C. (1984). *Sampling theory of surveys with applications* (3rd ed.). Ames: Iowa State University Press.
Westat. (2000). *WesVar 4.0 user's guide* (App. D). Rockville, MD: Author.

Unit Coverage

The proportion of the intended referential universe that is represented (on a weighted basis) in the sampling frame of a survey is referred to as the *coverage rate*. Unit coverage refers to how extensively the units (e.g., households, schools, businesses) in the universe are "covered" by (i.e., included in) the sampling frame, which includes the dynamic process whereby an enumerator (lister) or interviewer decides whether a household or person should be included in the frame.

For purposes of setting public policy, it is generally considered desirable to hear the voices of a broad swath of the public. Even in voter intention surveys, pollsters are more confident in their predictions if their screening survey for likely voters covers most of society. As such, survey researchers should strive to use sampling frames that cover the units of the population as well as is possible.

Coverage is a function of both how a sample is selected and how contact with sample units is attempted. Being "covered" does not necessarily mean that the person responds. But it does include whether they "cooperate" enough to confirm their existence. For example, an interviewer may approach a house that appears to be abandoned and knock on the door. If the occupant shouts out a demand that the interviewer leave, then he or she is covered. If, on the other hand, the occupant remains stealthily silent so that the interviewer erroneously classifies the house as vacant, then he or she is not covered. As another example, a person who answers the phone when contacted as part of a random-digit dialing survey and then hangs up without saying anything else is covered, but a person who never answers the phone because of a reaction to the caller ID is typically not covered. Errors in coverage that lead to households or people being "missing" from the frame make up *undercoverage.*

There are a variety of reasons for undercoverage. One is that some members of society are secretive, antisocial, or both. Examples include illegal migrants, squatters, fugitives, members of insular religious cults, and members of rebellion-like movements. Another reason is mental or physical illness that makes it impossible for someone to communicate with a survey interviewer. A third is high mobility, as in the case of migrant farm workers. A fourth is physical remoteness of dwellings. A fifth is shared addresses and improvised apartments. Electronic connectedness matters for some surveys. The desire to protect children also can be a factor. For example, it is known that overtly screening a sample for households with children can lead to much lower coverage of children than a general interview where information about children is collected as a secondary issue.

A continuum of eagerness and capacity for social engagement can range from schizophrenic homeless wanderers and misanthropic hermits at one extreme to politicians who live almost purely in the public eye at the other. Professional experience in the United States indicates that people in the top half of that continuum can be covered easily, provided that the survey has a legitimate social research purpose. People in the second quartile of the continuum require more effort but can still usually be covered with fairly low-cost methods. People between the 15th and 25th percentiles of the continuum can usually only be covered with fresh area samples conducted by door-to-door interviewers under government auspices. People between the 5th and 15th percentiles usually can be covered only in official surveys conducted by the Census Bureau. People between the 2nd and 5th percentiles can be covered only through heroic means, such as those employed in the decennial censuses. People in the first two percentiles are mostly not coverable by any procedure. Or rather, the extraordinary procedures that are required to try to cover them also result in *overcoverage* where some other people are

counted multiple times, so that it becomes practically impossible to determine the coverage rate.

Estimating unit coverage is difficult, but there are some fairly well-accepted conventions. In the United States, coverage measurement for demographic surveys usually starts with official population estimates published by the Census Bureau. These are synthesized from the count from the most recent decennial census, vital statistics, emigration and immigration statistics, tax statistics, and school enrollment statistics. A historical examination of coverage rates requires careful attention to benchmark methodology, as there have been occasional major shifts. One example concerned the counting of illegal aliens in the 1980s. Another concerned a period in the 1990s when there were parallel series: one adjusted for undercount in the decennial census, the other not.

Another difficulty in estimating coverage rates comes in separating undercoverage from nonresponse. If a combined adjustment is made for nonresponse and undercoverage, more effort is required to determine the coverage rate. A procedure preferred by some organizations is to use separate nonresponse and undercoverage adjustments. Weighted totals of the population before and after the undercoverage adjustment can then be compared to estimate the coverage rate.

In designing a survey, consideration must be given to the likely association between variables of interest and social attachment. Generally speaking, little is known about uncovered persons, so decisions about the targeted coverage rate must be based mostly on the survey designer's judgment. Surveys of antisocial behavior require the best coverage to be credible.

David Ross Judkins

See also Coverage; Nonresponse; Overcoverage; Undercoverage

Further Readings

Chromy, J. R., Bowman, K. R., Crump, C. J., Packer, L. E., & Penne, M. A. (1999). Population coverage in the National Household Survey on Drug Abuse. *Proceedings of the Section on Survey Research Methods* (pp. 575–580). Alexandria, VA: American Statistical Association.

Horrigan, M., Moore, W., Pedlow, S., & Wolter, K. (1999). Undercoverage in a large national screening survey for youths. *Proceedings of the Section on Survey Research Methods* (pp. 570–575). Alexandria, VA: American Statistical Association.

Judkins, D., DiGaetano, R., Chu, A., & Shapiro, G. (1999). Coverage in screening surveys at Westat. *Proceedings of the Section on Survey Research Methods* (pp. 581–586). Alexandria, VA: American Statistical Association.

Tourangeau, R., Shapiro, G., Kearney, A., & Ernst, L. (1997). Who lives here? Survey undercoverage and household roster questions. *Journal of Official Statistics, 13*(1), 1–18.

Unit Nonresponse

Unit nonresponse in a survey occurs when an eligible sample member fails to respond at all or does not provide enough information for the response to be deemed usable (not even as a "partial completion"). Unit nonresponse can be contrasted to item nonresponse (missing data) wherein the sample member responds but does not provide a usable response to a particular item or items. Unit nonresponse can be a source of bias in survey estimates, and reducing unit nonresponse is an important objective of good survey practice.

Reasons for Unit Nonresponse

Despite the best efforts of the survey practitioner, there are reasons why unit nonresponse will still occur.

Refusal: The sample member may refuse to participate in the survey. Often refusals are divided into *hard* refusals and *soft* refusals, depending on the intensity with which the sample member refuses to participate.

Sample member cannot be found: The sample member (whether a person, a household, or an establishment) may have moved or otherwise cannot be located. In the case of a telephone survey, the telephone may ring repeatedly with no answer or be picked up by an answering machine with an uninformative message.

Sample member may be temporarily away: The sample member may be known to be travelling and unavailable during the data collection period.

Communication difficulty: The sample member may speak a language that none of the interviewers speaks or into which the survey instrument has not been translated. In other instances, the sample member may have a physical or mental disability that interferes with communication.

Sample member provides inadequate data: The sample member provides some data, but after editing, the data are deemed inadequate to constitute a valid response.

Other: There are other reasons for unit nonresponse, such as quarantines, which although unlikely, do occur. (Detailed discussion of these other instances is available at www.aapor.org.)

It is important to distinguish sample members that are unit nonrespondents from those that are ineligible (out of scope). In the case of sample members that cannot be contacted, it may not be possible to know for certain if a particular sample member is a nonrespondent or ineligible, but the proportion of nonrespondents among the "noncontacts" can be estimated. An example is a random-digit dial telephone survey of households in which a selected telephone number is called repeatedly with no answer. The telephone number may belong to a household or an establishment, or it may not be an assigned number. Only in the first case is the sample member a unit nonrespondent.

Reducing Unit Nonresponse

Steps that may be taken to reduce unit nonresponse include the following:

- Keep the survey instrument (questionnaire, Web form, or interviewer protocol) short and relatively easy to complete. It helps if the items are interesting and salient.
- Use only thoroughly trained interviewers.
- Provide an advance letter or telephone call or other message. This helps the sample member to distinguish serious surveys from marketing and promotions. Including endorsements from respected organizations can also be beneficial.
- Provide a cash or other type of incentive.
- Allow proxy respondents. If the intended sample member is unavailable or uncooperative, someone else (e.g., a family member) may be able to respond for the person.
- Provide the sample member a choice of modes with which to respond. For example, the sample member may prefer to respond on the Web or by telephone rather than by mail in a paper questionnaire. Telephone follow-up to mail questionnaires is a frequently employed technique, to allow the respondent to be interviewed at that time.
- Assure the sample member of the confidentiality of the responses.

- If the sample member initially refuses to respond, make use of advanced refusal conversion techniques.
- Employ intense and well-designed follow-up techniques. For example, in telephone surveys, a large number of callbacks may be needed at varied times of the day and days of the week.
- In longitudinal surveys, make use of sophisticated tracking techniques to track sample members who may have moved between rounds of the survey.

Efforts to reduce unit nonresponse can have drawbacks. Incentives and follow-up activities are costly. If the follow-up is too intense, survey members may provide low-quality responses so as not to be bothered further. Proxy respondents may not be able to provide data as accurate as the intended respondent. In some cases, the disadvantages may even override the benefits of the reduced unit nonresponse, in part because not all unit nonresponse leads to unit nonresponse error.

In many surveys there are "hard-core" nonrespondents that are almost impossible to get to respond. In some cases, unfortunately, these nonrespondents may be of special interest. In household travel surveys, for example, there is great interest in recent immigrants because these individuals may not have obtained a driver's licence and hence may be dependent on public transportation, walking, and bicycling as modes of transportation. Yet because of possible language barriers, lack of telephone coverage, and other factors, recent immigrants may be especially difficult to get to respond.

Adjusting for Unit Nonresponse

Post-survey adjustments are usually made to ameliorate the effects of unit nonresponse. It is typically the case that unit nonresponse is not distributed evenly in the sample. In surveys of persons, for example, the rate of unit nonresponse is usually greater for younger adults than for older adults, for minorities than for whites, and especially among those with lower educational attainment compared to those with higher educational attainment. In establishment surveys, larger establishments may be more likely to respond than smaller ones. The most commonly employed adjustment is the weighting class method for adjusting the sample weights. The sample members are divided into groups, called *weighting classes*, which are deemed to be relatively homogeneous. Within a weighting class, the weights of all the unit respondents are multiplied by the same factor (at least one) so that they sum to the estimated population size for the weighting class.

The propensity scoring method of adjustment uses information available for all sample members to estimate each sample member's probability of responding. These probabilities of responding ("propensities") are then used to adjust the sample weights of the responding units.

Another adjustment method sometimes used is to impute all the items (or all the key items) for a unit nonrespondent. This method is particularly common in census data collections (where all sample members are selected with certainty), where sample weights are not employed.

Sometimes unit nonrespondents (at a particular point in time) are subsampled for intensive follow-up. The weights of the units in the subsample that eventually respond are increased to account for the subsampling. This procedure controls nonresponse bias at the expense of an increase in variance.

Michael P. Cohen

See also Advance Contact; Confidentiality; Eligibility; Incentives; Language Barrier; Missing Data; Noncontacts; Nonresponse; Nonresponse Bias; Partial Completion; Propensity Scores; Proxy Respondent; Refusal; Refusal Conversion; Respondent Burden; Unable to Participate; Unit; Weighting

Further Readings

Groves, R. M. (2004). *Survey errors and survey costs.* New York: Wiley.
Kalton, G. (1983). *Compensating for missing survey data.* Ann Arbor: University of Michigan, Institute for Social Research.
Lessler, J. T., & Kalsbeek, W. D. (1992). *Nonsampling error in surveys.* New York: Wiley.

UNIT OF OBSERVATION

A unit of observation is an object about which information is collected. Researchers base conclusions on information that is collected and analyzed, so using defined units of observation in a survey or other study helps to clarify the reasonable conclusions that can be drawn from the information collected.

An example of a unit of observation is an individual person. Other examples include a family or a neighborhood.

A survey or other type of study can involve many different levels of units of observation. For example, the U.S. Census 2000 used a hierarchical arrangement to describe the units of observation about which it collected information. These units range from "United States" to "region" to "census block."

Some researchers distinguish between the terms *unit of observation* and *unit of analysis*. For example, a unit of observation might be an individual person, but a unit of analysis might relate to the neighborhood in which the individual lives, based on data collected about individuals in the neighborhood. Clear articulations of units of observation through use of specific definitions lend clarity to survey and study efforts.

Focusing on the unit of observation throughout the course of a study—from inception to conclusions to dissemination of results—helps researchers later present an organized explanation of the phenomenon and helps keep the explanation relevant to the data collected.

Heather H. Boyd

See also Case; Unit

Further Readings

U.S. Census Bureau. (2003, June). *2000 Census of population and housing: Summary of social, economic, and housing characteristics, selected appendices, PHC-2-A*. Retrieved February 9, 2007, from http://www.census.gov/prod/cen2000/phc-2-a.pdf

UNIVERSE

The universe consists of all survey elements that qualify for inclusion in the research study. The precise definition of the universe for a particular study is set by the research question, which specifies who or what is of interest. The universe may be individuals, groups of people, organizations, or even objects. For example, research about voting in an upcoming election would have a universe comprising all voters. If the research was about political parties' sponsorship of candidates, the research would include all political parties. In research that involves taking a sample of

things for testing or review, the universe may include inanimate objects. For example, a researcher may want to determine the extent to which toys made in a particular country contain a certain type of paint. In this case, the universe would include all toys made in that country. Some survey research has a very small universe (e.g., a survey of individuals who have won 1 million dollars or more in the lottery), and some research has a large universe (a survey of the television-viewing habits of all adults in the United States).

Survey practitioners often do not expect to be able to measure the entire universe, because it is neither practical nor necessary. A survey of all the elements in a universe would not be a sample but would instead be a census. Taking a census is rarely practical because it is costly and it rarely is needed; that is, a good survey can gather as accurate (and sometimes more accurate) data about the universe.

Defining the universe is a key element in the design of an appropriate sampling strategy. The researcher must carefully consider precisely who or what is of interest and then how best to contact or include these individuals or things in the research. The importance of appropriately defining the universe should not be underestimated. A universe that has been too narrowly defined will exclude important opinions and attitudes, and a universe too broadly defined will include extraneous information that may bias or affect the overall results.

Once defined, the universe is used by the researcher to structure an appropriate sampling methodology, in particular by defining the target population and choosing a sampling frame or frames. Research being conducted with a universe of all adults who watch television, for example, can contact a random sample of such individuals using random-digit dialing or by sampling clusters of geographies and then sampling households within those geographies using addressed-based sampling or area probability sampling. Sometimes multiple frames are needed to adequately cover the universe. In many surveys, the researcher does not know (nor does she or he need to know in advance) how many individuals or things are qualified to be part of the universe. One way to estimate this information is to retain information from any screener used to identify and select qualified respondents. For example, imagine a researcher wanted to do a survey of all individuals who own *both* a dog and a cat in Australia. It is unlikely that there is any reliable information on the precise number of Australians who own both types of pets, and it is further unlikely that a listing of such pet owners exists. When screening randomly selected households, the researcher can determine how many of the individuals contacted qualify and can use this information to estimate the total universe size. For example, if the researcher randomly contacts 1,000 households and finds that 45 of these own both a dog and a cat, the researcher can then estimate that roughly between 3% and 6% of all households in Australia own both types of pets.

The universe sometimes is known as the *population of interest* or *target population*.

Sarah Butler

See also Address-Based Sampling; Area Probability Sample; Census; Population; Population of Inference; Population of Interest; Random-Digit Dialing (RDD); Research Question; Sampling Frame; Screening; Target Population

UNKNOWN ELIGIBILITY

Unknown eligible is a category of survey dispositions that is used in all survey modes (telephone, in-person, mail, and Internet) when there is not enough information known about the case to determine whether the case is eligible or ineligible. For this reason, most survey organizations make additional contact attempts on cases categorized into one of the unknown eligibility categories to try to definitively categorize the case into either the eligible or ineligible category. Because the unknown eligible category is broad, researchers usually use a more detailed set of survey disposition codes to better categorize the outcomes of cases that fall into the unknown eligible category.

In a telephone survey, cases are categorized as unknown eligibles under two circumstances: (1) when it is not known whether an eligible household exists at a telephone number and (2) when it is known that a household exists at the number, but it is unknown whether an eligible respondent exists at the number. For cases in which it is not known whether a household exists at the sampled telephone number, cases of unknown eligibility include those numbers that were included in the sample but never dialed by an interviewer. Another common subcategory of cases of unknown eligibility include numbers that always

ring busy, numbers that reach ambiguous answering machine or voicemail messages that do not indicate whether a household has been reached, privacy manager technologies that block interviewers from completing dialing attempts, and telephone line–related technical problems, such as "all circuits are busy." If it is known that a household exists at the sampled telephone number, cases of unknown eligibility also can occur when it is not possible to complete a screener, and thus it is not known whether a household has an eligible respondent.

In an in-person survey, cases are categorized into the unknown eligibility category when one of two circumstances exists: (1) when it is not known whether an eligible household exists at an address and (2) when it is known that a household exists at the sampled address, but it is not known whether an eligible respondent lives at the address. For cases in which it is not known whether a household exists at the address, cases of unknown eligibility include those in which a household was not contacted by an interviewer (i.e., the case was not worked), cases in which an interviewer was unable to reach the household (most commonly due to causes related to safety and building security), and cases in which an interviewer was not able to locate the sampled address. If it is known that a household exists at the sampled address, cases of unknown eligibility also can occur when it is not possible to complete a screener, and thus it is not known whether a household has an eligible respondent.

Cases of unknown eligibility occur for five principal reasons in mail surveys of specifically named respondents. One reason that a case of unknown eligibility might occur in a mail survey is that the questionnaire was never mailed out, and thus, nothing is known about the sampled address. A second, more common, reason for a case in a mail survey being included in the unknown eligibility category occurs when the questionnaire was mailed out but the addressee did not receive the mailing. These cases include "refused by addressee," cases in which the U.S. Postal Service will not deliver mail to the addressee, and cases in which the address on the outer envelope is incomplete or illegible. A third type of cases of unknown eligibility occurs in mail surveys when a case reaches a sampled address, but it is not known whether an eligible respondent resides at the address; this most often occurs when a screener is not completed. A fourth type of cases of unknown eligibility occurs in mail surveys when a questionnaire is returned as undeliverable but includes forwarding information. The fifth, and most common, case is those mailings for which the researcher never receives back any information on whether or not the mailing was received, including no returned questionnaire.

Cases of unknown eligibility occur for two principal reasons in an Internet survey: (1) when an invitation to complete the survey is sent, but nothing is known about whether the invitation was received, and (2) when the researcher learns that the invitation was never delivered. In the former case, many invitations to complete an Internet survey are sent via email, and researchers may receive no notification if the email address the invitation was sent to is incorrect, not working, or is not checked by the sampled respondent. In the latter case, researchers may receive a message that indicates that the email address is incorrect and that the invitation cannot be delivered. In either instance, usually nothing is known about the sampled respondent and his or her eligibility to complete the survey.

There tends to be variance across survey organizations in how cases of unknown eligibility are treated in computing surveys response and cooperation rates. The most conservative approach is to treat these cases as eligible cases; the most liberal approach, which makes the survey appear more successful, would treat cases of unknown eligibility as ineligible and thus exclude them from the response rate calculations. In most instances, neither of these extremes is prudent, and instead researchers often treat a proportion of unknown eligibility cases (referred to as "e") as being eligible in their response rate calculation. When doing this, the researcher should have an empirical basis upon which to calculate the proportion counted as eligible or ineligible.

Matthew Courser

See also *e*; Final Dispositions; Ineligible; Out of Sample; Response Rates; Temporary Dispositions

Further Readings

American Association for Public Opinion Research. (2006). *Standard definitions: Final dispositions of case codes and outcome rates for surveys* (4th ed.). Lenexa, KS: Author.

Weisberg, H. (2005). *The total survey error approach: A guide to the new science of survey research*. Chicago: University of Chicago Press.

UNLISTED HOUSEHOLD

An unlisted household is a residential unit that does not have a telephone number listed in published directories or one that would be given out by directory assistance. A telephone number may be unlisted for several reasons. Household residents actively may have chosen to keep their telephone number unlisted. Alternatively, although the residents of an unlisted household may not have specifically chosen to keep their telephone number unlisted, the number may be too new to be found in published directories or via directory assistance. This can be a result of a recent move or change in telephone number.

Although the literature suggests important differences between the characteristics of respondents who choose to keep their telephone numbers unlisted and respondents whose telephone numbers are unlisted for other reasons, consistent findings have been reported on the larger differences between the characteristics of households with listed numbers versus those with unlisted numbers. Directory-listed sampling frames have tended to exhibit an overrepresentation of (a) established households, (b) middle- and higher-income households, (c) two or more person households, (d) older householders, (e) married householders, (f) better-educated householders, (g) retired householders, (h) white-race households, and (i) home owners.

In general, sampling frames based on listed telephone numbers exclude unlisted households. This coverage shortfall has the potential to introduce bias into surveys that use a directory-listed sampling frame to construct a representative sample of the general population of telephone households. The coverage issue is most acute in urban areas and the western region of the United States, where unlisted telephone rates are higher. Additionally, as the proportion of households without listed telephone numbers in the general population increases, the potential for bias due to their exclusion from directory-listed sampling frames is likely to increase commensurately. Random-digit dialing (RDD) is an alternative sample design that can overcome this coverage limitation. However, although RDD sampling frames include both listed and unlisted households, the higher proportion of nonworking numbers in RDD sampling frames can reduce the efficiency of the sample as compared to that of a directory-listed sampling frame. It also may reduce the external validity of the sample, as respondents with an unlisted number are more prone to survey nonresponse due to both noncontact and refusal.

Adam Safir

See also Coverage Error; Directory Sampling; External Validity; List-Assisted Sampling; Noncontacts; Random-Digit Dialing (RDD); Refusal; Sampling Frame; Unpublished Number

Further Readings

American Association for Public Opinion Research. (2006). *Standard definitions: Final dispositions of case codes and outcome rates for surveys* (4th ed.). Lenexa, KS: Author. Retrieved April 24, 2008, from http://www.aapor.org/uploads/standarddefs_4.pdf

Brick, J. M., Waksberg, J., Kulp, D., & Starer, A. (1995). Bias in list-assisted telephone samples. *Public Opinion Quarterly, 59,* 218–235.

Currivan, D. (2003). Sampling frame. In M. Lewis-Beck, A. Bryman, & T. Futing Liao (Eds.), *The SAGE encyclopedia of social science research methods.* Thousand Oaks, CA: Sage.

Lavrakas, P. J. (1993). *Telephone survey methods: Sampling, selection, and supervision* (2nd ed.). Newbury Park, CA: Sage.

Tucker, C., Lepkowksi, J., & Piekarski, L. (2002). The current efficiency of list-assisted telephone sampling designs. *Public Opinion Quarterly, 66,* 321–338.

Unmatched Number

An unmatched telephone number is one that does not have a mailing address associated with it. Typically, it also does not have a name matched to it. The vast majority of unmatched telephone numbers are also unlisted telephone numbers. The proportion of unmatched numbers in a telephone survey that uses matching as a technique will depend upon the extent to which the survey organization uses multiple vendors to do their matching and the quality of the matching techniques and databases the vendor uses. However, in random-digit dialing surveys in the United States, regardless of how many matching vendors are used, a large minority of numbers can never be matched to an address because that information simply is not accessible to any matching company.

This is due to the privacy and confidentiality concerns of the households whose numbers cannot be matched to an accurate address.

Whether a telephone number can be "matched" to an address is predictive of the likelihood that a completed interview will be attained with that household in a telephone survey. A greater proportion of interviews are completed with numbers that are matched than are completed with unmatched numbers. A primary reason for this is that those with unmatched numbers are less likely to react positively when they are contacted by a stranger (i.e., the interviewer). Another primary reason for this is that matched numbers have an address associated with them. As such, researchers can send advance mailings to these households when they are sampled for a telephone survey to alert them ("warm them up") to the fact that an interviewer will be calling them. This cannot be done with unmatched numbers. Instead, calls to them are "cold calls," and response rates for them consistently have been shown to be lower than with matched numbers.

On average, unmatched telephone numbers require more callbacks than do matched numbers in order for them to reach a proper final disposition. Thus, the calling rules used by a survey center to process unmatched numbers should differ from the rules used to process matched numbers. However, unless a survey center has their telephone samples screened for matched/unmatched status or receives this information for each number in their sample from their sample vendor, it will not be possible for them to take the matched/unmatched status into account as their computer-assisted telephone interviewing system processes the callback attempts.

Paul J. Lavrakas

See also Advance Contact; Advance Letter; Calling Rules; Cold Call; Computer-Assisted Telephone Interviewing (CATI); Listed Number; Matched Number; Random-Digit Dialing (RDD); Telephone Surveys; Unpublished Number

Unpublished Number

The unpublished number disposition is used both in random-digit dialing (RDD) surveys of the general public and in telephone surveys of named people that use a list-based sample. Unpublished telephone numbers are numbers that are not listed in the local telephone directory, and the vast majority of these numbers also are unlisted and thus not available from directory assistance.

The unpublished number disposition is fairly rare in RDD surveys and is used only when an interviewer dials the telephone number of a case in the sampling pool and receives a recorded message from the local telephone company indicating that the telephone number dialed by the interviewer has been changed to an unpublished number—meaning that the original telephone number in the sampling pool is no longer in service. In RDD surveys of the general public, the new, unpublished number would not be called even in the unlikely possibility that it was known, because doing this would change the household's probability of selection to be included in the sampling pool— essentially doubling the household's chances of being included in the sample. Moreover, because RDD sampling techniques have a nonzero probability of reaching any household in a sampling area that has telephone service, the new, unpublished number also might be included in the sample already. In these cases, the unpublished number disposition would be considered a final disposition.

The unpublished number disposition is used more commonly in telephone surveys that use list-based sampling techniques. For example, if a researcher is sampling households from an address frame and then using reverse directory techniques to match telephone numbers to addresses in the sampling frame, there may be no telephone number available because the household or respondent may have designated his or her number as unpublished. In some cases the researcher may be able to contact directory assistance and obtain a telephone number. However, this does not happen very often because obtaining an unpublished number from directory assistance also requires that the number not also be designated as unlisted by the respondent or household.

The unpublished number disposition usually is considered a final disposition in telephone surveys of specifically named people (i.e., telephone surveys whose sample is a list of specific individuals), because it is highly unlikely that a researcher would be able to discover a telephone number for a sampled respondent or household if directory assistance and reverse directory techniques did not provide one. However, in a mixed-mode survey it might be possible to locate an address and to try to gather data by sending a mail questionnaire or an in-person interviewer to the address. As a result, researchers may consider the unpublished number disposition to be a temporary disposition in mixed-mode surveys.

Matthew Courser

See also Final Dispositions; Ineligible; Out of Order; Temporary Dispositions; Unlisted Household

Further Readings

American Association for Public Opinion Research. (2006). *Standard definitions: Final dispositions of case codes and outcome rates for surveys* (4th ed.). Lenexa, KS: Author.

Lavrakas, P. J. (1993). *Telephone survey methods: Sampling, selection, and supervision* (2nd ed.). Newbury Park, CA: Sage.

USABILITY TESTING

Although usability testing can apply to all types of products, for survey research, it can best be described as a method for measuring how well interviewers and respondents can use a computer-assisted interview such as a CAPI, CATI, CASI, or Web-based survey, for its intended purpose. It is important to separate usability testing from testing functionality, which focuses only on the proper operation of a computerized instrument (software and hardware), not the individual using the system. The purpose of usability testing is to determine whether or not the form being used to collect data helps or hinders a user's ability to deploy it.

In developing and designing survey instruments, researchers have always strived to ensure that data collection instruments are the best they can be through a variety of testing and evaluation methods put into place prior to data collection. Traditionally, cognitive interviewing and other cognitive methods have provided important tools for examining the thought processes that affect the quality of answers provided by survey respondents to survey questions. In addition, question appraisal systems are used to provide a structured, standardized instrument review methodology that assists a survey design expert in evaluating questions relative to the tasks they require of respondents, specifically with regard to how respondents understand and respond to survey questions. Focus groups can be used to obtain qualitative data that provide insight into the attitudes, perceptions, and opinions on a given topic or instrument. Although all of these efforts have long been important to understanding the way questions and the wording on a survey are perceived by respondents, the increased use of computer-assisted data collection has called for yet another form of testing instruments.

The general thought regarding computerized instruments is that they are easier on respondents and interviewers when compared with paper questionnaires. Pre-programmed skip patterns and automated progress through an instrument removes the time it takes to manually follow routing instructions, turn pages, and edit or calculate responses. But in practice, computer instruments can be more difficult to figure out than their paper counterparts because of complicated instructions, self-editing, navigational problems, and general layout. Usability testing can measure the time it takes to complete certain tasks in an instrument and whether or not these factors are contributing to increased respondent burden. Following the thought that burden is tied to stress or respondent fatigue, which could contribute to respondent attrition, identifying sources of burden and reducing them can contribute to improved response rates. In addition, usability testing can result in increased reliability and validity of survey instruments by examining features—such as error messages and other feedback, instructions, and placement of navigational features ("next buttons," etc.)— and assessing whether or not they help, confuse, encourage, or discourage respondents. The same examinations can also assist interviewers. Usability testing also can reveal how a computerized instrument affects the burden, emotions, and motivation of interviewers, which in turn, can have a positive impact on the quality of the data that they collect.

It is generally agreed that to properly conduct a high-quality usability test, a closed laboratory setting should be used. Many researchers use cognitive laboratories with common features such as one-way mirrors for observation to conduct usability testing. In addition, testing can be enhanced through the use of multiple cameras and recording devices. By using multiple cameras, researchers can capture users' hands on a computer keyboard as well as users' facial expressions. This practice is especially useful in allowing researchers to examine nonverbal cues that users may give, such as facial expressions or body language, that speak to burden or difficulties with a given task. By using microphones, researchers can record and analyze any comments that are made by users during testing. Devices such as scan converters or computers equipped with software allowing them to record images are useful for capturing images from a user's computer screen during testing. Video processors and editing equipment can also be used to capture images from all recording sources, synchronize them, and combine them so that the three images can either be viewed in real time or videotaped for later viewing, coding, and analysis.

Usability test subjects should reflect the population of interest. That said, it is important that usability tests focusing on interviewer-administered instruments are conducted with interviewers who are familiar with computer-assisted interviewing, while instruments to be used by the general public are tested among members of the general public. It is often recommended that tests are carried out with groups of 10 to 12 test subjects. Researchers will often prepare pre-scripted or mock interviews for test subjects to follow. By requiring test subjects to enter mock interview data, researchers can ensure that items of interest will be seen by test subjects. In addition, probes may be prepared in an effort to gain more detailed information about specific aspects of the instrument or task at hand that may not be mentioned spontaneously.

David James Roe

See also Cognitive Interviewing; Computer-Assisted Personal Interviewing (CAPI); Computer-Assisted Self-Interviewing (CASI); Computer-Assisted Telephone Interviewing (CATI); Contingency Question; Focus Group; Paper-and-Pencil Interviewing (PAPI); Questionnaire Design; Respondent Burden; Respondent Fatigue

Further Readings

Dumas, J. S., & Redish, J. (1999). *A practical guide to usability testing* (Rev. ed.). Portland, OR: Intellect.
Hanson, S., & Couper, M. (2004). Usability testing to evaluate computer assisted instruments. In S. Presser, J. Rothgeb, M. Couper, J. Lessler, E. Martin, J. Martin, et al. (Eds.), *Methods for testing and evaluating survey questionnaires* (pp. 337–360). New York: Wiley.

U.S. BUREAU OF THE CENSUS

The U.S. Bureau of the Census is a federal agency within the U.S. Department of Commerce. Most commonly known for conducting the enumeration of the U.S. population every 10 years, the bureau conducts activities that extend well beyond the decennial census. The largest federal statistical agency, the Census Bureau serves as the premier source of federal data on the U.S. population and economy. The Census Bureau is responsible for numerous surveys, including full censuses and sample surveys. The resulting data are used regularly not only by U.S. government officials but also by local governments, businesses, nonprofit organizations, and researchers in numerous disciplines.

Survey researchers in the United States are dependent on the accuracy of the decennial census and other Census Bureau surveys because they typically provide the population parameters (i.e., *universe estimates* [*UEs*]) to which other government, commercial, and academic survey data sets of the population often are weighted. Furthermore, because these other surveys are weighted to census data, the survey questionnaires used by these other organizations must use the same questionnaire wording used in census questionnaires so as to have equivalent variables for weighting purposes.

Census Bureau Surveys

The Census of Population and Housing (decennial census) is intended to count and collect information from all U.S. residents. First conducted in 1790, the decennial census is required by the U.S. Constitution for apportioning congressional representation. Conducting the census is a massive and multi-year effort. Major activities include finalizing content development, maintaining the Master Address File, printing and mailing paper questionnaires, conducting nonresponse follow-up, processing data, and disseminating results.

Modern population censuses are conducted largely through mailed paper questionnaires. In-person interviews occur when households do not have a usable mailing address or when residents do not return the mailed questionnaire (i.e., an in-person nonresponse follow-up). Recent decennial censuses have included short- and long-form questionnaires. With this design, long-form questionnaires included short-form questions as well as more detailed social, economic, and housing questions. Using statistical techniques, long forms were sent to a sample of U.S. residences (one in six for the year 2000), and results were projected to

the total population or universe. Starting with the 2010 Census, only short-form content will be included on the decennial questionnaire. Long-form data will be collected through the American Community Survey, an ongoing survey with a sample of 3 million households per year.

The Census Bureau also conducts censuses of U.S. businesses and government entities. Like the population enumeration, these censuses are intended to fully cover all entities that meet the criteria for inclusion. The Economic Census and the Census of Governments are conducted every 5 years (years ending in the numerals 2 and 7). Like the decennial population census, federal code requires these censuses and mandates participation. The purpose of the Economic Census is to compile data on the U.S. economy through surveys of business establishments. The Census of Governments is intended to supply information on government organization, employment, and finance.

The Census Bureau has extensive expertise in survey research and often conducts surveys for other federal government agencies. Designed to fulfill many different federal data needs, these sample-based surveys vary in terms of methodology, frequency, and collection mode(s).

The Current Population Survey (CPS) is conducted by the Census Bureau for the Bureau of Labor Statistics. Conducted since the 1940s, the CPS is the main source for national labor statistics, including unemployment rates and earnings measures. The CPS is a large (50,000-household) national survey that is conducted over the telephone and in person. The CPS program includes an Annual Social and Economic Supplement, which includes more extensive demographic variables than the monthly surveys. Researchers often rely on the supplement for annually updated information during the years between decennial censuses. Because of its very high quality and sophisticated design, the CPS is often studied by survey researchers, statisticians, and other social scientists.

Other examples of Census Bureau surveys are the American Housing Survey and the Consumer Expenditure Survey. Conducted for the Department of Housing and Urban Development, the American Housing Survey collects data on housing quality, availability, and characteristics for the United States and certain metropolitan areas. The Consumer Expenditure Survey is a periodic consumer survey designed to collect information on purchasing behaviors. The Bureau of Labor Statistics uses data from the Consumer Expenditure Survey when calculating the Consumer Price Index, a measure of inflation that tracks changes in the prices of products and services.

Applications for Survey Researchers

Survey researchers and social scientists rely on federal census results and sample-based estimates as valuable and comprehensive sources of information about the U.S. population and economy. Census data are subject to not only sampling error but also other survey errors, such as incomplete coverage and nonresponse. After the decennial census, the bureau publishes estimates of the net undercount or overcount as well as various nonresponse rates. Compared to other surveys, the error rates for the census are often very low. The sample-based surveys are subject to both sampling and nonsampling error. But the very large sample sizes and benefits of conducting ongoing surveys (such as professionally trained interviewers) often yield high-quality results.

Federal census results and sample-based estimates often serve as population or household controls for other sample-based surveys. The data can be used in various sampling phases such as design, stratification, and selection. Census data are commonly used as UEs in sample weighting adjustments, which reduce bias by accounting for differences in characteristics between a sample and the universe it is designed to represent.

Through extensive research on survey methods and statistical techniques, the Census Bureau strives to improve its own data collection and contribute to a wider knowledge base. Census Bureau reports cover topics such as survey design, questionnaire effects, and interviewing procedures. The resulting body of research provides very useful information to survey research professionals and students. Census Bureau technical reports and working papers are often accessible through federal Web sites or by request.

Christine Pierce

See also American Community Survey (ACS); Bureau of Labor Statistics (BLS); Census; Current Population Survey (CPS); Sample; Survey

Further Readings

Anderson, M. J. (1988). *The American census: A social history.* New Haven, CT: Yale University Press.

Anderson, M. J., & Fienberg, S. E. (1999). *Who counts? The politics of census-taking in contemporary America.* New York: Russell Sage Foundation.

Bureau of Labor Statistics. (2002, March). *Design and methodology* (Current Population Survey Tech. Paper No. 63RV). Retrieved January 10, 2007, from http://www.census.gov/prod/2002pubs/tp63rv.pdf

Executive Office of the President, Office of Management and Budget. (2006, September). *Statistical programs of the United States government: Fiscal year 2007.* Washington, DC: Author. Retrieved January 15, 2007, from http://www.whitehouse.gov/omb/inforeg/07statprog.pdf

Prewitt, K. (2003). *Politics and science in census taking.* New York: Russell Sage Foundation.

U.S. Census Bureau. (2008). *Statistical Abstract of the United States.* Washington, DC: U.S. Department of Commerce, Bureau of the Census, Government Printing Office. Retrieved April 24, 2008, from http://www.census.gov/compendia/statab/

U.S. Department of Commerce, Economics and Statistics Administration, & U.S. Census Bureau. (2007, June). *U.S. Census Bureau Strategic Plan FY 2007–2012.* Retrieved April 24, 2008, from http://www.census.gov/main/www/strategicplan/strategicplan.pdf

V

Validation

Within survey research, *validation* has more than one meaning, but this entry focuses on the concept of validating a completed interview, in particular one completed via paper and pencil, as soon as possible after it has been completed—that is, making certain that (a) all questions that should have been asked and answered were done so, and (b) answers that were written in for open-ended questions are legible, understandable, and relevant to the question being asked. The advantages of doing this type of validation as soon as possible after interviews are completed are three-fold. First, it allows for mistakes to be corrected soon after they have been made at a time when an interviewer's memory of the interview is still relatively fresh. Second, especially early in the field period of a survey, it helps to identify the need for retraining all or some interviewers if consistent problems are detected by the person doing the validation. Third, early in the survey period, it allows the researchers to modify their questionnaire if that is necessary—for example, fix a skip pattern that is not working as intended—before the problem negatively affects too many of the completed cases that otherwise may need to be reinterviewed.

With the advent of computer-assisted interviewing, whether the questionnaire is administered by an interviewer or is self-administered by the respondent, the need for manual validation of completed interviews is greatly reduced but not necessarily eliminated. It is reduced because the logic that is built into the computer interviewing software will not allow many of the problems to occur that are often present in paper-and-pencil interviewing (PAPI). These include erroneously skipped questions that should have been asked of a particular respondent and other questions that were asked when they should have been skipped. Problems like these in PAPI interviewing can be caught through manual validation and quickly corrected—whether they indicate the need to change the skipping instructions for certain contingency questions or the need to retrain particular interviewers.

Furthermore, the need for manual validation is not eliminated entirely by computer-assisted interviewing because the answers to open-ended questions cannot be checked for quality via computer software. Imagine a researcher who did not have open-ended answers validated until after all data were gathered, only to find significant problems in what was recorded by interviewers or respondents. Such problems could result from many reasons, including an open-ended question that was not well understood by most respondents. If this validation did not happen until all the data were gathered, the researcher may need to scrap this variable entirely. Instead, by having open-ended responses manually validated in the early stages of a survey, the researchers can catch such problems before they affect too many respondents. This will help ensure data quality and ultimately avoid disasters where those data for an entire variable are worthless.

Paul J. Lavrakas

See also Computer-Assisted Personal Interviewing (CAPI); Computer-Assisted Self-Interviewing (CASI); Computer-Assisted Telephone Interviewing (CATI); Contingency Question; Open-Ended Question; Quality Control; Verification

Further Readings

Groves, R. M., Fowler, F. J., Couper, M. P., Lepkowski, J. M., Singer, E., & Tourangeau, R. (2004). *Survey methodology.* Hoboken, NJ: Wiley.

Lavrakas, P. J. (1993). *Telephone survey methods: Sampling, selection, and supervision* (2nd ed.). Newbury Park, CA: Sage.

VALIDITY

The word *validity* is primarily a measurement term, having to do with the relevance of a measuring instrument for a particular purpose, but it has been broadened to apply to an entire study. A research investigation is said to have *internal validity* if there are valid causal implications and is said to have *external validity* if the results are generalizable.

As far as measurement is concerned, the most important property of a measuring instrument is the extent to which it has been validated with respect to some gold standard whose validity has been assumed to be taken for granted. For example, if scores on a test of mathematical aptitude (the instrument to be validated) correlate highly with scores on a subsequent test of mathematical achievement (the gold standard), all is well, and the aptitude test would be regarded as valid.

In the early 20th century, the methodological literature referred to three kinds of validity: (1) *content validity* (expert judgment, i.e., postulation of the gold standard itself), (2) *criterion-related validity* (the type of validity mentioned in the previous paragraph), and (3) *construct validity* (the extent to which the scores obtained using a particular measuring instrument agreed with theoretical expectations). There were also subtypes of criterion-related validity (*concurrent* and *predictive*) and construct validity (*convergent* and *discriminant*), but more recently the general label "construct validity" not only has become more popular but also has been alleged to include content validity and criterion-related validity as well.

Connection Between Reliability and Validity

Reliability is concerned with the consistency of results whether or not those results are valid. It is easy to imagine a situation in which ratings given to various contestants (in a figure skating event, for example) are consistent (reliable) from one judge to another, but that all the ratings are wrong due to the personal biases of the judges.

There is a way to investigate the validity of an instrument with respect to its reliability. Suppose that a survey researcher were interested in pursuing further the relationship between performance on an aptitude test (the predictor) and performance on an achievement test (the criterion with respect to which the predictor instrument is to be validated) in which a correlation between the two of .54 has been obtained. The researcher would like to estimate what the correlation would be if it were based upon true scores rather than observed scores. There is a formula called *the correction for attenuation* that can be used for that purpose. The obtained correlation is divided by the product of the square roots of the estimates of the respective reliability coefficients. If the reliability coefficient for the aptitude test were estimated to be .64 and the reliability coefficient for the achievement test were estimated to be .81, application of that formula would yield a value of .75, which is considerably higher than the .54. That makes sense, because the true correlation has been attenuated (i.e., reduced) by the less-than-perfect reliabilities of the two tests.

Validity of Instrument Versus Validity of Scores Obtained With Instrument

Just as for reliability, it is somewhat controversial whether researchers should refer to the validity of a measuring instrument or to the validity of the scores obtained with the instrument. Some authors even go so far as to insist that any investigation of the validity of a measuring instrument should address the consequences of any actions taken on the basis of such scores.

Thomas R. Knapp

See also Construct Validity; External Validity; Internal Validity; Reliability; True Value

Further Readings

Borsboom, D. (2005). *Measuring the mind: Conceptual issues in contemporary psychometrics.* Cambridge, UK: Cambridge University Press.

Campbell, D. T., & Stanley, J. C. (1963). *Experimental and quasi-experimental designs for research.* Chicago: Rand McNally.

Carmines, E. G., & Zeller, R. A. (1979). *Reliability and validity assessment* (Sage University Paper Series on Quantitative Applications in the Social Sciences, No. 07-017). Beverly Hills, CA: Sage.

Litwin, M. S. (1995). *Survey kit: Vol. 7. How to measure survey reliability and validity.* Thousand Oaks, CA: Sage.

Messick, S. (1989). Validity. In R. L. Linn (Ed.), *Educational measurement* (3rd ed., pp. 13–103). Washington, DC: American Council on Education.

VARIABLE

A variable is something that varies in value, as opposed to a constant (such as the number 2), which always has the same value. These are observable features of something that can take on several different values or can be put into several discrete categories. For example, respondents' scores on an index are variables because they have different values, and religion can be considered a variable because there are multiple categories. Scientists are sometimes interested in determining the values of constants, such as π, the ratio of the area of a circle to its squared radius. However, survey research involves the study of variables rather than constants.

A quantity X is a *random variable* if, for every number a, there is a probability p that X is less than or equal to a. A *discrete random variable* is one that attains only certain values, such as the number of children one has. By contrast, a *continuous random variable* is one that can take on any value within a range, such as a person's income (measured in the smallest possible fractions of a dollar).

Data analysis often involves hypotheses regarding the relationships between variables, such as "If X increases in value, then Y tends to increase (or decrease) in value." Such hypotheses involve relationships between *latent variables*, which are abstract concepts. These concepts have to be operationalized into *manifest variables* that can be measured in actual research. In surveys, this operationalization involves either using one question to tap the concept or combining several questions into an index that measures the concept.

A basic distinction in statistical analysis is between the dependent variable that the researcher is trying to explain and the independent variable that serves as a predictor of the dependent variable. In regression analysis, for example, the dependent variable is the Y variable on the left-hand side of the regression equation $Y = a + bX$, whereas X is an independent variable on the right-hand side of the equation.

The starting point in survey analysis is often looking at the distribution of the variables of interest, one at a time, including calculating appropriate univariate statistics such as percentage distributions. The changes in that variable over time can then be examined in a time-series analysis. Univariate analysis is usually just the jumping-off point for bivariate or multivariate analysis. For example, in survey experiments, the researcher examines the extent to which experimental manipulations in the survey (such as alternative wordings of a question) affect the variance in the variable of interest.

Herbert F. Weisberg

See also Dependent Variable; Experimental Design; Independent Variable; Null Hypothesis; Regression Analysis

Further Readings

Lewis-Beck, M. S. (1995). *Data analysis: An introduction.* Thousand Oaks, CA: Sage.

VARIANCE

Variance, or dispersion, roughly refers to the degree of scatter or variability among a collection of observations. For example, in a survey regarding the effectiveness of a political leader, ratings from individuals will differ. In a survey dealing with reading ability among children, the expectation is that children will differ. Even in the physical sciences, measurements might differ from one occasion to the next because of the imprecision of the instruments used. In a very real sense, it is this variance that motivates interest in statistical techniques.

A basic issue that researchers face is deciding how variation should be measured when trying to characterize a population of individuals or things. That is, if all individuals of interest could be measured, how should the variation among these individuals be characterized? Such measures are population measures of variation. A related issue is deciding how to estimate a population measure of variation based on a sample of individuals.

Choosing a measure of dispersion is a complex issue that has seen many advances during the past 30 years, and more than 150 measures of dispersion have been proposed. The choice depends in part on the goal of the investigator, with the optimal choice often changing drastically depending on what an investigator wants to know or do. Although most of these measures seem to have little practical value, at least five or six play an important and useful role.

Certainly the best-known measure of dispersion is the *population variance*, which is typically written as σ^2. It is the average (or expected) value of the squared difference between an observation and the population mean. That is, if all individuals in a population could be measured (as in a complete census), the average of their responses is called the population mean, μ, and if for every observation the squared difference between it and μ were computed, the average of these squared values is σ^2. In more formal terms, $\sigma^2 = E(X - \mu)^2$, where X is any observation the investigator might make and E stands for expected value. The (positive) square root of the variance, σ, is called the (population) standard deviation.

Based on a simple random sample of n individuals, if the investigator observes the values $X_1, \ldots, X_n$, the usual estimate of σ^2 is the sample variance:

$$s^2 = \frac{1}{n-1} \sum_{i=1}^{n} (X_i - \bar{X})^2,$$

where $\bar{X} = \sum_{i=1}^{n} X_i / n$ is the sample mean.

For some purposes, the use of the standard deviation stems from the fundamental result that the probability of an observation being within some specified distance from the mean, as measured by σ, is completely determined under normality. For example, the probability that an observation is within one standard deviation of the mean is .68, and the probability of being within two standard deviations is .954. These properties have led to a commonly used measure of effect size (a measure intended to characterize the extent to which two groups differ) as well as a frequently employed rule for detecting outliers (unusually

large or small values). Shortly after a seminal paper by J. W. Tukey in 1960, it was realized that even very small departures from normality can alter these properties substantially, resulting in practical problems that commonly occur.

Consider, for example, the two distributions shown in Figure 1. One is a standard normal, meaning it has a mean of zero (0) and a variance of one (1). The other is not a normal distribution, but rather something called a mixed or contaminated normal. That is, two normal distributions, both having the same mean but different variances, are mixed together. The important point is that despite the obvious similarity between the two distributions, their variances differ substantially: The normal has variance 1, but the mixed normal has variance 10.9. This illustrates the general principle that small changes in the tails of a distribution can substantially affect σ.

Now consider the property that under normality, the probability that an observation is within one standard deviation of the means is .68. Will this property hold under nonnormality? In some cases it is approximately true, but in other situations this is no longer the case, even under small departures from normality (as measured by any of several commonly used metrics by statisticians). For the mixed normal distribution in Figure 1, this probability exceeds .999.

The *sample variance* reflects a similar property: It is very sensitive to outliers. In some situations this can be beneficial, but for a general class of problems it is detrimental. For example, a commonly used rule is to declare the value X an outlier if it is more than

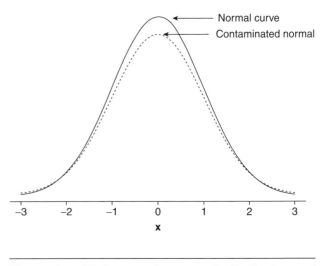

Figure 1 Variances of a normal distribution and a mixed normal distribution

two (sample) standard deviations from the mean, the idea being that under normality such a value is quite unusual from a probabilistic point of view. That is, declare X an outlier if

$$\frac{X - \bar{X}}{s} > 2.$$

This rule suffers from *masking*, however, meaning that even obvious outliers are not detected due to the sensitivity of s to outliers. Consider, for example, the values 2, 2, 3, 3, 3, 4, 4, 4, 100,000, 100,000. Then $\bar{X} = 20002.5$, $s = 42162.38$, and $(100,000 - 20002.5)/s = 1.9$. So the value 100,000 would not be declared an outlier based on the rule just given, yet it is clearly unusual relative to the other values.

For detecting outliers, two alternative measures of dispersion are typically used. The first is called the *median absolute deviation (MAD)* statistic. It is the median of the n values $|X_1 - M|, \ldots, |X_n - M|$, where M is the usual median of $X_1, \ldots, X_n$. Now X is declared an outlier if

$$\frac{|X - M|}{MAD/.6745} > 2.24.$$

The other is the *interquartile range*, which is just the difference between the upper and lower quartiles. (This latter measure of dispersion is used by *boxplot rules* for detecting outliers.) An important feature of both of these measures of dispersion is that they are insensitive to extreme values; they reflect the variation of the centrally located observations, which is a desirable property when detecting outliers with the goal of avoiding masking.

Another approach when selecting a measure of dispersion is to search for an estimator that has a relatively low standard error over a reasonably broad range of situations. In particular, it should compete well with s under normality, but it is desirable to maintain a low standard error under nonnormality as well. So, for example, if it is desired to compare two groups in terms of dispersion, the goal is to maintain high power regardless of whether sampling is from a normal distribution or from the mixed normal distribution in Figure 1.

Two measures of dispersion that satisfy this goal are called the *percentage bend midvariance* and the *biweight midvariance*. The tedious computational details are not given here, but they can be found in the further readings, along with easy-to-use software.

In terms of achieving a relatively low standard error, the sample standard deviation, s, competes well with these two alternative measures under normality, but for nonnormal distributions, s can perform rather poorly.

Effect Size

The variance has played a role in a variety of other situations, stemming in part from properties enjoyed by the normal distribution. One of these is a commonly used measure of *effect size* for characterizing how two groups differ:

$$\Delta = \frac{\mu_1 - \mu_2}{\sigma_p},$$

where μ_1 and μ_2 are the population means, and where, by assumption, the two groups have equal standard deviations, σ_p. The idea is that if $\Delta = 1$, for example, the difference between the means is one standard deviation, which provides perspective on how groups differ under normality. But concerns have been raised about this particular approach because under nonnormality it can mask a relatively large difference.

Standard Errors

The notion of variation extends to sampling distributions in the following manner. Imagine a study based on n observations resulting in a simple random sample mean, say $\bar{X}$. Now imagine the study is repeated many times (in theory, infinitely many times) yielding the sample means $\bar{X}_1, \bar{X}_2, \ldots$, with each sample mean again based on n observations. The variance of these sample means is called the *squared standard error of the sample mean*, which is known to be

$$E(\bar{X} - \mu)^2 = \sigma^2/n$$

under random sampling. That is, it is the variance of these sample means. Certainly the most useful and important role played by the variance is making inferences about the population mean based on the sample mean. The reason is that the standard error of the sample mean, $\sigma/\sqrt{n}$, suggests how inferences about μ should be made assuming normality, but the details go beyond the scope of this entry.

Winsorized Variance

Another measure of dispersion that has taken on an increasing importance in recent years is the *Winsorized variance*; it plays a central role when comparing groups based on *trimmed means*. It is computed as follows. Consider any γ such that $0 \leq \gamma < 1$. Let $g = \gamma n$, rounded down to the nearest integer. So if $\gamma n = 9.8$, say, $g = 9$. Computing a γ-trimmed mean refers to removing the g smallest and g largest observations and averaging those that remain. Winsorizing n observations refers to setting the g smallest values to the smallest value not trimmed and simultaneously setting the g largest values equal to the largest value not trimmed. The sample variance, based on the Winsorized values, is called the *Winsorized variance*. Both theory and simulation studies indicate that trimming can reduce problems associated with means due to nonnormality, particularly when sample sizes are small. Although not intuitive, theory indicates that the squared standard error of a trimmed mean is related to the Winsorized variance, and so the Winsorized variance has played a role when making inferences about a population trimmed mean. Also, it has been found to be useful when searching for robust analogs of Pearson's correlation.

Rand R. Wilcox

See also Mean; Outliers; Standard Deviation; Standard Error; Variance Estimation

Further Readings

Rousseeuw, P. J., & Leroy, A. M. (1987). *Robust regression and outlier detection*. New York: Wiley.

Staudte, R. G., & Sheather, S. J. (1990). *Robust estimation and testing*. New York: Wiley.

Wilcox, R. R. (2003). *Applying contemporary statistical techniques*. New York: Academic Press.

VARIANCE ESTIMATION

Variance refers to the degree of variability (dispersion) among a collection of observations. Although estimation of the size of the variance in a distribution of numbers often is a complex process, it is an extremely important endeavor for survey researchers, as it helps make valid inferences of population parameters.

Standard variance estimation formulas for simple random sampling, stratified sampling, and cluster sampling can be found in essentially any survey sampling textbook, such as those by William G. Cochran or Leslie Kish. However, most large survey samples use combinations of unequal probabilities, stratification, and clustering. Often, survey weights are used in estimation that account for unequal probabilities, nonresponse, and post-stratification. These are usually ratio estimates with the numerator being the weighted average and the denominator being the sum of the weights. Both the numerator and denominator are random variables. However, textbook variance formulas are not sufficient for these survey samples and estimation problems. Specialized variance estimation software packages have been required until only recently, but now general-purpose statistical analysis programs have started to include the special variance estimation techniques needed to correctly calculate variances for complex sample surveys.

Without correct variance estimates, users are unable to make valid inferences concerning population parameters. Most complex sample surveys have larger standard errors than do simple random samples. If inference is done using standard errors from simple random samples, the standard errors would be too small and any statistical procedures would be too liberal (e.g., p-values or confidence intervals would be too small, and test statistics would be too large).

Calculation Methods

The two most popular classes in the calculation of correct variance estimates for complex sample surveys are *replicate methods* for variance estimation and *Taylor series linearization methods*. A third class of techniques that are sometimes used are *generalized variance functions*.

Replicate methods for variance compute multiple estimates in a systematic way and use the variability in these estimates to estimate the variance of the full-sample estimator. The simplest replicate method for variance is the *method of random groups*. The method of random groups was originally designed for interpenetrating samples or samples that are multiple repetitions (e.g., 10) of the same sampling strategy. Each of these repetitions is a random group, from which an estimate is derived. The overall estimator is the average of these estimates, and the estimated variance of the estimator is the sampling variance of the estimators. Of course, this technique can be used for any complex sample survey by separating the sample into sub-samples that are as equivalent as possible (e.g., by sorting by design variables and using systematic sampling to divide into random groups). This simplest of replicate methods for variance is simple enough to do by hand, but is not as robust as more modern replication-based methods that can now be easily calculated by computers.

Balanced repeated replication (BRR), also known as *balanced half-samples*, was originally conceived for use when two primary sampling units (PSUs) are selected from each stratum. A half-sample then consists of all cases from exactly one primary sampling unit from each stratum (with each weight doubled). Balanced half-sampling uses an orthogonal set of half-samples as specified by a Hadamard matrix. The variability of the half-sample estimates is taken as an estimate of the variance of the full-sample estimator.

Jackknife variance calculation, also called *Jack-knife repeated replication (JRR)*, works in a similar way to BRR. The JRR method creates a series of replicate estimates by removing only one primary sampling unit from only one stratum at a time (doubling the weight for the stratum's other primary sampling unit).

For a simple example, let us use two strata (1 and 2) with two PSUs in each (1a, 1b, 2a, and 2b). BRR could form estimates by using only 1a and 2a, only 1b and 2b, only 1a and 2b, and only 1b and 2a (each orthogonal combination of PSUs). JRR drops only one PSU at a time and forms estimates by using 1b (doubly weighted), 2a, and 2b; or 1a (doubly weighted), 2a, and 2b; or 1a, 1b, and 2a (doubly weighted); or 1a, 1b, and 2b (doubly weighted).

Even if a complex sample survey does not have exactly two PSUs in each stratum, the BRR and JRR techniques can be used by defining pseudo-strata and pseudo-PSUs so that there are two pseudo-PSUs in each pseudo-stratum. Of course, these methods work only as well as these definitions work.

A more general replication method for variance is *bootstrapping*. The idea of bootstrapping is that, from the full original sample drawn, the researcher repeatedly draws simple random samples of the same sample size with replacement. With each draw, different observations will be duplicated, and these differences will result in different estimates. The variance of these estimates is the variance estimate.

Taylor series linearization methods work by approximating the estimator of the population parameter of interest by a linear function of the observations. These approximations rely on the validity of Taylor series or binomial series expansions. An estimator of the variance of the approximation is then used as an estimator of the variance of the estimator itself. Generally, first-order approximations are used (and are adequate), but second- and higher-order approximations are possible.

A third, but less commonly used, class of variance estimation methods is a *generalized variance function (GVF)*. Generalized variance functions are tables or formulas prepared by statistical experts as guidance for analysts who cannot directly calculate correct standard errors. The experts calculate variance estimates for as many variables as is practical and use the direct estimates as input into a regression model. The most common model states that the squared coefficient of variance is a linear function of the inverse of its expectation:

$$\frac{Var(\hat{X})}{X^2} = a + \frac{b}{X}.$$

Regression estimates for *a* and *b* can be done separately for multiple subgroups, or domains. Analysts can then input their estimate (X) and the two parameters *a* and *b* to calculate an estimated variance. GVFs are still being used, but as variance estimation tools become easier to use, the use of GVFs will continue to decline.

Choosing a method from among those described in this entry is an important and difficult decision. Software has improved so that those who can use standard statistical software now have the ability to calculate correct variance estimates. Empirical results from comparisons between the replicate methods for variance estimation and Taylor series linearization methods show only subtle differences (there is no difference asymptotically). Therefore, often the best solution is for researchers to use software with which they are already familiar. There seems a slight preference in the literature for the balanced repeated replication method on accuracy. However, Taylor series linearization methods are easier to set up and use. Jackknife variance calculations are less available through software, and bootstrapping software is very limited. The random groups method has been superseded by the other three replicate methods for variance estimation; its main advantage is its simplicity. Generalized variance functions are useful mostly for publication so that analysts can calculate reasonable (and stable) variance estimates without using the other statistical techniques; individual estimates of variance using the functions will be less accurate than other statistical methods. Finally, it is generally not acceptable to use simple random sample formulas to calculate variance estimates for complex sample surveys.

Software for Variance Estimation

Standard statistical software packages such as SAS, STATA, and Statistical Package for the Social Sciences (SPSS) used to only be able to calculate standard errors assuming a simple random sample. Standard routines in these packages still make this assumption. Such standard errors tend to be too small for a cluster sample design. However, these packages have recently added capability through new procedures or modules for calculating design-corrected standard errors for complex sample surveys.

Nevertheless, specialized variance estimation programs such as SUDAAN and WesVar are superior for variance estimation because they have wider sets of analyses for which correct variance estimation can be done, and the implementation is more robust after having such a head start on the general-use statistical software packages.

Steven Pedlow

See also Balanced Repeated Replication (BRR); Bootstrapping; Clustering; Cluster Sample; Cochran, W. G.; Complex Sample Surveys; Jackknife Variance Estimation; Kish, Leslie; Primary Sampling Unit; Replicate Methods for Variance Estimation; Sampling Variance; SAS; Simple Random Sample; Standard Error; Stata; Statistical Package for the Social Sciences (SPSS); Stratified Sampling; SUDAAN; Taylor Series Linearization; WesVar

Further Readings

Cochran, W. G. (1977). *Sampling techniques* (3rd ed.). New York: Wiley.
Kish, L. (1995). *Survey sampling.* New York: Wiley.
Wolter, K. (1985). *Introduction to variance estimation.* New York: Springer.

VERBATIM RESPONSES

A verbatim response refers to what an interviewer records as an answer to an open-ended question when writing down the *exact words* spoken by the respondent. Open-ended questions are those that do not provide a respondent with predetermined response choices and instead allow, expect, and encourage a respondent to answer in his or her own words.

Sometimes open-ended questions have "precoded" response categories for interviewers to use, but these are not read to a respondent. In these instances interviewers are trained to listen to the answer a respondent gives and then "fit" it into one of the precoded choices. However, this is not always possible to do for all given responses, so even with precoded open-ended questions, some verbatim responses that do not fit into any one of the precoded categories must be written down by the interviewer. Most open-ended questions do not have precoded response choices for interviewers to code; thus in most cases with an open-ended question, the interviewer must write down what the respondent says.

In some cases a researcher may allow interviewers to summarize the gist of what the respondent says in response to an open-ended question. However, in other cases it is important that the exact words spoken by the respondent are recorded by the interviewer. It is in these cases that interviewers are trained and expected to write down the complete verbatim response. Interviewers are trained to "slow down" respondents who are speaking too fast in answering an open-ended question for which a verbatim response must be recorded by the interviewer. Interviewers also are trained to use probing techniques to get more detailed replies to open-end questions.

After data collection has ended, the verbatim responses that interviewers have recorded often are coded (similar to content analysis) so that they then can be analyzed via quantitative statistical techniques. This is a labor-intensive and expensive process, if done reliably. Verbatim responses also are used in survey reports to help illustrate the statistical findings gleaned from coded open-ended variables by putting a "human face" to them. This is done without identifying the respondents whose verbatim responses are used, so as not to violate the confidentiality pledge given to the respondents.

Paul J. Lavrakas

See also Content Analysis; Open-Ended Question; Precoded Question; Probing; Standardized Survey Interviewing

Further Readings

Fowler, F. J., & Mangione, T. W. (1990). *Standardized survey interviewing.* Newbury Park, CA: Sage.

VERIFICATION

Within survey research, one of the meanings of *verification* refers to efforts that are made to confirm that a telephone or in-person interview was actually completed with a particular respondent. Within this context, verification is one of the techniques used to guard against interviewer falsification. Such verification often is done via telephone even if the interview was done in person. In most cases a small number (e.g., less than five) of randomly selected completed interviews of all interviewers are verified by having a person in a supervisory position contact the respondents and verify that they were, in fact, interviewed by the interviewer. In other instances, interviewers who may be under observation for previous interviewing infractions may have a greater number of their interviews verified. Oftentimes, interviewers are instructed to tell respondents at the end of an interview that someone may contact them to verify that the interview was completed.

Other meanings of verification, within the context of survey research, concern efforts that researchers sometimes make to verify whether a respondent's answer to a key variable is accurate. These procedures include so-called *record checks* in which the researcher gains access to an external database (such as those assembled by various government agencies) that can be used to officially verify whether the answer given by a respondent is correct. For example, in a survey conducted of voting behavior, if respondents are asked in a survey whether they voted in the past election, then researchers could go to public election records to learn if a given respondent did or did not vote in the last election, thereby verifying the answer given in the survey. However, in this entry, it is the former meaning of the term *verification* that is addressed.

In theory, informing interviewers that some of their completed interviews will be verified is assumed to motivate them against any falsification. However, little empirical work has been done to test this assumption. Nevertheless, many clients expect this will be done, and as such, verification is a process that many survey organizations build into their contracts. Of note, verification should not be confused with *interviewer monitoring*, which is a process used in real time to observe the behavior of interviewers as they interact with respondents in (a) gaining cooperation from the respondents and (b) gathering data from them.

Verification serves additional purposes beyond its primary purpose of confirming whether or not a given interview was conducted. In addition, a systematic and routine verification process provides information that a survey organization can use to evaluate the job performance of individual interviewers. For example, when respondents are contacted to verify a completed interview, they also can be asked a few additional questions, at very little additional cost to the survey organization, to help evaluate the quality of the interviewer's work. A system of routine verification can also serve as a check on the quality of the interviewer monitoring system a survey organization has instituted, as verification is a fail-safe approach to detecting falsification, which ideally should be detected via on-the-job monitoring.

Paul J. Lavrakas

See also Falsification; Interviewer Monitoring; Record Check; Reverse Record Check; Validation

Further Readings

Braun, J. R., & La Faro, D. (1968). Effectiveness of the California Study Methods Survey verification key in detecting faking. *Journal of Educational Measurement, 5*(2), 167–168.

Lavrakas, P. J. (1993). *Telephone survey methods: Sampling, selection, and supervision* (2nd ed.). Newbury Park, CA: Sage.

VIDEO COMPUTER-ASSISTED SELF-INTERVIEWING (VCASI)

Video computer-assisted self-interviewing (VCASI), sometimes referred to as audio-visual CASI (AVCASI), involves administration of an electronic self-administered questionnaire, which includes prerecorded video clips of an interviewer asking survey questions. This mode of data collection is an extension of audio computer-assisted self-interviewing (ACASI). Responses are recorded either by keyboard, mouse, or touch screen data entry. This technique is typically used in two settings. First is in conjunction with a face-to-face computer-assisted interview, where part of the interview is conducted by the interviewer and part is left to the respondent using the computer in a self-administered mode. Second is in a completely self-administered setting where the CASI questionnaire runs on a stand-alone terminal or kiosk. In an interviewer-administered setting, the respondent uses headphones for complete privacy. In a private kiosk setting the questions might be delivered to the respondent using built-in computer speakers.

VCASI was developed to collect information on sensitive topics, such as illegal drug use, sexual preference, criminal activity, in as valid and reliable a manner as possible. When responding to sensitive questions in the presence of a live interviewer or with other persons present, respondents are sometimes reluctant to answer certain questions completely and honestly. Instead, they tend to provide partial responses, socially desirable responses, or refuse to answer altogether. To overcome such resistance, interviewers equip respondents with headphones, which prevent others from overhearing the questions. The respondent then enters his or her response directly into the computer, thereby ensuring greater confidentiality. This approach is assumed to be less prone to social desirability bias and other response errors related to the presence of an interviewer or third parties. Unlike ACASI, in which the respondent typically hears only the questions being asked and sees text or a visual representation of the question on the computer screen, with VCASI the video of the interviewer is thought to mimic some of the benefits associated with face-to-face interviewing, such as personal interaction.

In addition, VCASI helps address the issue of illiteracy among some respondents, which can be a problem with some self-administered survey modes (such as mail surveys). Because the questions are asked in a video format, respondents do not need to be able to read the questions. They do, however, need to be able to enter the correct response category, which typically is an easier task requiring a lower level of reading competency.

VCASI also provides standardization of interviewer behaviors. Because the interviewer is prerecorded, there is no interviewer variation per se, such as interviewer mood or voice inflection, which might affect how a person responds. Conversely, interviewers cannot react to personal characteristics

of the respondent, the interview setting, or to the responses provided and thereby bias the data. In addition, because skip instructions and branching, as well as the sequence of the questions, are predefined and programmed into the VCASI system, no accidental or intentional omission of questions can occur, and all questions are administered exactly as worded. VCASI is not suitable, however, for complicated concepts and questions that require probing or clarification. Also, lengthy questionnaires that may require motivational efforts from an interviewer to maintain the respondent's interest in the survey are not good candidates for this approach.

In a kiosk setting (such as in a museum or shopping mall) where third parties cannot be excluded from the interview setting, the increased privacy provided by VCASI is less of a benefit. In such settings, however, it is a cost-efficient method of data collection, because no interviewers are needed and data entry is conducted by respondents at little to no cost, other than the fixed costs associated with system development, programming, and maintenance.

Marek Fuchs

See also Audio Computer-Assisted Self-Interviewing (ACASI); Interviewer Variance; Sensitive Topics; Social Desirability; Underreporting

Further Readings

Katz, L. M., Cumming, P. D., & Wallace, E. L. (2007). Computer-based blood donor screening: A status report. *Transfusion Medicine Reviews*, *21*(1), 13–25.

Kissinger, P., Rice, J., Farley, T., Trim, S., Jewitt, K., Margavio, V., et al. (1999). Application of computer-assisted interviews to sexual behaviour research. *American Journal of Epidemiology*, *149*(10), 950–954.

O'Reilly, J. M., Hubbard, M. L., Lessler, J. T., Biemer, P. P., & Turner, C. F. (1994). Audio and video computer assisted self-interviewing: Preliminary tests of new technologies for data collection. *Journal of Official Statistics*, *10*(2), 197–214.

VIDEOPHONE INTERVIEWING

Videophone interviewing enables researchers to closely reproduce face-to-face interviewing without requiring interviewers to physically enter respondent homes. A videophone enables real-time video and audio communication between two parties. There are two types of videophones: landline and mobile. Landline videophones are telephones with an LCD screen and a video camera. Mobile videophones are similar to landline phones with the exception of having a smaller screen. To transmit real-time video conversation, mobile phones should have 3G service—a wireless technology capable of transmitting a large amount of data.

Because videophone interviews closely mimic face-to-face interviews, the interaction between interviewer and respondent also shares the benefits of face-to-face interviewing. Specifically, the benefit of observing nonverbal communication, of allowing a slower pace than phone interviews, and of overcoming problems of respondent distraction are some examples. Because interviewers cannot observe the nonverbal communication of the respondent in a regular phone survey, it is more difficult to spot comprehension problems and to address issues of respondent motivation. Furthermore, interviewers cannot send nonverbal motivational cues or encouragement. Silences are also more difficult to handle on a regular telephone than face-to-face. In a videophone interview, the pace of the conversation can be reduced in comparison to a telephone interview. Breaking off would be more difficult than in a telephone survey. Lastly, multi-tasking, such as doing something else while being on the phone, can be discouraged in a videophone interview, as the norm of politeness is likely relevant. In other words, a videophone interview should elicit higher-quality data when compared to telephone interviews.

The videophone enables researchers to send text and multi-media material to the respondent. For example, show cards can be used when properly formatted for the small screen. In addition, still pictures, audio, and video can be sent to the respondent as is done nowadays with Web surveys.

Videophone interviewing is likely the most similar method to face-to-face interviewing, an interviewing technique that is still considered the most flexible and reliable, allowing for complex and long interviews, the reduction of missing data, and the increase response rates. Videophone interviewing, however, will potentially reintroduce some interviewer effects common in face-to-face interviews (e.g., social desirability bias).

Videophone interviews are still in the experimental phase. They are used in both the medical field and in psychological fields to communicate with and diagnose patients. Landline videophone penetration rates are extremely low or nonexistent in many countries, thus rendering landline videophone interviewing not feasible for surveys of the general population. On the other hand, the percentage of mobile phones equipped with videophone capabilities is growing in many industrialized countries, making videophone interviews a future possibility for survey researchers.

Mario Callegaro

See also Face-to-Face Interviewing; Show Card; Social Desirability; Telephone Surveys; Video Computer-Assisted Self-Interviewing (VCASI); Web Survey

Further Readings

Couper, M. P., Tourangeau, R., & Steiger, D. M. (2001, November). *Social presence in Web surveys.* Paper presented at the annual Federal Committee on Survey Methodology conference, Arlington, VA. Retrieved April 24, 2008, from http://www.fcsm.gov/01papers/Tourangeau.pdf

Demiris, G., Parker Oliver, D., & Courtney, K. (2006). A study of the suitability of videophone for psychometric assessment. *Behaviour & Information Technology, 25,* 233–237.

Holbrook, A. L., Green, M. C., & Krosnick, J. A. (2003). Telephone versus face-to-face interviewing of national probability samples with long questionnaires: Comparisons of respondent satisficing and social desirability response bias. *Public Opinion Quarterly, 67,* 79–125.

VIGNETTE QUESTION

A vignette is a sort of "illustration" in words. In survey research, a vignette question describes an event, happening, circumstance, or other scenario, the wording of which often is experimentally controlled by the researcher and at least one of the different versions of the vignette is randomly assigned to different subsets of respondents.

For example, imagine a vignette that describes a hypothetical crime that was committed, and the respondents are asked closed-ended questions to rate how serious they consider the crime to be and what sentence a judge should assign to the perpetrator. The researcher could experimentally alter the wording of the vignette by varying six independent variables: the gender, race, and age of both the victim and perpetrator. If two ages (e.g., 16 and 53), three races (Asian, black, and white) and both genders (female and male) were varied for both the victim and perpetrator, the resulting design—a $2 \times 3 \times 2 \times 2$ experiment—would yield 24 different versions of the vignette. In the typical use of this approach, one of these 24 versions would be randomly assigned to each respondent. This would allow the researcher to test for three main effects (age, gender, race), three two-way interaction effects, and one three-way interaction effect.

The experimental use of vignettes has been enhanced greatly with the advent of computer-assisted survey data collection such as CAPI, CASI, and CATI. No longer do researchers need to print hard copies of multiple versions of a questionnaire to deploy randomly to respondents. Instead, the computer software randomly serves up the version or versions of the vignette to any one respondent, thus balancing the allocation of the different versions easily and correctly across the entire sample.

Another way vignettes are used in survey research is illustrated as follows. A vignette question could describe a protagonist (or group of protagonists) faced with a realistic situation pertaining to the construct under consideration. The respondent is asked to make a judgment about the protagonist, the situation, or the correct course of action, using some form of closed-ended response. Sociologist Harry Triandis and colleagues developed a series of scenarios (vignettes) designed to measure respondents' cultural orientation. One vignette simply stated, *You and your friends decided spontaneously to go out to dinner at a restaurant. What do you think is the best way to handle the bill?* Four response options were provided: (a) *split it equally, without regard to who ordered what,* (b) *split it according to how much each person makes,* (c) *the group leader pays the bill or decides how to split it,* (d) *compute each person's charge according to what that person ordered.* For this particular measure, respondents were asked to rank their top two options. This particular study consisted of a series of 16 different vignettes, each with a unique set of response options, all designed to assess some aspect of cultural orientation.

Vignette questions are flexible and can be used to measure many different types of attitudes and beliefs or scenarios. They are especially useful when trying to measure complex concepts that may be best described by way of example.

Attitude measures may be classified in a variety of different ways, but one classic taxonomy remains remarkably useful. In the 1960s, Stuart Cook and Claire Selltiz classified measures in the following taxa: self-report, physiological, behavioral, partially structured, and measures based on the performance of objective tasks. Self-report, physiological, and behavioral measures remain conceptually and operationally (except for technological advances in the case of physiological measures) similar to those used nearly half a century ago. Measures based on the performance of objective tasks are those in which the respondent is asked to perform some task that is expected to be influenced by the respondent's attitude (e.g., when asked to draw a picture of a quarter, a respondent who has more favorable attitudes toward money may be expected to draw the quarter larger).

Partially structured measures are those in which respondents are presented with an ambiguous stimulus and asked to respond as they see fit. Responses to partially structured (e.g., vignette) measures are influenced by pertinent characteristics (e.g., attitudes) of the respondents and can therefore be used to infer characteristics about the respondents. One advantage of vignette measures is that they are more indirect than self-report measures. Although the topic under consideration is clearly present in the vignettes, responses to partially structured vignette questions do not require the intentional recollection of stored information, as with direct questions. Thus, vignette questions can be used to assess characteristics of the respondents that they may be either unwilling or unable to admit, even to themselves.

An example of this use may be seen in the psychology literature with an "older cousin" of the vignette question. This is the Thematic Apperception Test, in which respondents are presented with an actual illustration or pictographic image and are asked to write an imaginative story about the graphic. Respondents' stories are coded by trained judges and are used to infer motives, such as the needs for achievement, affiliation, or power. Respondents' achievement, affiliation, or power motives are generally considered to be consciously inaccessible to respondents and thus only available to researchers via administration of the Thematic Apperception Test.

Partially structured vignette measures may also be used with closed-ended response options. Patrick Vargas and his colleagues presented respondents with a series of vignettes describing different protagonists engaging in ambiguously conflicted behaviors; for example, in assessing attitudes toward being religious, one vignette described a woman who declared herself to be very religious but also admitted to not having attended religious services since starting college. Respondents were asked to judge how religious they believed the protagonists to be using 11-point scales. Respondents tended to contrast their judgments of the protagonists away from their own beliefs: Very religious people judged the woman to be more atheistic, whereas nonreligious people judged the woman to be more religious. Similar results were found with different vignettes assessing attitudes toward dishonesty, inequality, and politics. Of note, in all studies, responses to the vignette questions were uncorrelated with direct measures of the construct under consideration, and responses to the vignette questions reliably predicted both self-reported and actual behaviors, beyond what could be predicted by self-report measures.

The Internet, as a mode of survey data collection, is especially conducive for the deployment of vignette questions, as the vignettes can be displayed to respondents as text, with visuals, with audio stimuli, or all of these aids.

Patrick Vargas

See also Attitude Measurement; Computer-Assisted Personal Interviewing (CAPI); Computer-Assisted Self-Interviewing (CASI); Computer-Assisted Telephone Interviewing (CATI); Experimental Design; Factorial Design; Factorial Survey Method (Rossi's Method); Independent Variable; Interaction Effect; Main Effect; Random Assignment; Web Survey

Further Readings

Cook, S. W., & Selltiz, C. (1964). A multiple-indicator approach to attitude measurement. *Psychological Bulletin, 62*, 36–55.

Triandis, H. C., Chen, X. P., & Chan, D. K.-S. (1998). Scenarios for the measurement of collectivism and individualism. *Journal of Cross-Cultural Psychology, 29*, 275–289.

Vargas, P. T., von Hippel, W., & Petty, R. E. (2004). Using "partially structured" attitude measures to enhance the attitude-behavior relationship. *Personality and Social Psychology Bulletin, 30*, 197–211.

VISUAL COMMUNICATION

Visual communication involves the transmission of information through the visual sensory system, or the eyes and sense of sight. In surveys, visual communication relies heavily on verbal communication (i.e., written text) but can also include nonverbal communication (i.e., through images conveying body language, gestures, or facial expressions) and paralinguistic communication (i.e., through graphical language). Visual communication can be used to transmit information independently or in combination with aural communication. When conducting surveys, the mode of data collection determines whether information can be transmitted visually, aurally, or both. Whether survey information is transmitted visually or aurally influences how respondents first perceive and then cognitively process information to provide their responses.

Visual communication can consist of not only verbal communication but also nonverbal and paralinguistic forms of communication, which convey additional information that reinforces or modifies the meaning of written text. Nonverbal communication (i.e., information transferred through body language, gestures, eye contact, and facial expressions) is most common in face-to-face surveys but can also be conveyed with graphic images in paper and Web surveys. *Paralinguistic communication* is traditionally thought of as information transmitted aurally through the speaker's voice (e.g., quality, tone, pitch, inflection). However, recent literature suggests that graphical features, such as layout, spacing, font size, typeface, color, and symbols, that accompany written verbal communication can serve the same functions as aural paralinguistic communication. That is, these graphical features and images, if perceived and cognitively processed, can enhance or modify the meaning of written text in paper and Web surveys.

The process of perceiving visual information can be divided into two broad and overlapping stages: pre-attentive and attentive processing. In *pre-attentive processing*, the eyes quickly and somewhat effortlessly scan the entire visual field and process abstract visual features such as form, color, motion, and spatial position. The eyes are then drawn to certain basic visual elements that the viewer distinguishes as objects from other competing elements in the visual field that come to be perceived as background. Once the figure/ground composition is determined, the viewer can start discerning basic patterns among the objects. To distinguish such patterns, the viewer uses the graphical elements of proximity, similarity, continuity and connectedness, symmetry, and closure—as described by Gestalt psychology. During pre-attentive processing, the viewer uses a bottom-up model of processing where only stimuli from the visual field itself influence how objects and images are perceived. It is at this pre-attentive stage that graphical elements, strategically provided by survey designers, can help respondents perceive the basic navigational flow of the survey, including start of the survey, question order, and question groupings.

As respondents begin to recognize visual elements and patterns, *attentive processing* begins where they focus on the task of answering each question. Attentive processing is task oriented and involves the narrowing of one's vision to a limited visual field of attention known as the *foveal view*, which is 8 to 10 characters in width. During this stage, information is processed more slowly and often in a sequential order. It is also usually processed more deeply and committed to long-term memory rather than just reaching working memory as in pre-attentive processing. During attentive processing the viewer uses a top-down model of processing where his or her prior knowledge, experiences, and expectations about the particular situation influences how objects and images are perceived. It is at this stage that additional instructions or visual elements put in place to help facilitate the task of attending to, and answering, each individual question become useful to respondents. To be most effective, these elements should be located in the foveal view of attention near where they will be used.

Because visual and aural communication differ in how information is presented to survey respondents, the type of communication impacts how respondents initially perceive survey information. This initial step of perception influences how respondents cognitively process the survey in the remaining four steps (comprehension, retrieval, judgment formation, and answer reporting). Whereas paper surveys rely solely on visual communication, both Web and face-to-face surveys can utilize visual and aural communication. Web surveys rely extensively on visual communication and also have the potential to incorporate computer-mediated aural communication. In contrast, face-to-face surveys rely mostly on aural communication with the more occasional use of visual communication through show cards or other visual aids. Finally, telephone surveys rely on aural communication and generally do not incorporate any visual communication.

The specific effects that visual communication has on perception and the cognitive processing of information can contribute to mode effects during the survey response process. For example, visual communication allows the respondent to process a greater amount of information at once than does aural transmission; thus, survey designers can use more complex questions and response scales. However, the same questions and scales are not appropriate in aurally based surveys, and as a result, responses to survey modes may differ significantly.

*Leah Melani Christian
and Jolene D. Smyth*

See also Aural Communication; Comprehension; Gestalt Psychology; Graphical Language; Mode Effects; Mode of Data Collection; Retrieval

Further Readings

Dillman, D. A. (2007). *Mail and Internet surveys: The tailored design method* (2nd ed., 2007 update). Hoboken, NJ: Wiley.

Jenkins, C., & Dillman, D. A. (1997). Towards a theory of self-administered questionnaire design. In L. Lyberg, P. Biemer, M. Collins, E. de Leeuw, C. Dippo, N. Schwarz, et al. (Eds.), *Survey measurement and process quality* (pp. 165–196). New York: Wiley-Interscience.

Ware, C. (2004). *Information visualization: Perception for design*. San Francisco: Morgan Kaufmann.

VOICE OVER INTERNET PROTOCOL (VoIP) AND THE VIRTUAL COMPUTER-ASSISTED TELEPHONE INTERVIEW (CATI) FACILITY

Voice over Internet Protocol (VoIP) refers to real-time telecommunication using the Internet to carry the digitized versions of the voices that are speaking to each other. The world of telecommunications has been turned on its ear in the past few years with VoIP telephony challenging the regional telephone companies as broadband connections provided by cable TV vendors penetrate the market. This technological change has the potential to be a force to redesign computer-assisted telephone interviewing (CATI) and multi-modal survey interviewing efforts. For example, starting in 2002, the Center for Human Resource Research (CHRR) at Ohio State University began implementing such a redesign.

A number of survey organizations have converted their office phone systems to VoIP using large, well-established vendors of proprietary systems. These systems tend to be more costly to deploy than those obtainable from smaller companies offering a more open architecture. Moreover, because the "big name" systems are proprietary and targeted at the office environment, they are often harder to adapt and customize for survey research applications. A more open architecture allows for more creativity in designing the integration of survey interviewing and telephony.

Modern computing emphasizes the use of the Internet and relational database techniques. The CAPI (computer-assisted personal interviewing) and CATI technology used at CHRR for the past 2 years utilizes these technologies. For CATI, the client on the interviewer's machine communicates with the server at CHRR, and for CAPI, the client and "server" (an application that runs on several laptops) are both present on the interviewer's computer. This makes CATI/CAPI not two software systems but one. Whether for financial transaction processing, online shopping, or CATI interviewing, relational database tools are designed to support a high volume of queries and transaction processing. If a CATI interviewer can access a remote server via the Web from the telephone research facility, they can do so from home or from thousands of miles away. If they have a broadband connection, they can readily and inexpensively be connected to a VoIP system with a "softphone" (software that handles all the steps in placing or answering a call, and a USB connection for the interviewer's headset). The Internet carries the conversation from the interviewer's location to the central office where it crosses over to the public switched telephone network. A Web-based dialer schedules calls, presents cases to the interviewer, and places the calls.

With a VoIP connection to an interviewer's home (or to a research call center), he or she can log, record, and monitor calls just as in other traditional call centers. By using a client-server approach, the data are stored only in the central office, never at the remote location. Interviewers can be trained over the Internet, with utilities that allow the trainees to view the instructor's monitor as he or she instructs them on the use of the system and on proper interviewing techniques. During the venerable round-robin parts of interviewer training, where each trainee takes turns acting as the interviewer and the instructor acts as the respondent, the same utility allows the instructor to view the monitor of each trainee. As soon as someone falls behind or fails to follow directions, the trainer notices the nonconforming screen and brings that trainee back with the rest of the group. A single trainer can handle the groups of approximately eight trainees quite readily.

The VoIP branch of the call connecting the interviewer and the respondent is more secure than the connection from the central office to the respondent that is used over a public switched telephone network landline. First of all, VoIP converts the audio signal into data packets using a *codec*—a mathematical rule for digitizing and compressing audio signals. Unless one knows the codec—and there are many—one cannot reconvert the digital packets back to sound. Moreover, there are many ways of encrypting the digital packets, forcing a would-be eavesdropper to both break the encryption and reverse-engineer the codec. Second, the VoIP system conceals and encrypts the information on who is being called. The dialer communicates with the rest of the system over a separate data stream, which is itself encrypted, and the packets of data that make the connection between the interviewer and the central office VoIP server are channeled through separate servers using secure tunneling protocols. Using separate servers and data streams to handle the signaling that sets up the call from the data stream carrying the packets further complicates the task of a would-be eavesdropper. Cracking the voice packets does not allow one to know who is talking. There are rumors that some VoIP systems are so arcane and their functioning so ill-understood by outsiders that calls are, for practical purposes, immune from being logged let alone recorded by outsiders. Contrast these complications associated with compromising a VoIP conversation with what it takes to intercept a conversation over the public switched telephone network—calls that are well known to be vulnerable to intercept.

CHRR has used this virtual CATI shop technology for a variety of surveys including the National Longitudinal Surveys. The technology has several advantages. First, the virtual CATI facility technology allows survey organizations to use more effectively those remote interviewers who work in sparsely populated sampling areas. When not working face-to-face cases, they can work in a virtual CATI facility and achieve the same productivity metrics as in that more controlled environment. This technology will allow more survey organizations to train and use a skilled national field force because the volume of telephone work will keep remote staff employed and on the payroll between face-to-face engagements.

Second, this technology is valuable for tracking interviewer behavior for face-to-face surveys when the interviewers use the phone for contacting and making appointments. The technology allows for the tracking of interviewer calls to determine whether they are working as efficiently as they should. However, some interviewers shirk, and shirking can come in the form of not working when they say they are working or not placing the calls they say they are placing. When interviewers call from home over landlines, they currently cannot be monitored. With VoIP, they can be monitored and measured. Better monitoring will improve both technique and productivity.

Third, using VoIP allows for the implementation of sophisticated audio computer-assisted self-interviewing techniques by staff working from home on telephone interviews. The flexibility of VoIP and an open architecture allow the interviewer to switch the respondent to a system that uses voice recordings to ask a question and then, using voice recognition methods, record the answer and do the necessary branching.

Finally, this technology reduces the need to maintain a costly "bricks and mortar" call center to house all the call agents while still retaining the traditional call center's advantages in terms of monitoring, scheduling, and training. Although some call agents may not have a home environment that can serve as a virtual call center, many will. The virtual call center technology expands the labor pool (including the aged and infirm) and allows for the more flexible deployment of professional interviewers.

Randall Olsen and Carol Sheets

See also Audio Computer-Assisted Self-Interviewing (ACASI); Computer-Assisted Personal Interviewing (CAPI); Computer-Assisted Self-Interviewing (CASI); Computer-Assisted Telephone Interviewing (CATI); Data Management; Interviewer Monitoring

Further Readings

Bocklund, L., & Bengtson, D. (2002). *Call center technology demystified: The no-nonsense guide to bridging customer contact technology, operations and strategy.* Annapolis, MD: Call Center Press.

Olsen, R. J. (2004, May). *Does the Web doom traditional call centers?* Poster session presented at the annual meeting of the American Association for Public Opinion Research, Phoenix, AZ.

VOLUNTARY PARTICIPATION

Voluntary participation refers to a human research subject's exercise of free will in deciding whether to participate in a research activity. International law, national law, and the codes of conduct of scientific communities protect this right. In deciding whether participation is voluntary, special attention must be paid to the likely participants' socioeconomic circumstances in determining which steps must be put in place to protect the exercise of free will. The level of effort involved in clarifying voluntariness is not fixed and depends on several circumstances, such as the respondents' abilities to resist pressures like financial inducements, authority figures, or other forms of persuasion. Special care, therefore, must be taken to eliminate undue pressure (real and perceived) when research subjects have a diminished capacity to refuse.

Basic Requirements

The essential qualities of "voluntariness" include the following:

- The subject has a choice to participate.
- The choice is made without coercion.
- The choice is made without undue influence.
- The subject has foreknowledge of risks or benefits.

For a choice to occur, subjects must be of age and have the mental capacity to make such decisions. When this assumption cannot be upheld, this decision is left to the subjects' parents or legal guardians. For general-interest telephone surveys this prerogative may be largely implied, whereas in other situations it may have to be stated very precisely. The research director has the obligation to provide this choice at the outset, and the subject enjoys the prerogative to withdraw after data collection has begun.

Coercion refers to a threat that some type of harm will come to the research subject unless he or she participates. Such coercion might include an overt threat of violence, injury to reputation, or implied damage to career status. It may be important in some settings to take special precautions to ensure that participants do not perceive that they will face some retaliation from authority figures if they decline to participate.

Undue influence refers to excessive, improper, or immoral benefits. A frequent point of attention is cash incentives. To avoid undue influence, an incentive must be nominal, or so small that the subject can afford to refuse. This consideration is especially important when the indigent or children are the focus of data collection. The concept of voluntariness encompasses the realization that participants may perceive that persons in authority will reward their participation. Therefore, in some situations it may be necessary to take steps to dispel this explicitly.

For participation to be voluntary, subjects must have foreknowledge of likely risks and benefits of participation and of their option to withdraw from participation at any time. Subjects should have the opportunity to consider how the collected data will be used, whether confidentiality is being protected, who is sponsoring the research, how long they are expected to participate, and what costs or benefits they may expect from participation, refusal, or withdrawal. This means that information provided to subjects is without deceit about the project.

Some Exceptions

These requirements apply to research and should not be confused with taking tests, completing forms for employment, or filling out applications for public benefits.

Some data-collection activities are compulsory. Among these is the decennial Census of the United States and the Annual Survey of U.S. Direct Investment Abroad, the South Korean Monthly Industrial Production Survey, the British Surveillance of Healthcare Associated Infections, or the Canadian Survey of Innovations. The exceptions to voluntariness are made explicit in the respective countries' legislation.

Sean O. Hogan

See also Confidentiality; Deception; Ethical Principles; Informed Consent; Institutional Review Board (IRB)

Further Readings

American Association for Public Opinion Research. (2005). *Code of professional ethics and practices.* Retrieved April 24, 2008, from http://www.aapor.org/aaporcodeofethics

American Psychological Association. (2002). *Ethical principles of psychologists and code of conduct.* Retrieved January 2, 2007, from http://www.apa.org/ethics/code2002.html#8

The Nuremberg Code: Trials of war criminals before the Nuremberg military tribunals under control council Law No. 10. (1949–1953). Washington, DC: Government Printing Office. Retrieved January 2, 2007, from http://www.ushmm.org/research/doctors/Nuremberg_Code.htm

U.S. Department of Health and Human Services. Protection of Human Subjects (45 C.F.R. 46). Retrieved January 2, 2007, from http://www.hhs.gov/ohrp/humansubjects/guidance/45cfr46.htm

U.S. Department of Health, Education, and Welfare. (1979, April 18). *The Belmont report.* Retrieved January 2, 2007, from http://www.hhs.gov/ohrp/humansubjects/guidance/belmont.htm

World Medical Association. (2004). *Helsinki Declaration: Ethical principles for medical research involving human subjects.* Retrieved January 2, 2007, from http://www.wma.net/e/policy/b3.htm

W

WAVE

Within the context of survey research, a wave refers to each separate survey in a series of related surveys. If a survey is conducted only once, then the concept of a "wave" does not apply. It is when a survey is conducted two or more times, for example, once a year for 5 years in a row, that each repeated survey is called a *wave*. These waves may represent a panel survey in which the same respondents are tracked over time, often being asked some or all of the same questions in each wave. Other multi-wave (longitudinal) surveys use independent samples at each wave.

When a panel study is conducted and respondents who are interviewed in a prior wave are not successfully interviewed in a subsequent wave, even though they should have been, then *panel attrition* results. Common reasons for panel attrition at subsequent survey waves are refusals, moving, and illness or death. Some long-term survey designs rotate respondents in and out of being interviewed at various waves. Other long-term designs eliminate a random portion of the respondents that had been interviewed in previous waves and replace them with a random sample of "first time" respondents who likely will be contacted again in future waves.

Paul J. Lavrakas

See also Attrition; Longitudinal Studies; Panel; Panel Survey

Further Readings

Kasprzyk, D., Duncan, G., Kalton, G., & Singh, M. P. (1989). *Panel surveys.* New York: Wiley.

WEB SURVEY

Web surveys allow respondents to complete questionnaires that are delivered to them and administered over the World Wide Web. This offers advantages over other survey methods but also poses problems for quality data collection.

A main advantage of Web surveys, compared with other survey methods, is lower costs. Lower costs enable researchers to collect larger samples than affordable with other survey methods and have made Web surveys an option for many who cannot afford other survey methods. Technology allowing for complex questionnaire designs using features available in computer-assisted interviewing programs (such as CAPI, CASI, and CATI) is inexpensive. There are other advantages to Web surveys. The ability to quickly contact respondents over the Internet and process questionnaires through Web sites can shorten field periods compared to other survey methods. Web surveys can be used in conjunction with other methods, giving respondents another option for survey participation. The Web's role as an electronic meeting place has increased the ability to survey some rare, isolated, or marginal populations. In principle it is possible to conduct completely anonymous Web surveys, which may make surveying some populations easier.

Web surveys, however, have limitations that prevent them from being a simple substitute for other survey methods. A major limitation of Web surveys is their inability to represent the general population, or even the population of Internet users, without special efforts or techniques. Internet access, a requirement for participation in Web surveys, is more common among those with higher, as opposed to lower, socioeconomic status. This bias means that Web surveys are likely to have substantial coverage error for many survey topics (e.g., those related to health, finances, and education) if they are intended to represent the general population. Further, sampling those who have Internet access is problematic. There is no single sampling frame of the population of Internet users, and it is not possible to construct one because there is no standard system for assigning email addresses, the Internet counterpart to street addresses or telephone numbers.

Researchers have different approaches to dealing with these coverage and sampling issues. Mick Couper has categorized Web surveys according to their methods of respondent selection. Some approaches do not use probability sampling techniques for initial selection of respondents. A common approach is to rely on high traffic through Web sites to produce convenience samples. Another approach is to use Web sites to recruit pools of potential participants who are later sampled for Web surveys. Demographic information about those in a pool can be used for sampling quotas or for post-survey data weighting. These approaches rely on potential participants to opt into a survey or pool, which can produce a self-selection bias. The ability of such samples to represent a full population of Internet users is controversial. Other Web survey approaches use probability sampling methods for respondent selection. When Internet use is high among a population, email lists can serve as sampling frames (e.g., all students, staff, and faculty at a university). Web surveys based on these list samples are potentially representative of those populations. Another approach is to systematically sample users of Web sites using intercept or "pop-up" surveys; those data are potentially representative of users of those Web sites. A probability sampling approach for the population of Internet users could use random-digit dialing telephone surveys or in-person surveys of the general population to recruit Internet users who will then be sampled for Web surveys. Those without Internet access are considered out of the sample. Web surveys based on such samples are potentially representative of the population of Internet users. Finally, the last approach can be modified for conducting Web surveys of the general population. For example, random-digit dialing telephone surveys of a population are used to recruit potential participants for Web surveys. Those without Internet access are not considered out of the sample but are instead provided with Internet access and technology in order to participate in Web surveys. Web survey data collected from such samples are potentially representative of a population.

Web surveys may have unique sources of survey error that researchers must consider when evaluating data. For example, unique measurement error may be associated with the way Web questionnaires are displayed or controlled. Differences in Web browsers and display settings may alter the layout of questions, which could affect how respondents process them. Failing to answer questions or backing up through a questionnaire may disrupt programmed skip patterns, leading respondents to answer questions not meant for them or to skip questions they should receive. Web surveys may have unique sources of nonresponse error. Potential respondents may not be able to participate in a survey because their computer hardware or software may be inadequate for, or incompatible with, some Web survey programs. Web surveys that require high levels of computer literacy may discourage low-literacy respondents. Email requests for survey participation may be rejected or ignored as spam, preventing participation.

Finally, Web surveys may pose additional participant confidentiality issues. Security breaches of computer data, Web sites, and Internet communications are common and may threaten the confidentiality of Web survey participants. Measures should be in place to maximize respondent confidentiality.

Lew Horner

See also Computer-Assisted Self-Interviewing (CASI); Convenience Sampling; Coverage Error; Measurement Error; Nonresponse Error; Sampling Frame; Self-Selection Bias

Further Readings

Couper, M. P. (2000). Web surveys: A review of issues and approaches. *Public Opinion Quarterly, 64,* 464–494.

Dillman, D. A., & Bowker, D. K. (2001). The Web questionnaire challenge to survey methodologists. In U.-D. Reips & M. Bosnjak (Eds.), *Dimensions of Internet science* (pp. 159–178). Lengerich, Germany: Pabst Science.

WEIGHTING

Weighting is a correction technique that is used by survey researchers. It refers to statistical adjustments that are made to survey data after they have been collected in order to improve the accuracy of the survey estimates. There are two basic reasons that survey researchers weight their data. One is to correct for unequal probabilities of selection that often have occurred during sampling. The other is to try to help compensate for survey nonresponse. This entry addresses weighting as it relates to the second of these purposes.

Why Weighting for Nonresponse Is Necessary

Essentially all surveys suffer from nonresponse. This occurs either when elements (persons, households, companies) in the selected sample do not provide the requested information or when the provided information is useless. The situation in which all requested information on a sampled element is missing is called *unit nonresponse.*

As a result of unit nonresponse, estimates of population characteristics may be biased. This bias occurs if (a) some groups in the population are over- or underrepresented in the sample because of their differential response/nonresponse rates and (b) these groups are different with respect to the variables being measured by the survey. As a consequence, wrong conclusions are drawn from the survey results.

It is vital to try to reduce the amount of nonresponse in the field work as much as possible. Nevertheless, in spite of all these efforts, a substantial amount of nonresponse usually remains. To avoid biased estimates, some kind of correction procedure must be carried out. One of the most important correction techniques for nonresponse is weighting. It means that every observed object in the survey is assigned a weight, and estimates of population characteristics are obtained by processing weighted observations instead of the (unweighted) observations themselves.

Basics of Weighting to Correct for Nonresponse

Suppose that the objective of a survey is to estimate the population mean, $\bar{Y}$, of a variable Y. Suppose further that a simple random sample of size n is selected with equal probabilities and without replacement from a population of size N. The sample can be represented by a series of N indicators $t_1, t_2, \ldots, t_N$, where the k-th indicator t_k assumes the value 1 if element k is selected in the sample, and otherwise it assumes the value 0. In case of complete response, the sample mean,

$$\bar{y} = \frac{1}{n}\sum_{k=1}^{N} t_k Y_k, \qquad (1)$$

is an unbiased estimator of the population mean. In case of nonresponse, this estimator may be biased. Assuming that every element, k, in the population has an unknown probability, ρ_k, of response when invited to participate in the survey, the bias of the mean $\bar{y}_R$ of the available observations is equal to

$$B(\bar{y}_R) = \frac{R_{\rho Y} S_\rho S_Y}{\bar{\rho}}, \qquad (2)$$

where $R_{\rho Y}$ is the correlation between the values of the survey variable and the response probabilities, S_Y is the standard deviation of the Y, and S_ρ is the standard deviation of the response probabilities.

Weighting is a frequently used approach to reduce this nonresponse bias. Each observed element, k, is assigned a weight, w_k. Thus, the response mean, $\bar{y}_R$, is replaced by a new estimator,

$$\bar{y}_W = \frac{1}{n}\sum_{k=1}^{N} w_k t_k Y_k. \qquad (3)$$

Correction weights are the result of the application of some weighting technique. The characteristics of the correction weights should be such that the weighted estimator has better properties than the unweighted response mean.

Weighting is based on the use of auxiliary information. *Auxiliary information* is defined as a set of variables that have been measured in the survey and for which information on the population distribution (or the complete sample) is available. By comparing the population parameters for an auxiliary variable with its observed response distribution in the survey, it can be determined whether or not the sample is representative of the population (with respect to this variable). If these distributions differ in non-negligible ways, one must conclude that nonresponse has resulted in a biased sample.

The auxiliary information is used to compute adjustment weights. Weights are assigned to all records of the observed elements. These weights are defined in such a way that population characteristics for the auxiliary variables can be computed without error. So when weights are applied to the estimate population means of the auxiliary variables, the estimates must be equal to the true values, that is,

$$\bar{x}_W = \frac{1}{N} \sum_{k=1}^{N} w_k t_k X_k = \bar{X}. \qquad (4)$$

If this condition is satisfied, then the weighted sample is said to be *representative* with respect to the auxiliary variable used.

If it is possible to make the sample representative with respect to several auxiliary variables, and if these variables have a strong relationship with the survey variables, then the (weighted) sample will also be (approximately) representative with respect to these variables, and hence estimates of population characteristics will be more accurate.

Post-Stratification

The most frequently used weighting technique to correct for the effects of nonresponse is post-stratification. One or more qualitative auxiliary variables are needed to apply this technique. In the following explanation, only one such variable is considered. Extension to more variables is straightforward.

Suppose there is an auxiliary variable, X, having L categories. X divides the population into L strata. The number of population elements in stratum h is denoted by N_h, for $h = 1, 2, \ldots, L$. Hence, the population size is equal to $N = N_1 + N_2 + \cdots + N_L$.

Post-stratification assigns identical correction weights to all elements in the same stratum. The weight w_k for an element k in stratum h (in the case of a simple random sample with equal probabilities) is defined by

$$w_k = \frac{N_h/N}{n_h/n}, \qquad (5)$$

where n_h is the number of respondents in stratum h. If the values of the weights are substituted in Equation (4), the result is the well-known post-stratification estimator,

$$\bar{y}_{ps} = \frac{1}{N} \sum_{h=1}^{L} N_h \bar{y}_h, \qquad (6)$$

where $\bar{y}_h$ is the response mean in stratum h. So, the post-stratification estimator is equal to a weighted sum of response means in the strata.

The nonresponse bias disappears if there is no relationship between response behavior and the survey variable within strata. Two situations can be distinguished in which this is the case:

- The strata are homogeneous with respect to the target variable; that is, this variable shows little variation within strata.
- The strata are homogeneous with respect to the response behavior; that is, response probabilities show little variation within strata.

Linear Weighting

Even in the case of full response, the precision estimators can be improved if suitable auxiliary information is available. Suppose there are p auxiliary variables. The values of these variables for element k are denoted by the vector $X_k = (X_{k1}, X_{k2}, \ldots, X_{kp})'$. The vector of population means is denoted by $\bar{X}$. If auxiliary variables are correlated with the survey variable, Y, then for a suitably chosen vector $B = (B_1, B_2, \ldots, B_p)'$ of regression coefficients for a best fit of Y on X, the residuals, $E_k = Y_k - X_k B$, vary less than the values of target variable itself. The ordinary least squares solution B can be estimated, in the case of full response, by

$$b = \left(\sum_{k=1}^{N} t_k X_k X_k' \right)^{-1} \left(\sum_{k=1}^{N} t_k X_k Y_k \right). \qquad (7)$$

The generalized regression estimator is now defined by

$$\bar{y}_{GR} = \bar{y} + (\bar{X} - \bar{x})' b, \qquad (8)$$

in which $\bar{x}$ is the vector of sample means of the auxiliary variables. The generalized regression estimator is *asymptotically design unbiased*. This estimator reduces the bias caused by nonresponse if the underlying regression model fits the data well.

The generalized regression estimator can be rewritten in the form of the weighted estimator (4), where the correction weight, w_k, for observed element k is equal to $w_k = v'X_k$, and v is a vector of weight coefficients, which is equal to

$$v = \left(\sum_{k=1}^{N} \frac{t_k X_k X_k'}{n} \right)^{-1} \bar{X}. \qquad (9)$$

Post-stratification turns out to be a special case of linear weighting. If the stratification is represented by a set of dummy variables, where each dummy variable denotes a specific stratum, Equation 8 reduces to Equation 6.

Linear weighting can be applied in more situations than post-stratification. For example, post-stratification by age, class, and sex requires that the population distribution for the crossing of age and class by sex be known. If only the separate marginal population distributions of age, sex, or both, are known, then post-stratification cannot be applied. In that case in this example, only one variable can be used. However, linear weighting makes it possible to specify a regression model that contains both marginal distributions. In this way more information is used, and this generally will lead to better survey estimates.

Linear weighting has the disadvantage that some correction weights may turn out to be negative. Such weights are not wrong but simply a consequence of the underlying theory. Usually, negative weights indicate that the regression model does not fit the data well. Some analysis packages are able to work with weights, but they do not accept negative weights. This may be a reason not to apply linear weighting.

Multiplicative Weighting

Correction weights produced by linear weighting are the sum of a number of weighted coefficients. It is also possible to compute correction weights in a different way, namely, as the product of a number of weight factors. This weighting technique is usually called *raking* or *iterative proportional fitting*. Here this process is denoted by *multiplicative weighting*, because weights are obtained as the product of a number of factors contributed by the various auxiliary variables.

Multiplicative weighting can be applied in the same situations as linear weighting as long as only qualitative variables are used. Correction weights are the result of an iterative procedure. They are the product of factors contributed by all cross-classifications. To compute weight factors, the following scheme has to be carried out:

1. Introduce a weight factor for each stratum in each cross-classification term. Set the initial values of all factors to 1.

2. Adjust the weight factors for the first cross-classification term so that the weighted sample becomes representative with respect to the auxiliary variables included in this cross-classification.

3. Adjust the weight factors for the next cross-classification term so that the weighted sample is representative for the variables involved. Generally, this will disturb the representativeness of the other cross-classification terms in the model.

4. Repeat this adjustment process until all cross-classification terms have been dealt with.

5. Repeat steps 2, 3, and 4 until the weight factors do not change by any more than a negligible amount.

Multiplicative weighting has the advantage that computed weights are always positive. It has the disadvantage that there is no clear model underlying the approach. Moreover, there is no simple and straightforward way to compute standard errors of the weighted estimates. Linear weighting is based on a regression model, which allows for computing standard errors.

Calibration Estimation

Jean-Claude Deville and Carl-Erik Särndal have created a general framework for weighting of which linear weighting and multiplicative weighting are special cases. This framework is called *calibration*. Assuming simple random sampling with equal probabilities, the starting point is that adjustment weights have to satisfy two conditions:

1. The adjustment weights w_k have to be as close as possible to 1.

2. The weighted sample distribution of the auxiliary variables has to match the population distribution; that is,

$$\bar{x}_W = \frac{1}{n}\sum_{k=1}^{N} t_k w_k X_k = \bar{X}. \qquad (10)$$

The first condition sees to it that resulting estimators are unbiased, or almost unbiased, and the second condition guarantees that the weighted sample is representative with respect to the auxiliary variables used.

A distance measure, $D(w_k, 1)$, that measures the difference between w_k and 1 in some way, is introduced. The problem is now to minimize

$$\sum_{k=1}^{N} t_k D(w_k, 1) \qquad (11)$$

under the condition (10). This problem can be solved by using the method of Joseph Lagrange. By choosing the proper distance function, both linear and multiplicative weighting can be obtained as special cases of this general approach. For linear weighting the distance function D is defined by $D(w_k, 1) = (w_k - 1)^2$, and for multiplicative weighting the distance $D(w_k, 1) = w_k \log(w_k) - w_k + 1$ must be used.

Other Issues

There are several reasons why a survey statistician may want to have control over the values of the adjustment weights. One reason is that extremely large weights are generally considered undesirable. Use of such weights may lead to unstable estimates of population parameters. Another reason to have some control over the values of the adjustment weights is that application of linear weighting might produce negative weights.

The calibration approach allows for a weighting technique that keeps the adjustment weights within pre-specified boundaries and, at the same time, enables valid inference. Many surveys have complex sample designs. One example of such a complex design is a cluster sampling. Many household surveys are based on cluster samples. First, a sample of households is selected. Next, several or all persons in the selected households are interviewed. The collected information can be used to make estimates for two populations: the population consisting of all households and the population consisting of all individual persons. In both situations, weighting can be carried out to correct for nonresponse. This results in two

weights assigned to each record: one for the household and one for the individual. Having two weights in each record complicates further analysis.

The generalized regression estimation offers a solution. The trick is to sum the dummy variables corresponding to the qualitative auxiliary variables for the individuals over the household. Thus, quantitative auxiliary variables are created at the household level. The resulting weights are assigned to the households. Furthermore, all elements within a household are assigned the same weight, and this weight is equal to the household weight. This approach forces estimates computed using the element weights to be consistent with estimates based on the cluster weights.

Jelke Bethlehem

See also Auxiliary Variable; Bias; Cluster Sample; Differential Nonresponse; Nonresponse; Post-Stratification; Probability of Selection; Raking; Representative Sample; Unit Nonresponse

Further Readings

Bethlehem, J. G. (1988). Reduction of nonresponse bias through regression estimation. *Journal of Official Statistics, 4*(3), 251–260.

Bethlehem, J. G. (2002). Weighting nonresponse adjustments based on auxiliary information. In R. M. Groves, D. A. Dillman, J. L. Eltinge, & R. J. A. Little (Eds.), *Survey nonresponse* (pp. 275–288). New York: Wiley.

Bethlehem, J. G., & Keller, W. J. (1987). Linear weighting of sample survey data. *Journal of Official Statistics, 3*(2), 141–154.

Deville, J.-C., & Särndal, C.-E. (1992). Calibration estimators in survey sampling. *Journal of the American Statistical Association, 87*, 376–382.

Deville, J.-C., Särndal, C.-E., & Sautory, O. (1993). Generalized raking procedures in survey sampling. *Journal of the American Statistical Association, 88*, 1013–1020.

WesVar

WesVar is a Windows-based software package for analyzing data collected by surveys with complex sample designs. Sample designs that can be analyzed include stratified or unstratified designs, single- or multi-stage designs, one-time or longitudinal designs. A key aspect of WesVar is the calculation of design-based standard errors that take the complex sample design (e.g., stratification and clustering) into account.

WesVar calculates sampling variances using the jackknife and balanced repeated replication methods. WesVar users can calculate and use their own replicate weights or have WesVar calculate the replicate weights. WesVar can perform weight adjustments for nonresponse, post-stratification, and raking. Such weight adjustments are performed on both the full-sample weights and the replicate weights, so that calculated sampling variances take into account the effects of weight adjustments.

The estimates and standard errors calculated by WesVar take into account the sample design and adjustments to sampling weights. Statistical software that ignores the sample design and assumes simple random sampling typically underestimates standard errors.

WesVar can calculate all of the following:

- Multi-way tables containing totals, means, or proportions, along with estimated standard error, coefficient of variations, confidence intervals, and design effects
- Estimates of medians and other quantiles, along with estimated standard errors
- Complex functions of estimates, such as ratios, differences of ratios, and log-odds ratios, along with estimated standard errors
- Chi-square tests of independence for two-way tables of weighted frequencies
- Estimated coefficients and their standard errors for linear and logistic regression models and associated significance tests for linear combinations of parameters

WesVar was developed and is distributed by Westat. The program and user manual can be downloaded from the WesVar Web site.

Richard Sigman

See also Balanced Repeated Replication (BRR); Complex Sample Surveys; Design Effects (*deff*); Jackknife Variance Estimation; Multi-Stage Sample; Replicate Methods for Variance Estimation; Variance Estimation

Further Readings

Westat. (2007). *WesVar 4.3 user's guide*. Retrieved September 13, 2007, from http://www.westat.com/westat/wesvar/about/WV_4-3_Manual.pdf

WesVar: http://www.westat.com/westat/wesvar/index.html

WITHIN-UNIT COVERAGE

Within-unit coverage refers to the accuracy of selection of the respondent to be interviewed after a household is contacted, generally by phone or face-to-face methods, and the informant in the household identifies the prospective respondent, according to the interviewer's instructions. Theoretically, each eligible person living in the unit (e.g., all adults) should have a known and nonzero chance of selection. A number of probability, quasi-probability, and nonprobability methods exist for choosing the respondent, and only the probability methods allow estimation of chances of selection. Humans, however, do not always behave according to the logic of probability methods, and this leads to errors of within-unit coverage. Missed persons within households contribute more to noncoverage of the Current Population Survey, for example, than do missed housing units.

In general, methods that do not nominate the correct respondent by sex and age are more likely to produce within-unit coverage errors than are those that do specify those characteristics. Those methods that ask for a full listing of the household's adults, such as the Kish technique, can be time consuming and threatening to some informants. The last-birthday and next-birthday procedures were devised to be nonintrusive and yield within-unit probability samples; yet, between about 10% and 25% of the time, the informant chooses the wrong respondent. This can happen because of misunderstanding the question, not knowing all the birthdays of household members, or the informant's deliberate self-selection instead of the designated respondent. If birthdays do not correlate with the topics of survey questions, this is not very problematic. Training interviewers rigorously and having them verify the accuracy of the respondent's selection can help to overcome difficulties with the birthday methods. Rigorous training also helps considerably with the Kish procedure, an almost pure probability method.

Another problem is undercoverage of certain kinds of people, especially minorities, the poor, the less educated, inner-city dwellers, renters, young males (particularly young black or Hispanic males), and older women in single-person households, as well as omission of some household members inadvertently or deliberately. For example, some informants conceal the presence of males in households that would cause the loss of welfare eligibility if wage-earning adults, particularly males, were known to live there. Other informants do not mention members who stay there most of the time but not all the time. In some populations the composition of households changes frequently; this happens with inner-city black and Hispanic communities, migrant workers, or migrant populations such as American Indians who can divide their time between cities and their reservation on a seasonal basis. Sometimes the informant and the survey planners have different definitions of the word *household*. Another source of error is informants' thinking the interviewer wants a count of families in the unit instead of all individuals in the unit. The larger the household is, the greater is the chance for noncoverage error (discrepancy between the true number of persons and the number obtained on the roster). Sometimes within-household coverage problems stem from counting individuals more than once.

In many situations, obtaining a roster of household members by initials or other ways allowing more anonymity can improve representation within households. Methods exist that do not require a list. In addition, making the target population clear to informants at the outset improves accuracy of selection.

Cecilie Gaziano

See also Kish Selection Method; Last-Birthday Selection; Within-Unit Selection

Further Readings

Brogan, D. J., Denniston, M. M., Liff, J. M., Flagg, E. W., Coates, R. J., & Brinton, L. A. (2001). Comparison of telephone sampling and area sampling: Response rates and within-household coverage. *American Journal of Epidemiology, 153,* 1119–1127.

Lavrakas, P. J., Stasny, E. A., & Harpuder, B. (2000). A further investigation of the last-birthday respondent selection method and within-unit coverage error. *Proceedings of the Section on Survey Research Methods* (pp. 890–895). Alexandria, VA: American Statistical Association.

Maklan, D., & Waksberg, J. (1988). Within-household coverage in RDD surveys. In R. M. Groves, P. P. Biemer, L. E. Lyberg, J. T. Massey, W. L. Nicholls II, &

J. Waksberg (Eds.), *Telephone survey methodology* (pp. 51–72). New York: Wiley.

O'Rourke, D., & Lakner, E. (1989). Gender bias: Analysis of factors causing male underrepresentation in surveys. *International Journal of Public Opinion Research, 1,* 164–176.

Tourangeau, R., Shapiro, G., Kearney, A., & Ernst, L. (1997). Who lives here? Survey undercoverage and household roster questions. *Journal of Official Statistics, 13,* 1–18.

WITHIN-UNIT COVERAGE ERROR

Within-unit coverage error refers to the bias, variance, or both, that may result when the respondents who are selected from within a sampling unit, and from whom data are gathered, differ in non-negligible ways from those who were missed from being selected but in theory should have been selected.

Many probability sample surveys are made up of a target population of individuals that belong to one sampling unit. But often these surveys use a two-stage design in which the unit is sampled first, and then a respondent (or more than one) from within the unit is selected to be interviewed. One example is a household or a unit within an organization, from which one person or a subset of persons per sampling unit is surveyed. These surveys usually select randomly one or more persons among all eligible persons that belong to a certain sampling unit according to some a priori definition. Within-unit coverage error can occur when one or more eligible persons within a selected sampling unit have a zero chance of selection, have a 100% (certain) chance of being selected, or have some other disproportionate chance of being selected, for example, because they belong to more than one sampling unit.

Within-unit coverage problems that might lead to error can therefore be defined as the difference between the sampling frame and the target population at the level of the individual residents. Within-unit undercoverage problems occur if people that are in fact eligible and should be counted as sampling unit members have no chance or less chance of being selected because they are not "recognized" by the informant or the selection technique as being a sampling unit member or they are not mentioned at all when sampling unit members are listed for the respondent selection process. The undercoverage problem arises because these persons are part of the target population but do not have a correct chance (probability) of being part of the frame population. Persons are said to be overcovered if they are listed in the frame population more than once and therefore have more than one chance to be selected into the sample but are only represented once in the target population.

Within-unit coverage error includes a bias as well as an error variance component. In both cases, within-unit coverage error is a property of a statistic, not a survey. Within-unit coverage bias in a statistic of interest occurs only if the members of the population that are not covered (or are overcovered) are different from those who are covered (or are only covered once) with regard to the statistic of interest. Therefore, there are two conditions that have to be met to produce within-unit coverage bias in a statistic of interest. The first condition is a difference between the sampling frame and the target population—subsets of the population are overcovered or undercovered. The second condition entails a difference of those people overcovered or undercovered from the rest of the target population with regard to the statistic of interest. Each condition is necessary but not sufficient to produce coverage error.

The literature on coverage error has described a variety of reasons for undercoverage as well as overcoverage problems. With regard to undercoverage, two major theories have emerged. The first theory is that the informant listing the members of the sampling unit usually does not know, or has difficulties understanding, the complicated definitions and rules, such as the de jure and de facto residence rules, that determine who should be counted as a member of the sampling unit. Therefore the informant might erroneously, and without any intent, not list people who, per the definition, belong to the sampling unit. To improve the clarity of these rules and definitions, interviewers can be asked to administer additional questions, after an initial household listing has been established, that focus on situations that usually lead to within-unit undercoverage problems. The second theory of undercoverage claims that informants might intentionally not list members of the sampling unit because they fear that something bad will happen if they do, for example, that illegal activities might be detected or that providing information about members of the sampling unit could have negative consequences with regard to monetary support by the government. People might just be uncomfortable and suspicious if they are asked to list sampling unit members by a survey organization that just made contact with them and not list them at all. Because listing sampling unit members of a household by name can be perceived as intrusive, survey organizations have allowed the informant to use initials when listing the sampling unit members. Other respondent selection methods that do not require listing household members, but simply select the respondent based on a criterion, have been found to be helpful in increasing the coverage of subgroups of the population usually undercovered when listing is used and also in reducing unit nonresponse that is more likely to result when overly intrusive within-unit selection methods are deployed. The last-birthday selection method is the most used of these respondent selection methods within a household. This method asks the informant to identify the household member that most recently had his or her birthday.

There are also two main theories that exist about the occurrence of overcoverage. The first theory is again based on the informant's misunderstanding of the definition of or rules about whom to count as a member of the sampling unit. An informant who does not understand the definition of who is a member of the sampling unit may also list people that do not belong to this sampling unit, and therefore someone might be listed twice in the sampling frame if the other unit to which the person belongs also is sampled. An example of this occurrence is a child that goes to college and does not live at home anymore but still is counted by his or her parents as being a member of the household. The second explanation for overcoverage problems is the difficulty in establishing the sampling frame for a fixed point in time to define the residency of all members of the sampling units selected in the survey. Generally, the problem of undercoverage bias seems to be more serious than the problem of overcoverage bias.

Sonja Ziniel

See also Informant; Last-Birthday Selection; Overcoverage; Residence Rules; Sampling Frame; Target Population; Undercoverage; Within-Unit Selection

Further Readings

Gaziano, C. (2005). Comparative analysis of within-household respondent selection techniques. *Public Opinion Quarterly, 69,* 124–157.

Groves, R.M. (1989). *Survey errors and survey costs.* New York: Wiley.

Martin, E. (1999). Who knows who lives here? Within-household disagreements as a source of survey coverage error. *Public Opinion Quarterly, 63,* 220–236.

Tourangeau, R., Shapiro, G., Kearney, A., & Ernst, L. (1997). Who lives here? Survey undercoverage and household roster questions. *Journal of Official Statistics, 13,* 1–18.

WITHIN-UNIT SELECTION

In survey research, a sample of households usually must be converted into a sample of individuals. This often is accomplished by choosing respondents within households using methods intended to yield a sample similar to the population of interest. Ideally, this is done with a probability technique because all unit members will have a known, nonzero chance of selection, thus allowing generalization to a population. Probability methods, however, tend to be time consuming and relatively intrusive because they ask about household composition, potentially alienating prospective respondents and therefore increasing nonresponse.

Most researchers have limited resources, so often they need quicker, easier, and less expensive quasi-probability or nonprobability methods that they believe will yield samples adequately resembling the population being studied. Although surveyors wish to minimize nonresponse and reduce noncoverage, they have to balance these choices to fit their goals and resources. They have to decide if the benefits of probability methods outweigh their possible contributions to total survey costs or if departures from probability selection will contribute too much to total survey error. This does not mean that they tolerate substandard practices but that they consider which trade-offs will be the most acceptable within their budget and time restrictions. One paramount goal is to gain the respondent's cooperation in as short a time as possible, and a second is to obtain a reasonable balance of demographic (usually age and gender) distributions. Most households are homogeneous in other demographic characteristics, such as education and race. Many well-respected polling and other survey research organizations have to make these kinds of choices.

Selection of respondents within households is particularly important in telephone surveys because most refusals occur at the inception of contact. Although it might seem advantageous to take the first person who answers the phone or to let interviewers choose respondents, those persons who are often the most available or most willing to be interviewed also tend to be disproportionately female or older, which may bias results. In addition, patterns of telephone answering are not random; they can vary by gender and by region. Researchers need to control respondent selection in systematic ways, therefore, even if methods are quasi-probability or nonprobability. The well-known Kish selection procedure is almost a pure probability technique. Interviewers list all adult males in the household and their relationships to others in order of decreasing age, then make a similar list of adult females. Interviewers then randomly select one person by consulting a set of tables. This technique is criticized as being time consuming for large households and potentially threatening to informants, especially women who may be concerned about their safety.

The "last-birthday," or "most recent birthday" method is a popular quasi-probability selection scheme, considered to be less intrusive and time consuming than the Kish method. Interviewers ask to speak to the adult in the household who had the last birthday. A variation is the less frequently used "next-birthday" method. In theory (but not necessarily in practice), the birthday methods are probability methods because they assume the first stage of a two-stage selection process is birth (expected to be a random event), and a second stage is selection into the sample.

To further streamline the selection process, V. Troldahl and R. E. Carter offered a nonprobability method requiring only two questions: the number of persons 18 years or older living in the household and the number of men. The number of tables for interviewers to consult shrank to four, calling for selection of the oldest man, the youngest man, the oldest woman, or the youngest woman. Barbara Bryant later proposed a modification that could better represent women. Others suggested asking for women rather than men, further altering what became known as the Troldahl-Carter-Bryant respondent selection method.

D. E. Hagan and C. M. Collier offered a further simplified plan with four forms that asked only for (a) the youngest man in the household, (b) the oldest man, (c) the youngest woman, and (d) the oldest woman. Forms A, B, and C were used two times out of seven, and form D was used one time in seven. If no such individual was in the household, the interviewer asked for the opposite sex of the same age group. This method was condensed even further into the youngest male/oldest female technique, in which the interviewer asks first for the youngest adult male. If there isn't one, the interviewer requests the oldest woman. Frequently, surveyors add "now at home" to improve response rates. Although these methods are intended to save time and to obtain age and sex distributions that approximate the general population, some researchers believe they distort distributions of gender within age or gender by household composition.

Louis Rizzo, J. Michael Brick, and Inho Park suggested a potentially shorter probability technique that is relatively nonintrusive and easy to implement in computer-assisted telephone interviewing random-digit dialing surveys. Interviewers need to know only the number of adults in one-adult or two-adult households, which make up about 85% of U.S. households. If the household is larger, the interviewer determines whether or not the informant is sampled. If not, another method, such as Kish or last birthday, is applied.

A number of studies have compared two or more different within-unit selection methods to aid researchers in decisions about procedures that will best fit their needs, although more research on these issues is desirable. All of these methods rely on the selection process to be done by an interviewer. Little research has been conducted on how to utilize a within-unit selection process when the survey is not administered by an interviewer.

Cecilie Gaziano

See also Computer-Assisted Telephone Interviewing (CATI); Hagan and Collier Selection Method; Kish Selection Method; Last-Birthday Selection; Noncoverage; Nonresponse; Troldahl-Carter-Bryant Respondent Selection Method; Within-Unit Coverage

Further Readings

Gaziano, C. (2005). Comparative analysis of within-household respondent selection techniques. *Public Opinion Quarterly, 69*, 124–157.

Groves, R. M. (1989). *Survey errors and survey costs.* New York: Wiley.

Keeter, S., & Fisher, K. (1997–1998). Comparison of two respondent selection methods. *NNSP Newsletter, 31*(Winter), 1–3.

Lavrakas, P. J. (1993). *Telephone survey methods: Sampling, selection, and supervision* (2nd ed.). Newbury Park, CA: Sage.

Rizzo, L., Brick, J. M., & Park, I. (2004). A minimally intrusive method for sampling persons in random digit dial surveys. *Public Opinion Quarterly, 68*, 267–274.

Troldahl, V., & Carter, R. E., Jr. (1964). Random selection of respondents within households in phone surveys. *Journal of Marketing Research, 1*, 71–76.

Voss, D. S., Gelman, A., & King, G. (1995). Preelection survey methodology: Details from eight polling organizations, 1988 and 1992. *Public Opinion Quarterly, 59*, 98–132.

WORLD ASSOCIATION FOR PUBLIC OPINION RESEARCH (WAPOR)

The World Association for Public Opinion Research (WAPOR) is an international organization of individual members who are engaged in public opinion research and the development of survey research methods. It was founded in 1947 to promote and improve the quality of these kinds of activities around the world. WAPOR collaborates with both the American Association for Public Opinion Research (AAPOR) and the European Society for Opinion and Marketing Research (ESOMAR), with which it respectively shares its annual conferences every other year. This typically means that in alternating years, the WAPOR conference is held in North America and then in Europe. WAPOR is also affiliated with the United Nations' Educational, Scientific and Cultural Organization (UNESCO) through which it promotes a variety of social science efforts and projects. Members currently come from almost 60 different countries around the world.

WAPOR organizes a variety of activities to promote quality research around the world. It sponsors two or three regional seminars at different venues each year that focus on research methods, specific uses of public opinion research related to elections and democracy, and survey data quality. Recent regional conferences have been held in Latin America (Uruguay), the Middle East (Israel), Asia (India), and Europe (Italy). WAPOR is especially interested in promoting the training of journalists and others so that they can better report on public opinion. The organization has a long-standing interest in maintaining freedom to publish the results of public opinion polls, and it actively responds to legislation or attempts to legislate restrictions on the dissemination of such information. It disseminates a report on this topic, titled *Freedom to Publish Opinion Polls*, which is updated periodically to indicate where such restrictions are, and are not, in place.

In conjunction with ESOMAR, WAPOR promotes the *Guide to Opinion Polls*, which includes an international code of practice for publication of public opinion poll results. In recent years, the organization has turned its attention to setting broad standards for widely used or potentially adoptable public opinion methodologies. This began with the development of WAPOR Guidelines for Exit Polls and Election Forecasts, a set of desirable procedures for the conduct and dissemination of information about election results involving interviews with voters who have just cast ballots. It is also at work to develop a similar set of guidelines and standards for the conduct of "peace polls," studies of opinions about the sources and bases of conflict in locations around the world, including the need for wide dissemination of such information, through the media, to all affected communities.

The *International Journal of Public Opinion Research*, WAPOR's quarterly journal, publishes timely research on public opinion, especially in comparative perspective, and on research methodology. The content also includes summaries of recent public opinion findings and results published in books and other venues, as well as book reviews. WAPOR also produces a quarterly newsletter.

WAPOR is governed by an 11-person executive council, 5 of whom are elected by the membership at large; the remaining 6 council members are appointed. The executive council meets between annual conferences as necessary to conduct its business. The dues structure in WAPOR employs three tiers to take into account different national economic conditions around the world, and there is a special reduced fee for students.

Michael W. Traugott

See also American Association for Public Opinion Research (AAPOR); Election Night Projections; Exit Polls; *International Journal for Public Opinion Research* (IJPOR); Prior Restraint

Further Readings

European Society for Opinion and Marketing Research (ESOMAR). (n.d.). *ESOMAR/WAPOR Guide to Opinion Polls including the ESOMAR International Code of Practice for the Publication of Opinion Polls.* Retrieved April 7, 2008, from http://www.esomar .org/uploads/pdf/ESOMAR_Codes&Guidelines_ OpinionPolling_v5.pdf
World Association for Public Opinion Research: http://www.unl.edu/WAPOR/index.htm

Z

ZERO-NUMBER BANKS

Telephone numbers in the United States consist of 10 digits: The first three are the area code; the next three are the prefix or exchange; the final four digits are the suffix or local number. The 10,000 possible numbers for a suffix can be subdivided into banks of consecutive numbers: 1,000-banks (Nnnn); 100-banks (NNnn); or 10-banks (NNNn). Zero-number banks, or zero-listed banks, are banks that do not contain directory-listed residential numbers. Although including zero-number banks in a random-digit dialing frame allows for 100% coverage of landline residential telephone numbers, their inclusion can substantially reduce sample efficiency.

Based on regular analyses conducted by Survey Sampling International, only 29% of 100-banks in POTS (Plain Old Telephone Service) prefixes, and other prefixes shared by different types of service, have at least one directory-listed number. In prefixes that have at least one directory-listed telephone number, only 47% of the possible 100-banks contain at least one directory-listed number. Because of these inefficiencies, most random-digit dialing surveys today use list-assisted, truncated frames—that is, frames truncated to include only listed-banks or those 100-banks that contain at least one directory-listed residential telephone number.

This truncation introduces some coverage error by excluding 100-banks that contain residential numbers but are missing from the truncated frame. The most common reason for this omission is that newly opened banks have not yet been published in a telephone directory. Because directories are published only once a year, the time lag between number assignment and directory publication can result in new blocks not being represented. Another source of error is common in rural areas, particularly those serviced by small, local telephone companies. A formal directory may not be readily available to compilers, but numbers are listed in a paperback book that looks like the local real estate listings available at the supermarket.

Alternative sample designs are available for researchers that opt to include zero-listed banks. One approach, the Mitofsky-Waksberg method, takes advantage of the tendency of telephone numbers to cluster in 100-banks. It starts with a sample of primary numbers in prefixes available for landline residential use. If a primary number is determined to be a working residential number, a cluster of additional numbers in generated in the same 100-bank. Another approach is to use disproportionate stratified samples of both zero-listed banks and listed banks. For many years, this design was the sampling protocol for all surveys conducted as part of the U.S. Department of Health Behavioral Risk Factor Surveillance System.

Research by Michael Brick and others suggests that this coverage error is 3–4% of telephone households. However, work by Brick and by Clyde Tucker and Jim Lepkowski confirms that the efficiency gains of list-assisted designs make them preferable in most cases. In fact, in 2003 the Behavioral Risk Factor Surveillance System protocol was revised to include only the listed-bank stratum.

Linda Piekarski

See also Behavioral Risk Factor Surveillance System (BRFSS); Coverage; Coverage Error; Mitofsky-Waksberg Sampling; Random-Digit Dialing (RDD); Suffix Banks

Further Readings

Brick, J. M., Waksberg, J., Kulp, D., & Starer, A. (1995). Bias in list-assisted telephone samples. *Public Opinion Quarterly, 59*(2), 218–235.

District of Columbia Department of Health. (n.d.). *BRFSS survey protocol.* Retrieved December 2, 2006, from http://www.dchealth.dc.gov/doh/cwp/view,a,1374,q,601933.asp

Lepkowski, J. M. (1988). Telephone sampling methods in the United States. In R. M. Groves, P. P. Biemer, L. E. Lyberg, J. T. Massey, W. L. Nicholls II, & J. Waksberg (Eds.), *Telephone survey methodology* (pp. 73–98). New York: Wiley.

National Center for Chronic Disease Prevention and Health Promotion. (2003). *BRFSS policy memo 2003.1: Sampling and sampling information protocols.* Retrieved December 2, 2006, from http://www.cdc.gov/brfss/technical_infodata/memos/20031.htm

Tucker, C., Lepkowski, J. M., & Piekarski, L. (2002). The current efficiency of list-assisted telephone sampling designs. *Public Opinion Quarterly, 66,* 321–338.

Z-SCORE

The *z*-score is a statistical transformation that specifies how far a particular value lies from the mean of a normal distribution in terms of standard deviations. *z*-scores are particularly helpful in comparing observations that come from different populations and from distributions with different means, standard deviations, or both. A *z*-score has meaning only if it is calculated for observations that are part of a normal distribution.

z-scores are sometimes referred to as *standard scores.* When the values of a normal distribution are transformed into *z*-scores, the transformed distribution is said to be "standardized" such that the new distribution has a mean equal to 0 and a standard deviation equal to 1.

The *z*-score for any observation is calculated by subtracting the population mean from the value of the observation and dividing the difference by the population standard deviation, or $z = (x - \mu)/\sigma$. Positive *z*-scores mean that the observation in question is greater than the mean; negative *z*-scores mean that it is less than the mean. For instance, an observation with a *z*-score of 1.0 would mean that the observation is exactly one standard deviation above the mean of the distribution. An observation with a *z*-score equal to –0.5 would fall one-half of one standard deviation below the distribution's mean. An observation with a *z*-score equal to 0 would be equal to the mean of the distribution.

As an example, a researcher looking at middle school students' test scores might benefit from using *z*-scores as a way of comparing the relative performance of a seventh-grade student on a seventh-grade test to an eighth-grade student on an eighth-grade test. In this example, the researcher knows that the scores for the entire population of seventh graders and for the entire population of eighth graders are normally distributed. The average number of correct answers (out of 100 multiple choice questions) for the population of seventh graders on the seventh-grade test is 65 with a standard deviation of 10. The average score (out of 100 multiple choice questions) for the population of eighth graders on the eighth-grade test is 72 with a standard deviation of 12.

The seventh- and eighth-grade students of interest to this researcher scored 70 correct and 75 correct, respectively. Transforming each raw score into a *z*-score would be an appropriate way to determine which student scored better relative to his or her own population (cohort). The *z*-score for the seventh-grade student would be (70 − 65)/10, or 0.5, meaning that he or she scored 0.5 standard deviation above the average for seventh-grade students. The *z*-score for the eighth-grade student would be (75 − 72)/12, or 0.25, meaning that he or she scored 0.25 standard deviation above the average for eighth-grade students. Relative to his or her peers, the seventh-grade student performed better than the eighth-grade student, despite the eighth grader's higher raw score total.

Joel K. Shapiro

See also Percentile; Population of Interest; Population Parameter; Raw Data

Further Readings

Kvanli, A. H., Guynes, C. S., & Pavur, R. J. (1986). *Introduction to business statistics.* St. Paul, MN: West Publishing.

Wonnacott, T. H., & Wonnacott, R. J. (1990). *Introductory statistics* (5th ed.). New York: Wiley.

Index

Entry titles and their page numbers are in bold; illustrative material is identified by (figure) and (table).

Newspaper, call-in polls and, **1:**77–78

News polls. *See* **Media polls**

New York Times, **1:**49, **2:**600
    methods boxes used in, **1:**464
    on nonresponse, **2:**528
    on protection of human subjects, **2:**630

***New York Times*/CBS News poll, 2:**507–509

New York Times Co. v. United States, **2:**612

Next-birthday (NB) selection method, **1:**417

Neyman, Jerzy, **1:**284, **2:**783, **2:**820

Neyman allocation, 2:509–510, **2:**850–851

Nicholls, William, **1:**352

Nichols, Jack, **1:**417–418

Nie, Normal, **2:**843

Nielsen Media Research, **1:**9

Nielsen TV Diary, **1:**198

Niemi, Richard, **1:**150

900 poll, 2:510

Nisbet, Matthew, **1:**315

Nixon, Richard, **1:**20–21, **1:**149

Noelle, Neumann, Elisabeth, **2:**830–833

No interaction effect, **1:**341, **1:**341 (figure)

Nominal measure, 1:421–422, **2:**510–511, **2:**511
    (table)

Nonattitude, 2:511–513, **2:**512

Noncash incentives, **1:**330

Noncausal covariation, 2:513–514

Noncontact rate, 1:217, **1:**283,
    2:514–515, **2:**522, **2:**760

Noncontacts, 2:515–516

Noncontingent incentives, 1:329–330, **2:**516–517

Noncooperation. *See* **Refusal**

Noncooperation rate (NCR), 2:517–519

Noncoverage, 1:159–160, **1:**310, **2:**519–520

Nondifferentiation, 2:520–521

Nondirectional hypothesis. *See* **Research hypothesis**

Nondirective probing, 2:521–522

Nonequivalent control group designs, **2:**727

Nonexperimental research designs, **2:**728–729

Nonignorable nonresponse, 2:522–523

Noninstitutional facilities, defined, **2:**738

Nonobservational errors, **2:**897

Nonprobability sampling, 2:523–526, **2:**621,
    2:645, **2:**668–669, **2:**783–784
    convenience sampling, **2:**525
    purposive sampling, **2:**524–525
    quota sampling, **2:**523–524
    recent developments in, **2:**526
    weighting and drawing inferences from, **2:**525

Nonrandom error, **2:**679

Nonresearch call centers, **2:**722–723

Nonresidential dispositions, 2:526–527

Nonresponse, 2:527–530, **2:**927–928
    current theories, **2:**529–530
    declining response rates and implications, **2:**529
    history of survey nonresponse, **2:**528–529
    nonignorable, **2:**522–523
    predictability, **2:**528
    unit nonresponse, **2:**927–928
    weighting and, **2:**959–960

Nonresponse bias, 1:59–60, **2:**531–533, **2:**751
    maximizing response rates, **2:**531
    recent research and, **2:**531–532
    reducing, **2:**532

Nonresponse error, 1:256, **2:**533–536, **2:**898
    basic concepts, **2:**533–534
    classification of final fieldwork outcomes, **2:***534*
    error of nonobservation, **1:**237
    information to evaluate, **2:**534–535
    in mail surveys, **1:**444
    nonsampling error and, **2:**539
    reducing, **2:**535–536
    simple model, **2:**533

Nonresponse rates, 2:536–539
    formulae to calculate, **2:**538
    ineligible cases, **2:**537–538
    nonresponses, **2:**537
    responses, **2:**537
    unknown eligibility, **2:**537

Nonsampling error, 2:539
    in censuses, **1:**92
    coder variance, **1:**101–102

Nontelephone household, 2:539–540

Nonverbal behavior, 2:540–541

"No opinion," **1:**38, **2:**511–512

Normative-judgment equation, **1:**264

North American Numbering Plan (NANP), **2:**608

North Carolina State University, **2:**796

Northwestern University, **2:**600–601

"No time/no interest," **1:**219

Not missing at random (NMAR), **1:**323, **1:**467–468

Null hypothesis, 2:541–542
    alternative hypothesis and, **1:**19, **2:**732–733
    ANOVA and, **1:**26

Number changed, 2:542–543

Numbering Plan Area (NPA), **2:**607

Number portability, 2:543–545

Number verification, 2:545

Nuremburg Code. *See* **Ethical principles**

Observational error. *See* **Total survey error (TSE)**

Occupational Outlook Handbook (BLS), **1:**71

Office of Management and Budget (OMB), **1:**22
    Bureau of Labor Statistics (BLS) and, **1:**70